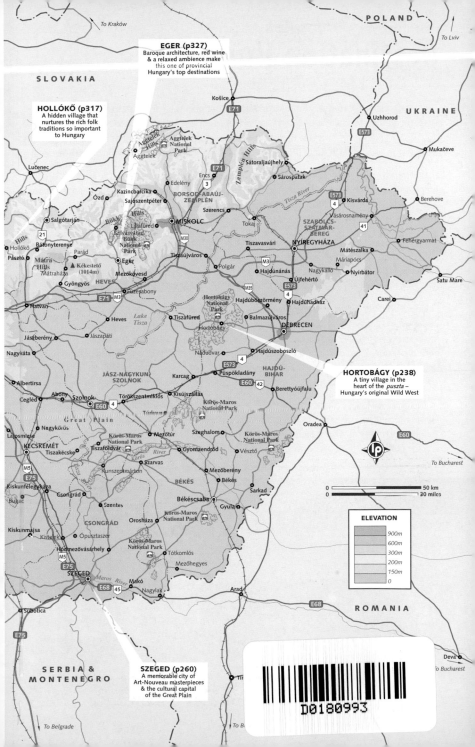

POLAND

To Kraków

To Lviv

EGER (p327)
Baroque architecture, red wine
& a relaxed ambience make
this one of provincial
Hungary's top destinations

SLOVAKIA

UKRAINE

HOLLÓKŐ (p317)
A hidden village that
nurtures the rich folk
traditions so important
to Hungary

Košice

E71

Uzhhorod

Mukačeve

Aggtelek
Hills

Aggtelek
National
Park

Sátoraljaújhely

Sárospatak

E573

Berehove

Lučenec

Aggtelek

Edelény

Encs

E71
3

Zemplén Hills

Tisza River

Kisvárda

Vásárosnamény

Ózd

Kazincbarcika

Sajószentpéter

BORSOD-ABAÚJ-
ZEMPLÉN

Szerencs

Tokaj

SZABOLCS-
SZATMÁR-
BEREG

E573
4

Mátészalka

Fehérgyarmat

Salgótarján

Bükk
Hills

MISKOLC

Tiszavasvári

NYÍREGYHÁZA

41

Máriapócs

Lillafüred

Szilvásvárad

M30

Pásztó

Hollókő

21

Bátonyterenye

Parád

Bükk
National
Park

Tiszaújváros

Polgár

Hajdúnánás

M3

Nagykálló

Nyírbátor

Satu Mare

Mátra
Hills

Mátraháza

Kékestető
(1014m)

Eger

Mezőkövesd

Füzesabony

Újfehértó

E573

Hatvan

Gyöngyös

HEVES

E71

M3

M35

Hortobágy
National
Park

Hajdúböszörmény

Hajdúhadház

Carei

Heves

Lake
Tisza

Tiszafüred

Hortobágy

Balmazújváros

DEBRECEN

Jászberény

Jászapáti

Nádudvar

Hajdúszoboszló

HORTOBÁGY (p238)
A tiny village in the
heart of the *puszta* –
Hungary's original Wild West

Nagykáta

JÁSZ-NAGYKUN-
SZOLNOK

Karcag

E573
4

HAJDÚ-
BIHAR

Albertirsa

Abony

Szolnok

E60

Törökszentmiklós

Püspökladány

E60
42

Berettyóújfalu

Cegléd

Great Plain

E60

Kisújszállás

Körös-Maros
National Park

Oradea

E60

Nagykőrös

Mezőtúr

Szeghalom

Körös-Maros
National Park

To Bucharest

Lajosmizse

KECSKEMÉT

Tiszakécske

Körös-Maros
National Park

Tiszaföldvár

River

Gyomaendrőd

Vésztő

Kunszentmárton

Szarvas

Bugac

M5

Csongrád

BÉKÉS

Mezőberény

Békés

Kiskunfélegyháza

Kiskunmajsa

Kistelek

Szentes

CSONGRÁD

Orosháza

Körös-Maros
National Park

Sarkad

Gyula

Békéscsaba

0   50 km

0   30 miles

ELEVATION

900m
600m
300m
200m
150m
0

Ópusztaszer

Körös-Maros
National Park

Hódmezővásárhely

M5

Tótkomlós

Mezőhegyes

SZEGED

Makó

E68
45

Maros River

Nagylak

Arad

E68

ROMANIA

Subotica

E75

Deva

To Bucharest

SERBIA &
MONTENEGRO

SZEGED (p260)
A memorable city of
Art-Nouveau masterpieces
& the cultural capital
of the Great Plain

D0180993

To Belgrade

To B...

Destination Hungary

There is no place like Hungary (Magyarország) . Situated in the very heart of Europe, this kidney-shaped country can claim a unique place in the continent's soul. Doubters need only listen to the music of Franz Liszt and Béla Bartók, view the romantic Danube River as it dramatically splits Budapest in two or taste the nation's unique (and paprika-infused) cuisine to be convinced.

Hungary's impact on Europe's history and development has been far greater than its present size and population would suggest. Hungarians, who call themselves Magyars, speak a language and form a culture unlike any other in the region – a distinction that has been both a source of pride and an obstacle for more than 1100 years.

Hungary is the best place to enter both Central and Eastern Europe. While some of its neighbours may have more dramatic scenery or older and more important monuments, Hungary abounds in things to see and do, and those with special interests – fishing, horse riding, botany, bird-watching, cycling, thermal spas, Jewish culture – will find a treasure-trove here.

Under the old communist regime, most of the government's focus and money went to Budapest. As a result, foreign visitors rarely ventured beyond this splendid city on the Danube River, except on a day trip to the Danube Bend or to Lake Balaton. These places should be visited, of course, but don't ignore other towns and regions off the beaten track: the *tanya világ* (farm world) of the Southern Plain, the ethnically rich Northeast, the Villány Hills in Southern Transdanubia covered in vineyards and the traditional Őrség region in the far west.

The '90s were not a stellar time for the reborn republic. Its economic development was in limbo and serious economic problems affected all aspects of daily life. Thankfully, those days are past and many now view Hungary, with its intelligent, hard-working populace, and rich and vibrant culture, as the star performer and most interesting destination of the new Europe.

MARTIN MOO

Highlights

A bird's-eye view of Sopron's Fő tér rewards those who climb the 200 steps to the top of the firewatch tower (p164)

MARTIN MOOS

KIM GRANT

Visit the chapels and crypt at the neo-Romanesque Basilica of St Peter in Pécs (p297)

Castle Hill has a treasure-trove of medieval monuments and museums (p69)

MARTIN MOOS

Kecskemét's town hall is a pastiche of architectural styles (p244)

The grand and opulent Esterházy Palace in Fertőd is fit for royalty (p169)

Brush up on the history of Nyíregyháza at the András Jósa Museum (p357)

The grape is king in the town of Tokaj (p345)

DAVID GREEDY

MARTIN MOOS

Tickle your taste buds with the big-bodied *barrique* reds of Villány (p292)

A visit to picturesque Hollókő is like stepping back in time (p317)

ROBERTO SONCIN GEROMETTA

8

Join the action on Lake Balaton, a water-lover's paradise (p188)

The thermal lake at Hévíz is a sure-fire way of curing all aches and pains (p197)

Cowboys race bareback 'five-in-hand' in horseshows on the *puszta* (p247)

Contents

Regional Map Contents

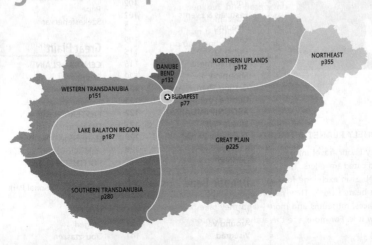

WESTERN TRANSDANUBIA p151

DANUBE BEND p132

NORTHERN UPLANDS p312

NORTHEAST p355

BUDAPEST p77

LAKE BALATON REGION p187

GREAT PLAIN p225

SOUTHERN TRANSDANUBIA p280

The Authors

STEVE FALLON   Coordinating Author, Budapest, Western Transdanubia

Steve, who has worked on every edition of Hungary, first visited Magyarország in the early 1980s with three things on his 'to do' list: visit a thermal spa, drink masses of Tokaj wine and buy fruit for friends in Poland whose children, born under the neofascist regime of General Wojciech Jaruzelski, had never seen (much less tasted) such 'exotics' as bananas. Having accomplished all three, he returned again and again, moving to Budapest in 1992, where he learned to love the Hungarian language, *pálinka* more than Tokaj and very hot thermal water – not necessarily in that order. Now based in London, Steve goes back to Hungary regularly for a fix of all three.

Steve's Favourite Trip

The problem with getting into Budapest (p63) is getting out, but after a couple of days (and nights) of nonstop frolicking, I'm ready for something 'high'. The drive through the Mátra Hills (p322), Hungary's most picturesque upland area, fulfils all my requirements: wine at Gyöngyös (p322), thermal water at Parádsasvár (p326) and superlatives at Kékestető (p326; Hungary's highest point) and Eger (p327; Hungary's most beautiful town). If I'm feeling 'low', I head south to Veszprém (p214) and follow the northern shore of Lake Balaton via Balatonfüred (p210), Tihany (p207) and Badacsony (p198). I may not find many superlatives here, but there is plenty of wine and enough thermal water to float a ship at my destination, Hévíz (p197).

NEAL BEDFORD   Danube Bend, Lake Balaton Region, Great Plains, Southern Transdanubia, Northern Uplands, Northeast

Neal had visited Hungary many times from his home in Vienna for cheap dental work and even cheaper wine. However, taking advantage of the savings in Sopron and Budapest doesn't amount to actually seeing Magyarország. This soon became apparent on his first proper exploration of the country for Lonely Planet a number of years ago. After clocking up thousands of kilometres, avoiding mad drivers, horse-drawn carts and parking inspectors, Neal now believes he can truly say he's seen Hungary, but in his heart he knows this kidney-shaped country still holds some surprises for him.

LONELY PLANET AUTHORS

Why is our travel information the best in the world? It's simple: our authors are independent, dedicated travellers. They don't research using just the Internet or phone, and they don't take freebies in exchange for positive coverage. They travel widely, to all the popular spots and off the beaten track. They personally visit thousands of hotels, restaurants, cafés, bars, galleries, palaces, museums and more – and they take pride in getting all the details right, and telling it how it is. For more, see the authors section on www.lonelyplanet.com.

Getting Started

A trip to Hungary actually requires very little advance planning. Free tourist literature abounds, maps are excellent and readily available, and staff at tourist offices, travel agencies, hotels, train stations and so on are generally helpful and knowledgeable. In fact, almost anything can be arranged after you've arrived. And as most experienced travellers know, the problems that occurred to you at home usually turn out to be irrelevant or sort themselves out once you're on the road.

See Climate Charts (p368) for more information.

But all this applies only if you have unlimited time and budget, you don't have an interest in a particular activity, type of architecture or kind of music, and you'll eat or drink anything set down in front of you. If you have to watch what you spend or want better value for your money while travelling, you will benefit greatly from careful planning. And if you have specific interests, you'll certainly want to make sure that the things you came to see and do will be possible when you visit.

WHEN TO GO

Hungary has a temperate climate with three climatic zones so there is a certain amount of variation across the country: Mediterranean in the south, Continental in the east and Atlantic in the west. The main tourist season is discussed in Directory (p365).

DON'T LEAVE HOME WITHOUT...

There are no particular items of clothing to remember when packing – an umbrella in spring and autumn, perhaps, and a warm hat in winter – unless you plan to do some serious hiking or other sport. In general, Hungarians dress very casually – their summer fashions and beachwear are daringly brief, even by Continental European standards – and many attend even the opera in denim. Men needn't bother bringing a tie; it will never be used.

A swimsuit for use in the mixed-sex thermal spas and pools is a good idea as are plastic sandals or thongs (flip-flops). If you plan to stay in hostels, pack a towel and soap. Bedclothes are usually provided, though you might want to bring your own sleeping sheet, as well as a padlock for storage lockers.

Other items you might need include:

- a compass to help orient yourself while rambling (or even while driving)
- a torch/flashlight if you intend on camping or visiting caves
- an adaptor plug for electrical appliances that don't have a standard two-pin European plug (eg, an immersion water heater or small kettle for an impromptu cup of tea or coffee)
- a universal bath/sink plug (a plastic film canister sometimes works)
- sunglasses and sun block, even in the cooler months
- premoistened towelettes or a large cotton handkerchief to soak in fountains and use to cool off in the hot summer months
- a Swiss Army knife (or equivalent), with such essentials as a bottle opener and strong corkscrew (don't forget to pack it with your check-on luggage, though)
- binoculars for trekking, bird-watching or viewing detail on churches and other buildings
- photocopies of important documents (passport data page, credit cards, travel insurance policy, air/bus/train tickets, driving licence etc), with a copy left with someone at home

Without taking regional differences into consideration, every season has its attractions in Hungary. But do yourself a favour and drop the 'romantic' notion of a winter on the *puszta* (Great Plain). Aside from being cold and often bleak, winter sees museums and other tourist sights closed or their hours sharply curtailed.

Although it can be pretty wet in April and May, spring is just glorious throughout Hungary. The weather is usually mild and – a boon for independent travellers – the crowds of tourists have not yet arrived.

The Hungarian summer is warm, sunny and unusually long, and the resorts can get very crowded in late July and August. If you avoid Lake Balaton and the ever-popular Mátra Hills, you should be OK. As elsewhere in Europe, Budapest and other Hungarian cities come to a grinding halt in August, which Hungarians traditionally call 'the cucumber-growing season' (because that's about the only thing happening here).

Autumn is beautiful, particularly in the hills around Budapest and in the Northern Uplands. In Transdanubia and on the Great Plain it's harvest and vintage time. November is one of the rainiest months of the year in certain parts of the country, however.

COSTS & MONEY

Hungary is no longer the bargain-basement destination for foreign travellers that it was even five years ago, but it is still cheaper by a third or even a half than most Western European countries. If you bunk down in private rooms, eat at medium-priced restaurants and travel on public transport, you should get by on €30 a day in the provinces without too much scrimping, though Budapest will cost you closer to €40 a day.

Travelling in more style and comfort – restaurant splurges with bottles of wine, a fairly active nightlife, stay in small hotels/guesthouses with 'character' – will cost you twice as much (€60 in the provinces and €80 in the capital). Those putting up at hostels or college dormitories, eating *burek* street food for lunch and at self-service restaurants for dinner could squeak by for €20 a day.

For information about discounts, see p369.

TRAVEL BOOKS

Travellers writing diary accounts usually treat Hungary rather cursorily as they make tracks for 'more exotic' Romania or places beyond. A few classic – and very personal accounts – are still available in bookshops, libraries or on Amazon.com.

- *Between the Woods and the Water* (Patrick Leigh Fermor) Describing his 1933 walk through Western and Central Europe to Constantinople as a young man, Fermor wrote the classic account of Hungary.
- *Stealing from a Deep Place* (Brian Hall) Sensitive but never cloying, the author describes his tempered love affair with the still communist Budapest of the 1980s while completing a two-year cycle tour of Hungary, Romania and Bulgaria.
- *The City of the Magyar or Hungary and Her Institutions in 1839–40* (Julia Pardoe) One of the best sources for early 19th-century Hungary in English, this three-volume part-travelogue, part-history by a British spinster is priceless for its vivid descriptions of contemporary events such as the devastating Danube floods of 1838.
- *Under the Frog* (Tibor Fischer) An amusing account of the antics of two members of Hungary's elite national basketball team from the end of WWII through the 1956 Uprising.

HOW MUCH?

Cheap/good bottle (75cL) of wine in supermarket 600/2000Ft

Bed in private room in provinces/Budapest from 2000/4500Ft

Cup of coffee in café 200–380Ft

Local English-language newspaper 395–590Ft

Dinner for two at good restaurant in provinces/Budapest 9000/15,000Ft

LONELY PLANET INDEX

1L petrol 265–273Ft

1L bottled water 150Ft

Korsó (0.5L) of Dreher beer in pub/café 350–600Ft

Souvenir T-shirt 1500Ft

TOP TENS

Castles & Palaces
Hungary's most celebrated castles and palaces:

- Boldogkő Castle at Boldogkőváralja (p344)
- Sümeg Castle (p203)
- Hollókő Castle (p318)
- Eger Castle (p329)
- Zrínyi Castle at Szigetvár (p305)

- Jurisics Castle in Kőszeg (p183)
- Siklós Castle (p287)
- Esterházy Palace at Fertőd (p169)
- Royal Mansion at Gödöllő (p129)
- Festetics Palace at Keszthely (p193)

Churches & Synagogues
Hungary's most beautiful houses of worship:

- Art Nouveau synagogue in Szeged (p263)
- Church of the Ascension in Sümeg (p204)
- Gothic Calvinist church and the Minorite church in Nyírbátor (p360)
- Abbey Church in Tihany (p208)
- Baroque Minorite church in Eger (p330)
- Baroque cathedral at Kalocsa (p247)

- Pécs synagogue (p297)
- Romanesque church at Őriszentpéter (p185)
- Gothic Old Synagogue in Sopron (p165)
- Romantic Nationalist synagogue in Szolnok (now the Szolnok Gallery; p227)

Outdoor Activities
Among Hungary's top outdoor activities:

- Horse riding around Szilvásvárad in the Northern Uplands (p336)
- Canoeing or kayaking on the Tisza River (p231)
- Cycling in the Danube Bend area (p148)
- Bird-watching in the Hortobágy region (p239)
- Swimming in the thermal lake at Hévíz (p197)

- Riding the narrow-gauge railway from Miskolc into the Bükk Hills (p339)
- Hiking in the Zemplén Hills (p345)
- Sailing (or windsurfing) on Lake Balaton (p190)
- Caving in Aggtelek (p343)
- Fishing in Lake Tisza (p231)

- *Homage to the Eighth District* (Giorgio and Nicola Pressburger) A poignant account of life in what was a Jewish working-class section of Budapest during and after WWII by twin brothers who emigrated to Italy in 1956.
- *In Time of Trouble* (Claud Cockburn) An enlightening, often very funny, autobiography by the celebrated British journalist who spent several years in Budapest as a young man in the 1920s with his government servant father. The account of the aborted orgy by the banks of the Danube is classic.
- *Hungary & the Hungarians: The Keywords* (István Bart) Subtitled 'A Concise Dictionary of Facts, Beliefs, Customs, Usage & Myths', this book will prepare you for (and guide you through) just about everything Magyar – from ABC (a kind of greengrocer under the old regime) to Zsolnay.
- *Living in Hungary* (Jean-Luc Soule and Alain Fleischer) This lavishly photographed coffee-table book takes you into the country's finest and most elegant cafés, bathhouses, palaces, castles, hotels, restaurants and private homes.

INTERNET RESOURCES

Hungarian Home Page (www.fsz.bme.hu/hungary/homepage.html) Reference site and search engine for everything and anything Hungarian

Hungarian National Tourism Organisation (www.hungary.com) Without a doubt the best single website on Hungary and should be your first portal of call

Hungarian Youth Hostels (www.youthhostels.hu) An excellent site for tracking down budget accommodation across Hungary as well as for practical and background information about the country

Inside Hungary (www.insidehungary.com) National news and a myriad of excellent links on everything from business to culture

Hungary.hu (www.hungary.hu) Government portal with key data but not always as up-to-date as it should be

Museums in Hungary (www.museum.hu) A complete list of every museum in the land currently open to the public

Travelport (www.hotels.hu) A great source of information for accommodation to suit every pocket

Check out www
.lonelyplanet.com for
summaries on Hungary,
links to Hungary-related
sites and travellers trading information on the
Thorn Tree.

Itineraries
CLASSIC ROUTES

IN THE WAKE OF THE LAKE
One week

Combining the highlights of Transdanubia and the Lake Balaton regions will give you a taste of Hungary's historical wealth and natural beauty. From **Budapest** (p63) make your way through the rolling **Pilis Hills** (p144) and turn off for **Esztergom** (p144), Hungary's holiest city. The road continues west along the Danube to **Győr** (p155), an industrial city surprisingly rich in historical buildings and monuments. From here you can detour south to **Pannonhalma** (p160), whose awesome abbey is on Unesco's World Heritage List, or carry on westwards via Hungary's own 'Versailles' at **Fertőd** (p169) to delightful **Sopron** (p162). Next head south to **Kőszeg** (p181), so pretty it's called the nation's jewellery box, and then make your way southeast via **Sárvár** (p177), where Hungary's 'Dracula' had her nip and suck, to **Sümeg** (p203) and its dramatic castle. Lake Balaton is just 20km south; follow the scenic northern coast road past the costal settlements of **Badacsony** (p198), **Tihany** (p207) and **Balatonfüred** (p210) to **Veszprém** (p214), the 'city of queens'. From here you can make your way back to Budapest and, to be fair, stop at **Székesfehérvár** (p220), the 'city of kings'.

This 545km trip has something for everyone: castles, historic churches, palaces, thermal spas, rolling hills and Hungary's biggest lake. For the most part it's an easy drive, and you could do it in a few days. But with so much to see and time to recharge on the Balaton, we'd recommend at least a week.

OVER HILL & BEYOND DALE   One week

Hungary's uplands to the north are hardly what you could call dramatic. But they have a gentle beauty all their own and nestling within the hills are important historical towns and traditional villages. From **Budapest** (p63) head north to **Vác** (p137), arguably the most attractive town on the Danube Bend, and then on to **Balassagyarmat** (p313), the capital of the traditional Palóc region. Continue due east to **Szécsény** (p315), site of a pivotal battle and a delightful manor house. Dip down through the rolling Cserhát Hills to **Hollókő** (p317), a 'museum town' of Hungarian traditions. From here the road winds through the eastern Cserhát and foothills of the Mátra Hills to **Gyöngyös** (p322), where you'll start an almost tortuous drive through the hills past **Kékestető** (p326), Hungary's highest point, and scary **Recsk** (p327), site of what was once Hungary's most brutal forced-labour camp. Lovely baroque **Eger** (p327) awaits you at the end of the high road. For a taste of Hungary's 'lowlands' – the Great Plain – head southeast via **Tiszafüred** (p230) and **Hortobágy National Park** (p238) to **Debrecen** (p233), nicknamed 'Calvinist Rome', the country's second-largest city.

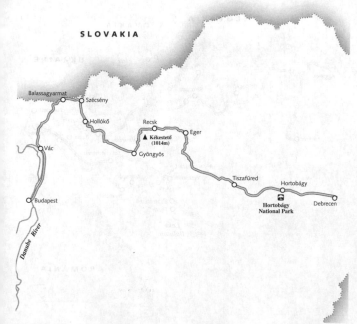

You'll get both the 'ups' and the 'downs' of northern and eastern Hungary – the so-called Northern Uplands and the Great Plain – on this 345km trip. There's plenty to do – from exploring historical cities like Eger and Debrecen to wine-tasting in Gyöngyös and bird-watching in the Hortobágy region.

ROADS LESS TRAVELLED

FORGOTTEN CORNER IN MIND   Three days

Hungary's northeast corner, encompassing parts of the Northern Uplands and a region appropriately called the Northeast, is an area often overlooked by travellers and all the more attractive for it. For a good overview of the region, start in **Miskolc** (p337), Hungary's third-largest city, and head north to **Aggtelek** (p342), gateway to an enormous karst cave system and a Unesco World Heritage Site. From here head east via **Boldogkőváralja** (p344), site of a 'Disneyesque' hilltop castle, to **Sárospatak** (p348), renowned for its college and castle. Then continue on to **Vásárosnamény** (p362), the gateway to traditional villages and sights of the Northeast, including **Tákos** (p362) and **Csaroda** (p362) to the east, and **Tarpa** (p362), **Szatmárcseke** (p363) and **Túristvándi** (p363) to the south. Once back on the main road, carry on to **Nyírbátor** (p359), famed for its Gothic churches. Head west, stopping briefly at **Máriapócs** (p361) and **Nagykálló** (p359), pilgrimage sites for the Catholic and Jewish faithful respectively, before reaching the Northeast's regional centre and your destination, **Nyíregyháza** (p355).

For a look at how things used to be – when the world was governed by the seasons and powered by the horse – this is the ideal itinerary. At 415km, with relatively few major centres and places to stay en route, it's a trip that could be done in just a few days if you plough straight through. But you might like to pause and, well, smell the roses.

TAILORED TRIPS

MIXING WINE & WATER

Nothing beats a glass of wine and nothing beats a sauna and/or soak after one glass too many. So why not combine the two – wine and water – and indulge and detox as you go?

Eger (p327) is home to Hungary's famous Egri Bikavér (Eger Bull's Blood) and Pinot Noir and boasts thermal baths of its own. A mere 8km to the southwest is **Egerszalók** (p334), a hot spring set to become one of northern Hungary's biggest spas.

The celebrated **Tokaj region** (p345) nestling in the foothills of the Zemplén Hills to the northeast is awash with sweet wine and sweet water. You won't find much thermal water in these parts but there's swimming in the Tisza River, and the curative waters of the Cave Bath at **Miskolctapolca** (p340) and the Végardó recreational complex in **Sárospatak** (p348) are only a hop, skip and plunge away.

Sopron (p162) is one of the most important wine regions of western Hungary and the surrounding hills produce such notable red wines as Kékfrankos and Merlot. Here you'll also find the large **Lővér Baths** (p169), a great place to relax after a night on the town. To the southeast, on the way to Lake Balaton, is the **Somló region** (p58), which has two great and indigenous grape varieties: Hárslevelű (Linden Leaf) and Juhfark (Sheep's Tail).

The northern shore of the Balaton – particularly around **Badacsony** (p198) – produces some of Hungary's finest wines, notably Olaszrizling (Italian Riesling) and Kéknyelű (Blue Stalk). Swimming in the lake from Badacsonytomaj is pleasant but if you want to 'take the waters' in what is one of the world's largest thermal lakes, head to **Hévíz** (p197).

The **Villány-Siklós region** (p57), in southwest Hungary, is home to the nation's best reds: Kékoportó (Blauer Portugieser), Cabernet Franc, Cabernet Sauvignon and Merlot. They are almost always big-bodied Bordeaux-style wines that are high in tannins. Should you have over-indulged, get thee to the spa town of **Harkány** (p290), a short distance to the west, where everything centres round the cure-all thermal baths.

Snapshot

At the end of its first full year as a fully-fledged member of the EU (May 2005), Hungary was at something of a crossroads politically, economically and, at the risk of sounding overly dramatic, historically.

Parliamentary elections loomed in May 2006, and incumbent prime minister Ferenc Gyurcsány of the socialist MSZP party was still trying to convince the electorate of the benefits of adopting the euro. Gyurcsány succeeded Péter Medgyessy in August 2004 when the government's popularity was at its lowest in three years, having curbed salary increases, cut housing subsidies and raised some taxes. But it remained a hard sell. For one thing, it was going to require a longer wait than anticipated for all those riches from the 'drunken uncles' in Brussels; in May 2004 Medgyessy had been forced to push back the proposed adoption date (2008) by two years when it became clear he could not reduce the budget deficit by 2.5% as required by the EU in time. Now Gyurcsány faced the same unattractive choice: scale back social programmes established during communism or delay adoption of the euro yet again – thereby eroding the benefits of joining the EU in the first place.

By late 2005 inflation had been contained at 3.5%, down from double-digit figures 10 years before, and annual growth remains a respectable 4%. The unemployment rate nationwide hovers just under 6% but that figure is deceptive. While the rate is only about 5% in Budapest, it is as high as 20% in the Northeast.

Waiting in the wings in late 2005 was Viktor Orbán, head of the centre-right Fidesz-MPP party. Orbán, who became prime minister in 1998 but was ousted as much for his arrogance as anything else in 2002, was pitted against Medgyessy, his nemesis and junior by just a year. And in a world turned upside-down the 'socialist' Gyurcsány, who cut his political teeth in the communist youth movement, ranked among the 100 wealthiest Hungarians and advocated the sale of the national carrier Malév and Ferihegy International Airport. The conservative Orbán meanwhile, opposed the sale of such state assets and backs an increase in social spending.

Amid all the wrangling a news item that seemed to go unnoticed in much of the Western press was the rejection by the Hungarian electorate in the December 2004 plebiscite to grant ethnic Hungarians living outside the borders – a total of 2.5 million, with an estimated 1.45 million in Romania alone – the right to hold Hungarian as well as Romanian, Slovakian, Serbian or Ukrainian citizenship. Many saw this as the final nail in the coffin of 'Greater Hungary' – the nation of the swollen borders that nationalists had dreamed of returning to throughout the 1930s and took the nation to the wrong side in WWII. In 1992 the late Prime Minister József Antall alienated people at home and abroad with his claim to be the 'emotional and spiritual' prime minister of the Magyar minorities in those countries.

FAST FACTS

Population: 10.083 million

GDP per head: US$10,400; GDP per head at purchasing power parity: US$14,900

Inflation: 3.5%

Unemployment: 5.9%

Size: 93,030 sq km

Population identifying themselves as Roman Catholics: 52%

Internet domain: hu

Suicide rate: 60.1 per 100,000 people (UK: 15.1% per 100,000 people; USA: 21.7% per 100,000 people)

National anthem: *Himnusz*, with the music composed by Ferenc Erkel and the lyrics written by poet Ferenc Kölcsey

Number of government employees: 800,000 (20% of the total workforce)

History

EARLY INHABITANTS

The Carpathian Basin, in which Hungary lies, has been populated for hundreds of thousands of years. Bone fragments found at Vértesszőlős, about 5km southeast of Tata (p151), in the 1960s are believed to be half a million years old. These findings suggest that Palaeolithic and later Neanderthal humans were attracted to the area by the hot springs and the abundance of reindeer, bears and mammoths.

During the Neolithic period (3500–2500 BC), climatic changes forced much of the indigenous wildlife to migrate northward. As a result the domestication of animals and the first forms of agriculture appeared, simultaneously with the rest of Europe. Remnants of the Körös culture in the Szeged area of the southeast (p261) suggest that these goddess-worshipping people herded sheep, fished and hunted.

Indo-European tribes from the Balkans stormed the Carpathian Basin in horse-drawn carts in about 2000 BC, bringing with them copper tools and weapons. After the introduction of the more durable metal bronze, forts were built and a military elite began to develop.

Over the next millennium, invaders from the west (Illyrians, Thracians) and east (Scythians) brought iron, but it was not in common use until the Celts arrived at the start of the 4th century BC. They introduced glass and crafted some of the fine gold jewellery that can still be seen in museums throughout Hungary.

Some three decades before the start of the Christian era the Romans conquered the area west and south of the Danube River and established the province of Pannonia – later divided into Upper (Superior) and Lower (Inferior) Pannonia. Subsequent victories over the Celts extended Roman domination across the Tisza River as far as Dacia (today's Romania). The Romans brought writing, viticulture and stone architecture, and established garrison towns and other settlements, the remains of which can still be seen in Óbuda (Aquincum in Roman times; p74), Szombathely (Savaria; p174), Pécs (Sophianae; p297) and Sopron (Scarabantia; p165). They also built baths near the region's thermal waters and their soldiers introduced the new religion of Christianity.

THE GREAT MIGRATIONS

The first of the so-called Great Migrations of nomadic peoples from Asia reached the eastern outposts of the Roman Empire late in the 2nd century AD, and in 270 the Romans abandoned Dacia altogether. Within less than two centuries they were also forced to flee Pannonia by the Huns, whose short-lived empire was established by Attila; he had previously conquered the Magyars near the lower Volga River and for centuries these two groups were thought – erroneously – to share a common ancestry. Attila remains a very common given name for males in Hungary, however.

Germanic tribes such as the Goths, Gepids and Longobards occupied the region for the next century and a half until the Avars, a powerful Turkic people, gained control of the Carpathian Basin in the late 6th

Millennium in Central Europe: A History of Hungary by Lászlo Kontler is recent, definitive and dry. Nonhistorians should turn to Paul Lendvai's more lively The Hungarians: A Thousand Years of Victory in Defeat.

TIMELINE **AD 895–96** | **1000**

| Nomadic Magyar tribes enter and settle in the Carpathian Basin | Stephen (István) is crowned 'Christian King' of Hungary at Esztergom on Christmas Day |

century. They in turn were subdued by Charlemagne in 796 and converted to Christianity. By that time, the Carpathian Basin was virtually unpopulated except for groups of Turkic and Germanic tribes on the plains and Slavs in the northern hills.

THE MAGYARS & THE CONQUEST OF THE CARPATHIAN BASIN

The origin of the Magyars is a complex issue, not in the least helped by the similarity in English of the words 'Hun' and 'Hungary', which are *not* related. One thing is certain: Magyars are part of the Finno-Ugric group of peoples who inhabited the forests somewhere between the middle Volga River and the Ural Mountains in western Siberia as early as 4000 BC.

By about 2000 BC population growth had forced the Finnish-Estonian branch of the group to move westward, ultimately reaching the Baltic Sea. The Ugrians migrated from the southeastern slopes of the Urals into the valleys, and switched from hunting and fishing to primitive farming and raising livestock, especially horses. The Magyars' equestrian skills proved useful half a millennium later when climatic changes brought drought, forcing them to move north to the steppes.

On the plains, the Ugrians turned to nomadic herding. After 500 BC, by which time the use of iron had become commonplace, some of the tribes moved westward to the area of Bashkiria in central Asia. Here they lived among Persians and Bulgars and began referring to themselves as Magyars (from the Finno-Ugric words *mon*, 'to speak', and *e*, 'man').

Several centuries later another group split away and moved south to the Don River under the control of the Khazars, a Turkic people. Here they lived among various groups under a tribal alliance called *onogur*, or '10 peoples'. This is the derivation of the word 'Hungary' in English and 'Ungarn' in German. Their penultimate migration brought them to what modern Hungarians call the Etelköz, the region between the Dnieper and lower Danube Rivers just north of the Black Sea.

Small nomadic groups of Magyars probably reached the Carpathian Basin as early as the mid-9th century AD, acting as mercenaries for various armies. It is believed that while the men were away on a campaign in about 889, the Pechenegs, a fierce people from the Asiatic steppe, allied themselves with the Bulgars and attacked the Etelköz settlements. When they were attacked again in about 895, seven tribes under the leadership of Árpád – the *gyula* (chief military commander) – upped stakes. They crossed the Verecke Pass (in today's Ukraine) into the Carpathian Basin.

The Magyars met almost no resistance and the tribes dispersed in three directions: the Bulgars were quickly dispatched eastward; the Germans had already taken care of the Slavs in the west; and Transylvania was wide open. Known for their ability to ride and shoot, and no longer content with being hired guns, the Magyars began plundering and pillaging. Their raids took them as far as Spain, northern Germany and southern Italy, but in the early 10th century they began to suffer a string of defeats. In 955 they were stopped in their tracks for good by the German king Otto I at the Battle of Augsburg.

This and subsequent defeats – the Magyars' raids on Byzantium ended in 970 – left the tribes in disarray, and they had to choose between their more powerful neighbours – Byzantium to the south and east or the Holy

If you'd like to learn more about the nomadic Magyars, their civilisation and art, go to http://studentorgs.utexas.edu/husa/origins/magyarhist/magyar.art.html.

The early Magyars were such fierce fighters that a common Christian prayer during the Dark Ages was: 'Save us, O Lord, from the arrows of the Hungarians.'

King Andrew II signs the Golden Bull, according the nobility more rights and powers

The Mongols sweep across Hungary, reducing the population by up to one-half

Roman Empire to the west – to form an alliance. In 973 Prince Géza, the great-grandson of Árpád, asked the Holy Roman emperor Otto II to send Catholic missionaries to Hungary. Géza was baptised along with his son Vajk, who took the Christian name Stephen (István), after the first martyr. When Géza died, Stephen ruled as prince. Three years later, he was crowned 'Christian King' Stephen I, with a crown sent from Rome by Otto's erstwhile tutor, Pope Sylvester II. Hungary the kingdom – and the nation – was born.

KING STEPHEN I & THE ÁRPÁD DYNASTY

Stephen set about consolidating royal authority by siezing the land of the independent-minded clan chieftains and establishing a system of *megye* (counties) protected by fortified *vár* (castles). The crown began minting coins and, shrewdly, Stephen transferred much land to his most loyal (mostly Germanic) knights. The king sought the support of the church throughout and, to hasten the conversion of the population, ordered that one in every 10 villages build a church. He also established 10 episcopates, two of which – Kalocsa and Esztergom – were made archbishoprics. Monasteries were set up around the country and staffed by foreign – notably Irish – scholars. By the time Stephen died in 1038 – he was canonised less than half a century after his death – Hungary was a nascent Christian nation, increasingly westward-looking and multiethnic.

Despite this apparent consolidation, the next two and a half centuries until 1301 – the reign of the House of Árpád – would test the kingdom to its limit. The period was marked by continuous struggles between rival pretenders to the throne, weakening the young nation's defences against its more powerful neighbours. There was a brief hiatus under King Ladislas I (László; r 1077–95), who ruled with an iron fist and fended off attacks from Byzantium; and also under his successor Koloman the Booklover (Könyves Kálmán; r 1095–1116), who encouraged literature, art and the writing of chronicles until his death in 1116.

Tensions flared again when the Byzantine emperor made a grab for Hungary's provinces in Dalmatia and Croatia, which it had acquired by

---

BLAME IT ON THE BIRD

The ancient Magyars were strong believers in magic and celestial intervention, and the *táltos* (shaman) enjoyed an elevated position in society. Certain animals – for example, bears, stags and wolves – were totemic and it was taboo to mention them directly by name. Thus the wolf was 'the long-tailed one' and the stag the 'large-antlered one'. In other cases the original Magyar word for an animal deemed sacred was replaced with a foreign loan word: *medve* for 'bear' comes from the Slavic *medved*.

No other ancient totemic animal is better known to modern Hungarians than the turul, a hawk-like bird that supposedly impregnated Emese, the grandmother of Árpád. The legend can be viewed in many ways: as an attempt to foster a sense of common origin and group identity in the ethnically heterogeneous population of the time; as an effort to bestow a sacred origin on the House of Árpád and its rule; or just as a good story.

In the recent past, the fearsome-looking turul has been used as a symbol by the far right – much to the distress of average Hungarians, who simply look upon it as their heraldic 'eagle' or 'lion'.

1458–90	1514
Medieval Hungary enjoys a golden age under the enlightened reign of King Matthias Corvinus	A peasant uprising is crushed, with 70,00 people – including leader György Dózsa – killed

the early 12th century. Béla III (r 1172–96) successfully resisted the invasion and had a permanent residence built at Esztergom (p146), which was then the alternative royal seat to Székesfehérvár. Béla's son, Andrew II (András; r 1205–35), however, weakened the crown when, to help fund his crusades, he gave in to local barons' demands for more land. This led to the Golden Bull, a kind of Magna Carta signed at Székesfehérvár in 1222, which limited some of the king's powers in favour of the nobility.

When Béla IV (r 1235–70) tried to regain the estates, the barons were able to oppose him on equal terms. Fearing Mongol expansion and realising he could not count on the support of his subjects, Béla looked to the west and brought in German and Slovak settlers. He also gave asylum to Turkic Cuman (Kun) tribes displaced by the Mongols in the east. In 1241 the Mongols arrived in Hungary and swept through the country, burning it virtually to the ground and killing an estimated one-third to one-half of its two million people.

To rebuild the country as quickly as possible Béla, known as the 'second founding father', again encouraged immigration, inviting Germans to settle in Transdanubia, Saxons in Transylvania and Cumans on the Great Plain. He also built a string of defensive hilltop castles, including the ones at Buda (p69) and Visegrád (p142). But in a bid to appease the lesser nobility, he handed them large tracts of land. This strengthened their position and demands for more independence even further; by the time of Béla's death in 1270, anarchy had descended upon Hungary. The rule of his reprobate son and heir Ladislas the Cuman (so-called because his mother was a Cuman princess) was equally unsettled. The Árpád line died out in 1301 with the death of Andrew III, who left no heir.

'In 1241 the Mongols arrived in Hungary... killing an estimated one-third to one-half of its two million people'

MEDIEVAL HUNGARY

The struggle for the Hungarian throne following the death of Andrew III involved several European dynasties, but it was Charles Robert (Károly Róbert) of the French House of Anjou who, with the pope's blessing, finally won out in 1308 and ruled for the next three and a half decades. Charles Robert was an able administrator who managed to break the power of the provincial barons (though much of the land remained in private hands), sought diplomatic links with his neighbours and introduced a stable gold currency called the florin (or forint). In 1335 Charles Robert met the Polish and Bohemian kings at the new royal palace in Visegrád to discuss territorial disputes and to forge an alliance that would smash Vienna's control of trade.

Under Charles Robert's son, Louis I the Great (Nagy Lajos; r 1342–82), Hungary returned to a policy of conquest. A brilliant military strategist, Louis acquired territory in the Balkans as far as Dalmatia and Romania and as far north as Poland. He was crowned king of Poland in 1370, but his successes were short-lived; the menace of the Ottoman Turks had begun.

As Louis had no sons, one of his daughters, Mary (r 1382–87), succeeded him. This was deemed unacceptable by the barons, who rose up against the 'petticoat throne'. Within a short time Mary's husband, Sigismund (Zsigmond; r 1387–1437) of Luxembourg, was crowned king. Sigismund's 50-year reign brought peace at home, and there was a great flowering of Gothic art and architecture in Hungary (p40). But while he

1526	1541
Hungary is defeated at the Battle of Mohács; the Turkish occupation lasting more than a century and a half begins	Buda falls to the Ottomans; Hungary is partitioned and shared between the Turks, the Habsburgs and the Transylvanian princes

managed to procure the coveted crown of Bohemia and was made Holy Roman emperor in 1433, he was unable to stop the Ottoman onslaught and was defeated by the Turks at Nicopolis (now Bulgaria) in 1396.

There was an alliance between Poland and Hungary in 1440 that gave Poland the Hungarian crown. When Vladislav I (Ulászló) of the Polish Jagiellon dynasty was killed fighting the Turks at Varna in 1444, János Hunyadi was declared regent. A Transylvanian general born of a Wallachian (Romanian) father, János Hunyadi began his career at the court of Sigismund. His 1456 decisive victory over the Turks at Belgrade (Hungarian: Nándorfehérvár) checked the Ottoman advance into Hungary for 70 years and assured the coronation of his son Matthias (Mátyás), the greatest ruler of medieval Hungary.

Wisely, Matthias (r 1458–90), nicknamed Corvinus (the Raven) from his coat of arms, maintained a mercenary force of 8000 to 10,000 men by taxing the nobility, and this 'Black Army' conquered Moravia, Bohemia and even parts of lower Austria. Not only did Matthias Corvinus make Hungary one of central Europe's leading powers, but under his rule the nation enjoyed its first golden age. His second wife, the Neapolitan princess Beatrice, brought artisans from Italy who completely rebuilt and extended the Gothic palace at Visegrád (p142); the beauty and sheer size of the Renaissance residence was beyond compare in the Europe of the time.

But while Matthias, a fair and just king, busied himself with centralising power for the crown, he ignored the growing Turkish threat. His successor Vladislav II (Ulászló; r 1490–1516) was unable to maintain even royal authority, as the members of the diet (assembly), which met to approve royal funds and decrees, squandered royal funds and expropriated land. In May 1514, what had begun as a crusade organised by the power-hungry archbishop of Esztergom, Tamás Bakócz, turned into a peasant uprising against landlords under the leadership of one György Dózsa.

The revolt was brutally repressed by noble leader John Szapolyai (Zápolyai János). Some 70,000 peasants were tortured and executed; Dózsa himself was fried alive on a red-hot iron throne. The retrograde Tripartitum Law that followed the crackdown codified the rights and privileges of the barons and nobles, and reduced the peasants to perpetual serfdom. By the time Louis II (Lajos) took the throne in 1516 at the tender age of nine, he couldn't count on either side.

THE BATTLE OF MOHÁCS & TURKISH OCCUPATION

The defeat of Louis' ragtag army by the Ottoman Turks at Mohács (p286) in 1526 is a watershed in Hungarian history. On the battlefield near this small town in Southern Transdanubia a relatively prosperous and independent medieval Hungary died, sending the nation into a tailspin of partition, foreign domination and despair that would be felt for centuries afterward.

It would be unfair to lay all the blame on the weak and indecisive teenage King Louis or on his commander-in-chief, Pál Tomori, the archbishop of Kalocsa. Bickering among the nobility and the brutal response to the peasant uprising a dozen years before had severely diminished Hungary's military might, and there was virtually nothing left in the royal coffers. By 1526 the Ottoman sultan Suleiman the Magnificent occupied

> 'The defeat of Louis' ragtag army by the Ottoman Turks at Mohács in 1526 is a watershed in Hungarian history'

much of the Balkans, including Belgrade, and was poised to march on Buda and then Vienna with a force of 100,000 men.

Unable – or, more likely, unwilling – to wait for reinforcements from Transylvania under the command of his rival John Szapolyai, Louis rushed south with a motley army of 26,000 men to battle the Turks and was soundly thrashed in less than two hours. Along with bishops, nobles and an estimated 20,000 soldiers, the king was killed – crushed by his horse while trying to retreat across a stream. John Szapolyai, who had sat out the battle in Tokaj, was crowned king six weeks later. Despite grovelling before the Turks, Szapolyai was never able to exploit the power he had sought so single-mindedly. In many ways greed, self-interest and ambition had led Hungary to defeat itself.

> 'After Buda Castle fell to the Turks in 1541, Hungary was torn into three parts'

After Buda Castle fell to the Turks in 1541, Hungary was torn into three parts. The central section, including Buda, went to the Turks, while parts of Transdanubia and what is now Slovakia were governed by the Austrian House of Habsburg and assisted by the Hungarian nobility based at Bratislava. The principality of Transylvania, east of the Tisza River, prospered as a vassal state of the Ottoman Empire, initially under Szapolyai's son John Sigismund (Zsigmond János; r 1559–71). Though heroic resistance continued against the Turks throughout Hungary, most notably at Kőszeg (see boxed text, p181) in 1532, Eger (see boxed text, p330) 20 years later and Szigetvár (see boxed text, p307) in 1566, this division would remain in place for more than a century and a half.

The Turkish occupation was marked by constant fighting among the three divisions; Catholic 'Royal Hungary' was pitted against both the Turks and the Protestant Transylvanian princes. Gábor Bethlen, who ruled Transylvania from 1613 to 1629, tried to end the warfare by conquering 'Royal Hungary' with a mercenary army of Heyduck peasants and some Turkish assistance in 1620. But both the Habsburgs and the Hungarians themselves viewed the 'infidel' Ottomans as the greatest threat to Europe since the Mongols and blocked the advance.

As Ottoman power began to wane in the 17th century, Hungarian resistance to the Habsburgs, who had used 'Royal Hungary' as a buffer zone between Vienna and the Turks, increased. A plot inspired by the palatine Ferenc Wesselényi was foiled in 1670 and a revolt (1682) by Imre Thököly and his army of *kuruc* (anti-Habsburg mercenaries) was quelled. But with the help of the Polish army, Austrian and Hungarian forces liberated Buda from the Turks in 1686. An imperial army under Eugene of Savoy wiped out the last Turkish army in Hungary at the Battle of Zenta (now Senta in Serbia) 11 years later. Peace was signed with the Turks at Karlowitz (now in Serbia) in 1699.

HABSBURG RULE

The expulsion of the Turks did not result in a free and independent Hungary, and the policies of the Habsburgs' Counter-Reformation and heavy taxation further alienated the nobility. In 1703 the Transylvanian prince Ferenc Rákóczi II assembled an army of *kuruc* forces against the Austrians at Tiszahát in northeastern Hungary. The war dragged on for eight years and in 1706 the rebels 'dethroned' the Habsburgs as the rulers of Hungary. Superior imperial forces and lack of funds, however, forced

1848–49	1867
War of Independence; Lajos Batthyány and 13 of his generals are executed for their role	Act of Compromise creates the Dual Monarchy: Austria (the empire) and Hungary (the kingdom)

the *kuruc* to negotiate a separate peace with Vienna behind Rákóczi's back. The 1703-11 war of independence had failed, but Rákóczi was the first leader to unite Hungarians against the Habsburgs.

The armistice may have brought the fighting to an end, but Hungary was now little more than a province of the Habsburg Empire. Five years after Maria Theresa ascended the throne in 1740, the Hungarian nobility pledged their 'lives and blood' to her at the diet in Bratislava in exchange for tax exemptions on their land. Thus began the period of 'enlightened absolutism' that would continue under the rule of Maria Theresa's son Joseph II (r 1780-90).

Under both Maria Theresa and Joseph, Hungary took great steps forward economically and culturally. Depopulated areas in the east and south were settled by Romanians and Serbs, while German Swabians were sent to Transdanubia. Joseph's attempts to modernise society by dissolving the all-powerful (and corrupt) religious orders, abolishing serfdom and replacing 'neutral' Latin with German as the official language of state administration were opposed by the Hungarian nobility, and he rescinded most (but not all) of these orders on his deathbed.

Dissenting voices could still be heard and the ideals of the French Revolution of 1789 began to take root in certain intellectual circles in Hungary. In 1795 Ignác Martonovics, a former Franciscan priest, and six other prorepublican Jacobites were beheaded at Vérmező (Blood Meadow) in Buda for plotting against the crown.

Liberalism and social reform found their greatest supporters among certain members of the aristocracy, however. Count György Festetics (1755-1819), for example, founded Europe's first agricultural college at Keszthely. Count István Széchenyi (1791-1860), a true Renaissance man and called 'the greatest Hungarian' by his contemporaries (see boxed text, p171), advocated the abolition of serfdom and returned much of his own land to the peasantry.

The proponents of gradual reform were quickly superseded by a more radical faction that demanded more immediate action. The group included Miklós Wesselényi, Ferenc Deák and Ferenc Kölcsey, but the predominant figure was Lajos Kossuth (1802-94). It was this dynamic lawyer and journalist who would lead Hungary to its greatest-ever confrontation with the Habsburgs.

THE 1848-49 WAR OF INDEPENDENCE

Early in the 19th century the Habsburg Empire began to weaken as Hungarian nationalism increased. Suspicious of Napoleon's motives and policies, the Hungarians ignored French appeals to revolt against Vienna and certain reforms were introduced: the replacement of Latin, the official language of administration, with Magyar; a law allowing serfs alternative means of discharging their feudal obligations of service; and increased Hungarian representation in the Council of State.

The reforms carried out were too limited and far too late, however, and the Diet became more defiant in its dealings with the crown. At the same time, the wave of revolution sweeping Europe spurred on the more radical faction. In 1848 the liberal Count Lajos Batthyány was made prime minister of the new Hungarian ministry, which counted

Do you have Habsburg blood – from either the Austrian or the Hungarian branch – flowing through your veins? Find out by logging on to http://worldroots.com /brigitte/royal/royal10 .htm.

Habsburg emperor Joseph was called the 'hatted king' because he was never actually crowned in Hungary.

Deák, Kossuth and Széchenyi among its members. The Habsburgs also reluctantly agreed to abolish serfdom and proclaim equality under the law. But on 15 March a group calling itself the Youth of March, led by the poet Sándor Petőfi, took to the streets to press for even more radical reforms and revolution. Habsburg patience was wearing thin.

In September 1848 the Habsburg forces, under the governor of Croatia, Josip Jelačić, launched an attack on Hungary, and Batthyány's government was dissolved. The Hungarians hastily formed a national defence commission and moved the government seat to Debrecen, where Kossuth was elected governor-president. In April 1849 the parliament declared Hungary's full independence and the Habsburgs were 'dethroned' for the second time.

> 'This 'Age of Dualism' would continue until 1918 and would spark an economic, cultural and intellectual rebirth in Hungary'

The new Habsburg emperor, Franz Joseph (r 1848–1916), was not at all like his feeble-minded predecessor Ferdinand V (r 1835–48). He quickly took action, seeking the assistance of Russian tsar Nicholas I, who obliged with 200,000 troops. Support for the revolution was waning rapidly, particularly in areas of mixed population where the Magyars were seen as oppressors. Weak and vastly outnumbered, the rebel troops were defeated by August 1849.

A series of brutal reprisals ensued. In October Batthyány and 13 of his generals – the so-called 'Martyrs of Arad' – were executed, and Kossuth went into exile in Turkey. (Petőfi died in battle in July of that year.) Habsburg troops then went around the country systematically blowing up castles and fortifications lest they be used by resurgent rebels.

THE DUAL MONARCHY

Hungary was again merged into the Habsburg Empire as a conquered province and 'neoabsolutism' was the order of the day. Passive local resistance and disastrous military defeats for the Habsburgs in 1859 and 1865, however, pushed Franz Joseph to the negotiating table with liberal Hungarians under Deák's leadership.

The result was the Act of Compromise of 1867 (German: Ausgleich), which created the Dual Monarchy of Austria (the empire) and Hungary (the kingdom) – a federated state with two parliaments and two capitals: Vienna and Pest (Budapest when Buda, Pest and Óbuda were merged in 1873). Only defence, foreign relations and customs were shared. Hungary was even allowed to raise a small army.

This 'Age of Dualism' would continue until 1918 and would spark an economic, cultural and intellectual rebirth in Hungary. Agriculture developed, factories were established, and the composers Franz Liszt and Ferenc Erkel wrote beautiful music. The middle class, dominated by Germans and Jews in Pest, burgeoned and the capital entered into a frenzy of building. Much of what you see in Budapest today – from the grand boulevards with their Eclectic-style apartment blocks to the Parliament building and Matthias Church in the Castle district – was built at this time. The apex of this golden age was the six-month exhibition in 1896 celebrating the millennium of the Magyar conquest of the Carpathian Basin, *honfoglalás*.

But all was not well in the kingdom. The city-based working class had almost no rights and the situation in the countryside remained as dire as

1920	1941
Treaty of Trianon carves up much of central Europe, reducing historical Hungary by almost two-thirds	Hungary joins the Axis led by Germany and Italy against the Allies in WWII

it had been in the Middle Ages. Minorities under Hungarian control – Czechs, Slovaks, Croatians and Romanians – were under increased pressure to 'Magyarise', and many viewed their new rulers as oppressors. Increasingly they worked to dismember the empire.

WWI, THE REPUBLIC OF COUNCILS & TRIANON

On 28 July 1914, a month to the day after the assassination of Archduke Franz Ferdinand, the heir to the Habsburg throne, by a Bosnian Serb in Sarajevo, Austria-Hungary declared war on Serbia and entered WWI allied with the German Empire. The result was disastrous, with widespread destruction and hundreds of thousands killed on the Russian and Italian fronts. At the armistice in 1918 the fate of the Dual Monarchy – and Hungary as a multinational kingdom – was sealed.

A republic under the leadership of Count Mihály Károlyi was declared five days after the armistice was signed, but the fledgling republic would not last long. Destitution, the occupation of Hungary by the Allies and the success of the Bolshevik Revolution in Russia had radicalised much of the working class in Budapest. In March 1919 a group of Hungarian communists under a former Transylvanian journalist called Béla Kun seized power. The so-called *Tanácsköztársaság*, or Republic of Councils, set out to nationalise industry and private property and build a fairer society, but mass opposition to the regime led to a brutal reign of 'red terror'. Kun and his comrades, including Minister of Culture Béla Lugosi of *Dracula* fame, were overthrown in just five months by Romanian troops, who occupied the capital.

In June 1920 the Allies drew up a postwar settlement under the Treaty of Trianon that enlarged some countries, truncated others and created several new 'successor states'. As one of the defeated nations with large numbers of minorities demanding independence within its borders, Hungary stood to lose more than most – and it did. The nation was

Miklós Jancsó's film *Csend és Kiáltás* (Silence and Cry; 1967) is a political thriller about a 'red' who takes refuge among politically dubious peasants after the overthrow of Béla Kun's Republic of Councils in 1919.

HUNGARY BEFORE THE 1920 TRIANON TREATY

1944	1945
Germany invades and occupies Hungary; most Hungarian Jews are deported to Nazi concentration camps	Budapest is liberated by the Soviet army in April, a month before full victory in Europe

reduced to about 40% of its historical size and, while it was now largely a homogeneous nation-state, for millions of ethnic Hungarians in Romania, Yugoslavia and Czechoslovakia, the tables had turned: they were now in the minority.

'Trianon' became the singularly most hated word in Hungary, and the *diktátum* is still reviled today as if it were imposed on the nation just yesterday. Many of the problems it created remained for decades and it has coloured Hungary's relations with its neighbours for more than 40 years.

THE HORTHY YEARS & WWII

In March 1920, in Hungary's first-ever election by secret ballot, parliament chose a kingdom as the form of state and – lacking a king – elected as its regent Admiral Miklós Horthy, who would remain in the position until the latter days of WWII. Horthy embarked on a 'white terror' – every bit as fierce as the red one of Béla Kun – that attacked communists and Jews for their roles in supporting the Republic of Councils. As the regime was consolidated it showed itself to be extremely rightist and conservative. Though the country had the remnants of a parliamentary system, Horthy was all-powerful and very few reforms were enacted. On the contrary, the lot of the working class and the peasantry worsened.

One thing on which everyone agreed was that the return of the 'lost' territories was essential for Hungary's development and '*Nem, Nem, Soha!*' (No, No, Never!) became the rallying cry. Early on Prime Minister István Bethlen was able to secure the return of Pécs, illegally occupied by Yugoslavia, and the citizens of Sopron voted in a plebiscite to return to Hungary from Austria, but that was not enough. Hungary obviously could not count on France, Britain and the USA to help recoup its land; instead, it sought help from the fascist governments of Germany and Italy.

Hungary's move to the right intensified throughout the 1930s, though it remained silent when WWII broke out in September 1939. Horthy hoped an alliance would not actually mean having to enter the war, but after recovering northern Transylvania and part of Croatia with Germany's help, he was forced to join the German and Italian–led Axis in June 1941. The war was as disastrous for Hungary as WWI had been, and hundreds of thousands of Hungarian troops died while retreating from Stalingrad, where they'd been used as cannon fodder. Realising too late that his country was on the losing side again, Horthy began negotiating a separate peace with the Allies.

When Germany caught wind of this in March 1944 it sent in its army, which occupied all of Hungary. Under pressure, Horthy installed Ferenc Szálasi, the deranged leader of the pro-Nazi Arrow Cross Party, as prime minister in October before being deported to Germany. (Horthy would later find exile in Portugal, where he died in 1957. Despite some public outcry, his body was taken to Hungary in September 1993 and buried in the family plot at Kenderes, east of Szolnok.)

The Arrow Cross Party moved quickly to quash any opposition, and thousands of liberal politicians and labour leaders were arrested. At the same time, its puppet government introduced anti-Jewish legislation similar to that in Germany and Jews, relatively safe under Horthy, were

The Siege of Budapest: 100 Days in World War II by Krisztián Ungváry examines the battle to overrun a major European capital often forgotten in favour of Warsaw or Berlin.

1949	1956
Communists are in complete control; Hungary is declared the 'People's Republic of Hungary'	Hungary is in revolution in October; János Kádár is installed as leader

rounded up into ghettos by Hungarian Nazis. In May 1944, less than a year before the war ended, some 430,000 Jewish men, women and children were deported to Auschwitz and other labour camps in just over eight weeks, where they starved to death, succumbed to disease or were brutally murdered by the German fascists and their henchmen.

Hungary now became an international battleground for the first time since the Turkish occupation, and bombs began falling on Budapest. The resistance movement drew support from many sides, including the communists. Fierce fighting continued in the countryside, especially near Debrecen and Székesfehérvár, but by Christmas 1944 the Soviet army had encircled Budapest. When the Germans and Hungarian Nazis rejected a settlement, the siege of the capital began. By the time the German war machine had surrendered in April 1945, many of Budapest's homes, historic buildings and churches had been destroyed.

A perplexed US president Franklin D Roosevelt once asked: 'Hungary is a kingdom without a king, run by a regent who's an admiral without a navy?'

THE PEOPLE'S REPUBLIC OF HUNGARY

When free parliamentary elections were held in November 1945, the Independent Smallholders' Party (FKgP) received 57% (245 seats) of the vote. In response, Soviet political officers, backed by the occupying Soviet army, forced three other parties – the Communists, Social Democrats and National Peasants – into a coalition. Limited democracy prevailed, and land-reform laws, sponsored by the communist Minister of Agriculture Imre Nagy, were enacted, doing away with the prewar feudal structure.

Within a couple of years, the Communists were ready to take complete control. After a rigged election (1947) held under a complicated new electoral law, they declared their candidate, Mátyás Rákosi, victorious. The following year the Social Democrats merged with the communists to form the Hungarian Workers' Party.

Rákosi, a big fan of Stalin, began a process of nationalisation and unfeasibly rapid industrialisation at the expense of agriculture. Peasants were forced into collective farms and all produce had to be delivered to state warehouses. A network of spies and informers exposed 'class enemies' (such as Cardinal József Mindszenty; see boxed text, p147) to the secret police called the ÁVO (ÁVH after 1949). The accused were then jailed for spying, sent into internal exile or condemned to labour camps, like the notorious one at Recsk in the Mátra Hills (p327).

Bitter feuding within the party began, and purges and Stalinist show trials became the norm. László Rajk, the communist minister of the interior (which also controlled the secret police), was arrested and later executed for 'Titoism'; his successor János Kádár was tortured and jailed. In August 1949, the nation was proclaimed the 'People's Republic of Hungary'.

After the death of Stalin in March 1953 and Krushchev's denunciation of him three years later, Rákosi's tenure was up and the terror began to abate. Under pressure from within the party, Rákosi's successor Ernő Gerő rehabilitated Rajk posthumously and readmitted Nagy, who had been expelled from the party a year earlier for suggesting reforms. But Gerő was ultimately as much a hardliner as Rákosi and, by October 1956 during Rajk's reburial, whisperings for a genuine reform of the system – 'socialism with a human face' – could already be heard.

1958	1962
Imre Nagy and others are executed by the communist regime for their role in the Uprising	Amnesty is extended to those involved in the 1956 Uprising by the communist government

THE 1956 UPRISING

The nation's greatest tragedy – an event that rocked communism, pitted Hungarian against Hungarian and shook the world – began on 23 October, when some 50,000 university students assembled at Bem tér in Buda shouting anti-Soviet slogans and demanding that Nagy be named prime minister. That night a crowd pulled down the colossal statue of Stalin near Heroes' Square, and shots were fired by ÁVH agents on another group gathering outside the headquarters of Hungarian Radio in Pest. Overnight, Hungary was in revolution.

The next day Nagy, the reform-minded minister of agriculture, formed a government while János Kádár was named president of the Central Committee of the Hungarian Workers' Party. At first it appeared that Nagy might be successful in transforming Hungary into a neutral, multiparty state. On 28 October the government offered amnesty to all those involved in the violence and promised to abolish the ÁVH. On 31 October hundreds of political prisoners were released and widespread reprisals began against ÁVH agents. The next day Nagy announced that Hungary would leave the Warsaw Pact and proclaimed its neutrality.

At this, Soviet tanks and troops crossed into Hungary and within 72 hours began attacking Budapest and other centres. Kádár, who had slipped away from Budapest to join the Russian invaders, was installed as leader.

Fierce street fighting continued for several days – encouraged by Radio Free Europe broadcasts and disingenuous promises of support from the West, which was embroiled in the Suez Canal crisis at the time. When the fighting was over, 25,000 people were dead. Then the reprisals – the worst in Hungarian history and lasting several years – began. About 20,000 people were arrested and 2000 – including Nagy and his associates – were executed. Another 250,000 refugees fled to Austria.

HUNGARY UNDER KÁDÁR

After the revolt, the ruling party was reorganised as the Hungarian Socialist Workers' Party, and Kádár, now both party president and premier, launched a programme to liberalise the social and economic structure, basing his reforms on compromise. (His most quoted line was: 'Whoever is not against us is with us' – a reversal of the Stalinist adage: 'Those not with us are against us'.) In 1968, he and the economist Rezső Nyers unveiled the New Economic Mechanism (NEM) to introduce elements of a market to the planned economy. But even this proved too daring for many party conservatives. Nyers was ousted and the NEM was all but abandoned.

Kádár managed to survive that power struggle and went on to introduce greater consumerism and market socialism. By the mid-1970s Hungary was light years ahead of any other Soviet bloc country in its standard of living, freedom of movement and opportunities to criticise the government. People may have had to wait seven years for a Lada car or 12 years for a telephone, but most Hungarians could at least enjoy access to a second house in the countryside through work or other affiliation and a decent standard of living. The 'Hungarian model' attracted much Western attention – and investment.

The website of the Institute for the History of the 1956 Hungarian Revolution (www.rev.hu) will walk you through the build-up, outbreak and aftermath of Hungary's greatest modern tragedy.

1988	1989
János Kádár is forced to retire in May after more than three decades in power	The electrified fence separating Hungary and Austria is removed in July; the Republic of Hungary is declared in October

But things began to sour in the 1980s. The Kádár system of 'goulash socialism', which seemed so 'timeless and everlasting' (as one Hungarian writer put it) was incapable of dealing with such 'unsocialist' problems as unemployment, soaring inflation and the largest per-capita foreign debt in Eastern Europe. Kádár and the 'old guard' refused to hear talk about party reforms. In June 1987 Károly Grósz took over as premier and less than a year later Kádár was booted out of the party and forced to retire.

RENEWAL & CHANGE

A group of reformers – among them Nyers, Imre Pozsgay, Miklós Németh and Gyula Horn – took charge. Party conservatives at first put a lid on real change by demanding a retreat from political liberalisation in exchange for their support of the new regime's economic policies. But the tide had already turned.

Throughout the summer and autumn of 1988 new political parties were formed and old ones revived. In January 1989 Pozsgay, seeing the handwriting on the wall as Mikhail Gorbachev launched his reforms in the Soviet Union, announced that the events of 1956 had been a 'popular insurrection' and not the 'counter-revolution' that the regime had always called it. Four months later some 250,000 people attended the reburial of Imre Nagy and other victims of 1956 in Budapest.

In July 1989, again at Pozsgay's instigation, Hungary began to demolish the electrified wire fence separating it from Austria. The move released a wave of East Germans holidaying in Hungary into the West and the opening attracted thousands more. The collapse of the communist regimes around the region had become unstoppable.

THE REPUBLIC OF HUNGARY AGAIN

At their party congress in February 1989 the Communists had agreed to give up their monopoly on power, paving the way for free elections in March or April 1990. On 23 October 1989, the 33rd anniversary of the 1956 Uprising, the nation once again became the Republic of Hungary. The party's name was changed from the Hungarian Socialist Workers' Party to the Hungarian Socialist Party (MSZP).

The MSZP's new programme advocated social democracy and a free-market economy, but this was not enough to shake off the stigma of its four decades of autocratic rule. The 1990 vote was won by the centrist Hungarian Democratic Forum (MDF), which advocated a gradual transition to capitalism. The social-democratic Alliance of Free Democrats (SZDSZ), which had called for much faster change, came second and the Socialists trailed far behind. As Gorbachev looked on, Hungary changed political systems with scarcely a murmur and the last Soviet troops left Hungarian soil in June 1991.

In coalition with two smaller parties – the Independent Smallholders and the Christian Democrats (KDNP) – the MDF provided Hungary with sound government during its painful transition to a full market economy. Those years saw Hungary's northern (Czechoslovakia) and southern (Yugoslavia) neighbours split along ethnic lines. Prime Minister József Antall did little to improve Hungary's relations with Slovakia, Romania or Yugoslavia by claiming to be the 'emotional and spiritual'

'In February 1989 the Communists had agreed to give up their monopoly on power'

1990	1991
The centrist MDF wins the first free elections in 43 years in April; Árpád Göncz is elected the first president in August	The last Soviet troops leave Hungarian soil in June

prime minister of the large Magyar minorities in those countries. Antall died in December 1993 after a long fight with cancer and was replaced by interior minister Péter Boross.

Despite initial successes in curbing inflation and lowering interest rates, a host of economic problems slowed the pace of development, and the government's laissez-faire policies did not help. Like most people in the region, Hungarians had unrealistically expected a much faster improvement in their living standards. Most of them – 76% according to a poll in mid-1993 – were 'very disappointed'.

In the May 1994 elections the Socialist Party, led by Gyula Horn, won an absolute majority in parliament. This in no way implied a return to the past, and Horn was quick to point out that it was in fact his party that had initiated the whole reform process in the first place. Árpád Göncz of the SZDSZ was elected for a second five-year term as president in 1995.

'In April 2002 the largest turnout of voters in Hungarian history unseated the government in the country's most closely fought election ever'

THE ROAD TO EUROPE

After its dire showing in the 1994 elections, the Federation of Young Democrats (Fidesz) – which until 1993 limited membership to those aged under 35 in order to emphasise a past untainted by communism, privilege and corruption – moved to the right and added 'MPP' (Hungarian Civic Party) to its name to attract the support of the burgeoning middle class. In the elections of 1998, during which it campaigned for closer integration with Europe, Fidesz-MPP won by forming a coalition with the MDF and the agrarian conservative Independent Smallholders' Party. The party's youthful leader, Viktor Orbán, was named prime minister.

Despite the astonishing economic growth and other gains made by the coalition government, the electorate grew increasingly hostile to Fidesz-MPP's – and Orbán's – strongly nationalistic rhetoric and perceived arrogance. In April 2002 the largest turnout of voters in Hungarian history unseated the government in the country's most closely fought election ever and returned the MSZP, allied with the SZDSZ, to power under Prime Minister Péter Medgyessy, a free-market advocate who had served as finance minister in the Horn government. In August 2004, amid revelations that he had served as a counterintelligence officer in the late 1970s and early 1980s while working in the finance ministry and with the government's popularity at a three-year low, Medgyessy tendered his resignation – the first collapse of a government in Hungary's postcommunist history. Sports Minister Ferenc Gyurcsány of the MSZP was named in his place.

Hungary became a fully fledged member of NATO in 1999 and, with nine so-called accession countries, was admitted into the EU in May 2004. In June 2005 parliament elected László Sólyom, a law professor and founding member of the MDF, as the third president of the republic to succeed the outgoing Ferenc Mádl.

1999	2004
Hungary joins NATO	Hungary is admitted to the EU along with nine other new member-nations

The Culture

THE NATIONAL PSYCHE

When the Italian-American Nobel Prize–winning physicist Enrico Fermi (1901–54), was asked whether he believed extraterrestrials actually existed, he replied: 'They are among us, but they call themselves Hungarians.' Dr Fermi was, of course, referring to the Magyars, an Asiatic people of obscure origins who do not speak an Indo-European language and make up the vast majority of Hungary's population.

On the whole, Hungarians are not uninhibited souls like the extroverted Romanians or the sentimental Slavs, who will laugh or cry at the drop of a hat (or drink). Forget about the impassioned, devil-may-care Gypsy-fiddling stereotype – it doesn't exist. Hungarians are a reserved and somewhat formal people. They are almost always extremely polite in social interaction and the language can be very courtly – even when doing business with the butcher or having a haircut. The standard greeting for a man to a woman (or youngsters to their elders, regardless of sex) is *Csókolom* ('I kiss it' – 'it' being the hand). People of all ages – even close friends – shake hands with gusto when meeting.

The national anthem calls Hungarians 'a people torn by fate' and the overall mood is one of *honfibú*, literally 'patriotic sorrow' but really a penchant for the blues with a sufficient amount of hope to keep most people going. This mood certainly predates what Hungarians call '*az átkos 40 év*' (the accursed 40 years) of communism. To illustrate what she saw as the 'dark streak in the Hungarian temperament', the late US foreign correspondent Flora Lewis recounted a story in *Europe: A Tapestry of Nations* that was the talk of Europe in the early 1930s. 'It was said', she wrote, 'that a song called *Gloomy Sunday* so deeply moved otherwise normal people (in Budapest) that whenever it was played, they would rush to commit suicide by jumping off a Danube bridge.' The song has been covered in English by many artists, including Billie Holiday, Sinéad O'Connor and Björk, and is the subject of German director Rolf Schübel's eponymous romantic drama.

Hungary is a highly cultured and educated society, with a literacy rate of over 99% among those 15 years and over. School is compulsory until the age of 16. About 65% of the population have completed secondary-school and 10% are university graduates. There are currently 19 universities.

WHERE THE FIRST COME LAST

Following a practice unknown outside Asia, Hungarians reverse their names in all uses, and their 'last' name (or surname) always comes first. For example, John Smith is never János Kovács but Kovács János, while Elizabeth Taylor is Szabó Erzsébet and Francis Flour is Liszt Ferenc.

Most titles also follow the structure: Mr John Smith is Kovács János úr. Many women follow the practice of taking their husband's full name. If Elizabeth were married to John, she might be Kovács Jánosné (Mrs John Smith) or, increasingly popular among professional women, Kovácsné Szabó Erzsébet.

To avoid confusion, all Hungarian names in this guide are written in the usual Western manner – Christian name first – including the names of museums, theatres etc if they are translated into English: Budapest's Arany János színház is the János Arany Theatre in English. Addresses are always written in Hungarian as they appear on street signs: Kossuth Lajos utca, Dísz tér etc.

For lots more names
that you may or may
not have known were
Magyar, get hold of
Eminent Hungarians by
Ray Keenoy, a 'light-
hearted look' at the
subject, or check out
www.webenetics.com
/hungary/famous.htm.

Hungary's contributions to specialised education and the sciences have been far greater than its present size and population would suggest. A unique method of music education devised by the composer Zoltán Kodály (1882–1967) is widespread, and the Pető Institute in Budapest has a very high success rate in teaching children with cerebral palsy to walk. Albert Szent-Györgyi (1893–1986) won the Nobel Prize for Medicine or Physiology in 1937 for his discovery of vitamin C; Georg von Békésy (1899–1972) won the same prize in 1961 for his research on the inner ear; and Eugene Paul Wigner (1902–95) received a Nobel Prize in 1963 for his research in nuclear physics.

LIFESTYLE

About two-thirds of all Hungarians now live in towns (opposite) though many retain some connection with the countryside – be it a *nyaralóház* (summer cottage) in the hills or by the lake, or a hut in one of the wine-growing regions.

That's not to say traditional culture is exactly thriving in Hungary. Apart from the Busójárás festival in Mohács (p371), Farsang and other pre-Lenten carnivals are now celebrated at balls and private parties, and only some people go in costume. The sprinkling of water or perfume on young girls on Easter Monday is now rare except in the village of Hollókő (p317) in the Northern Uplands, though the Christmas tradition of Betlehemzés, where young men and boys carry model churches containing a manger from door to door, can still be seen in some parts of the countryside. A popular event for city folk, with tenuous ties to the countryside, is the *disznótor*, which involves the slaughtering of a pig followed by an orgy of feasting and drinking. (The butchering, thankfully, is done somewhere out the back by an able-bodied *paraszt* or peasant.)

Like Spaniards, Poles and many others with a Catholic background, Hungarians celebrate *névnap* (name days) rather than (or as well as) birthdays. Name days are usually the Catholic feast day of their patron saint, but less holy names have a date, too. Most calendars in Hungary list them and it's traditional for men to give women – colleagues, class-mates and neighbours as well as spouses and family members – at least a single blossom.

By and large Hungarians tend to meet their friends and entertain outside the home at cafés and restaurants. If you are invited to a Hungarian home, bring a bunch of flowers (available in profusion all year and very inexpensive) or a bottle of good local wine (p55).

You can talk about anything under the sun – from religion and politics to whether the Hungarian language really is more difficult than Japanese and Arabic – but money is a touchy subject. Traditionally, the discussion of wealth – or even wearing flashy jewellery and clothing – was considered gauche in Hungary. Though it's almost impossible to calculate (the 'black economy' being so widespread and important), the average monthly salary in Hungary at the time of writing was 146,000/94,000Ft gross/net (or €599/386). The minimum wage was 57,000Ft (€235) a month.

Drinking is an important part of social life in a country that has produced wine and fruit brandies for thousands of years. Consumption is high; only Luxembourg and Ireland drink more alcohol per capita in Europe. Alcoholism in Hungary is not as visible to the outsider as it is in, say, Poland or Russia, but it's there nonetheless; official figures suggest that as much as 9% of the population are fully fledged alcoholics.

Hungarian men can be sexist in their thinking, but women do not suffer any particular form of harassment (though domestic violence and rape get little media coverage here). Most men – even drunks – are effusively polite to women. Women may not be made to feel especially welcome when eating or drinking alone, but it's really no different from most other countries in Europe.

Life expectancy in Hungary is very low by European standards: just over 68 years for men and almost 77 for women. The nation also has one of Europe's lowest birth rates – 9.76 per 1000 population, with a population growth of -0.26% – and, sadly, one of the highest rates of suicide (see boxed text, below). Currently 57% of all Hungarian marriages end in divorce.

The lesbian and gay communities keep a low profile outside Budapest. Both groups can enter into domestic partnerships, but such arrangements carry very few legal rights. At the time of writing, the government was considering introducing partnership legislation similar to that of the UK by perhaps as early as 2007.

POPULATION

According to the 2001 census just over 92% of the population is ethnically Magyar. Non-Magyar minorities who make their home here include Germans (2.6%), Serbs and other South Slavs (2%), Slovaks (0.8%), Romanians (0.7%) and others. The number of Roma is officially put at 1.9% of the population (or 193,800 people), though in some sources the figure is twice as high.

The population density is about 109 people per sq km and just under 65% of the total live in towns or cities. Almost a quarter of the population live in one of the nation's six largest cities: Budapest (1.75 million), Debrecen (205,000), Miskolc (178,000), Szeged (161,000), Pécs (157,000) and Győr (129,000). More than half – 54% in fact – of the total 3150 communities in Hungary are in Transdanubia.

For the most part, ethnic minorities in Hungary aren't discriminated against and their rights are inscribed in the constitution. Yet this has not stopped the occasional attack on non-white foreigners, a rise in anti-Semitism and the widespread hatred of and discrimination against Roma.

Significantly almost half as many Magyars (or descendants of ethnic Hungarians) – about five million people – live outside the country's national borders as within them, mostly as a result of the Trianon Treaty (1920), WWII and the 1956 Uprising. The estimated 1.45 million Hungarians in Transylvania (now Romania) constitute the largest ethnic minority in Europe, and there are another 580,000 Magyars

> Cleveland, Ohio, was once the largest 'Hungarian' city outside Hungary and more than 200,000 ethnic Hungarians live in Ohio (www.clevelandmemory .org/hungarian/).

A DUBIOUS DISTINCTION

Hungary has one of the world's highest suicide rates – 60.1 per 100,000 people, surpassed only by Russia and several other former Soviet republics. Psychologists still differ as to why. Some say that Hungarians' inclination to gloom leads to an ultimate act of despair. Others link it to a phenomenon not uncommon here in the late 19th century. As the Hungarian aristocracy withered away, the *kisnemesség* (minor nobility), some of whom were no better off than the local peasants, would do themselves in to 'save their name and honour'. As a result, suicide was – and is – not looked upon dishonourably as such. Victims may be buried in hallowed ground and the euphemistic sentence used in newspaper obituaries is: 'János Kádár/Erzsébet Szabó died suddenly and tragically.' About 60% of suicides are by hanging.

in Slovakia, 295,000 in Serbia, 170,000 in Ukraine, 70,000 in Austria, 16,500 in Croatia, 14,500 in the Czech Republic and 10,000 in Slovenia. Hungarian immigrants to the USA, Canada, Australia and Israel total more than one million.

SPORT

Hungary finished 13th overall at both the 2004 Olympic Games in Athens and the games at Sydney in 2000, with exactly the same number of medals: 17 (eight gold, six silver and three bronze).

Hungarians enjoy attending sporting matches and watching them on TV as much as they do participating. The most popular spectator sports are football and water polo, though auto and horse racing and even chess have their fans.

Football is far and away the nation's favourite sport, and people still talk about the 'match of the century' at Wembley in 1953 when the Magic Magyars beat England 6-3 – the first time England lost a home match. There are a dozen premier league football teams in Hungary, with four of them based in the capital (p120).

In water polo, Hungary has dominated the European Championships (12 times) and the Olympic Games (eight times) for decades, so it's worthwhile catching a professional or amateur game of this exciting seven-a-side sport. For details, see p120.

The Formula One Hungarian Grand Prix (p371), *the* sporting event of the year, takes place near Budapest in August.

MEDIA

As in most European countries, printed news has strong political affiliations in Hungary. Almost all the major broadsheets have left or centre-left leanings, with the exception of the conservative *Magyar Nemzet* (Hungarian Nation).

The most respected publications are the weekly news magazine *Heti Világgazdaság* (World Economy Weekly), known as HVG, and the former Communist Party mouthpiece *Népszabadság* (People's Freedom). This daily broadsheet is now completely independent and has the highest paid circulation (198,000) of any Hungarian newspaper. Hard on its heels is the Swiss-owned *Blikk*, a brash tabloid that focuses on sport, stars and sex – not necessarily in that order. Specialist publications include the weekly intellectual *Élet és Irodalom* (Life and Literature), the satirical biweekly *Hócipő* (Snowshoe) and the mass-circulation *Nemzeti Sport* (National Sport).

With the sale of the state-owned TV2, Magyar Televízió (MTV) controls only one channel (MTV-1) though there is a public terrestrial channel (M2) and a public satellite one (Duna TV). A second private terrestrial channel (RTL Klub) and some 20 private cable and satellite channels nationwide broadcast everything from game and talk shows to classic Hungarian films. Most midrange and top-end hotels and *pensions* have satellite TV, mainly in German.

The public Magyar Rádió (MR; Hungarian Radio) has three stations, and they are named after famous Hungarians: Lajos Kossuth (jazz and news; 98.6AM), the most popular station in the country; Sándor Petőfi (1960s to 1980s music, news and sport; 94.8FM); and Béla Bartók (classical music and news; 105.3FM). Budapest Rádió, the external arm of Hungarian Radio, broadcasts on 88.1FM and 91.9FM.

Juventus (89.5FM), a music station popular with youngsters, claims the second-highest audience in Hungary. Szeged-based Rádió 88 (95.4FM) plays the greatest hits from the 1980s and 90s – just what students want. Danubius Rádió (98.3FM and 103.3FM) is a mixture of popular music and news.

MADONNA, THE MIGHTY TEST MOUSE

When director Alan Parker was scouting around for locations for his film *Evita* in the mid-1990s, he chose that European destination so well known for its swarthy citizens and Latino temperament – Budapest – and lead actress Madonna started packing her Louis Vuittons. While in the Hungarian capital, *az anyagias lány* (the Materialistic Girl) agreed to be interviewed by *Blikk* and the script has since become a cult favourite. *Blikk* asked the questions in Hungarian, which were translated into English for Madonna, then back into Hungarian and published. At the request of *USA Today* – bless 'em – the interview was translated back into English for publication in the USA. The result was, well, a *kupleráj*, literally a 'whorehouse' – slang in Hungarian for one mighty mess. Herewith some snippets:

Blikk: 'Madonna, Budapest says hello with arms that are spread-eagled. Are you in good odour? You are the biggest fan of our young people who hear your musical productions and like to move their bodies in response.'

Madonna: 'Thank you for saying these compliments.' (She holds up her hands.) 'Please stop with taking sensationalist photographs until I have removed my garments for all to see.' (She laughs.) 'This is a joke I have made.'

Blikk: 'Madonna, let's cut toward the hunt. Are you a bold hussy-woman that feasts on men who are tops?'

Madonna: 'Yes, this is certainly something that brings to the surface my longings. In America it is not considered to be mentally ill when a woman advances on her prey in a discotheque setting with hardy cocktails present. And there is a more normal attitude toward leather play-toys.'

Blikk: 'Tell us how you met Carlos, your love servant who is reputed? Did you know he was heaven-sent right off the stick? Or were you dating many other people in your bed at the same time?'

Madonna: 'No, he was the only one I was dating in my bed then, so it is a scientific fact that the baby was made in my womb using him. But as regards those questions, enough! I am a woman and not a test mouse!'

Blikk: 'May we talk about your other "baby", your movie, then? Please do not be denying that the similarities between you and the real Evita are grounded in basis. Power, money, tasty food, Grammys – all these elements are afoot.'

Madonna: 'What is up in the air with you? Evita never was winning a Grammy!'

Blikk: 'OK, here's a question from left space. What was your book *Slut* about?'

Madonna: 'It was called *Sex*, my book.'

Blikk: 'Not in Hungary. Here it was called *Slut*... There is much interest in you from this geographical region, so I must ask this final question. How many Hungarian men have you dated in bed? Are they No 1? How are they comparing to Argentine men, who are famous for being tip-top as well?'

Madonna: 'Well, to avoid aggravating global tension, I won't say. It's a tie.' (She laughs.) 'No, no, I am serious now. See here I am working like a canine all the way around the clock! I am too busy even to try the goulash that makes your country for the record books.'

Blikk: 'Thank you for your candid chitchat.'

Madonna: 'No problem, friend who is a girl.'

Blikk is available at quality newsstands nationwide.

RELIGION

Hungarians tend to have a more pragmatic approach to religion than most of their neighbours, and almost none of the bigotry. It has even been suggested that this generally sceptical view of matters of faith has led to Hungarians' high rate of success in science and mathematics. Except in villages and on the most important holy days (Easter, the Assumption of Mary, and Christmas), churches are never full. The Jewish community in Budapest, on the other hand, has seen a great revitalisation in recent years – mostly due to an influx of Orthodox Jews from the USA and Israel.

Of those Hungarians declaring religious affiliation in the 2001 census, about 52% said they were Roman Catholic, 16% Reformed (Calvinist) Protestant and nearly 3% Evangelical (Lutheran) Protestant. There are also small Greek Catholic (2.5%), and Orthodox and other Christian (1%) congregations. Hungary's Jews (though not always practicing) number about 80,000, down from a prewar population of nearly 10 times that amount, with almost 90% living in Budapest.

ARTS

The arts in Hungary have been both starved and nourished by the pivotal events in the nation's history. King Stephen's conversion to Catholicism brought Romanesque and Gothic art and architecture to Hungary, while the Turkish occupation nipped most of Hungary's Renaissance in the bud. The Habsburgs opened the doors to baroque influences. The arts thrived under the Dual Monarchy (Austro-Hungarian Empire), through truncation and even under fascism. The early days of communism brought socialist-realist art celebrating wheat sheaves and muscle-bound steelworkers to a less-than-impressed populace, but much money was spent on music and 'correct art' such as classical theatre.

Painting & Architecture

The abbey church at Ják (p177) is a fine example of Romanesque architecture, and there are important Gothic churches in Nyírbátor (p360) and Sopron (p165). For Gothic art, have a look at the 15th-century altarpieces done by various masters at the Christian Museum in Esztergom (p147). The Corpus Christi Chapel in the basilica at Pécs (p297), the Bakócz Chapel in Esztergom Basilica (p145) and the Royal Palace at Visegrád (p142) contain exceptional examples of Renaissance masonry.

The dynamic Association of Young Artists (www .c3.hu/fkse), a branch of the Hungarian Artists' National Association that only allows those under 35 to join it, is a showcase for contemporary Hungarian art.

Baroque abounds in Hungary; you can see architectural examples in virtually country town. For something on a grand scale, visit the Esterházy Palace at Fertőd (p169) or the Minorite church in Eger (p330). The ornately carved altars in the Minorite church at Nyírbátor (p360) and the Abbey Church in Tihany (p208) are baroque masterpieces. The greatest painters of this period were the 18th-century artists Anton Maulbertsch (frescoes in the Ascension Church at Sümeg; p204) and István Dorffmeister (frescoes in the Bishop's Palace in Szombathely; p174).

Distinctly Hungarian art and architecture didn't come into its own until the mid-19th century when Mihály Pollack, József Hild and Miklós Ybl were changing the face of Budapest, or racing around the country building mansions and cathedrals. The Romantic Nationalist school of heroic paintings, best exemplified by Bertalan Székely (1835–1910) and Gyula Benczúr (1844–1920), fortunately gave way to the realism of Mihály Munkácsy (1844–1900), the 'painter of the *puszta*'. The greatest painters from this period were Tivadar Kosztka Csontváry (1853–1919), who has been compared with Van Gogh, and József Rippl-Rónai (1861–1927), the key exponent of Secessionist art in Hungary. There are museums dedicated to their work in Pécs (p297) and Kaposvár (p303), respectively. Favourite artists of the 20th century include Victor Vasarely (1908–97), the so-called father of Op Art who began life as Győző Vásárhelyi but changed his name when he emigrated to Paris in 1930, and the sculptor Amerigo Tot (1909–84). There are museums dedicated to Victor Vasarely in Pécs (p298) and Budapest (p74), and one with Amerigo Tot's work in Pécs (p298).

The Romantic Eclectic style of Ödön Lechner (Budapest Museum of Applied Arts; p94) and Hungarian Secessionist or Art Nouveau (Reök Palace in Szeged; p261) brought unique architecture to Hungary at the

HUNGARIAN FOLK ART

Hungary has one of the richest folk traditions in Europe and this is where the country often has come to the fore in art. Many urban Hungarians probably wouldn't want to hear that, considering folk art a bit *déclassé* and its elevation the work of the communist regime, but it's true.

As segments of the Hungarian peasantry became more prosperous in the early 18th century, they tried to make their world more attractive by painting and decorating objects and clothing. It's important to remember two things when looking at folk art. First, with very few exceptions (such as the 'primitive' paintings in Kecskemét's Hungarian Museum of Naive Artists; p244), only practical objects were decorated. Second, this was not 'court art' or the work of artisans making Chinese brocade or Fabergé eggs. It was the work of ordinary people trying to express the simple world around them in a new and different way.

The main centre of cottage weaving has always been the Sárköz region (p284), near Szekszárd in Southern Transdanubia – its distinctive black and red fabric is copied everywhere. Simpler homespun material can be found in the Northeast, especially around the Tiszahát. Because of the abundance of reeds in these once marshy areas, the people here became skilled at cane weaving as well.

Three groups of people stand out for their embroidery, the acme of Hungarian folk art: the Palóc of the Northern Uplands, especially around the village of Hollókő (p317); the Matyó from Mezőkövesd (p334); and the women of Kalocsa (p248). The various differences and distinctions are discussed in the appropriate chapters, but to our minds no-one works a needle like a Matyó seamstress. Also impressive are the woollen waterproof coats called *szűr*, once worn by herders on the Great Plain, which were masterfully embroidered by men using thick, 'furry' yarn.

Folk pottery is world-class here and no Hungarian kitchen is complete without a couple of pairs of matched plates or shallow bowls hanging on the walls. The centre of this industry is the Great Plain – Hódmezővásárhely, Karcag and Tiszafüred, in particular – though fine examples also come from Transdanubia, especially from the Őrség region. There are jugs, pitchers, plates, bowls and cups, but the rarest and most attractive are the *írókázás fazékok* (inscribed pots), usually celebrating a wedding day, or in the form of animals, or people such as the *Miskai kancsó* (Miska jugs), not unlike English Toby jugs, from the Tisza River region. Nádudvar near Hajdúszoboszló on the Great Plain specialises in black pottery – striking items and far superior to the greyish stuff produced in Mohács in Southern Transdanubia.

Objects carved from wood or bone – mangling boards, honey-cake moulds, mirror cases, tobacco holders, saltcellars – were usually the work of herders or farmers idle in winter. The shepherds and swineherds of Somogy County south of Lake Balaton and the cowherds of the Hortobágy excelled at this work, and their illustrations of celebrations and local 'Robin Hood' outlaws like Horseshoe Steve are always fun to look at.

Most people made and decorated their own furniture in the old days, especially cupboards for the *tiszta szoba* (parlour) and *tulipán ládák* (trousseau chests with tulips painted on them). Among the finest traditional furniture in Hungary are the tables and chairs made of golden spotted poplar from the Gemenc Forest near Szekszárd. The oaken chests decorated with geometrical shapes from the Ormánság region of Southern Transdanubia are superior to the run-of-the-mill tulip chests.

end of the 19th century and the start of the 20th. Art Nouveau fans will find in cities such as Budapest, Szeged and Kecskemét some of the best examples of the style outside Brussels, Nancy and Vienna.

Postwar architecture in Hungary is almost completely forgettable. One exception is the work of Imre Makovecz, who has developed his own 'organic' style (not always popular locally) using unusual materials like tree trunks and turf. His work is everywhere, but among the best (or strangest) examples are the cultural centres at Sárospatak (p350) and Szigetvár (p306), and the Evangelist church in Siófok (p190).

A turning point for modern art in Hungary came in 2005 when the Ludwig Museum (p94) moved from Castle Hill to its new purpose-built premises in the Palace of Arts, opposite the National Theatre.

Music & Dance

Hungary has produced many leading musicians in the world of classical music, but one person stands head and shoulders above the rest: Franz (or, in Hungarian, Ferenc) Liszt (1811–86). Liszt established the Academy of Music in Budapest and liked to describe himself as 'part Gypsy'. Some of his works, notably the 20 *Hungarian Rhapsodies,* do in fact echo the traditional music of the Roma.

Ferenc Erkel (1810–93) is the father of Hungarian opera, and two of his works – the nationalistic *Bánk Bán,* based on József Katona's play of that name, and *László Hunyadi* – are standards at the Hungarian State Opera House. Erkel also composed the music for the national anthem, *Himnusz.*

Imre Kálmán (1882–1953) was Hungary's most celebrated composer of operettas. The *Queen of the Csárdás* and *Countess Marica* are two of his popular works.

Béla Bartók (1881–1945) and Zoltán Kodály (1882–1967) made the first systematic study of Hungarian folk music, travelling together and recording throughout the Magyar linguistic region in 1906. Both used their findings in some of their compositions – Bartók in *Bluebeard's Castle,* for example, and Kodály in the *Peacock Variations.*

There are many symphony orchestras both in the capital and provincial cities. Among the finest are the Budapest Festival Orchestra and the Hungarian Radio Symphony Orchestra, which uses the name Budapest Symphony Orchestra on certain domestic and on all of its foreign recordings.

Pop music is as popular here as anywhere – indeed, Hungary has one of Europe's biggest pop spectacles, the annual Sziget Music Festival (p371). It attracts more then 200 bands and an audience of almost 370,000 people.

It is important to distinguish between 'Gypsy' music and Hungarian folk music. Gypsy music as it is known and heard in Hungarian restaurants from Budapest to Boston is urban schmaltz and based on tunes called *verbunkos* played during the Rákóczi independence wars. At least two fiddles, a bass and a cymbalom (a curious stringed instrument played with sticks) are *de rigueur.* You can hear this saccharine *csárdas* (Hungarian-style restaurant/ inn) music at almost any fancy hotel restaurant in the provinces or get hold of a recording by Sándor Déki Lakatos and his band.

Hungarian folk musicians play violins, zithers, hurdy-gurdies, bagpipes and lutes on a five-tone diatonic scale. Watch out for Muzsikás (with the inimitable Marta Sebestyén or on her own); Ghymes, a Hungarian folk band from Slovakia; and the Hungarian group Vujicsics that mixes elements of South Slav music. The music of the Csángó people, an ethnic group of Hungarians living in eastern Transylvania and Moldavia, is particularly haunting and is performed during the 10-day Jászberény Summer (p371), which attracts folk aficionados from all over. For something more contemporary – Western beats with East European tonal flavours – listen to Anima Sound System, in particular their *Hungarian Astronaut* CD.

To confuse matters, Roma – as opposed to Gypsy – music traditionally sung a cappella (though sometimes it is backed with percussion and even guitar). Two of the best-known modern Roma groups are Kalyi Jag (Black Fire), from northeastern Hungary and led by Gusztav Várga, and Romano Drom. Check out the latter's *Romano Trip: Gypsy Grooves from Eastern Europe,* where Roma folk meets world music, with an electronic twist.

Attending a *táncház* (dance house; p118) is an excellent way to hear Hungarian folk music and even to learn to dance. It's all good fun and they're relatively easy to find, especially in Budapest where the dance house revival began. Hungary also has ballet companies based in Budapest, Pécs and Szeged, but the best by far is the Győr Ballet (p159).

When Almásy (Ralph Fiennes) plays a Hungarian folk song on the phonograph for Katharine (Kristin Scott Thomas) in Anthony Minghella's film *The English Patient* (1996) it is Marta Sebestyén singing *Szerelem, Szerelem* (Love, Love).

For times, dates and places of *táncház* meetings and performances in Budapest and around the rest of the country, check out the website www .tanchaz.hu/.

Literature

No-one could have put it better than the poet Gyula Illyés (1902–83), who wrote: 'The Hungarian language is at one and the same time our softest cradle and our most solid coffin.' The difficulty and subtlety of the Magyar tongue has excluded most outsiders from Hungarian literature for centuries and, though it would be wonderful to be able to read the swashbuckling odes and love poems of Bálint Balassi (1554–94) or Miklós Zrínyi's *Peril of Sziget* (1651) in the original, most people will have to make do with their works in translation (see boxed text, p44).

Sándor Petőfi (1823–49) is Hungary's most celebrated and accessible poet and a line from his work *National Song* became the rallying cry for the 1848–49 War of Independence, in which Petőfi fought and died. A deeply philosophical play called *The Tragedy of Man* by Imre Madách (1823–64), published a decade after Hungary's defeat in the War of Independence, is still considered to be the country's greatest classical drama.

Hungary's defeat in 1849 led many writers to look to Romanticism for inspiration and solace: winners, heroes and knights in shining armour became popular subjects. Petőfi's comrade-in-arms, János Arany (1817–82), whose name is synonymous with impeccable Hungarian, wrote epic poetry (including the *Toldi Trilogy*) and ballads.

Another friend of Petőfi, the prolific novelist and playwright Mór Jókai (1825–1904), gave expression to heroism and honesty in such wonderful works as *The Man with the Golden Touch* and *Black Diamonds*. This 'Hungarian Dickens' still enjoys widespread popularity. Another perennial favourite, Kálmán Mikszáth (1847–1910), wrote satirical tales such as *The Good Palóc People* and *St Peter's Umbrella*, in which he poked fun at the gentry in decline. Apparently the former US president Theodore Roosevelt (1858–1919) enjoyed the latter so much that he insisted on visiting the ageing novelist during a European tour in 1910.

Zsigmond Móricz (1879–1942) was a very different type of writer. His works, in the tradition of Émile Zola, examined the harsh reality of peasant life in Hungary in the late 19th century. His contemporary Mihály Babits (1883–1941), poet and editor of the influential literary magazine *Nyugat* (West), made the rejuvenation of Hungarian literature his lifelong work.

Two 20th-century poets are unsurpassed in Hungarian letters: Endre Ady (1877–1919), sometimes described as a successor to Petőfi, was a reformer who ruthlessly attacked Hungarians' growing complacency and materialism, provoking a storm of protest from right-wing nationalists. The work of socialist poet Attila József (1905–37) expressed the alienation felt by individuals in the modern age; *By the Danube* is brilliant even in English. József ran afoul of both the underground communist movement and the Horthy regime. Tragically, he threw himself under a train near Lake Balaton at the age of 32. A recent 'discovery' is the late Sándor Márai (1900–89), whose crisp style has encouraged worldwide interest in Hungarian literature.

Among Hungary's most important contemporary writers are Imre Kertész (1929–), György Konrád (1933–), Péter Nádas (1942–) and Péter Esterházy (1950–). Konrád's *A Feast in the Garden* (1985) is an almost autobiographical account of a Jewish community in a small eastern Hungarian town. *A Book of Memoirs* by Nádas traces the decline of communism written in the style of Thomas Mann and has been made into a film. In *The End of a Family Story,* Nádas uses a child narrator as a filter for the adult experience of 1950s communist Hungary. Esterházy's partly autobiographical *Celestial Harmonies* (2000) paints a favourable portrait of the protagonist's father. His later *Revised Edition* (2002) is based on documents revealing his father to have been a government informer during the communist regime.

Culture Shock! Hungary: A Guide to Customs & Etiquette by Zsuzsanna Ardo goes beyond the usual anecdotal information and observations offered in this series and is virtually an anthropological and sociological study of the Magyar race.

Hungarian Literature Online (www.hlo.hu) leaves no page unturned in the world of Hungarian books, addressing everyone from writers and editors to translators and publishers.

HUNGARIAN WRITERS IN ENGLISH

The following is a small selection of key Hungarian literary works available in English at Bestsellers or the Writers' Bookshop in Budapest (p65).

■ The Tragedy of Man (Imre Madách, 1859–60) This lyrical drama, inspired by Milton and Goethe, puts a different spin on human history and examines the limitations of science and technology in dealing with moral issues.

■ The Man with the Golden Touch (Mór Jókai, 1872) Jókai's best work is a realistic portrait of the cruel world of finance, which is conquered by a hero with the 'Midas touch', and an attack on the commercialism of modern civilisation.

■ St Peter's Umbrella (Kálmán Mikszáth, 1895) This delightful novel is a mixture of legend, fairy tale and social satire woven into the upbeat tale of a successful search for happiness.

■ Eclipse of the Crescent Moon (Géza Gárdonyi, 1901) This Boys Own–style page-turner tells the story of the siege of Eger by the Turks in 1552 and an orphaned peasant boy who grows up to become one of the greatest (fictional) heroes in Hungarian history.

■ Be Faithful unto Death (Zsigmond Móricz, 1921) This moving story of a bright and sensitive schoolboy being educated at an old, very established boarding school in Debrecen is a microcosm of Hungary truncated after the treaty of Trianon.

■ Skylark (Dezső Kosztolányi, 1924) The story of a spinster living in the back of beyond of provincial Hungary conceals tensions and the purposeless of life.

■ The Story of My Wife (Milan Füst, 1942) This complex tale of obsession concerns a Dutch captain's attempts to learn the truth about his coquettish French wife.

■ Embers (Sándor Márai, 1942) The story of a lifelong grievance that consumed the lives and friendship of two men for more than four decades.

Novelist and Auschwitz survivor Kertész won the Nobel Prize for Literature in 2002, the first time a Hungarian has gained this distinction. Of his eight novels, only three – Fateless (1975), Kaddish for a Child Not Born (1990) and Liquidation (2003) – have been translated into English.

Cinema

Scarce government grants has limited the production of recent Hungarian films to under 20, but there are a handful of good (and even great) ones. For classics, look out for films by Oscar-winning István Szabó (Sweet Emma, Dear Böbe, The Taste of Sunshine), Miklós Jancsó (Outlaws) and Péter Bacsó (The Witness, Live Show). Other favourites are Simon Mágus, the surrealistic tale of two magicians and a young woman in Paris from Ildikó Enyedi, and her Tender Interface about the brain-drain from Hungary after WWII.

Péter Timár's Csinibaba is a satirical look at life – and film production quality – during communism. Zimmer Feri, set on Lake Balaton, pits a young practical joker against a bunch of loud German tourists; the typo in the title is deliberate. Timár's 6:3 takes viewers back to that glorious moment when Hungary defeated England in football (p38). Gábor Herendi's Something America is the comic tale of a filmmaking team trying to profit from an expatriate Hungarian who pretends to be a rich producer.

Of more recent vintage is Hungarian-American director Nimród Antal's Kontroll, a high-speed romantic thriller set almost entirely in the Budapest metro in which assorted outcasts, lovers and dreamers interact. And if it's unusual you want, try Hukkle by György Pálfi, a curious film where a bizarre cacophony of hiccups, belches, buzzing and grunting replaces dialogue. A sinister David Lynch-like classic or lad's movie? You decide.

Environment

THE LAND

Hungary occupies the Carpathian Basin in the very centre of Eastern Europe. It covers 93,030 sq km – about the same size as Portugal or the US state of Indiana – and shares 2171km of border with seven countries: Austria, Slovakia, Ukraine, Romania, Serbia, Croatia and Slovenia.

The country has three basic topographies: the low-lying regions of the Great Plain (Nagyalföld) in the east, centre and southeast, and of the Little Plain (Kisalföld) in the northwest, which together account for two-thirds of Hungary's territory; the mountain ranges in the north; and the hilly regions of Transdanubia in the west and southwest. The longest rivers are the Tisza (596km in Hungary) and the Danube (417km), which divide the country into three parts. The country has well over 1000 lakes, of which the largest by far is Lake Balaton (596 sq km) followed by Lake Tisza (127 sq km).

> If you want to learn more about what the Hungarians called the *szőke* (blond) Danube, check out Claudio Magris' *The Danube*. Part history, part philosophy and part travelogue, it's an overall excellent read.

Regions

Hungary's topographical divisions do not accurately reflect the country's cultural and subtler geographical differences, nor do the 19 administrative *megye* (counties) help travellers much. Instead, Hungary can be divided into eight main regions: Budapest and environs, the Danube Bend, Western Transdanubia, the Lake Balaton region, Southern Transdanubia, the Great Plain, the Northern Uplands and the Northeast (see map, p10).

Greater Budapest, by far Hungary's largest city with about 1.75 million people and the most exciting spot in Hungary for travellers, has for its borders Csepel Island in the Danube River to the south, the start of the Great Plain to the east, the Buda Hills to the west and the Danube Bend to the north. The Danube splits the city in two, with flat Pest on the east side and hilly Buda on the west.

> Budapest is the sixth-largest city in the EU, after London, Berlin, Madrid, Rome and Paris.

The Danube Bend, an area of great beauty and historical significance, is the point at which the river, flowing eastward across Europe, is forced southward by two small ranges of hills. Its main city is Esztergom.

Transdanubia – the area 'across the Danube' to the west – is a region of striking contrasts. Western Transdanubia is both hilly and flat – the Little Plain is to the north – and its chief centres are the historical cities of Győr, Sopron and Szombathely, all rich in art and architecture. Central Transdanubia is dominated by Lake Balaton, the nation's watery playground. Székesfehérvár is the largest city here. Southern Transdanubia, with almost Mediterranean-like Pécs as its 'capital', is less hilly and a treasure-trove of traditional architecture and culture. Wine is produced throughout Transdanubia but the reds of the south are the best.

> The mean depth of Balaton, the largest lake in Europe outside Scandinavia, is only 3m, though the lake floor drops to 12m in the Tihany Strait.

The Great Plain, often called the *puszta,* is a prairie scarcely 200m above sea level that stretches for hundreds of kilometres east of the Danube River. The central part, the most industrialised area of the plain, has Szolnok as its major town. The Eastern Plain is largely saline grassland and given over to the breeding of livestock, though some of the land is national parkland and ideal for bird-watching. Debrecen is the principal city. The Southern Plain is agriculturally rich, with cereal crops and fruit in abundance, and the occasional farmstead breaking the scenic monotony. Kecskemét and Szeged, both with more than their share of things to see and do, are market towns that have grown into cities on the plain. Horse riding is a major pastime here.

There are three distinct Magyar dog breeds: the giant white komondor, a sheepdog with a corded coat; the short-haired vizsla pointing dog; and the unforgettable mop-like puli herding dog.

The Northern Uplands is Hungary's 'mountainous' region and has a number of peaks averaging between 400m and 800m, the highest of which is Kékes (1014m) in the Mátra Hills. Abutting the forested hills and valleys of the Northern Uplands are lush vineyards and sprawling factories, many now in decline. Industrial Miskolc and lovely Eger are the region's main cities.

Northeast Hungary is much lower than the Northern Uplands but not quite as flat as the Great Plain. It is a fruit-growing region and ethnically quite heterogeneous, with the bulk of the nation's Roma population living here. This is the place to come if you are interested in indigenous folk culture and architecture, especially wooden churches. Nyíregyháza is the main centre.

WILDLIFE
Animals

While there are a lot of common European animals in Hungary (deer, hare, wild boar, foxes, and wolves) as well as some rare species (wild cat, lake bat, and Pannonian lizard), wildlife is not a major attraction unless you count our fine-feathered friends. Well over half of the country's 450 known vertebrates are birds, for the most part waterfowl attracted by the rivers, lakes and wetlands. For details on the best places to watch birds in Hungary, see boxed text, p51.

Plants

In addition to national parks, Hungary maintains 1300 'landscape protection' and 'nature conservation' areas that range from such places as the Tihany peninsula on Lake Balaton to a clump of ancient oak trees in Hajdúböszörmény.

Just over 50% of Hungary is under cultivation of some form or another; 19% of it is forested but only 10% is natural forest. It is home to some 2200 flowering plant species and, because of its topography and transitional climate, many of them are not normally found at this latitude. Much of the flora in the Villány and Mecsek Hills of Southern Transdanubia, for example, is usually seen only around the Mediterranean. The salty Hortobágy region on the Eastern Plain has many plants normally found by the seashore, and the Nyírség area is famous for meadow flowers. The Gemenc Forest on the Danube near Szekszárd, the Little Balaton in the centre of Transdanubia and the Tisza River backwater east of Kecskemét are all important wetlands. Most of the trees in the nation's forested areas are deciduous (beech, oak and birch); only a small percentage are fir.

NATIONAL PARKS

Hungary currently counts nine Unesco World Heritage sites, of which two (the caves of the Aggtelek and Slovak Karst and Lake Fertő) are shared with neighbouring Slovakia and Austria, respectively.

Hungary now has 11 national parks, up from just five a decade ago. The three on the Great Plain – Hortobágy National Park (also a Unesco World Heritage site; p238), Kiskunság National Park (p246) and Körös-Maros National Park (p273) – protect the wildlife, fragile wetlands and marsh and saline grasslands of the *puszta*. In Western Transdanubia there are three largely forested parks: Őrség National Park in the Őrség region (p185), the Írottkő Forest near Kőszeg (p183), which calls itself a 'nature park', and Fertő-Hanság National Park at Lake Fertő (p162), which Hungarians share with Austrians (who call it Neusiedlersee). The Northern Uplands counts two national parks: one in the almost completely wooded Bükk Hills (p327) and the other in the Aggtelek karst region (Aggtelek National Park; p342), with its extensive system of caves and streams hewn into the limestone that spills into Slovakia.

Hungary's other national parks are Danube-Dráva National Park, which incorporates the Gemenc Forest (p283) in Southern Transdanubia; Balaton Uplands National Park (p195), within the hilly areas north of Lake Balaton; and Danube-Ipoly National Park (p141), on the Danube Bend.

RESPONSIBLE TOURISM

The rules and regulations in most national parks and nature reserves are fairly obvious: no littering, no picking flowers, no collecting insects (eg butterflies), no open fires except in designated areas, no loud noises or music and so on. Bear in mind that the flora and fauna of certain ecosystems – Hortobágy National Park, for example – are very fragile, and you should never stray from marked hiking trails and paths.

Minimise the waste you carry out of protected areas by removing packaging and taking no more food than you need. Don't use detergents or toothpaste in or near watercourses, even if they are biodegradable.

Traffic congestion on Hungary's roads is a problem in peak season, and visitors will do themselves and residents a favour if they forgo driving and use public transport, especially in the cities. Also remember to use the recycling banks on the streets of larger towns and the litter bins.

ENVIRONMENTAL ISSUES

Pollution is a large and costly problem, particularly because Hungary has had to hasten the pace of cleaning up its act before joining the EU. Low-grade coal that fuels some power plants and industries creates sulphur dioxide and acid rain. Nitrogen oxide emitted by cars on highways and in city centres causes severe air pollution. Over-use of nitrate fertilisers in agriculture has caused groundwater to become contaminated with phosphates.

There has been a marked improvement since the creation of the Ministry of the Environment in the 1990s. Between 1990 and 1997, for example, sulphur dioxide emissions fell by one-third and are expected to decrease further following the closure or conversion to gas turbines of all but one or possibly two – in Oroszlány south of Tata and the Mátra Hills in the Northern Uplands – of the nation's coal-fired power stations. At the same time nitrogen oxide levels dropped by only one-fifth. Vehicles are burning cleaner fuel but there are a lot more of them on the roads. The Soviet-designed nuclear power generator at Paks in Southern Transdanubia produces about one-third of the nation's electricity. And the total amount of annual waste produced has dropped from 106 million tonnes to between 75 and 80 million tonnes, which corresponds to the EU average.

Log on to www.rec.org to learn about the Regional Environmental Center for Central and Eastern Europe, a Szentendre-based body developing a common ecosystem strategy and solving environmental problems in the region.

Activities

A visit to Hungary is not just an educational or cultural experience – there are plenty of outstanding outdoor activities on offer, too. Indeed, you could forsake many of the country's sights and spend your entire time boating, cycling, bird-watching or taking the waters.

Urbanites love a day out in the country to escape their relatively cramped living quarters and the pollution of the towns and cities, and nothing is more sacred than the *kirándulás* (outing), which can be a day of hiking, swimming, horse riding or just a picnic of *gulyás* (beef goulash soup) cooked in a *bogrács*, a kettle suspended over a fire with a tripod, in the open air by a river or lake.

THERMAL BATHS

Since the Romans settlers have enjoyed Hungary's thermal waters; some 1300 springs are registered and 300 used for bathing purposes. Many of the 150 or so spas open to the public, such as those at Balatonfüred (p211), Hajdúszoboszló (p241), Hévíz (p197) and Gyula (p277), are very serious affairs indeed, with people coming to 'take the waters' for specific maladies: respiratory, muscular, cardiac or gynaecological. Most hotels at these spas offer cure packages (including accommodation, use of the spa and other facilities, medical examination, treatments etc) that last a week or longer. **Danubius Travels** (☎ 1-888 8200; www.danubiusgroup.com; V Szervita tér 8) in Budapest is the expert in the field and books packages. **Tourinform** (☎ 1 438 8080, 24hr information hotline 06 80 630 800; www.tourinform.hu), with offices nationwide, distributes the useful *Health and Wellness* brochure listing spa centres across Hungary.

One of the biggest growth industries in Hungarian tourism is the emergence (or rather conversions from old outdated spas) of huge wellness centres such as the new modern complex at Sárvár (p180) and the Raba Quelle at Győr (p158). They remain serious centres for those seeking a cure, of course, but they also offer holistic and beauty treatments.

HORSE RIDING

There's a Hungarian saying that the Magyars were 'created by God to sit on horseback'. Judging from the number of stables, riding schools and trails around the country, that is still true today.

A lot of riding in Hungary is the follow-the-leader variety up to a castle, through open fields, or in horse-drawn coaches. Larger schools, however, have horses that can be taken into the hills or across the *Puszta* (Great Plain) by more experienced riders. These schools also offer lessons. Not surprisingly, the best centres are on the Great Plain – at Máta (p239) near Hortobágy and Bugacpuszta (p246) near Kecskemét and Solt (p257), north of Kalocsa. In Transdanubia you'll find good a school in Orfű (p302) while around Lake Balaton they're at Sümeg (p205) and Keszthely (p195). However, nothing compares with mounting a Lipizzaner at the stud farm at Szilvásvárad (p336) in the Northern Uplands.

The nonprofit **Hungarian Equestrian Tourism Association** (MLTSZ; ☎ 1-456 0444; www.equi.hu; IX Ráday utca 8) in Budapest can provide you with a list of recommended riding schools nationwide. Also in the capital, **Pegazus Tours** (☎ 1-317 1644; www.pegazus.hu; V Ferenciek tere 5) organises riding tours of between three and five days (€300 to €350) and one week to nine days (€750 to €850) in Transdanubia, the Great Plain and around Lake Balaton.

The word 'coach' comes from Kocs, a small village southwest of Tata in Western Transdanubia where light horse-drawn vehicles were first used in place of more cumbersome wagons for journeys between Budapest and Vienna.

For more information about the distinctive Hungarian breed of horse called the Nonius, see http://horsecare.stablemade.com/_articles/nonius.htm. For the Lipizzaner, go to www.imh.org/imh/bw/lip.html.

CANOEING & KAYAKING

As Hungary is in a basin, it has many rivers of varying sizes; there are some 4000km of passable waterways, most of which are navigable by canoe or kayak at some point during the year, though April to September is probably the best time. Boat rental, food and camping along the rivers and lakes are cheap; in fact an *evezőstúra* (rowing excursion) is considered the 'poor man's holiday' in Hungary and is popular with students.

There are many canoe and kayak trips available. Following the Danube from Rajka to Mohács (386km) or the Tisza River from Tisza becs to Szeged (570km) are popular runs, but there are less congested waterways and shorter trips such as the 210km stretch of the Körös and Tisza Rivers from Békés to Szeged or the Rába River from Szentgotthárd to Győr (205km).

Cartographia (www.cartographia.hu) has several water-sports maps (*vízitúrázók térképei*; 800Ft to 1100Ft) to the rivers and lakes of Hungary (eg the 1:50,000 *Rába*, the 1:40,000 *Tisza-tó* etc).

You can find all the kayak and canoe clubs in Hungary listed on the website of the **Hungarian Kayak-Canoe Association** (MKKSZ; www.mkksz.hu), and many of them can provide information or help you with the routing in their area. The water tours section of the **Hungarian Friends of Nature Federation** (MTSZ; ☎ 1-332 7177, 331-2467; www.fsz.bme.hu/mtsz; VI Bajcsy-Zsilinszky út 31) in Budapest can also be of assistance.

Vizitura (☎ 1-280 8182; info@vizitura.hu; IX Hurok utca 1), based in Budapest, organises tours on most of Hungary's rivers. A four-seat canoe rents for 1400Ft to 2000Ft a day, and a guide is 15,000Ft (Hungarian-speaking) or 30,000Ft (English-speaking) per day.

SWIMMING

Swimming is extremely popular in Hungary, and most towns have both a covered and outdoor pool, allowing enthusiasts to get into the water year-round. The entry fee is generally low (from 550Ft), and you can often rent swimming costumes and bathing caps (the latter are mandatory in most indoor pools) for roughly the same price. All pools have a locker system. Find one, get changed in it (or beside it) and call over the attendant. He or she will lock the door with your clothes inside and hand you a numbered tag to tie on your costume. Note: in order to prevent theft lest you lose or misplace the tag, the number is not the same as the one on the locker, so commit the *locker* number to memory.

Lakes and rivers of any size have a grassy *strand* (beach), often with showers and changing facilities.

The first Hungarian Olympic medallist was swimmer Alfréd Hajós, who took two golds at the first modern Olympic Games in Athens in 1896.

HIKING

There is good hiking in the forests around Visegrád (p144), Esztergom (p148), Badacsony (p200), Kőszeg (p183) and Budapest (p74). North of Eger are the Bükk Hills (p327) and, south of Kecskemét, the Bugac (p246), both national parks with marked hiking trails. The best time to go hiking is in spring and autumn.

Cartographia publishes 30 hiking maps (average scales 1:40,000 and 1:60,000; 900/2350Ft folded/spiral-bound) to the hills, plains and forests of Hungary. Most are available from its outlet in Budapest (p65). On all hiking maps, paths appear as a red line and with a letter, or an abbreviation in Hungarian, indicating the colour-coding of the trail. Colours are painted on trees or the letter of the colour in Hungarian appears on markers: 'K' for *kék* (blue), 'P' for *piros* (red), 'S' for *sárga* (yellow) and 'Z' for *zöld* (green).

Contact the nonprofit Hungarian Friends of Nature Federation (see above) in Budapest for information and advice.

Walking in Hungary: 32 Routes through Upland Areas by Tom Chrystal and Beata Dosa leads hikers through the hills and forests of northern Hungary and Transdanubia.

CYCLING

Hungary's flat terrain makes it ideal for cycling, and cycle lanes in towns and regions (Budapest, Szeged, along the Danube and Tisza Rivers, around Lake Balaton) now total upward of 2000km, with more on the way. In addition, there are thousands of kilometres of roads with light traffic and dikes suitable for cycling. Among the choicest areas to explore on two wheels are the Danube Bend (p136), the Kál Basin southeast of Tapolca (p201), the Hortobágy National Park (p238), the Őrség region (p185) the Sopron region (p169) and the Zemplén Hills (p344).

Frigoria (www.frigoriakiado.hu) publishes the very useful 1:250,000-scale *Cycling around Hungary* (*Kerékpártúrák Magyarországon*; 2950Ft), with 100 tours outlined and places of interest and service centres listed in several languages, including English. It also produces similar map guides (average price 1800Ft) to a dozen different regions, including Lake Balaton, Southern Transdanubia and the Danube Bend.

For information and advice on cycling, contact the very helpful **Hungarian Cyclists' Club** (MK; ☎ 1-206 6223, 06 30 922 9052; www.kerosz.hu) or the **Hungarian Bicycle Touring Association** (MKTSZ; ☎ 1-311 2467; mktsz@dpg.hu; VI Bajcsy-Zsilinszky út 31, 2/F), which are in Budapest. Mountain bikers should get in touch with the **Hungarian Mountain Bike Association** (MMBSZSZ; ☎ 1-278 0946; mktsz@dpg.hu), also based in the capital.

Remember when planning your itinerary that bicycles are banned from motorways as well as national highways Nos 0 to 9, and they must be fitted with lights and reflectors. On certain train lines, bicycles can be transported in special carriages holding up to 58 bikes.

Balázs and Friends Cyclists' Sport Association (BBBSE; ☎ 1-227 6236, 06 30 991 6327; info@bbbse.hu; XXII Háros utca 47-49) in Budapest has cycling trips of one to three days (2000Ft to 15,000Ft, including transport and accommodation) throughout the year.

Happy Bike (☎ 06 20 556 8686; www.happybike.hu), in association with the Hungarian Cyclists' Club, has five more ambitious week-long trips in Transdanubia, including Lake Balaton, the Danube Bend and the Őrség region for €397 to €467, including bicycle rental, accommodation, three meals a day and luggage transport.

Also in the capital, **Velo-Touring** (☎ 1-319 0571; www.velo-touring.hu; XI Előpatak utca 1; ☻ 9am-5pm Mon-Fri) is a large cycling travel agency that has an eight-day spa tour from Hajdúszoboszló on the Great Plain to various spa towns (€655), a 10-day Lake Balaton–Vienna circuit (€729) and a 10-day tour of the Danube Bend and beyond (€736). Prices include a bike, accommodation and two meals a day; groups can range from eight to 20 cyclists.

BIRD-WATCHING

Gerard Gorman's *The Birds of Hungary* is the birder's Bible for assistance in spotting the best of Hungary's feathered friends. His *Where to Watch Birds in Eastern Europe* will set your sights further afield but is difficult to find.

Hungary, the ornithological crossroads of Europe, has some of the best bird-watching sites in Europe. Indeed, some 380 of the continent's 400-odd species have been sighted here, and a full 250 are resident or regular visitors. The country's indigenous populations of great white egrets (over 2000 pairs), spoonbills (several hundred pairs) and red-footed falcons (800 pairs), as well as white-tailed eagles (70 pairs), aquatic warblers (600 singing males), saker falcons (150 pairs) and great bustards (1200 birds) are among the most important in Europe, and more eastern imperial eagles (80 pairs) nest here than anywhere else in Europe. The arrival of the storks to the Great Plain, the Northern Uplands and the Northeast in April and May is a wonderful sight to behold.

If you prefer a guided rather than a DIY outing, look no further than **Birding Hungary** (☎ 06 70 214 0261; www.birdinghungary.com), owned and operated

THE BIRDS OF HUNGARY

There are dozens of excellent sites for bird-watching in Hungary, but the best ones are the Hortobágy region, the Kiskunság, Lake Fertő, Aggtelek, the Little Balaton (Kis-Balaton) and Tisza Lake. The Pilis, Bükk and Buda Hills and even small lakes like the ones at Tata and Fehér, north of Szeged, attract a wide variety of bird life. Spring and autumn are always good seasons for sightings, but the best month is May, when breeding is in full swing.

Hortobágy (p238)

This region of grassy, saline steppe, large fish ponds and marshes on the Great Plain is one of the best bird areas of Europe, with more than 300 species sighted, including great bustards, red-footed falcons and aquatic warblers. Almost any time of year is good for saker falcons, long-legged buzzards and white-tailed eagles; September/October is when geese and up to 70,000 cranes pass through. The Hortobágy fishponds are home to four species of grebe and eight species of heron, as well as several varieties of tern. In winter they host white-tailed eagles.

Lake Fertő (p162)

Some 210 nesting and migrant species have been registered at Fertő-Hanság National Park, which includes the southern end of shallow, saline Lake Fertő, near the Austrian border in Western Transdanubia. April to June sees the most activity in the lake's reedbeds, August sees the arrival of white storks, and autumn is the best time to sight white-fronted and bean geese.

Aggtelek (p342)

The hilly karst region of Aggtelek is a breeding ground for black storks, corncrakes, Ural owls, rock buntings, honey buzzards and various types of woodpecker. The best time to visit is April to September.

Little Balaton (p195)

This vast wetland, which is composed of impenetrable reed-choked ponds and a reservoir created in 1984, is home to about 100 breeding species. The best place to view little egrets, spoonbills terns and warblers is from Kányavári Island (Kányavári-sziget), a tiny island with two observation towers. The optimum season is April to August. In autumn tens of thousands of birds stop here on passage.

Lake Tisza (p230)

The northern third of this vast artificial lake, the area just east of Poroszló, is a bird reserve under the jurisdiction of Hortobágy National Park. The reedbeds and forests along the Tisza River attract large numbers of purple herons, little bitterns, great white egrets, cormorants and black kites. Any time of year is good for birding at Lake Tisza, but May and June are best for breeding birds and August and September for storks and raptors on passage.

Bükk Hills (p327)

This range of wooded hills east of Budapest, which forms Bükk National Park, supports a good variety of woodpeckers and flycatchers from May to July, as well as imperial eagles and woodland birds.

Tata (p153)

Old Lake (Öreg-tó), a nature conservation area at this Western Transdanubia city, attracts a considerable number and variety of waterfowl from October to February; between 20,000 and 40,000 white-fronted and bean geese can pass through in February alone. The best viewing spot is the southern end of the lake, where a thermal spring prevents that part of the lake from freezing over. The adjoining park and woodland attracts waxwings, hawfinches, bramblings and various woodpeckers in winter.

by Gerard Gorman, Hungary's most experienced bird guide. He runs between one and four organised birding tours a month from spring to late autumn that usually take in parts of the Northern Uplands and the Hortobágy, and last between four and eight days. Tailor-made tours and daily guiding are also available for around €100 a day.

Another experienced company with a solid reputation is Debrecen-based **Aquila Nature Tours** (☎ 52-456 744; aquila@hu.inter.net), which offers bird-watching tours in the Hortobágy and Zemplén Hills for about €65 a day.

The **Hungarian Ornithological & Nature Conservation Society** (MME; ☎ 1-275 6247; mme@mme.hu; XII Költő utca 21) in Budapest can help with general information, too. They also have a **birder shop** (☎ 1-270 2920; XIII Katona József utca 35; ☿ 8am-6pm Mon-Fri, 10am-2pm Sat) in the capital, which stocks books and guides, binoculars, clothing and bird-watching accessories.

SAILING & WINDSURFING

For sailing, you might try Lake Velence or Tisza Lake, but the real centre is Lake Balaton. Qualified sailors can rent boats at locations around Lake Balaton (p186), including Balatonfüred, Siófok, Balatonaliga, Balatonalmádi, Balatonkenese and Tihany. You'll find **Sail & Surf** (☎ 0630 227 8927; www.wind99.com), a sailing and windsurfing centre at **Club Tihany** (p209), with rental and both group and private lessons available. They also charter yachts. Expect to pay from €270 to €300 per weekend and €590 to €690 per week for a yacht sleeping four to six people.

Wherever there's water, a bit of wind and a camp site, you'll find sailboards for rent – on Lake Tisza at Abádszalók (p231), Lake Velence (p222) at Gárdony and Velence town, and Lake Fertő (p162) near Fertőrákos. The main place for windsurfing, however, is Lake Balaton (p186), especially at Kesthely, Balatonszabadi, Balatonvilágos and Balatonaliga. The best time for it is early and late summer, as the wind tends to die down in July and August.

The **Hungarian Windsurfing Association** (MSZSZ; ☎ 1-488 0312; husurf@windsurfing .hu; XII Krisztina körút 3) in Budapest can answer any questions you may have.

FISHING

Hungary's lakes and sluggish rivers are home to pike, perch, carp and other coarse fish. You'll see people fishing in waterways everywhere, but Lake Balaton and the Tisza River – especially at the Kisköre Reservoir southwest of Tiszafüred – are particularly popular venues. The water surface area of Hungary measures 130,000 sq km, and anglers make use of more than half of it.

In order to fish, you need a state fishing license valid for a year as well as a local one issued by the day, week or year for the area that interests you. You can usually buy them at the same place – anglers' clubs and associations, tackle shops, or even ticket booths by the water at more popular venues. The best source of information is the **National Federation of Hungarian Anglers** (MOHOSZ; ☎ 1-248 2590; www.mohosz.hu; XII Korompai utca 17) in Budapest.

Only sailing and rowing boats and craft with electric motors are allowed on Lake Balaton.

Food & Drink

Much has been written about Hungarian food – some of it silly, a lot of it downright false. It's true that Hungarian cuisine has had many outside influences and that it makes great use of paprika. But even that spice's hottest variety (called *csípős*) is pretty mild; a taco with salsa or a chicken vindaloo tastes a lot more 'fiery'.

Although still relatively inexpensive by Western standards and served in huge portions, Hungarian food is heavy and can be unhealthy. Meat, sour cream and fat abound and, except in season, *saláta* (salad) means a plate of pickled vegetables. Things are changing, however, at least in Budapest. A number of vegetarian (or partially vegetarian) restaurants have opened, more places now offer a wider selection of 'real' vegetarian dishes and ethnic food is very popular. And even Hungarian food itself is undergoing a long-awaited transformation. *Kortárs magyar konyha* (modern Hungarian cuisine) is being touted at more and more restaurants and, judging from the bookings at the establishments serving it, it's here to stay.

Culinaria Hungary by Aniko Gergely et al is a beautifully illustrated, 320-page tome on all things involving Hungarian food, from soup to nuts and more. It is as prized for its recipes as the history and traditions it contains.

STAPLES & SPECIALITIES

Hungarians are for the most part not big eaters of *reggeli* (breakfast), preferring a cup of tea or coffee with a plain bread roll at the kitchen table or on the way to work. *Ebéd* (lunch), eaten at 1pm, is traditionally the main meal in the countryside. *Vacsora* (dinner) – supper, really – is less substantial when eaten at home, often just sliced meats, cheese and some pickled vegetables.

Bread & Pasta

It is said that Hungarians will eat bread with bread. *Kenyér* (leavened bread) has been used to thicken soups and stews since at least the reign of King Matthias; *kifli* (crescent-shaped rolls) have been popular since the Turkish occupation. But, frankly, bread in Hungary is not as memorable as the flour-based *galuska* (dumplings) and *tarhonya* (egg barley pasta) served with dishes such as *pörkölt* (stew), *paprikás* and *tokány* (p54).

For a good selection of Hungarian recipes online, go to http://lingua.arts.klte.hu/hungary/konyha.htm.

Soup

Most Hungarian meals start with *leves* (soup). This is usually something like *gombaleves* (mushroom soup) or *gombócleves* (meat-filled dumplings in consommé). More substantial fare is beef *gulyásleves* (p54) and *bableves*, a thick bean soup, which are sometimes eaten as a main course. Another favourite is *halászlé* (fisherman's soup), a rich soup of poached carp, fish stock, tomatoes, green peppers and paprika.

Meat & Fish

Hungarians eat an astonishing amount of meat, and 'meat-stuffed meat' is a dish often on menus here. Pork, beef, veal and poultry are the meats most commonly used. They can be breaded and fried, baked, turned into some paprika-flavoured concoction or simmered in *lecsó*, a tasty mix of peppers, tomatoes and onions (and one of the few Hungarian sauces that does not include paprika). Lamb and mutton are rarely eaten in Hungary.

A typical menu will have up to 10 pork and beef dishes, a couple of fish ones and usually only one poultry dish. Goose livers and legs and turkey breasts – though not much else of the birds – make it onto most menus.

The early Magyars were so successful in battle because, unlike other armies, which fed from an accompanying (and very slow) herd of cattle, the Hungarian horsemen carried dried meat and pasta and turned it into nourishing *gulyás* when they reached a water source.

Freshwater fish, such as the indigenous *fogas* (great pike-perch) and the smaller *süllő* from Lake Balaton, and *ponty* (carp) from the nation's rivers and streams, is plentiful but can be expensive and often overcooked.

Paprika

Many dishes are seasoned with paprika, a spice as Magyar as King Stephen; indeed, not only is it used in cooking but it also appears on restaurant tables as a condiment beside the salt and pepper shakers. It's generally quite a mild spice and is used predominantly with sour cream or in *rántás*, a heavy roux of pork lard and flour added to cooked vegetables. *Töltött,* things stuffed with meat and/or rice, such as cabbage or peppers, are cooked in *rántás* as well as in tomato sauce or sour cream.

There are four major types of meat dish that use paprika. The most famous is *gulyás* or *gulyásleves,* a thick beef soup cooked with onions, cubed potatoes and paprika, and usually eaten as a main course. *Pörkölt,* or 'stew', is closer to what foreigners call 'goulash'; the addition of sour cream, less paprika and white meat, such as chicken, makes the dish *paprikás. Tokány* is similar to *pörkölt* and *paprikás* except that the meat is not cubed but cut into strips, black pepper is on equal footing with the paprika, and bacon, sausage or mushroom are added as flavouring.

Vegetables

Fresh salad as it's usually known around the world is called *vitamin saláta* here and is usually available when lettuce is in season; almost everything else is *savanyúság* (literally 'sourness'), which can be anything from mildly sour-sweet cucumbers and pickled peppers to almost acid sauerkraut.

Zöldség (boiled vegetables), when available, are 'English-style' or *angolos zöldség.* The traditional way of preparing vegetables – real Hungarian 'comfort food' – is in *főzelék,* where peas, green beans, lentils or marrow are fried or boiled and then mixed into a roux with milk.

Desserts

Hungarians love sweets and eat them with great gusto. Intricate pastries such as *Dobos torta,* a layered chocolate and cream cake with a caramelised brown sugar top, and *rétes* (strudel) filled with poppy seeds or cherry preserves are usually consumed mid-afternoon in one of Hungary's ubiquitous *cukrászda* (cake shop or patisserie). Desserts more commonly found on restaurant menus include *somlói galuska,* a sponge cake with chocolate and whipped cream, and *Gundel palacsinta,* flambéed pancake with chocolate and nuts.

DRINKS

A *kávéháv,* literally a 'coffee house' or 'café', is the best place to get something hot or nonalcoholic and cold. An *eszpresszó,* along with being a type of coffee, is essentially a coffee house too, but it usually also sells alcoholic drinks and light snacks.

To sample the local brew or vintage try visiting: a *söröző,* a pub with draught beer *(csapolt sör)* on tap; a *borozó,* an establishment (usually a dive) serving wine; and a *pince,* which can be a beer or wine cellar but is usually the latter and also called *bor pince.*

Nonalcoholic Drinks

Hungarians drink a tremendous amount of *kávé* (coffee) – as a *fekete* (single black), a *dupla* (double) or with milk, *tejes kávé.* Decaffeinated coffee is *koffeinmentes kávé.*

Hungary produces about 10,000 tonnes of paprika a year and exports 55% of it while each Hungarian consumes an average of 500g of the spice annually.

The 1971 film *Szindbád* (Sinbad), based on the eponymous novel by Gyula Krúdy (1878–1933) and directed by Zoltán Huszárik, featured a scene of a diner eating bone marrow on toast, which had the audience spellbound and salivating at a time when such luxuries were at a premium in socialist Hungary.

Black tea (*tea*; *tay*-ah) is not as popular as coffee in Hungary, though
teaházk (teahouses) serving every imaginable type of tea and tisane have
become very trendy in recent years.

Alcoholic Drinks

Hungarians are big drinkers and enjoy a tipple at the drop of a hat (or a
forint or a glass).

BEER

Hungary produces a number of its own beers for national distribution, and
the most common three are Dreher, Kőbányai and Arany Ászok. Some,
however, are found only in the vicinity of where they are brewed, such as
Borsodi near Miskolc, Kanizsai in Nagykanizsa and Szalon in Pécs. Bottled
Austrian, German and Czech beers are readily available. Locally brewed
and imported beer in Hungary is almost always *világos sör* (lager), though
occasionally you'll come across Dreher Barna (Dreher Brown), which is
stout. At a pub, beer is served in a *pohár* (0.3L) or a *korsó* (0.4L or 0.5L).

BRANDY & LIQUEUR

Pálinka is a strong (about 40%), uniquely Hungarian, brandy or *eau de
vie* distilled from a variety of fruits but most commonly from apricots
or plums. There are many different types and qualities, but among our
favourites are *Óbarack,* the double-distilled 'Old Apricot', the kind made
with *málna* (raspberry) and anything with *kóser* (kosher) on the label.

Hungarian liqueurs are usually unbearably sweet and artificial tasting,
though the Zwack brand is good. Zwack also produces Unicum, a bitter
aperitif that has been around since 1790.

Habsburg Emperor
Joseph II supposedly gave
Hungary's most famous
liqueur its name when he
first tasted it, exclaiming:
'Das ist ein Unikum!'
(This is a unique drink!).

WINE

Wine has been made in Hungary for thousands of years and is sold by the
glass or bottle everywhere – at very basic wine bars, food stalls, restaurants,
supermarkets and 24-hour grocery stores – and usually at reasonable prices.
Old-fashioned wine bars ladle it out by the *deci* (decilitre, 0.1L), but in more
modern places it comes by the undefined *pohár* (glass). If you're seriously
into wine, you should visit Budapest's speciality wine shops (p121).

When choosing a Hungarian wine, look for the words *minőségi bor* (quality wine) or *különleges minőségű bor* (premium quality wine), Hungary's
version of the French quality regulation *appellation controlée*. Generally
speaking, the vintage or *évjárat* has become important only recently; see
boxed text, p57. On a wine label the first word indicates the region, the
second the grape variety (eg Villányi Kékfrankos) or the type or brand of
wine (eg Tokaji Aszú, Szekszárdi Bikavér). Other important words that
you'll see include: *édes* (sweet), *fehér* (white), *féledes* (semisweet), *félszáraz*
(semidry or medium), *pezsgő* (sparkling), *száraz* (dry) and *vörös* (red).

The single best website
for Hungarian wines is
www.bortarsasag.hu/en/.
It also lists prices from
the Bortársaság (Wine
Society), Hungary's
foremost wine club.

One very surprising development since Hungary joined the EU in 2004
is that locals are still overwhelmingly buying their own wine despite the
great increase in prices (at least in top-shelf wines) and the steady stream
of cheaper wines from other parts of the union. Are they being loyal to
the local product or just too familiar with the Magyar varieties to switch?
As they say in the trade, only time will tell.

Tokaj

The volcanic soil, sunny climate and protective mountain barrier of the
Tokaj-Hegyalja region in the Northern Uplands make it ideal for growing
grapes and making wine.

WINE REGIONS

0 — 100 km
0 — 50 miles

Wine-growing Areas
Selected Regions

TOKAJ
MISKOLC • Tokaj
Eger • NYÍREGYHÁZA
EGER Tisza River
Danube River
Sopron • GYŐR Gyöngyös Heves DEBRECEN •
BUDAPEST
Etyek Jászberény
Somló Mór SZÉKESFEHÉRVÁR
SOMLÓ Veszprém KECSKEMÉT
Zalaegerszeg BADACSONY Lake Balaton
Badacsony Balatonboglár
SZEKSZÁRD
Szekszárd Tolna • Hajós
TOLNA Baja • SZEGED
PÉCS • VILLÁNY
Villány
Siklós

Hungary now counts 22
distinct wine-growing
areas in Transdanubia,
the Balaton region, the
Northern Uplands and on
the Great Plain.

Tokaj dessert wines are rated according to the number – from three to six – of *puttony* (butts, or baskets for picking) of sweet Aszú grapes added to the base wines. These are grapes infected with 'noble rot', a mould called *Botrytis cinera* that almost turns them into raisins on the vine. Aszú Eszencia, an essence even sweeter than six-*puttony* wine, is added – very judiciously – to improve the wine. Some six-*puttony* Aszú sells for as little as 6000Ft.

Tokaj also produces less-sweet wines, including dry Szamorodni (an excellent aperitif) and sweet Szamorodni, which is not unlike an Italian *vin santo*. Of the four grape varieties grown here Furmint and Hárslevelű (Linden Leaf) are the driest. Some Hungarian wine connoisseurs believe dry Furmint, with a flavour recalling apples, has the potential to become the best white wine in the country.

For Tokaji Aszú the name to look out for is István Szepsy, who concentrates on the upscale six-*puttony* variety as well as the Aszú Eszencia itself. His 2000 six-*puttony* Aszú currently retails for a cool 19,950Ft a bottle and his 1999 Eszencia is 45,000Ft for a mere 37.5cL. Szepsy Cuvée, aged in stainless steel barrels for a year or two (against the usual five for Tokaji Aszú) was first bottled in 1999 and is a complex, elegant blend comparable to Sauternes. A bottle of his excellent 2002 vintage is around 10,900Ft. Disznókő produces a six-*puttony* Aszú (about 9000Ft) reminiscent of apricots, and a fine, sweet Szamorodni (3010Ft). Other names to watch out for in quality Tokaj wines are Hétszőlő, Degenfeld and, for Furmint, Oremus and Béres. Oremus' Mandolás Furmint 2003 (2050Ft) and Béres' single Furmint 2003 (2850Ft) are both excellent value for money.

Louis XIV famously called
Tokaj, 'the wine of kings
and the king of wines',
while Voltaire wrote that
'this wine could be only
given by the boundlessly
good God'.

Vintage has always played a more important role in Tokaj than elsewhere in Hungary, and it is said that there is only one truly excellent year each decade. The wines produced in 1972, 1988, 1999, 2000 and 2003 were all superb, though 1993 was almost as good.

Eger

Flanked by two of the Northern Uplands' most beautiful ranges of hills and on the same latitude as Burgundy, Eger is the home of the celebrated Egri Bikavér (Eger Bull's Blood). By law, Hungarian vintners must spell out the blend of wine on their label; the sole exception is Bikavér, though it's usually Kékfrankos (Blaufränkisch) mixed with other reds, sometimes including Kadarka. One of the few wineries whose blend of Bikavér is known for sure is Tibor Gál's. Its blend is 50% Kékfrankos and 50% Cabernet and it is excellent (2150Ft). Another producer of Bikavér to watch out for is István Toth. His 1999 Bikavér (3150Ft) can easily compare with any of the 'big' reds from Villány.

Eger produces Pinot Noir and some experts think Vilmos Thummerer's 1999 vintage (3500Ft) is on par with the *premiers crus* from Burgundy. His Vili Papa Cuvée, a blend of Cabernet Franc, Cabernet Sauvignon and Merlot, is a monumental wine aged in new wood, with fleshy fruit flavours. It's priced from 9900Ft for the 1999 vintage. You'll also find several decent whites in Eger, including Leányka (Little Girl), Olaszrizling (Italian Riesling) and Hárslevelű from Debrő. Something new is Tibor Gál's Viognier 2003 (4350Ft; a delicate floral white), a variety once limited to 2 hectares and now planted on 10.

> Two excellent sources on Hungarian wines are the richly illustrated *Terra Benedicta: Tokaj and Beyond* by Gábor Rohály et al and *The Wines of Hungary* by Alex Liddell. These books don't just look at the wines but the whole winemaking process.

Villány

Villány-Siklós, in Hungary's southernmost and warmest region – it is on the same latitude as Bordeaux – is one of Hungary's principal producers of wine, noted especially for its red Kékoportó (Blauer Portugieser), Cabernet Franc, Cabernet Sauvignon and Merlot wines. They are almost always big-bodied Bordeaux-style wines and are high in tannin. The region is also now experimenting in Pinot Noir.

Among the best vintners in Villány is József Bock, whose Cuvée Barrique (6980Ft) is a smoky, earthy special blend of Kékfrankos (Blaufränkisch), Cabernet Franc and Merlot. Other vintners to watch out for are Márton Mayer and Alajos Wunderlich, especially the latter's Cabernet Sauvignon (3150Ft). Wines to try from this region include Attila Gere's elegant and complex Cabernet Sauvignon (2950Ft) and his Kopár (9500Ft), a blend of Cabernet Sauvignon, Cabernet Franc and Merlot, as well as Ede Tiffán's austere, tannic Kékoportó and Cabernet Franc.

Szekszárd

Mild winters and warm, dry summers combined with favourable loess soil help Szekszárd in Southern Transdanubia to produce some of the best affordable red wines in Hungary. They are not like the big-bodied reds of Villány, but softer and less complex, with a distinctive paprika flavour, and are easy to drink. In general they are much better value. An excellent, premium-quality Szekszárd retails for 2000Ft to 3000Ft.

THE BEST YEARS OF THEIR LIVES

1997 Excellent year for reds across the board, but especially in Eger and Szekszárd.

1998 Very mediocre year, except for producers of the very best reds (eg those in Villány).

1999 Superb year; biggest vintage for both whites and reds ever.

2000 Very hot summer raises alcohol levels in whites, impairing acids and lowering quality; excellent year for reds in Eger, Sopron, Szekszárd and Villány.

2001 Decent year for whites in general; very good for some top-end reds (eg from Eger and Villány).

2002 No great whites, but the reds are firm and cellar well, depending on the grower.

2003 Very hot year, with a long, very even ripening season. The whites suffer from burned acids and preponderant alcohol; however, the reds are even more promising than in 2000 – full-bodied and big, almost with a California flair.

2004 Inferior year throughout, with aggressive whites and thin reds.

2005 Very wet summer is catastrophic for whites, but red-wine growers are hopeful at the time of writing (mid-September).

WINE & FOOD

The pairing of food with wine is as great an obsession in Hungary as it is in, say, France. Everyone agrees that sweets like strudel go very well indeed with a glass of Tokaji Aszú, but what is less appreciated is the wonderful synergy that this wine enjoys with savoury foods like foie gras and cheeses such as Roquefort, Stilton and Gorgonzola. A bone-dry Olaszrizling from Badacsony is a superb accompaniment to any fish dish, but especially the pike-perch indigenous to nearby Lake Balaton. Villány Sauvignon Blanc is excellent with goat's cheese.

It would be a shame to 'waste' a big wine like a Vili Papa Cuvée on traditional but simple Hungarian dishes like *gulyás* or *pörkölt*; save it for a more complex or sophisticated meat dish. Try Kékfrankos or Szekszárd Kadarka with these simpler dishes. Cream-based dishes stand up well to late-harvest Furmint and pork dishes are nice with new Furmint or Kékfrankos. Try Hárslevelű with poultry.

The premier grape here is Kadarka, a late-ripening variety, which is produced in limited quantities. The best Kadarka is made by Ferenc Takler (2590Ft). Kadarka originated in the Balkans (the Bulgarian Gamza grape is a variety of it) and is a traditional ingredient in making Szekszárd Bikavér, a wine usually associated with Eger. In fact, many wine aficionados in Hungary prefer the Szekszárd variety of 'Bull's Blood'; try the Heimann 1999 variety (2750Ft) or his much praised Stílusgyakorlat Cuvée 2003 (3250Ft), which is six parts Merlot and one part Syrah, Hungary's 'newly discovered' variety of grape. The best Merlot (2350Ft) and Kékfrankos from Szekszárd is produced by Ferenc Vesztergombi, who also makes an excellent Bikavér (2970Ft). Tamás Dúzsi is acknowledged to be the finest producer of Hungarian rosés; sample his tried and true (and very dry) 1999 Zweigelt.

The website www .wineportal.hu is excellent for basic and background information on Hungarian wine. It also lists the dates and locations of wine events and blind tastings throughout the country.

Badacsony

The Badacsony region is named after the 400m-high basalt massif that rises like a bread loaf from the Tapolca Basin, along the northwestern shore of Lake Balaton. Wine has been produced here for centuries and the region's Olaszrizling, especially that produced by Huba Szeremley (1850Ft), is among the best dry white wines for everyday drinking available in Hungary. Olaszrizling, a straw-blond Welschriesling high in acid that is related to the famous Rhine vintages in name only and is actually French in origin, is drunk young – in fact, the younger, the better. Szeremley's 2000 late harvest Olaszrizling (6750Ft) is almost as sweet as Tokaj.

The area's volcanic soil gives the unique Kéknyelű (Blue Stalk) wine its distinctive mineral taste; it is a complex tipple wine of very low yield that ages well. Szeremley's Kéknyelű (3300Ft) is the only reliably authentic example. A big name producer of quality white wines (eg Nagykúti Chardonnay 2003; 2550Ft) is Jásdi in the nearby Balaton wine region of Csopak.

Somló

The entire region of Somló is a single volcanic dome and the soil (basalt talus and volcanic tuff) helps to produce wine that is mineral-tasting, almost flinty. The region boasts two great and indigenous grape varieties: Hárslevelű and Juhfark (Sheep's Tail); the latter takes its name from the shape of its grape cluster. Firm acids give 'spine' to this wine and it reaches its peak at five years old.

Foremost among the producers of Somlói Hárslevelű and Juhfark is Béla Fekete (3390Ft). Another big name in these parts is Imre Györgykovács, whose Olaszrizling (2490Ft) is a big wine with a taste vaguely reminiscent of burnt almonds. His Hárslevelű (2490Ft) is a brilliant golden wine, with a tart, mineral flavour.

WHERE TO EAT & DRINK

An *étterem* is a restaurant with a large selection, including international dishes. A *vendéglő* or *kisvendéglő* is smaller and is supposed to serve inexpensive regional dishes or 'home cooking', but the name is now 'cute' enough for a lot of large places to use it. An *étkezde* is something like a *vendéglő* but cheaper, smaller and often with counter seating. The overused term *csárda* originally signified a country inn with a rustic atmosphere, Gypsy music and hearty local dishes. Now any place that strings dry paprikas on the wall and a couple of painted plates is one. Most restaurants offer a good-value *menü* (set menu) of two or three courses at lunch.

A *bisztró* is a much cheaper sit-down place that is often *önkiszolgáló* (self-service). A *büfé* is cheaper still with a very limited menu. Here you eat while standing at counters.

Other useful words include *élelmiszer* (grocery store), *csemege* (delicatessen) and *piac* (market).

Quick Eats

Many *hentesáru bolt* (butchers) have a *büfé* selling boiled or fried *kolbász* (sausage), *wirsli* (frankfurters), *hurka* (blood sausage or liverwurst), roast chicken, bread and pickled vegetables. Point to what you want; the staff will weigh it all and hand you a slip of paper with the price. You usually pay at the *pénztár* (cashier) and hand the stamped receipt back to the staff for your food. Here you pay for everything, including a slice of rye bread and a dollop of mustard for your *kolbász*.

Food stalls, known as a *Laci konyha* (Larry's kitchen) or *pecsenyesütő* (roast oven), sell the same sorts of things, as well as fish when located beside lakes or rivers. One of the more popular snacks is *lángos*, deep-fried dough with various toppings (usually cheese and sour cream), available at food stalls throughout Hungary.

VEGETARIANS & VEGANS

Such a carnivorous country as Hungary is naturally suspicious of non-meat eaters. 'You don't want meat?!?' we overheard a waiter snarl at an optimistic vegetarian, 'Then go to Romania!' Places around the country that serve good vegetarian meals have been listed in the regional chapters. Where there are no vegetarian restaurants, you'll have to make do with what's on the regular menu or shop for ingredients in the markets. The selection of fresh vegetables and fruit is not great in the dead of winter,

---

HUNGARY'S TOP FIVE

- Halászcsárda, Szeged (p265) – *the* place for paprika-infused *szegedi halászlé* (Szeged-style fish soup) by the cauldron

- Kéhli, Budapest (p109) – this ancient eatery's marrow (animal) on toast is celebrated in Hungarian literature

- Kisfaludy House, Badacsony (p201) – the food (especially the fish dishes) is good and the view of Lake Balaton is spectacular

- Jégverem, Sopron (p166) – the charming 'Icehouse Pension' restaurant is known for the quality and quantity (as only Hungarians know how to dish it out) of its food

- Csülök Csárda, Esztergom (p149) – the 'Pork Knuckle Inn' serves the real McCoy and other good home cooking to both visitors and locals

but come spring and a cycle of bounty begins: from strawberries and raspberries and cherries through all the stone fruits to apples and pears and nuts. Large supermarket chains such as Kaiser's and Rothschild usually sell takeaway salads in plastic containers.

In restaurants, vegetarians can usually order *gombafejek rántva* (fried mushroom caps), pasta and noodle dishes with cheese, such as *túrós csusza* and *sztrapacska,* and an infinite variety of *főzelék.*

Other vegetarian dishes include *rántott sajt* (fried cheese), *gombaleves* (mushroom soup), *gyümölcsleves* (fruit soup) and *sajtos kenyér* (sliced bread with soft cheese). *Bableves* (bean soup) usually (but not always) contains meat. *Palacsinta* (pancakes) may be savoury and made with *sajt* (cheese) or *gomba* (mushrooms), or sweet and prepared with *dió* (nuts) or poppy seeds *(mák).*

EAT YOUR WORDS

For pronunciation guidelines, see p394.

Useful Phrases

I'm hungry/thirsty.
Éhes/szomjas vagyok.   ay·hesh/sawm·yosh vo·dyawk
The menu, please.
Az étlapot, kérem.   az ayt·lo·pawt kay·rem
Is there an English-language menu?
Van angol nyelvű étlap?   von on·gawl nyel·vēw ayt·lop
What would you recommend?
Mit ajánlana?   mit o·yaan·lo·no
I'd like a local speciality.
Valamilyen helyi specialitást szeretnék.   vo·lo·mi·yen he·yi shpe·tsi·o·li·taasht se·ret·nayk
I'm (a) vegetarian.
Vegetáriánus vagyok.   ve·ge·taa·ri·aa·nush vo·dyawk
Do you have vegetarian food?
Vannak önöknél vegetáriánus ételek?   von·nok eu·neuk·nayl ve·ge·taa·ri·aa·nush ay·te·lek
I'm allergic to (nuts/peanuts).
Allergiás vagyok a (diófélékre/mogyoróra).   ol·ler·gi·aash vo·dyawk o (di·āw·fay·layk·re/maw·dyaw·rāw·ro)
Is service included in the bill?
A kiszolgálás díja benne van a számlában?   o ki·sawl·gaa·laash dee·ya ben·ne von o saam·laa·bon
I'd like ..., please.
Legyen szíves, hozzon egy ...   le·dyen see·vesh hawz·zawn ej ...
Another ... please.
Még (egy) ... kérek szépen.   mayg (ej) ... kay·rek say·pen
Please bring the bill.
Kérem, hozza a számlát.   kay·rem hawz·zo o saam·laat

Menu Decoder

Restaurant menus are often translated into German and English, with mixed degrees of success. The following is a sample menu as it would appear in a 'generic' Hungarian restaurant. It's far from complete but gives a good idea of what to expect.

ELŐÉTELEK (APPETISERS)

hortobágyi palacsinta	hawr·taw·baa·dyi po·lo·chin·to	meat-filled pancakes with paprika sauce
libamájpástétom	li·bo·maa·y·paash·tay·tawm	goose-liver pâté
rántott gombafejek	raan·tawtt gom·bo·fe·y·ek	breaded, fried mushroom caps

LEVESEK (SOUPS)

csontleves	chont·le·vesh	consommé
jókai bableves	yāw·kai bob·le·vesh	bean soup with meat
meggyleves	mejj·le·vesh	cold sour-cherry soup (in summer)
tyúkhúsleves	tyūk·hūsh·le·vesh	chicken soup with carrot, kohl-rabi, parsley and celery roots

SALÁTÁK (SALADS)

cékla saláta	tsay·klo sho·laa·to	pickled beetroot salad
ecetes almapaprika	e·tse·tesh ol·mo pop·ri·ko	pickled (apple) peppers
paradicsom saláta	po·ro·di·chawm sho·laa·to	tomato salad
uborka saláta	u·bawr·ko sho·laa·to	sliced pickled cucumber salad
vegyes saláta	ve·dyesh sho·laa·to	mixed salad of pickles

KÖRETEK (SIDE DISHES)

rizi-bizi	ri·zi·bi·zi	rice with peas
sült hasábburgonya	shewlt ho·saa·bur·gon'	chips (French fries)

KÉSZÉTELEK (READY-MADE DISHES)

csirke paprikás	chir·ke pop·ri·kaash	chicken paprika
(marha)pörkölt	(mor·ho)·peur·keult	(beef) stew (many types)
töltött paprika/káposzta	teul·teutt pop·ri·ko/kaa·paws·to	stuffed peppers/cabbage

FRISSENSÜLTEK (DISHES MADE TO ORDER)

borjú bécsiszelet	bawr·yū bay·chi se·let	Wiener schnitzel
brassói aprópecsenye	bra·shāwy a·prāw pe·che·nye	braised pork Braşov-style
cigánypecsenye	tsi gawn·y·pe·che·nye	roast pork Gypsy-style
csülök	chew·leuk	smoked pork knuckle
hagymás rostélyos	hoj·maash rawsh·tay·yawsh	beef sirloin fried with onions
rántott hátszínszelet	raan·tawtt haat·seen·se·let	breaded, fried rump steak
rántott pulykamell	raan·tawtt pu·y·ko·mell	breaded, fried turkey breast
sertésborda	sher·taysh·bawr·do	pork chop
sült csirkecomb	shewlt chir·ke·tsawmb	roast chicken thigh
sült libacomb	shewlt li·bo·tsawmb	roast goose leg

ÉDESSÉGEK (DESSERTS)

Dobostorta	daw·bawsh·tawr·to	multilayered 'Dobos' chocolate and cream cake with caramel-ised brown sugar top
Gundel palacsinta	gun·del po·lo·chin·to	'Gundel' flambéed pancake with chocolate and nuts
rétes	ray·tesh	strudel
somlói galuska	shawm·lāw·i go·lush·ko	Somló-style sponge cake with chocolate and whipped cream

Food Glossary
BASICS

bors	bawrsh	pepper
cukor	tsu·kawr	sugar
cukorral/cukor nélkül	tsu·kawr·ol/tsu·kawr nayl·kewl	with/without sugar
ennivaló	en·ni·vo·law	food
étel	ay·tel	dish
étlap	ayt·lop	menu
gyümölcs	dyew·meulch	fruit

hús	hüsh	meat
jéggel/jég nélkül	yay-gel/yayg nayl-kewl	with/without ice
meleg/forró/hideg	me-leg/fawr-rāw/hi-deg	warm/hot/cold
sajt	sho·y·t	cheese
só	shāw	salt
tojás	taw-yaash	egg
vaj	vo·y	butter
zöldség	zeuld-shayg	vegetables

MEAT & FISH

borjúhús	bawr·yū·hüsh	veal
csirke	chir-ke	chicken
disznóhús	dis-nāw·hüsh	pork
hal	hol	fish
hús	hüsh	meat
marhahús	mor·ho·hüsh	beef
pulyka	pu·y·ko	turkey

VEGETABLES

gomba	gawm-bo	mushroom
káposzta	kaa·paws·to	cabbage
karfiol	kor·fi·awl	cauliflower
sárgarépa	shaar·go·ray·po	carrot
spenót	shpe-nāwt	spinach
zöldbab	zeuld·bob	string (green) bean
zöldborsó	zeuld·bawr·shāw	pea

FRUIT

alma	ol·mo	apple
banán	bo·naan	banana
cseresznye	che·res·nye	(sweet) cherry
(földi)eper	(feul·di)·e·per	strawberry
körte	keur·te	pear
meggy	mejj	sour (Morello) cherry
narancs	no·ronch	orange
őszibarack	ēū·si·bo·rotsk	peach
sárgabarack	shaar·go·bo·rotsk	apricot
szőlő	sēū·lēū	grape

NONALCOHOLIC DRINKS

almalé	ol·mo·lay	apple juice
ásvány víz	aash·vaan'·veez	mineral water
gyümölcslé	dyew·meulch lay	fruit juice
narancslé	no·ronch·lay	orange juice
üdítőital	ew·dee·tēū·i·tal	soft drink
tej	te·y	milk
víz	veez	water

BEER & SPIRITS

barackpálinka	bo·rotsk·paa·lin·ko	apricot brandy
barna sör	bor·no sheur	dark beer/stout
fél barna sör	fayl bor·no sheur	dark lager
korsó sör	kawr·shāw sheur	mug (half litre) of beer
pohár sör	paw·haar sheur	glass (one-third litre) of beer
sör	sheur	beer

Budapest

Budapest is unique in Hungary. No other city is as beautiful, as rich, as well endowed in fine art and architecture or, frankly, as crowded. As Hungary's *főváros* (main city or capital), it is the administrative, business and cultural centre; virtually everything in Hungary starts, finishes or is currently taking place here.

Straddling a curve in the Danube River (Duna), Budapest is flanked by the Buda Hills on the western bank and what is essentially the start of the Great Plain to the east. And the human legacy is just as remarkable as Mother Nature's. Architecturally, Budapest is a gem, with a surfeit of baroque, neoclassical, Eclectic and Art-Nouveau (or Secessionist) buildings. Overall, however, Budapest has a *fin-de-siècle* feel to it, for it was then – during the industrial boom and the capital's 'golden age' in the late 19th century – that most of today's city was built.

To retain its well-deserved title of *világváros* (world-class city), Budapest has taken on all the baggage that such a status usually demands: organised crime, faceless modern architecture, a mobile phone at the ear of every 'suit', international fast-food eateries at every corner. Yet Budapest remains Hungarian: exotic, sometimes inscrutable, often passionate, with its two feet firmly planted in Europe, but with a glance every now and then eastward to the spawning grounds of its citizens. It is unmissable.

HIGHLIGHTS

- Taking views of the Danube while above it (from **Castle Hill**, p69, or **Gellért Hill**, p71), while on it (from **Vigadó tér**, p102) or while in it (from **Margaret Island**, p75)

- Letting your mind wander over the sinuous curves and asymmetrical forms of the city's incomparable Art-Nouveau architecture, such as the **Museum of Applied Arts** (p94)

- Soaking the afternoon away in a thermal bath – Turkish-style (**Rudas**, p99, or **Király**, p97), in a 'cathedral' (**Gellért**, p97) or while playing board games afloat (**Széchenyi**, p97)

- Taking in an evening of music at the **Hungarian State Opera House** (p95) or the **Liszt Academy of Music** (p93)

- Sizing up the monumental socialist mistakes on display at **Statue Park** (p127)

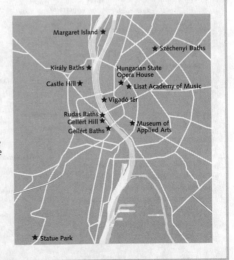

| ■ TELEPHONE CODE: 1 | ■ POPULATION: 1.75 MILLION | ■ AREA: 525 SQ KM |

HISTORY

Strictly speaking, the story of Budapest begins only in 1873 when hilly, largely residential Buda and historic Óbuda on the western bank of the Danube merged with flat, industrial Pest on the eastern side to form what was at first called Pest-Buda. But like so much in Hungary, it's not that simple.

The Romans had an important colony here called Aquincum until the 5th century, when they were forced to flee the settlement by the Huns. The Magyars arrived nearly half a millennium later, but Buda and Pest were no more than villages until the 12th century, when foreign merchants and tradespeople settled. In the late 13th century King Béla IV built a fortress in Buda, but it was King Charles Robert (Károly Róbert) who moved the court from Visegrád to Buda 50 years later. His son Louis the Great (Nagy Lajos) began the construction of a royal palace.

The Mongols had burned Buda and Pest to the ground in 1241–42, and thus began a pattern of destruction and rebuilding that would last until the 20th century. Under the Turks the two towns lost most of their populations, and when the Turks were defeated by the Habsburgs in the late 17th century Buda Castle was in ruins. The 1848 Revolution, WWII and the 1956 Uprising all took their toll. In 1944–45, for example, the retreating Germans even blew up every bridge spanning the Danube.

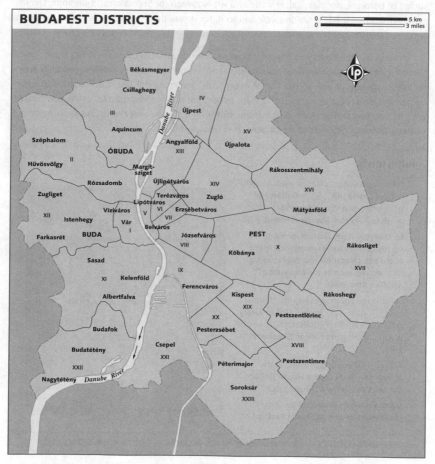

BUDAPEST DISTRICTS

0 ─────── 5 km
0 ─────── 3 miles

Békásmegyer
Csillaghegy
III
IV
Újpest
Aquincum
XV
Széphalom
Angyalföld
Újpalota
ÓBUDA
XIII
Hüvösvölgy
II
Margit-
sziget
Rózsadomb
Újlipótváros
XIV
Rákosszentmihály
Zugliget
Terézváros
Zugló
XVI
Lipótváros
Vizíváros
V
VI
Erzsébetváros
Mátyásföld
XII
Istenhegy
Vár
VII
I
Belváros
Farkasrét
BUDA
Józsefváros
PEST
X
Rákosliget
VIII
Köbánya
Sasad
IX
XVII
XI
Kelenföld
Ferencváros
Albertfalva
Kispest
Rákoshegy
XIX
Pestszentlőrinc
XX
Budafok
Pesterzsébet
XVIII
Budatétény
Csepel
XXII
XXI
Péterimajor
Pestszentimre
Nagytétény Danube River
Soroksár
XXIII

ORIENTATION

Budapest lies in the north-central part of Hungary, some 250km southeast of Vienna. The Danube River, the city's historical artery, is crossed by nine bridges that link hilly, historic Buda with bustling, commercial and very flat Pest.

It's a large, sprawling city but, with few exceptions (the Buda Hills, City Park and some excursions), the areas beyond the Nagykörút (literally, 'Big Ring road') in Pest and west of Moszkva tér in Buda are residential or industrial and of little interest to visitors. It is a well laid-out city, so much so that it is almost difficult to get lost.

If you look at a map of the city you'll see that two ring roads – the Nagykörút and the semicircular Kiskörút ('Little Ring road') – more or less link all of the most important bridges across the Danube and define central Pest. The Nagykörút consists of Szent István körút, Teréz körút, Erzsébet körút, József körút and Ferenc körút. The Kiskörút comprises Károly körút, Múzeum körút and Vámház körút. Important boulevards such as Bajcsy-Zsilinszky út, Andrássy út, Rákóczi út and Üllői út, fan out from the ring roads, creating large squares and circles.

Buda is dominated by Castle and Gellért Hills; its busiest square is Moszkva tér. Important roads on this side are Margit körút (the only part of either ring road to cross the river), Fő utca and Attila út on either side of Castle Hill, and Hegyalja út and Bartók Béla út running westerly and southwesterly.

Budapest is divided into 23 *kerüle*, or districts, which usually also have traditional names, such as Lipótváros (Leopold Town) in district V or Víziváros (Watertown) in district I. The Roman numeral appearing before each street address indicates the district.

For information on getting to/from Budapest's Ferihegy International Airport, 24km southeast of the city centre, see p123.

Maps

Lonely Planet's *Budapest City Map* covers the more popular parts of town in detail.

The best folding maps of the city are Cartographia's 1:22,000 (690Ft) and 1:28,000 (570Ft) ones. If you plan to explore the city thoroughly, the *Budapest Atlas*, also from Cartographia, is indispensable. It comes in the same scale (1:20,000) but two sizes: a smaller format (1950Ft) and a larger one (2600Ft). There is also a 1:25,000 pocket atlas of just the Inner Town available for 1210Ft.

Many bookshops, including Libri Könyvpalota (p66), stock a wide variety of maps. **Cartographia** (Map p84; ☎ 312 6001; www.carto graphia.hu; VI Bajcsy-Zsilinszky út 37; ☼ 10am-6pm Mon-Fri; Ⓜ M3 Arany János utca) has its own outlet in Budapest, but it's not self-service, which can be annoying. A better bet is **Térképkirály** (Map King; Map p84; ☎ 472 0505; VI Bajcsy-Zsilinszky út 23; ☼ 10am-6pm Mon-Fri; Ⓜ M3 Arany János utca) or the smaller **Párisi Udvar Könyvesbolt** (Párisi Udvar Bookshop; Map p86; ☎ 235 0379; V Petőfi Sándor utca 2; ☼ 9am-7pm Mon-Fri, 10am-2pm Sat; Ⓜ M3 Ferenciek tere) in the Párisi Udvar.

INFORMATION
Bookshops

Bestsellers (Map p86; ☎ 312 1295; V Október 6 utca 11; ☼ 9am-6.30pm Mon-Fri, 10am-5pm Sat, 10am-4pm Sun; Ⓜ M1/2/3 Deák Ferenc tér) Top of the pops for English-language books in Budapest is this recently expanded bookshop, which has novels, travel guides and lots of Hungarica, as well as a large selection of magazines and newspapers.

A STREET BY ANY OTHER NAME

After WWII most streets, squares and parks were renamed after people, dates or political groups that have since become anathema to an independent and democratic Hungary. From April 1989 names were changed with a determination that some people felt was almost obsessive; Cartographia's street atlas of Budapest lists almost 400 street name changes in the capital alone. Sometimes it was just a case of returning a street or square to its original (perhaps medieval) name – from Lenin útja, say, to Szent korona útja (Street of the Holy Crown). Other times the name was new.

The new (or original) names are now in place after more than a decade and a half; the old street signs with a red 'X' drawn across them have all but disappeared, and virtually no one refers to Ferenciek tere (Sq of the Franciscans) in the capital, for example, as Felszabadulás tér (Liberation Sq), which honoured the Soviet Army's role in liberating Budapest in WWII.

Central European University Bookshop (Map p86; ☎ 327 3096; V Nádor utca 9; ⏰ 10am-6pm Mon-Fri; 🚌 15) Under the same management as Pendragon is this two-floor bookshop at the Central European University, which has a good selection of academic and business titles with a regional focus, as well as some second hand stock.

Írók Boltja (Writers' Bookshop; Map p84; ☎ 322 1645; VI Andrássy út 45; ⏰ 10am-6pm Mon-Fri, 10am-1pm Sat; M M1 Oktogon, 🚊 4 or 6) For Hungarian authors in translation, this is the place to go.

Központi Antikvárium (Map p86; ☎ 317 3514; V Múzeum körút 13-15; ⏰ 10am-6.30pm Mon-Fri, 10am-2pm Sat; M M3 Kálvin tér) For antique and second-hand books in Hungarian, German and English try the 'Central Antiquarian', which was established in 1885 and is the largest antique bookshop in Budapest.

Libri Könyvpalota (Map p84; ☎ 267 4844; VII Rákóczi út 12; ⏰ 10am-7.30pm Mon-Fri, 10am-3pm Sat; M M2 Astoria) Huge and spread over two floors, the 'Book Palace' has a selection of English-language novels, art books, guidebooks, maps, music and a café on the 1st floor.

Libri Stúdium (Map p86; ☎ 318 5680; V Váci utca 22; ⏰ 10am-7pm Mon-Fri, 10am-3pm Sat & Sun; M M3 Ferenciek tere) For books in English and other languages on Hungarian subjects, the more central Stúdium is among the best bets.

Pendragon (Map pp80-1; ☎ 340 4426; XIII Pozsonyi út 21-23; ⏰ 10am-6pm Mon-Fri, 10am-2pm Sat; 🚊 4 or 6) This English-language bookshop has an excellent selection of books and guides (including Lonely Planet titles).

Red Bus (Map p86; ☎ 337 7453; V Semmelweiss utca 14; ⏰ 11am-6pm Mon-Fri, 10am-2pm Sat; M M2 Astoria) Below the popular hostel (p104) of the same name, this is the only shop in town selling used English-language books.

Szőnyi Antikváriuma (Map p84; ☎ 311 6431; www.szonyi.hu; V Szent István körút 3; ⏰ 10am-6pm Mon-Fri, 9am-1pm Sat; 🚊 4 or 6) This long-established antiquarian bookshop has an excellent selection of antique prints and maps (look in the drawers), as well as books.

Világsajtó Háza (World Press House; Map p86; ☎ 317 1311; V Városház utca 3-5; ⏰ 7am-7pm Mon-Fri, 7am-2pm Sat, 8am-noon Sun; M M3 Ferenciek tere) This is the best place in Budapest for foreign-language newspapers, magazines and other periodicals.

BUDAPEST IN ...

Two Days

If you've got just a couple of days in Budapest spend most of the first day on **Castle Hill** (p69), taking in the views and sights and visiting a museum or two. In the afternoon ride the **Sikló** (p69) down to Clark Ádám tér and, depending on the day of the week, make your way to the **Király Baths** (p97) or **Gellért Baths** (p97) for a relaxing soak. In the evening head for Liszt Ferenc tér for drinks and dinner at **Menza** (p111). The following day concentrate on the two icons of Hungarian nationhood and the places that house them: the **Crown of St Stephen** (p91) in the Parliament building and the saint-king's mortal remains in **St Stephen's Basilica** (p91). Take a late afternoon coffee (and cake) break at **Gerbeaud** (p113) in Vörösmarty tér, and try to attend a performance at the **Liszt Academy of Music** (p93) or the **Hungarian State Opera House** (p95).

Four Days

With another couple of days to look around the city, consider taking our walking tour (p100) up Andrássy út, stopping off and visiting whatever interests you along the way – be it the **House of Terror** (p95) or the **Museum of Fine Arts** (p96). **Lukács** (p113), the café and cake shop, is conveniently located en route, and you could take the waters at the **Széchenyi Baths** (p97) in City Park. **Robinson** (p111) or **Bagolyvár** (p111) are convenient places for an evening meal. The following day why not take in destinations further afield, such as **Statue Park** (p127), a ride up into the Buda Hills on the **Cog Railway** (p75) or a hike? Be back in time for a farewell pub and club crawl or, if it's the right season, a well-watered tour of the city's best 'gardens' (p117).

One Week

If you have a week in Budapest you could manage to see most of the sights listed in this chapter, including 'secondary' gems, such as the **Tomb of Gül Baba** (p73) and the **Ferenc Hopp Museum of East Asian Art** (p95), or markets like the **Nagycsarnok** (p114) and **Ecseri Piac** (p120), and do a little shopping (p120). You could even leave Budapest for a couple of days' excursion to the **Danube Bend** (p131), **Lake Balaton** (p186) or even the **Hortobágy** (p238) on the Great Plain.

Emergency

If you need to report a crime or a lost or
stolen passport or credit card, first call the
central emergency number (☎ 112), the **police**
(☎ 107) or the **English-language crime hotline**
(☎ 8am-8pm 438 8080, 8pm-8am 06 80 660 044). Any
crime must then be reported at the police
station of the district you're in. In central
Pest that would be the **Belváros-Lipótváros Police Station** (Map p84; ☎ 373 1000; V Szalay utca 11-13;
🚇 15). If possible, bring along a Hungarian
speaker.

Other useful numbers:
Ambulance (☎ 105)
Fire (☎ 104)

Internet Access

Ami Internet Coffee (Map p86; ☎ 267 1644; www.
amicoffee.hu in Hungarian only; V Váci
utca 40; per 15/30/60min 200/400/700Ft, per 5/10hr
3250/6400Ft; 🕐 9am-2am; Ⓜ M3 Ferenciek tere)
This Internet café in the university area has 40 terminals.
Electric Cafe (Map p84; ☎ 413 1803; www.electric
café.hu; VII Dohány utca 37; per 30/60min 100/200Ft;
🕐 9am-midnight; Ⓜ M2 Blaha Lujza tér) This place is
very popular with travellers.
Narancs (Map p84; ☎ 413 6071; VII Akácfa utca 5; per
30/60min 100/200Ft; 🕐 10am-midnight; Ⓜ M2 Blaha
Lujza tér) This is a small but charming French-run 'neighbourhood' Internet café.
Parknet (Map p86; ☎ 270 2249; www.parknetcafé.hu;
V Váci utca 23; per 15/30/60min 170/270/500Ft, per
5/10hr 1800/3000Ft; 🕐 9am-8pm Mon-Sat, 10am-8pm
Sun; Ⓜ M3 Ferenciek tere) This place is about as central
as you'll find in Pest.
Private Link (Map pp80-1; ☎ 334 2057; www.private
-link.hu; VIII József körút 52; per 1/5/10hr 690/2000/
3500Ft; 🕐 24hr; Ⓜ M3 Ferenc körút) This is Budapest's
largest and most comfortable Internet café, and one of the
very few open round the clock.

Internet Resources

For Hungarian websites with Budapest links,
see p15.
Budapest Sun Online (www.budapestsun.com) Popular
English weekly online, with local news, interviews and
features.
Budapest Tourism Office (www.budapestinfo.hu)
Budapest's best overall website.
Budapest Week (www.budapestweek.com) An excellent
source for events, arts and entertainment.
Pestiside (www.pestiside.hu) Subtitled 'The Daily Dish of
Cosmopolitan Budapest', this acerbic and often very funny
take on the capital (and nation, for that matter) will have
you culturally and politically fluent before you even arrive.
Visitors' Guide Budapest (www.visitorsguide.hu)
This is the *Budapest Sun's* very own website for visitors.

Left Luggage

Budapest's three major train stations, two
bus stations and Ferihegy International Airport (Terminal 2B) all have left-luggage offices or lockers. For more information, see
the appropriate sections in the Transport
chapter (p378).

Medical Services

CLINICS

FirstMed Centers (Map p83; ☎ 224 9090; www.first
medcentres.com; I Hattyú utca 14, 5/F; 🕐 appointments
8am-7pm Mon-Thu, 8am-6pm Fri, urgent care 24hr;
Ⓜ M2 Moszkva tér) This is a modern private medical
clinic with round-the-clock emergency treatment, but it's
not cheap: a basic consultation costs 12,600/25,200Ft for
up to 10/20 minutes.
SOS Dental Services (Map p86; ☎ 267 9602, 269
6010; VI Király utca 14; 🕐 24hr; Ⓜ M1/2/3 Deák Ferenc
tér) This dental surgery charges 2000Ft for a consultation,
5000Ft to 6000Ft for extractions and 6000Ft to 10,000Ft
for fillings.

PHARMACIES

All of Budapest's 23 districts have a rotating
all-night pharmacy; a sign on the door of any
pharmacy will help you locate the nearest
24-hour place. Other conveniently located
pharmacies:
Csillag Patika (Map p84; ☎ 314 3695; VIII Rákóczi
út 39; 🕐 7.30am-9pm Mon-Fri, 7.30am-2pm Sat; Ⓜ M2
Blaha Lujza tér)
Déli Gyógyszertár (Map pp80-1; ☎ 355 4691; XII
Alkotás utca 1/b; 🕐 8am-8pm Mon-Fri, 8am-2pm Sat;
Ⓜ M2 Déli pályaudvar)
Teréz Patika (Map p84; ☎ 311 4439, 475 0295;
VI Teréz körút 41; 🕐 8am-8pm Mon-Fri, 8am-2pm Sat;
Ⓜ M3 Nyugati pályaudvar)

Money

There are ATMs everywhere in Budapest, including in the train and bus stations, and quite a few foreign-currency exchange machines, too.

K&H bank (Map p86; V Váci utca 40; 8am-5pm Mon, 8am-4pm Tue-Thu, 8am-3pm Fri; M3 Ferenciek tere) Conveniently located on the main shopping drag; offers fairly good rates.

OTP bank (Map p86; V Deák Ferenc utca 7-9; 7.45am-6pm Mon, 7.45am-5pm Tue-Fri; M1/2/3 Deák Ferenc tér) The National Savings Bank offers among the best exchange rates for cash and travellers cheques, but arrive at least an hour before closing to ensure the bureau de change counter is still open.

Post

Main post office (Map p86; V Petőfi Sándor utca 13-15; 8am-8pm Mon-Fri, 8am-2pm Sat; M1/2/3 Deák Ferenc tér) A few minutes' walk from Deák Ferenc tér and the main Tourinform office, the main post office is where you can buy stamps, mail letters, and send packages and faxes all from the same place.

Main post office annexe (Map p86; V Városház utca 18; 8am-8pm Mon-Fri, 8am-2pm Sat; M1/2/3 Deák Ferenc tér) Poste restante service around the corner from the main post office.

Post office Keleti train station (Map pp80-1; VIII Kerepesi út 2-6; 7am-9pm Mon-Fri, 8am-2pm Sat; M2 Keleti pályaudvar); Nyugati train station (Map p84; VI Teréz körút 51-53; 7am-9pm Mon-Sat, 10am-5pm Sun; M3 Nyugati pályaudvar)

Telephone & Fax

You can buy SIM cards and rent hand units from various mobile-phone outlets throughout the city:

Pannon GSM (Map p86; 311 8416; www.pgsm.hu; V Arany János utca 17; 9am-8pm Mon-Fri, 9am-2pm Sat; M3 Arany János utca)

T-Mobile (Map p86; 266 5723; www.t-mobile.hu; V Petőfi Sándor utca 12; 9am-7pm Mon-Fri, 10am-1pm Sat; M3 Ferenciek tere)

Vodafone (Map p84; 238 7281; www.vodafone.hu; West End City Centre, VI Váci út 3; 10am-9pm Mon-Sat, 10am-6pm Sun; M Nyugati pályaudvar)

Tourist Information

Budapest Tourist Office (BTO; 266 0479; www.budapestinfo.hu; Castle Hill Map p83; 488 0475; I Szentháromság tér; 9am-8pm May-Sep, 10am-7pm Oct-Apr; 16 or Várbusz; Nyugati train station Map p84; 302 8580; Nyugati pályaudvar, platform No 10; 9am-7pm Apr-Oct, 9am-6pm Nov-Mar; M3 Nyugati pályaudvar; Oktogon Map p84; 322 4098;

VI Liszt Ferenc tér 11; 9am-7pm Apr-Oct, 10am-6pm Nov-Mar; M1 Oktogon) These are less frantic options than Tourinform for tourist information. BTO also maintains offices at Ferihegy International Airport's Terminals 1, 2A (arrivals) and 2B (departures).

Tourinform (Map p86; 438 8080, 24hr information hotline 06 80 630 800; www.tourinform.hu; V Sütő utca 2; 8am-8pm; M1/2/3 Deák Ferenc tér) This is usually the single best source of information on Budapest, but it can get hopelessly crowded in summer, and the staff are not always very patient or even helpful.

Travel Agencies

Many of the offices listed here also provide information, and dispense brochures and maps. For details on commercial outfits that can book private accommodation, see Private Rooms (p104).

Express (Map p86; 327 7290, 266 3277; www.express-travel.hu; V Semmelweiss utca 4; 8.30am-5pm Mon-Fri, 9am-1pm Sat; M2 Astoria) The main office of this youth- and student-orientated agency can book accommodation in Budapest, particularly hostels and colleges, and sells transport tickets.

Ibusz (Map p86; 485 2700; www.ibusz.hu; V Ferenciek tere 10; 9am-6pm Mon-Fri, 9am-1pm Sat; M3 Ferenciek tere) The main office of this travel-agency giant supplies travel brochures, changes money, books all types of accommodation and accepts credit-card payments.

Mellow Mood (Map p86; 411 2390; www.youthhostels.hu, www.mellowmood.hu; V Molnár utca 3; 9am-6pm Mon-Fri; M3 Ferenciek tere) This new kid on the block run by the hostel group of the same name (p104) can organise accommodation in private rooms and hostels, book tours, sell you discounted air tickets etc.

Vista (Map p86; 429 9751; www.vista.hu; VI Paulay Ede utca 2; M1/2/3 Deák Ferenc tér; 9am-6.30pm Mon-Fri, 9am-2.30pm Sat) Vista is an excellent one-stop shop for all your travel needs, both outbound (air tickets, package tours etc) and incoming (room bookings, organised tours, study and ecological tours in Hungary etc).

Wasteels (Map pp80-1; 210 2802, 343 3492; VIII Kerepesi út 2-6; 8am-8pm Mon-Fri, 8am-6pm Sat; M2 Keleti pályaudvar) This agency at the top of platform No 9 at Keleti train station sells Billet International de Jeunesse (BIJ) tickets (p381), but you must have a student or youth card (p370) to get the discounted fares.

DANGERS & ANNOYANCES

No parts of Budapest are 'off limits' to visitors, although some locals now avoid Margaret Island after dark during the low season, and both residents and visitors give the dodgier parts of the VIII and IX districts (areas of prostitution) a wide berth.

Pick pocketing is most common in markets, the Castle District, Váci utca and Hősök tere, near major hotels, and on certain popular buses (eg 7) and trams (2, 4, 6, 47 and 49).

Catching a taxi in Budapest can be an expensive and even unpleasant experience. Never hail a taxi on the street; instead order one from a phone – private, mobile or public – and give the number (almost always posted somewhere in the phone box) to the dispatcher. For more information about taxis, see p127.

If you've left something on any form of public transport in Budapest, contact the **BKV lost & found office** (Map p84; ☎ 267 5299; VII Akácfa utca 18; ☺ 8am-5pm Mon & Tue, Thu & Fri, 8am-6pm Wed; Ⓜ M2 Blaha Lujza tér).

Scams

Scams involving attractive young women, gullible guys, expensive drinks in nightclubs and a frog-marching to the nearest ATM by gorillas-in-residence have been all the rage in Budapest for a decade now, and we get stacks of letters from male readers complaining they've been ripped off. Guys, please, do us all a favour. If it seems too good to be true, it is. Trust us and the mirror; such vanity has cost some would-be Lotharios hundreds, even thousands, of dollars.

SIGHTS

For more details on the many museums and other sights listed here, see the **Museums in Hungary** (www.museum.hu) website.

Buda

Leafy and unpolluted, Buda as seen from Pest isn't just a pretty face. The city's more majestic western side fronting the Danube has some of its most important and historical landmarks (eg Castle Hill, the Citadella) and museums (National Gallery, Budapest History Museum) and, to the north, the original Roman settlement at Aquincum.

CASTLE HILL

Castle Hill (Várhegy), also called the Castle District, a 1km-long limestone plateau towering 170m above the Danube, contains Budapest's most important medieval monuments and museums, and is a Unesco World Heritage Site. Below it is a 28km-long network of caves formed by thermal springs.

The walled area consists of two distinct parts: the Old Town, where commoners lived in the Middle Ages (today's owners of the burgher houses here are anything but 'common'), and the Royal Palace, the original site of the castle built in the 13th century.

The easiest way to get to Castle Hill from Pest is to take bus 16 from Deák Ferenc tér to Dísz tér, midway between the Old Town and the Royal Palace. Much more fun, though, is to stroll across Chain Bridge and board the **Sikló** (☺ 7.30am-10pm, closed 1st & 3rd Mon of month), a funicular railway (uphill/downhill ticket adult 650/550Ft, child aged three to 14 350Ft) built in 1870 that ascends from Clark Ádám tér to Szent György tér near the Royal Palace.

Alternatively, you can walk up the Király lépcső, the 'Royal Steps' that lead from Clark Ádám tér to the northwest, or the wide staircase that goes to the southern end of the Royal Palace from I Szarvas tér.

Another option is to take metro M2 to Moszkva tér, go up the stairs in the northeastern part of the square and walk up I Várfok utca to Vienna Gate. A minibus with a logo of a castle and labelled 'Várbusz' (or 'Dísz tér') follows the same route from the start of Várfok utca.

Vienna Gate

The medieval entrance to the Old Town, **Vienna Gate** (Map p83; Bécsi kapu; ☺ 24hr) was rebuilt in 1936 to mark the 250th anniversary of the retaking of the castle from the Turks. You can climb to the top at any time. It's not all that huge, but when children in Budapest are loquacious or noisy, their parents tell them: 'Your mouth is as big as the Vienna Gate!'

Medieval Jewish Prayer House

The **Medieval Jewish Prayer House** (Középkori Zsidó Imaház; Map p83; ☎ 225 7815; I Táncsics Mihály utca 26; adult/child 400/150Ft; ☺ 10am-5pm Tue-Sun May-Oct), parts of which date from the 14th century, contains documents and items linked to the Jewish community of Buda, as well as Gothic stone carvings and tombstones from the Great Synagogue in Pest.

Museum of Military History

The **Museum of Military History** (Hadtörténeti Múzeum; Map p83; ☎ 356 9522; I Tóth Árpád sétány 40; admission free; ☺ 10am-6pm Tue-Sun Apr-Sep, 10am-4pm

Tue-Sun Oct-Mar), loaded with weaponry dating from before the Turkish conquest, also does a pretty good job with uniforms, medals, flags and battle-themed fine art. Exhibits focus on the 1848–49 War of Independence and the Hungarian Royal Army under Admiral Miklós Horthy (1918–43).

Buda Castle Labyrinth

The **Buda Castle Labyrinth** (Budavári Labirintus; Map p83; ☎ 489 3281; www.labirintus.com; cnr I Úri utca 9 & Lovas út 4; adult/child 1400/1100Ft; ☺ 9.30am-7.30pm), a 1200m-long cave system some 16m under the Castle District, looks at how the caves have been used since prehistoric times in nine halls and chambers. The admission fee is very high by Budapest standards, but it's all good fun, and a relief from the heat and the crowds above on a hot summer's day.

House of Hungarian Wines

The **House of Hungarian Wines** (Magyar Borok Háza; Map p83; ☎ 212 1030; www.winehouse.hu; I Szentháromság tér 6; sampling 3800Ft; ☺ noon-8pm) offers the chance of a crash course in Hungarian viticulture in the heart of the Castle District. But with over 700 wines on display from Hungary's 22 wine regions and as many as 55 to sample, 'crash' may soon become the operative word.

Matthias Church

Parts of the **Matthias Church** (Mátyás-templom; Map p83; ☎ 355 5657; www.matyas-templom.hu; I Szentháromság tér 2; adult/child/family 600/300/1000Ft, audioguide 300Ft; ☺ 9am-5pm Mon-Fri, 9am-1pm Sat, 1-5pm Sun) date back some 500 years, notably the carvings above the southern entrance. But basically the church (so named because King Matthias Corvinus married Beatrix here in 1474) is a neo-Gothic creation designed by the architect Frigyes Schulek in 1896. In April 2005 the government began a US$20 million restoration of the church that will last two years.

Steps to the right of the main altar inside the church lead to the crypt. The **Matthias Church Collection of Ecclesiastical Art** (Mátyás-templom Egyházművészeti Gyűjteménye; Map p83; ☎ 488 0717), which is included in the church admission fee, has ornate monstrances, reliquaries, chalices and other church plates, as well as a copy of the coronation regalia. There are some interesting views of the chancel from high up in the Royal Oratory.

Fishermen's Bastion

The **Fishermen's Bastion** (Halászbástya; Map p83; adult/child 330/165Ft; ☺ 9am-11pm) is another neo-Gothic masquerade that most visitors (and Hungarians) believe to be much older. But who cares? It looks medieval and still offers views that are among the best in Budapest. Built as a viewing platform in 1905 by Schulek, the bastion's name was taken from the guild of fishermen responsible for defending this stretch of the wall in the Middle Ages. The seven gleaming white turrets represent the Magyar tribes that entered the Carpathian Basin in the late 9th century. In front of the bastion is an ornate equestrian **statue of St Stephen** by sculptor Alajos Stróbl.

Golden Eagle Pharmacy Museum

The **Golden Eagle Pharmacy Museum** (Arany Sas Patikamúzeum; Map p83; ☎ 375 9772; I Tárnok utca 18; admission free; ☺ 10.30am-5.30pm Tue-Sun mid-Mar–Oct, 10.30am-3.30pm Tue-Sun Nov–mid-Mar), just north of Dísz tér on the site of Budapest's first pharmacy (1681), contains an unusual mixture of displays on medieval medicine, including a mock-up of an alchemist's laboratory.

Royal Palace

The former Royal Palace (Budavári Palota; Map p83) has been burned, bombed, razed, rebuilt and redesigned at least a half-dozen times over the past seven centuries. Béla IV established a royal residence here in the mid-13th century and subsequent kings either rebuilt their own residences or added on to them. The palace was destroyed in the battle to rout the Turks in 1686; the Habsburgs rebuilt it, but spent very little time here. Today the Royal Palace contains not royal residences but two museums (the Hungarian National Gallery and the Budapest History Museum) and the **National Széchenyi Library**.

There are two entrances to the Royal Palace. The first is via the **Habsburg Steps**, southeast of Szent György tér and through an ornamental gateway dating from 1903. The other way in is via **Corvinus Gate** (☺ 6am-midnight), with its big black raven symbolising King Matthias Corvinus, southwest of the square.

The **Hungarian National Gallery** (Magyar Nemzeti Galéria; Map p83; ☎ 201 9082, 06 20 439 7325; Royal Palace, Wings B, C & D; admission free, special exhibitions adult/child/family 1500/800/3000Ft; ☺ 10am-6pm Tue-Sun) is an overwhelmingly large collection over four floors that traces the development of Hungarian art from the 10th century to the present day. The largest collections include medieval and Renaissance stonework, Gothic wooden sculptures and panel paintings, late-Gothic winged altars, and late Renaissance and baroque art.

The museum also has an important collection of Hungarian paintings and sculpture from the 19th and 20th centuries. You won't recognise many names, but keep an eye open for the harrowing depictions of war and the dispossessed by László Mednyánszky, the unique portraits by József Rippl-Rónai, the mammoth canvases by Tivadar Csontváry, the paintings of carnivals by the modern artist Vilmos Aba-Novák and works by the realist Mihály Munkácsy, the 'painter of the *puszta*'.

The **Budapest History Museum** (Budapesti Történeti Múzeum; Map p83; ☎ 225 7815, 375 7533; Royal Palace, Wing E; adult/child/family 900/450/1500Ft; audioguide 800Ft; ☼ 10am-6pm mid-May–mid-Sep, 10am-6pm Wed-Mon Mar–mid-May & mid-Sep–Oct, 10am-4pm Wed-Mon Nov-Feb), also known as the Castle Museum (Vár Múzeum), traces the 2000 years of the city on three floors of jumbled exhibits. Restored palace rooms dating from the 15th century can be entered from the basement, which contains an exhibit on the Royal Palace in medieval Buda.

In the basement three vaulted halls, one with a magnificent Renaissance door frame in red marble bearing the seal of Queen Beatrice and tiles with a raven and a ring (the seal of her husband King Matthias Corvinus), lead to the **Gothic Hall**, the **Royal Cellar** and the 14th-century **Tower Chapel**.

On the ground floor is an exhibit entitled 'Budapest in the Middle Ages' as well as Gothic statues discovered during excavations in 1974. The exhibit on the 1st floor – 'Budapest in Modern Times' – traces the history of the city from the expulsion of the Turks in 1686 to Hungary's entry into the EU. On the 2nd floor the exhibits reach way back – Budapest from prehistoric times to the arrival of the Avars in the late 6th century.

GELLÉRT HILL & THE TABÁN

Gellért-hegy (Map p83), a 235m-high rocky hill southeast of the Castle District, is crowned with a fortress of sorts and the Independence Monument, Budapest's unofficial symbol. From Gellért Hill, you can't beat the views of the Royal Palace and the Danube. The Tabán (Map p83), the leafy area between Gellért and Castle Hill, is associated with the Serbs, who settled here after fleeing from the Turks in the early 18th century. Later it became known for its restaurants and wine gardens – a kind of Montmartre for Budapest. Most of them burned to the ground at the turn of the 20th century.

Today Gellért Hill and the Tabán are given over to private homes, parks and three thermal spas that make good use of the hot springs gushing from deep below Gellért Hill. The **Gellért Baths** (Map pp80–1) are open to the public (see p97); the **Rác Baths** (Map p83) were still under renovation at the time of writing.

Szent Gellért tér

Szent Gellért tér faces **Independence Bridge** (Szabadság híd; Map pp80–1 and Map pp88–9) and is dominated by the **Danubius Gellért Hotel** (Map pp80–1), an Art-Nouveau pile (1918) and the city's favourite old-world hotel and spa.

Cave Chapel (Sziklakápolna; Map pp80–1; ☎ 385 1529; ☼ 9am-8pm), on a small hill directly north of the hotel, was built into a cave in 1926. It was the seat of the Pauline order until 1951, when the priests were arrested and imprisoned by the communists, and the cave sealed off. It was reopened in 1992 and reconsecrated. The chapel is closed to the public during Mass services.

Gellért tér can be reached from Pest on bus 7 or tram 47 or 49, and from the Buda side on bus 86 or tram 18 or 19.

Citadella

The **Citadella** (Map pp80–1; ☎ 365 6076; www.citadella.hu; ☼ 24hr) is a fortress that never did battle. Built by the Habsburgs after the 1848–49 War of Independence to 'defend' the city from further insurrection, by the time it was ready (1851) the political climate had changed and the Citadella had become obsolete. It was given to the city in the 1890s and parts of it were symbolically blown to pieces. Today the Citadella contains some big guns and dusty displays in the central courtyard, the new **1944 Waxworks** (1944 Panoptikum; Map pp80–1; ☎ 279 1963; admission 1200Ft; ☼ 9am-9pm Mon Fri, 8am-10pm Sat,

8am-9pm Sun) inside a bunker used during WWII, a hotel/hostel (p105), a restaurant and a dance club.

To get here from Pest cross Elizabeth Bridge and take the stairs leading up behind the statue of St Gellért, or cross Independence Bridge and follow Verejték utca through the park starting at the Cave Chapel. Bus 27 runs almost to the top of the hill from Móricz Zsigmond körtér, southwest of the Danubius Gellért Hotel (and accessible on trams 18, 19, 47 and 49).

Independence Monument

The **Independence Monument** (Szabadságszobor; Map pp80–1), the lovely lady with the palm frond proclaiming freedom throughout the city, is to the east of the Citadella. Some 14m high, it was erected in 1947 in tribute to the Soviet soldiers who died liberating Budapest in 1945.

Statues & Bridges

The **Elizabeth Bridge** (Erzsébet híd; Map p86) is the gleaming white (though rather generic-looking) suspension bridge northeast of Gellért Hill. It enjoys a special place in the hearts of Budapesters, as it was the first newly designed bridge to reopen after WWII (1964).

Looking down on Elizabeth Bridge from Gellért Hill is the **St Gellért statue** (Map p83), an Italian missionary invited to Hungary by King Stephen to convert the natives. The monument marks the spot where the bishop was hurled to his death in a spiked barrel in 1046 by pagan Hungarians resisting the new faith.

To the north of the bridge and through the underpass is a **Queen Elizabeth statue** (Map p86), the Habsburg empress and Hungarian queen. The consort of Franz Joseph, she was much-loved by Magyars because, among other things, she learned to speak Hungarian. Sissi, as she was affectionately known, was assassinated by an Italian anarchist in Geneva in 1898.

VÍZIVÁROS

Víziváros (Watertown; Map p83 and Map pp80–1) is the narrow area between the Danube and Castle Hill that widens as it approaches Óbuda to the north and Rózsadomb (Rose Hill) to the northwest, spreading as far west as Moszkva tér, one of Buda's

main transport hubs. In the Middle Ages those involved in trades, crafts and fishing lived here. Under the Turks many of the district's churches were used as mosques, and baths were built, one of which is still functioning. Víziváros is today the heart of urban Buda.

You can reach Víziváros on foot from the metro M2 Batthyány tér stop by walking south along the river or via tram 19, which links the neighbourhood with Szent Gellért tér. Bus 16 from Deák Ferenc tér stops here on its way to/from Castle Hill.

Clark Ádám tér

Clark Ádám tér (Map p83) is named after the 19th-century Scottish engineer who supervised the building of the **Széchenyi Chain Bridge** (Széchenyi lánchíd; Map p83), leading from the square, and who designed the **tunnel** (*alagút*; Map p83) under Castle Hill, which took eight months to carve out of the limestone. The bridge was actually the idea of Count István Széchenyi – see p171 – and when it opened in 1849 it was unique for two reasons: it was the first dry link between Buda and Pest; and the aristocracy, previously exempt from all taxation, had to pay the toll like everybody else. The curious sculpture, which looks like an elongated doughnut, hidden in the bushes to the south is the **0km stone** (Map p83); all Hungarian roads to and from the capital are measured from this exact spot.

Fő utca

Fő utca (Map p83) is the 'Main Street' running through Víziváros and dates from Roman times. At the former **Capuchin church** (Map p83; 1 Fő utca 30-32), used as a mosque during the Turkish occupation, you can see the remains of two Islamic-style ogee-arched doors and windows on the southern side. Around the corner there's the seal of King Matthias Corvinus – a raven and a ring – and the little square with the delightful **Louis Fountain** (Lajos kútja; 1904) is called **Corvin tér**. The Eclectic building on the north side is the **Buda Concert Hall** (Budai Vigadó; Map p83; Corvin tér 8).

Batthyány tér (Map p83 and Map pp80–1), a short distance to the northeast, is the centre of Víziváros and the best place to snap a picture of the Parliament building across the river. In the centre of this rather shabby square is the entrance to both metro

M2 and the HÉV suburban line to Szentendre. On the southern side is **St Anne's Church** (Szent Ana templom; Map p83; II Batthyány tér 7), with one of the loveliest baroque interiors of any church in Budapest.

A couple of streets north is **Nagy Imre tér** (Map pp80–1), with the enormous **Military Court of Justice** (Map pp80–1; II Fő utca 70-78) on the northern side. Here Imre Nagy and others were tried and sentenced to death in 1958 (see p32). It was also the site of the notorious **Fő utca prison**, where many other victims of the regime were incarcerated and tortured.

The **Király Baths** (Király Gyógyfürdő; Map pp80–1; II Fő utca 82-86), parts of which date from 1580, are one block to the north (see p97). Across pedestrianised Ganz utca is the Greek Catholic **St Florian Chapel** (Szent Flórián kápolna; Map pp80–1; II Fő utca 88-90), built in 1760 and dedicated to the patron saint of fire-fighters.

Millennium Park

One of the more successful urban redevelopment projects on either side of the Danube in the past decade, **Millennium Park** (Millenáris Park; Map pp80–1; ☎ 438 5312; www.millenaris.hu; II Kis Rókus utca 16-20 & Lövőház utca 37; ☷ 6am-1am; Ⓜ M2 Moszkva tér, ⓐ 4 or 6) is a large landscaped complex behind the Mammut shopping mall comprising fountains, ponds, little bridges, a theatre and the **Millennium Exhibition Hall** (Millenáris Kiállítócsarnok; ☎ 438 5335; admission varies; ☷ 10am-6pm or 8pm), which hosts some unusual cultural exhibits.

Frankel Leó út

At Bem tér, Fő utca turns into Frankel Leó út, a tree-lined street of antique shops and boutiques. At its northern end is the **Lukács Baths** (Lukács Gyógyfürdő; Map pp80–1; II Frankel Leó út 25-29; ☷ 17, ⓐ 60 or 86), which caters to an older and quite serious crowd of bath enthusiasts (see p97). A short distance north and tucked away in an apartment block is the **Újlak Synagogue** (Újlaki zsinagóga; Map pp80–1; II Frankel Leó út 49), built in 1888 on the site of an older prayer house and not open to the public.

Tomb of Gül Baba

The overly reconstructed **Tomb of Gül Baba** (Gül Baba türbéje; Map pp80–1; ☎ 326 0062; II Türbe tér 1; adult/child/student 500/250/500Ft; ☷ 10am-6pm Mar-Oct, 10am-4pm Nov-Feb; HÉV station Margit híd, ⓐ 4, 6 or 17) contains the remains of one Gül Baba, an

Ottoman Dervish who took part in the capture of Buda in 1541, and is known in Hungary as the 'Father of Roses'. To reach it from Török utca, which runs parallel to Frankel Leó út, walk west along steep (and cobbled) Gül Baba utca to the set of steps just past No 16. You can also reach here along Mecset utca, which runs north from Margit utca. The tomb is a pilgrimage place for Muslims, especially from Turkey, and you must remove your shoes before entering. There's a pleasant café here with fine views.

ÓBUDA

'Ó' means 'ancient' in Hungarian; as its name suggests, Óbuda is the oldest part of Buda. The Romans settled at Aquincum north of here (see p21) and when the Magyars arrived, they named it Buda, which became Óbuda when the Royal Palace was built on Castle Hill.

You can reach the heart of Óbuda on the HÉV commuter train – get off at the Árpád híd stop – from Batthyány tér, which is on the M2 metro line, or bus 86 from Fő utca and other points along the Danube on the Buda side. If you're near City Park (Városliget) in Pest, walk southeast to the intersection of Hungária körút and Thököly út and catch the No 1 tram, which avoids Buda and crosses Árpád Bridge into Óbuda.

Florián tér & Surrounds

Florián tér (Map pp78–9), split in two by the Árpád Bridge flyover and encircled by mammoth housing blocks, is not the best introduction to Óbuda, but it remains the district's historic centre.

The yellow baroque **Óbuda Parish Church** (Óbudai plébániatemplom; Map pp78-9; III 168 Lajos utca), built in 1749 and dedicated to Sts Peter and Paul, dominates the easternmost side of Flórián tér. There's a massive rococo pulpit inside. To the south, the large neoclassical building beside the Corinthia Aquincum Hotel is the former **Óbuda Synagogue** (Óbudai zsinagóga; Map pp78-9; III Lajos utca 163), dating from 1821. It now houses the sound studios of MTV (Hungarian TV).

Opposite, the **Budapest Gallery Exhibition House** (Budapest Galéria Kiállítóháza; Map pp78–9; ☎ 388 6771; III Lajos utca 158; adult/child 400/200Ft; ☷ 10am-6pm Tue-Sun) hosts some of the most interesting avant-garde exhibitions in town. It also has a standing exhibit of works by

Pál Pátzay, whose sculptures can be seen throughout the city (eg the fountain on Tárnok utca in Buda's Castle District and the *Serpent Slayer* in honour of Raoul Wallenberg in Szent István Park in Pest).

To explore the **Roman Military Amphitheatre** (Római katonai amfiteátrum; Map pp78-9; Pacsirtamező utca), built in the 2nd century for the garrisons, archaeology and classical history buffs taking bus 86 to Flórián tér should get off at Nagyszombat utca (for HÉV passengers, it's the Tímár utca stop), about 800m south of Flórián tér. The amphitheatre could accommodate up to 15,000 people and was larger than the Colosseum in Rome. The rest of the military camp extended north to Flórián tér.

Housed in an 18th-century monastery, later a barracks that was badly damaged in WWII and again in 1956, to the southwest of Flórián tér, the exhibits at the **Kiscell Museum** (Kiscelli Múzeum; Map pp78-9; ☎ 388 8560, 250 0304; III Kiscelli utca 108; adult/child 600/300Ft; ☒ 10am-6pm Tue-Sun Apr-Oct, 10am-4pm Nov-Mar; ☒ 17, ☒ 60) attempt to tell the story (from the human side) of Budapest since liberation from the Turks. The museum counts among its best exhibits a complete 19th-century apothecary moved here from Kálvin tér, ancient signboards advertising shops and other concerns, and rooms furnished in Empire, Biedermeier and Art-Nouveau furniture and bric-a-brac. The **Municipal Gallery** (Fővárosi Képtár), with its impressive art collection (József Rippl-Rónai, Lajos Tihanyi, István Csók, Béla Czóbel etc) is housed upstairs.

Szentlélek tér & Fő tér

Two contiguous squares lying east of Flórián tér – Szentlélek tér (Holy Spirit Sq; Map pp78-9), a transport hub, and Fő tér (Main Sq; Map pp78-9), a quiet restored square of baroque houses, public buildings and restaurants – contain Óbuda's most important museums.

The **Vasarely Museum** (Map pp78-9; ☎ 388 7551; III Szentlélek tér 6; admission free, temporary exhibitions adult/child 400/200Ft; ☒ 10am-5.30pm Tue-Sun), housed in the crumbling Zichy Mansion, is devoted to the works of Victor Vasarely (or Vásárhelyi Győző before he emigrated to Paris in 1930), the late 'Father of Op Art'. The works are excellent and fun to watch as they swell and move around the canvas. On the 1st floor are exhibits of works by Hungarian artists working abroad.

The **Imre Varga Exhibition House** (Varga Imre kiállítóháza; Map pp78-9; ☎ 250 0274; III Laktanya utca 7; adult/child 250/100Ft; ☒ 10am-6pm Tue-Sun), part of the Budapest Gallery, includes sculptures, statues, medals and drawings by Varga (1923–), one of Hungary's foremost sculptors, who seems to have sat on both sides of the fence politically for decades – sculpting Béla Kun and Lenin as dextrously as he did St Stephen, Béla Bartók and even Imre Nagy (p91). En route to the museum from Fő tér, you'll pass some of Varga's work: a group of odd metal sculptures of rather worried-looking women holding umbrellas in the middle of the road.

AQUINCUM

The most complete Roman civilian town in Hungary and now a museum, Aquincum (Map pp78–9) had paved streets and fairly sumptuous single-storey houses with courtyards, fountains and mosaic floors, as well as sophisticated drainage and heating systems. Not all that is easily apparent today as you walk among the ruins, but you can see its outlines, as well as those of the big public baths, the market, an early-Christian church and a temple dedicated to the god Mithra. Across the road to the northwest is the **Roman Civilian Amphitheatre** (Római polgári amfiteátrum; Map pp78-9; Szentendrei út), about half the size of the one reserved for the garrison.

You can reach Aquincum on the HÉV (Aquincum stop) or on bus 34 or 42 from Szentlélek tér.

The **Aquincum Museum** (Aquincumi Múzeum; Map pp78-9; ☎ 250 1650, 430 1081; www.aquincum.hu; III Szentendrei út 139; archaeological park adult/child 400/150Ft, park & museum adult/child/family 700/300/1200Ft; ☒ park 9am-6pm Tue-Sun May-Sep, 9am-5pm Tue-Sun 15-30 Apr & Oct, museum 10am-6pm Tue-Sun May-Sep, 10am-5pm Tue-Sun 15-30 Apr & Oct), in the centre of what remains of this Roman civilian settlement, puts the ruins in perspective with some success. Most of the big sculptures and stone sarcophagi are outside to the left of the museum or behind it in the lapidary. Look out for the replica of a 3rd-century portable organ called a hydra (and the mosaic illustrating how it was played) and the mock-up of a Roman bath.

BUDA HILLS

With 'peaks' reaching over 500m, a comprehensive system of trails and no lack of unusual conveyances, the Buda Hills (Map p77) are the city's playground and a welcome respite from hot, dusty Pest in the warmer months; some families actually have summer homes here. If you're planning to ramble, take along a copy of Cartographia's 1:30,000 *A Budai-hegység* map (No 6; 900Ft). Apart from the Béla Bartók Memorial House, under renovation at the time of writing, there are few sights, though you might want to poke your head in one of the Buda Hills' pair of caves (p99).

With all the unusual transport options, heading for the hills is more than half the fun. From the Moszkva tér metro station on the M2 line in Buda, walk westward along Szilágyi Erzsébet fasor for 10 minutes (or take tram 18 or 56 for two stops) to the circular high-rise Hotel Budapest at Szilágyi Erzsébet fasor 47. Directly opposite is the terminus of the **Cog Railway** (Fogaskerekű vasút; Map p77; ☎ 355 4167; admission 1 BKV ticket; ⏰ up 5am-11pm, down 5.20am-11.30pm). Built in 1874, the cog climbs for 3.6km in about 16 minutes to **Széchenyi-hegy** (427m), one of the prettiest residential areas in the city.

At Széchenyi-hegy, you can stop for a picnic in the attractive park south of the old-time station or board the narrow-gauge **Children's Railway** (Gyermekvasút; Map p77; ☎ 397 5394; adult/child 300/100Ft; ⏰ 10am-5pm Mon-Fri, 9.45am-5.30pm Sat & Sun mid-Mar late Oct, 10am-4pm Tue-Fri, 10am-5pm Sat & Sun late Oct–mid-Mar), two minutes to the south on Hegyhát út. The railway was built in 1951 by Pioneers (socialist Scouts) and is staffed entirely by schoolchildren aged 10 to 14 – the engineer excepted. The little train chugs along for 12km, terminating at **Hűvösvölgy** (Chilly Valley). There are walks fanning out from any of the stops along the way, or you can return to Moszkva tér on tram 56 from Hűvösvölgy. The train operates about once an hour (every 45 minutes on weekends in season).

A more interesting way down from the hills, though, is to get off at **János-hegy**, the fourth stop on the Children's Railway and the highest point (527m) in the hills. About 700m due east is the **chairlift** (libegő; ☎ 394 3764; adult/child 450/200Ft; ⏰ 9.30am-5pm mid-May–mid-Sep, 9.30am-4pm mid-Sep–mid-May), which will take you down to Zugligeti út. (Note the chairlift is closed on the Monday of every even-numbered week.) From here bus 158 returns to Moszkva tér (last one just after 10.15pm).

Margaret Island

Neither Buda nor Pest, 2.5km-long Margaret Island (Margit-sziget; Map pp80–1 and Map pp78–9) in the middle of the Danube River was always the domain of one religious order or another until the Turks came and turned what was then called the Island of Rabbits into – appropriately enough – a harem, from which all 'infidels' were barred. It's been a public park open to everyone since the mid-19th century.

Cross over to Margaret Island from Pest or Buda via trams 4 or 6. Bus 26 covers the length of the island as it makes the run between Nyugati train station (Nyugati pályaudvar) and Árpád Bridge bus station. Cars are allowed on Margaret Island from Árpád Bridge only as far as the two big hotels at the northeastern end; the rest is reserved for pedestrians, cyclists and horse-drawn carriages.

MEDIEVAL RUINS

The ruins of the **Franciscan church and monastery** (Ferences templom és kolostor; Map pp80–1) – no more than a tower and a wall dating from the late 13th century – are almost in the exact geographical centre of Margaret Island. The Habsburg archduke Joseph built a summer residence here when he inherited the island in 1867. It was later converted into a hotel that operated until 1949.

The former **Dominican convent** (Domonkos kolostor; Map pp78–9) lies to the northeast of the Franciscan church and monastery. It was built by Béla IV, whose scribes played an important role in the continuation of Hungarian scholarship. Its most famous resident was Béla's own daughter, St Margaret (1242–71). As the story goes, the king promised to commit his daughter to a life of devotion in a nunnery if the Mongols were driven from the land. They were and she was – at nine years of age. Still, she seemed to enjoy it – if we're to believe the *Lives of the Saints* – especially the mortification-of-the-flesh parts and never bathing above her ankles. St Margaret, not canonised until 1943, commands something of a cult following in Hungary. A red marble sepulchre cover surrounded by a wrought-iron grille marks her original resting place, and there's a much visited shrine with votives nearby.

ISLAND ON THE GO

The Romans used mineral springs as both drinking water and therapy, and so do the modern Magyars. Kristályvíz, one of the more popular brands of mineral water in Hungary, is sourced and bottled here, and the thermal spa at the Danubius Grand Hotel Margitsziget (p97), to the northeast, is one of the most modern spas in Budapest.

You can hire a bicycle from one of several stands, including **Sétacikli** (Map pp80-1; ☎ 06 30 966 6453; 3-speed per 30min/hr/day 400/600/1800Ft, pedal coach per hr for 3/5 people 1800/2700Ft; ☒ 10am-dusk Mar-Oct), which is on the western side just before the athletic stadium as you walk from Margaret Bridge. **Bringóhintó** (Map pp78-9; ☎ 329 2073, 06 30 881 0983; www.bringohinto.hu; mountain bike per 30min/ hr 590/990Ft, pedal coach for 4 people 1480/3380Ft, inline skates 880/1480Ft; ☒ 8am-dusk) rents equipment from the refreshment stand near the Japanese Garden in the north of the island.

A twirl around the island in one of the **horse-drawn coaches** (Map pp78–9), stationed just south of the Bringóhintó bike-rental stand, costs from about 2000Ft per person.

WATER TOWER & OPEN-AIR THEATRE

The octagonal **water tower** (víztorony; Map pp78–9), erected in 1911 in the north-central part of the island, rises 66m above the **open-air theatre** (szabadtéri színpad; ☎ 340 4883), which is used for opera, plays and concerts in summer. The tower now houses the **Lookout Gallery** (Kiállító Galéria; ☎ 340 4520; adult/child 200/100Ft; ☒ 11am-7pm May-Oct), which exhibits some interesting folk craft and contemporary art on the ground floor. But the main reason for entering is to climb the 153 steps for a stunning 360-degree view of the island, Buda and Pest from the cupola terrace.

Pest

While Buda can often feel like a garden, Pest is an urban jungle, with a wealth of architecture, museums, historic buildings and broad boulevards that are unmatched on the other side of the Danube. And while there's nothing like the Buda Hills here, there's no shortage of open green spaces either – City Park (Map pp80-1) at the end of Andrássy út is the largest park in Budapest.

INNER TOWN

The Inner Town (Belváros; Map p86) is the heart of Pest and has the most valuable commercial real estate in the city. The area north of Ferenciek tere is full of flashy boutiques and well-touristed bars and restaurants; you'll hear more German, Italian, Spanish and English spoken here than Hungarian. The neighbourhood south of Ferenciek tere was until recently studenty, quieter and much more local. Now parts of it, too, have been reserved for pedestrians, and there is no shortage of trendy pubs, cafés and restaurants.

Ferenciek tere, which divides the Inner Town at Szabadsajtó út (Free Press Avenue), is on the M3 metro line and can be reached by bus 7 from Buda or points east in Pest.

Around Egyetem tér

The centre of the Inner Town south of Szabadsajtó út is Egyetem tér (University Sq; Map p86), a five-minute walk south along Károly Mihály utca from Ferenciek tere. The square's name refers to the branch of the prestigious **Loránd Eötvös Science University** (ELTE; Map p86; V Egyetem tér 1-3). Next to the university building to the west is the **University Church**, a lovely baroque structure built in 1748. Over the altar inside is a copy of the **Black Madonna of Częstochowa** so revered in Poland.

Leafy Kecskeméti utca runs southeast from the square to **Kálvin tér** (Map p86). At the end of it, near the Korona Hotel, there's a plaque marking the location of the **Kecskemét Gate** (Kecskeméti-kapu), part of the medieval city wall that was pulled down in the 1700s. **Ráday utca** (Map p86 and Map pp80-1), which leads south from Kálvin tér and is full of cafés, clubs and restaurants, is where university students and travellers entertain themselves these days.

Along Váci utca

The best way to see the posher side of the Inner Town is to walk up pedestrian Váci utca, the capital's premier – and most expensive – shopping street, with designer clothes, expensive jewellery shops, pubs and some bookshops for browsing. This was the total length of Pest in the Middle Ages. To gain

(Continued on page 90)

0 _____ 2 km
0 _____ 1 mile

Óbuda, Aquincum & Angyalföld (pp78–9)

Esztergom (46km);
Komárom (85km)
Bp-Üröm vá

Aranyhegy
Rómaifürdő
Csillaghegy
To Szentendre (11km)
To Vác (26km)
Újpest
IV

Óbuda vá
Aquincum felső vm
Aquincum

Kaszásdűlő

Aquincum
Nép sziget
Újpest-Városkapu

To Gödöllő (24km);
Gyöngyös (69km);
Miskolc (179km)

ármashatár-
egy (495m)
II
Kaszásdűlő
Filatorigát

Óbuda Island
(Óbudai-sziget)
Gyöngyösi u
Angyalföld vá
Istvántelek

Felső-Kecske-
hegy (443m)
Tábor-hegy (396m)
Remetehgy
Remete-hegy (351m)
ÓBUDA
III
Árpád híd
Forgách u
Angyalföld
XIII

Buda Hills
Mátyás-hegy (300m)
Tímár u
Árpád híd
XIV

Chairlift & Zugligeti
the Camping
cm);
vösvölgy
5km);
vascentrum (3km)
Zöldmál
Ferenc-hegy (265m)
Újlak
Szépvölgyi út
Vizafogó
Dózsa György út
Löportárdűlő
Rákosrendező
Buda & Pest (pp80–2)

Törökvész
Felhévíz
Margaret Island
(Margit-sziget)
Mexikói út
Herminamező

Vérhalom
Rózsadomb
Margit híd
Széchenyi fürdő
Nagy Lajos király útja
To Favorit Lovarda (5km)

Rézmal
BUDA
Central Pest (pp84–5)
Nyugati Train Station
Hősök tere
City Park (Városliget)
Zugló Train Station

Kútvölgyi út
Castle Hill & Watertown (p83)
Lipótváros
Kossuth Lajos tér
Bajza utca
Kodály körönd
Andrássy út
VI
Terézváros
VII
Vörösmarty utca

Children's Railway
Istenhegy
Széchenyi-gy (1.2km)
tyos
Moszkva tér
Vízivárós
Batthyány tér
Arany János utca
Oktogon
PEST
Ferenc Puskás Stadium
To Gödöllő (27km);
Miskolc (179km)

Déli Train Station
Royal Palace
Belváros (Inner Town) (pp86–7)
Vörösmarty tér
Deák Ferenc tér
VIII
Keleti Train Station
Stadionok
7

Farkasrét
Tabán
Ferenciek tere
Belváros
Astoria
Blaha Lujza tér
Józsefváros
X
Ligettelek

Farkasréti temető
Németvölgy
Gellért-hegy
Kálvin tér
Józsefvárosi pu

Törökbálinti út
XII
Citadella
IX
Ferenc krt
Klinikák
South Buda & Ferencváros (pp88–9)
Néplíget

Sasad
Villányi út
Boráros tér
Ferencváros
Nagyvárad tér
Néplíget
Ecseri út

Győr (123km);
enna (275km)
XI
Kelenföldi pu
Haller u
National Theatre
Könyves Kálmán krt
To Europark Market (2km);
Ferihegy International Airport (20km);
Debrecen (226km)

M1 M7
Budaörsi út
Vágóhíd vá
To Ecseri Piac (2km);
József Bozsik Stadium (2km);
Kecskemét (72km)

Siófok (106km);
ake Balaton
Kelenvölgy
Beöthy u f vm
Csepel Island
(Csepel-sziget)
M5
E75
Pesterzsébet

Péterhegy
Szabadkikötő vm

Rózsavölgy
Budafok-Albertfalva vá
Ófalu
To Ráckeve (36km)
Pesterzsébet vm

INFORMATION	
Slovenian Consulate	1 A2
South African Embassy	2 A2

SIGHTS & ACTIVITIES	(pp69–101)
Cog Railway Terminus	3 A3
Statue Park	4 A6

SLEEPING	(pp103–8)
Beatrix Panzio	(see 5)
IBS Garden Hotel	5 A3

EATING	(pp109–15)
Remíz	6 A3

ENTERTAINMENT	(pp116–20)
International Buda Stage	(see 5)
Kincsem Park	7 D4

TRANSPORT	(pp122–7)
Queenybus	8 A4

To Százhalombatta (16km);
Siófok (106km);
Lake Balaton
To Fox Autorent (2km); Balázs & Friends Cyclists'
Sports Association (2.5km); Anselport (3km);
Siófok (106km); Lake Balaton
To Kecskemét (72km);
Baja (132km)

A B C D

1

6
Csillaghegy

20

Rómaifürdő
Rozgonyi Piroska u
29
Monostori út

Aranyhegy

Óbuda vá

Óbudai temető

Aquincum
21

Aquincum
felső vm
Keled út
Pók u

2

Kaszásdülő

3

Záhony u

10

Kunigunda útja
Bojtár u

Aquincum

3

ÓBUDA

Farkastorki út

Kaszásdülő

Filatorigát

33

Hévízi út
Meggyfa u

Május 9 park

Óbuda Island
(Óbudai-sziget)

Raktár u

4

Remetehegy
Buda Hills

Remetehegyi út
Bécsi út

Váradi u

Hunor u

Velence u

Vörösvári út

Szentendrei út

Vöröskereszt u
11
12

Kórház u

Laktanya u

Danube River

Szabadsá
strand

Reménység u
1

Szél u

San Marco u

Flórián
tér
Fő
tér
24

30
9

Szentlélek
tér
Árpád híd

Árpád Bridge (Árpád híd)

14

Kiscelli u

Kenyeres u

Szőlő u

Zápor u

San Marco u

Serfőző u
16
Pacsirtamező u
Korvin u
5
31
Tél u

Perc u

7

5

Mátyás-hegy
(300m)

Mátyáshegyi út

Szépvölgyi út
19

Dévai Bíró
M tér

Szőnyeg u

Selmeci u

Bécsi út

Beszterce u

32

Tímár u

Fényes

Fecske u

Textilgyár u

Tímár u
Tímár u

4
13
10
27
26

Csatárka út

Szépvölgyi út

Viador u

Nagyszombat u

22
Újlak

25
34
8

Zöldlomb út
Felső Zöldmáli út
23

Zöldmál

6

Bokor u

Ürömi u

Derogie u

18

Kolosy
tér
Szépvölgyi út

Lajos u

Hűvösvölgyi út

Hajós Alfréd sétány

Margaret Island
(Margit-sziget)

Vizafogó

Kő
tér

Csejfa u

Pusztaszeri út

Orbán u

Újlak u

Zsigmond
tér

INFORMATION
Hungarian Federation of Disabled
　Persons' Associations.........................**1** B4
Slovak Consulate.....................................**2** H6

SIGHTS & ACTIVITIES (pp73–5)
Aquincum Museum.................................**3** C2
Bringóhintó Bike Rentals.......................**4** D5
Budapest Gallery Exhibition House.....**5** C5
Csillaghegy Swimming Complex..........**6** C1
Dagály Swimming Complex...................**7** D5
Former Dominican Convent...................**8** D6
Former Óbuda Synagogue.....................**9** C5
Horse-Drawn Coaches.........................**10** C5
Imre Varga Exhibition House..............**11** C4
Imre Varga Sculptures.........................**12** C4
Japanese Garden..................................**13** D5
Kiscell Museum & Municipal Gallery..**14** B5
KSH Canoe Club....................................**15** E1
Lookout Gallery.............................(see 25)
Óbuda Parish Church...........................**16** C5
Óbuda Sport Club.................................**17** E1
Palatinus Strand...................................**18** C6
Pálvölgy Cave.......................................**19** A5
Rómaifürdő Strandfürdő......................**20** D1
Roman Civilian Amphitheatre.............**21** C2
Roman Military Amphitheatre.............**22** C4
Szemlő-hegy Cave................................**23** A6
Thermal Bath.................................(see 26)
Vasarely Museum.................................**24** C4
Water Tower..**25** C5

SLEEPING 🛏 🏠 (pp103–8)
Danubius Grand Hotel Margitsziget.**26** D5
Danubius Thermal Hotel Margitsziget
　& Thermal Bath.................................**27** D5
Flandria Hotel.......................................**28** F6
Római Camping.....................................**29** C1

EATING 🍴 (pp109–11)
Corinthia Aquincum Hotel...................**30** C5
Kéhli..**31** C5
Kisbuda Gyöngye.................................**32** B5

ENTERTAINMENT 🎭 (pp116–20)
Mokka Cuka..**33** D3
Open-Air Theatre..................................**34** C6
UTE Stadium..**35** F1

TRANSPORT (pp122–7)
Árpád Bridge Bus Station.....................**36** E5

A B C D

1 2 3 4 5 6

Zöldmál
Felső Zöldmáli út
Bécsi
Derögvie
73
Csemete u
Kolosy tér
Szepvölgyi út
Kő tér
27
Pusztaszeri
Cserfa u
23
Viza u
Révész u
Gábor Áron u
Törökvész út
Kupeczky u
Zsigmond tér
Margaret Island
(Margit-sziget)
Drávc u
Tisza u
Vérhalom
Mandula u
Felhévíz
Harcsa u
45
53
Bessenyei u
Garam u
Rózsadomb
17
52
31
67
16
48
39
Szent István Park
Victor Hugó u
Lehel tér
Rézmal
Római Flórís u
43
Türbe tér
Vibra u
80
41
69
9
62
Újlipótváros
93
Ribáry u
84
Marczibányi tér
55
29
92
Margit híd
Margaret Bridge
(Margit híd)
87
Katona József u
Nyugati Train Station
Nyugati pu
34
35
Margit krt
Bem József tér
3
Ganz u
64
Szent István krt
Lipótváros
Szilágyi Erzsébet fasor
Cog Railway Terminus
Fény u
63
91
95
90
61
BUDA
30
Kacsa u
32
89
Honvéd u
Márkó u
Kossuth Lajos tér
Nyugati pu
Vérosmajor
Moszkva tér
Toldy Ferenc u
Szabó Ilonka u
Mátray u
Mária tér
Batthyány tér
Batthyány tér
Danube River
Kossuth Lajos tér
Alkotmány u
Kálmán Imre u
Báthory u
Arany János utca
Magyar jakobinusok tere 6
Vérmező
Déli pu
Déli Train Station
Országház u
Úri u
Szentháromság tér
Toldy Ferenc u
Szilágyi Dezső tér
Corvin tér
Lipótváros
Roosevelt tér
Szent István tér
Opera
Andrássy út
To Hungarian Ornithological & Nature Conservation Society (7.5km)
Királyhágó tér
68
Márvány u
Attila u
Krisztina tér
Alagút u
Várfok u
Disz tér
Clark Ádám tér
Széchenyi Chain Bridge (Széchenyi lánchíd)
Eötvös tér
József Attila u
Erzsébet tér
Bajcsy-Zsilinszky út
Deák Ferenc tér
Vörösmarty tér
Viágodi tér
Szervita tér
Astoria
Apor Vilmos tér
Németvölgy
Csörsz u
Mészáros u
Royal Palace
Ybl Miklós u
Tabán
Belváros
Petőfi tér
Ferenciek tere
Váci u
Kossuth u
Hegyalja út
Gellért-hegy
Elizabeth Bridge (Erzsébet híd)
77
Orom u
Citadella
20
28
Jubilee Park
Kelenhegyi út
19
Szent Gellért tér
49
25
Fővám tér
18
Németvölgyi út

CASTLE HILL & WATERTOWN

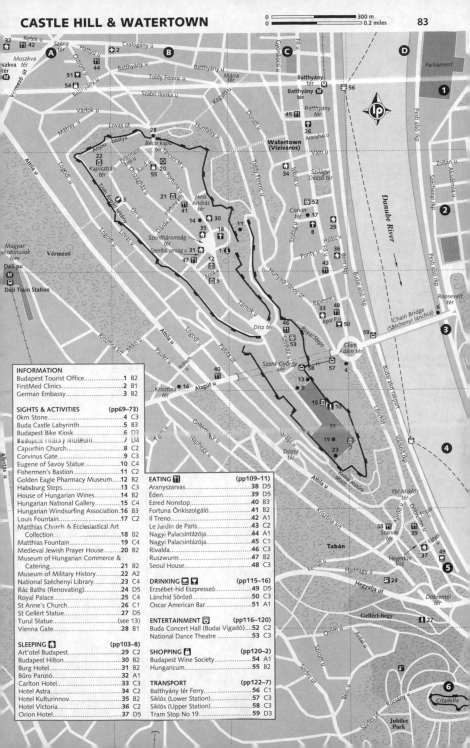

See Belváros (Inner Town) Map (p86–7)

A   B   C   D

Citadella

Otthon u

Helbélia út

Ramvány u

Schweider u

Szirtes út

Bécsi u

Szirtes út

Kelenhegyi út

Jubilee Park

Independence Bridge (Szabadság híd)

Citadella

Menesi út

Somlói út

Mányoki út

Verejték u

Kelenhegyi út

Orlay u

Szent Gellért tér

Buda alsó ráp

Műegyetem rkp

Danube River

Mátyás u

Csuczor u

Kökraklu u

1

Sas-hegy (266m)

Nedecvár u

Alkotás út

Karolina út

Diószegi út

Villányi út

Firsz

Csurét

Balogi u

Himfy u

Bartók Béla u

Mínerva u

Mátyás u

Bartalan Lajos u

Krusper u

Sztoczek József u

Petőfi Bridge (Petőfi híd)

Goldman György tér

2

9

6

10

18

David Ferenc u

Tarjent u

Ménesi út

Móricz Zsigmond körtér

Karinthy Frigyes út

Bersenyi u

Nagyszőlős u

Feketekő u

Fenekeetlen-tó

Kosztolányi Dezső tér

Október 23 u

Kőrösy József u

Irínyi József u

Bogdánfy u

ELTE

Takés Mu

Bocskai út

3

Bartók Béla út

Hamzsabégi út

Kanizsai u

Baranyai u

Sárbogárdi u

Budafoki út

Magyar tudósok körútja

2

Halmi utca

Bartók Béla út

Frakno u

Bártfai u

Hamzsabégi út

14

Dombóvári u

Andaló u

3

To Statue Park (7km)

To Velo-Touring (1km)

Budaörsi út

Vasút u

Kelenföldi Train Station

Ildikó tér

Etele tér

20

Vahot u

Tétenyi u

Mérnök u

Etele út

Kelenföld

Fehérvári út

Galambóc u

Bánát u

Lecke u

Hengermalom u

Menyecske u

Bikszádi út

Borszék u

Major u

Sztregova u

Nádportehajó u

Szerém u

Lágymányos

11

Barazda u

Budafoki út

Sopron u

4

Egér út

Kadihegyi út

Allende Park

Andor u

Csurgói út

Zsombor u

Galvani u

6

Kelenvölgy

Hunyadi Mátyás út

Adács u

Letanca Sándor u

Szabados Sándor u

Temesvár út

Danube River

Kondorosi út

Fehérvári út

5

Fehér- hegyi út

Körmend u

Építész u

Kunhegyes u

Albertfalva

Vegyész u

Szerém u

Hunyadi János út

Ady Endre út

17

6

Ady Endre út

Budafok-Albertfalva vá

Kítérő út

Anna u

Rózsavölgy

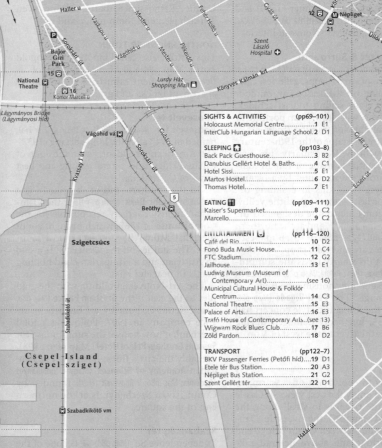

(Continued from page 76)

access from Ferenciek tere, walk through **Párisi Udvar** (Parisian Court; Map p86; V Ferenciek tere 5), a gem of a Parisian-style arcade built in 1909, and into tiny Kigyó utca. Váci utca is immediately to the west.

Many of the buildings on Váci utca are worth closer inspection, but as it's a narrow street you'll have to crane your neck or walk into one of the side streets for a better view. **Thonet House** (Map p86; V Váci utca 11/a) is a masterpiece built by Ödön Lechner (1890) and the flower shop called **Philanthia** (Map p86; V Váci utca 9) has an original Art-Nouveau interior.

Vörösmarty tér & Surrounds

Váci utca ends at Vörösmarty tér (Map p86), a large square of smart shops, galleries, cafés and, depending on the season, an outdoor market with stalls selling tourist schlock, and artists who will draw your portrait or caricature suitable for framing (maybe).

In the centre is a statue of the 19th-century poet after whom Vörösmarty tér was named. The statue is made of Italian marble and is protected in winter by a bizarre plastic 'iceberg' that kids love sliding on. The first – or last – stop of the little yellow (or Millennium) metro line designated the M1 is also in the square, and at the northern end is **Gerbeaud** (Map p86; p113), Budapest's most famous café and cake shop.

South of Vörösmarty tér is the sumptuous **Bank Palace** (Bank Palota; Map p86; Deák utca 5), built in 1915 and now housing the Budapest Stock Exchange. The **Pesti Vigadó** (Map p86; V Vigadó tér 1), the Romantic-style concert hall built in 1865, but badly damaged during WWII, faces the river to the west of Vörösmarty tér.

Duna korzó

An easy way to cool down on a warm afternoon (and enjoy the best views of Castle Hill across the river) is to stroll along the Duna korzó (Map p86), the riverside 'Danube Promenade' between Chain Bridge and Elizabeth Bridge and above Belgrád rakpart. It's full of cafés, musicians and handicraft stalls, and leads into **Petőfi tér** (Map p86), named after the poet of the 1848–49 War of Independence and the scene of political rallies (both legal and illegal) over subsequent years. **Március 15 tér** (Map p86),

which marks the date of the outbreak of the revolution, abuts it to the south.

On the eastern side of Március 15 tér, sitting uncomfortably close to the Elizabeth Bridge flyover, is the **Inner Town parish church** (Belvárosi plébániatemplom; Map p86; V Március 15 tér 2), where a Romanesque church was first built in the 12th century within a Roman fortress. You can see a few bits of the fort, **Contra Aquincum** (Map p86), in the small park to the north. The church was rebuilt in the 14th and 18th centuries, and you can easily spot Gothic, Renaissance, baroque, and even Turkish elements, both inside and out.

NORTHERN INNER TOWN

This district, also called Lipótváros (Leopold Town; Map p84 and Map p86), is full of offices, government ministries, 19th-century apartment blocks and grand squares.

Roosevelt tér

Roosevelt tér (Map p86; 🚍 16 or 105, 🚃 2 or 2/a), named in 1947 after the long-serving (1933–45) American president, is at the foot of Chain Bridge and offers among the best views of Castle Hill.

On the southern end of the square is a **statue of Ferenc Deák** (Map p86), the Hungarian minister largely responsible for the Compromise of 1867, which brought about the Dual Monarchy of Austria and Hungary. The statues on the western side are of an Austrian and a Hungarian child holding hands in peaceful bliss.

The Art-Nouveau building with the gold tiles to the east is the **Gresham Palace** (Map p86; V Roosevelt tér 5-6), built by an English insurance company in 1907. Following a total overhaul, it now houses the sumptuous **Four Seasons Gresham Palace Hotel** (Map p86; p108), arguably the city's finest hostelry. The **Hungarian Academy of Sciences** (Magyar Tudományos Akadémia; Map p86; V Roosevelt tér 9), founded by Count István Széchenyi, is at the northern end of the square.

Szabadság tér

'Independence Sq' (Map p84; 🚍 15), one of the largest squares in the city, is a few minutes' walk northeast of Roosevelt tér. In the centre is a **monument to the Soviet army** (Map p84), one of the very few still left in Budapest.

South of the US embassy is the former **Royal Postal Savings Bank** (Map p84; V Hold utca 4), a Secessionist extravaganza of colourful tiles and folk motifs built by Ödön Lechner in 1901 and now part of the **National Bank of Hungary** (Map p84; Magyar Nemzeti Bank; V Szabadság tér 8) next door.

Kossuth Lajos tér

Northwest of Szabadság tér is Kossuth Lajos tér (Map p84; Ⓜ M2 Kossuth Lajos tér), the site of Budapest's most photographed building and the best museum in the country for traditional arts and crafts. Southeast of the square in Vértanúk tere is a **statue of Imre Nagy**, the reformist Communist prime minister executed in 1958 for his role in the Uprising two years before (see p32). It was unveiled with great ceremony in the summer of 1996.

The Eclectic **Parliament** (Országház; Map p84; ☎ 441 4904, 441 4415; V Kossuth Lajos tér 1-3, Gate X; admission free for EU citizens, other adult/child 2300/1150Ft; Ⓜ M2 Kossuth Lajos tér), designed by Imre Steindl and completed in 1902, has almost 700 sumptuously decorated rooms, but you'll only get to see three on a guided tour of the North Wing: the main staircase and landing, where the **Crown of St Stephen** (see boxed text, below), the nation's most important national icon, is on display; the Loge Hall; and the Congress Hall, where the House of Lords of the one-time bicameral assembly sat until 1944. The building is a blend of architectural styles – neo-Gothic, neo-Romanesque, neobaroque – and in sum works very well. Members of Parliament sit in the National Assembly Hall in the South Wing from February to June and again

from September to December. Tours of the North Wing depart at 10am, 12pm, 1pm, 2pm and 6pm.

The **Ethnography Museum** (Néprajzi Múzeum; Map p84; ☎ 473 2400; www.hem.hu; V Kossuth Lajos tér 12; admission free, temporary exhibitions adult/child/family from 500/200/1000Ft; Ⓒ 10am-6pm Tue-Sun; Ⓜ M2 Kossuth Lajos tér), opposite the Parliament building, offers visitors an easy introduction to traditional Hungarian life, with thousands of displays in 13 rooms on the 1st floor. The mock-ups of peasant houses from the Örség and Sárköz regions of Western and Southern Transdanubia are well done, and there are some priceless objects collected from Transdanubia. On the 2nd floor, most temporary exhibitions deal with other peoples of Europe and further afield.

BAJCSY-ZSILINSZKY ÚT

Bajcsy-Zsilinszky út (Map p84 and Map p86) is the arrow-straight boulevard that stretches from central Deák Ferenc tér, the only place in the city where all three metro lines converge, and Nyugati tér, where the Nyugati train station is located.

St Stephen's Basilica

The neoclassical **St Stephen's Basilica** (Szent István Bazilika; Map p86; ☎ 311 0839, 338 2151; V Szent István tér; Ⓒ 9am-5pm & 7-8pm Mon-Fri, 9am-1pm & 7-8pm Sat, 1-5pm & 7-8pm Sun; Ⓜ M2 Arany János utca), built over the course of half a century, was not completed until 1905. Much of the interruption had to do with the fiasco in 1868 when the dome collapsed during a storm,

---

THE CROWN OF ST STEPHEN

Legend tells us that it was Asztrik, the first abbot of the Benedictine monastery at Pannonhalma (p161), who presented a crown to Stephen as a gift from Pope Sylvester II around AD 1000, thus legitimising the new king's rule and assuring his loyalty to Rome over Constantinople. It's a nice story, but it has nothing to do with the object on display in the Parliament building. That two-part crown, with its characteristic bent cross, pendants hanging on either side and enamelled plaques of the Apostles, dates from the 12th century. Regardless of its provenance, the Crown of St Stephen has become the very symbol of the Hungarian nation.

The crown has disappeared several times over the centuries, only to appear again later. During the Mongol invasions of the 13th century the crown was dropped while being transported to a safe house, giving it that slightly jaunty, skewed look. More recently in 1945 Hungarian fascists fleeing the Soviet army took it to Austria. Eventually the crown fell into the hands of the US Army, which transferred it to Fort Knox in Kentucky. In January 1978 the crown was returned to Hungary with great ceremony – and relief. Because legal judgments in Hungary had always been handed down 'in the name of St Stephen's Crown', it was considered a living symbol and had thus been 'kidnapped'.

BUDAPEST

and the structure had to be demolished and rebuilt. The basilica is rather dark and gloomy inside, but take a trip to the top of the **dome** (adult/child 500/400Ft; ⏱ 10am-4.30pm Apr & May, 9.30am-6pm Jun-Aug, 10am-5.30pm Sep & Oct), which can be reached by lift and 146 steps, and offers one of the best views in the city.

To the right as you enter the basilica is a small **treasury** (kincstár; ⏱ 9am-5pm Apr-Sep, 10am-4pm Oct-Mar) of ecclesiastical objects. Behind the main altar and to the left is the basilica's major drawing card: the **Holy Right Chapel** (Szent Jobb kápolna; ⏱ 9am-4.30pm Mon-Sat, 1am-4.30pm Sun May-Sep, 10am-4pm Mon-Sat, 1am-4.30pm Sun Oct-Apr). It contains the Holy Right (also known as the Holy Dexter), the mummified right hand of St Stephen and an object of great devotion. To view it, you have to put a 100Ft coin into a little machine in front of it, which lights up the glass casket containing the relic.

English-language guided tours of the basilica (with/without dome visit 2000/1500Ft) depart Monday to Friday at 9.30am, 11am, 2pm and 3.30pm, and on Saturday at 9.30am and 11am.

SZENT ISTVÁN KÖRÚT

Szent István körút (Map p84), the north-ernmost stretch of the Big Ring road (Nagykörút) in Pest, runs in a westerly direction from Nyugati tér to Margaret Bridge and the Danube. It's an interesting street to stroll along, with many fine Eclectic-style buildings decorated with Atlases, reliefs and other details. Don't hesitate to explore the inner courtyards here and further on.

You can reach Jászai Mari tér (Map p84), at the western end of Szent István körút, on tram 4 or 6 from either side of the river or via tram 2 from the Inner Town in Pest. The eastern end of the boulevard is best reached by metro (M3 Nyugati pályaudvar).

Újlipótváros

The area north of Szent István körút is known as Újlipótváros (New Leopold Town; Map pp80–1 and Map p84) to distinguish it from Lipótváros (Leopold Town) in the Northern Inner Town. (Archduke Leopold was the grandson of Empress Maria Theresa.) The area was upper middle class and Jewish before the war, and many of the 'safe houses' organised by the Swedish diplomat Raoul Wallenberg during WWII were here (see boxed text, below). A street named after this great man, two blocks to the north, bears a commemorative plaque, and a **statue of Wallenberg** (Map pp80–1) doing battle with a snake, was erected in Szent István Park in 1999.

ERZSÉBETVÁROS

The Big Ring road slices district VII – also called Erzsébetváros (Elizabeth Town; Map p84 and Map p86) – in half between two busy squares: Oktogon and Blaha Lujza tér.

RAOUL WALLENBERG, RIGHTEOUS GENTILE

Of all the 'righteous gentiles' honoured by Jews around the world, the most revered is Raoul Wallenberg, the Swedish diplomat and businessman who rescued as many as 35,000 Hungarian Jews during WWII.

Wallenberg began working in 1936 for a trading firm whose president was a Hungarian Jew. In July 1944 the Swedish Foreign Ministry, at the request of Jewish and refugee organisations in the USA, sent the 32-year-old Wallenberg on a rescue mission to Budapest as an attaché to the embassy there. By that time almost half a million Jews in Hungary had been sent to Nazi death camps in Germany and Poland.

Wallenberg immediately began issuing Swedish safe-conduct passes (called 'Wallenberg pass-ports') and set up 'safe houses' flying the flag of Sweden and other neutral countries where Jews could seek asylum. He even followed German 'death marches' and deportation trains, distrib-uting food and clothing, and actually pulling some 500 people off the cars along the way.

When the Soviet army entered Budapest in January 1945, Wallenberg went to report to the authorities, but in the wartime confusion was arrested for espionage and sent to Moscow. In the early 1950s, responding to reports that Wallenberg had been seen alive in a labour camp, the Soviet Union announced that he had in fact died of a heart attack in 1947. Several reports over the next two decades suggested Wallenberg was still alive, but none was ever confirmed. Many believe Wallenberg was executed by the Soviets, who suspected him to be a spy for the USA.

The eastern side is a rather poor area, with little of interest to travellers except the Keleti train station (Map pp80–1) on Baross tér. The western side, bounded by the Little Ring road, has always been predominantly Jewish, and this was the ghetto where Jews were forced to live behind wooden fences when the Nazis occupied Hungary in 1944.

Oktogon is on the M1 metro line, Blaha Lujza tér on the M2. You can also reach this area via trams 4 and 6 from both Buda and the rest of Pest.

Liszt Academy of Music

The **Liszt Academy of Music** (Liszt Zeneakadémia; Map p84; ☎ 342 0179; VI Liszt Ferenc tér 8; Ⓜ M2 Oktogon), one block southeast of Oktogon, was built in 1907. It attracts students from all over the world and is one of the top venues for concerts in Budapest. The interior, with large and small concert halls richly embellished with Zsolnay porcelain and frescoes, is worth a look even if you're not attending a performance.

Jewish Quarter

The heart of the old Jewish quarter, **Klauzál tér** (Map p84; Ⓖ 4 or 6), and its surrounding streets retain a feeling of prewar Budapest. Signs of a continued Jewish presence are still evident – in a **kosher bakery** (Map p86; Kazinczy utca 28), the **Frölich cake shop** (Map p86; Dob utca 22), which has old Jewish favourites, and a **wigmaker** (Map p86; Kazinczy utca 32).

There are about half a dozen synagogues and prayer houses in the district, which were reserved for different sects and ethnic groups: conservatives, the Orthodox, Poles, Sephardics and so on. The **Orthodox Synagogue** (Ortodox zsinagóga; Map p86; VII Kazinczy utca 29-31; Ⓖ 4 or 6), which is also accessed from Dob utca 35, was built in 1913 for Budapest's Orthodox community, and the Moorish **Rumbach Sebestyén utca Synagogue** (Rumbach Sebestyén utcai zsinagóga; Map p86; VII Rumbach Sebestyén utca 11; Ⓜ M1/2/3 Deák Ferenc tér) in 1872 by Austrian Secessionist architect Otto Wagner for the conservatives.

The **Great Synagogue** (Nagy zsinagóga; Map p86; VII Dohány utca 2-8; Ⓜ M2 Astoria) is the largest Jewish house of worship in the world outside New York City and can seat 3000 of the faithful. Built in 1859 and containing both Romantic-style and Moorish architectural elements, the copper-domed synagogue was renovated with funds raised by the Hungarian government and a New York–based charity headed by the actor Tony Curtis, whose parents emigrated from Hungary in the 1920s. In an annexe of the synagogue is the **Jewish Museum** (Zsidó Múzeum; Map p86; ☎ 342 8949; VII Dohány utca 2; synagogue admission 300Ft, synagogue & museum adult/child 1000/400Ft; ☽ 10am-5pm Mon-Thu, 10am 2pm Fri, 10am-2pm Sun mid-Apr–Oct, 10am-3pm Mon-Thu, 10am-2pm Fri, 10am-2pm Sun Nov–mid-Apr), which contains objects related to religious and everyday life, and an interesting handwritten book of the local Burial Society from the 18th century. The Holocaust Memorial Room – dark and sombre – relates the events of 1944–45, including the infamous mass murder of doctors and patients at a hospital on Maros utca.

On the synagogue's north side, the **Holocaust Memorial** (Map p86; VII Wesselényi utca) stands over the mass graves of those murdered by the Nazis in 1944–45. On the leaves of the metal 'tree of life' are the family names of some of the 400,000 victims.

Blaha Lujza tér & Rákóczi út

The subway (underpass) below Blaha Lujza tér (Map p84), the square named after a leading 19th-century stage actress, is one of the liveliest in the city, with hustlers, beggars, peasants selling their wares, musicians and, of course, pickpockets. Just north of the square is the Art-Nouveau **New York Palace** (New York Palota; Map p84; VII Erzsébet körút 9-11), erstwhile home of the celebrated **New York Kávéház**, scene of many a literary gathering over the years. It has been almost completely restored and will soon reopen as a hotel.

Rákóczi út (Map pp80–1 and Map p84), a busy shopping street, cuts across Blaha Lujza tér and ends at Baross tér and Keleti train station (Keleti pályaudvar; Map pp80–1), built in 1884 and renovated a century later.

JÓZSEFVÁROS & FERENCVÁROS

From Blaha Lujza tér, the Big Ring road runs through district VIII, also called Józsefváros (Joseph Town; Map pp80–1 and Map p84). The western side transforms itself from a neighbourhood of lovely 19th-century townhouses and villas around the Little Ring road to a large student quarter. East of the boulevard is the once rough-and-tumble district where much of the fighting in October 1956 took place. Today it is being developed at breakneck speed and the sound of bulldozers is constant nowadays.

The neighbourhood south of Üllői út is Ferencváros (Francis Town; Map pp80–1), home of the city's most popular football team, Ferencvárosi Torna Club (p120), and many of its tough, green-and-white-clad supporters. Most of the area was washed away in the Great Flood of 1838. Today there is a tremendous amount of building going on in Ferencváros too.

The Józsefváros and Ferencváros districts are best served by trams 4 and 6.

Hungarian National Museum

The **Hungarian National Museum** (Magyar Nemzeti Múzeum; Map p86; ☎ 338 2122, 317 7806; www.mnm .hu; VIII Múzeum körút 14-16; admission free, temporary exhibitions adult/child 700/350Ft; ☺ 10am-6pm Tue-Sun; Ⓜ M3 Kálvin tér, ☒ 47 or 49) contains the nation's most important collection of historical relics in a large neoclassical building purpose-built in 1847. On the 1st floor exhibits trace the history of the Carpathian Basin from earliest times to the arrival of the Avars in the 9th century, and on the 2nd floor of the Magyar people to 1849 and of Hungary in the 19th and 20th centuries. Look out for the enormous 3rd-century Roman mosaic from Balácapuszta, near Veszprém, at the foot of the central staircase; the crimson silk royal coronation robe (or mantle) stitched by nuns at Veszprém in 1031; the reconstructed 3rd-century Roman villa from Pannonia; the treasury room with pre-Conquest gold jewellery; a second treasury room with later gold objects (including the 11th-century Monomachus crown); the Turkish tent; the stunning baroque library; and Beethoven's Broadwood piano.

Museum of Applied Arts

The galleries of the **Museum of Applied Arts** (Iparművészeti Múzeum; Map pp80-1; ☎ 456 5100; IX Üllői út 33-37; admission free, temporary exhibitions adult/child 600/300Ft; ☺ 10am-6pm Tue-Sun; Ⓜ M3 Ferenc körút), which surround a central hall of white marble supposedly modelled on the Alhambra in southern Spain, usually contain a wonderful array of Hungarian furniture dating from the 18th and 19th centuries, Art-Nouveau and Secessionist artefacts, and objects related to the history of trades and crafts (glass making, bookbinding, goldsmithing, leatherwork etc). However, the last time we visited there were only temporary exhibitions on display and the permanent collections were closed. The building, designed by Ödön Lechner and decorated with Zsolnay ceramic tiles, was completed for the Millenary Exhibition (1896), but was badly damaged during WWII and again in 1956.

Holocaust Memorial Center

The new **Holocaust Memorial Center** (Holokauszt Emlékközpont; Map pp88-9; ☎ 455 3348; www.hdke .hu; IX Páva utca 39; admission free; ☺ 10am-6pm Tue-Sun), housed in a striking modern building in a working-class neighbourhood of Ferencváros, opened in 2004 on the 60th anniversary of the start of the holocaust in Hungary. Both a museum and an educational foundation, the centre displays pages from the harrowing 'Auschwitz Album', an unusual collection of photographs documenting the transport, internment and extermination of Hungarian Jews that was found by a camp survivor after liberation. In the central courtyard, a sublimely restored synagogue designed by Leopold Baumhorn and completed in 1924 hosts temporary exhibitions, such as a recent one on the genocide of the Roma people during WWII.

Ludwig Museum (Museum of Contemporary Art)

Just across from the National Theatre, the Ludwig Museum, which is also called the **Museum of Contemporary Art** (Kortárs Művészeti Múzeum; Map pp88-9; ☎ 555 3444; www.ludwigmuseum .hu; IX Komor Marcell utca 1; admission free, temporary exhibitions adult/child 1000/500Ft; ☺ 10am-6pm Tue, Fri & Sun, noon-6pm Wed, noon-8pm Thu, 10am-8pm Sat; ☒ 2 or 2/a) and was until 2005 housed in the Royal Palace on Castle Hill, is clearly enjoying its new and vastly expanded exhibition space in the equally architecturally controversial **Palace of Arts** (Művészetek Palotája; p118). The museum is the only one collecting and exhibiting international contemporary art and works by American, Russian, German and French contemporary artists over the past 50 years, and Hungarian, Czech, Slovakian, Romanian, Polish and Slovenian works from the 1990s onward. In the past dozen years the museum has held some 150 temporary exhibitions, many of them on the cutting edge.

ANDRÁSSY ÚT
Andrássy út (Map pp80–1 and Map p84) starts a short distance north of Deák Ferenc tér and stretches for 2.5km to the northeast, ending at Heroes' Sq (Hősök tere) and Városliget, Pest's sprawling 'City Park'. Andrássy út is such a pretty boulevard and there's so much to enjoy en route that the best way to see it is on foot (see p100), although the M1 metro runs beneath Andrássy út from Deák Ferenc tér as far as the City Park.

Hungarian State Opera House
The neo-Renaissance **Hungarian State Opera House** (Magyar Állami Operaház; Map p84; ☎ 332 8197; www.operavisit.hu; VI Andrássy út 22; adult/student 2400/1200Ft; M M1 Opera) was designed by Miklós Ybl in 1884 and is among the city's most beautiful buildings. If you cannot attend a concert or an opera at least join one of the guided tours (held at 3pm and 4pm), which include a brief musical performance. Tickets are available from the souvenir shop on the eastern side of the building facing Hajós utca.

House of Terror
The **House of Terror** (Terror Háza; Map p84; ☎ 374 2600; www.terrorhaza.hu; Andrássy út 60; adult/child 1200/600Ft; ☯ 10am-6pm Tue-Fri, 10am-7.30pm Sat & Sun; M M1 Vörosmarty utca), in what was once the headquarters of the dreaded ÁVH secret police (p31), purports to focus on the crimes and atrocities committed by both Hungary's fascist and Stalinist regimes, but the latter, particularly the years after WWII leading up to the 1956 Uprising, gets the lion's share of the exhibition space (almost three-dozen rooms, halls and corridors over three floors). The tank in the central courtyard is a jarring introduction and the wall displaying many of the victims' photos speaks volumes. But even more harrowing are the reconstructed prison cells and the final Perpetrators' Gallery, featuring photographs of the turncoats, spies, torturers and 'cogs-in-the-wheel', many of them still alive, who allowed or caused these atrocities to take place. May they never forget their crimes.

Franz Liszt Memorial Museum
The **Franz Liszt Memorial Museum** (Liszt Ferenc Emlékmúzeum; Map p84; ☎ 322 9804; VI Vörosmarty utca 35; adult/child 400/250Ft; ☯ 10am-6pm Mon-Fri, 9am-5pm Sat; M M1 Vörösmarty utca) is situated in the building where the great composer lived in a 1st-floor apartment from 1881 until his death in 1886. The four rooms are filled with his pianos (including a tiny glass one), the composer's table, portraits and personal effects.

Asian Art Museums
This area has two fine museums devoted to Asian arts and crafts, within easy walking distance of one another.

The **Ferenc Hopp Museum of East Asian Art** (Hopp Ferenc Kelet-Ázsiai Művészeti Múzeum; Map pp80–1; ☎ 322 8476; VI Andrássy út 103; adult/child 400/200Ft; ☯ 10am-6pm Tue-Sun; M M1 Bajza utca) is in the former villa of its benefactor and namesake. Founded in 1919, the museum has a good collection of Indonesian *wayang* puppets, Indian statuary, and lamaist sculpture and scroll paintings from Tibet. There's an 18th-century Chinese moon gate in the back garden, but most of the Chinese and Japanese collection of ceramics and porcelain, textiles and sculpture is housed in the **György Ráth Museum** (Ráth György Múzeum; Map pp80–1; ☎ 342 3916; VI Városligeti fasor 12; adult/child 400/250Ft; ☯ 10am-6pm Tue-Sun; M M1 Bajza utca), in a gorgeous Art-Nouveau residence a few minutes' walk southwards down Bajza utca.

HEROES' SQUARE
Andrássy út ends at Heroes' Sq (Hősök tere; Map pp80–1), which in effect forms the entrance to City Park and is on the M1 metro line (Hősök tere stop).

Millenary Monument
In the centre is the Millenary Monument (Ezeréves emlékmű; Map pp80–1), a 36m-high pillar backed by colonnades to the right and left. Topping the pillar is the Angel Gabriel, who is holding the Hungarian crown and a cross. At the base are Árpád and the six other Magyar chieftains who occupied the Carpathian Basin in the late 9th century.

The 14 statues in the colonnades behind are of rulers and statesmen – from King Stephen on the left to Lajos Kossuth on the right. The reliefs below show a significant scene in the honoured man's life. The four allegorical figures atop are (from left to right): Work & Prosperity, War, Peace and Knowledge & Glory.

Museum of Fine Arts

The **Museum of Fine Arts** (Szépművészeti Múzeum; Map pp80-1; ☎ 469 7100, 363 2675; www.szep muveszeti.hu; XIV Dózsa György út 41; admission free, temporary exhibitions adult/child 1200/600Ft; ◐ 10am-5.30pm Tue-Sun), on the northern side of the square, houses the city's outstanding collection of foreign art works in a renovated building dating from 1906. The Old Masters collection is the most complete, with thousands of works from the Dutch and Flemish, Spanish, Italian, German, French and British schools between the 13th and 18th centuries, including seven paintings by El Greco. Other sections include Egyptian and Greco-Roman artefacts and 19th- and 20th-century paintings, watercolours, graphics and sculpture, including some important impressionist works. Free tours of key galleries are available in English at 11am Tuesday to Friday.

Palace of Art

The **Palace of Art** (Műcsarnok; Map pp80-1; ☎ 460 7014, 363 2671; www.mucsarnok.hu; XIV Dózsa György út 37; 3-D film adult/child 1000/500Ft, exhibitions & film 1500/500Ft; ◐ 10am-6pm Tue-Sun) is among the city's largest exhibition spaces, and hosts temporary exhibitions of works by Hungarian and foreign artists in fine and applied art, photography and design. Concerts are sometimes staged here, too. A 3-D film that whisks you around Hungary in 25 minutes (with commentary available in seven languages) is screened continuously from 10am to 5pm Tuesday to Sunday from mid-March to September and from 10am to 4.30pm Friday to Sunday from October to mid-March.

CITY PARK

City Park (Városliget; Map pp80-1) is Pest's green lung, an open space measuring almost a square kilometre that hosted most of the events during Hungary's 1000th anniversary celebrations in 1896. It's not so cut and dry, but in general museums lie to the south of XIV Kós Károly sétány, while activities of a less cerebral nature – including the Municipal Great Circus (p120) and the Széchenyi Baths (opposite) are to the north.

City Park is served by the M1 metro (Széchenyi fürdő stop), as well as by trolleybuses 70, 72, 75 and 79.

Transport Museum

The **Transport Museum** (Közlekedési Múzeum; Map pp80-1; ☎ 273 3840; XIV Városligeti körút 11; admission free, temporary exhibitions adult/child 400/200Ft; ◐ 10am-5pm Tue-Fri, 10am-6pm Sat & Sun May-Sep, 10am-4pm Tue-Fri, 10am-5pm Sat & Sun Oct-Apr) may not sound like a crowd pleaser, but it is one of the most enjoyable in Budapest and great for children. In an old and a new wing there are scale models of ancient trains (some of which run), classic late-19th-century automobiles and lots of those old wooden bicycles called 'bone-shakers'. There are a few hands-on exhibits and lots of show-and-tell from the attendants. Outside are pieces from the original Danube bridges that were retrieved after the bombings of WWII and a café in an old MÁV coach.

City Zoo & Botanical Garden

The large **City Zoo and Botanical Garden** (Városi Állatkert és Növénykert; Map pp80-1; ☎ 273 4900, 363 3701; www.zoobudapest.com; XIV Állatkerti út 6-12; adult/child/student/family 1300/900/1000/4100Ft; ◐ 9am-6.30pm Mon-Thu, 9am-7pm Fri-Sun May-Aug, 9am-5.30pm Mon-Thu, 9am-6pm Fri-Sun Apr & Sep, 9am-5pm Mon-Thu, 9am-5.30pm Fri-Sun Mar & Oct, 9am-4pm Nov-Feb) has a good collection of animals (big cats, rhinos, hippopotamuses), but some visitors come here just to look at the Secessionist animal houses built in the early part of the 20th century, such as the Elephant House with pachyderm heads in beetle-green Zsolnay ceramic and the Palm House (with aquarium 300Ft extra) erected by the Eiffel Company of Paris.

Funfair Park

The **Funfair Park** (Vidámpark; Map pp80-1; ☎ 363 8310, 363 2660; www.vidampark.hu; XIV Állatkerti körút 14-16; admission free or 300Ft, rides 300-600Ft; ◐ 10am-8pm Jul & Aug, 11am-7pm Mon-Fri, 10am-8pm Sat & Sun May & Jun, 11am-6.30pm Mon-Fri, 10am-7pm Sat & Sun Apr & Sep, 11am-6pm Mon-Fri, 10am-6.30 Sat & Sun Mar & Oct) is a 150-year-old luna park on 2½ hectares next to the Municipal Great Circus. There are a couple of dozen thrilling rides, including the heart-stopping Ikarus Space Needle, the looping Star roller coaster and the Hip-Hop freefall tower, as well as go-karts, dodgem cars and a carousel built in 1906.

ACTIVITIES

Though Budapest may not seem like a destination for activities, it is chock-a-block with things to keep you occupied outdoors. From swimming, taking the waters and cycling to caving and canoeing, it's all within easy access of the capital.

Thermal Baths

Budapest lies on the geological fault separating the Buda Hills from the Great Plain; more than 30,000 cubic metres of warm to scalding (21°C to 76°C) mineral water gush forth daily from some 120 thermal springs. As a result, the city is a major spa centre and 'taking the waters' at one of the many *gyógyfürdő* (thermal baths) is a real Budapest experience. Some baths date from Turkish times, some are Art-Nouveau wonders and others are spick-and-span modern establishments.

Generally, entry to those baths without a deposit or voucher system (such as Gellért, Lukács and Szécheny) allows you to stay for two hours on weekdays and 1½ hours on weekends, though this rule is not always enforced. Most of the baths offer a full range of serious medical treatments, plus more indulgent treatments, like massage (15/30 minutes 1900/2700Ft) and pedicures (2000Ft). Specify what you want when buying your ticket.

The procedure for getting into the warm water is similar to the one for swimming pools (p98), though in Budapest's baths you will sometimes be given a number and will have to wait until it is called or appears on the electronic board. Though some of the local spas and baths look a little rough around the edges, they are clean and the water is changed regularly. You might consider taking along a pair of plastic sandals or flip-flops, however. Most bathhouses now require you to wear a bathing suit and no longer distribute those strange drawstring loincloths. Most hire out swimming costumes (around 800Ft) if you don't have your own.

Please note that some of the baths become gay venues on male-only days – especially the Király. Not much actually goes on, except for some intensive cruising, but those not into it may feel uncomfortable.

An excellent source of information is **Budapest Spas and Hot Springs** (www.spasbudapest .com).

Soaking in the Art-Nouveau **Gellért Baths** (Gellért Gyógyfürdő; Map pp80-1; ☎ 466 6166;

XI Kelenhegyi út 4; admission deposit before/after 3pm 3000/2800Ft; ☒ 6am-7pm May-Sep, 6am-7pm Mon-Fri, 6am-5pm Sat & Sun Oct-Apr; ☒ 18, 19, 47 or 49), open to both men and women in separate sections, has been likened to taking a bath in a cathedral. The pools maintain a constant temperature of 44°C, and the water, high in calcium, magnesium and hydrogen carbonate, is good for pains in the joints, arthritis and blood circulation. The entrance fee is actually a kind of deposit; you get back 700/400/200Ft if you leave within two/three/four hours before 3pm, and 500/200Ft if you exit within two/three hours after 3pm. Just make sure you hold on to your receipts.

The four pools at the **Király Baths** (Király Gyógyfürdő; Map pp80-1; ☎ 202 3688, 201 4392; II Fő utca 84; admission 1100Ft; ☒ men 9am-8pm Tue, Thu & Sat, women 7am-6pm Mon, Wed & Fri; ☒ 60 or 86), with water temperatures of between 26°C and 40°C, are genuine Turkish baths erected in 1570 and they have a wonderful skylit central dome.

The **Lukács Baths** (Lukács Gyógyfürdő; Map pp80-1; ☎ 326 1695; II Frankel Leó út 25-27; admission deposit locker/cabin 1500/1700Ft; ☒ 6am-7pm May-Sep, 6am-7pm Mon-Fri, 6am-5pm Sat & Sun Oct-Apr; ☒ 17, ☒ 60 or 86), housed in a sprawling, 19th-century complex, are popular with older, very keen spa aficionados, and include everything from thermal and mud baths (temperatures 22°C to 40°C) to a swimming pool. The thermal baths are open to men on Tuesday, Thursday and Saturday, and women on Monday, Wednesday and Friday. You get back 500/300/100Ft if you leave two/three/four hours after you enter.

At the northern end of City Park, the **Széchenyi Baths** (Széchenyi Gyógyfürdő; Map pp80-1; ☎ 363 3210; XIV Állatkerti út 11; admission deposit before/after 3pm 2300/1400Ft; ☒ 6am-7pm; ☒ M1 Széchenyi fürdő) is unusual for three reasons: its immense size (a dozen thermal baths and three swimming pools); its bright, clean atmosphere; and its water temperatures (up to 38°), which really are what the wall plaques say they are. It's open to both men and women at all times, and you get back 800/500/200Ft on your deposit if you leave within two/three/four hours before 3pm and 600/300Ft if you exit within two/three hours after 3pm.

The **Thermal Bath** (Map pp78-9; ☎ 889 4737; XIII Margit-sziget; admission Mon-Fri 5200Ft, Sat & Sun 6300Ft; ☒ 6.30am-9.30pm; ☒ 26) is a modern-style thermal spa in the Danubius Grand Hotel Margitsziget on leafy Margaret Island. The baths are open to men and women in separate sections.

Cycling

Parts of Budapest, including City and Népliget Parks, Margaret Island and the Buda Hills, are excellent places for cycling. At present dedicated bike lanes in the city total about 140km, including the path along Andrássy út, but that number is expected to double in the next decade. To contact Budapest-based cycling associations for information and advice, see p50.

For places to rent bicycles on Margaret Island, see boxed text p76).

Long-established and very reliable **Yellow Zebra Bikes** (Deák Ferenc tér Map p86; ☎ 266 8777, 06 30 211 8861; www.yellowzebrabikes.com; V Sütő utca 2; per hr/half-day/day 500/2000/3000Ft; ⏰ 10am-6pm Nov-Mar, 9am-8pm Apr-Oct; Ⓜ M1/2/3 Deák Ferenc tér; Opera House Map p84; ☎ 269 3843; VI Lázár utca 16; ⏰ 10am-5pm Nov-Mar, 9.30am-7.30pm Apr-Oct; Ⓜ M1 Opera) rents out bikes year-round from outlets just behind the Tourinform office and the Opera House.

Budapest Bike (Erzsébetváros Map p86; ☎ 06 30 944 5533; www.budapestbike.hu; VII Wesselényi utca 18; per 2hr/half-day/day 600/1500/3000Ft; ⏰ 9am-midnight; 🚌 4 or 6 or trolleybus 74; Inner Town Map p83; ☎ 06 30 944 5533; V Lánchíd; ⏰ 9am-midnight May-Sep) rents bikes from its main outlet, as well as from a kiosk at the Pest end of Chain Bridge. Another outfit is **Bike Base** (Map p84; ☎ 269 5983, 06 70 625 8501; www‧.bikebase.hu; VI Podmaniczky utca 19; per 1/2/3 days €8/12/16; ⏰ 9am-7pm; Ⓜ M3 Nyugati pályaudvar).

Frigoria (www.frigoriakiado.hu) publishes a number of useful guides and maps, including one called *Kerékparral Budapest környékén* (By Bike around Budapest; 2200Ft) that takes in the surrounding areas and describes 30 different routes. The tourist offices distribute the free but less ambitious *Budapest & Surroundings Bicycle Route Map*, with 20 recommended tours that range in length from 24km to 177km.

Bicycles can be transported on the HÉV, all Mahart boats and the Cog and Children's Railways, but not on the metro, buses or any trams.

Swimming

Every town of any size in Hungary has at least one indoor and outdoor *úszoda*

(swimming pool), and Budapest boasts dozens. They're always excellent places to get in a few laps (if indoor), cool off on a hot summer's day (if outdoor) or watch all the posers strut their stuff.

The system inside is similar to that at the baths, except that rather than a cabin or cubicle you store your gear in lockers. Get changed and call the attendant, who will lock it, write the time on a chalkboard and hand you a key. Many pools require the use of a bathing cap, so bring your own or wear the plastic one provided or sold for a nominal fee. Most pools rent bathing suits and towels.

Following are the best outdoor and indoor pools in the city. Some are attached to thermal baths reviewed previously, others part of hotel wellness centres.

The popular **Csillaghegy swimming complex** (Map pp78-9; ☎ 250 1533; III Pusztakúti út 3; adult/child 1000/800Ft; ⏰ 9am-7pm mid-May–Sep, 7am-7pm Mon-Fri, 7am-5pm Sat, 7am-4pm Sep–mid-May; HÉV Csillaghegy) north of Óbuda is the oldest open-air bath in Budapest. There are three pools in a 90-hectare terraced park; in winter they are covered by a heated canvas tent.

The huge **Dagály swimming complex** (Map pp78-9; ☎ 452 4500; XIII Népfürdő utca 36; adult admission deposit 1800/1500Ft with/without cabin, child admission deposit 1300Ft; ⏰ outdoor pools 6am-7pm May-Sep, indoor pools 6am-7pm Mon-Fri, 6am-5pm Sat & Sun Oct-Apr; Ⓜ M3 Árpád híd, 🚌 1) has a total of 10 pools, with plenty of grass and shade. If you leave the complex two/three hours after entering you get 500/300Ft back.

The indoor pools at the **Gellért Baths** (Gellért Gyógyfürdő; Map pp80-1; ☎ 466 6166; XI Kelenhegyi út 4; admission deposit to swimming pool & thermal baths with locker/cabin 2500/3000Ft, 2400/2800Ft after 5pm May-Sep, after 5pm Mon-Fri & after 2pm Sat & Sun Oct-Apr; ⏰ 6am-7pm May-Sep, 6am-7pm Mon-Fri, 6am-5pm Sat & Sun Oct-Apr; 🚌 18, 19, 47 or 49) are the most beautiful in Budapest. The outdoor pools (May to September) have a wave machine and nicely landscaped gardens.

The pools at the **Alfréd Hajós swimming complex** (Map pp80-1; ☎ 450 4214, 340 4946; XIII Margit-sziget; adult/child 900/550Ft; ⏰ outdoor pools 6am-7pm May-Sep, indoor pools 6am-7pm Mon-Fri, 6am-5pm Sat & Sun Oct-Apr; 🚌 4 or 6, 🚢 26), one indoor and three outdoor, form the National Sports Pool where Olympic swimming and water-polo teams train.

The ultramodern **Helia swimming and spa centre pool** (Map pp80-1; ☎ 889 5800; XIII Kárpát utca 62-64; admission before/after 3pm Mon-Fri 3500/4500Ft, Sat & Sun 4900Ft; ☼ 7am-10pm; Ⓜ M3 Dózsa György út or trolleybus 79), in the four-star Danubius Helia Hotel on the Danube, boasts three pools, sauna and steam room.

The **Béla Komjádi Swimming Pool** (Map pp80-1; ☎ 212 2750; II Árpád fejedelem útja 8; adult/child 900/550Ft; ☼ 6am-7pm; 🚇 17, 🚌 60 or 86) is used by very serious swimmers and fitness freaks so don't come here for fun and games.

Use of the three swimming pools at the **Lukács Baths** (Lukács Gyógyfürdő; Map pp80-1; ☎ 326 1695; II Frankel Leó út 25-27; ☼ 6am-7pm May-Sep, 6am-7pm Mon-Fri, 6am-5pm Sat & Sun Oct-Apr; 🚇 17, 🚌 60 or 86) is included in the general admission price (p97).

The largest series of pools in the capital, the **Palatinus Strand** (Palatinus Beach; Map pp78-9; ☎ 340 4505; XIII Margit-sziget; adult/child locker 1500/1300Ft, admission with cabin 1900Ft; ☼ 10am-6pm Mon-Fri, 9am-7pm Sat & Sun May & Jun, 9am-7pm Mon-Sun Jul & Aug; 🚌 26) on Margaret Island has a total of 11 pools (two or three with thermal water), wave machines, water slides etc.

The outdoor pools at the **Rómaifürdő Strandfürdő** (Rómaifürdő Beach; Map pp78-9; ☎ 388 9740; III Rozgonyi Piroska utca 2; adult/child locker 1200/1000Ft, admission with cabin 1600Ft; ☼ 9am-7pm May-Aug; HÉV Rómaifürdő or 🚌 34) are just north of Aquincum.

The indoor pools at the **Rudas Baths** (Map p86; ☎ 356 1322, 356 1010; I Döbrentei tér 9, admission with locker/cabin 900/1100Ft; ☼ 6am-6pm Mon-Fri, 6am-1pm Sat & Sun; 🚇 18 or 19, 🚌 7 or 86), close to the river, were built by the Turks in 1566 and retain a strong Turkish atmosphere. The thermal baths are currently under renovation.

Use of the three enormous thermal swimming pools at the **Széchenyi Baths** (Széchenyi Gyógyfürdő; Map pp80-1; ☎ 363 3210; XIV Állatkerti út 11; ☼ 6am-10pm May-Sep, 6am-7pm Oct-Apr; Ⓜ M1 Széchenyi fürdő) is included in the baths' general admission fee (p97).

Hiking

Budapest is an excellent springboard for hiking. If you plan on doing any walking in the Buda Hills, get hold of a copy of Cartographia's 1:30,000 *A Budai-hegység* map (No 6; 900Ft).

The tourist offices distribute a useful free map called *Budapest & Surroundings Hiking Tours*, with a dozen hikes and walks from the capital.

Caving

Budapest has a number of caves, two of which are open for walk-through guided tours in Hungarian. **Pálvölgy Cave** (Pálvölgyi-barlang; Map pp78-9; ☎ 325 9505; II Szépvölgyi út 162; adult/child 750/450Ft; 🚌 65 from Kolosy tér in Óbuda), the second-largest cave in Hungary, is noted for its stalactites and bats; be advised that the 500m route involves climbing some 400 steps and a ladder, so it may not be suitable for children. Hourly tours depart between 10am and 4pm Tuesday to Sunday.

A more beautiful cave, with stalactites, stalagmites and weird grapelike formations, is **Szemlő-hegy Cave** (Szemlőhegyi-barlang; Map pp78-9; ☎ 325 6001; II Pusztaszeri út 35; adult/child 650/400Ft; ☼ 10am-4pm Wed-Mon; 🚌 29 from III Kolosy tér), about 1km southeast of Pálvölgy Cave.

Boating

The best place for canoeing and kayaking in Budapest is on the Danube at Rómaipart (Map pp78-9); take the HÉV suburban line to Rómaifürdő (Map pp78-9) and walk eastwards towards the river. Two reliable places to rent kayaks and/or canoes are from **Óbuda Sport Club** (ÓSE; Map pp78-9; ☎ 240 3353; III Rozgonyi Piroska utca 28; canoes per day 1400Ft; ☼ 8am-6pm) and the **KSH canoe club** (Map pp78-9; ☎ 368 8967; III Királyok útja 31; canoes per day 1000/1300Ft, 1-/2-person kayaks per day 1300/1500Ft, 3-/4-person canoes per day 1800/1900Ft; ☼ 8am-6pm mid-Apr–mid-Oct).

Horse Riding

The Hungarian Equestrian Tourism Association (Map p86; p48) has a list of recommended riding schools within striking distance of Budapest, but bear in mind that Hungary has just introduced a new system of rating riding schools and centres, and things are (to say the least) in a state of flux.

One of the closest riding schools to Budapest is the long-established **Petneházy Lovascentrum** (☎ 397 5048, 06 20 588 3571; petnehazy@net .hu; Feketefej utca 2-4; ☼ 9am-4pm Sat & Sun; 🚌 63 from Hűvösvölgyi út) at Adyliget near Hűvösvölgy. It may have resumed lessons, paddock practice and trail riding by the time you read this. In the meantime there are pony rides (1500Ft per 15 minutes) for the kiddies and carriage rides (15,000Ft per 30 minutes for eight people).

Pegazus Tours (☎ 317 1644; www.pegazus.hu; V Ferenciek tere 5) can book riding programmes (for details, see p48), as can the highly respected **Favorit Lovarda** (☎ 257 1065, 06 30 966 9992; XVI Mókus utca 23; HÉV Szabadságtelep) in the Csömör district.

WALKING TOUR

This is a fairly straightforward walk that starts just a little north of Deák Ferenc tér and follows Andrássy út, the most attractive boulevard in Budapest, to Heroes' Sq (Hősök tere) and the enormous City Park (Városliget). It's not a very long walking tour, but there's a tremendous amount to see and do along the way so choose judiciously unless you want to make a whole day of it. The little yellow metro (M1) runs just beneath the boulevard, so if you begin

---

WALK FACTS

Start Ⓜ M1 Opera
End Ⓜ M1 Hősök tere
Distance 2.6km
Duration Two hours (or more)
Fuel Stop Művész or Lukács café

---

to lose your stamina, just go down and jump on.

Andrássy út splits away from Bajcsy-Zsilinszky út some 200m north of Deák Ferenc tér. This section of Andrássy út is lined with plane trees – cool and pleasant on a warm day. The first major sight is the **Hungarian State Opera House** (**1**; p95). The interior, which can be visited on tour, is especially lovely and sparkles after a total overhaul in the 1980s.

Opposite the Opera House, the so-called **Drechsler House** (**2**; VI Andrássy út 25), was designed by Art-Nouveau master builder Ödön Lechner in 1882. Until recently it housed the Hungarian State Dance Institute but it now stands empty, another victim of 'development' that never happened. For something even more magical, walk down Dalszínház utca to the **New Theatre** (**3**; Új Színház; ☎ 351 1406; VI Paulay Ede utca 35), a Secessionist gem embellished with monkey faces, globes and geometric designs that opened as the Parisiana music hall in 1909.

The old-world café **Művész** (**4**; p113) is in the next block. The next cross street is

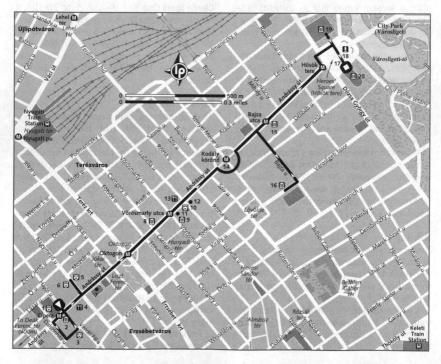

Nagymező utca, 'the Broadway of Budapest', counting a number of theatres, such as the **Budapest Operetta** (5; p119) at No 17 and, just opposite, the **Thália** (6; ☎ 331 0500; VI Nagymező utca 22-24), lovingly restored in 1997.

On the right-hand side of the next block, the so-called **Fashion House** (7; Divatcsarnok; VI Andrássy út 39), the fanciest emporium in town when it opened as the Grande Parisienne (or Párisi Nagyaruház in Hungarian) in 1912, contains the ornate Ceremonial Hall (Díszterem) on the mezzanine floor, a room positively dripping with gilt, marquetry and frescoes by Károly Lotz. It is currently being redeveloped, so it may be closed when you pass by.

Andrássy út meets the Nagykörút – the Big Ring road – at Oktogon, a busy intersection full of fast-food outlets, shops, honking cars and pedestrians. Just beyond it, the former secret police building, which now houses the **House of Terror** (8; p95), has a ghastly history, for it was here that many activists of whatever political side was out of fashion before and after WWII were taken for interrogation and torture (including Cardinal Mindszenty; see boxed text, p147). The walls were apparently double thickness to mute the screams. A plaque on the outside of this house of shame reads in part: 'We cannot forget the horror of terror, and the victims will always be remembered.' The **Franz Liszt Memorial Museum** (9; p95) is diagonally opposite.

Along the next two blocks you'll pass some very grand buildings housing such institutions as the **Budapest Puppet Theatre** (10; p119) at No 69, the **Academy of Fine Arts** (11; Magyar Képzőművészeti Egyetem; VI Andrássy út 71) and the headquarters of **MÁV** (12; V Andrássy út 73), the national railway. The **Lukács** (13; p113) café and cake shop is just opposite.

The next square (more accurately a circus) is **Kodály körönd** (14), one of the most beautiful in the city, with the façades of the four neo-Renaissance townhouses still in desperate need of a massive face-lift.

The last stretch of Andrássy út and the surrounding neighbourhoods are packed with stunning old mansions that are among the most desirable addresses in the city. It's no surprise to see that embassies, ministries, multinationals and even political parties (eg FIDESZ-MPP at VI Lendvay utca 28) have moved in.

The **Ferenc Hopp Museum of East Asian Art** (15; p95) is in the former villa of its eponymous collector and benefactor at No 103. More of the collection is on display at the nearby **György Ráth Museum** (16; p95), a few minutes' walk southwest.

Andrássy út ends at **Heroes' Sq** (17; Hősök tere; p95), which leads to City Park. The city's most flamboyant monument and two of its best exhibition spaces are in the square.

The **Millenary Monument** (18; Ezeréves emlékmű; p95) in effect defines Heroes' Sq. Beneath the tall column and under a stone slab is an empty coffin representing the unknown insurgents of the 1956 Uprising. To the north of the monument is the **Museum of Fine Arts** (19; p96) and its rich collection while to the south is the ornate **Palace of Art** (20; Műcsarnok; p96), which was built around the time of the millenary exhibition in 1896 and renovated a century later.

The M1 Hősök tere metro stop is conveniently just across the square.

COURSES
Language
The most prestigious Hungarian-language school in the country, the Debrecen Summer University (p368) now has a **Budapest branch** (Map p84; ☎ 320 5751; www.nyariegyetem.hu/bp; Jászai Mari tér 6, 2/F), with intensive courses lasting three weeks (60 hours) for €282 and regular evening classes of 72/96 hours for €236/322.

In addition, the following Hungarian-language schools are recommended for either classroom study or one-to-one instruction.
Hungarian Language School (Map p86; ☎ 266 2617; www.hls.hu; VIII Brody Sándor utca 4, 1/F)
InterClub Hungarian Language School (Map pp88-9; ☎ 279 0831; www.interclub.hu; XI Bertalan Lajos utca 17)
International House (Map pp80-1; ☎ 212 4010; www.ih.hu; II Bimbó út 7)

BUDAPEST FOR CHILDREN
Budapest abounds in places that will delight children and there is always a special child's entry rate to paying attractions (though ages of eligibility may vary). Family visits to many areas of the city can be designed around a rest stop (or picnic) at, say, City Park, on Margaret Island or along the Danube.

Kids love transport and the city's many (some might say unusual) forms of conveyance – from the **Cog Railway** (p75) and **Children's Railway** (p75) in the Buda Hills and the **Sikló** (p69) funicular climbing up to Castle Hill, to the trams, trolleybuses and M1 metro – will fascinate and entertain. Specific places to take children include the **Municipal Great Circus** (p120), the **Funfair Park** (p96), the **City Zoo** (p96) and the **Budapest Puppet Theatre** (p119). And don't forget the **Transport Museum** (p96). It's got an embarrassment of hands-on displays for kids of all ages.

Lonely Planet's *Travel with Children* by Cathy Lanigan includes all sorts of useful information and advice for those travelling with their little ones.

TOURS
Boat
From early May to mid-September **Mahart PassNave** (Map p86; ☎ 484 4013, 318 1223; www.mahartpassnave.hu; V Belgrád rakpart) has 1½- to two-hour cruises at noon and 7.30pm along the Danube (adult/child under 12 high season 1900/950Ft, low season 1600/800Ft). In the low season, from April to early May and mid-September to mid-October, only the evening cruise sails (on Friday and the weekend). A ticket with a meal on board costs 2800/1400Ft per adult/child, except in the evening in high season when it costs 3200/1600Ft, with music and dancing on board.

There are other, more expensive, cruises that also operate on the river, including those offered by **Legenda** (Map p86; ☎ 266 4190, 06 30 944 5216; www.legenda.hu; V Vigadó tér, pier No 7), which runs tours by day (3600Ft) and night (4200Ft), with taped commentary in up to 30 languages. Check the website for its schedule.

Bus
Many travel agencies, including **Cityrama** (Map p84; ☎ 302 4382; www.cityrama.hu; V Báthory utca 22) and **Program Centrum** (Map p86; ☎ 317 7767, 06 20 944 9091; www.programcentrum.hu; V Erzsébet tér 9-10), next to Le Meridien Budapest, offer three-hour city tours with three stops from 6500/3000Ft per adult/child under 12. They also have trips to the Danube Bend, Lake Balaton, the Great Plain, the Eger wine region etc. For more information, see p387.

Budatours (Map p86; ☎ 353 0558, 374 7070; www.budatours.hu; VI Andrássy út 2) runs nine city

bus tours daily in both open and covered coaches in July and August (between three and eight buses the rest of the year) from V Andrássy út 3 across the street (adult/student 4300/3000Ft). It's a two-hour tour with one stop (Gellért Hill) and with taped commentary in 16 different languages.

Queenybus (Map p77; ☎ 247 7159; queenybus@queenybus.hu; XI Törökbálinti út 28) has buses departing three times daily (10am, 11am and 2.20pm) from in front of St Stephen's Basilica on V Bajcsy-Zsilinszky út (Map p86) for three-hour city tours (adult/student/child under 14 6000/3200/3000Ft, open-deck 4300/3000/1500Ft).

Cycling
Run by the same people behind Absolute Walking Tours (below), **Yellow Zebra Bikes** (Map p86; ☎ 266 8777, 06 30 211 8861; www.yellowzebrabikes.com; V Sütő utca 2; Ⓜ M1/2/3 Deák Ferenc tér) has cycling tours (adult/student 5500/5000Ft) of the city that take in Heroes' Sq, City Park, inner Pest and Castle Hill. Tours include the bike and a drink, and depart from in front of the yellow Lutheran church in Deák Ferenc (Map p86) at 11.30am in May, June, September and October, and 11.30am and 4pm in July and August.

Walking
Among other tours, **Absolute Walking Tours** (☎ 266 8777, 06 30 211 8861; www.absolutetours.com) has a 3½-hour guided promenade through City Park, central Pest and Castle Hill (adult/student or under 26 4000/3500Ft). Tours depart at 9.30am and 1.30pm from mid-May to September and at 10.30am the rest of the year from the steps of the yellow Lutheran church on Deák Ferenc tér (Map p86). It also has some cracker specialist tours, including the Hammer & Sickle Tour (6000/5000Ft) and the Hungaro Gastro Food & Wine Tour (6500/5500Ft).

FESTIVALS & EVENTS
Many festivals and events are held in and around Budapest; look out for the tourist board's annual *Events Calendar* for a complete listing.

January
New Year Concert (www.hungariaconcert.hu) This is an annual event usually held in Pesti Vigadó (Map p86; p119) on January 1 to herald the new year.

February
Opera Ball (www.operabal.com) This annual, very prestigious event is held at the Hungarian State Opera House (Map p84 p95).

March
Budapest Spring Festival (www.festivalcity.hu) The capital's largest (200 events at 60 venues) and most important cultural event takes place at venues throughout the city.

April
Spring Marathon (www.marathon.hu) Marathon between Budapest and Visegrád.

May
Budapest Early Music Forum (www.festivalcity.hu) A festival focusing on ancient music – classical music as it was played when first composed at the Liszt Academy of Music (Map p84; p93) and at churches around Budapest.

June
Budapesti Búcsú (www.festivalcity.hu) City-wide 'Budapest Fair' festival of concerts and street theatre marking the departure of Soviet troops from Hungarian soil in 1991.

Danube Folklore Carnival (www.dunart.hu) Pan-Hungarian international 10-day carnival of folk and world music and modern dance held in Vörösmarty tér (Map p86; p90) and on Margaret Island.

August
Formula One Hungarian Grand Prix (www.hungaroring.hu) Hungary's prime sporting event held in Magyoród, 24km northeast of the capital.

Sziget Music Festival (www.sziget.hu) Now one of the biggest and most popular music festivals in Europe, held on Budapest's Óbuda Island (Map pp78–9; p73).

September
Budapest International Wine & Champagne Festival (www.winefestival.hu) Hungary's foremost winemakers introduce their wine to festival goers in the Castle District (Map p83; p69).

October
Budapest International Marathon (www.budapestmarathon.com) Eastern Europe's most celebrated foot race goes along the Danube and across its bridges.

December
New Year's Gala & Ball (www.viparts.hu) Gala dinner and ball held at the Hungarian State Opera House (Map p84) on 31 December.

SLEEPING
Budapest accommodation options run the gamut from basic but comfortable hostels cobbled from a couple of old apartments high above the Big Ring road to five-star palaces staring at (or down on) the Danube.

Budget
In Budapest budget accommodation – hostels, private rooms, *pensions* and camp sites – costs anything under 12,000Ft (€49).

HOSTELS
Hostelling International (HI) cards or their equivalents (p369) are not required at any hostels in Budapest, but they'll often get you a discount of up to 10%; make sure to ask beforehand. Prices almost always include a simple (continental) breakfast.

Hostels usually have laundry facilities (1000Ft to 1500Ft for a wash and dry), a fully equipped kitchen, storage lockers, TV lounge, no curfew and computers for Internet access (free or from about 10Ft per minute).

While you can go directly to all the hostels mentioned here, the Express and Mellow Mood travel agencies (p68) are the best contact for budget accommodation information. In fact, the latter, which is affiliated with HI, runs two year-round hostels and budget hotels, as well as a half-dozen hostels that are open in summer only. Mellow Mood also maintains three kiosks at **Keleti train station** (Map pp80-1; VIII Kerepesi út 2-4; **M** M3 Keleti pályaudvar), where staff make bookings, and can advise you about transport from there or arrange it for you:

Platform No 9 kiosk (☎ 353 2722; ☼ 7am-6pm)

Rail/Bus office (☎ 461 0948; ☼ 6am-10pm) Along platform No 6.

U Tours travel agency (☎ 303 9818; www.utours.hu; ☼ 7am-8pm) At the end of platform No 6.

Buda
Martos Hostel (Map pp88-9; ☎ 209 4883, 06 30 911 5755; reception@hotel.martos.bme.hu; XI Sztoczek József utca 5-7; s 4000Ft, d/tr/q 5000/7500/10,000Ft, apt 15,000Ft; 🚊 4 or 6) Though primarily a summer hostel with 200 beds, the independent Martos has around 20 beds available year-round. It's reasonably well located, near the Danube, and just a few minutes' walk from Petőfi Bridge.

BUDAPEST

AUTHOR'S CHOICE

Back Pack Guesthouse (Map pp88-9; ☎ 385 8946; www.backpackbudapest.hu; XI Takács Menyhért utca 33; bed in large/small dm 2500/3000Ft, d 7000Ft; ☒ black-numbered 7 or 7A, ☒ 19 or 49; ☒) The laid-back Back Pack is in a colourfully painted suburban 'villa' in south Buda and is relatively small, with a mere 50 beds (large dormitories with between seven and 11 beds, and small ones with four to five), but therein lies its charm. There is a super garden in the back, with a Thai-style lounging/sleeping platform – they call it a gazebo – as well as hammocks. Internet access is free and there is low-cost massage available. The upbeat attitude of the friendly, much travelled manager seems to permeate the place and the welcome is always warm.

Pest

Red Bus Hostel (Red Bus I Map p86; ☎ 266 0136; www.redbusbudapest.hu; V Semmelweiss utca 14, 1/F; dm 2800-3000Ft, s & d 7900Ft, tr 11,000Ft; ☒ M2 Astoria; Red Bus II Map pp80-1; ☎ 321 7100; VII Szövetség utca 2, 2/F; dm 2800Ft; trolleybuses 73, 74 or 76; ☒) Red Bus Hostel is a very friendly, central and well-managed place, with four large and airy rooms with four to five beds, as well as private rooms for up to three people. The new Red Bus II has four rooms of four to five beds.

Green Bridge Hostel (Map p86; ☎ 266 6922; www.greenbridgehostel.com; V Molnár utca 22-24; bed in 8-bed dm €11-14, bed in 2/3/4/5-bed dm €25/19/18/17; ☒ M3 Kálvin tér; ☒) Few hostels truly stand out in terms of comfort, location and reception, but Green Bridge has it all – in spades. Bunks are nowhere to be seen, it's on a quiet street just one block in from the Danube and coffee is on offer gratis throughout the day.

Station Guesthouse (Map pp80-1; ☎ 221 8864; www.stationguesthouse.hu; XIV Mexikói út 36/b; bed in 14-/8-bed dm 2300/2800Ft, d & t per person 3600Ft, q per person 3800Ft; red-numbered ☒ 7, ☒ 1 or 1A; ☒) This guesthouse in suburban Zugló is a real party place, with a 24-hour bar, pool table and occasional live entertainment. It has between 42 and 56 beds, depending on the season. For those intending to stay a while, rates drop by 100Ft a night from the second to the sixth night.

Best Hostel (Map p84; ☎ 332 4934; www.besthostel.hu; VI Podmaniczky utca 27, 1st fl; dm 3000Ft, d/q per person 4200/3600Ft; ☒ M3 Nyugati pályaudvar; ☒) This is a six-room hostel put together from several apartments, with parquet floors, very high ceilings and big, airy rooms. It's a quiet place with a fair number of rules (drugs, booze or tobacco), so don't expect to party here.

Caterina Hostel (Map p84; ☎ 269 5990, 06 20 992 8854; www.caterinahostel.hu; VI Teréz körút 30, 3rd fl; bed in 6-/8-/10-bed dm 2800/2600/2500Ft, s/d/t per person 6800/3400/3400Ft, 5-bed apt per person 3200Ft; ☒ M1 Oktogon; ☒) Long a key player on the Budapest budget accommodation scene, this hostel has moved from Oktogon in the past year or so, but continues to offer reliable, cheap accommodation in a 3rd-floor, 27-bed walk-up apartment above the celebrated Művész Cinema.

Hostel Marco Polo (Map p84; ☎ 413 2555; www.marcopolohostel.com; VII Nyár utca 6; bed in 12-bed dm €20, s €54, d/tr/q per person €38/28/26; ☺ year-round; ☒ M2 Blaha Lujza tér; ☒) The Mellow Mood group's very central flagship hostel is a swish, powder-blue, 47-room place, with telephones and TVs in all the rooms, except the dorms, and a lovely courtyard. Even the five spotless dorms (one reserved for women during the low season) are 'private', with beds separated by lockers and curtains.

Mellow Mood Central Guesthouse (Map p86; ☎ 411 1310; www.mellowmoodhostel.com; V Bécsi utca 2; bed in 6-/8-bed dm 5000/4500Ft, d/tr/q per person 6800/5700/5400Ft; ☒ M1/2/3/Deák Ferenc tér; ☒) This place will put you right in the heart of town. With 179 beds on four floors, it's the largest hostel in Budapest, so don't expect the personal treatment. Still, it's clean and upbeat, and there's a 24-hour bar.

PRIVATE ROOMS

Private rooms in Budapest generally cost 4500Ft to 6000Ft for a single, 6500Ft to 8000Ft for a double and 8000Ft to 15,000Ft for a small apartment. There's usually a 30% supplement on the first night if you stay less than four nights. To get a room in the city centre, you may have to try several offices. You might need an indexed city map (p65) to find the block where your room is located, though.

Tourinform in Budapest does not arrange private accommodation, but will send you to a travel agency, such as **To-Ma** (Map p86; ☎ 353 0819; www.tomatour.hu; V Október 6 utca 22; ☺ 9am-noon & 1-8pm Mon-Fri, 9am-5pm Sat & Sun; ☒ M1/2/3 Deák Ferenc tér). Among the best places to try for private rooms are Ibusz and Vista (p68), and U Tours (p103) in Keleti train station. After hours, try the imaginatively named **Nonstop Hotel Service** (Map p86; ☎ 266 8942; www .non-stophotelservice.hu; V Apáczai Csere János utca 1; ☽ 9am-10pm; Ⓜ M1 Vörösmarty tér) near the Budapest Marriott Hotel.

PENSIONS & GUESTHOUSES
Budapest has scores of *panzió* (*pensions* and guesthouses), but most of them are in the outskirts of Pest or in the Buda Hills and not very convenient unless you have your own (motorised) transport.

Pest
Dominik Panzió (Map pp80-1; ☎ 460 9428; domin ikpanzio@axelero.hu; XIV Cházár András utca 3; s/d/5-bed apt €28/36/75; 🚗 7) Just off Thököly út and located beside a large church, Dominik Panzió is on a leafy street lined with 19th-century villas and just two stops northeast of Keleti train station by bus. The 36 rooms, which could use an upgrade, come with shared bathroom and there is a five-person apartment available.

　Garibaldi Guesthouse & Apartments (Map p84; ☎ 302 3457, 06 30 951 8763; garibaldiguest@hotmail .com; V Garibaldi utca 5, 5th fl; s/d €28/32, apt per person €25-45; Ⓜ M2 Kossuth Lajos tér) Arguably the most welcoming hostel-cum-guesthouse in Budapest, the Garibaldi has five rooms with shared bathroom and kitchen in a flat just around the corner from Parliament. In the same building, the gregarious owner has at least a half-dozen apartments available.

HOTELS
A room in a budget (ie one- or two-star) hotel will cost more than a private room, though the management won't mind if you stay only one night.

Buda
Papillon Hotel (Map pp80-1; ☎ 212 4750; www .hotels.hu/papillon; II Rózsahegy utca 3/b; s/d/tr €38/48/58, apt for 3/5 people €60/75; 🚗 4 or 6; Ⓟ 🛏 🐕) One of Buda's best-kept accommodation secrets, this small 20-room hotel in Rózsa-domb has a delightful back garden with a small swimming pool. There are also two apartments available in the block just across the road.

　Hotel Császár (Map pp80-1; ☎ 336 2640; www .csaszarhotel.hu; II Frankel Leó utca 35; s/d/q €42/53/84, ste €116; 🚗 17, 🚇 86; ✖ 🛏) The huge yellow

building in which the 'Emperor' is located was built in the 1850s as a convent, which might explain the size of the 34 cel-like rooms. Request one of the larger superior rooms that look onto the nearby outdoor Olympic-size pools of the huge Béla Komjádi Swimming Pool (p99).

　Hotel Citadella (Map pp80-1; ☎ 466 5794; www .citadella.hu; XI Citadella sétány; dm 2200Ft, s & d with shared shower/shower/bath 10,000/11,000/12,000Ft; 🚇 27; Ⓟ) This hotel in the fortress atop Gellért-hegy is pretty threadbare and though most of the dozen guestrooms share their facilities, they are extra large and retain some of their original features. The one dorm room with 14 beds is usually booked by groups a week ahead, so call in advance.

Margaret Island
Hotel Margitsziget (Map pp80-1; ☎ 329 2949; www .hotelmsz.hu; XIII Margit-sziget; s €43-53, d €45-55; 🚇 26; Ⓟ 🛏) This 11-room budget hotel in the centre of Margaret Island is surrounded by greenery and feels almost like a resort. If you really want to get away from it all on a budget but remain within easy striking distance of the action, choose this place.

Pest
KM Saga Guest Residence (KM Saga I Map pp80-1; ☎ 217 1934; www.km-saga.hu; IX Lónyay utca 17, 3rd fl; s €38-63, d €50-75; 🚇 15, 🚃 47 or 49, KM Saga II Map p86; ☎ 217 1934; IX Vámház körút 11, 6th fl; 🛏) This unique place has five themed rooms, an eclectic mix of 19th-century furnishings and a hospitable, multilingual Hungarian-American owner. It's essentially a gay B&B, but everyone is welcome. KM Saga II is somewhat more modern but less atmospheric and has three rooms.

　Radio Inn (Map pp80-1; ☎ 342 8347; www.ra dioinn.hu; VI Benczúr utca 19; s/d €52/75, 2-room apt €92; Ⓜ M1 Bajza utca; 🛏) Just off leafy Andrássy út, this place is a real find, with 33 large one-bedroom apartments with bath and kitchen, 10 with two bedrooms and one with three bedrooms measuring between 44 and 60 sq metres, all spread over five floors. The garden courtyard is a delight.

　Flandria Hotel (Map pp78-9; ☎ 350 3181; hotel flandria@axelero.hu; XIII Szegedi út 27; s/d/tr/q with wash basin 5100/6300/7400/8600Ft, with shower 9500/ 9500/12,000/14,000Ft; 🚇 4; Ⓟ) The Flandria is a classic example of a former workers' hostel that has been turned into a budget hotel.

Don't expect anything within a couple of light years of luxury, but the 116 guestrooms, which have from one to four beds, a TV and refrigerator, are both clean and serviceable.

CAMPING
Buda
Római Camping (Map pp78-9; ☎ 388 7167; www .hotels.hu/romaicamping; III Szentendrei út 189; camp sites per person/tent site/campervan/caravan 990/2250/ 2390/3580Ft, 1st-class cabins for 6 people 15,000Ft, 2nd-/3rd-class cabins per person 2500/1800Ft; ⌚ site & cabins year-round; P 🚊) Located in a leafy park north of the city opposite a popular swimming complex, Római is the city's largest camp site. To get there, take the HÉV suburban railway from the Batthyány tér metro station in Buda to the Rómaifürdő station, which is almost opposite the camp site. Use of the adjacent strand and swimming pool is included.

Zugligeti Niche Camping (☎ 200 8346; www .campingniche.hu; XII Zugligeti út 101; camp sites per person/tent/caravan 1200/3800/4600Ft; ⌚ year-round; 🚌 158; P) This is a small camp site in the Buda Hills for 200 campers at the bottom station of the chairlift.

Midrange
Budapest is not bereft of midrange options altogether, but they are not as plentiful as in Western European cities. Midrange – usually *pensions* and hotels – means anything between 12,500Ft (€50) and 25,000Ft (€102) during any season.

BUDA
Hotel Astra (Map p83; ☎ 214 1906; www.hotelastra .hu; I Vám utca 6; s/d/ste €90/105/135; M M2 Batthyány tér, 🚌 86) Tucked away in a small street just west of Fő utca and just below the Castle District is this hotel-cum-guesthouse in a centuries-old townhouse. It has seven double rooms, two suites and a family apartment – essentially two doubles separated by a shared bathroom.

IBS Garden Hotel (Map p77; ☎ 274 2088; www .ibsgardenhotel.hu; II Tárogató út 2-4; s & d €59; 🚌 29, 🚊 56; P 🖳) This newly opened midrange hotel on the way to the Buda Hills, with 100 rooms spread over five floors, is an excellent option for those who want to be very close to the city but not exactly in it.

Orion Hotel (Map p83; ☎ 356 8583; www.best western-ce.com/orion; I Döbrentei utca 13; s/d/tr/ste €88/112/132/150; 🚊 18 or 19) Hidden away in the Tabán district, this is a cosy place with a relaxed atmosphere and within easy walking distance of the Castle District. The 30 rooms are bright and of a good size.

Beatrix Panzió (Map p77; ☎ 275 0550; www.beatrix hotel.hu; II Széher út 3; s/d/tr €60/65/75, apt €75-90; 🚌 5, 🚊 56; P) Up in the Buda Hills but easily accessible by public transport, this is an attractive *pension* with 18 rooms. Surrounding the *pension* is a lovely garden with fishpond, sun terraces and a grill; you might even organise a BBQ during your stay.

Burg Hotel (Map p83; ☎ 212 0269; www.burghotel budapest.com; I Szentháromság tér 7-8; s/d €105/115, 2-person ste €127; 🚌 16 or Várbusz; ✖ 🖳) This place with all the mod cons is in the Castle District, just opposite Matthias Church. The 26 rooms are no more than just ordinary but, as they say, location is everything and midrange options are as scarce as hen's teeth on Castle Hill.

Carlton Hotel (Map p83; ☎ 224 0999; www.carlton hotel.hu; I Apor Péter utca 3; s/d/tr €90/115/126; 🚌 86; ✖ 🖳) A total revamp at the start of 2005 has given this 95-room hotel at the foot of Castle Hill and at the end of a narrow cul-de-sac in Víziváros a cleaner, fresher look and an extra star.

Hotel Victoria (Map p83; ☎ 457 8080; www.vic toria.hu; I Bem rakpart 11; s/d/tr €102/107/148; 🚌 86, 🚊 19; P 🖳) This hotel has 27 comfortable and spacious rooms with larger-than-life views of Parliament and the Danube. It gets special mention for its friendly service and facilities, despite its small size. The best rooms are on floor Nos 7 to 9.

Hotel Kulturinnov (Map p83; ☎ 224 8102, 06 20 544 5396; www.mka.hu; I Szentháromság tér 6; s/d/tr €64/80/100; 🚌 16 or Várbusz; P) A 16-room hotel in the former Finance Ministry, a neo-Gothic structure dating back to 1904, the Kulturinnov can't be beat for location and price in the Castle District. The guestrooms, though clean and with private bathrooms, are not as nice as the opulent public areas.

Büro Panzió (Map p83; ☎ 212 2929; http://buro -panzio.Internettudakozo.hu; II Dékán utca 3; s/d/tr/q 8000/12,000/16,000/20,000Ft; M M2 Moszkva tér) A *pension* just a block off the northern side of Moszkva tér, this place looks basic from the outside, but its 10 rooms are comfortable and have TV and telephone. They were recently renovated, so they retain that just-off-the-assembly-line look.

PEST

Hotel Hold (Map p84; ☎ 472 0480; www.hotelhold
.hu, V Hold utca 5, s/d €88/99, ste €121-165; Ⓜ M3 Árany
János; Ⓟ) Housed in what was once a Jewish
school, the 'Moon' is an excellent choice if
you want to stay in an affordable and romantic hotel right in the city centre. The 28
rooms on two floors – there is no lift – look
down onto a central covered courtyard or
onto Hold utca.

Hotel Sissi (Map pp88-9; ☎ 215 0082; www.hotel
sissi.hu; IX Angyal utca 33; s/d €110/120, ste from €195;
Ⓜ M3 Ferenc körút; Ⓟ) Named in honour of
Elizabeth, the Habsburg empress, Hungarian queen and consort of Franz Joseph much
beloved by Hungarians, the Hotel Sissi is
decorated in a minimalist-cum-elegant sort
of style, and the 44 guestrooms spread over
six floors are of a good size.

Hotel Baross (Map pp80-1; ☎ 461 3010; www.ba
rosshotel.hu; VII Baross tér 15; s/d/tr/q €78/90/102/114, apt
for 4/6/8 people €120/145/160; Ⓜ M2 Keleti pályaudvar;
Ⓧ Ⓠ) The flagship hotel of the Mellow
Mood hostel group (p104), the Hotel Baross
is a comfortable, 40-room caravanserai
conveniently located directly opposite Keleti train station. The bluer-than-blue inner
courtyard is a delight, and reception, which
is on the 5th floor, is clean and bright, with
a dramatic central staircase.

Leó Panzió (Map p86; ☎ 266 9041; www.leopanzio
.hu, V Kossuth Lajos utca 2/a, 2nd floor; s/d/tr €66/82/100,
Ⓜ M3 Ferenciek tere) This place would be a 'find'
just on the strength of its central location,
but when you factor in the low cost, this
B&B is a 'discovery'. A dozen of its 14 immaculate rooms look down on busy Kossuth
Lajos utca, but they all have double-glazing
and are quiet.

Boat Hotel Fortuna (Map pp80-1; ☎ 288 8100;
ww.fortunahajo.hu; XIII Szent István Park, Pesti alsó rakpart;
s/d/tr with washbasin €20/30/40, with shower €65/80/100;
trolleybuses 76 or 79; Ⓟ) Sleeping on a one-time
river ferry anchored in the Danube that
goes nowhere may not be everyone's idea
of a good time, but it's a unique experience. This 'boatel' has 44 single and double
rooms with shower and toilet at water level,
and 14 rooms with two or three beds and
wash basin below deck.

Erzsébet Hotel (Map p86; ☎ 889 3700; www.dan
ubiusgroup.com/erzsebet; V Károlyi Mihály utca 11-15; s €75-
95, d €95-105; Ⓜ M2 Ferenciek tere; Ⓟ) One of Budapest's first independent hotels, the Erzsébet
is in a very good location in the centre of the

university district, and within easy walking
distance of the pubs and bars of Ráday utca.
The 123 guestrooms – mostly twins – spread
across eight floors are small and dark, with
generic hotel furniture.

Carmen Mini Hotel (Map p86; ☎ 352 0798; carmen@
axelero.hu; Károly körút 5/b, 2nd floor; s/d/tr €50/60/75;
Ⓜ M1/2/3 Deák Ferenc tér; Ⓟ) With nine rooms,
this hotel is about the closest thing to a B&B
in Budapest. It's very close to Deák Ferenc tér
and convenient to all forms of transport.

Benczúr Hotel (Map pp80-1; ☎ 479 5650; www
.hotelbenczur.hu; VI Benczúr utca 35; s €49-79, d €69-99;
Ⓜ M1 Bajza utca; Ⓟ Ⓧ) This rather faded
place done up in creams and oranges has
96 serviceable rooms (some of which look
down on a leafy garden) spread over seven
floors. It's just minutes away from Andrássy
út, Heroes' Sq and City Park.

Hotel Medosz (Map p84; ☎ 374 3001; www.me
doszhotel.hu; VI Jókai tér 9; s/d/tr €55/65/7, ste from €93;
Ⓜ M1 Oktogon) One of the most central cheap
hotels in Pest, the Medosz is just opposite
the restaurants and bars of Liszt Ferenc tér.
The 67 rooms are well worn but clean, and
have private bath and satellite TV; the best
ones are in the main block, not in the laby-
rinthine wings.

Thomas Hotel (Map pp88-9; ☎ 218 5505; www
.hotels.hu/hotelthomas; IX Liliom utca 44; s €55-65, d €75-
85; Ⓜ M3 Ferenc körút; Ⓟ) A brightly coloured
place in an odd location, this hotel has 45
rooms and is a real bargain for its location in
up-and-coming Ferencváros. Some rooms –
including No 14 – have balconies looking
onto an inner courtyard.

Star Hotel (Map pp80-1; ☎ 479 0400; www.star
hotel.hu; VII István utca 14; s/d/tr/apr €64/80/90/120 late
Mar-Oct, €50/64/90/120; trolleybus 74 or 79; Ⓧ Ⓠ) A
recent addition to the Mellow Mood hostel group's stable is this 48-room midrange
hotel just a few minutes' walk north of Keleti train station. The ground floor lobby is
quite spacious and a popular meeting place
for travellers; most of the guestrooms are
doubles spread over four floors.

Top End

Double-room rates at top-end hotels start
at around 25,500Ft. From there the sky's
the limit.

BUDA

Art'otel Budapest (Map p83; ☎ 487 9487; www
.artotel.hu; I Bem rakpart 16-19; s/d/ste €198/218/298, with

Danube view €218/238/318; ⊜ 86, ⌨ 19; ✕ ⊠ ⊑) The Art'otel is a minimalist hotel that would not look out of place in London or New York. But what makes this 165-room place unique is that it cobbles together a seven-story modern building (views of the Castle District and the Danube) and an 18th-century baroque building; they're separated by a leafy courtyard-cum-atrium.

Danubius Gellért Hotel (Map pp80-1; ☎ 889 5500; www.danubiusgroup.com/gellert; XI Szent Gellért tér 1; s €75-130, d €170-210, ste €270; ⌨ 18, 19, 47 or 49; Ⓟ ✕ ⊠ ⓡ) Budapest's *grande dame* is a 234-room, four-star hotel with loads of character. The gorgeous thermal baths are free for guests, but overall its other facilities are forgettable. Prices depend on which way your room faces and what sort of bathroom it has.

PEST

Andrássy Hotel (Map pp80-1; ☎ 462 2195; www.andrassyhotel.com; VI Andrássy út 111; standard s & d €134-240, ste from €161; Ⓜ M1 Hősök tere; Ⓟ ✕ ⊠ ⊑) This stunning, five-star hotel just off leafy Andrássy út has 70 tastefully decorated rooms (almost half of which have balconies) in a listed building. The lobby and ground-floor restaurant were renovated in 2004; the use of etched glass and mirrors as well as wrought iron is inspired.

Kempinski Hotel Corvinus (Map p86; ☎ 429 3777; www.kempinski-budapest.com; V Erzsébet tér 7-8; s €260-410, d €300-450, ste from €570; Ⓜ M1/2/3 Deák Ferenc tér; ✕ ⊠ ⊑) Essentially for business travellers on hefty expense accounts, the Kempinski Hotel has European service, American efficiency and Hungarian charm. A recent (and very thorough) renovation has given both the hotel's public areas and 369 guestrooms and suites a fresh new look and colour scheme.

Corinthia Grand Hotel Royal (Map p84; ☎ 479 4000; www.corinthia.hu; VII Erzsébet körút 43-49; s €180-240, d €220-280, ste from €300; ⌨ 4 or 6; ✕ ⊠ ⊑) The erstwhile Royal Hotel on the Big Ring road has reopened as a very grand 414-room, five-star hotel, and its lobby – a double atrium with massive marble staircase – is among the most impressive in the capital. The hotel truly is 'a legend reborn'.

Four Seasons Gresham Palace Hotel (Map p86; ☎ 268 6000; www.fourseasons.com/budapest; V Roosevelt tér 5-6; s €250-740, d €280-770, ste from €950; Ⓜ M1 Vörösmarty tér, ⊜ 15; ✕ ⊠ ⊑) After much

angst and sweat, this magnificent 179-room hotel has been created out of the long derelict Art-Nouveau Gresham Palace (1907). No expense was spared to piece back together the palace's Zsolnay tiles, famous wrought-iron Peacock Gates and splendid mosaics, and the hotel is truly worthy of its name.

K+K Hotel Opera (Map p84; ☎ 269 0222; www.kkhotels.com/hotel_HO_en.aspx; VI Révay utca 24; s/d/ste from €168/209/336; Ⓜ M1 Opera; ✕ ⊑) This upbeat, Austrian-owned place just behind the Hungarian State Opera House has 206 rooms spread over seven floors. They're on the smallish side and decorated in unusually cheerful colours – predominantly yellows, blues and reds – which raises the tenor of the whole place.

MARGARET ISLAND

Danubius Grand Hotel Margitsziget (Map pp78-9; ☎ 889 4700; www.danubiusgroup.com/grandhotel; XIII Margit-sziget; s/d/ste €153/168/198; ⊜ 26; Ⓟ ✕ ⊠ ⊑ ⓡ) Built in the late 19th century on Margaret Island, this comfortable (rather than grand) and tranquil hotel has 164 rooms with all the mod cons, and is connected to the Danubius Thermal Hotel Margitsziget, via a heated underground corridor, where you can take the waters for free.

AUTHOR'S CHOICE

Residence Izabella (Map p84; ☎ 475 5900; www.residenceizabella.com; VI Izabella utca 61; 1-bedroom apt €180-330, 2-bedroom apt €440-605; Ⓜ M1 Vörösmarty utca; ✕ ⊠ ⊑) Beg, borrow and/or steal to stay at this fabulous conversion of a 19th-century Eclectic building with 38 apartments just off swanky Andrássy út. The apartments, measuring between 45 and 97 sq metres, surround a delightful and very tranquil central courtyard garden, and the décor mixes materials such as wood, terracotta and basketry to great success. Some might find the colour scheme of the guestrooms a tad too 'oatmeal with cream', but we love the use of wrought-iron furniture and room dividers to increase the feeling of spaciousness. The kitchenettes have everything – did we notice a potato peeler? – and the deluxe units are equipped with washing machines and dishwashers. Long-term rentals earn big discounts.

EATING

Very roughly, a two-course sit-down meal for one person with a glass of wine or beer for under 2500Ft in Budapest is 'cheap', while a 'moderate' meal will cost up to 5000Ft. There's a big jump to an 'expensive' meal (5000Ft to 7500Ft), and 'very expensive' is anything above that. Most restaurants are open from 10am or 11am to 11pm or midnight; if there are no times listed under a particular entry, you can expect the place to be open between those hours. It's always best to arrive by 9pm or 10pm at the latest, though, to ensure being served. It is advisable to book tables at medium-priced to expensive restaurants.

Buda

HUNGARIAN RESTAURANTS

Kisbuda Gyöngye (Map pp78-9; ☎ 368 6402; III Kenyeres utca 34; soups 880-1180Ft, starters 920-2980Ft, mains 2380-4880Ft; ✆ noon-midnight Mon-Sat; 🚌 60, 🚃 17) This is a traditional and very elegant Hungarian restaurant in Óbuda; the antique-strewn dining room and attentive service manage to create a *fin-de-siècle* atmosphere. Try the excellent goose liver dishes (around 3400Ft) and more pedestrian items, like *csirke paprikás* (chicken paprika; 2380Ft).

Aranyszarvas (Golden Stag; Map p83; ☎ 375 6451; I Szarvas tér 1; soups 150-890Ft, starters 1100-2900Ft, mains 2180-3500Ft; ✆ noon-11pm; 🚌 86, 🚃 19) Set in an old 18th-century inn literally at the foot of Castle Hill, this place serves – what else? – game dishes. There's piano music on Thursday to Saturday evenings. The covered outside terrace is lovely in summer, when grills are available.

Kéhli (Map pp78-9; ☎ 250 4241; III Mókus utca 22; soups 580-880Ft, starters 980-2880Ft, mains 1480-6280Ft; ✆ noon-midnight; HÉV Árpád híd) A rustic but stylish place in Óbuda, Kéhli has some of the best traditional Hungarian food in town. In fact, one of Hungary's best-loved writers, the novelist Gyula Krúdy (1878–1933), who lived in nearby Dugovits Titusz tér, moonlighted as a restaurant critic and enjoyed Kéhli's bone marrow on toast (980Ft as an entrée – and better than it sounds!) so much, he included it in one of his novels.

Kacsa (Map pp80-1; ☎ 201 9992; II Fő utca 75; soups 450-750Ft, starters 800-2300Ft, mains 1200-3600Ft; ✆ noon-midnight; 🚌 86) 'Duck' is the place to go 'quackers', though you need not restrict yourself to duck dishes (2200Ft to 2800Ft).

It's a fairly elegant place, with art on the walls and piano music in the evening.

INTERNATIONAL RESTAURANTS

Rivalda (Map p83; ☎ 489 0236; I Színház utca; starters 975-1800Ft, mains 3000-4500Ft; ✆ 11.30am-11.30pm; 🚌 16 or Várbusz) An international café-restaurant in an old convent next to the National Dance Theatre with some modern Hungarian favourites, Rivalda has a thespian theme and delightful garden courtyard. This is one of the very few places we'd choose to visit in the generally touristy and expensive Castle District.

Remíz (Map p77; ☎ 275 1396; II Budakeszi út 5; soups 780-1240Ft, starters 980-2620Ft, mains 1980-3220Ft; ✆ 9am-midnight; 🚌 22, 🚃 56) Next to an old *remíz* (tram depot) in the Buda Hills, this virtual institution remains excellent for its food (try the grilled dishes, especially the ribs; 1980Ft to 2880Ft), prices and verdant garden terrace.

FRENCH RESTAURANTS

Le Jardin de Paris (Map p83; ☎ 201 0047; II Fő utca 20; soups 900-1900Ft, starters 1500-3000Ft, mains 1950-4650Ft; ✆ noon-midnight; 🚌 86) A regular haunt of staff from the French Institute across the road (who should know their *cuisine française*), 'The Parisian Garden' is in a wonderful old townhouse abutting an ancient castle wall. The back garden ablaze in fairy lights is a delight in summer.

ITALIAN RESTAURANTS

Marcello (Map pp88-9; ☎ 466 6231; XI Bartók Béla út 40; soup 450Ft, pizza & pasta 820-950Ft, mains 1680-2880Ft; ✆ noon-10pm Mon-Sat; 🚃 18, 19, 47 or 49) Popular with students from the nearby university since it opened some 15 years ago, this father-and-son-owned eatery has good Italian fare at affordable prices. The salad bar (large/small 780/580Ft) is great value and the lasagne (950Ft) is legendary in these parts.

Sole d'Italia (Map p86; ☎ 483 0186; V Molnár utca 15; pizza & pasta 990-1790Ft, mains 1190-2380Ft; ✆ 11am-10pm; 🚌 15) This place has super-friendly service, good, inexpensive pizza and pasta dishes and – wait for it – some of the cleanest toilets in town. It's convenient to the nightlife strip along Ráday utca.

ASIAN RESTAURANTS

Seoul House (Map p83; ☎ 201 9607; I Fő utca 8; soups 400-1000Ft, rice & noodle dishes 2200Ft, mains 2100-2700Ft;

noon-3pm & 6-11pm Mon-Sat; 🚇 86) This place serves excellent Korean food from barbecue grills to spicy *kimchi* cabbage. Not the most atmospheric place in town, but very authentic.

Mongolian Barbecue (Map pp80-1; ☎ 212 1859, 212 3743; XII Márvány utca 19/a; buffet before 5pm 2590Ft, after 5pm & Sat & Sun 4390Ft; ⏰ noon-5pm & 6pm-midnight; 🚌 61) This is one of those all-you-can-eat pseudo-Asian places, but this one includes as much beer and wine as you can sink for the price. In summer seating is also available in an attractive, tree-filled courtyard.

VEGETARIAN RESTAURANTS

Éden (Map p83; ☎ 375 7575; I Döbrentei utca 9; soups 590-690Ft, mains 990-1490Ft; ⏰ noon-11pm Sun-Thu; 🚇 86) This place in a mid-18th century townhouse below Castle Hill must have the classiest location of any vegetarian restaurant anywhere. Seating is in the 1st-floor dining room or, in warmer months, in the lovely courtyard.

CAFÉS & TEAHOUSES

For the past two centuries Budapest has been as famous as Vienna for its cafés, cake shops and café culture; at the start of the 20th century the city counted more than 500 cafés, but by the time of the change in 1989 (ie the collapse of communism) there were scarcely a dozen left. The majority of the traditional cafés are in Pest, but Buda can still lay claim to several.

Surprisingly, teahouses have made a big splash in recent years in Budapest, the capital of a country not normally associated with that beverage.

Auguszt (Map pp80-1; ☎ 356 8931; II Fény utca 8, 1st fl; cakes 150-350Ft; ⏰ 10am-6pm Tue-Fri, 9am-6pm Sat; Ⓜ M2 Moszkva tér) Tucked away on the 1st floor of a building behind the Fény utca market and Mammut shopping mall, this is the original Auguszt café (there are imitators), and only sells its own cakes, pastries and biscuits.

Ruszwurm (Map p83; ☎ 375 5284; I Szentháromság utca 7; cakes 190-440Ft; ⏰ 9am-8pm; 🚌 16 or Várbusz) This is the perfect place for coffee and cakes in the Castle District, though it can get pretty crowded and it's almost always impossible to get a seat.

Angelika (Map pp80-1; ☎ 212 3784; I Batthyány tér 7; salads 490-1490Ft, sandwiches 750-850Ft, cakes 310Ft;

⏰ 9am-2am; Ⓜ M2 Batthyány tér) Angelika is another charming café – this time attached to an 18th-century church – with a lovely terrace overlooking the Danube. The food is just so-so; come here for the cakes and the views.

Demmer's Teaház (Buda Map pp80-1; 345 4150; II Lövőház utca 12; teas 180-400Ft; ⏰ 9.30am-7.30pm; Ⓜ M2 Moszkva tér; Pest Map p84; ☎ 302 5674; VI Podmaniczky utca 14; ⏰ 11am-9pm Mon-Sat, 1-9pm Sun; Ⓜ M3 Nyugati pályaudvar) This cosy little teahouse next to the Mammut shopping mall is the place to come in Buda if you're serious about your cuppa cha. There's also a branch in Pest.

QUICK EATS

International fast-food places are a dime a dozen in Budapest, but old-style self-service restaurants, the mainstay of both white- and blue-collar workers in the old regime, are disappearing fast. As everywhere else, pizzerias are on an upward spiral.

Fortuna Önkiszolgáló (Fortuna Self-Service Restaurant; Map p83; ☎ 375 2401; I Fortuna utca 4; soups 200-300Ft, mains 500-700Ft; ⏰ 11.30am-2.30pm Mon-Fri; 🚌 16 or Várbusz) You'll find cheap and quick weekday lunches in the Castle District at this very basic but clean and cheerful self-service restaurant. Reach it via the stairs on the left side as you enter the Fortuna Passage.

Íz-É Faloda (Drink-Eat Snack Bar; Map pp80-1; ☎ 345 4130, 238 0282; II Lövőház utca 12; soups 250-380Ft, mains 320-590Ft; ⏰ 11am-6pm Mon-Fri, 11am-4pm Sat; Ⓜ M2 Moszkva tér) This is a clean, modern and very cheap self-service place in the Fény utca market next to the Mammut shopping mall. It has excellent *főzelék* dishes (comfort food; when peas, green beans, lentils or marrow are fried or boiled and then mixed into a roux with milk).

Nagyi Palacsintázója (Granny's Palacsinta Place; Buda Map p83; ☎ 201 5321; I Hattyú utca 16; set menus 780-1060Ft; ⏰ 24hr; Ⓜ M2 Moszkva tér; Buda Map p83; ☎ 212 4866; I Batthyány tér 5; ⏰ 24hr; Ⓜ M2 Batthyány tér; Pest Map p86; ☎ 418 0721; V Petőfi Sándor tér 17-19; ⏰ 24hr; Ⓜ M1/2/3 Deák Ferenc tér) This place, with branches in Buda and another across the river in Pest, serves Hungarian pancakes – both the savoury (218Ft to 398Ft) and sweet (118Ft to 398Ft) varieties – round the clock and is always packed.

Il Treno (Map p83; ☎ 356 2846; II Retek utca 12; pizza 820-1790Ft, pasta 990-1290Ft; ⏰ 11am-11pm; Ⓜ M2 Moszkva tér) With a cheap set menu (950Ft),

AUTHOR'S CHOICE

Malomtó (Map pp80-1; ☎ 330 1030; II Frankel Leó utca 48; soups 750-1100Ft, starters 1400-2100Ft, mains 2400-4200Ft; ⌚ noon-10pm; 🚋 17) The 'Mill Lake', north of Margit körút in Buda and just across from the Lukács Baths, is a welcome arrival, with up-to-date, fresh décor, and an inspired menu of modern Hungarian and international – especially game and seafood – dishes, many with an Asian spin. But its major draw is its unique position at the foot of a tiny lake filled with water lilies and croaking green frogs; a seat on the terrace in the warmer months is not just recommended, it's mandatory. We especially liked the goose-liver sampler with the bird's organ prepared in three different ways, the Japanese pork wrap with plum and the lamb duet (minced wrapped in cabbage and grilled chops). The roaring fire in winter is a nice touch. It's obviously a place for all seasons and we'll keep going back.

a half-dozen branches throughout the city and a thriving **takeaway service** (☎ 814 1414), Il Treno is one of the most popular pizzerias in town. Seating at this branch is in the neighbouring Trombitás restaurant or, in warmer months, a positive oasis of a courtyard off busy Moszkva tér.

MARKETS & SELF-CATERING

Budapest counts some 20 large food markets, with the lion's share of them in Pest. **Fény utca market** (Fény utcai piac; Map pp80-1; II Fény utca; ⌚ 6am-6pm Mon-Fri, 6am-2pm Sat), one of the largest in Buda, is just next to the Mammut shopping mall.

Supermarkets and 24-hour nonstop shops selling everything from cheese and cold cuts to cigarettes and beer abound in Buda. Following are two central ones:

Ezred Nonstop (Map p83; I Attila utca 57; ⌚ 24hr)

Kaiser's Supermarket (Map pp88-9; cnr XI Október 23 utca & Bercsényi utca; ⌚ 7am-8pm Mon-Fri, 7am-4pm Sat, 8am-3pm Sun; 🚋 4)

Pest

HUNGARIAN RESTAURANTS

Múzeum (Map p86; ☎ 338 4221, 267 0375; VIII Múzeum körút 12; soups 700-800Ft; starters 1400-3400Ft, mains 2400-4400Ft; ⌚ noon-midnight Mon-Sat; 🚋 47 or 49) This is the place to come if you like to dine in old-world style. It's a café-restaurant that is still going strong after more than a century at the same location near the National Museum. There's a good selection of Hungarian wine.

Firkász (Hack; Map pp80-1; ☎ 450 1118; Tátra utca 18; soups 590-790Ft, starters 1150-1690Ft, mains 1990-3600Ft; ⌚ noon-midnight; 🚌 15) Set up by former journalists (thus the name), this is a retro Hungarian restaurant with lovely old mementoes on the walls, excellent home cooking and a great wine list.

Móri Kisvendéglő (Map pp80-1; ☎ 349 8390; XIII Pozsonyi út 37; dishes 480-1500Ft; ⌚ 10am-8pm Mon-Thu, 10am-3pm Fri; trolleybuses 76 or 79) This simple *borozó* (wine bar) and restaurant, a short walk north of Szent István körút, has some of the best home-cooked Hungarian food in Budapest. But, as the owner warns our 'dear readers', get here by 3pm if you want to eat *főzelék*.

Menza (Map p84; ☎ 413 1482; VI Liszt Ferenc ter 2; soups 590-650Ft, starters 990-1390Ft, mains 1390-2790Ft; ⌚ 10am-midnight; 🚋 4 or 6) This upmarket Hungarian restaurant on Budapest's most lively square takes its name from the Hungarian for a drab school canteen – something it is anything but. Book a table; it's fabulously stylish and always packed by diners who come for its simply but perfectly cooked Hungarian classics with a modern spin. Weekday two-course set lunches are a snip at 790Ft.

Bagolyvár (Map pp80-1; ☎ 468 3110; XIV Állatkerti út 2; soups 500-880Ft, mains 1330-2400Ft; ⌚ noon-11pm; Ⓜ M1 Hősök tere) With reworked Hungarian classics that make it a winner, the 'Owl's Castle' attracts the Budapest cognoscenti, who leave its sister restaurant next door, Gundel, to the expense-account brigade.

INTERNATIONAL RESTAURANTS

Robinson (Map pp80-1; ☎ 422 0222; XIV Városligeti-tó; soups 790-890Ft, starters 1990-2890Ft, mains 2790-4800Ft; ⌚ noon-4pm & 6pm-midnight; Ⓜ M1 Hősök tere) Located in leafy City Park, Robinson is the place to secure a table on the lakeside terrace on a warm summer's evening. Starters include sliced goose liver (2890Ft) and home-made venison pâté, and mains feature *fogas* (Balaton pike-perch; 3790Ft), grilled tuna and smoked duck breast cooked on lava stones.

Café Kör (Map p86; ☎ 311 0053; V Sas utca 17; salads 730-2110Ft, mains 1590-3190Ft; ⌚ 10am-10pm Mon-Sat; 🚌 15) Just behind St Stephen's Basilica, the

'Circle Café' is a great place for a light meal at any time, including late breakfast (460Ft to 590Ft). Salads, desserts and daily specials are very good; there is also a three-/four-course wine-tasting menu for 4900/6900Ft.

Mokka (Map p86; ☎ 328 0081; V Sas utca 4; soups 890-960Ft, mains 2450-5950Ft; ☯ noon-midnight; ☐ 15 or red-numbered 4) It's 'ethno-cuisine' here, with a mishmash of dishes; you'll need a map to read the menu. But we love the space and the great African décor, and there's a good wine list. The three-course set menu (7000Ft), including wine, is good value.

Marquis de Salade (Map p84; ☎ 302 4086; VI Hajós utca 43; soups 800-1700Ft, salads 1200-1600Ft, mains 2500-3400Ft; ☯ 11am-1am; trolleybuses 72 or 73) This is a serious hybrid of a place, with dishes from Russia and Azerbaijan as well as Hungary. There are lots of quality vegetarian choices, too, in the basement restaurant.

Soul Café (Map p86; ☎ 217 6986; IX Ráday utca 11-13; starters 590-1890Ft, mains 1980-2980Ft; ☯ noon-11.30pm; ☐ M3 Kálvin tér) One of the better choices along a street heaving with so-so restaurants and iffy cafés, the Soul has inventive Continental food and décor, and you can order anything from a sandwich (850Ft) or a pizza (890Ft to 1500Ft) to a full meal, including many vegetarian dishes (590Ft to 1890Ft). It has a great terrace.

FRENCH RESTAURANTS

Lou Lou (Map p86; ☎ 312 4505; V Vigyázó Ferenc utca 4; soups 800Ft, starters 1600-2800Ft, mains 2300-4400Ft; ☯ noon-3pm & 7-11pm Mon-Fri, 7-11pm Sat; ☐ 15) One of the most popular places with expatriate *français* in Budapest is this lovely bistro with excellent daily specials. Two signature dishes are the marinated grilled breast of duck with orange and Arabica coffee sauce (3100ft), and the rack of lamb with garlic and haricots verts (3600Ft).

ITALIAN RESTAURANTS

Trattoria Toscana (Map p86; ☎ 327 0045; V Belgrád rakpart 13; starters 990-3200Ft, pasta & pizza 1350-2690Ft, mains 1500-3390Ft; ☯ noon-midnight; ☐ 15) Hard by the Danube, this trattoria serves rustic and very authentic Italian and Tuscan food, including *ribollito alla chiantigiana*, a hearty vegetable soup stewed with *cannellini* (white Tuscan beans) and Parmesan cheese. The focaccia is excellent, too.

Fausto's (Map p86; ☎ 269 6806; VII Dohány utca 5; soups 1300-3300Ft, starters 2400-4200Ft, mains 3200-6400Ft;

☯ noon-3pm & 7-11pm Mon-Sat; trolleybus 74) Still the most upmarket (and expensive) Italian restaurant in town, Fausto's has brilliant pasta dishes, daily specials and desserts; there are lots of choices for vegetarians. The yellow walls and antique furniture provide an elegant touch, and the Italian wine selection is huge.

Okay Italia (Pest Map p84; ☎ 349 2991; XIII Szent István körút 20; pizza 1320-1790Ft, pasta 1460-2290Ft, mains 1680-3050Ft; ☯ 11am-midnight Mon-Fri, noon-midnight Sat & Sun; ☒ 4 or 6; Nyugati tér Map p84; ☎ 332 6960; V Nyugati tér 6; ☐ M3 Nyugati pályaudvar) This is a perennially popular place run by Italians, with a nearby Nyugati tér branch serving just pasta and pizza. Most people come just for either of those, in any case. Both restaurants have terraces.

GREEK & MIDDLE EASTERN RESTAURANTS

Al-Amir (Map p86; ☎ 352 1422; VII Király utca 17; meze 650-850Ft, mains 1490-2300Ft; ☯ noon-11pm; ☐ M1 Bajcsy-Zsilinszky út 17) Arguably the most authentic Middle Eastern (in this case, Syrian) place in town, and light years from the gyros and falafel outlets found along the Big Ring road. It has a window selling takeaway gyros (500Ft) and falafels (450Ft), too, but we're talking quality here.

Taverna Pireus Rembetiko (Map p86; ☎ 266 0292; V Fóvám tér 2-3; starters 590-1590Ft, mains 1690-2290Ft; ☯ noon-midnight; ☒ 47 or 49) Overlooking a patch of green and facing the Nagycsarnok (Great Market), this place serves reasonably priced and pretty authentic Greek fare. *Rembetiko* is a folk music school and a style of traditional Greek music; there are live performances on Friday and Saturday evening.

SPANISH & MEXICAN RESTAURANTS

Pata Negro (Map p86; ☎ 215 5616; IX Kálvin tér 8; tapas 250-650Ft, plates 500-1200Ft; ☯ 11am-midnight Mon-Wed, 11am-1am Thu & Fri, noon-1am Sat, noon-midnight Sun; ☐ M3 Kálvin tér) The 'Black Foot' (it's a kind of ham) is a new cellarlike Spanish tapas bar and restaurant at the (almost) top of trendy Ráday utca. Good cheese and an excellent wine selection, too.

Iguana (Map p84; ☎ 331 4352; V Zoltán utca 16; starters 430-1590Ft; mains 1890-3990Ft; ☯ 11.30am-12.30am; ☐ 15) Iguana serves decent-enough Mexican food (not a difficult task in this *cantina* desert), but it's hard to say whether the pull is the chilli (1050Ft to 1490Ft), the enchilada and burrito combination *platos* (plates; 2090Ft to 2290Ft), or the frenetic and boozy we-party-every-night atmosphere.

JEWISH & KOSHER RESTAURANTS
Kinor David (David's Harp; Map p86; ☎ 512 8783; VII Dohány utca 10; soup 800-1300Ft; mains 2800-3200Ft; ☙ 11am-11pm Mon-Fri & Sun, noon-2pm Sat; Ⓜ M2 Astoria or trolleybus 74) Budapest's largest kosher restaurant is a cut above the usual. There are special fish dishes (3000Ft to 4500Ft) and Israeli treats (2600Ft to 3100Ft). You pay in advance for Friday dinner and Saturday lunch.

ASIAN RESTAURANTS
Bangkok House (Map p86; ☎ 266 0584; V Só utca 3; soups & Thai salads 550-2250Ft, mains 1450-4550Ft; ☙ noon-11pm; Ⓔ 47 or 49) Bangkok House is done up in kitsch, Asian-esque décor that recalls takeaway places on any UK High St. The Thai and Laotian-inspired dishes are acceptable, and service all but seamless. A tourist menu (1460Ft) is available from noon to 4pm.

Sushi An (Map p86; ☎ 317 4239; V Harmincad utca 4; sushi 300-600Ft per piece, hand rolls 900-1400Ft, sets 1900-3900Ft; ☙ noon-10pm; Ⓜ M1/2/3 Deál tér) A tiny sushi bar next to the British embassy in central Pest. It's great for sushi and sashimi, but even better for Japanese sets served with miso soup.

VEGETARIAN RESTAURANTS
Napfényes Ízek (Map pp80-1; ☎ 351 5649; VII Rózsa utca 39; soups 450-850Ft, pasta & pizza 1190-1490Ft, mains 1190-1650Ft; ☙ 10am-11pm Mon-Fri, 12-10.30pm Sat & Sun; trolleybuses 73 or 76) 'Sunny Tastes' is a bit out of the way (unless you're staying near Andrássy út), but the wholesome foods and the speciality cakes are worth the trip. There is an organic shop here, too.

Govinda (Map p86; ☎ 269 1625, 473 1309; V Vigyázó Ferenc utca 4; soups 350Ft, dishes 240-450Ft; ☙ noon-9pm Mon-Sat; Ⓔ 15) Run by a Buddhist and blessed by the Dalai Lama, Govinda is in a basement near Chain Bridge. As well as wholesome salads, soups and desserts, it serves a daily set menu plate (large/small 1600/1280Ft).

CAFÉS & TEAHOUSES
Along with traditional cafés in Pest, a new breed of café has emerged on the scene – all polished chrome, halogen lighting and straight lines. Leafy VI Liszt Ferenc tér is surrounded by these hip cafés, and there are a few on IX Ráday utca and V Szent István tér behind St Stephen's Basilica.

Lukács (Map p84; ☎ 302 8747; VI Andrássy út 70; cakes 200-500Ft; ☙ 9am-8pm Mon-Fri, 10am-8pm Sat & Sun; Ⓜ M1 Vörösmarty utca) This café is dressed up in the finest of divine decadence – all mirrors and gold and soft piano music (on weekday evenings), with a nonsmoking section, too. The selection of cakes is small but good; try the creamy Lukács *szelet*.

Művész (Map p84; ☎ 352 1337; VI Andrássy út 29; cakes 280-480Ft; ☙ 9am-11.45pm; Ⓜ M1 Opera) Almost opposite the State Opera House, this is a more interesting place to people-watch than most (especially from the terrace), though its cakes are not what they used to be, with the exception of the *almás torta* (apple cake).

Centrál Kávéház (Map p86; ☎ 266 4572, 266 2110; V Károlyi Mihály utca 9; cakes 290-350Ft, mains 1990-3590Ft; ☙ 8am-midnight; Ⓜ M3 Ferenciek tere) This *grande dame* that reopened a couple of years ago after extensive renovations is still jostling to reclaim her title as *the* place to sit and look intellectual in Pest. It serves meals as well as lighter fare, like sandwiches (750Ft to 1190Ft) and omelettes (890Ft to 990Ft).

Gerbeaud (Map p86; ☎ 429 9020; V Vörösmarty tér 7-8; cakes 580-850Ft; ☙ 9am-9pm; Ⓜ M1 Vörösmarty tér) This is the most famous of the famous cafés in Budapest – bar none. Founded in 1858, it has been a fashionable meeting place for the city's elite on the northern side of Pest's busiest square since 1870. It serves a Continental breakfast (2880Ft) and sandwiches (1300Ft to 2500Ft).

Café Vian (Map p84; ☎ 268 1154; VI Liszt Ferenc tér 9; cakes 300-470Ft; ☙ 9am-1am; Ⓜ M1 Oktogon) This comfortable café – done up in warm peach tones and serving breakfast all day – remains the anchor tenant on the sunny side of 'the tér' and the court of Pest's arty aristocracy.

Negro (Map p86; ☎ 302 0136; V Szent István tér 11; breakfast 320-908Ft; ☙ 8am-1am Mon-Wed, 8am-3am Thu & Fri, 8am-4am Sat, 8am-midnight Sun; Ⓔ 15) This stylish café just behind the basilica (views!) attracts Budapest's über trendy crowd, dressed to the nines (or did we see 10s?) and sipping whatever is the latest concoction.

Teaház a Vörös Oroszlánhoz (Jókai tér Map p84; ☎ 269 0579; VI Jókai tér 8; teas 480-630Ft; ☙ 11am-11pm

Mon-Fri, 3-11pm Sat, 5-11pm Sun; Ⓜ M1 Oktogon; Ráday utca Map p86; ☎ 215 2101; IX Ráday 9; ☽ 11am-11pm Mon-Sat, 3-11pm Sun) This serene place with a mouthful of a name (it just means 'Teahouse at the Sign of the Red Lion') and two branches is a funky and quite serious teahouse north of Liszt Ferenc tér.

QUICK EATS

Middle Eastern fast-food is as popular in Budapest as Indian is in London and Chinese in New York.

Szeráj (Map p84; ☎ 311 6690; XIII Szent István körút 13; salads & meze 200-400Ft, mains 1100-1250Ft; ☽ 9am-5am; 🚋 4 or 6) A very inexpensive self-service Turkish place for felafels and kebabs (700Ft), with some 10 varieties on offer.

Három Testvér (Erzsébet körút Map p84; ☎ 342 2377; VII Erzsébet körút 17; salads 350-450Ft, gyros & kebabs 500-900Ft; ☽ 9am-3am; Szent István körút Map p84; ☎ 329 2951; XIII Szent István körút 20-22; ☽ 9am-3am Sun-Wed, 9am-4am Thu, 9am-5am Fri & Sat; 🚋 4 or 6; Teréz körút Map p84; ☎ 312 5835; VI Teréz körút 60-62; ☽ 9am-3am; 🚋 4 or 6) Great any time but especially for a late-night snack or post-club bit of blotter, the 'Three Brothers' has branches throughout Pest, including these three on the Big Ring road.

If you're looking for places like McDonald's, Burger King and KFC, you'll find them everywhere in Pest – especially around Oktogon. Much better are the new-style self-service restaurants that cater to students and office workers, including **Pick Ház** (Map p84; ☎ 331 7783; V Kossuth Lajos tér 9; sandwiches & salads 140-180Ft, mains 210-580Ft; ☽ 8am-4pm Mon-Fri; Ⓜ M2 Kossuth Lajos tér), above the famous salami manufacturer's central showroom near Parliament, and **Central European University caféteria** (Map p86; ☎ 327 3000; V Nádor utca 9; soups 190-235Ft, pizza 220-250Ft, mains 380-495Ft; ☽ 11.30am-4pm Mon-Fri; 🚌 15), which is open to all.

Much more interesting places serving tastier dishes are the little restaurants called *étkezdék* – canteens not unlike British 'cafs' that serve simple dishes that change every day. A meal can easily cost under 1000Ft. Some of the better ones:

Kádár (Map p84; ☎ 321 3622; X Klauzál tér 9; soups 400Ft, mains 580-1100Ft; ☽ 11.30am-3.30pm Tue-Sat; 🚋 4 or 6) In the Jewish area and probably the most popular of its type in town.

Kisharang (Map p86; ☎ 269 3861; V Október 6 utca 17; soups 145-230Ft, mains 290-850Ft; ☽ 11am-8pm Mon-Fri, 11.30am-4.30pm Sat & Sun; 🚌 15)

The centrally located 'Little Bell' is popular with students and staff of the nearby Central European University.

Frici Papa Kifőzdéje (Papa Frank's Canteen; Map p84; ☎ 351 0197; VI Király utca 55; soups 279-439Ft, mains 429-529Ft; ☽ 11am-9pm Mon-Sat; 🚋 4 or 6) Excellent *főzelék* dishes cost 289Ft to 339Ft.

MARKETS & SELF-CATERING

Most of Budapest's 20-odd food markets are in Pest. The vast majority are closed on Sunday, and Monday is always very quiet (if the market isn't closed altogether). Two of the better ones are the **Rákóczi tér market** (Map pp80-1; VIII Rákóczi tér 8; ☽ 6am-4pm Mon, 6am-6pm Tue-Fri, 6am-1pm Sat; 🚋 4 or 6) and the **Hold utca market** (Map p84; V Hold utca 11; ☽ 6am-5pm Mon, 6.30am-6pm Tue-Fri, 6.30am-2pm Sat; Ⓜ M3 Arany János utca) near V Szabadság tér. Following are two much larger and very colourful markets.

Nagycsarnok (Great Market; Map p86; IX Vámház körút 1-3; ☽ 6am-5pm Mon, 6am-6pm Tue-Fri, 6am-2pm Sat; 🚋 47 or 49) This is Budapest's biggest market, though it has become a bit of a tourist trap since its renovations in 1996. Still, plenty of locals head here for fruit, vegetables, deli items, fish and meat. There are good food stalls on the west side of the 3rd level.

Lehel Csarnok (Map pp80-1; XIII Lehel tér; ☽ 6am-6pm Mon-Fri, 6am-2pm Sat, 6am-1pm Sun; Ⓜ M3 Lehel tér) This is one of Pest's more interesting traditional markets, recently rehoused in a hideous boatlike structure designed by László Rajk, son of the Communist Minister of the Interior executed for 'Titoism' in 1949. This is apparently his revenge.

Mézes Kuckó (Map p84; XIII Jászai Mari tér 4; ☽ 10am-6pm Mon-Fri year-round, 9am-1pm Sat Oct-May; 🚋 4 or 6) The 'Honey Nook' is the place to go if you've got the urge for something sweet; its nut and honey cookies (180Ft per 10dg) are to die for. A colourfully decorated *mézeskalács* (honey cake) in the shape of a heart (400Ft to 600Ft) makes a lovely gift.

Butterfly (Map p84; VI Teréz körút 20; 90Ft per scoop; ☽ 10am-7pm Mon-Fri, 10am-2pm Sat; 🚋 4 or 6) The Butterfly – and *not* the pastry shop next door called Vajassütemények boltja – is *the* place in Pest for ice cream, as you'll be able to deduce from the queues outside.

Large supermarkets are everywhere in Pest. We recommend:

Match Supermarket (Map p84; VIII Rákóczi út; ☽ 6am-9pm Mon-Fri, 7am-8pm Sat, 7am-3pm Sun; Ⓜ M3 Blaha Lujza tér) This supermarket faces Blaha Lujza tér.

Kaiser's Supermarket (Map p84; VI Nyugati tér 1-2; 7am-8pm Mon-Sat, 7am-4pm Sun; M3 Nyugati pályaudvar) Opposite Nyugati train station.

Rothschild Supermarket (Map p84; XIII Szent István körút 4; 24hr; 4 or 6) Sells a good supply of kosher products.

There are nonstop shops open till very late or even 24 hours in Pest. Recommended shops:

Nyugati ABC (Map p84; track No 13; 24hr; M3 Nyugati pályaudvar) Located at the Nyugati train station.

Keleti Csarnok (Map pp80-1; VIII Baross tér 3; 6am-midnight; M2 Keleti pályaudvar) Near Keleti train station.

DRINKING

Budapest – particularly Pest – is loaded with pubs and bars and there are enough to satisfy all tastes. In summer the preferred drinking venues are the outdoor *kertek* (see boxed text, p117).

Buda

Lánchíd Söröző (Map p83; 214 3144; I Fő utca 4; 10am-midnight; 86) The 'Chain Bridge Pub' has a wonderful retro Magyar feel to it, with old movie posters and advertisements on the walls and red-checked cloths on the tables. Friendly service, too.

Erzsébet-híd Eszpresszó (Map p83; 214 2785; I Döbrentei tér 1; 10am-10pm, 15, 80) If you're in the mood for a relaxing drink in simple surrounds, the 'Elizabeth Bridge Espresso Bar' is a wonderful old dive with a large terrace under a big plane tree and views of the bridge.

Oscar American Bar (Map p83; 212 8017; I Ostrom utca 14; 5pm 2am Sun-Thu, 5pm-4am Fri & Sat; M2 Moszkva tér) The décor is cinema-inspired – film memorabilia on the wood-panelled walls, leather directors' chairs on the floor – and the beautiful crowd often act like they're on camera. Not to worry – the powerful cocktails (some 150, in fact) go down a treat. There's music most nights.

Café Rolling Rock (Map pp80-1; 368 2298; III Bécsi út 53-55; 9am-1am Mon-Thu, 9am-2am Fri, 9am-4am Sat, noon-midnight Sun; 17 or HÉV Szépvölgyi út) If you find yourself in Óbuda in need of a libation, you could do worse than this place, a revamped pub where the trendies of Óbuda (not necessarily a contradiction in terms) gather for some of the peculiar American brew in the little green bottles.

Pest

Kultiplex (Map pp80-1; 219 0706; IX Kinizsi utca 28; 10am-5am; M3 Ferenc körút) This huge complex has something for everyone – performance space, cinema, grill restaurant – and a simple inside/outside bar where you can enjoy an unreconstructed drink.

Szimpla (Map p84; 342 1034; VII Kertész utca 46; noon-midnight Jun-Aug, 10am-2am Sep May; 4 or 6) This is a distressed-looking, very un-flashy place, just a hop, skip and a tumble from the stilettos south of Liszt Ferenc tér. There's live music three nights a week.

Paris, Texas (Map pp80-1; 218 0570; IX Ráday utca 22; 10am-1am Sun & Mon, 10am-3am Tue-Sat; M3 Kálvin tér) One of the original bars on the Ráday utca nightlife strip, this place has a coffee-house feel to it with old sepia-tinted photos on the walls and pool tables downstairs. The cocktail list is huge.

Darshan Udvar (Map p84; 266 5541; VIII Krúdy utca 7; 11am-1am Mon-Fri, 6pm -1am Sat & Sun; 4 or 6) This cavernous complex of two bars, a restaurant and a courtyard terrace vegetarian café with décor that combines Euro-techno with Eastern flair is a great escape from the bars of VI Liszt Ferenc tér and the dull sophistication of IX Ráday utca.

Becketts (Map p84; 311 1033; V Bajcsy-Zsilinszky út 72; 10am-1am Sun-Thu, 10am-3am Fri & Sat; M3 Nyugati pályaudvar) Of the capital's ubiquitous 'Irish' pubs, this is the best (and largest) of the lot, with all-day breakfast (1600Ft), as well as sandwiches (850Ft to 1700Ft) and salads (1200Ft to 1300Ft). The new cocktail bar in the rear is an added attraction.

Champs Sport Pub (Map p86; ☎ 413 1655; VII Dohány utca 20; ☒ noon-midnight Sun-Thu, noon-2am Fri & Sat; Ⓜ M2 Astoria) Owned by five Olympic medallists, Champs is the place for sports fans and the vicarious, with two huge screens and 35 TVs. The menu tells you how many calories and how much fat each dish contains – and what you need to do to lose it.

ENTERTAINMENT

For a city of its size, Budapest has a huge choice of things to do and places to go after dark – from opera and folk dancing to jazz and mee(a)t-market clubs. It's usually not difficult getting tickets or getting in; the hard part is deciding what to do.

Your best sources of information for what's on in the city are the weekly freebie **PestiEst** (www.est.hu in Hungarian), published every Thursday, and available at bars, cinemas and fast-food joints; and the more thorough weekly – with everything from clubs and films to art exhibits and classical music – **Pesti Műsor** (Budapest Program; www.pesti musor.hu in Hungarian), also called *PM Program Magazin*, available at newsstands every Thursday for 149Ft.

Other freebies include the vastly inferior (though English- and German-language) *Programme in Ungarn/in Hungary* and its scaled-down monthly version for the capital, *Budapest Panorama*. The free *Koncert Kalendárium*, published monthly (bimonthly in summer), has more serious offerings: concerts, opera, dance etc. A welcome arrival is *Mr Gordonsky's Budapest City Spy Map*, a hip little publication with all sorts of insider's tips. It's available free at pubs and bars.

Booking Agencies

The most important and/or useful booking agencies in Budapest include those listed here. You can book almost anything online at www.jegymester.hu and www.kultur info.hu.

Ticket Express (Inner Town Map p86; ☎ information 312 0000, bookings 06 30 303 0999; www.tex.hu; Andrássy út 18; ☒ 9.30am-6.30pm Mon-Fri; Ⓜ M1 Opera; Józsefváros Map p84; ☎ 334 0369; MCD Zeneáruház, VIII József körút 50; ☒ 9.30am-6.30pm Mon-Fri; 🚋 4 or 6) The largest ticket-office network in the city, with eight outlets.

Central Ticket Office (Központi Jegyiroda; Map p86; ☎ 267 9737, 267 1267; VI Andrássy út 15; Ⓜ M1 Opera; ☒ 10am-6pm Mon-Fri) This is the busiest theatrical ticket agency, with tickets to plays and other events at theatres around Budapest.

Symphony Ticket Office (Szimfonikus Jegyiroda; Map p84; ☎ 302 3841; VI Nagymező utca 19; Ⓜ M1 Opera; ☒ 10am-7pm Mon-Fri) Come here for tickets to the philharmonic and other classical-music concerts.

Nightclubs

Piaf (Map p84; ☎ 312 3823; VI Nagymező utca 25; ☒ 7pm-6am; Ⓜ M3 Arany János utca or trolleybuses 70 or 78) Piaf is the place to go when everything else slows down. There's dancing and action well into the new day. Most of the action – and characters – are in the smoky cavern below.

Sark (Map p84; ☎ 06 30 282 9625; VII Klauzál tér 14; ☒ 10am-3am Sun-Thu, 10am-5am Fri & Sun; 🚋 4 or 6) This popular alternative music pub and club on three floors has a big cellar with a dance floor, where bands occasionally perform. It's all a bit student-clubbish.

Süss Fél Nap (Map p84; ☎ 374 3329; V Honvéd utca 40; ☒ 5pm-5am; 🚋 4 or 6) This cellar club attracts a student crowd, and hosts lots of student bands and visiting talent. It's a lot of fun and less expensive than many of the other clubs.

Közgáz Pince Klub (Map pp80-1; ☎ 215 4359, 218 6855; IX Fővám tér 8; ☒ 9pm-5am Tue-Sat; 🚋 47 or 49) With few frills and cheap covers at the Economics University, this is the pick-up venue of choice for many a student. Avoid Wednesday unless you like karaoke.

Kaméleon (Map pp80-1; ☎ 345 8547; Mammut II, 4th fl, II Lövőház utca 2-6; ☒ 5pm-midnight Sun-Thu, 5pm-3am Fri & Sat; Ⓜ M3 Moszkva tér) This throbbing club in the newer wing of Buda's massive Mammut shopping mall is a true chameleon, with a different party every night – from La Noche Cubana on Friday to live bands on Monday.

Bank Dance Hall (Map p84; ☎ 06 20 344 4888; VI Teréz körút 55; ☒ 10pm-4am Sun-Thu, 10pm-5am Fri & Sat; Ⓜ M3 Nyugati pályaudvar) In the southern wing of Nyugati train station next to McDonald's, this enormous disco has rhythm and blues on the 1st floor, house and trance on the 2nd, Dance on the 3rd and funkhouse (a Hungarian thing) on the 4th.

Gay & Lesbian Venues

Angel (Map p84; ☎ 351 6490; VII Kazinczy utca 2; ☒ 10pm-5am Fri-Sun; Ⓜ M2 Astoria) Also known by its Hungarian name, Angyal, this is

THE HEAT IS ON

During Budapest's (usually) very long and very hot summer, so-called *kertek*, literally 'gardens' but in Budapest any outdoor spot that has been converted into an entertainment zone (including courtyards and any available stretch along the river), empty out even the most popular indoor bars and clubs. The venues (and their locations) can change from year to year and a definitive list is usually not available until about May; the best single source of information is **Pestiside** (www.pestiside.hu). Some of the venues listed under Drinking (p115) and Nightclubs (opposite) have their own outside equivalent – 'gardens' that only blossom in summer. Some of the more popular ones in recent years:

Café del Rio (Map pp88–9; ☎ 06 30 297 2158; www.rio.hu in Hungarian; XI Goldman György tér; ☻ 2pm-4.30am; ☒ 4 or 6) On the northern side of Petőfi Bridge on the Buda side, Rio is stylish but not up itself, with a pseudo tropical/carnival theme.

Cha Cha Cha Terasz (Map pp80–1; ☎ 215 0545; www.chachacha.hu in Hungarian; XIII Margit-sziget; ☻ 4pm-4am; ☒ 26, ☒ 4 or 6) In the stadium at the southern tip of Margaret Island, Cha Cha Cha Terasz is an attitude-free venue, with great music and dance space.

Holdudvar (Map p86; ☎ 485 5270; VIII Múzeum körút 6-8; ☻ 8am-4am; Ⓜ M2 Astoria) A large courtyard on the grounds of the city's largest university has a predictably split personality: earnest and coffee-drinking, wild and out of control.

Mokka Cuka (Map pp78–9; ☎ 453 2120; www.mokkacuka.hu; III Óbudai-sziget; ☻ 24hr; HÉV Filatorigát) On the island that attracts the capital's beautiful people, Mokka Cuka is a leading outdoor underground venue showcasing great indie DJs.

Szimpla Kert (Map p84; ☎ 321 5880; www.szimpla.hu; VII Kazinczy 14; ☻ noon-midnight; trolleybus 74) One of the capital's first *kertek*, Szimpla is just that – a simple, low-key affair that keeps itself to itself.

Szóda Udvar (Map p86; ☎ 461 0007; V József nádor tér 1; ☻ noon-late; Ⓜ M1/2/3 Deák Ferenc tér) This rather well-heeled venue – a former bank headquarters – pulls in a subdued crowd that lets loose on the basement dancefloor in the wee hours.

Tűzraktár (Map pp88–9; ☎ 06 70 523 1593; www.tuzraktar.hu; IX Tűzoltó utca 54-56; ☻ 5pm-3am; Ⓜ 3 Klinikák) This abandoned factory building called the Fire Warehouse and its big courtyard plays host to all sorts of cultural and party events.

Zöld Pardon (Map pp88–9; www.zp.hu; XI Goldman György tér; ☻ 9am-6am; ☒ 4 or 6) What bills itself as the world's longest summer festival is a rocker's paradise just opposite the Café del Rio.

Budapest's flagship gay club. It welcomes girls on Friday and Sunday.

CoXx (Map p84; ☎ 344 4884; VII Dohány utca 38; ☻ 9pm-4am Sun-Thu, 9pm-5am Fri & Sat; ☒ 7 or 7/a) This cellar bar has a DJ and small dance floor, but it's more of a pub than a club. There's a gallery and **Internet café** (☻ noon to 4am Mon-Fri, 9pm-4am Sat & Sun) at street level just to let you know this place has a serious side, too.

Action (Map p86; ☎ 266 9148; V Magyar utca 42; ☻ 9pm-4am; Ⓜ M3 Kálvin tér) Action is where to head if you want just that. Take the usual precautions and have a ball.

There are no specific girl bars in Budapest, though we recommend:

Café Eklektika (Map p86; ☎ 266 1226; V Semmelweis utca 21; ☒ 47 or 49; ☻ noon-midnight Mon-Fri, 5pm-midnight Sat & Sun) Attracts a mixed crowd.

Candy (Map p86; ☎ 789 2130, V Kossuth Lajos utca 17; Ⓜ M2 Astoria) Lesbian parties are held on the last Saturday of the month.

Jailhouse (Map pp88–9; ☎ 06 30 989 4905, 218 1368; IX Tűzoltó utca 22; Ⓜ M3 Ferenc körút) Lesbian parties are held on the first Friday of the month. For more details, see below.

Live Music
ROCK & POP

Wigwam Rock Blues Club (Map pp88–9; ☎ 208 5569; XI Fehérvári utca 202; ☻ 8pm-5am; ☒ 41 or 47) This place is one of the best of its kind in Hungary, and hosts some big-name Hungarian rock and blues bands on Friday and Saturday.

Gödör Klub (Map p86; ☎ 06 20 943 5464; V Erzsébet tér; ☻ 9am-late; Ⓜ M1/2/3 Deák Ferenc tér) This new arrival in the old bus bays below Elizabeth Sq in central Pest is a real mixed bag, offering everything from folk and jazz but especially rock.

Jailhouse (Map pp88–9; ☎ 06 30 989 4905, 218 1368; IX Tűzoltó utca 22; ☻ 10pm-5am Fri & Sat; Ⓜ M3 Ferenc körút) A small venue next to the Trafó House of Contemporary Arts (opposite), with a friendly atmosphere, underground DJs and live music.

Budapest Sportcsarnok (Map pp80-1; ☎ 422 2600; www.budapestarena.hu; XIV Stefánia út 2; Ⓜ M2 Stadionok) This new arena named after the Hungarian pugilist László Papp is where the likes of Phil Collins, Duran Duran, Rod Stewart and Simply Red warble.

Petőfi Csarnok (Map pp80-1; ☎ 363 3730, 251 7266; www.petoficsarnok.hu; XIV Zichy Mihály út 14; Ⓜ M1 Széchenyi fürdő or trolleybuses 72 or 74) The city's main youth centre, in City Park, is the place for smaller rock concerts as the hall is intimate enough to get really close to the performers.

JAZZ & BLUES

Columbus Jazzklub (Map p86; ☎ 266 9013; V Pesti alsó rakpart; ⏰ noon-midnight; ▣ 2 or 2/a) This place located on a boat moored in the Danube, just north of V Vigadó tér opposite the Budapest Inter-Continental Hotel, has transformed itself from being 'just another Irish pub' to a jazz club of note with big-name local and international bands.

Fat Mo's Music Club (Map p86; ☎ 267 3199; V Nyáry Pál utca 11; ⏰ noon-2am Mon & Tue, noon-3am Wed, noon-4am Thu & Fri, 6pm-4am Sat, 6pm-2am Sun; Ⓜ M3 Ferenciek tere, ▣ 15) With a speakeasy 1920s Prohibition theme, this club has jazz (and sometimes country) from 9pm or 9.30pm. DJs take over at midnight Thursday to Saturday.

Jazz Garden (Map p86; ☎ 266 7364; V Veres Pálné utca 44/a; ⏰ 6pm-1am Sun-Thu, 6pm-2am Fri & Sat; ▣ 47 or 49) A sophisticated venue with traditional, vocal and Latin jazz, and odd décor: a faux cellar 'garden' with street lamps and a night 'sky' bedecked with blinking stars. Book a table (starters 1420Ft to 2250Ft, mains 2250Ft to 3490Ft) in the dining room; music starts at 9.30pm.

FOLK & TRADITIONAL

Authentic *táncház*, literally 'dance house' but really folk-music workshops, are held at various locations throughout the week, but less frequently in summer. Times and venues often change; consult one of the publications earlier in this section (p116) or check out **Dance House Guild** (www.tanchaz.hu). The best local *klezmer* (Jewish folk music) is the **Budapest Klezmer Band** (www.budapestklezmer.hu).

Fonó Buda Music House (Fonó Budai Zeneház; Map pp88-9; ☎ 206 5300; www.fono.hu; XI Sztregova

utca 3; ▣ 41 or 47) This place has regular programmes – always at 8pm on Wednesday and the second Friday of each month, as well as other days. Consult its website.

Almássy tér Recreation Centre (Almássy téri Szabadidő Központ; Map pp80-1; ☎ 352 1572; VII Almássy tér 6; trolleybus 74) This is a venue for just about anything that's in and/or interesting, from rock and blues to folk music. There's Hungarian dance house every second Saturday at 7.30pm.

Pótkulcs (Spare Key; Map p84; ☎ 269 1050; VI Csengery utca 65/b; Ⓜ M3 Nyugati pályaudvar) This wonderful little venue, with a varied menu of music most nights, has dance house at 8pm every Tuesday.

Two city cultural houses in Buda have frequent folk programmes.

Municipal Cultural House (Fővárosi Művelődési Háza; Map pp88-9; ☎ 203 3868; XI Fehérvári út 47; ▣ 41 or 47) The Folklór Centrum based here has folk music every Friday at 7.30pm and a children's dance house hosted by the incomparable Muzsikás (p42) every Tuesday from 5pm to 6.30pm.

Marczibányi tér Cultural Centre (Marczibányi téri Művelődési Központ; Map pp80-1; ☎ 212 0803, 212 2820; II Marczibányi tér 5/a; ▣ 4, 6 or 49) Offers Hungarian, Moldavian and Slovakian dance and music every Wednesday from 8pm.

Aranytíz Cultural Centre (Aranytíz Művelődési Központ; Map p86; ☎ 354 3400, 311 2248; V Arany János utca 10; ▣ 15) At this new cultural centre in Pest the wonderful Kalamajka Táncház has programmes from 5pm on Saturday that frequently run to well after 2am.

CLASSICAL

The *Koncert Kalendárium* highlights all concerts in Budapest monthly. The main concert halls are the National Concert Hall (Nemzeti Hangversenyterem) and the smaller Festival Theatre (Fesztivál Színház) at the new **Palace of Arts** (Művészetek Palotája; Map pp88-9; ☎ information 555 3000, tickets 555 3301; www.mupa.hu; IX Komor Marcell utca; ⏰ ticket office 1-6pm Mon-Sat, 10am-3pm Sun; ▣ 2 or 2/a) and the stunning **Liszt Academy of Music** (Liszt Zeneakadémia; Map p84; ☎ 342 0179; www.zeneakademia.hu; VI Liszt Ferenc tér 8; ⏰ ticket office 10am-8pm Mon-Fri, 2-8pm Sat & Sun; Ⓜ M2 Oktogon) in Pest, and the modern **Budapest Congress Centre** (Budapesti Kongresszusi Központ; Map pp80-1; ☎ information 372 5700, tickets 372 5429; www.bcc.hu; XII Jagelló út 1-3; ▣ 8 or 112) in Buda, which has just had a total renovation.

The **Pesti Vigadó** (Map p86; ☎ 318 9903, 318 9167; V Vigadó tér 2; Ⓜ M1 Vörösmarty tér, ☒ 2 or 2/a) and the **Duna Palota** (Map p86); ☎ 235 5500, 317 2790; V Zrínyi utca 5; ☒ 15) have light classical music, and touristy musical revues in summer.

Opera

Hungarian State Opera House (Magyar Állami Operaház; Map p84; ☎ information 353 0170, tickets 332 7914; www.opera.hu; VI Andrássy út 22; ☺ ticket office 11am-7pm Mon-Sat, 4-7pm Sat & Sun; Ⓜ M1 Opera) The opera house should be visited at least once – to admire the incredibly rich decoration inside as much as to view a performance and hear the perfect acoustics.

Erkel Theatre (Erkel Színház; Map pp80-1; ☎ 333 0540; VIII Köztársaság tér 30; ☺ ticket office 11am-7pm Tue-Fri, 11am-3pm Sat, 10am-1pm & 4-7pm Sun; Ⓜ M2 Keleti pályaudvar, ☒ 7 or 7/a) Budapest's modern (and ugly) second opera house is southwest of Keleti train station.

Budapest Operetta (Budapesti Operettszínház; Map p84; ☎ 472 2030, 269 3870; www.operettszinhaz.hu; VI Nagymező utca 17; ☺ ticket office 10am-7pm Mon-Fri, 1-7pm Sat & Sun; Ⓜ M1 Opera) This theatre presents operettas – always a riot, especially campy ones like the *Queen of the Csárdás* by Imre Kálmán.

Dance
CLASSICAL
Budapest's two so-so ballet companies – the Hungarian National and the Hungarian Festival Ballet troupes – perform at the Hungarian State Opera House, the Erkel Theatre and at the National Dance Theatre.

For modern dance fans there are several good options, including the **Trafó House of Contemporary Arts** (Trafó Kortárs Művészetek Háza; Map pp88-9; ☎ information 456 2040, tickets 215 1600; www .trafo.hu; IX Liliom utca 41; Ⓜ M3 Ferenc körút), which presents the cream of the crop, including a good pull of international acts, as well as the **Central Europe Dance Theatre** (Közép-Európa Táncszínház; Map pp80-1; ☎ 342 7163, 06 30 526 1024; www .cedt.hu; VII Bethlen Gábor tér 3; trolleybuses 74 or 78).

FOLK
The 30 dancers of the Hungarian State Folk Ensemble (Magyar Állami Népi Együttes) perform at the **Buda Concert Hall** (Budai Vigadó; Map p83; ☎ 201 3766 I Corvin tér 8; ☒ 86, ☒ 19) in Buda on Tuesday, Thursday and Sunday from May to mid-October, and on Saturday and/or Sunday only the rest of the year. In addition the Rajkó Folk Ensemble (Rajkó Népi Együttes) stages folk dance performances at the Budapest Puppet Theatre (below) on Saturday, and the Duna Folk Ensemble (Duna Népi Együttes) dances at the Duna Palota (left) just off Roosevelt tér in Pest on Monday and Wednesday. The 1½-hour programmes begin at 8pm, and tickets cost from 4600/4200Ft per adult/student. Contact **Hungaria Koncert** (☎ 317 2754, 201 5928; www .ticket.info.hu) for information and bookings.

National Dance Theatre (Nemzeti Táncszínház; Map p83; ☎ information 201 4407, tickets 375 8649; www .nemzetitancszinhaz.hu; I Színház utca 1-3; ☺ ticket office 1-6pm; ☒ 16 or Várbusz) The National hosts at some point every troupe in the city, including the two ballet companies and the Honvéd Ensemble, one of the city's best folk troupes and now experimenting with modern choreography as well.

Theatre
Merlin Theatre (Map p86; ☎ 317 9338, 266 4632; www.merlinszinhaz.hu; V Gerlóczy utca 4; Ⓜ M1/2/3 Deák Ferenc tér, ☒ 47 or 49) This theatre, in Pest, stages numerous plays in English, often performed by the Merlin's Atlantis Company and the local Madhouse troupe. Usually pretty serious stuff, with little scenery and few props.

International Buda Stage (IBS; Map p77; ☒ 391 2525; www.ibs-b.hu; II Tárogató út 2-4; ☒ 56, ☒ 29) Further afield in Buda, the Buda Stage is a more recent arrival, with occasional performances – often comedies – in English.

National Theatre (Nemzeti Színház; Map pp88-9; ☎ information 476 6800, tickets 476 6868; www .nemzetiszinhaz.hu; IX Bajor Gizi park 1; ☺ ticket office 10am-6pm Mon-Fri, 2-6pm Sat & Sun; ☒ 2 or 2/a) This rather eclectic venue is the place to go if you want to brave a play in Hungarian or just check out the bizarre architecture (p94).

Budapest Puppet Theatre (Bábszínház; Map p84; ☎ information 342 2702, 321 5200; www.budapest-babszinhaz.hu; VI Andrássy út 69; tickets 500-1100Ft; Ⓜ M1 Vörösmarty utca) The puppet theatre, which usually doesn't require fluency in Hungarian, presents shows designed for children on weekdays (usually at 10am or 10.30am and 4pm) and folk programmes for adults occasionally in the evening.

Cinemas
A couple of dozen cinemas screen English-language films with Hungarian subtitles.

Consult the listings in the *Budapest Sun* newspaper, *Pesti Est* or *Pesti Műsor* (p116).

Corvin Film Palace (Corvin Filmpalota; Map pp80-1; ☎ 459 5050; VIII Corvin köz 1; Ⓜ M3 Ferenc körút) This cinema, which saw a lot of action during the 1956 Uprising, has been fantastically renovated and is worth a visit. Note the two wonderful reliefs outside.

Örökmozgó Film Museum (Örökmozgó Filmmúzeum; Map p84; ☎ 342 2167; VII Erzsébet körút 39; 🚊 4 or 6) Part of the Hungarian Film Institute, this cinema (whose name vaguely translates as 'moving picture') screens an excellent assortment of foreign classic films in their original languages.

Művész (Map p84; ☎ 332 6726; VI Teréz körút 30; Ⓜ M1 Oktogon, 🚊 4 or 6) Shows artsy and cult films.

Puskin (Map p86; ☎ 429 6080; V Kossuth Lajos utca 18; 🚊 7 or 7/a) Screens a mix of arthouse and popular releases.

Uránia National Cinema (Uránia Nemzeti Filmszínház; Map p84; ☎ 486 3413; VIII Rákóczi út 21; 🚊 7 or 7/a) This all-Art Deco/neo-Moorish extravaganza is a tarted-up film palace. It has an excellent café.

Circus

Municipal Great Circus (Fővárosi Nagycirkusz; Map pp80-1; ☎ 343 8300, 343 6002; www.maciva.hu in Hungarian; XIV Állatkerti körút 7; adult 1200-1900Ft, child 900-1500Ft; Ⓜ Széchenyi fürdő) Europe's only permanent big top has everything one would expect from a circus, including acrobats, dare devils on horseback and ice shows in season. Performances are at 3pm Wednesday to Sunday, with additional shows at 10.30am on Saturday and Sunday and at 7pm on Saturday.

Sport

WATER POLO

The **Hungarian Water Polo Association** (MVLSZ; ☎ 412 0041; www.waterpolo.hu in Hungarian) is based at the Alfréd Hajós swimming complex (p98) on Margaret Island. Matches take place here and at two other pools: the Béla Komjádi Swimming Pool (p99) in Buda and the **BVSC** (Map pp80-1; ☎ 251 3888; XIV Szőnyi út 2; trolleybuses 74 or 74/a) in Pest from September to May. If you want to see a match or watch the lads in training in summer, call the MVLSZ for times and dates, or get someone to check schedules for you in the daily *Nemzeti Sport* (National Sport; 99Ft) available at newsstands everywhere.

FOOTBALL

Hungary's descent from the top of the heap of European football to *a béka segge alatt* – literally, 'under the arse of the frog' as the Hungarians describe something *really* far down – remains as great a mystery as the allure of Cliff Richard. Hungary's defeat of the England team both at Wembley (6-3) in 1953 and at home (7-1) the following year, are still talked about as if the winning goals were scored yesterday.

There are four premier league football teams in Budapest out of a total of 12 nationwide, including: Kispest-Honvéd, which plays at **József Bozsik Stadium** (☎ 282 9791, 282 9789; XIX Új temető út 1-3; 🚊 36), accommodating 15,000 spectators; MTK at **Hungária Stadium** (Map pp80-1; ☎ 219 0300; VIII Salgótarjáni utca 12-14; 🚊 1 or 1/a), accommodating 8000 spectators; and UTE at **UTE Stadium** (Map pp78-9; ☎ 369 7333; IV Megyeri út 13; 🚊 47 or 96), accommodating 15,000 fans. But no club dominates Hungarian football like Ferencváros (FTC), the country's loudest and brashest team, and its only hope. You either love the Fradi boys in green and white or you hate them. Watch them play at **FTC stadium** (Map pp88-9; ☎ 215 1013; IX Könyves Kálmán körút 26; Ⓜ M3 Népliget), with space for 18,000 spectators. Check *Nemzeti Sport* for game schedules.

HORSE RACING

The descendants of the nomadic Magyars are keen on horse racing. **Kincsem Park** (Map p77; ☎ 433 0522; www.kincsempark.com; X Albertirsai út 2; Ⓜ M2 Pillangó utca) is the place to go for both *ügető* (trotting) and *galopp* (flat racing). Schedules can change, but in general three trotting meetings of 10 to 11 races take place weekly, usually 3pm on Saturday and Sunday, and 4pm or 5pm on Wednesday. Flat racing usually takes place from 2pm on Thursday and Sunday between May and early November.

SHOPPING

Budapest is a great place to satisfy that urge to buy, and you'll find all the products described in the Directory (p375) in full supply here. But some people consider the city's flea markets their highlight – not just as places to indulge their vice, but as the consummate Budapest experience.

Flea markets

Ecseri Piac (Map pp88-9; ☎ 282 9563; XIX Nagykőrösi út 156; 🕒 8am-4pm Mon-Fri, 6am-3pm Sat, 8am-1pm Sun) Often called the *piac* (market), it's one of the biggest and best flea markets in Central Europe, selling everything from antique jewellery and Soviet army watches to Fred Astaire–style top hats. Saturday is said to be the best day to go. To get there, take bus 54 from Boráros tér in Pest or, better, the red express bus 54 from the Határ utca stop on the M3 metro line and get off at the Fiume utca stop. Then follow the crowds over the pedestrian bridge.

City Park flea market (Városligeti bolhapiac; Map pp80-1; ☎ 363 3730, 251 7266; www.bolhapiac.com; XIV Zichy Mihály utca 14; ⏰ 7am-2pm Sat & Sun; 🚋 1 or 1/a or trolleybuses 70, 72 or 74) This is a huge outdoor flea market – a kind of Hungarian boot or garage sale – held next to the Petőfi Csarnok (p118) in City Park. The usual diamonds-to-rust stuff is on offer – from old records and draperies to candles, honey and herbs. Sunday is the better day to visit.

If you don't have time to get to the Ecseri or City Park flea markets, check out any of the **BÁV stores** (Bizományi Kereskedőház és Záloghitel; ☎ 325 2600; ⏰ 10am-6pm Mon-Fri, 9am-1pm Sat), essentially a chain of pawn and second-hand shops with many branches around town. Try the **VI Andrássy út branch** (Map p84; ☎ 342 9143; VI Andrássy út branch 43; Ⓜ M1 Opera) for old jewellery, watches and silver; the **V Bécsi utca branch** (Map p86; ☎ 318 4403; V Bécsi utca 1-3; Ⓜ M1/2/3 Deák Ferenc tér) for knick-knacks, porcelain and glassware, the **XIII Szent István körút branch** (Map p84; ☎ 473 0666; XIII Szent István körút 3; 🚋 4 or 6) for chinaware, textiles and artwork; and the **II Margit körút branch** (Map pp80-1; ☎ 315 0417; II Margit körút 4; 🚋 4 or 6) for furniture, lamps and fine porcelain.

Gifts & Souvenirs

Holló Atelier (Map p86; ☎ 317 8103; V Vitkovics Mihály utca 12; ⏰ 10am-6pm Mon-Fri, 10am-noon Sat; Ⓜ M1/2/3 Deák Ferenc tér) Off the northern end of Váci utca, this place sells attractive folk art with a modern look and remains a personal favourite place to shop for gifts.

Hungaricum (Map p83; ☎ 487 7306; I Fortuna utca 1; ⏰ 9am-9pm; 🚌 16 or Várbusz) This shop conveniently located in the Castle District sells quality Hungarian handicrafts, as well as foodstuffs (eg potted goose liver and honey), wines and *pálinka* (brandy).

Intuita (Map p86; ☎ 266 5864; V Váci utca 67; ⏰ 11am-6pm Mon-Fri, 10am-2pm Sat; 🚌 15) You're not about to find painted eggs and *pálinka* here, but modern Hungarian folk craft, like

handmade glasses, ceramics and bound books.

Folkart Centrum (Népművészet; Map p86; ☎ 318 5840; V Váci utca 58; ⏰ 10am-7pm; 🚌 15) This is a large shop where everything Magyar-made is available – folk costumes, dolls, painted eggs, embroidered tablecloths – and prices are clearly labelled. The staff are very helpful and will advise.

Glassware & Porcelain

Herend (Map p86; ☎ 317 2622; V József nádor tér 11; ⏰ 10am-6pm Mon-Fri, 9am-1pm Sat; Ⓜ M1 Vörösmarty tér) For both contemporary and traditional fine porcelain, there is no other place but Herend.

Herend Village Pottery (Map pp80-1; ☎ 356 7899; II Bem rakpart 37; ⏰ 9am-5pm Mon-Fri, 9am-noon Sat; Ⓜ M2 Batthyány tér) Stocks hard-wearing pottery and dishes decorated with bold fruit patterns; an unusual alternative to what some might describe as rather prissy (and fragile) Herend flatware.

Zsolnay (Map p86; ☎ 266 6305; V Váci utca 19-21; ⏰ 10am-7pm; Ⓜ M3 Ferenciek tere) For both contemporary and traditional fine Zsolnay porcelain from Pécs, check out this place. We like the iridescent green frogs.

Haas & Czjzek (Map p84; ☎ 311 4094; VI Bajcsy-Zsilinszky út 23; ⏰ 10am-7pm Mon-Fri, 10am-3pm Sat; Ⓜ M3 Arany János utca) Just up from Deák Ferenc tér, this chinaware and crystal shop sells Zsolnay, as well as more affordable Hungarian-made Hollóháza and Alföldi porcelain.

Ajka Kristály (Map p84; ☎ 332 4541; VI Teréz körút 50; ⏰ 10am-6pm Mon-Fri, 10am-1pm Sat; Ⓜ M3 Nyugati pályaudvar) Established in 1878, Ajka has Hungarian-made lead crystal pieces and stemware. Most of it is very old fashioned, but there are some more contemporary pieces.

Wine & Spirits

Budapest Wine Society (Batthyány utca Map p83; ☎ 212 2569; www.bortarsasag.hu; I Batthyány utca 59; ⏰ 10am-8pm Mon-Fri, 10am-6pm Sat; Ⓜ M2 Moszkva tér; Ráday utca Map p86; ☎ 219 5647; IX Ráday utca 7; ⏰ noon-8pm Mon-Fri, 10am-3pm Sat; Ⓜ M3 Kálvin tér) This society has retail outlets with an exceptional selection of fine Hungarian wines. No-one, but no-one, knows Hungarian wines like these guys do.

La Boutique des Vins (Map p86; ☎ 317 5919; V József Attila utca 12; ⏰ 10am-6pm Mon-Fri,

10am-3pm Sat; Ⓜ M1/2/3 Deák Ferenc tér) Owned by the former sommelier at Gundel, the ingeniously named 'Wine Shop' (sounds better than 'Bor Boltja') has an excellent selection of Hungarian wines. Ask the staff to recommend a label if – when – you feel lost.

Hungarian Pálinka House (Magyar Pálinka Ház; Map p84; ☎ 338 4219; www.magyarpalinkahaza.hu; VIII Rákóczi út 17; ☼ 9am-7pm Mon-Sat; Ⓜ M2 Astoria) If you're into Hungarian *pálinka*, the exquisite brandy flavoured with everything from apricot and sour cherry to (be still, our heart) raspberry, make a beeline for this place. It stocks hundreds of varieties.

GETTING THERE & AWAY
Air
The main **Malév Customer Service Centre** (Map pp80-1; ☎ 235 3222; www.malev.hu; XIII Váci út 26; ☼ 8.30am-7pm Mon-Fri, 10am-6pm Sat & Sun; Ⓜ M3 Nyugati pályaudvar) is 100m northwest of Nyugati train station. Malév also has ticket-issuing desks at **Terminal 2A** (☎ 296 7211; ☼ 5am-11pm) and another one at **Terminal 2B** (☎ 296 5767; ☼ 6am-8.30pm). For contact telephone numbers and websites of other carriers with offices in the capital, see p378.

Boat
Hydrofoils to Bratislava and Vienna run by **Mahart PassNave** (Map p86; ☎ 484 4013; www.mahart passnave.hu; V Belgrád rakpart; ☼ 8am-6pm) arrive at and depart from the **International Ferry Pier** (Nemzetközi hajóállomás; Map p86; V Belgrád rakpart). For more information, see p383.

From April to late October Mahart Pass Nave also runs excursion boats on the Danube from Budapest to Szentendre, Vác, Visegrád and Esztergom, and between late May and early September hydrofoils from Budapest to Visegrád, Nagymoros and Esztergom. Boats usually leave from the **Legenda Boat Tours Office & pier** (Map p86; ☎ 318 1223; Ⓜ M1 Vörösmarty tér) off V Vigadó tér on the Pest side, and sometimes pick up and discharge passengers from the ferry stop at I Batthyány tér (Map p83) on the Buda side, which is on the M2 metro line.

Bus
All international buses and some – but not all – domestic ones (especially to/from north and north-central Hungary) arrive at and depart from **Népliget bus station** (Map pp88-9; ☎ 219 8080; IX Üllői út 131; Ⓜ M3 Népliget) in

Pest. The **international ticket office** (☼ 6am-6pm Mon-Fri Sep-May, 6-8pm Mon-Fri Jun-Aug, 6am-4pm Sat & Sun) is upstairs. **Eurolines** (☎ 219 8021; www .eurolines.com) is represented here, as is its Hungarian associate **Volánbusz** (☎ 382 0888; www.volanbusz.hu). There's a **left-luggage office** (☼ 6am-9pm) downstairs that charges 190Ft per piece per day.

Stadionok bus station (Map pp80-1; ☎ 251 0125; XIV Hungária körút 48-52; ☼ ticket office 6am-6pm Mon-Fri, 6am-4pm Sat & Sun; Ⓜ M3 Stadionok) serves cities and towns to the east of Budapest. The ticket office and the **left-luggage office** (☼ 6am-7pm; per piece 200Ft) are on the ground floor. Buses to southwest Hungary use **Etele tér bus station** (Map pp88-9; ☎ 382 4900; XI Etele tér; ☼ 6am-6pm; red 🚌 7) in Buda.

The **Árpád Bridge bus station** (Map pp78-9; ☎ 329 1450; XIII Róbert Károly körút; ☼ ticket office 6am-8pm; Ⓜ M3 Árpád híd), on the Pest side of Árpád Bridge, is the place to catch buses for the Danube Bend and parts of the Northern Uplands (eg Balassagyarmat, Szécsény, Salgótarján etc). The small **Széna tér bus station** (Map pp80-1; ☎ 201 3688; I Széna tér 1/a; ☼ ticket office 6.30am-4.30pm; Ⓜ M3 Moszkva tér) in Buda handles some traffic to and from the Pilis Hills and towns northwest of the capital, with a half-dozen departures to Esztergom (from bay No 5) as an alternative to the Árpád Bridge bus station.

For details of international bus services, see p380.

Car & Motorcycle
All the international car-rental firms have offices in Budapest, but don't expect many bargains. An Opel Corsa from **Avis** (Map p86; ☎ 318 4158; www.avis.hu in Hungarian; V Szervita tér 8; ☼ 9am-6pm Mon-Fri, 9am-3pm Sat; Ⓜ 1/2/3 Deák Ferenc tér), for example, costs €33/198 per day/week, plus €0.33 per kilometre and €23 Collision Damage Waiver (CDW) and theft protection insurance. The same car with unlimited kilometres and insurance costs from €99/88 per day/weekend. The 25% ÁFA (value-added tax) doesn't apply to nonresidents paying with foreign currency or credit card.

One of the cheapest and most reliable outfits for renting cars is **Anselport** (☎ 362 6080, 06 20 945 0279; www.anselport.hu; XXII V utca 22; ☼ 9am-6pm; 🚌 14 or 114) in south Buda. Its Suzuki Swift costs €19 to €43 per day, including unlimited mileage and insurance, depending on the length of the rental (one day to three weeks). Another good bet is **Fox Autorent** (☎ 382 9000; www.fox-autorent.com; XXII Nagytétényi út 48-50; ☻ 8am-8pm; ◙ 3, 14 or 114), which charges from €46/230 per day/week for a Fiat Seicento, €55/320 for a Smart car and €59/349 for a Fiat Punto (kilometres and insurance included).

Assistance and/or advice for motorists is available from the **Hungarian Automobile Club** (Magyar Autóklub; Map pp80-1; ☎ 212 2821, 24hr helpline 345 1755; II Rómer Flóris utca 4/a; ◙ 4 or 6) off Margit körút near Margaret Bridge. Motorists anywhere in Hungary can call the automobile club on ☎ 188 for assistance.

For information on traffic and public road conditions in the capital, ring **Főinform** (☎ 317 1173).

Hitching

The ride service **Kenguru** (Map p84; ☎ 266 5837, 483 0105; www.kenguru.hu; VIII Kőfaragó utca 15; ☻ 9am-6pm Mon-Fri, 10am-2pm Sat) matches up drivers and riders for a fee – mostly to points abroad. Sample destinations and approximate one-way fares include Amsterdam (14,200Ft), London (15,700Ft), Munich (7500Ft), Paris (14,900Ft), Prague (8600Ft) and Vienna (3000Ft).

Train

Budapest has three main train stations. Most international trains arrive and depart from **Keleti train station** (Keleti train station; Map pp80-1; ☎ 313 6835; VIII Kerepesi út 2-6; Ⓜ M3 Keleti pályaudvar). Trains to certain destinations in the east (eg Romania) leave from **Nyugati train station** (Western train station; Map p84; ☎ 349 0115; VI Teréz körút 55-57; Ⓜ M3 Nyugati pályaudvar), while **Déli train station** (Southern train station; Map p83; ☎ 375 6293, 355 8657; I Krisztina körút 37; Ⓜ M2 Déli pályaudvar) handles trains to some destinations in the south (eg Osijek in Croatia and Sarajevo in Bosnia). These are not hard-and-fast rules, so always make sure you check which station your train leaves from when you buy a ticket. The handful of secondary train stations are of little importance to long-distance travellers. Occasionally, though, a through train will stop at **Kelenföldi train station** (Map pp88-9; ☎ 203 1687; XI Etele tér 5-7; ◙ 19 or 49) in Buda. For 24-hour information on international train services call ☎ 461 5500 in Budapest or ☎ 06 40 49 49 49 nationwide.

The train stations are generally pretty dismal places, with unsavoury-looking characters hanging about day and night, but all have some amenities. The left-luggage office at **Keleti train station** (☻ 24hr) is next to platform No 6. At **Nyugati train station** (☻ 4am-midnight) and **Déli train station** (☻ 3.30am-11.30pm) it's beside the information and ticketing hall. They charge 150/300Ft for a normal/large piece for six hours and 300/600Ft per day. You'll also find post offices and grocery stores that are open late or even round the clock.

The three main train stations are on metro lines and night buses serve them when the metro is closed. If you need to take a taxi, avoid the sharks hovering around the stations. At Déli train station, cross over to I Alkotás utca and hail one there. At Keleti train station, get into one of the legal taxis at the rank on VIII Kerepesi út, just south of the Eastern (Keleti) train station. Nyugati tér is a major intersection, so you'll have no problem finding a legitimate taxi there.

You can buy tickets at the three international train stations in Budapest, but the queues are often long, passengers are in a hurry and sales staff are not the most patient in the city. It's easier at the **MÁV international information and ticket centre** (Map p84; ☎ 461 5500, 352 2800; www.mav.hu in Hungarian; VI Andrássy út 35; ☻ 9am-6pm Mon-Fri Apr-Sep, 9am-5pm Mon-Fri Oct-Mar). For fares, check www.elvira.hu.

For more information on international train travel, see p381.

GETTING AROUND
To/From the Airport

Budapest's **Ferihegy International Airport** (☎ 296 7000; www.bud.hu), 24km southeast of the city centre, has two modern terminals side by side and within easy walking distance of one another, and an older one about 5km to the west. For information on which airlines use which terminal, see p378. Terminal 2B has an **OTP bank** (☻ 5.30-10pm) and an ATM, seven car-rental desks, a hotel booking office, a **post office** (☻ 8am-3.30pm Mon-Fri) and a **left-luggage office** (☻ 24hr), which charges 350/1050/1400Ft for one/three/six hours, 2200/6500Ft per day/week.

With much cheaper options for getting to/from Ferihegy, it would be senseless to take a taxi and risk a major rip-off. If you want to take a taxi, do *not* hail one

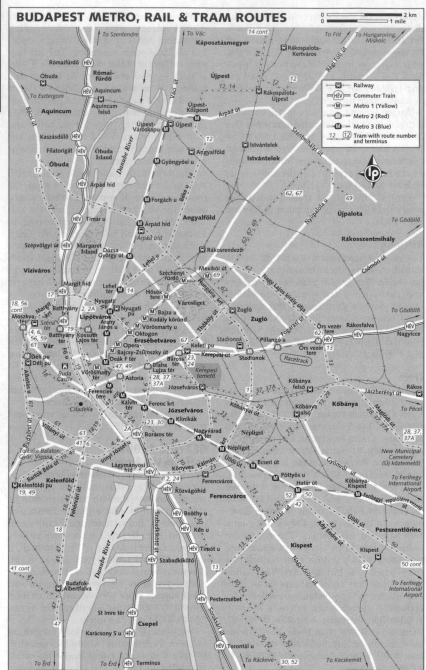

BUDAPEST METRO, RAIL & TRAM ROUTES

from outside. Instead call one of the recommended companies (p127) with a mobile phone or from a phone box at arrivals (dispatchers understand English) and expect to pay about 5000Ft. Several taxi companies have a flat, discounted fare to/from Ferihegy. **Tele 5** (☎ 355 5555) charges 3490Ft between the airport and Pest, and 3990Ft between Ferihegy and Buda. Its taxis are just down the road waiting for your call.

The **Airport Minibus Service** (☎ 296 8555; minibus@bud.hu) ferries passengers in eight-seater vans from all three of the airport's terminals directly to their hotel, hostel or residence (one way/return 2300/3900Ft). Tickets are available at a clearly marked desk in the arrival halls. You need to book your journey *to* the airport 24 hours in advance, but remember that, with up to seven pick-ups en route, this can be a nerve-wracking way to go if you're running late.

The cheapest way – but probably the most time-consuming – to get into the city centre is to take the airport bus (look for the stop marked 'BKV Plusz Reptér Busz' on the footpath between terminals 2A and 2B), which terminates at the Kőbánya-Kispest metro station. From there take the M3 metro into the city centre. The total cost is 320Ft.

Bicycle

More and more cyclists are seen on the streets and avenues of Budapest these days, taking advantage of the growing network of bike paths. The main roads in the city might be a bit too busy and nerve-wracking to allow enjoyable cycling, but the side streets are fine and there are some areas (City Park, Margaret Island etc) where cycling is positively ideal. For ideas on where to cycle and information on where to rent bikes, see p98.

Boat

Between May and mid-September passenger ferries run by **BKV** (Budapest Transport Company; ☎ 369 1359; www.bkv.hu) depart from IX Boráros tér (Map pp88–9) beside Petőfi Bridge between six and eight times daily and head for III Rómaifürdő and Csillaghegy in Óbuda, a two-hour trip with 10 stops along the way. Tickets (adult/child 600/300Ft from end to end or between 500/250Ft and 200/150Ft for intermediate stops) are sold on board. The ferry stop

closest to the Castle District is I Batthyány tér (Map p83), and V Petőfi tér is not far from the pier just west of Vörösmarty tér (Map p86), a convenient place to pick up the boat on the Pest side. Transporting a bicycle costs 500Ft.

For information on river cruises, see p102.

Car & Motorcycle

Though it's not so bad at night, driving in Budapest during the day can be a nightmare: ongoing road works reduce traffic to a snail's pace; there are more serious accidents than fender-benders; and parking spots are difficult to find. The public transport system is good and cheap. Use it.

Parking costs 120Ft to 400Ft on the street, generally between 8am and 6pm Monday to Friday and 8am and noon Saturday. There are 24-hour covered car parks charging up to 500/5000Ft per hour/day at V Váci utca 25 (below the Millennium Center; Map p86); V Szervita tér 8 (Map p86) and at V Aranykéz utca 4-6 (Map p86) in the Inner Town, and at VII Nyár utca 20 (Map p84).

Illegally parked cars are not normally towed in Budapest these days but 'booted'. If you are trying to trace a vehicle you believe has been towed, ring ☎ 383 0700 or 383 0770. To have a boot removed, which is going to cost you 15,000Ft, ring the telephone number on the sticker placed on the windscreen or ☎ 313 0810.

Drink-driving is taken very seriously in Hungary; see p372.

Public Transport

Budapest has an ageing but safe, efficient and inexpensive public transport system that will never have you waiting more than five or 10 minutes for any conveyance. There are five types of vehicle in general use: metro trains on three city lines, green HÉV trains on four suburban lines, blue buses, yellow trams and red trolleybuses. All are run by **BKV** (Budapest Transport Company; ☎ 342 2335, 06 80 406 688; www.bkv.hu). Anyone planning to travel extensively by public transport in Budapest should invest in the invaluable *Budapesti Közlekedési Hálózata Térképe* (Budapest Transport Network Map; 380Ft) available at most metro ticket booths.

Daytime public transport in Budapest runs from about 4.30am to between 9pm and 11.30pm, depending on the line. From 11.30pm to 4am a network of some 30 night buses kicks in, running every 10 to 60 minutes, again depending on the line.

FARES & TRAVEL PASSES

To ride the metro, trams, trolleybuses, buses and the HÉV (as far as the city limits, which is the Békásmegyer stop to the north) you must have a valid ticket, which you can buy at kiosks, newsstands or metro entrances. Children up to the age of six travel free when accompanied by an adult. Bicycles can only be transported on the HÉV.

The basic fare for all forms of transport is 185Ft (1665/3145Ft for a block of 10/20 tickets), allowing you to travel as far as you like on the same metro, bus, trolleybus or tram line without changing. A ticket allowing unlimited stations with one change within 1½ hours costs 320Ft.

On the metro exclusively, the base fare drops to 130Ft if you are just going three stops within 30 minutes. For 200Ft you can travel five stops and transfer at Deák Ferenc tér to another metro line within one hour. Unlimited stations travelled with one change within one hour costs 300Ft.

You must always travel in one continuous direction on any ticket; return trips are not allowed. Tickets have to be validated in machines at metro entrances and aboard other vehicles – inspectors will fine you for not validating your ticket.

Life will most likely be much simpler if you buy a travel pass. Passes are valid on all trams, buses, trolleybuses, HÉV (within the city limits) and metro lines, and you don't have to worry about validating your ticket each time you get on. The most central places to buy them are ticket offices at the Deák Ferenc tér metro station (Map p86), the Nyugati pályaudvar metro station (Map p84) and the Déli pályaudvar metro station (Map pp80–1), all of which are open from 6am to 8pm daily.

A one-day pass is poor value at 1150Ft, but the three-day pass (*touristajegy,* or tourist ticket) for 2500Ft and seven-day pass (*hetijegy,* or one week) for 3400Ft are worthwhile for most people. You'll need a photo for the fortnightly/monthly passes (4500/6900Ft). All but the monthly passes are valid from midnight to midnight, so buy them in advance and specify the date(s) you want.

Travelling 'black' (ie without a valid ticket or pass) is risky; with increased surveillance (especially in the metro), there's an excellent chance you'll get caught. (NB: Tickets are *always* checked by a conductor on the HÉV.) The on-the-spot fine is 2500Ft, which rises to 7000Ft if you pay at the **BKV office** (Map p84; ☎ 461 6800; VII Akácfa utca 22; 🕐 6am-8pm Mon-Fri, 8am-1.45pm Sat; Ⓜ M2 Blaha Lujza tér) up to 30 days later and 14,000Ft after that.

METRO & HÉV

Budapest has three underground metro lines that converge (only) at Deák Ferenc tér: the little yellow (or Millennium) line designated M1 that runs from Vörösmarty tér to Mexikoi út in Pest; the red M2 line from Déli train station in Buda to Örs vezér tere in Pest; and the blue M3 line from Újpest-Központ to Kőbánya-Kispest in Pest. A possible source of confusion on the M1 is that one station is called Vörösmarty tér and another, five stops later, is Vörösmarty utca. The HÉV suburban train line, which runs on four lines (north from Batthyány tér in Buda via Óbuda and Aquincum to Szentendre, south to both Csepel and Ráckeve and east to Gödöllő), is almost like an additional above-ground metro line.

BUS, TRAM & TROLLEYBUS

An extensive system of trams, trolleybuses and buses serve greater Budapest. On certain bus lines the same number bus may have a black or a red number. In such cases, the red-numbered one is an express, which makes limited stops and is, of course, faster.

Buses and trams are much of a muchness, though the latter are often faster and generally more pleasant for sightseeing. Trolleybuses go along cross streets in central Pest and are of little use to most visitors, with the sole exception of the ones to City and Népliget Parks.

Following are the most important tram lines (always marked with red lines on a Budapest map, while a broken red line signifies a trolleybus).

Nos 2 & 2/a Scenic trams that travel along the Pest side of the Danube as far as V Jászai Mari tér.

Nos 4 & 6 Extremely useful trams that start at XI Fe-hérvári út and XI Móricz Zsigmond körtér in south Buda respectively, and follow the entire length of the Big Ring road in Pest before terminating at II Moszkva tér in Buda.

No 18 Runs from southern Buda along XI Bartók Béla út through the Tabán to II Moszkva tér.

No 19 Covers part of the same route as No 18, but then runs along the Buda side of the Danube to I Batthyány tér.

Nos 47 & 49 Link V Deák Ferenc tér in Pest with points in southern Buda via the Little Ring road.

No 61 Connects XI Móricz Zsigmond körtér with Déli train station and II Moszkva tér in Buda.

Some buses (always shown with a blue line on a Budapest map) you might find useful:

Black No 4 Runs from northern Pest via VI Hősök tere to V Deák Ferenc tér (the red No 4 follows the same route but crosses over Chain Bridge into central Buda).

No 7 Cuts across a large swathe of central Pest from XIV Bosnyák tér and down VII Rákóczi út before crossing Elizabeth Bridge to Kelenföld train station in southern Buda.

No 86 Runs the length of Buda from XI Kosztolányi Dezső tér to Óbuda.

No 105 Goes from V Deák Ferenc tér to XII Apor Vilmos tér in central Buda.

Night bus 906 Follows tram 6's route along the Big Ring road.

Night bus 907 Traces an enormously long route from Örs vezér tere M2 metro stop in Pest to Kelenföld train station in Buda.

Taxi

Taxis in Budapest are still not expensive compared with other European countries, but with such an excellent public transport network available, you don't really have to use them very often. We've heard from many readers who were grossly overcharged and even threatened by taxi drivers in Budapest, so taking a taxi in this city should be approached with caution. However, the reputable firms we've listed have caught on to the concept of customer service and take complaints very seriously nowadays.

Avoid taxis with no name on the door and only a removable taxi light box on the roof; these are just guys with cars and the ones most likely to rip you off. Never get into a taxi that does not have a yellow licence plate and an identification badge displayed on the dashboard (as required by law), the logo of one of the reputable taxi firms on the side doors and a table of fares clearly visible.

Not all taxi meters are set at the same rates, and some are much more expensive

than others, but there are price ceilings under which taxi companies are free to manoeuvre. From 6am to 10pm the highest flag-fall fee that can be legally charged is 300Ft, the per-kilometre charge 240Ft and the waiting fee 60Ft. From 10pm to 6am the equivalent fees are 420/330/80Ft.

Budapest residents – local or foreign – rarely flag down taxis on the street. They almost always ring for them, and fares are actually cheaper if you book over the phone. Make sure you know the number of the landline phone you're calling from, as that's how they establish your address (though you can, of course, call from a mobile phone, too).

Following are the telephone numbers of reputable taxi firms:

Buda ☎ 233 3333
City ☎ 211 1111
Fő ☎ 222 2222
Rádió ☎ 377 7777
Tele 5 ☎ 355 5555

AROUND BUDAPEST

Let's be honest: an awful lot in Hungary is 'around Budapest', and many of the towns and cities in the Danube Bend, Transdanubia, Northern Uplands and even the Great Plain could be relatively easy day trips from the capital. You can be in Szentendre (19km) in half an hour, for example, and Gyöngyös, the gateway to the bucolic Mátra Hills, is only 80km to the east. Here are several easy day or even half-day trips from the capital.

STATUE PARK

A truly mind-blowing excursion is a visit to **Statue Park** (Szoborpark; Map p77; ☎ 424 7500; www .szoborpark.hu; cnr XXII Szabadkai út & Balatoni út; adult/child 600/400Ft; ☯ 10am-dusk), 10km southwest of the city centre. It's home to more than 40 busts, statues and plaques of Lenin, Marx, Béla Kun and 'heroic' workers that have ended up on rubbish heaps in other former socialist countries, but get an airing here to remind everyone how tawdry and dishonest the *ancien régime* was. Ogle at the social-ist realism and try to imagine that at least four of these monstrous monuments were erected as recently as the late 1980s; a few of them, including the Béla Kun memorial of our 'hero' in a crowd by fence-sitting sculptor Imre Varga (p74), were still in place when one of us moved to Budapest in early 1992. The museum shop sells fabulously kitsch communist memorabilia – statues, pins, CDs of revolutionary songs etc.

To reach this socialist Disneyland, take tram 19 from I Batthyány tér in Buda, tram 49 from V Deák Ferenc tér in Pest or red-numbered bus 7 from V Ferenciek tere in Pest to the terminus at XI Etele tér. From there catch a yellow Volán bus from stand No 7 to Diósd/Érd (133Ft, 15 minutes, 8km, every 15 to 20 minutes); you'll want the fifth stop.

A direct bus (adult/child return 1950/1350Ft) departs from in front of the Le Meridien Budapest Hotel on Deák Ferenc tér at 11am year-round, with an extra departure at 3pm from March to October, and at 10am and 4pm as well in July and August.

SZÁZHALOMBATTA
☎ 23 / pop 17,500
Some 28km southwest of Budapest in the unattractive town of Százhalombatta, site of a huge heat and power plant, is **Archaeological Park** (Régészeti Park; ☎ 350 537; http://matrica.battanet.hu; István király út 4; park adult/child/family 600/300/1600Ft, park & museum 805/415/2070Ft; ◷ 10am-6pm Tue-Sun Apr-Oct), the only open-air prehistoric museum in Hungary. The six-hectare park sits in the middle of Iron Age tumuli – Százhalombatta means '100 Mounds' – and is still undergoing excavation and expansion. What can be seen at present are reconstructed Bronze and Iron Age settlements, plus replicas of pottery, cooking utensils, musical instruments and clothing. The highlight of the park is a 2700-year-old oak-timber burial mound that houses an incredibly detailed 5.5 sq m burial chamber rebuilt from archaeological finds and floor plans. An 18-minute film (in English, Hungarian and German) briefly delves into the history of the Bronze and Iron Age in Central Europe, before moving onto the burial process and a step-by-step explanation of the reconstruction of the burial crypt.

The **Matrica Museum** (☎ 354 591; www.matrica .battanet.hu; Gesztenyés út 1-3; adult/child/family 415/210/1035Ft; ◷ 10am-6pm Tue-Sun Apr-Oct, 10am-4pm Tue-Fri, 10am-6pm Sat & Sun Nov-Mar), part of the Archaeological Park but closer to town,

traces the history of the settlement from prehistoric times till today.

Getting There & Away
Over two dozen trains leaving Budapest's Déli and Kelenföld train stations for Pécs every day stop at Százhalombatta (248Ft, 40 minutes, 28km, every 20 minutes); the last train returns at just before 10.30pm. A bus links the train station at Százhalombatta with the park, but it's rather infrequent – the last leaves for the station at around 4pm.

Buses bound for Százhalombatta (363Ft, 45 minutes, 28km, half-hourly) leave frequently throughout the day from the Kelenföld train station at XI Etele tér in southern Buda.

RÁCKEVE
☎ 24 / pop 9250
The lures of this attractive town on the southeastern end of Csepel Island, the long island in the Danube south of Budapest, are its pretty riverside park and strand, a Gothic Serbian Orthodox church (rác is the old Hungarian word for 'Serb') and the former Savoy Mansion, now a lovely hotel. **Tourinform** (☎ 429 747; www.tourinform.rackeve.hu; Kossuth Lajos utca 51; ◷ 9am-5pm Mon-Sat mid-Jun–mid-Sep, 8am-4pm Mon-Fri mid-Sep–mid-Jun) is in the Károly Ács Cultural Centre, about 1km south of the train station.

Sights
SAVOY MANSION
From the HÉV station in Ráckeve, walk south along Kossuth Lajos utca to the **Savoy Mansion** (Savoyai-kastély; ☎ 485 253; Kossuth Lajos utca 95), now a 30-room hotel facing the Ráckeve-Danube River branch. The domed manse with two wings was finished in 1722 in the baroque style for Prince Eugene of Savoy, who drove out the last of the Turkish occupiers from Hungary at the Battle of Zenta in 1697, by an Austrian architect who would later go on to design Schönbrunn Palace in Vienna. The mansion was completely renovated and turned into a pricey hotel and conference centre in 1982. Concerts are held here in July and August.

ÁRPÁD MUSEUM
This small **museum** (☎ 485 364; Kossuth Lajos utca 34; adult/child 400/200Ft; ◷ 10am-6pm Tue-Sun mid-Mar–Oct,10am-4pm Mon-Fri Nov–mid-Mar), a couple

of hundred metres south of the mansion, has exhibits focusing on the Danube, with an emphasis on water mills of various types, along with a lot of old photographs.

SERBIAN ORTHODOX CHURCH

From Kossuth Lajos utca you can't miss the blue clock tower of the **Serbian Orthodox Church** (Görög-keleti szerb templom; Viola utca 1; ⊗ 10am-noon & 2-5pm Tue-Sat, 2-5pm Sun) to the southeast. The late Gothic church was originally built in 1487 by Serbs who fled their town of Keve ahead of the invading Turks, and many street signs in this area are in Serbian. It was enlarged in the following century. The free-standing clock tower was added in 1758.

The walls and ceiling of the church interior are covered with colourful frescoes painted by a Serbian master from Albania in the mid-18th century. The walls depict scenes from the Old and New Testaments and a panoply of saints; they were meant to teach the Bible to illiterate parishioners. The first section of the nave is reserved for women; the part beyond the separating wall is for men. Only the priest and his servers enter the sanctuary beyond the iconostasis, the richly carved and gilded gate festooned with icons.

Eating

Savoyai Kastély (☎ 424 189; Kossuth Lajos utca 95; soups 350-450Ft, starters 600-2200Ft, mains 1200-3500Ft; ⊗ noon-11pm) This cellar restaurant at the Savoy Mansion is one of the better eateries in Ráckeve. Dining here is a good way to get a look at the mansion's interior without actually staying there.

Cadran (☎ 485 470; Hősök tere 1; pizza 520-980Ft; ⊗ 10am-10pm Mon-Sat, 12.30-10pm Sun) A popular pizzeria and pub in the centre of town and facing the Árpád Bridge, Cadran is recommended for a lunch stop before or after visiting the Serbian church. There's outside seating in a back courtyard.

Getting There & Away

The easiest way to reach Ráckeve is on the HÉV suburban train (520Ft, 70 minutes, 40km, half-hourly), departing from the Vágóhíd HÉV terminus in district IX on the Pest side. You can get to that train station from the Inner Town on tram 2 or from Keleti train station on tram 24.

The last HÉV train back to Budapest leaves Ráckeve at 10.30pm.

GÖDÖLLŐ

☎ 28 / pop 32,400

Just 27km northeast of the Inner Town and easily accessible on the HÉV, Gödöllő (pronounced – roughly – good-duh-ler) is an easy day trip from the capital. The main draw here is the Royal Mansion, which rivalled Esterházy Palace at Fertőd in Western Transdanubia (p169) in splendour and size when it was completed in the 1760s, and is the largest baroque manor house in Hungary. But the town itself, full of lovely baroque buildings and monuments and home to the seminal Gödöllő Artists Colony (1901–20), is worth the trip in itself.

Tourinform (☎ 415 402; www.godollotourinform .hu; ⊗ 10am-6pm Tue-Sun Apr-Oct, 10am-5pm Tue-Sun Nov-Mar) has an office just inside the entrance to the Royal Mansion.

Sights

The **Royal Mansion** (Királyi Kastély; ☎ 410 124; www.kiralyikastely.hu; Szabadság tér 1; adult/child/family 1400/700/2800Ft; ⊗ 10am-6pm Tue-Sun Apr-Oct, 10am-5pm Tue-Sun Nov-Mar), sometimes called the Grassalkovich Mansion after its commissioner, Antal Grassalkovich (1694–1771), count and confidante of Empress Maria Theresa, was designed by Antal Mayerhoffer in 1741. After the formation of the Dual Monarchy, the mansion (or palace) was enlarged as a summer retreat for Emperor Franz Joseph, and soon became the favoured residence of his consort, the much beloved Habsburg empress and Hungarian queen, Elizabeth (1837–98), affectionately known as Sissi. Between WWI and WWII the regent, Admiral Miklós Horthy, also used it as a summer residence, but after the communists came to power part of the mansion was used as a Soviet barracks, as an old people's home and as temporary housing. The rest was left to decay.

Partial renovation of the mansion began in 1994, and today some 26 rooms are open to the public as the Palace Museum on the ground and 1st floors. The rooms have been restored (some would say with too much enthusiasm) to when the imperial couple were in residence, and on the 1st floor Franz Joseph's suites, done up in 'manly' greys and golds, and Sissi's lavender-coloured private apartments are impressive, if not as evocative of the past as the rooms at the Esterházy Palace. Check out the **Decorative Hall**, all gold tracery and chandeliers, where chamber-music concerts are held throughout the year but especially in late June and early July during the **Palace Concerts Chamber Music Festival**; the **Queen's Salon**, with a Romantic-style oil painting of Sissi patriotically repairing the coronation robe of King Stephen with needle and thread; and the **Study Annexe**, with a restored ceiling painting and an 18th-century tapestry of the huntress Diana.

A number of other recently opened rooms and buildings can be visited on a guided tour only at extra cost, including the baroque **Palace Theatre** (adult/child 960/550Ft or 2500Ft with museum) in the southern wing; the **Royal Hill Pavilion** (admission 2750Ft with theatre & museum) in the park built in the 1760s; and the **Royal Baths** (adult/child 1200/700Ft with theatre & pavilion, 2600/1250Ft with museum, theatre & pavilion).

Eating

Tourinform at the palace has sample menus from restaurants around town and also distributes discount vouchers.

Pizza Palazzo (☎ 420 688; Szabadság tér 2; pizza & pasta 750-1250Ft, mains 950-1590Ft; ☒ 11am-11pm) This popular pizzeria with some more substantial main courses is conveniently attached to the Szabadság tér HÉV station.

Mei Shi Lin (☎ 412 658; Kossuth Lajos utca 33; rice & noodle dishes 450-1680Ft, mains 950-2150Ft; ☒ 11am-10pm Sun-Thu, 11am-11pm Fri & Sat) This pleasant eatery, to the northwest of the mansion, serves surprisingly good Chinese food.

Kastélykert (☎ 527 020; Szabadság tér 4; starters 480-1990Ft, mains 1000-1840Ft; ☒ noon-11pm) The 'Castle Garden', situated in a lovely old baroque house opposite the mansion (and still apparently on its grounds) is an excellent and much more upmarket choice for an evening meal.

Getting There & Away

HÉV trains from Örs vezér tere at the terminus of the M2 metro link Budapest with Gödöllő (326Ft, 40 minutes, 27km, half-hourly) throughout the day. Make sure you get off at the Szabadság tér stop, which is the third from the last stop. The last train leaves this stop for Budapest just before 10.45pm.

In addition, buses from Stadionok bus station in Budapest also serve Gödöllő (302Ft, 23km, 40 minutes, half-hourly). The last bus back is just after 7.15pm Monday to Friday (shortly after 8pm on Saturday and Sunday). The bus station is due east of the Szabadság tér HÉV station next to the colossal cultural centre.

Danube Bend

The Danube, Hungary's dustless highway and the second-largest river in Europe, cuts a path through the hills to the north of Budapest. Over the millennia the unrelenting mass of the Börzsöny Hills on the left bank and the Pilis Hills on the right have forced the river into a handful of tight, bunched curves, creating arguably the prettiest stretch of the Danube.

Of course places like this don't stay uninhabited for long. First the Romans then the Magyars decided the area needed to be settled and fought over, and this legacy of human endeavour is plain for all to see along the river's banks. Esztergom, for so many years the Pope's 'eyes and ears' in Hungary, is now a sleepy town with the biggest basilica this side of the Balkans, a mammoth edifice containing artwork and a crypt worthy of age-old bishops. Not far to the east is Visegrád, once the seat of Hungary's kings and queens; nowadays it plays host to the ruins of a 15th-century palace and hilltop castle, with a position so intimidating would-be attackers must have thought their generals suicidal.

The town of Szentendre is another kettle of fish altogether. Embracing newcomers and unorthodox religions, it sports more church spires than seems practical and lives quite well on a legacy of artists' colonies dating from the early 20th century.

And this is only to mention the highlights of the west bank. On the east, the atmosphere changes again. Vác, a small town with a big history, is a lovely spot with a Mediterranean feel and a laid back attitude, but scratch the surface and you'll find a macabre crypt of bodies. To the north of Vác are the Börzsöny Hills, a wild stretch of nature and an outdoor playground.

HIGHLIGHTS

- Taking in the expansive views of the Danube Bend from Visegrád's medieval **hilltop citadel** (p143)

- Exploring Esztergom's **Christian Museum** (p147), with its incomparable collection of medieval art and sculpture

- Picking through the plethora of art galleries in **Szentendre** (p133) in hope of finding that perfect piece

- Soaking up the relaxed atmosphere in little-visited **Vác** (p137)

- Escaping the hustle, bustle and tussle in the lush green **Börzsöny** (p141) or **Pilis Hills** (p144)

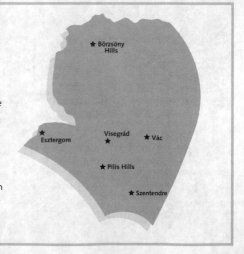

History

The Danube Bend may look either sleepy or overrun with tourists, but it has a rich and varied history. It was the northernmost region of Rome's colonies for centuries, and Esztergom was the first seat of the Magyar kings and has been the centre of Roman Catholicism in the region for more than a millennium.

Visegrád, Central Europe's 'Camelot', was the royal seat during Hungary's short-lived flirtation with the Renaissance in the 15th century. Szentendre has many of its roots in Serbian culture, and became an important centre for art and culture early in the 20th century. Vác, on the Danube's eastern bank, is not to be outdone by its western counterparts. It was an important river crossing during Roman times and King Stephen himself thought the town valuable enough to establish an episcopate there in the 11th century.

Getting There & Around

Being so close to Budapest, the Danube Bend has good connections to the rest of Hungary. Regular buses serve towns on the western bank of the Danube, but trains only go as far as Szentendre with a separate line running to Esztergom; the eastern bank has the luxury of excellent bus and train links. The river itself is a perfect highway, and regular boats ferry tourists to and from Budapest over the summer months.

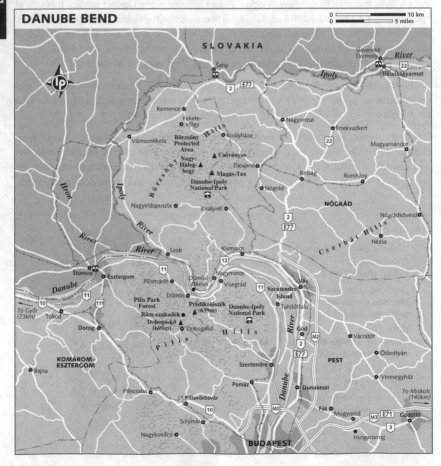

From May to August, one daily Mahart ferry plies the Danube to/from Budapest's Vigadó tér, departing at 9am and calling at Szentendre (one way/return 990/1485Ft, 10.40am) and Visegrád (one way/return 1090/1635Ft, 12.30am), before returning from Visegrád at 4pm. The service dwindles to weekends only in April, September and October. From June to mid-September two extra boats depart from Budapest at 10.30am and 2pm bound for Szentendre (one way 1400Ft), returning at 12.20pm and 5pm; in the last half of May and September only the 10.30am and 5pm services run.

On weekends and holidays from mid-May to mid-September, a hydrofoil service links Budapest with Visegrád (one way 1990Ft) and Esztergom (one way 2490Ft), departing at 9.30am and calling on Visegrád (10.30am) and Esztergom (11.30am). Slower boats leave Budapest's Vigadó tér in Pest at 7.30am daily from May to August and weekends and holidays in April, September and October, stopping at Batthyány tér in Buda, and going on to Vác (one way/return 490/735Ft, 9.50am), Visegrád (1090/1635Ft, 10.50am) and Esztergom (1490/2235Ft, 1pm). The return trip from Esztergom leaves at 4pm. From June to August a daily boat connects Esztergom with Visegrád (one way 1400Ft), leaving at 9am and arriving at 10.25am; boats return from Visegrád at 4pm.

SZENTENDRE
☎ 26 / pop 22,700

Szentendre is a town that has changed little in appearance since the 18th century. For some this is a blessing, and for others a curse; its cobblestone alleyways and skyline of church spires are indeed something special, but the hoards of tourists jostling you as you attempt to appreciate the scene can at times simply be too much. Either way you look at it, Szentendre is worth visiting – however brief – and if its architecture doesn't impress, its plethora of art museums and galleries should. Note that Szentendre is best avoided on weekends in summer, and between November and mid-March much of the town shuts down on weekdays.

History

Like most towns along the Danube Bend, Szentendre was home first to the Celts and then the Romans, who built an important border fortress here called Wolf's Castle (Ulcisia Castra). The Magyars arrived late in the 9th century and established a colony here and by the 14th century Szentendre was a prosperous estate under the supervision of the royal castle at Visegrád.

It was about this time that the first wave of Serbian Orthodox Christians came from the south in advance of the Turks, but the Turkish occupation of Hungary over the ensuing centuries brought the town's peaceful coexistence to an end, and by the end of the 17th century the town was deserted. Though Hungary was liberated from the Ottomans soon afterwards, fighting continued in the Balkans and a second wave of Serbs, together with Greeks, Dalmatians and others, fled to Szentendre. Believing they would return home, but enjoying complete religious freedom under the relatively benevolent rule of the Habsburgs (a right denied Hungary's Protestants at the time), half a dozen Orthodox clans each built their own churches and gave the town its unique Balkan feel.

Szentendre's delightful location began to attract day-trippers and painters from Budapest early last century; an artists' colony was established here in the 1920s. The town has been known for its art and artists ever since.

Orientation

The HÉV commuter train and bus stations lie side by side south of the town centre at the start of Dunakanyar körút (Danube Bend Ring road). From here it's a short walk north along Kossuth Lajos utca and Dumtsa Jenő utca to Fő tér, the heart of Szentendre. The Duna korzó promenade along the Danube and the ferry to Szentendre Island are a few minutes' walk east and northeast, respectively, of Fő tér. The **Mahart ferry pier** (Czóbel Béla sétány) is about a kilometre northeast, off Duna korzó.

Information
Game Planet (Petőfi Sándor utca 1; per hr 400Ft; ☯ 10am-10pm) Internet access.
OTP bank (Dumtsa Jenő utca 6) Has change machine and ATM.
Post office (Kossuth Lajos utca 23-25)
Surgery (☎ 312 650; Bükkös part 27) In case of medical emergencies.
Tourinform (☎ 317 965; szentendre@tourinform.hu; Dumtsa Jenő utca 22; ☯ 9.30am-4.30pm Mon-Fri

DANUBE BEND

DANUBE BEND

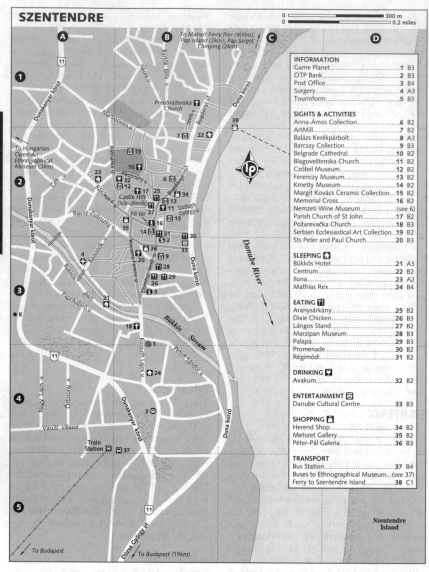

SZENTENDRE

0 ——————— 300 m
0 ——————— 0.2 miles

To Mahart Ferry Pier (400m);
Pap Island (2km); Páp Sziget
Camping (2km)

To Hungarian
Open-Air
Ethnographical
Museum (3km)

Preobraženska
Church

Castle Hill
(Vár-domb)

Bükkös Stream

Danube River

To Budapest

To Budapest (19km)

Train
Station

Szentendre
Island

INFORMATION

Game Planet	1	B3
OTP Bank	2	B3
Post Office	3	B4
Surgery	4	A3
Tourinform	5	B3

SIGHTS & ACTIVITIES

Anna-Ámos Collection	6	B2
ArtMill	7	B2
Balázs Kerékpárbolt	8	A3
Barcsay Collection	9	B3
Belgrade Cathedral	10	B2
Blagoveštenska Church	11	B2
Czóbel Museum	12	B2
Ferenczy Museum	13	B2
Kmetty Museum	14	B2
Margit Kovács Ceramic Collection	15	B2
Memorial Cross	16	B2
Nemzeti Wine Museum	(see 6)	
Parish Church of St John	17	B2
Požarevačka Church	18	B3
Serbian Ecclesiastical Art Collection	19	B2
Sts Peter and Paul Church	20	B3

SLEEPING

Bükkös Hotel	21	A3
Centrum	22	A2
Ilona	23	A2
Mathias Rex	24	B4

EATING

Aranysárkány	25	B2
Dixie Chicken	26	B2
Lángos Stand	27	B2
Marzipan Museum	28	B3
Palapa	29	B2
Promenade	30	B2
Régimódi	31	B2

DRINKING

Avakum	32	B2

ENTERTAINMENT

Danube Cultural Centre	33	B3

SHOPPING

Herend Shop	34	B2
Metzset Gallery	35	B2
Péter-Pál Galéria	36	B3

TRANSPORT

Bus Station	37	B4
Buses to Ethnographical Museum	(see 37)	
Ferry to Szentendre Island	38	C1

year-round, 10am-2pm Sat & Sun mid-Mar–Oct) Helpful centre with stacks of information.
www.szentendre.hu In Hungarian only.

Sights
INNER TOWN

A good starting point on your tour of Szentendre is the **Požarevačka Church** (☎ 310 554; Kossuth Lajos utca 1; admission 200Ft; ☼ by appointment), which you'll pass on the way from the stations. Dedicated in 1763, this Serbian Orthodox church has a lovely iconostasis inside (1742).

To the north, the **Sts Peter and Paul Church** (Péter-Pál utca 6; admission free; ☼ 10am-4pm Tue-Sun) began life as the Čiprovačka Orthodox

Church in 1753, but was later taken over by Dalmatian Catholics. The **Barcsay Collection** (Barcsay Gyűjtemény; ☎ 310 790; Dumtsa Jenő utca 10; adult/child 400/200Ft; ☉ 10am-6pm Tue-Sun Apr-Oct), to the east, contains the work of one of the founders of Szentendre's art colony, Jenő Barcsay (1900–88).

Moving onto Fő tér, the colourful heart of Szentendre surrounded by 18th- and 19th-century burghers' houses, you'll find the **Memorial Cross** (1763), an iron cross decorated with icons on a marble base. The **Kmetty Museum** (☎ 310 790; Fő tér 21; adult/child 400/200Ft; ☉ 10am-6pm Tue-Sun Apr-Oct) on the southwestern side of the square displays the work of the cubist János Kmetty (1889–1975).

However, the square's highlight is the **Blagoveštenska Church** (☎ 310 554; admission 200Ft; ☉ 10am-5pm Tue-Sun), built in 1754. The church, with fine baroque and rococo elements, hardly looks 'eastern' from the outside, but the inside gives the game away. The small but powerful nave is lined with an ornate iconostasis and elaborate 18th-century furnishings. It is a sight to behold.

The **Ferenczy Museum** (☎ 310 790; Fő tér 6; adult/child 400/200Ft; ☉ 10am-6pm Tue-Sun Apr-Oct) next to the Blagoveštenska Church is devoted to Károly Ferenczy (1862–1917), the father of plein-air painting in Hungary, and his three children: a painter, a sculptor and a weaver.

Descending Görög utca and turning right onto Vastagh György utca, you'll reach the **Margit Kovács Ceramic Collection** (Kovács Margit Kerámiagyűjtemény; ☎ 310 244; Vastagh György utca 1; adult/child 600/300Ft; ☉ 9am-5pm Mar, 10am-6pm Apr-Oct) in an 18th-century salt house. Kovács (1902–77) was a ceramicist who combined Hungarian folk, religious and modern themes to create Gothic-like figures. Some of Kovács' works are overly sentimental, but many are very powerful, especially the later ones in which she became obsessed with mortality.

Castle Hill (Vár-domb), which can be reached via Váralja lépcső, the narrow steps between Fő tér 8 and 9, was the site of a fortress in the Middle Ages. All that's left of it today is the walled **Parish Church of St John** (Templom tér; admission free), from where you get splendid views of the town. Unfortunately the church entrance (which is early Gothic) is often locked, but you can peer through the bars at the frescoes which were painted by members of the artists' colony in the 1930s. West of the church the **Czóbel Museum** (☎ 310

790; Templom tér 1; adult/child 400/200Ft; ☉ 10am-6pm Tue-Sun Apr-Oct), contains the works of the impressionist Béla Czóbel (1883–1976), a friend of Pablo Picasso and student of Henri Matisse.

Just north of Castle Hill you'll notice the red tower of **Belgrade Cathedral** (Belgrád Székesegyház; Alkotmány utca; adult/child including art collection 300/150Ft; ☉ 10am-6pm Tue-Sun Mar-Oct, 10am-4pm Fri-Sun Jan & Feb), completed in 1764 and seat of the Serbian Orthodox bishop in Hungary. One of the church buildings beside it now contains the **Serbian Ecclesiastical Art Collection** (Szerb Egyházművészeti Gyűjtemény; ☎ 312 399; Pátriárka utca 5; adult/child 400/200Ft; ☉ 10am-6pm Tue-Sun Apr-Oct), a treasure trove of icons, vestments and other sacred objects in precious metals. A 14th-century glass painting of the crucifixion is the oldest item on display; a 'cotton icon' of the life of Christ from the 18th century is unusual. Take a look at the defaced portrait of Christ upstairs on the right-hand wall. The story goes that a drunken *kuruc* (anti-Habsburg) mercenary slashed it and, told what he had done next morning, drowned himself in the Danube.

Bogdányi utca, Szentendre's busiest pedestrian street, leads north from Fő tér, where you'll find the excellent **Anna-Ámos Collection** (☎ 310 790; Bogdányi utca 10-12; adult/child 400/200Ft; ☉ 10am-6pm Tue-Sun Apr-Oct), displaying the symbolist paintings of husband-and-wife team Margit Anna and Imre Ámos. Next door the **Nemzeti Wine Museum** (Nemzeti Bormúzeum; ☎ 317 054; Bogdányi utca 10; admission 100Ft, tastings 1600Ft; ☉ 10am-10pm) traces the development of wine-making in Hungary and charges quite a bit more to sample various vintages. Housed in a 19th-century industrial complex at the northern end of Bogdányi utca is the **ArtMill** (MűvészetMalom; ☎ 301 701; Bogdányi utca 32; adult/child 500/250Ft; ☉ 10am-6pm), Szentendre's bid to recapture its past as a serious centre for artists and the arts. Its extensive exhibition space is used for paintings, sculpture, graphics and applied arts, and its grounds are possibly the quietest spot in the touristy centre.

HUNGARIAN OPEN-AIR ETHNOGRAPHICAL MUSEUM

The collection of buildings at this **museum** (Magyar Szabadtéri Néprajzi Múzeum; ☎ 502 500; Sztaravodai út; Tue & Wed admission free, Thu & Fri adult/child 600/400Ft, Sat & Sun 800/400Ft; ☉ 9am-5pm Tue-Sun

Apr-Oct), about 3km northwest of the centre, is Hungary's most ambitious *skanzen* (open-air museum). Situated on a 46-hectare tract of rolling land, the museum was founded in 1967 to introduce urban Hungarians and tourists alike to traditional Magyar culture by bringing bits and pieces of villages, farms and towns to one site. The plans call for some 300 farmhouses, churches, bell towers, mills and so on ultimately to be set up in 10 regional units, but so far there are only five regional units.

Highlights include the Calvinist church and 'skirted' belfry from the Erdőhát region of the Northeast, the German 'long house' from Harka outside Sopron, the curious heart-shaped gravestones from the Buda Hills and the lovely whitewashed façade of the thatched house from Sükösd on the Great Plain. Craftspeople and artisans do their thing on random days from late March to early November (generally on Sundays and holidays), and the open-air museum hosts festivals throughout the season.

See Getting Around (opposite) for information on buses to the museum.

Activities

Pap Island (Pap-sziget), 2km north of the centre, is Szentendre's playground and has a grassy *strand* for sunbathing, a **swimming pool** (adult/child 500/250Ft; 8am-7pm May-Sep), and **tennis courts** and **rowing boats** for hire.

Bicycles can be rented from **Balázs Kerékpárbolt** (312 111; Elód utca 2a; 1 hr/day 500/3000Ft; 10am-6.30pm Mon-Fri, 9am-2pm Sat); take the hourly ferry across to Szentendre Island to enjoy kilometres of uncrowded cycling paths. Canoes and motor boats can be rented from **Dunabogdány** (390 086) for 2000/7000Ft per day, respectively; boats are delivered to a place you request on the river, and a minimal fee is charged for the delivery.

Sleeping

With Budapest so close, there's no point overnighting here unless you plan to push on to the rest of the Danube Bend. There are, however, a couple of worthwhile options.

Ilona (313 599; Rákóczi Ferenc utca 11; s/d 5000/6600Ft; P) A perfect little *pension*, with plenty going for it: superb central location, locked parking, inner courtyard for breakfast and rooms in very good nick (although on the small side).

Centrum (302 500; www.hotelcentrum.hu; Bogdányi utca 15; s/d from 9000/10,000Ft; P) This quaint *pension* occupies a beautifully renovated house, a stone's throw from the Danube. Rooms are bright, large and filled with antique furniture; breakfast is optional.

Bükkös Hotel (312 021; Bükkös part 16; s/d 8500/11,000Ft; P) Bükkös is a hotel with a touch of style about it that has warm and cosy rooms; ask for one overlooking Bükkös stream. The town centre is a very short walk from the front door.

Mathias Rex (505 570; Kossuth Lajos utca 16; s/d 8500/12,500Ft; P) This relatively new *pension* has rooms so clean they border on sterile. The décor is modern and minimalist and an inexpensive cellar-restaurant occupies the basement.

Pap-sziget Camping (310 697; www.pap-sziget .hu; camp sites per adult/child/tent 1000/600/2000Ft, bungalows 12,000Ft; May–mid-Oct; P) This big, leafy camping site takes up most of Pap Island, some 2km north of Szentendre. Motel and *pension* rooms are very basic, as are the bungalows; facilities include a small supermarket, a snack bar and a restaurant. See Getting Around (opposite) for information on getting here by bus.

Eating & Drinking

Aranysárkány (Golden Dragon; 301 479; Alkotmány utca 1/a; mains over 2000Ft) It may sound Chinese but this place serves superb Hungarian and Austrian dishes and is big on steaks. Laura Bush has graced this place with her presence, so it must be good.

Promenade (312 626; Futó utca 4; mains 1500-2500Ft) Vaulted ceilings, whitewashed walls and a wonderful terrace overlooking the Danube are all highlights of this, one of Szentendre's best restaurants. The menu is a selection of Hungary's favourites and a smattering of international cuisine.

Palapa (302 418; Batthyány utca 4; mains 1000-1500Ft; 5pm-midnight Mon-Fri, noon-midnight Sun) This colourful Mexican restaurant, which serves all the Mexican favourites, is the perfect place for a change from heavy Hungarian fare; there's also garden seating.

Régimódi (311 105; Dumtsa Jenő utca 2; set menu 1800Ft) The best of the tourist traps in the centre. With a menu heavy on poultry, there are enough vegetarian, fish and game dishes to keep everyone satisfied. Choose a table on the main square or the quieter back terrace.

Marzipan Museum (☎ 311 931; Dumtsa Jenő utca 12; 10am-7pm May-Oct, 10am-6pm Nov-Apr) This is a good place to stop for cake and ice cream, and kids will love the marzipan creations inside the museum (adult/child 300/200Ft).

Avakum (☎ 500 145; Alkotmány utca 14) Dive into this place, a cellar bar near Castle Hill, to escape the tourist hordes and rehydrate.

For a quick bite to eat, try the food stalls at the bus and HÉV stations, the small **lángos stand** (lángos from 200Ft; Váralja lépcső) halfway up the steep steps from Fő tér to Castle Hill or **Dixie Chicken** (Dumtsa Jenő utca 16; burgers from 240Ft), a standard fast-food joint with the added bonus of a salad bar.

Entertainment

Danube Cultural Centre (☎ 312 657; Duna korzó 11/a) This centre stages theatrical performances, concerts and folk dance gatherings and can tell you what's on elsewhere in Szentendre.

Shopping

Szentendre is a shopper's town – from souvenir embroidery to the latest fashions – and although prices are at Budapest levels, not everything you see is available in the capital.

Péter-Pál Galeria (☎ 311 182; Péter-Pál utca 1; 10am-6pm Thu-Sun) For ceramics and lace, try this place.

Metszet Gallery (☎ 312 577; Fő tér 14; 11am-6pm Tue-Sun) This shop has wonderful old engravings, prints and a handful of maps.

Herend Shop (☎ 505 288; Bogdányi út 1; 10am-6pm Mon-Sat, 10am-4pm Sun) If you don't make it to Herend (p218), you can pick up an expensive piece of porcelain here.

Getting There & Away
BOAT
See Getting Around at the beginning of the chapter for more information.

BUS
Buses from Budapest's Árpád híd station, which is on the blue metro line, run to Szentendre at least once an hour throughout the day (241Ft, 30 minutes, 16km). Onward service to Visegrád (302Ft, 45 minutes, 23km, eight daily) and Esztergom (606Ft, 1½ hours, 48km, hourly) is good.

TRAIN
The easiest way to reach Szentendre from Budapest is to catch the HÉV suburban

train from Batthyány tér in Buda (160Ft, 40 minutes, every 10 to 20 minutes). Remember that a yellow city bus/metro ticket is good only as far as the Békásmegyer stop; you'll have to pay extra to get to Szentendre. Also, many HÉV trains run only as far as Békásmegyer, where you must cross the platform to board the train for Szentendre. The last train leaves Szentendre for Budapest at 11.10pm.

Getting Around
Any bus heading north on Rte 11 to Visegrád and Esztergom will stop near Pap-sziget Camping (opposite); ring the bell after you pass the Danubius hotel at Ady Endre utca 28 on the left. Between 14 and 17 buses daily leave bus stop No 7 (located at the town's bus station) for the Hungarian Open-Air Ethnographical Museum.

Ferries run hourly to Szentendre Island (5am to 7.30pm daily from March to October) and cost 130/65Ft for an adult/child one way.

You can also book a **taxi** (☎ 311 111) in town.

VÁC
☎ 27 / pop 35,000
Lying to the east of the Danube, Vác is generally forgotten by the majority of visitors who cling to the more tourist-orientated towns on the far side of the river. This is quite unfortunate, for this unpretentious town, with its quiet ambience, multitude of churches and rich history, has something to offer most people. And it has one distinct advantage over its west-bank counterparts – glorious sunsets over the Börzsöny Hills, reflected in the Danube.

History
Unlike most Hungarian towns, Vác can prove its ancient origins without putting a spade into the ground: Uvcenum – the town's Latin name – is mentioned in Ptolemy's 2nd-century *Geographia* as a river crossing on an important road. King Stephen established an episcopate here in the 11th century, and within 300 years Vác was rich and powerful enough for its silver mark to become the realm's legal tender. The town's medieval centre and Gothic cathedral were destroyed during the Turkish occupation; reconstruction under several bishops

in the 18th century gave Vác its present baroque appearance.

No more than a sleepy provincial centre in the middle of the 19th century, Vác was the first Hungarian town to be linked with Pest by train (1846), but development didn't really come until after WWII. Sadly, for many older Hungarians the name Vác conjures up a single frightening image: the notorious prison on Köztársaság út, where political prisoners were incarcerated and tortured both before the war under the rightist regime of Miklós Horthy and in the 1950s under the Communists. Today you'd scarcely be aware of it as you enjoy the breezes along the embankment of the Danube, a more prominent feature here than in the Bend's other towns.

Orientation

The train station is at the northeastern end of Széchenyi utca, the bus station is a few steps southwest. Following Széchenyi utca toward the river for about 500m will take you across the ring road (Dr Csányi László körút) and down to Március 15 tér, the main square. The Mahart ferry pier is at the northern end of Liszt Ferenc sétány; the car and passenger ferry to Szentendre Island is just south of it.

Information

DunaWeb (☎ 301 571; Széchenyi utca 8; per hr 400Ft) Internet access directly opposite the OTP ATM.
Main post office (Posta Park 2) Off Görgey Artúr utca.
OTP ATM (Dunakanyar shopping centre) Just around the corner from Tourinform.

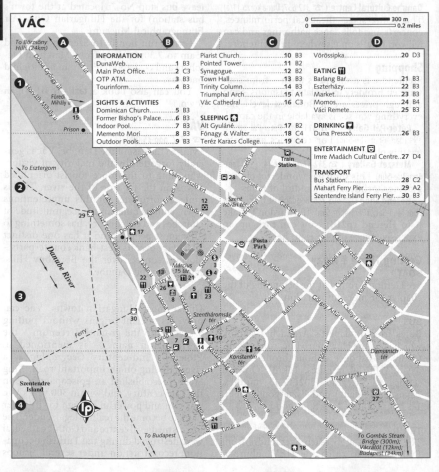

VÁC

INFORMATION			
DunaWeb	1	B3	
Main Post Office	2	C3	
OTP ATM	3	B3	
Tourinform	4	B3	

SIGHTS & ACTIVITIES		
Dominican Church	5	B3
Former Bishop's Palace	6	B3
Indoor Pool	7	B3
Memento Mori	8	B3
Outdoor Pools	9	B3

Piarist Church	10	B3
Pointed Tower	11	B2
Synagogue	12	B2
Town Hall	13	B3
Trinity Column	14	B3
Triumphal Arch	15	A1
Vác Cathedral	16	C3

SLEEPING		
Alt Gyuláné	17	B2
Fónagy & Walter	18	C4
Teréz Karacs College	19	C4

Vörössipka	20	D3

EATING		
Barlang Bar	21	B3
Eszterházy	22	B3
Market	23	B3
Momos	24	B4
Váci Remete	25	B3

DRINKING		
Duna Presszó	26	B3

ENTERTAINMENT		
Imre Madách Cultural Centre	27	D4

TRANSPORT		
Bus Station	28	C2
Mahart Ferry Pier	29	A2
Szentendre Island Ferry Pier	30	B3

Tourinform (☎ 316 160; vac@tourinform.hu; Március 15 tér 16-18; ☺ 10am-6pm Mon-Fri, 10am-2pm Sat & Sun mid-Jun–Aug, 9am-5pm Mon-Fri, 10am-noon Sat Sep–mid-Jun) Overlooking the main square.

Sights

Március 15 tér has the most colourful buildings in Vác, although the square itself looks like a building site; excavations are currently underway to unearth ruins dating from the 13th and 14th centuries. The **Dominican church** (Fehérek temploma; ☎ 305 988; Március 15 tér 19; adult/child 300/150Ft; ☺ 10am-6pm Tue-Sun), with temporary exhibitions by local artists, is 18th-century baroque, as is the magnificent **Town Hall** (1764; Március 15 tér 11). Note the seals held by the two figures on the gable – they represent Hungary and Bishop Kristóf Migazzi, the driving force behind Vác's reconstruction more than 200 years ago. The building next door at No 9 has been a hospital since the 18th century. Opposite is the former **Bishop's Palace** (☎ 319 494; Március 15 tér 6; admission 100Ft; ☺ 2-6pm Wed-Fri, 10am-6pm Sat & Sun mid-May–Oct), parts of which belong to the oldest building in Vác; it's now used as a school and temporary exhibition space.

North of the main square is the **Triumphal Arch** (Diadalív-kapu), the only such structure in Hungary. It was built by Bishop Migazzi in honour of a visit by Empress Maria Theresa and her husband Francis of Lorraine (both pictured in the arch's oval reliefs) in 1764. From here, dip down one of the narrow side streets (such as Molnár utca) to the west for a stroll along the Danube. The **old city walls** and Gothic **Pointed Tower** (now a private home) are near Liszt Ferenc sétány 12.

If you climb up Fürdő utca near the pool complex, you'll reach tiny Szentháromság tér and its renovated **Trinity Column** (1755). The **Piarist church** (Piarista templom; admission free), completed in 1741, with a stark white interior and marble altar, is to the east across the square.

Tree-lined Konstantin tér to the southeast is dominated by colossal **Vác Cathedral** (Váci székesegyház; admission free), which dates from 1775 and was one of the first examples of neoclassical architecture in Hungary. This imposing grey church designed by the French architect Isidore Canevale isn't to everybody's liking, but the frescoes on the vaulted dome and the altarpiece by Franz Anton Maulbertsch are worth the look inside. There's a display of stone fragments from the medieval cathedral in the crypt, but it is normally closed; Tourinform can arrange tours.

If you continue walking south along Budapesti főút, you'll reach the small stone **Gombás Stream Bridge** (Gombás-patak hídja; 1757), lined with the statues of seven saints – Vác's modest response to Charles Bridge in Prague.

Near the bus stop is the town's newly renovated 19th-century **synagogue** (Eötvös utca 5). The interior is yet to be finished, but when complete it will be used as an exhibition hall.

THE MUMMIES OF VÁC

Through sheer forgetfulness and perfect micro-climatic conditions, Vác became the very proud owner of its own crypt of mummies (minus the curses).

Between 1731 and 1801 the original crypt of the Dominican church functioned as a place of burial for the general public but, for reasons unknown, it was later bricked up and promptly forgotten. The micro-climatic conditions underground were perfect for mummification – a cool temperature year-round and minimal ventilation allowed the bodies and clothes of the deceased to remain in exceptional condition for centuries. When renovation work on the church began in 1994, the crypt was rediscovered and a total of 262 bodies were exhumed over the ensuing months 166 of which were easily identified through church records. It was a veritable gold mine for historians; the clothing, jewellery and general appearance of the corpses helped to shed light on the burial practices and way of life in the 18th century.

The majority of mummies now reside in the vaults of the Hungarian National Museum in Budapest (p94) but three – a man (who has a disturbing likeness to Michael Jackson), woman and baby – are on display in the **Memento Mori** (☎ 316 160; Március 15 tér 19; adult/child or student 400/200Ft; ☺ 10am-6pm Tue-Sun). It also showcases some colourfully painted coffins, clothes and jewellery of the deceased, a registry of those buried and a brief history of the church and its crypt.

Activities

The Vác **Strandfürdő** (Szentháromság tér 3) has **outdoor pools** (adult/child or student 600/360Ft; ☼ 7am-7pm Jun-Sep) and an **indoor pool** (adult/child or student 600/360Ft; ☼ 6am-8pm Mon-Fri, 7am-8pm Sat & Sun Oct-Apr, 6am-8pm Mon-Fri, 6am-7pm Sat, 7am-5pm Sun Oct-Apr) on the southern edge of the 'beach', accessible from Ady Endre sétány.

Sleeping

Alt Gyuláné (☎ 316 860; Tabán utca 25; s/d without bath room 6000/8000Ft) This exceptionally friendly *pension* (it's more like overnighting with nice relatives) makes a perfect base for exploring the eastern side of the Danube region. Rooms are very cosy, there's a fully equipped kitchen and private garden for guests; bikes can be rented.

Fónagy & Walter (☎ 310 682; www.fonagy.hu; Budapesti főút 36; r 9500Ft; (P)) Fónagy & Walter is another *pension* from the 'homely' mould – rooms are lovingly prepared, the hosts love to sit and chat, the wine selection from the private cellar is outstanding and the outdoor grill may be fired up just for you.

Other recommendations:

Vörössipka (☎ 501 055; okktart@netelek.hu; Honvéd utca 14; r 8000/12,000Ft; (P)) Most business-like of Vac's hotels, with newish rooms.

Teréz Karacs College (☎ 510 045; Budapesti főút 2/8; dm 1024Ft; ☼ Jul & Aug) The most central of six colleges.

Eating & Drinking

Barlang Bar (Cave Bar; ☎ 501 760; Március 15 tér 12; dishes 1000-1500Ft; ☼ to 11pm Sun-Thu, to 1am Fri & Sat) With its florescent lighting and red booths, Barlang looks as though it would be more at home in New York than Vác. Its international menu is appealing, as are the medieval wine-cellar surroundings.

Duna Presszó (☎ 310 569; Március 15 tér 13) Duna is the quintessential café: dark-wood furniture,

---

chandeliers, excellent cake and ice cream, the occasional drunk, and good for coffee during the day and something stronger at night.

Vác's colourful, lively market is to the southeast of the main square.

Also try the following:

Momos (Tímár utca 9; mains 1500-2000Ft) Huge terrace overlooking parkland and the river; excellent for fish and anything from the grill.

Eszterházy (Eszterházy utca; ice cream 100Ft; ☼ 9am-8pm) Perfect spot for refreshments on your stroll along the Danube.

Entertainment

Imre Madách Cultural Centre (☎ 316 411; Dr Csányi László körút 63) This circular centre can help you with what's on in Vác, such as theatre, concerts and kid's shows.

Concerts are occassionally held in Vác Cathedral, the Dominican church and at the arboretum in **Vácrátót** at 7pm on certain Sundays in June, July and August (tickets 1600-2000Ft).

Getting There & Away

BOAT

Car ferries (1100/300/300/240Ft per car/bicycle/adult/child, hourly 6am to 9pm) cross over to Szentendre Island; a bridge connects the island's west bank with the mainland at Tahitótfalu. From there hourly buses run to Szentendre. See Getting Around (p132) for more information.

BUS

Buses depart for Árpád híd station in Budapest frequently (363Ft, one hour, 30km). From Vác count on up to 18 services Monday to Saturday to Vácrátót (182Ft, 30 minutes, 14km), at least a dozen to Balassagyarmat (605Ft, 1¼ hours, 45km) and between two and eight to Diósjenő (363Ft, 50 minutes, 25km) and Nógrád (241Ft, 30 minutes, 20km). You can also reach Salgótarján (1150Ft, 2½ hour, 95km, four daily).

TRAIN

Trains depart from Nyugati station in Budapest almost every half-hour for Szob via Vác (346Ft, 34km), and three of these continue along the eastern bank of the Danube to Štúrovo, across from Esztergom, in Slovakia. Slow trains north to Balassagyarmat (up to 10 a day) from Vác stop at Nógrád and Diósjenő in the Börzsöny Hills.

AUTHOR'S CHOICE

Váci Remete (☎ 302 199; Fürdő utca; mains 1500Ft) Váci Remete is more than inviting, it's a must: its shady terrace is backed by flower beds, there are views of the Danube and the wine selection is top-notch. Surprisingly, there's not a fish dish in sight, but the Hungarian specialities are complimented by a small selection of vegetarian choices.

From the last Saturday in April to the first one in October, **MÁV Nostalgia** (☎ 1-269 5242; www.mavnosztalgia.hu; adult/child 1020/870Ft) runs a *nosztalgiavonat* (vintage steam train) from Nyugati station in Budapest (departing at 9.40am) to Szob (two hours) via Vác and Nagymaros-Visegrád; the train returns from Vac at 5pm. But verify this service and schedule with MÁV Nostalgia, or check its website before making plans.

AROUND VÁC
Börzsöny Hills

These hills begin the series of six ranges that make up Hungary's Northern Uplands, and – along with the Pilis Hills (p144) on the opposite bank of the Danube – form Hungary's 600-sq-km **Danube-Ipoly National Park**. There's very good hiking, but make sure you get hold of Cartographia's 1:40,000 map *A Börzsöny* (No 5; 800Ft), which is available from Vác **Tourinform** (☎ 316 160; Március 15 tér 16-18, Vác).

Nógrád, with the ruins of a hilltop castle dating from the 12th century, could be considered the gateway to the Börzsöny. Diósjenő, 6km north, is a good base for exploring the hills and has a few accommodation options, including **Diósjenő Camping** (☎ 35-364 134; www .patakpart.hu; camp sites per person/tent 750/750Ft, bungalows 5000-15 000Ft; ᠁ May-Sep; P). It's rather disorganised and overgrown, but on the plus side the staff are welcoming. There are a variety of bungalows, and repairs were underway at the time of research. From here you can strike out west along marked trails to **Nagy Hideg** (864m) or **Magas-Tax** (739m). The Börzsöny's highest peak, **Csóványos** (938m), lies to the west of Diósjenő and is a much more difficult climb.

If you're under your own steam, take the beautiful restricted road from Diósjenő to Kemence via Királyháza; it follows the Kemence Stream almost the entire way – a great place for a cool dip or a picnic in summer. Just before you reach Kemence, there is a turn-off south to the beautiful **Fekete-völgy**, 'Black Valley', and **Feketevölgy Pension** (☎ 27-365 153; www.feketevolgy.hu; r 9200-14,000Ft; P ᠁), a peaceful oasis set well into the forest. Otherwise, head onto Kemence, a nondescript town with a few *pensions* and restaurants, Internet access and an ATM.

The southern end of the Börzsöny is bereft of any tourist infrastructure, aside from

the **Szent Orbán** (☎ 27-378 034; www.szentorban.hu; s/d from 15,200/16,900Ft; P ᠁ ᠁) in the heart of the forest at tiny **Nagyirtáspuszta**. The wood cabin–like rooms at this large, ecofriendly hotel are spacious and come with plenty of modern amenities; there's also a restaurant, with an extensive wine list. There's no public transport to the hotel and it often caters to conferences, so call ahead rather than turn up on the doorstep.

VISEGRÁD
☎ 26 / pop 1650

Situated on the Danube's abrupt loop, Visegrád (from the Slavic words for 'high castle') is the most beautiful section and the very symbol of the Bend. Most tourists, however, don't come here for the views (which are reason enough to visit) but rather to explore what remains of the town's history – its Renaissance palace and accompanying citadel.

History

The Romans built a border fortress on Sibrik Hill just a little north of the present castle in the 4th century, and it was still being used by Slovak settlers 600 years later. After the Mongol invasion in 1241, King Béla IV began work on a lower castle by the river and then on the hilltop citadel. Less than a century later, King Charles Robert of Anjou, whose claim to the local throne was being fiercely contested in Buda, moved the royal household to Visegrád and had the lower castle converted into a palace.

For almost 200 years, Visegrád was Hungary's 'other' (often summer) capital and an important diplomatic centre. But Visegrád's real golden age came during the reign of King Matthias Corvinus (r 1458–90) and Queen Beatrice, who had Italian Renaissance craftsmen rebuild the Gothic palace. The sheer size of the residence, its stonework, fountains and hanging gardens were the talk of 15th-century Europe.

The destruction of Visegrád came with the Turks and later in 1702, when the Habsburgs blew up the citadel to prevent Hungarian independence fighters from using it as a base. All trace of the palace was lost until the 1930s when archaeologists, following descriptions in literary sources, uncovered the ruins.

Orientation

The Mahart ferry pier, just south of the city gate and opposite the Vár hotel, is one of two stops where buses from Szentendre or Budapest will drop you off. To the right of the Vár hotel are steps to Salamon-torony utca, which go to the lower castle and the citadel. There are also bus stops near the village centre and the car ferry is about a 1km south on Rte 11.

Information

OTM bank (Rév utca 9) Not far from Visegrád Tours.
Post office (Fő utca 77; 8am-noon, 12.30-4pm Mon-Fri) In the village centre.
Visegrád Tours (398 160; www.visegradtours.hu; Rév utca 15; 8am-5.30pm) This office, near the ferry to

Nagymaros centre has limited information on Visegrád, but it's the only source in town.

Sights

A perfect place to start your tour of Visegrád is the **Royal Palace** (Visegrádi királyi palota; 398 026; Fő utca 29; admission free; 9am-4.30pm Tue-Sun), situated not far south of the Mahart ferry pier. The palace's foundations were laid in 1323 by King Charles Robert but it was King Matthias and his Neopolitan second wife Queen Beatrice who, in the 15th century, truly breathed life into the place. The Gothic structure was given a Renaissance makeover and the finished product was unrivalled in Europe at that time.

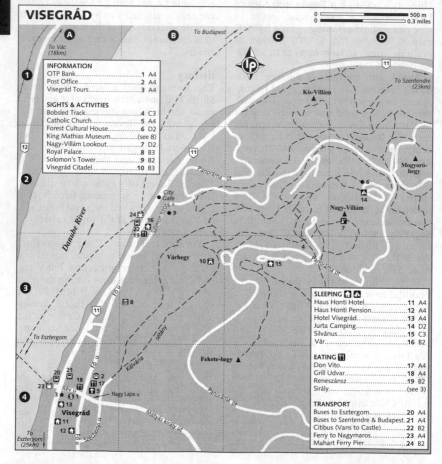

VISEGRÁD

INFORMATION
OTP Bank..............................1 A4
Post Office...........................2 A4
Visegrád Tours.....................3 A4

SIGHTS & ACTIVITIES
Bobsled Track......................4 C3
Catholic Church...................5 A4
Forest Cultural House...........6 D2
King Mathias Museum.........(see 8)
Nagy-Villám Lookout............7 D2
Royal Palace........................8 B3
Solomon's Tower...................9 B2
Visegrád Citadel.................10 B3

SLEEPING
Haus Honti Hotel................11 A4
Haus Honti Pension............12 A4
Hotel Visegrád...................13 A4
Jurta Camping...................14 D2
Silvánus............................15 C3
Vár...................................16 B2

EATING
Don Vito...........................17 A4
Grill Udvar........................18 A4
Reneszánsz.......................19 B2
Sirály.............................(see 3)

TRANSPORT
Buses to Esztergom............20 A4
Buses to Szentendre & Budapest..21 A4
Citibus (Vans to Castle).......22 B2
Ferry to Nagymaros............23 A4
Mahart Ferry Pier...............24 B2

Once featuring a massive 350 rooms, the palace today is a shadow of its former self and only a small section has been reconstructed; the rest has been overrun with weeds and still lies in ruin. The handful of rooms that can be visited – the royal suites – are centred on the Court of Honour and its **Hercules Fountain**, a replica of the original Renaissance piece. Moving from room to room, you'll discover more reconstructions and replicas: a cold and clammy royal bedchamber from the 1400s, a warmer kitchen, and the **Lion Fountain**, famed for its red marble. Also of note is the petite **St George's Chapel** (1366), but once again, it's not the original. The history of the palace and its reconstruction, along with architectural finds, including richly carved stones dating from the 14th century, is told in the **King Mathias Museum**, occupying one of the rooms.

If you walk back to the ferry pier and north up Salamon-torony utca, the first thing you'll see is the 13th-century **Solomon's Tower** (☎ 398 233; adult/child or student 500/300Ft; 🕑 9am-4.30pm Tue-Sun May-Sep), a stocky, hexagonal keep with walls up to 8m thick. Once used to control river traffic, it now houses many of the precious objects unearthed at the Royal Palace, such as the original pieces of the Hercules and Lion fountains.

North of the tower, a trail marked 'Tellegvár' turns southeast at a fork and leads up to **Visegrád Citadel** (☎ 398 101; adult/child or student 800/350Ft; 🕑 9.30am-5.30pm daily mid-Mar–mid-Oct, 9.30am-5.30pm Sat & Sun mid-Oct–mid-Mar), sitting atop a 350m hill and surrounded by moats hewn from solid rock. Completed in 1259, the citadel was the repository for the Hungarian crown jewels until 1440, when Elizabeth of Luxembourg, the daughter of King Sigismund, stole them with the help of her lady-in-waiting and hurried off to Székesfehérvár to have her infant son László crowned king. (The crown was returned to the citadel in 1464 and held here – under a stronger lock, no doubt – until the Turkish invasion.)

There's a small pictorial exhibit in the residential rooms on the west side of the citadel and two smaller displays near the east gate: one on hunting and falconry, the other on traditional occupations in the region (stone-cutting, charcoal-burning, beekeeping and fishing). However, the real highlight is just walking along the ramparts of this eyrie, admiring the views of the Börzsöny

Hills and the Danube, which are arguably the best in the region.

If you're walking to the citadel from the village centre, Kálvária sétány, a trail beginning from behind the 18th-century **Catholic church** (Fő tér), is less steep than the trail from Solomon's Tower. You can also reach it by minibus (p144).

Activities

There are some easy **walks** and **hikes** in the immediate vicinity of Visegrád Citadel – to the 377m high **Nagy-Villám Lookout Tower**, for example. Across from the Jurta camping ground is the sod and wood **Forest Cultural House** designed by Imre Makovecz; it's set up to educate Hungarian children about nature and the environment.

A 750m **bobsled track** (bob-pálya; ☎ 397 397; Mon-Fri 280Ft, Sat & Sun 320Ft; 🕑 9am-6pm Mon-Fri, 9am-7pm Sat & Sun Apr-Sep, 11am-4pm Oct-Mar), on which you wend your way down a metal chute while sitting on a felt-bottomed cart, is on the hillside below the lookout.

Sleeping

Visegrád Tours (☎ 398 160; Rév utca 15) can arrange private rooms (single/double from 4000/6500Ft), or strike out on your own along Fő utca and Széchenyi utca.

Silvánus (🖵 398 311, hotelsilvanus@mail.matav.hu; s/d from €67/96; P 🐾) Silvánus is easily the best option in town if you're looking for a hotel with extras. Count on spotless rooms, extensive views, a terrace restaurant and bar with conservatory, an indoor pool plus a sauna, squash courts and tenpin bowling. Rooms with views of the Danube River cost more.

Haus Honti (☎ 398 120; Fő utca 66; hotel s/d €40/50, pension s/d €30/35; P) This friendly and hospitable establishment has modern hotel rooms near Rte 11 and more simple *pension* rooms on quieter Fő utca. Bicycles are also available for rent.

Jurta Camping (☎ 398 217; Mogyoróhegy; camp sites per adult/child/tent or car 650/400/500Ft; P) About 2km northeast of the citadel is this nicely situated camp ground near meadows and woods. It is, however, far from the centre, and the shuttle service is infrequent (p144).

Also worth recommending:

Vár (☎ 397 522; varhotelvisegrad@axelero.hu; Fő utca 9; s/d €40/50; P) Small, old-fashioned rooms in a lovely renovated building. Its 100-year old cellar is a treat.

Hotel Visegrád (☎ 397 034; hotelvisegrad@visefrado urs.hu; Rév utca 15; s/d €50/60; P 🐾) Modern, warm dark rooms with balcony and partial views of the castle or the Danube.

Eating

Sirály (☎ 597 088; Rév utca 15; mains 1500-2000Ft) This is a flash, popular restaurant with tourists and locals alike. It has big bay windows and an enormous terrace facing the Danube.

Don Vito (☎ 397 230; Fő utca 83; pizzas from 500Ft; 🐾 Apr-Oct) Big, bright, new Don Vito is an attractive pizzeria-cum-pub, with outdoor seating and a convivial atmosphere in the evening.

Grill Udvar (Rév utca 6; pizzas & mains 500-1000Ft; 🐾 10am-9pm) This simple place is good for a quick sit-down meal with no fuss involved. On hot, stuffy days its small covered courtyard is a blessing.

Reneszánsz (☎ 398 081; Fő utca 11; mains 2000Ft) Reneszánsz is the epitome of the tourist trap; busload after busload of tourists file through its doors to be greeted by a medieval banquet and men in tights with silly hats. But in the right mood, it can be quite a hoot.

Getting There & Away

BOAT

Hourly ferries cross the Danube to Nagymaros (280/280/1050Ft per person/bicycle/car) from around 5.30am to 8.30pm. The ferry operates all year except when the Danube freezes over or fog descends.

BUS & TRAIN

Buses are very frequent (423Ft, 1¼ hours, 34km, up to 14 daily) to/from Budapest's Árpád híd station, Szentendre (302Ft, 45 minutes, 25km) and Esztergom (302Ft, 40 minutes, 25km). No train line reaches Visegrád, but you can take one of two dozen daily trains to Szob (658Ft, 65km) from Nyugati station in Budapest. You'll need to get off at Nagymaros-Visegrád, and then hop on the ferry to Visegrád.

Getting Around

Citibus (☎ 397 372; up to 6 people 2000Ft) operates a taxi van service between the Mahart ferry pier and the citadel via the Nagymaros ferry pier and Jurta Camping on request from April to September.

AROUND VISEGRÁD
Pilis Hills

Directly to the south and southwest of Visegrád are the Pilis Hills, an area of rolling hills blanketed in oak and beech woods. Once the private hunting grounds of Matthias Corvinus, it's now Budapest's outdoor playground, criss-crossed by a lot more hiking trails (including Hungary's first, laid in 1869) than roads. The entire region, which covers 250 sq km, falls within the scope of the **Danube-Ipoly National Park**; the Börzsöny Hills (p141), north of the Danube, make up the rest of the park.

A good starting point for exploring the hills is Dömös, 6km west of Visegrád. From close by, marked trails lead to **Prédikálószék** (Pulpit Seat), a 639m crag for experienced hikers and climbers only, and to **Dobogókő** (699m), a much easier ascent of about three hours via the **Rám-szakadék** (Rám Precipice). Some of the best bird-watching in western Hungary is in these hills. A *Pilis és a Visegrádi-helység*, the 1:40,000 Pilis and Visegrád Hills map (No 16; 800Ft) from Cartographia, outlines the many hiking possibilities for the entire area.

In Dömös you'll find an excellent river beach and **Dömös Camping** (☎ 33-482 319; www .domoscamping.hu; camp sites per adult/child/tent/car 780-830/580-620/700-830/350-420Ft, cottages 9900-12200Ft; 🐾 May–mid-Sep; P 🐾), with tent sites and well-equipped cottages that sleep up to four.

At Dobogókő there's an excursion centre with further trails mapped out, or you can catch a bus to Esztergom (241Ft, 40 minutes, 20km, four or five daily) or to the HÉV station in Pomáz, two stops before Szentendre.

Alternatively, you can take the small ferry (400Ft; runs on demand) across the Danube from Dömös to Dömösi átkelés (on the train line two stops from Nagymaros-Visegrád), then climb to the caves that are visible on the hillside and hike back into the hills behind Nagymaros.

ESZTERGOM
☎ 33 / pop 28,785

Esztergom, 25km west of Visegrád and 66km from Budapest via Rte 11, is one of Hungary's most historical cities and, as the effective 'capital' of the Danube Bend, well worth a visit. For more than 1000 years it has been the seat of Roman Catholicism; the archbishop of Esztergom is the primate – the highest ranking cleric – of Hungary. The country's first king, St Stephen, was born here in 975, and it was a royal seat from the late 10th to the mid-13th centuries. As a result, Esztergom has both great spiritual and temporal significance for Hungarians.

History

Vár-hegy (Castle Hill), towering over the city centre, was the site of the Roman settlement of Solva Mansio in the 1st century, and it is thought that Marcus Aurelius finished his *Meditations* in a camp nearby during the second half of the 2nd century.

Prince Géza chose Esztergom as his capital, and his son Vajk (later Stephen) was crowned king here in 1000. Stephen founded one of the country's two archbishoprics at Esztergom and built a basilica, bits of which can be seen in the palace.

Esztergom (German: Gran) lost its political significance when King Béla IV moved the capital to Buda after the Mongol invasion in 1241. It remained the ecclesiastical seat, however, vying with the royal court for power and influence. Esztergom's capture by the Turks in 1543 interrupted the church's activities, and the archbishop fled to Nagyszombat (now Trnava in Slovakia) to the northwest.

The church did not reestablish its base in this Hungarian Rome until the early 19th century. It was then that Esztergom went on a building spree that transformed it into a city of late baroque and, in particular, neoclassical buildings.

Orientation

Esztergom lies on a high point above a slight curve of the Danube across from the Slovakian city of Štúrovo (Hungarian: Párkány), to which it is linked by the Mária Valéria Bridge. The centre of Esztergom today is Rákóczi tér, a few steps east of the Little Danube (Kis-Duna), the tributary that branches off to form Primate Island (Prímás-sziget). From the square Bajcsy-Zsilinszky utca leads northwest to Castle Hill; to the southwest of Rákóczi tér is Széchenyi tér, the town centre in the Middle Ages and site of the rococo town hall.

Esztergom's bus station (Simor János utca) is beyond the street market, 700m south of Rákóczi tér. The train station (Bem József tér) is another 1.2km further south.

Mahart boats dock at the pier just south of Mária Valéria Bridge on Primate Island.

Information

Ágost Bajor Cultural Centre (☎ 313 888; Bajcsy-Zsilinszky utca 4; per hr 400Ft; ☯ 8am-9pm Mon-Fri, 9am-1pm & 5-10pm Sat, 5-10pm Sun) Internet access on one computer.

Atek Computers (☎ 501 320; atekcomp@axelero.hu; Bajcsy-Zsilinszky utca 5; per hr 500Ft; 9am-5pm Mon-Fri, 9am-noon Sat) In a small courtyard, this shop has Internet access on two machines.

Cathedralis Tours (☎ 403 603; fax 520 261; Bajcsy-Zsilinszky utca 26; ☯ 8am-5pm Mon-Fri) Useful for information and private rooms.

Gran Tours (☎ 502 001; grantours@freemail.hu; Széchenyi tér 25; ☯ 8am-5pm Mon-Fri, 9am-noon Sat Jun-Aug, 8am-4pm Mon-Fri Sep-May) Visitor centre run by the city of Esztergom.

K&H bank (cnr Rákóczi tér & Simor János utca; ☯ 8am-5pm Mon, 8am-4pm Tue-Thu, 8am-3pm Fri)

OTP bank (Rákóczi tér 2-4; ☯ 7.45am-5pm Mon, 7.45am-4pm Tue-Fri)

Post office (Arany János utca 2) Enter from Széchenyi tér.

www.esztergom.hu Hungarian only, but with English-language links.

Sights

ESZTERGOM BASILICA

The **basilica** (Bazilika; ☎ 411 895; www.bazilika-esztergom.hu; Szent István tér 1; admission free; ☯ 6am-6pm), the largest church in Hungary, is on Castle Hill, and its 72m-high central dome can be seen for many kilometres around. The building of the present neoclassical church was begun in 1822 on the site of a 12th-century one destroyed by the Turks. József Hild, who designed the cathedral at Eger, was involved in the final stages, and the basilica was consecrated in 1856 with a sung Mass composed by Franz Liszt.

The grey church is colossal (117m long and 47m wide) and rather bleak inside, but the red-and-white marble **Bakócz Chapel** on the south side is a splendid example of Italian Renaissance stone-carving and sculpture. It was commissioned by Archbishop Tamás Bakócz who, having failed in his bid for the papacy, launched a crusade that turned into the peasant uprising under György Dózsa in 1514 (see p25). The chapel escaped most – though not all – of the Turks' axes; notice the smashed-in faces of Gabriel and other angels above the altar. It was dismantled into 1600 separate pieces and then reassembled

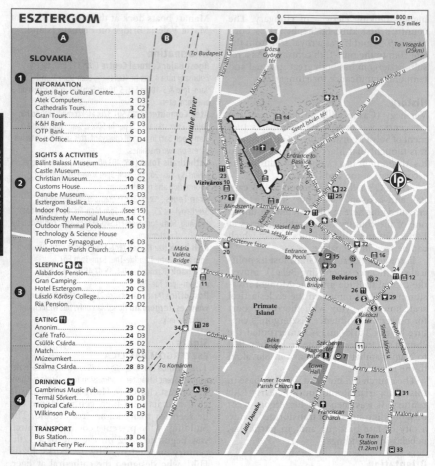

ESZTERGOM

in its present location in 1823. The copy of Titian's *Assumption* over the church's main altar is said to be the world's largest painting on a single canvas.

On the northwest side of the church is the entrance to the basilica's **treasury** (kincstár; ☎ 402 354; adult/child/family 450/220/1000Ft; ☼ 9am-4.30pm daily Mar-Oct, 11am-3.30pm Sat & Sun Nov & Dec, closed Jan & Feb), an Aladdin's cave of vestments and religious plate in gold and silver and studded with jewels. It is the richest ecclesiastical collection in Hungary and contains Byzantine, Hungarian and Italian objects of sublime workmanship and great artistic merit.

The door to the left as you exit the basilica leads to the **crypt** (altemplom; admission 100Ft;

☼ 9am-4.30pm), a series of spooky vaults with tombs guarded by monoliths representing Mourning and Eternity. Among those at rest here are János Vitéz, Esztergom's enlightened Renaissance archbishop, and József Mindszenty, the conservative primate who opposed the former regime (see boxed text, opposite). It's worth making the tortuous climb up to the **cupola** (admission 200Ft; ☼ 9am-4.30pm) for the outstanding views over the city; the stairs leading up to it are to the left of the crypt entrance.

CASTLE HILL MUSEUMS

The small **Castle Museum** (Vármúzeum; ☎ 415 986; Szent István tér 1; admission free; ☼ 10am-6pm Tue-Sun Apr-Oct, 10am-4pm Tue-Sun Nov-Mar) at the southern

CARDINAL MINDSZENTY

Born József Pehm in 1892 in the village of Csehimindszent near Szombathely, Mindszenty was politically active from the time of his ordination in 1915. Imprisoned under the short-lived regime of communist Béla Kun in 1919 and again when the fascist Arrow Cross came to power in 1944, Mindszenty was made archbishop of Esztergom – and thus primate of Hungary – in 1945 and cardinal the following year.

In 1948, when he refused to secularise Hungary's Roman Catholic schools under the new communist regime, Mindszenty was arrested, tortured and sentenced to life imprisonment for treason. Released during the 1956 Uprising, he took refuge in the US Embassy on Szabadság tér when the communists returned to power. He remained there until September 1971.

As relations between the Kádár regime and the Holy See began to improve in the late 1960s, the Vatican made several requests for the cardinal to leave Hungary, which he refused to do. Following the intervention of US President Richard Nixon, Mindszenty left for Vienna, where he continued to criticise the Vatican's relations with the regime in Hungary. He retired in 1974 and died the following year. But as he had vowed not to return to his homeland until the last Soviet soldier had left Hungarian soil, Mindszenty's remains were not returned until May 1991. This was actually several weeks before the last soldier had been repatriated.

end of Castle Hill is housed in the former Royal Palace, which was built mostly by French architects under Béla III (r 1172–96) during Esztergom's golden age. The palace was the king's residence until the capital was relocated to Buda – at which time the archbishop moved in. Most of the palace was destroyed and covered with earth for defensive purposes under the Turks; excavations only began in the 1930s.

The museum concentrates on archaeological finds from the town and its surrounding area, the majority of which is pottery dating from the 11th century onwards. Other points of interest include some of the basilica's original ornate capitals and a fantastic view across the Danube to Slovakia. Outside are 15 enormous church bells no longer in use.

Northeast of the basilica, in the former Seminary building (Szeminárium), is the new **Mindszenty Memorial Museum** (Mindszenty Emlékmúzeum; ☎ 403 162; Szent István tér 4; admission free; ☼ 9am-5pm Tue-Sun), which examines the life and times of one of Hungary's most controversial figures.

OTHER SIGHTS

Below Castle Hill on the banks of the Little Danube is **Víziváros**, the colourful 'Watertown' district of pastel town houses, churches and museums. The fastest way to get there is to walk down steep Macskaút, which can be accessed from just behind the basilica. An easier route is to cross the palace

drawbridge, walk down the grassy hill to Batthyány Lajos utca and then turn west onto Pázmány Péter utca.

The **Bálint Balassi Museum** (☎ 412 584; Pázmány Péter utca 13; adult/child or student 100/50Ft; ☼ 9am-5pm Tue-Sun), in an 18th-century baroque building, has objects of local interest, with much emphasis on the churches and monasteries of medieval Esztergom. The museum is named in honour of the general and lyric poet who was killed during an unsuccessful attempt to retake Esztergom Castle from the Turks in 1594.

Just north of the Italianate **Watertown Parish Church** (Víziváros plébániatemplom; 1738), which is vaguely reminiscent of the glorious Minorite church in Eger, is the former Bishop's Palace. Today it houses the **Christian Museum** (Keresztény Múzeum; ☎ 413 880; www.christianmuseum.hu; Mindszenty hercegprímás tere 2; adult/child or student 500/250Ft; ☼ 10am-6pm Tue-Sun Apr-Oct, 10am-5pm Tue-Sun Mar, 11am-3pm Tue-Sun Nov & Dec) – the finest collection of medieval religious art in Hungary and one of the best museums in the country. Established by Archbishop János Simor in 1875, it contains Hungarian Gothic triptychs and altarpieces; later works by German, Dutch and Italian masters; tapestries; and what is arguably the most beautiful object in the nation: the sublime *Holy Sepulchre of Garamszentbenedek* (1480), a sort of wheeled cart in the shape of a cathedral, with richly carved figures of the 12 Apostles (above) and Roman soldiers (below) guarding

Christ's tomb. It was used at Easter Week processions and was painstakingly restored in the 1970s.

Be sure to see Tamás Kolozsvári's Calvary altar panel (1427), which was influenced by Italian art; the late Gothic *Christ's Passion* (1506) by 'Master M S'; the gruesome *Martyrdom of the Three Apostles* (1490) by the so-called Master of the Martyr Apostles; and the *Temptation of St Anthony* (1530) by Jan Wellens de Cock, with its drug-like visions of devils and temptresses. A free guided tour in English can be booked by ringing the museum in advance.

Cross the bridge south of Watertown Parish Church and around 100m further south is the **Mária Valéria Bridge**, connecting Esztergom with the Slovakian city of Štúrovo. Destroyed during WWII, the bridge only reopened in 2002. The bridge's original **Customs House** (Vámház) now houses an EU information office.

The so-called **Technology & Science House** (Technika és Tudomány Háza; Imaház utca 4) built in 1888, once served as a synagogue for Esztergom's Jewish community, the oldest in Hungary, and now contains a regional government office. It was designed in Moorish Romantic style by Lipót Baumhorn, the master architect who was also responsible for the synagogues in Szeged, Szolnok and Gyöngyös. Close by is the **Danube Museum** (Duna Múzeum; ☎ 500 250; www.dunamuzeum.hu; Kölcsey utca 2; admission free; ☉ 10am-6pm Wed-Mon May-Oct, 10am-4pm Wed-Mon Nov-Apr), with displays on – you guessed it – Hungary's mightiest river and life on it. With all the hands-on exhibits, it's a great place for kids.

Activities

Just east of the Little Danube are **outdoor thermal pools** (☎ 312 249; Kis-Duna sétány 1; adult/child 550/350Ft; ☉ 9am-7pm Mon-Sat, 8am-7pm Sun May-Sep) and stretches of grass 'beach'. You can use the **indoor pool** (☉ 6am-7pm Tue-Fri, 6am-6pm Sat, 8am-4pm Sun) throughout the year.

Esztergom is an excellent base for hiking, cycling and other outdoor pursuits. Ask Gran Tours for a copy of the free *Activities for Tourists in the Komárom-Esztergom Region*.

Sleeping

BUDGET

Contact **Gran Tours** (☎ 502 001; Széchenyi tér 25) or **Cathedralis Tours** (☎ 403 603; Bajcsy-Zsilinszky utca 26) about private rooms (2500Ft to 3500Ft per person) or apartments (8000Ft to 12,000Ft).

László Kőrösy College (☎ 400 005; korosy-koll@freemail.hu; Szent István tér 6; dm 2830Ft; ☉ Jul & Aug; P) This school dormitory just a stone's throw from the basilica opens its doors during the college's summer break.

Gran Camping (☎ 402 513; fortanex@t-online.hu; Nagy-Duna sétány 3; camp sites per adult/child/tent/tent & car 1100/600/900/1100Ft, bungalows 12,000-16,000Ft, d/tr pension 8500/9500Ft; ☉ May-Sep; P ☼) Small but centrally located on Primate Island, this camping ground has space for 500 souls in various forms of accommodation, as well as a good-sized swimming pool. It also has a hostel, with dormitory accommodation for 2200Ft per person.

MIDRANGE

Ria Pension (☎ 313 115, 401 428; www.riapanzio.com; Batthyány Lajos utca 11-13; s/d 10,500/12,500Ft; P) This family-run place just down from the basilica has cosy rooms, a small sauna and bicycles to rent.

Alabárdos Pension (☎ /fax 312 640; Bajcsy-Zsilinszky utca 49; s/d 8500/11,000Ft) This *pension* has rooms arranged within a pleasant courtyard, and a covered car park. It's somewhat up a hill, off the main street.

Hotel Esztergom (☎ 412 555; www.hotels.hu/esztergom; Nagy-Duna sétány; s/d €41/63; P ☒ ☐ ☼) This uninspiring block on leafy Primate Island has modern guest rooms, a rather fancy restaurant and a roof terrace. There's a sports centre with a tennis court, bikes for rent (600/4000Ft per hour/day) and hotel guests get to use a nearby swimming pool.

Eating

Anonim (☎ 411 880; Berényi Zsigmond utca 4; mains 1250-3500Ft; ☉ noon-10pm Tue-Sat) Housed in an attractive old townhouse in Watertown, 'Anonymous' serves small but excellent and very tasty dishes. The garden seating is a real plus in the warmer months.

Szalma Csárda (Thatched Inn; ☎ 315 336; soups 350-850Ft, mains 900-4550Ft; ☉ noon-11pm) Done up in HHK (High Hungarian Kitsch) – with lots of chillies and plates on the walls – Szalma is very popular with tourists. Opposite the Mahart pier, it may be just the spot for a provincial meal before sailing back to Budapest.

Café Trafó (☎ 403 980; Vörösmarty utca 15; coffee 150-400Ft; ☉ 7am-11pm) This little café opposite the

---

AUTHOR'S CHOICE

Csülök Csárda (☎ 412 420; Batthyány Lajos utca 9; soups & starters 690-1490Ft, mains 1290-3220Ft; ☯ noon-10pm) The 'Pork Knuckle Inn' – guess the speciality here – is a charming eatery that is popular with visitors and locals alike. It serves up good home cooking (try the bean soup), the portions are huge and we remember a delightful winter Sunday in Esztergom long ago that began at the Christian Museum and ended with a Dreher-fuelled porky lunch here. Highly recommended.

Danube Museum is a leafy oasis with modern décor; a great place to take a breather, sit back and relax. We could spend all day here.

Múzeumkert (☎ 403 775; Batthyány Lajos utca 1; cakes 180-300Ft; ☯ 9am-midnight Apr-Oct, 9am-10pm Nov-Mar) This restaurant-cum-cocktail lounge called the 'Museum Garden' also serves some of the best cakes and pastries in Esztergom. It attracts a mixed crowd of tea drinkers and boozers.

Match (Bajcsy-Zsilinszky utca; ☯ 6.30am-8pm Mon-Fri, 6.30am-6pm Sat) In the centre of Esztergom, next to the OTP bank, is this branch of the supermarket chain.

Drinking

Wilkinson Pub (☎ 06 70 515 3583; Bajcsy-Zsilinszky utca 25-27; ☯ 8am-10pm Mon-Thu, 8am-2am Fri, 8am-3am Sat, 9am-10pm Sun) This friendly pub should be your first choice for a sundowner in Esztergom. It has a terrace overlooking busy Bajcsy-Zsilinszky utca.

Termál Sörkert (Kis-Duna sétány; ☯ 9am-10pm) The 'Thermal Beer Garden' in the outdoor thermal pool grounds is a great place to be on a balmy summer evening; its outdoor seating area is jam-packed with a young crowd trying to be heard over the music.

Gambrinus Music Pub (Vörösmarty utca 3; ☯ 11am-2am Mon-Thu, 11am-3am Fri, 3pm-3am Sat, 3pm-2am Sun) If you want to kick your heels up, head for this popular pub-bar with the retro Hungarian look (curios and 'antiqued' stuff) and canned music.

Tropical Café (☎ 417 354; Simor János utca 46; ☯ 10am-10pm Mon-Thu, 10am-midnight Fri & Sat, noon-8pm Sun) This pub by the bus station has

cheap beer and is popular with students from the nearby trade school.

Entertainment

For up-to-date entertainment information on what's on, check the listings in the biweekly freebie *Komárom-Esztergomi Est*.

Organ concerts take place in the basilica over summer, the Esztergom Chroniclers sometimes perform ancient Hungarian music at the palace, and a bunch of concerts and plays are held in the town from mid-July to mid-August. Check with **Gran Tours** (☎ 502 001; Széchenyi tér 25), the **Ágost Bajor Cultural Centre** (☎ 313 888; Bajcsy-Zsilinszky utca 4) or visit www.esztergominyarijatekok.hu.

Getting There & Away

BUS

From Esztergom there are frequent buses to Budapest's Árpád híd bus station (544Ft, 70 minutes to two hours, 45km, every 20 minutes) in Pest between 4am and 9.30pm Monday to Saturday, or 4.20am and 8.10pm Sunday, and a handful to Széna tér bus station (766Ft, two hours, 65km, four daily) in Buda. The buses to Árpád híd bus station go via Dorog (70 minutes) or Visegrád (two hours). Buses to Visegrád (302Ft, 45 minutes, 25km) and Szentendre (606Ft, 1¼ hours, 50km) leave every hour or so between 6.45am and 9pm.

Other important destinations served:

Destination	Price	Duration	Km	Frequency
Balatonfüred	2060Ft	4hr	165	1 daily at 5am
Dobogókő	241Ft	40min	20	2-4 daily
Komárom	795Ft	1½hr	60	3-4 daily
Sopron	2300Ft	4hr	190	1 daily at 5am
Tata	665Ft	1hr 40min	55	hourly
Veszprém	1820Ft	3½-4hr	145	3 daily

TRAIN

Trains for Budapest's Nyugati train station in Budapest (512Ft, 1½ hours, 55km, up to two dozen on weekdays and 20 at the weekend) are frequent. To get to Western Transdanubia and points beyond from Esztergom, take a train to Komárom (512Ft, 1½ to two hours, up to six daily), where you can change for Győr, Székesfehérvár and Vienna.

Western Transdanubia

The aptly named region of Western Transdanubia (Nyugat-Dunántúl) lies 'across the Danube' from Budapest, extending west and southwest as far as the borders with Austria and Slovenia. It is an area of plains and rolling hills, with the vineyards of Etyek, Mór and especially Sopron producing some excellent wines. As the nation's 'window on the West', Western Transdanubia has always been the richest and most developed region of Hungary, and it contains some of the most historically important towns, castles, churches and monuments in the country.

HIGHLIGHTS

- Watching one of the best sights in **Tata** (p153) – birds in flight – at Öreg-tó (Old Lake) in winter

- Reliving (as it were) the life and bloodsucking times of Erzsébet Báthory at Sárvár's **Nádasdy Castle** (p179)

- Exploring colourful **Jurisics tér** (p182), dubbed 'the nation's jewellery box', in Kőszeg

- Hiking in the **Őrség National Park** (p185), one of the most unspoiled and traditional areas of Hungary

- Checking out Sopron's **Storno Collection** (p165) of Romanesque and Gothic furnishings and deciding where the Storno family got it right or wrong

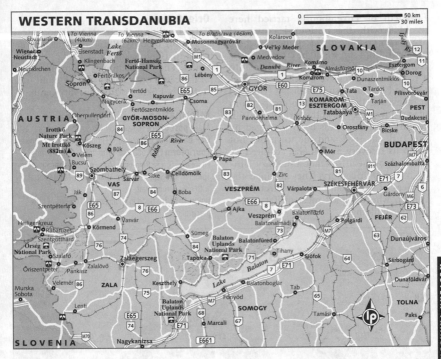

WESTERN TRANSDANUBIA

History

The Danube River was the limit of Roman expansion in what is now Hungary, and most of today's Western Transdanubia formed the province of Pannonia Superior, or 'Upper Pannonia'. The Romans built some of their most important military and civilian towns here, including Arrabona (Győr), Scarbantia (Sopron), Savaria (Szombathely), Adflexum (Mosonmagyaróvár) and Brigetio (Komárom). Because of their positions on the trade route from northern Europe to the Adriatic Sea and Byzantium, and the influx of such ethnic groups as Germans and Slovaks, these towns prospered in the Middle Ages. Episcopates were established, castles were built and many of the towns were granted special royal privileges.

A large part of Western Transdanubia remained in the hands of the Habsburgs during the Turkish occupation, and it was thus spared the ruination suffered in the south and on the Great Plain. As a result, some of the best examples of Romanesque and Gothic architecture in the country can be found here. Because of Vienna's authority and influence throughout the 16th and 17th centuries, Western Transdanubia received Hungary's first baroque churches and civic buildings.

TATA

☎ 34 / pop 23,900

Tata (German: Totis), situated west of the Gerecse Hills, is a pleasant town of springs, canals and lakes, a castle and much history; for a town of its size, there's lots for travellers to see and do. Tata's two lakes offer ample opportunities for sport – including bird-watching – and there's a spa complex north of town. Tata is also a convenient springboard from Budapest and the Danube Bend for other Western Transdanubian towns.

History

Tata's Öregvár (Old Castle), perched on a rock at the northern end of a large lake, has been the focus of the town since the 14th century. It was a favourite residence of King Sigismund, who added a palace to it in the early 15th century, and his daughter,

Elizabeth of Luxembourg, tarried here in 1440 with the purloined crown of St Stephen, en route to Székesfehérvár where her newly born son would be crowned king. King Matthias Corvinus turned Tata into a royal hunting reserve attached to Visegrád, and his successor, Vladislav (Úlászló) II, convened the diet here to escape from plague-ravaged Buda at the turn of the 16th century. The castle was badly damaged by the Turks in 1683, and the town did not begin its recovery until it was acquired by a branch of the aristocratic Esterházy family in the 18th century. They retained the services of Moravian-born architect Jakab Fellner, who designed most of Tata's fine baroque buildings.

Orientation

Tata's bustling main street (Ady Endre utca), a section of busy Rte 1, separates larger Öreg-tó (Old Lake) from Cseke-tó (Tiny Lake). The bus station is 200m northwest of the castle on Május 1 út. The main train station is 1.5km north of the city centre.

Information

Main post office (Kossuth tér 19) Southwest of the castle.
OTP bank (Ady Endre utca 1-3) Opposite the clock tower.
Tourinform (☎ 586 046; tata@tourinform.hu; Ady Endre utca 9; ⊙ 9am-6pm Mon-Fri, 9am-3pm Sat, 9am-1pm Sun Jun-Sep, 8am-4pm Mon-Fri Oct-May) Central, with very helpful staff.
www.tata.hu Good introduction to Tata but of little practical use.

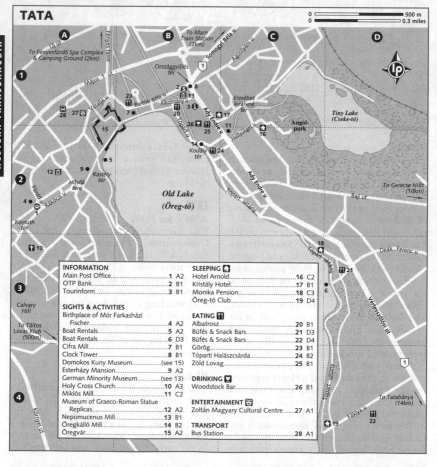

TATA

| 0 | 500 m |
| 0 | 0.3 miles |

INFORMATION	
Main Post Office	1 A2
OTP Bank	2 B1
Tourinform	3 B1

SIGHTS & ACTIVITIES	
Birthplace of Mór Farkasházi Fischer	4 A2
Boat Rentals	5 A2
Boat Rentals	6 D3
Cifra Mill	7 B1
Clock Tower	8 B1
Domokos Kuny Museum	(see 15)
Esterházy Mansion	9 A2
German Minority Museum	(see 13)
Holy Cross Church	10 A3
Miklós Mill	11 C2
Museum of Graeco-Roman Statue Replicas	12 A2
Nepomucenus Mill	13 B1
Öregkálló Mill	14 B2
Öregvár	15 A2

SLEEPING	
Hotel Arnold	16 C2
Kristály Hotel	17 B1
Monika Pension	18 C3
Öreg-tó Club	19 D4

EATING	
Albatrosz	20 B1
Büfés & Snack Bars	21 D3
Büfés & Snack Bars	22 A4
Görög	23 B1
Tóparti Halászcsárda	24 B2
Zöld Lovag	25 B1

| DRINKING | |
| Woodstock Bar | 26 B1 |

| ENTERTAINMENT | |
| Zoltán Magyary Cultural Centre | 27 A1 |

| TRANSPORT | |
| Bus Station | 28 A1 |

Sights

ÖREGVÁR

The remains of the medieval Old Castle – one of four original towers and a palace wing – were rebuilt in neo-Gothic style at the end of the 19th century to mark a visit by Emperor Franz Joseph. Today they house the **Domokos Kuny Museum** (☎ 381 251; adult/senior or student 500/250Ft; ☉ 10am-6pm Tue–Sun mid-Apr–mid-Oct, 10am-2pm Wed-Fri, 10am-4pm Sat & Sun mid-Oct–mid-Apr). On the ground floor are archaeological finds from nearby Roman settlements, bits of the 12th-century Benedictine monastery near Oroszlány and contemporary drawings of the castle in its heyday. The 'Life in the Old Castle' exhibit on the 1st floor is interesting; don't miss the cathedral-like green-tiled Gothic stove that takes pride of place in the **Knights' Hall**. Material on the 2nd floor examines the work of a dozen 18th-century artisans, including Kuny, a master ceramist. Tata porcelain was well known for centuries (the crayfish, once abundant in the lake, was a common motif) and the craft indirectly led to the foundation of the porcelain factory at Herend near Veszprém.

MILLS

Öregvár is surrounded by a moat, and a system of locks and sluices regulates the flow of water into nearby canals: Tata was once known as the 'town of mills'. The 16th-century **Cifra Mill** (Cifra-malom; Váralja utca 3), east of the castle, is interesting only for its red marble window frames and five, rapidly deteriorating, water wheels visible from the north side.

The magnificently restored **Nepomucenus Mill** (Alkotmány utca 2), built in 1758, now houses the **German Minority Museum** (Német Nemzetiségi Múzeum; ☎ 487 888; adult/child or student 200/100Ft; ☉ 10am-6pm Tue-Sun mid-Apr–mid-Oct, 10am-2pm Wed-Fri, 10am-4pm Sat & Sun mid-Oct–mid-Apr). Like Pécs and Székesfehérvár, Tata was predominantly German-speaking for centuries, and the exhibition ('Living Together for 1100 Years') explores all aspects of the German experience in Hungary. Other mills around the lake include the **Öregkálló Mill** (Tópart sétány) and the **Miklós Mill** (Ady Endre utca 26).

OTHER SIGHTS

Walking southwest from the castle for a few minutes through leafy Kastély tér to Hősök tere, you'll pass the Zopf-style former **Esterházy Mansion** (Eszterházy Kastély; Kastel tér; ☎ 708 106; adult/student or child 300/150Ft; ☉ 10am-6pm Wed-Sun May-Sep). Designed by Jakab Fellner in 1764 and used as a hospital for many years, it has now been restored and hosts temporary exhibitions. In the renovated Romantic-style former synagogue is the **Museum of Graeco-Roman Statue Replicas** (Görög-Római Szobormásolatok Múzeuma; ☎ 381 251; Hősök tere 7; adult/student or child 200/150Ft; ☉ 10am-6pm Tue-Sun Apr-Oct). Here you'll find displays of plaster copies of stone sculptures that lined the walkways of Cseke-tó in the 19th century. At Bercsényi utca 1, just before you enter Kossuth tér, is the **birthplace of Mór Farkasházi Fischer**, founder of the Herend porcelain factory (see boxed text, p218) and Tata's most famous son. Dominating the square is another of Fellner's works, the 18th-century **Holy Cross Church** (Szent Kereszt-templom), also called the Great Church.

Cseke-tó, surrounded by the protected 200-hectare Angolpark, built in 1780 and Hungary's first 'English park', is a relaxing place for a walk or a day of fishing.

The octagonal wooden **clock tower** (óratorony; Országgyűlés tér) is a lot older than it looks. Designed by Fellner in 1763, it once housed the town's tiny prison.

Activities

Öreg-tó, a 'Wetland of International Importance' and protected by the Ramsar Convention, attracts a considerable number and variety of waterfowl (see boxed text, p51).

The lake has several **swimming beaches**, and **pleasure boats** (☎ 383 136; adult/child 400/300Ft) depart from the pier just southwest of the castle and on the eastern shore of the lake. **Táltos Lovas Klub** (☎ 06 30 242 2233; Fekete utca 2/a) is a horse-riding school south of Calvary Hill, with horses for hire and coach rides.

The **Fényesfürdő** (☎ 588 144; www.fenyesfurdo .hu; Fényes fasor; adult/child or student 800/500Ft, after 3pm 500/300Ft; ☉ 9am-7pm May-Sep) spa complex and camping ground north of the city centre has thermal spas and several huge pools.

Ask Tourinform for a copy of the free *Activities for Tourists in the Komárom-Esztergom Region*. If you do plan on **hiking** in the Gerecse Hills east of Tata, get a head start by taking a bus to Tardos, Tarján or Dunaszentmiklós. Cartographia publishes a 1:40,000-scale map of the area called *Gerecse Turistatérkép* (No 10; 900Ft).

WESTERN TRANSDANUBIA

Sleeping

BUDGET

Öreg-tó Club (☎ /fax 487 960; Fáklya utca 4; bungalows per person 1200Ft, hotel d 9300Ft; **P** **⚥**) Near the big lake, it has 19 basic bungalows with shared facilities and a 24-room hotel.

Fényesfürdő Camping (☎ /fax 481 208; www.fenyes furdo.hu; Fényes fasor; camp sites per large tent/ small tent/adult/child May–mid-Jun & late Aug–mid-Sep 1100/800/1100/900Ft, mid-Jun–late Aug 1400/1000/ 1300/1000Ft, bungalows for 4/6 people 8500/10,500Ft & 11,000/13,000Ft; **⚥** May–mid-Sep; **P** **⚥**) This place is about 2km north of the city centre and connected to the spa complex. It also has motel rooms for two/four people costing 6500/9000Ft.

MIDRANGE

Hotel Arnold (☎ 588 028; www.hotels.hu/arnold; Erzsébet királyné tér 8; s/d/tr €40/54/65; **P** **⚥**) In an older building on the edge of Angolpark just metres from the small lake, this lovely 25-room hotel leaves the Kristály Hotel in the dust in terms of comfortable, stylish and tranquil accommodation.

Kristály Hotel (☎ 383 577; www.hotels.hu/kristaly_ tata; Ady Endre utca 22; old building s/d/tr €40/50/68, new building s/d €44/54; **P**) This atmospheric (though well-worn) place has 20 rooms in a 200-year-old former Esterházy holding and 17 rooms in a sympathetically designed new wing. It has a lovely back garden, but the front rooms can be rather noisy.

Monika Pension (☎ /fax 383 208; www.hotels.hu /monikapanzio; Tópart sétány 9; d €45; **P** **⚥**) Eight-room Monika is not the most modern *pension*, but it's right on the big lake (ask for a room with balcony) and the price is right.

Eating & Drinking

Büfés and snack bars line Fáklya utca near Öreg-tó Camping and along Deák Ferenc utca near the pier where you can rent boats.

Tóparti Halászcsárda (☎ 380 136; Tópart sétány 10; starters 500-1400Ft, mains 860-1800Ft; **⚥** noon-10pm Sun-Thu, noon-midnight Fri & Sat) South of Kodály tér, the 'Lakeside Fisherman's Inn' is a quaint little eatery serving scaly things. Try its famous *halászlé* (fish soup; 860Ft). The *csárda* (Hungarian-style inn or restaurant) may be closed on Monday and Tuesday in winter.

Görög (☎ 480 980; Váralja utca 20; starters 750-1100Ft, mains 1100-1500Ft; **⚥** noon-10pm) In a restored Esterházy mansion, the 'Greek' serves, well, Greek-ish food in pseudo-Hellenic surrounds. It does make for a change from goulash.

Zöld Lovag (Green Knight; ☎ 481 681; Ady Endre utca 17; mains 1200-2700Ft; **⚥** noon-11pm Sun-Thu, noon-midnight Fri & Sat) This courtyard eatery is another one of those 'medieval-style' restaurants, with colourful banners, large rough-hewn tables and chairs, a menu in Old Hungarian script and men in tights. But the food ain't half bad at this particular one.

Albatrosz (Tópart utca 3; soups 450-700Ft, starters 500-1050Ft, mains 1050-1400Ft) This restaurant and (sometimes lively) bar is in an attractive old house overlooking the lake near the castle. It attracts a young crowd.

Woodstock Bar (Ady Endre utca 13; **⚥** 10am-midnight Sun-Thu, 10am-6am Fri & Sat) At the end of a courtyard just off Ady Endre utca, this is a modern joint with outdoor seating. The crowd is often young and exuberant.

Entertainment

Zoltán Magyary Cultural Centre (☎ 380 811; Váralja utca 4), between the castle and the bus station, can provide you with brochures and up-to-date information on what's going on. Also consult the listings in the biweekly freebie *Komárom-Esztergomi Est*, which includes Tata.

Getting There & Away

BUS

Buses leave very frequently for Tatabánya (133Ft, 20 minutes, 10km, every 20 minutes), Dunaszentmiklós (182Ft, 23 minutes, 11km, at least hourly) and Komárom (423Ft, 30 to 50 minutes, 31km, at least hourly), and there are regular departures to Tarján (302Ft, one hour, 31km, six daily) in the Gerecse Hills and Oroszlány (423Ft, one hour, 32km, every 45 minutes to one hour), which is the gateway to the Vértes Hills. You can also reach Győr (907Ft, 1½ hours, 72km, two daily Monday to Saturday), Budapest (907Ft, 1½ hours, 75km, two daily via Visegrád or Tatabánya) and Esztergom (665Ft, one hour and 40 minutes, 54km, hourly) from here.

TRAIN

Tata is on the main train line linking Budapest with Győr (512Ft, 55 to 90 minutes, 57km, half-hourly) and Vienna (5294Ft, 2½ to three hours, 189km, up to four with just one change). There are direct trains to Sopron (1350Ft, two hours and 10 minutes, 142km, three or four daily) and Szombathely (1730Ft, three hours, 174km, two or three daily) via Tata, but you usually have to change at Győr. If you're travelling by train to Esztergom (512Ft, two hours, 51km, up to six daily with change), you must change at Almásfüzitő. To get to Slovakia, take the train to Komárom (170Ft, 15 to 20 minutes, 20km, half-hourly) and walk across the border.

Getting Around

Bus 1 links the main train station with the bus station and Kossuth tér. Bus 3 will take you to Fényesfürdő; bus 5 gets you close to Fáklya utca. For a local taxi call ☎ 489 808 or 489 080.

GYŐR

☎ 96 / pop 129,000

Győr is usually pegged as 'that big industrial city with the funny name' and neither can be denied. Pronounced something like 'jyeur', Győr (German: Raab) is an important producer of trucks, rolling stock and textiles, and is the nation's third-largest industrial centre.

But Győr is also a historical city; in fact, after Budapest and Sopron, no place in the country can boast as many important buildings and monuments, and no traveller to Transdanubia should miss it. Stroll 100m up pedestrian Baross Gábor utca from the bus or train station and you'll enter a world that has, in some regards, changed little since the 17th and 18th centuries.

History

Situated in the heart of the so-called Little Plain, or Kisalföld, at the meeting point of the Mosoni-Danube and Rába Rivers, Győr was settled first by the Celts and then by the Romans who called it Arrabona. The Avars came here, too, and built a circular fort (called a *gyűrű* from which the town took its name) before the arrival of the Magyars.

King Stephen established a bishopric at Győr in the 11th century, and 200 years later the town was granted a royal charter, allowing it to levy taxes on goods passing through.

A castle was built here in the 16th century and, being surrounded by water, was an easily defended outpost between Turkish-held Hungary and Vienna, the seat of the Habsburg Empire, until late in the century. When the Ottomans captured Győr, they were able to hold on to it for only four years and were evicted in 1598. For that reason Győr is known as the 'dear guard', watching over the nation through the centuries.

Orientation

Győr's train station lies south of Honvéd liget (Soldier Park) on Révai Miklós utca. To reach the bus station in Hunyadi utca on the other side of the train line, go through the subway (underpass) east of the main entrance. Baross Gábor utca leads to the Belváros, the historic Inner Town, and the rivers run to the north and northwest.

Information

Different Internet Café (☎ 516 810; Zichy Palace, Liszt Ferenc utca 20; per 30min 250Ft; ☼ 8am-9pm Mon-Fri, 2-9pm Sat) Internet access on six machines in the basement of a stunning 18th-century mansion.
Ibusz (☎ 311 700; Kazinczy utca 3; ☼ 8am-5pm Mon-Fri, 8am-1pm Sat) More useful for accommodation than general information.
Main post office (Bajcsy-Zsilinszky út 46; ☼ 8am-6pm Mon-Fri) Opposite the Győr National Theatre; train station branch (Révai Miklós utca 8) South of the colossal city hall.
OTP bank (Baross Gábor utca 10, ☼ 7.45am-4pm Mon, 7.45am-3pm Tue-Thu, 7.45am-1.30pm Fri)
Tourinform (☎ /fax 311 771; gyor@tourinform.hu; Árpad út 32; ☼ 8am-8pm Mon-Fri, 9am-6pm Sat & Sun Jun–mid-Sep, 8am-6pm Mon-Fri, 9am-2pm Sat Apr & May, 9am-4pm Mon-Fri, 9am-2pm Sat mid-Sep–Mar) In a kiosk, just north of the county hall.
www.gyor.hu Has both background and practical information but doesn't seem to be updated very often.

Sights

BÉCSI KAPU TÉR

Baroque 'Viennese Gate Sq' is dominated to the south by the **Carmelite church** built in 1725. On the north and northwest side of the square and cutting it off from the river are the fortifications built in the 16th century to stop the Turkish onslaught, and a bastion that has served as a prison, a chapel, a shop and, until recently, even a restaurant.

In the casemates is the **lapidarium** (☎ 310 588; Bécsi kapu tér 5; adult/senior or student 400/200Ft; ☼ 10am-6pm Tue-Sun Apr-Oct), a rich collection of Roman and medieval bits and pieces (the majority of which is stone remains); it is

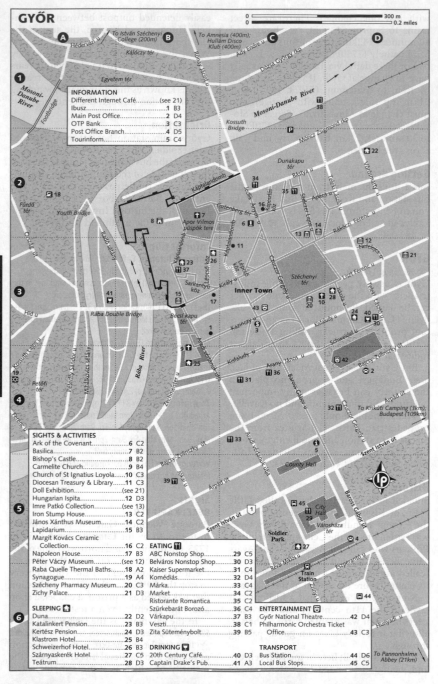

GYŐR

0 — 300 m
0 — 0.2 miles

INFORMATION
Different Internet Café............(see 21)
Ibusz..**1** B3
Main Post Office.....................**2** D4
OTP Bank.................................**3** C3
Post Office Branch...................**4** D5
Tourinform..............................**5** C4

SIGHTS & ACTIVITIES
Ark of the Covenant.................**6** C2
Basilica....................................**7** B2
Bishop's Castle........................**8** B2
Carmelite Church.....................**9** B4
Church of St Ignatius Loyola....**10** C3
Diocesan Treasury & Library.....**11** C3
Doll Exhibition.......................(see 21)
Hungarian Ispita....................**12** D3
Imre Patkó Collection............(see 13)
Iron Stump House..................**13** C2
János Xánthus Museum...........**14** C2
Lapidarium.............................**15** B3
Margit Kovács Ceramic
  Collection.............................**16** C2
Napoleon House.....................**17** B3
Péter Váczy Museum.............(see 12)
Raba Quelle Thermal Baths.....**18** A2
Synagogue..............................**19** A4
Széchény Pharmacy Museum...**20** C3
Zichy Palace............................**21** D3

SLEEPING
Duna.......................................**22** D2
Katalinkert Pension.................**23** B3
Kertész Pension.......................**24** D3
Klastrom Hotel........................**25** B4
Schweizerhof Hotel.................**26** B3
Szárnyaskerék Hotel................**27** C5
Teátrum...................................**28** D3

EATING
ABC Nonstop Shop..................**29** C5
Belváros Nonstop Shop...........**30** D3
Kaiser Supermarket.................**31** C4
Komédiás.................................**32** D4
Márka......................................**33** C4
Market....................................**34** C2
Ristorante Romantica..............**35** C2
Szürkebarát Borozó.................**36** C4
Várkapu...................................**37** B3
Veszti......................................**38** C1
Zita Süteménybolt...................**39** B5

DRINKING
20th Century Café...................**40** D3
Captain Drake's Pub................**41** A3

ENTERTAINMENT
Győr National Theatre.............**42** D4
Philharmonic Orchestra Ticket
  Office....................................**43** C3

TRANSPORT
Bus Station..............................**44** D6
Local Bus Stops.......................**45** C5

NAPOLEONIC PAUSE

Known only to pedants and Lonely Planet guidebook writers is the 'footnote fact' that Napoleon actually spent a night in Hungary – at Király utca 4, due east of Bécsi kapu tér, on 31 August 1809. The building is now called Napoleon-ház (Napoleon House), appropriately enough, and contains a branch of the City Museum. And why did NB choose Győr to make his grand entrée into Hungary? Apparently the city was near a battle site and an inscription on the Arc de Triomphe in Paris recalls 'la bataille de Raab'.

a branch of the János Xánthus Museum. To the north but still within the fortified walls is the **Bishop's Castle** (Püspökvár), a fortress-like structure with parts dating from the 13th century; the foundations of an 11th-century Romanesque chapel are on the south side.

KÁPTALAN-DOMB

From Bécsi kapu tér, Káptalan-domb (Chapter Hill) leads to Apor Vilmos püspök tere, the oldest part of the city. The **basilica** (Bazilika; admission free; ☉ 8am-noon & 2-6pm), whose foundations date back to the 11th century, is an odd amalgam of styles, with Romanesque apses (have a look from the outside), a neoclassical façade and a Gothic chapel riding piggyback on the south side. But most of what you see inside, including the stunning frescoes by Franz Anton Maulbertsch, the main altar, the bishop's throne and the pews hewn from Dalmatian oak, is baroque and dates from the 17th and 18th centuries.

The Gothic **Hédervary Chapel** contains one of the most beautiful (and priceless) examples of medieval gold work in Hungary, the **Herm of László**. It's a bust reliquary of one of Hungary's earliest king-saints (r 1077–95) and dates from the early 15th century. If you're looking for miracles, though, move to the north aisle and the **Weeping Icon of Mary**, an altarpiece brought from Galway by the Irish Bishop of Clonfert in 1649, who had been sent packing by Oliver Cromwell. Some 40 years later – on St Patrick's Day no less – it began to cry tears of blood and is still a pilgrimage site.

To the east of the Basilica is the **Diocesan Treasury and Library** (Egyházmegyei kincstár

és könyvtár; ☎ 525 090; adult/senior or student/family 300/150/500Ft; ☉ 10am-4pm Tue-Sun mid-Mar–Oct), one of the richest in Hungary and labelled in English.

As you descend narrow Gutenberg tér to the east of the Basilica, you'll pass the outstanding **Ark of the Covenant** (Frigyszekrény szobor; Jedlik Ányos utca), a large statue dating from 1731. Local tradition has it that King Charles (Károly) III erected the ark, the city's finest baroque monument, to appease the angry people of Győr after one of his soldiers accidentally knocked a monstrance containing the Blessed Sacrament out of the bishop's hands during a religious procession. Just opposite the ark but entered from Káposztás köz 8 is the **Margit Kovács Ceramic Collection** (Kovács Margit kerámiagyűjtemény; ☎ 326 739; Apáca utca 1; adult/senior or student/family 400/200/1000Ft; ☉ 10am-6pm Tue-Sun), a branch of the City Art Museum devoted to the celebrated ceramicist Margit Kovács (1902–77) who was born in Győr.

SZÉCHENYI TÉR

A couple of blocks southeast of Káptalan-domb is enormous Széchenyi tér, which was the town's marketplace in the Middle Ages. On the south side, the Jesuit and later Benedictine **Church of St Ignatius Loyola**, the city's finest, dates from 1641. The 17th-century white-stucco side chapels and the ceiling frescoes painted by the Viennese baroque artist Paul Troger in 1744 are worth a look. Next door, the **Szécheny Pharmacy Museum** (Széchény Patikamúzeum; ☎ 320 954; Széchenyi tér 9; admission free; ☉ 7.30am-4pm Mon-Fri) was established by the Jesuits in 1654 and is a fully operational baroque institution. You can inspect the rococo vaulted ceiling and its fabulous frescoes with religious and herbal themes.

If time is limited, skip the main branch of the **János Xánthus Museum** (☎ 310 588; Széchenyi tér 5; adult/senior or student 500/250Ft; ☉ 10am-6pm Tue-Sun Apr-Sep, 10am-2pm Tue-Sun Oct-Mar), with exhibits on local history, stamps, coins, antique furniture and natural history, and head next door to the **Imre Patkó Collection** (☎ 310 588; Széchenyi tér 5; adult/senior or student 400/200Ft; ☉ 10am-6pm Tue-Sun Apr-Sep, with advance booking 10am-2pm Tue-Sun Oct-Mar) in the 17th-century **Iron Stump House** (Vastuskós Ház), a former caravanserai entered from Stelczer Lajos utca that still sports the log into which itinerant artisans would drive a nail to mark their visit. The museum has an excellent collection of 20th-century fine art on the first two floors; the 3rd floor is given over to objects collected by the journalist and art historian Imre Patkó during his travels in India, Tibet, Vietnam and west Africa.

OTHER SIGHTS

The late Renaissance **Hungarian Ispita** (Magyar Ispita; 3 Nefelejcs köz), once a charity hospital, now houses the **Péter Váczy Museum** (☎ 318 141; adult/senior or student/family 400/200/1000Ft; ☒ 10am-6pm Tue-Sun). Váczy, a history professor and avid antiques collector, managed to assemble quite an eclectic assortment of pieces, from Greek and Roman relics to Chinese terracotta figures, all of which are on display.

In the stunning **Zichy Palace** (Zichy palota; Liszt Ferenc utca 20) is the **Doll Exhibition** (Baba Kiállítás; ☎ 320 289; adult/child 200/100Ft; ☒ 8am-3.30pm Mon-Thu, 8am-1pm Fri), consisting of some 72 19th-century dolls and furniture. It's worth a visit just to see the 18th-century baroque palace, which is also used sometimes for concerts and plays.

Across the river the richly decorated octagonal cupola, galleries and tabernacle of the city's erstwhile **synagogue** (Kossuth Lajos utca 5), built in 1870, are worth a look if you can get into the partially restored building; try at the entrance to the music academy (formerly a Jewish school) next door.

Activities

On the left bank of the Rába River is **Raba Quelle** (☎ 514 900; www.gyortermal.hu; Fürdő tér 1; adult/child or student per day 1600/1000Ft, per 3hr 1300/800Ft; ☒ thermal baths 9am-10pm year-round, covered pool 6am-8pm Mon-Sat year-round, open-air pool 8am-8pm May-Aug), Győr's renovated complex of thermal baths, pools, and fitness and wellness centres, offering every treatment imaginable.

Festivals & Events

The prestigious **Hungarian Dance Festival** (www.nemzetitancszinhaz.hu/english/festivals.php) is held biannually in Győr in late June.

Sleeping

BUDGET

A limited number of private rooms (4200Ft per two people) are available from Ibusz.

István Széchenyi College (☎ 503 447; Hédervári út 3; dm 2300Ft) Dormitory accommodation is available year-round at this huge school north of the city centre.

Szárnyaskerék Hotel (☎ 314 629; fax 317 844; Révai Miklós utca 5; d without/with bathroom 5500/7800Ft) Within stumbling distance of the train and bus stations is the 'Winged Wheel', a four-storey, 30-room hotel that could do with some TLC before it totally disintegrates. The two dozen or so rooms without private bathrooms have washbasins.

Kiskúti Camping (☎ 318 986, 06 30 600 7905; camp sites incl tent & adult 1600Ft, bungalows for 2/4 people 2400/4000Ft, motel d/tr/q 4000/6000/8000Ft; ☒ bungalows mid-Apr–mid-Oct; ℗) Some 3km northeast of town in Kiskútliget (Little Well Park) and near the stadium is this camping ground for 300 people. It also has bungalows and a 32-room heated motel.

MIDRANGE

Unusually for a Hungarian city, Győr is full of small private *pensions*. Very central and in some of the city's most colourful old buildings, they're very good value but seldom have lifts.

Teátrum (☎ /fax 310 640; www.teatrum.hu in Hungarian; Schweidel utca 7; s/d/tr 7500/9500/11,500Ft) An excellent choice, this very central *pension* on an attractive pedestrian street has 10 rooms.

Duna (☎ /fax 329 084; paarhotels@mail.arrabonet .hu; Vörösmarty utca 5; s/d/tr 6500/8500/10,400Ft) Teátrum's sister-*pension* and equally recommended, the powder-blue 14-room Duna has antique furniture in some of the common rooms.

Katalinkert Pension (☎ /fax 542 088; katalinkert@ axelero.hu; Sarkantyú köz 3; s/d 7100/9100Ft; ℗) This lovely place has six modern rooms tucked away above a pleasant courtyard restaurant. The staff here are exceptionally friendly and helpful.

Kertész Pension (☎ /fax 317 461; sometimes love@freemail.hu; Iskola utca 11; s/d/tr/q 6900/9900/13,000/15,000Ft) The friendly 'Gardener' has nine cheery rooms, a tiny sauna and some fitness machines.

TOP END

Schweizerhof Hotel (☎ 329 171; www.schweizerhof .hu; Sarkantyú köz 11-13; s €68, d €73-82; ℗ ☒ ☒ ☒) This is Győr's finest top-end hotel and about as plush as you'll find here. There's a wellness centre, wine cellar, and quality restaurant and bar within the hotel.

Klastrom Hotel (☎ 516 910; www.klastrom.hu; Zechmeister utca 1; s/d/tr €55/70/80; P ☒) This delightful three-star hotel is in a 300-year-old Carmelite convent south of Bécsi kapu tér. It boasts a sauna, solarium, pub with a vaulted ceiling, and a restaurant with seating in a leafy and peaceful inner garden. The best rooms face the courtyard.

Eating
RESTAURANTS & CAFÉS

Várkapu (☎ 328 625; Bécsi kapu tér 7; dishes 700-2400Ft; ☽ 10am-11pm Tue-Sun) Overlooking the Carmelite church, this is a charming little eatery, particularly when dining is available on the terrace. It has a limited but excellent menu of Hungarian favourites.

Komédiás (☎ 527 217; Czuczor Gergely utca 30; soups 350-750Ft, starters 500-1900Ft, mains 960-2720Ft; ☽ 11am-midnight Mon-Sat) A very upscale cellar eatery decorated in postmodern greys and blacks, the 'Comedian' is opposite the Béla Bartók Cultural Centre. It has courtyard seating, which is a delight in the warmer months, and there are good-value set menus (570Ft and 670Ft).

Ristorante Romantica (☎ 314 127; Dunakapu tér 5; starters 1125-3750Ft, pasta 1250-1875Ft, mains 1850-3850Ft) The name might be hyperbole but the RR is a lovely restaurant just down from the river, with superb Italian food and an eye for detail.

Szürkebarát Borozó (☎ 311 548; Arany János utca 20; soups & starters 250-600Ft, mains 750-2600Ft; ☽ 9am-10pm Mon-Fri, 9am-4pm Sat) A decent wine cellar–restaurant in a small courtyard, where you'll also find a small kiosk selling very popular

---

AUTHOR'S CHOICE

Veszti (☎ 337 700; Móricz Zsigmond rakpart 3; soups 440-640Ft, starters 460-1690Ft, mains 990-1990Ft; ☽ 10.30am-10pm Mon-Thu, 10.30am-midnight Fri, 10.30am-2am Sat, 10.30am-3pm Sun) It hardly serves what you'd call *haute gourmande* food, but this jack-of-all-trades eatery, on an atmospheric old riverboat on the Mosoni-Danube River, has everything from Hungarian mains to pizza (490Ft to 1490Ft) and Tex-Mex (1290Ft to 1690Ft). It attracts a fun crowd and the service is right on the ball.

---

ice cream for 100Ft per scoop. The restaurant also does breakfast (350 Ft to 600Ft) and there's a set menu at lunch (530Ft).

Zita Süteménybolt (☎ 323 180; Jókai utca 6/a; cakes 100-120Ft; ☽ variable) For something sweet don't go by this window dispensing cakes and pastries. It's so popular that people sometime have to queue up along the footpath.

QUICK EATS & SELF-CATERING

Márka (☎ 320 800; Bajcsy-Zsilinszky út 30; dishes 250-540Ft; ☽ 11am-5pm Mon-Sat) A modernised cafeteria and a good choice for a cheap self-service meal in the centre of town.

A very small but colourful open-air **market** (Dunakapu tér) is held most mornings. Shops selling foodstuffs and sundries:

ABC nonstop shop (Révai Miklós utca; ☽ 24hr) Next to the train station.

Belváros nonstop shop (Schweidel utca 27; ☽ 10am-6am)

Kaiser supermarket (Arany János utca 16; ☽ 7.30am-7pm Mon, 6.30am-7pm Tue-Fri, 6.30am-3pm Sat)

Drinking

Captain Drake's Pub (☎ 312 686; Radó sétány 1; ☽ noon-midnight Sun-Thu, noon-2am Fri & Sat) A relaxing spot for a drink on the little island in the Rába River.

20th Century Café (☎ 312 819; Schweidel utca 25; ☽ 7am-midnight Sun-Thu, 7am-5am Fri & Sat) This very central café promotes itself as a cocktail bar and caters to a more mature crowd.

Entertainment

A good source of information for what's on in Győr is the free fortnightly magazine *Győri Est*.

Győr National Theatre (Győri Nemzeti Színház; ☎ 520 600, 314 800, ticket office 520 611; www.gyoriszinhaz.hu in Hungarian; Czuczor Gergely utca 7; ☽ 10am-1pm Mon, 10am-1pm & 2-6pm Tue-Fri) This is a modern, technically advanced though rather unattractive structure covered in Op Art tiles by the promoter of the style Victor Vasarely. The celebrated **Győr Ballet** (www.gyoribalett.hu), the city's opera company and the **philharmonic orchestra** (☎ ticket office 326 323; Kisfaludy utca 25; ☽ 8am-noon & 1-4.30pm Mon-Wed & Fri, 8am-noon & 1-5pm Thu) all perform here.

Amnésia (☎ 06 30 402 2411; Szövetség utca 12; ☽ 10am-midnight Mon-Wed, 10am-2am Thu & Fri, 2pm-2am Sat, 4pm-midnight Sun) A popular bar-cum-club with theme nights – 'Italo Disco Night' anyone? – that attracts a student crowd.

Hullám Disco Klub (☎ 315 276; Hédervári utca 22; ☼ 10pm-5am Fri & Sat) This weekend-only dance club just a few metres away from Amnésia has DJs and a Moroccan-themed restaurant, with food available till 4am.

Getting There & Away

BUS

Buses depart from Győr for the following places:

Destination	Price	Duration	Km	Frequency
Balatonfüred	1210Ft	2½hr	100	7 daily
Budapest	1570Ft	1hr 5min	128	12-16 daily
Dunaújváros	1690Ft	2½-3hr	137	5 daily
Esztergom	1210Ft	2½hr	99	1-2 daily
Hévíz	1570Ft	3hr	124	2 daily
Kapuvár	605Ft	1hr 10min	50	half-hourly
Keszthely	1570Ft	3¼hr	129	4 daily
Lébény	302Ft	30min	23	8-12 daily
Mosonmagyaróvár	484Ft	50min	39	up to 12 daily
Pannonhalma	302Ft	30min	21	half-hourly
Pápa	605Ft	1hr	48	10 daily
Pécs	3020Ft	4-5hr	243	2 daily
Sümeg	1210Ft	2¼hr	99	4 daily
Székesfehérvár	1090Ft	1½hr	86	7 daily
Szombathely	1330Ft	2½hr	110	5-7 daily
Tapolca	1330Ft	2½hr	106	2-3 daily
Tata	786Ft	1½hr	64	3 daily
Veszprém	968Ft	1½hr	79	9 daily
Vienna	1918Ft	2hr	129	2-3 daily
Zalaegerszeg	2060Ft	4hr	165	5 daily

TRAIN

Győr is the main train junction after Budapest. It has convenient connections with Budapest (1338Ft, 1½ to two hours, 131km, half-hourly) and Vienna (4750Ft, 1½ hours, 119km, six to eight daily) via Hegyeshalom. Trains to Ebenfurth in Austria via Sopron are run by GySEV, which isn't part of the MÁV system; they are less frequent.

You can also reach Szombathely (1142Ft, 1½ to two hours, 117km, eight daily) by train via Celldömölk or Csorna and the gateway to the Balaton region, Veszprém (739Ft, two hours, 79km, four or five daily) via Pannonhalma and Zirc. If heading for Slovakia, change trains at Komárom (326Ft, 30 minutes, 37km, hourly).

Getting Around

You can easily reach Kiskúti Camping on bus 8 from beside the city hall on Városház

tér, where a number of other local buses also stop.

Parking is difficult (and costly) in Győr and the one-way system very confusing for the uninitiated. Avoid driving in the city if at all possible. Local taxis are available on ☎ 444 444.

PANNONHALMA
☎ 96 / pop 4090

Since the late 10th century, this small village 21km southeast of Győr has been the site of a Benedictine abbey, which even managed to continue functioning during the darkest days of Stalinism. Its secondary school, founded in 1802 and attended by more than 300 students, is among the best in the country. In 1996 the abbey received the distinction of being added to Unesco's World Heritage List and is now one of the most impressive historical complexes in Hungary.

History

The monastery was founded by monks from Venice and Prague with the assistance of Prince Géza. The Benedictines were considered a militant order, and Géza's son, King Stephen, used them to help convert the Magyars to Christianity.

The abbey and associated buildings have been razed, rebuilt and restored many times over the centuries; it escaped damage during the Turkish occupation when it was used as a mosque. As a result, the complex is a patchwork of architectural styles.

Orientation

Pannonhalma is dominated by Várhegy (Castle Hill) and the abbey. Most buses from Győr stop in the village centre; from here follow Váralja up to the abbey. About four or five buses continue up the eastern side of the hill and stop at the abbey's main entrance.

The train station is a few kilometres west of the village off Petőfi utca in the direction of Rte 82.

Information

Main post office (Dózsa György utca 7; ☼ 8am-4pm Mon-Fri) Also does foreign exchange.

OTP bank (Dózsa György utca 1)

Tourinform (☎ /fax 471 733; pannonhalma@tourinform.hu; Petőfi utca 25; ☼ 9am-4pm Mon-Fri) Inconveniently located about 600m south of Szabadság tér at the Ferenc Kazinczy Cultural Centre.

Sights

Pannonhalma Abbey (Pannonhalmi főapátság; ☎ 570 191; www.bences.hu; Vár utca 1; ☺ 9am-4pm Tue-Sun late Mar-May & Oct–mid-Nov, 9am-5pm Jun-Sep, 10am-3pm Tue-Sun mid-Nov–late Mar) was spruced up for its 1000th birthday in 1996. After buying your ticket at the reception building opposite the car park and watching a 15-minute film about life in the monastic community, follow the overhead walkway to the central courtyard, where the tour begins. In the centre you'll see a statue of the first abbot, Asztrik, who brought the crown of King Stephen to Hungary from Rome, and a relief of King Stephen himself presenting his son Imre to the tutor Bishop Gellért. To the north are dramatic views of the Kisalföld, while looming behind you are the abbey's modern wings and a neoclassical clock tower built in the early 19th century.

The entrance to **St Martin's Basilica** (Szent Márton-bazilika), built early in the 12th century, is through the **Porta Speciosa**. This arched doorway in red limestone was re-carved in the mid-19th century by the Stornos, a controversial family of restorers who imposed 19th-century Romantic notions of Romanesque and Gothic architecture on medieval buildings (see p165); it is beautiful despite the butchery. The fresco above the doorway by Ferenc Storno depicts the church's patron, St Martin of Tours, giving half his cloak to a crouching beggar. Look down to the right below the columns and you'll see what is probably the oldest graffiti in Hungary: 'Benedict Padary was here in 1578', in Latin.

As you walk along the cloister arcade, you'll notice the little faces carved in stone on the wall. They represent human emotions and vices, such as wrath, greed and conceit, and are meant to remind monks of the baseness and transitory nature of human existence. In the cloister garden a Gothic sundial offers a sobering thought: 'Una Vestrum, Ultima Mea' (One of you will be my last).

The most beautiful part of the abbey is the neoclassical **abbey library** (főapátság könyvtára) built in 1836 by János Packh, who was involved in designing the Esztergom Basilica. It contains some 300,000 volumes – many of them priceless historical records – making it the largest private library in Hungary. But the rarest and most important document is in the abbey archives.

It is the *Deed of Foundation* of Tihany Abbey and dates from 1055. It is written in Latin, but also contains about 50 Hungarian place names, making it the earliest surviving example of written Hungarian. The library's interior may look like marble, but it is actually wood made to look like the more expensive stone. An ingenious system of mirrors within the skylights reflects and redirects natural light throughout the room.

The **art gallery** *(képtár)* off the library contains works by Dutch, Italian and Austrian masters from the 16th to 18th centuries. The oldest work, however, goes back to 1350.

Because it still functions as a monastery, the abbey must be visited with a guide. Tours in Hungarian (with foreign-language text) go on the hour between 9am and 5pm daily from June to September, and in English and four other languages (Italian, German, French and Russian) at 11.20am, 1.20 and 3.20pm. From late March to May and October to mid-November they leave on the hour between 9am and 4pm Tuesday to Sunday, with tours in other languages only available at 11.20am and 1.20pm. In winter tours in Hungarian occur five times daily Tuesday to Sunday (10am to 3pm); those in other languages are by request only.

Activities

Oázis Bikerent at the Familia *pension* has **bicycles** (per day 1500Ft) for hire. Ask Tourinform for a copy of *Cycling in West Transdanubia: Pannonhalma-Sokoró*, which includes three cycle tours of the area between 45km and 56km long.

Festivals & Events

Six **organ and choral concerts** are scheduled between April and December in the basilica – always at the same time, 3.30pm, and on the same dates: Easter Monday, Whit Monday, St Stephen's Day (20 August), Virgin Mary's Birthday (Saturday before/after 8 September), National Day (23 October) and 26 December. See www.bences.hu for details.

Sleeping

Pannon (☎ /fax 470 041; www.hotels.hu/pannon; Hunyadi út 7/c; s/d/tr/q 6200/8300/9800/11,000Ft; Ⓟ) A relatively large guesthouse – with 16 rooms, it's almost a small hotel – on the way up the hill to the abbey. The surrounding garden is a plus.

Família (☎ /fax 570 592; http://w3.enternet.hu/fa
miliap; Béke utca 61; s/d/tr/q 3750/5500/6750/9000Ft;
P) This seven-room, very homey *pension*
has a small kitchen and lounge available for
guests' use, and there are bicycles for rent.
You'll find it on Rte 82 as you enter the
town from the north.

Fazekas Vendégház (☎ /fax 470 157; Kisfaludy
utca 1; d/tr 4300/5800Ft; **P**) This very simple
B&B, with four rooms just opposite the
Tourinform office, is about the closest Pan-
nonhalma has to budget accommodation.
It's comfortable but basic.

Eating & Drinking

Pannon (☎ /fax 470 041; Hunyadi út 7/c; mains 900-
1950Ft; ☼ 12.30-9.30pm Tue-Sun) The restaurant
at this *pension* is a convenient place for a
meal going to or coming from the abbey.

Kolostor (☎ 470 012; Szabadság tér 1; soups 380-550Ft,
starters 680-1500Ft, mains 950-2680Ft; ☼ 10am-9pm Mon-
Thu, 10am-10pm Fri & Sat, 10am-5pm Sun) In a historic
building in the centre of town, this is the best
place in Pannonhalma for a meal.

Szent Márton (☎ 470 793; Vár utca 1; soups 400-
700Ft, starters 900-1500Ft, mains 800-2400Ft; ☼ 10am-
4pm) Below the abbey and at the back of the
car park, this place has a snack bar, pub and
gift shop, as well as a decent – if not ground-
breaking – restaurant.

While in town try some of the wine from
the nearby Pannonhalma-Sokoróalja region,
which produces some excellent white whites,
notably Rieslings; the abbey's vineyard produces some 300,000 bottles annually from
vines planted only in 2001.

Borbirodalom (Wine Empire; ☎ 471 240; Szabadság
tér 27; ☼ 11am-7pm) A good place to start is
this wine cellar and restaurant, diagonally
across from the Kolostor restaurant in the
town centre. It has an extensive selection
available for tasting (140Ft to 200Ft per
10cL, 350Ft to 500Ft per 25cL).

Getting There & Away

There are frequent buses to/from Győr
(302Ft, 30 minutes, 21km, half-hourly). The
first bus from Győr leaves for Pannonhalma
at 7.20am (8.50am Saturday and Sunday)
and the last bus from Pannonhalma to Győr
departs at 5.35pm daily.

Trains stop at Pannonhalma on their way
to Veszprém (512Ft, 1¾ hours, 58km, six
daily), usually from Győr (248Ft, 30 minutes, 21km, six to eight daily).

SOPRON

☎ 99 / pop 55,600

At the foot of the Lővér Hills and only
a couple of kilometres from Lake Fertő,
Fertő-Hanság National Park and Austria,
Sopron (German: Ödenburg) is one of the
most charming medieval cities in Hungary. With its preponderance of Gothic
and early baroque architecture, Sopron
is the closest city Hungary has to Prague
(though admittedly on a much smaller
scale), and exploring the backstreets and
courtyards of the Inner Town is like stepping back in time.

History

Sopron has had more wars, difficult deci-
sions and political rulings thrust upon it
than most other Hungarian cities. Indeed
as recently as 1921 its citizens had to vote
whether to stay in Austria's Bürgenland as
a result of the Trianon Treaty (see p29) or
be reannexed by Hungary. They resound-
ingly chose the latter, which explains the
little knot of Hungarian territory that juts
into Austria.

First to arrive in the area were the
Celts, then came the Romans, who lived
in a settlement called Scarbantia (now Sopron's Inner Town) between the 1st and
4th centuries. The Germans, Avars, Slavs
and the Magyars followed in succession.
In medieval times Sopron was ideally situated for trade along the so-called Amber
Route from the Baltic Sea to the Adriatic
and Byzantium. By the 1300s, after a century of struggle between the Hungarians
and the Austrians for hegemony over the
city, Sopron had been made a royal free
town – its mixed population able to pursue
their trades without pressure from feudal
landlords. Thus a strong middle class of
artisans and merchants emerged here, and
their wealth contributed to making Sopron
a centre of science and education.

Neither the Mongols nor Turks were able
to penetrate the heart of Sopron, which is
why so many old buildings still stand. But
damage during WWII was extensive – the
area saw much restoration work done in
the 1960s.

Orientation

The medieval Belváros, or Inner Town,
shaped vaguely like a shoeprint, contains

almost everything of interest, though there are a few worthy sights across the narrow Ikva Stream to the northeast, just beyond the city walls. The Lővér Hills start about 4km southwest of the city. Várkerület and Ógabona tér form a ring around the Inner Town, roughly following the city's Roman and medieval walls.

Sopron's main train station (Map p167) is on Állomás utca, about 800m south of the Inner Town. Sopron-Déli train station (Map p167), through which trains to/from Szombathely also pass, is to the northwest of the Sopron train station. The bus station is just northwest of the Inner Town on Lackner Kristóf utca.

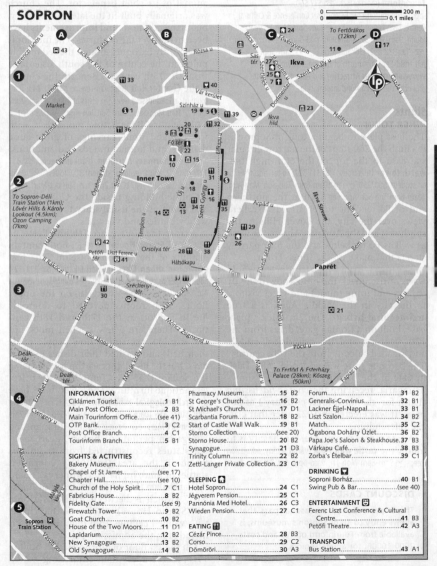

INFORMATION	
Ciklámen Tourist	1 B1
Main Post Office	2 B3
Main Tourinform Office	(see 41)
OTP Bank	3 C2
Post Office Branch	4 C1
Tourinform Branch	5 B1

SIGHTS & ACTIVITIES	
Bakery Museum	6 C1
Chapel of St James	(see 17)
Chapter Hall	(see 10)
Church of the Holy Spirit	7 C1
Fabricius House	8 B2
Fidelity Gate	(see 9)
Firewatch Tower	9 B2
Goat Church	10 B2
House of the Two Moors	11 D1
Lapidarium	12 B2
New Synagogue	13 B2
Old Synagogue	14 B2

Pharmacy Museum	15 B2
St George's Church	16 B2
St Michael's Church	17 D1
Scarbantia Forum	18 B2
Start of Castle Wall Walk	19 B1
Storno Collection	(see 20)
Storno House	20 B2
Synagogue	21 D3
Trinity Column	22 B2
Zettl-Langer Private Collection	23 C1

SLEEPING	
Hotel Sopron	24 C1
Jégverem Pension	25 C1
Pannónia Med Hotel	26 C3
Wieden Pension	27 C1

EATING	
Cézár Pince	28 B3
Corso	29 C2
Dömöröri	30 A3

Forum	31 B2
Generalis-Corvinius	32 B1
Lackner Éjjel-Nappal	33 B1
Liszt Szalon	34 B2
Match	35 C2
Ógabona Dohány Üzlet	36 B2
Papa Joe's Saloon & Steakhouse	37 B3
Várkapu Café	38 B3
Zorba's Ételbar	39 C1

DRINKING	
Soproni Borház	40 B1
Swing Pub & Bar	(see 40)

ENTERTAINMENT	
Ferenc Liszt Conference & Cultural Centre	41 B3
Petőfi Theatre	42 A3

TRANSPORT	
Bus Station	43 A1

Information

Ciklámen Tourist (☎ 312 694; fax 311 480; Ógabona tér 8; ☼ 8am-4.30pm Mon-Fri, 8am-noon Sat) On the road leading to the bus station.

Main post office (Széchenyi tér 7-8) South of the Inner Town; Inner Town branch (Várkerület 37; ☼ 8am-4pm Mon-Fri)

OTP bank (Várkerület 96/a)

Tourinform (main branch ☎ 517 560; sopron@tourinform.hu; Ferenc Liszt Conference & Cultural Centre, Liszt Ferenc utca 1; ☼ 9am-5pm Mon-Fri year-round, 9am-3pm Sat & Sun Jun–mid-Sep; Inner Town branch ☎ /fax 338 892; Előkapu utca 11; ☼ 9am-5pm Mon-Fri Jun–mid-Sep) Just north of the Inner Town.

www.sopron.hu Attractive and easy-to-use, with practical and background information.

Sights

INNER TOWN

The best place to begin a tour of Sopron is to climb the 200 steps of the narrow circular staircase to the top of the 60m-high **fire-watch tower** (tűztorony; ☎ 311 327; Fő tér; adult/senior or student 500/250Ft; ☼ 10am-8pm Tue-Sun May-Aug, 10am-6pm Tue-Sun Apr, Sep & Oct) at the northern end of Fő tér. The tower affords excellent views over the city, the Lővér Hills to the southwest and the Austrian Alps to the west, as well as Fő tér below and the four narrow streets that make up the Inner Town.

The tower, from which trumpeters would warn of fire, mark the hour (now done by chimes and tinny music) and greet visitors to the city in the Middle Ages, is a true architectural hybrid. The 2m-thick square base, built on a Roman gate, dates from the 12th century, and the cylindrical middle and arcaded balcony from the 16th century. The baroque spire was added in 1681. **Fidelity Gate** at the bottom of the tower shows 'Hungaria' receiving the *civitas fidelissima* (Latin for 'the most loyal citizenry') of Sopron. It was erected in 1922 after that crucial referendum.

Another way to get a feel for the city is to follow the **castle wall walk** (várfal sétány; admission free; ☼ 9am-8pm Mon-Fri, 9am-6pm Sat & Sun), but

---

DISCOUNT CARDS

The **Sopron Ticket**, a seasonal pass that allows entry to 10 of Sopron's museums, is available from Tourinform offices and costs 2000/1000Ft for adults/seniors.

---

since so much of it goes behind or between buildings you won't see as much.

The focal points of graceful Fő tér are the **Trinity Column** (1701), the best example of a 'plague pillar' in Hungary, and, on the south side of the square, the old **Goat Church** (Kecsketemplom; Templom utca 1; admission free; ☼ 8am-6pm), whose name comes from the heraldic animal of its chief benefactor. The church was originally built in the late 13th century, but many additions and improvements have been made over the centuries. The interior is now mostly baroque, though the red marble pulpit in the centre of the south aisle dates from the 15th century. Beneath the church is the **Chapter Hall** (Káptalan-terem; ☎ 338 843; Templom utca 1; admission free; ☼ visits at 10am, 11am, 2pm, 3pm & 4pm Mon-Sat, 11am Sun Jun-Aug) – part of a 14th-century Benedictine monastery, with frescoes and stone carvings of grotesques, demons, and human moods and emotions.

The **Pharmacy Museum** (Patikamúzeum; ☎ 311 327; Fő tér 2; adult/senior or student 300/150Ft; ☼ 10am-6pm Tue-Sun Apr-Sep, 10am-2pm Tue-Sun Oct-Mar) is in a Gothic building beside the Goat Church and contains the usual scary things in cobwebby bottles and vile vials.

Across the square are **Fabricius House** (Fő tér 6) and **Storno House** (Fő tér 8); both contain exhibits of the Sopron Museum. The first contains **urban flats** (polgári lakások; ☎ 311 327; adult/senior or student 500/250Ft; ☼ 10am-6pm Tue-Sun Apr-Sep, 10am-2pm Tue-Sun Oct-Mar) on the upper floors, with rooms devoted to domestic life in Sopron in the 17th and 18th centuries. There are a few kitchen mock-ups and exhibits explaining how people made their beds and washed their dishes in those days, but the highlights are the rooms facing the square that are crammed with priceless antique furniture. The lower floors have an **archaeological exhibition** (adult/senior or student 500/250Ft; ☼ 10am-6pm Tue-Sun Apr-Sep, 10am-2pm Tue-Sun Oct-Mar) covering Celtic, Roman and Hungarian periods of history. Scarbantia-era statues reconstructed from fragments found in the area (including enormous statues of Juno, Jupiter and Minerva), guard the **lapidarium** *(kőtár)* in the cellar of house No 7 (which is between Fabricius House and Storno House), once a Gothic chapel with vaulted ceilings 15m high. Entrance is included in the admission price.

On the 1st floor of Storno House, built in 1417, there's a less-than-enthralling exhibit on Sopron's more recent history, but on the floor above is the wonderful **Storno Collection** (Storno Gyűjtemény; ☎ 311 327; adult/senior or student 800/400Ft; ◷ 10am-6pm Tue-Sun Apr-Sep, 10am-2pm Tue-Sun Oct-Mar), which belonged to a 19th-century Swiss-Italian family of restorers whose re-carving of Romanesque and Gothic monuments throughout Transdanubia is frowned upon today. To their credit, the much ma-ligned Stornos did rescue many altarpieces and church furnishings from oblivion, and their house is a Gothic treasure-trove. High-lights include the beautiful enclosed balcony with leaded windows and frescoes, leather chairs with designs depicting Mephisto with his dragons, and door frames made from pews taken from 15th-century St George's Church on Szent György utca. Franz Liszt played a number of concerts in this house in the mid-19th century.

The **Scarbantia Forum** (☎ 321 804; Új utca 1; adult/senior or student 240/120Ft; ◷ 8am-5pm Mon-Thu, 8am-1.30pm Fri) is an original Roman-era mar-ketplace recently discovered under – and accessible through – an office block. If you carry on walking down Új utca – known as Zsidó utca (Jewish St) until the Jews were evicted from Sopron in 1526 – you'll reach the **Old Synagogue** (Ó Zsinagóga; ☎ 311 327; Új utca 22; adult/senior or student 400/200Ft; ◷ 10am-5pm Tue-Sun May-Sep, 10am-2pm Tue-Sun Oct) and the **New Syna-gogue** (Új Zsinagóga; Új utca 11). Both were built in the 14th century, and are among the greatest Jewish Gothic monuments in Europe; they are unique in Hungary. The Old Synagogue, now a museum, contains two rooms, one for each sex (note the women's windows along the west wall). The main room con-tains a medieval 'holy of holies' with geo-metric designs and trees carved in stone, and some ugly new stained-glass windows. The inscriptions on the walls date from 1490. There's a reconstructed *mikvah* (ritual bath) in the courtyard. The New Synagogue, which once formed part of a private house and of-fices, was recently renovated with EU funds and may soon be open to the public.

OTHER SIGHTS

Sopron's sights are not entirely confined to the Inner Town. Walk back to Fő tér, past the old Roman walls, under Előkapu and over a small bridge leading to Ikva, once a district of merchants and artisans. Your first stop should be the excellent **Zettl-Langer**

Private Collection (Zettl-Langer Magángyűjtemény; ☎ 311 136; Balfi út 11; admission 300Ft; ◷ 10am-noon Tue-Sun Apr-Oct, 10am-noon Fri-Sun Nov-Mar), contain-ing ceramics, paintings and furniture. It's the largest and most significant private col-lection on display in Hungary.

Heading northwards, on Dorfmeister utca, is the 15th-century **Church of the Holy Spirit** (Szentlélek-templom), worth a peek for its wall and ceiling frescoes. Further north at Szent Mihály utca 9 is the **House of the Two Moors** (Két mór ház). It was fashioned from two 17th-century peasant houses and is guarded by two large statues, which are now painted PC-white.

At the top of the hill, along Szent Mihály utca, is **St Michael's Church** (Szent Mihály-templom), built between the 13th and 15th centuries, and behind it to the south is the little Romanesque-Gothic **Chapel of St James** (Szent Jakab-kápolna), the oldest structure in Sopron and originally an ossuary. Not much escaped the Stornos' handiwork when they 'renovated' St Michael's – they even added the spire. Check out the lovely polychrome Stations of the Cross (1892) in the churchyard and the large number of tombstones with German family names.

If you return to the House of the Two Moors and walk west along Fövényverem utca, you'll soon reach Bécsi út and the **Bakery Museum** (Pékmúzeum; ☎ 311 327; Bécsi út 5; adult/senior or student 300/150Ft; ◷ 10am-2pm Tue-Sun May-Aug), a fantastic reminder of a bygone era. It's actually the completely restored home, bakery and shop of a successful 19th-century bread and pastry maker named Weissbeck, and contains some interesting gadgets and work-saving devices.

There's a crumbling **synagogue** (Paprét 14) east of the Inner Town. A new plaque tells passers-by that '1640 martyrs' were taken from here to Auschwitz on 5 July 1944.

Activities

Tóth & Fia (Map p167; ☎ 334 001, 06 20 935 7625; Bécsi utca 13; ◷ 9am-noon & 1-5pm Mon-Fri Nov-Mar, 8am-noon & 1-5pm Mon-Fri Apr-Oct, 9am-noon Sat), a cycle shop just down the hill from Bástya *pension*, rents bicycles for 1500Ft per day (3300/5500Ft three/five days).

Festivals & Events

Sopron is a musical town, and the high-lights of the season are the **Spring Days** in late

March, the **Sopron Festival Weeks** from mid-June to mid-July and the **International Choir Festival** in early July. Tickets to the various events are available from the ticket office in the Ferenc Liszt Conference and Cultural Centre. For details check the Events Calendar under Tourism at **Sopron** (www.sopron.hu).

Sleeping
BUDGET
Enquire at Ciklámen Tourist about private rooms (2500Ft per person), though there are very few available in the city centre.

Vakáció Vendégház Sopron (Map p167; ☎ 338 502; Ady Endre út 31; dm 2200Ft; P ✕) This brightly coloured place is one of the new brand of hostels in Hungary, with decent accommodation in 16 clean and well-furnished rooms of two to 10 beds. Bus 10 will drop you off right outside.

Özon Camping (☎ /fax 331 144; ozoncamping@sopron.hu; Erdei Malom köz 3; camp sites per large tent/small tent adult/child 1600/800/1200/850Ft; ✺ mid-Apr–mid-Oct; P) This delightful camping ground with 60 sites has everything you could want from fridges and washing machines to a pool and other sports facilities. Özon Camping is set in a leafy valley about 4.5km west of the Inner Town.

MIDRANGE
Jégverem Pension (☎ /fax 510 113; www.jegverem.hu; Jégverem utca 1; s 4990-5790Ft, d 7990-9590Ft, tr 9990-11,590Ft) This is an excellent and central bet, with five suite-like rooms in an 18th-century ice cellar in the Ikva district. The staff are exceptionally accommodating, and the restaurant comes highly recommended whether you're staying here or not.

Wieden Pension (☎ 523 222; www.wieden.hu; Sas tér 13; s €26-29, d €39-43, tr €55-61, apt for 4 people €61-70, apt for 8 people €106-115; P) This guesthouse is in a lovingly renovated old townhouse, and is the most plush of Sopron's *pensions* (though the dormer windows in most of the rooms are a minus). There are seven rooms and six apartments, four of them in the building opposite.

Bástya Pension (Map p167; ☎ 325 325; info@bastya-panzio.hu; Patak utca 40; s/d/tr/q 6000/9000/11,000/14,000Ft; P) A modern *pension* with 16 rooms, it's approximately a 10-minute walk north of the Inner Town up Szélmalom

utca. If you're coming by car, parking is easy here.

TOP END
Pannónia Med Hotel (☎ 312 180; www.pannonia-hotel.com; Várkerület 75; s €75, d €85-115, ste €115-130; P ⧆ ⧈ ✕) Sopron's grand century-old hotel and now part of the Best Western stable. The Pannónia has 62 renovated rooms and, on the 1st floor, a very green (as in the colour) wellness centre with pool, sauna and gym. If you really want to splash out, ask for one of the 14 suites with antique furnishings. The prices of the doubles depend on the room.

Hotel Sopron (☎ 512 261; www.hotelsopron.hu; Fövényverem utca 7; s €56-75, d €65-83, ste €145-250; P ✕ ⧈ ⧆) This sprawling place is up on Korońzó-domb (Coronation Hill), with views of the city and the Lővér Hills. It has 100 rooms as well as bars, a restaurant and the Vinosseum wine cellar. There are clay tennis courts and a small outdoor swimming pool to boot.

Eating
RESTAURANTS
Cézár Pince (☎ 311 337; Hátsókapu 12; dishes 340-850Ft; ✺ 11am-midnight Mon-Sat, 1-11pm Sun) Located in a medieval cellar in a historic building off Orsolya tér, 'Caesar's Cellar' is the best restaurant in Sopron for an inexpensive lunch or light meal. The platter of sausages and salad (850Ft) attracts the locals; chase it with a glass of Soproni Kékfrankos (a red) or a young white Zöldveltelini. There is courtyard seating over the summer months.

Generális-Corvinus (☎ 505 035; Fő tér 7-8; mains 990-2100Ft; ✺ 9am-11pm) With its café tables on

---

AUTHOR'S CHOICE

Jégverem (☎ /fax 510 113; www.jegverem.hu; Jégverem utca 1; soups 170-550Ft, starters 620-1550Ft, mains 860-1790Ft) This rustic *pension* restaurant, whose slogan is 'The Restaurant for Guzzle-guts' (we think they mean 'greedy-guts'), serves a huge selection of reasonably priced Hungarian dishes, some of them quite inventive, in portions that are enormous even by Hungarian standards. If you want to skip breakfast *and* lunch tomorrow, eat here tonight. And order the half-portions (where available).

the Inner Town's main square, the GC is a great place for a pizza (650Ft to 1700Ft) in the warmer months.

Corso (☎ 340 990; 1st fl, Várkerület 73; soups 290-320Ft, starters 440-740Ft, mains 990-1990Ft; ☒ 11am-10pm Mon-Thu, 11am-midnight Fri & Sat, 11am-5pm Sun) In the Korona shopping arcade next to the Pannónia Med Hotel, this place serves above-average Hungarian fare. Its two-course set menus (780Ft to 1290Ft) are excellent value.

Forum (☎ 340 231; Szent György utca 3; starters 350-1050Ft, mains 1090-2290Ft; ☒ 11am-10pm) This popular spot is great in the warmer months when tables spread out into a courtyard between two Inner Town streets. It serves the whole range, but we'd stick to pizza (650Ft to 1350Ft), pasta dishes (550Ft to 1100Ft) and/or the self-serve salad bar (small/large 350/420Ft).

Papa Joe's Saloon & Steak House (☎ 340 933; Várkerület 108; soups 270-520Ft, starters 650-1150Ft, mains 950-3200Ft; ☒ 11am-midnight Sun-Wed, 11am-2am Thu-Sat) If you're feeling ravenous (but don't fancy Hungarian at the Jégverem), head to Joe's for a steak (1500Ft to 3200Ft)

or some passable Tex-Mex (1210Ft to 1600Ft).

CAFÉS

Várkapu Café (☎ 311 523; Várkerület 108/a & Hátsókapu 3; cakes 140-260Ft; ☒ 7.30am-8pm Mon-Fri, 7.30am-10pm Sat) This old world–style coffeehouse is an excellent place for both cakes and coffee, and a relaxing oasis from the summer crowds.

Dömöröri (☎ 506 623; Széchenyi tér 13; ice cream per scoop 100Ft, cakes from 250Ft; ☒ 7am-10pm Mon-Thu, 7am-11pm Fri & Sat, 8am-10pm Sun) The queues lining up to get ice cream or a table here testify to the quality of its products. Don't miss out!

Liszt Szalon (☎ 323 407; Szent György utca 12; hot drinks 190-490Ft; ☒ 10am-10pm) Very stylish indeed is this new/old (just opened/ancient building) café serving a wide range of hot chocolates (with chilli, anyone?) as well as teas and coffees.

QUICK EATS & SELF-CATERING

Zorba's Ételbár (☎ 06 70 249 5454; Várkerület 40; gyros 490-690Ft, burgers 350-390Ft; ☒ 10am or 10.30am-1am)

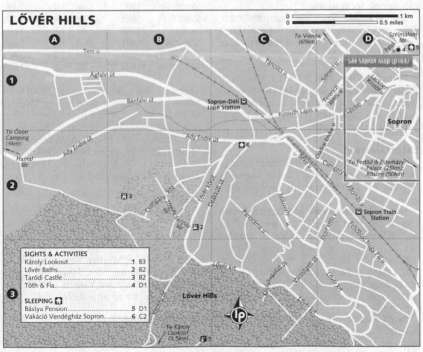

LŐVÉR HILLS

0 ———————— 1 km
0 ———————— 0.5 miles

See Sopron Map (p163)

SIGHTS & ACTIVITIES	
Károly Lookout............................1	B3
Lővér Baths.................................2	B2
Taródi Castle..............................3	B2
Tóth & Fia.................................4	D1

SLEEPING	
Bástya Pension...........................5	D1
Vakáció Vendégház Sopron............6	C2

WESTERN TRANSDANUBIA

This fast-food eatery serves passable gyros as well as burgers till the wee – for Sopron – hours, and there's a sitting area just opposite by the road.

Match (Várkerület 100-102; ☯ 6.30am-7pm Mon-Fri, 6.30am-4pm Sat) This is a central branch of the supermarket chain.

Sopron handily has two shops open round the clock within staring distance of one another:

Ógabona Dohány Üzlet (Ógabona tér 12; ☯ 24hr) Essentially a tobacconist and drinks shop.

Lackner Éjjel-Nappal (Lackner Kristóf utca 2; ☯ 24hr) The usual necessities available here.

Drinking

The Sopron region is noted for its red wines, especially Kékfrankos and Merlot. Many – but not all by any means – are cheap and high in acid and tannin, so watch your intake if you don't want a massive *macskajaj* ('cat's wail' – Hungarian for 'hangover') the next day. Tourinform distributes a pamphlet called *A Soproni Bor Útja* (The Sopron Wine Road), which lists vintners throughout the region where you can sample local wines.

Soproni Borház (Sopron Wine House; ☎ 510 022; Várkerület 15; ☯ 11am-11pm Tue-Sat) Sopron's largest cellar and wine shop, and the best place in town to try the local vintages and/or buy a bottle.

Swing Pub & Bar (☎ 06 20 214 8029; Várkerület 15; ☯ 5pm-midnight Sun-Fri, 5pm-2am Sat) This popular place in the same courtyard as the Soproni Borház is a good spot to catch live music, particularly jazz, nightly.

Entertainment

For more up-to-date entertainment listings on Sopron, get hold of freebie biweekly *Soproni Est* or the monthly *Soproni Program Ajánló*.

Ferenc Liszt Conference and Cultural Centre (☎ 517 500, ticket office 517 517; www.prokultura .hu; Liszt Ferenc utca 1; ☯ 9am-5pm Mon-Fri, 9am-noon Sat) This newly renovated venue facing Széchenyi tér contains a theatre, concert hall, casino and restaurant, and hosts some of the most important music and other cultural events in Sopron. Contact Tourinform for details.

Petőfi Theatre (☎ 511 738; Petőfi tér 1) This beautiful theatre with National Romantic–style mosaics on the front façade is just

around the corner from the Ferenc Liszt Conference and Cultural Centre.

Getting There & Away

BUS

The bus service to/from Sopron:

Destination	Price	Duration	Km	Frequency
Balatonfüred	1930Ft	4hr	158	2 daily
Budapest	2660Ft	3¾hr	218	4 daily
Esztergom	2300Ft	4hr	190	1 daily
Fertőd	363Ft	45min	28	half-hourly
Fertőrákos	182Ft	20min	11	half-hourly
Győr	1150Ft	1½hr	94	half-hourly
Hévíz	1690Ft	2½-3hr	132	1-2 daily
Kaposvár	2780Ft	4½hr	220	1 daily
Kapuvár	544Ft	1hr	45	half-hourly
Keszthely	1690Ft	2½-3hr	138	1-2 daily
Komárom	1690Ft	2¾hr	137	1 daily
Kőszeg	725Ft	1hr 20min	59	6 daily
Nagycenk	241Ft	20min	15	half-hourly
Nagykanizsa	2170Ft	4¼hr	179	2 daily
Pécs	3510Ft	5½hr	285	1 daily
Sárvár	786Ft	1½hr	62	3 daily
Sümeg	1330Ft	2½-3½hr	107	3 daily
Székesfehérvár	2170Ft	4½hr	182	2 daily
Szombathely	968Ft	1¾hr	76	up to 6 daily
Tapolca	2060Ft	4hr	170	1 daily
Tatabánya	1930Ft	2¾hr	160	1 daily
Veszprém	1690Ft	3½hr	138	3 daily
Zalaegerszeg	1570Ft	3hr	129	2 daily

There are also buses to Vienna (2000Ft, 1¼ hours, 66km), with an 8am bus on Monday to Friday (Saturday late June to September only) and extra departures at 9.25am Monday, Thursday and Friday. Also, buses go to Munich (9300Ft, seven hours, 496km) and Stuttgart (13,700Ft, 10½ hours, 728km) on Thursday (8.05pm) and Sunday (9.05pm).

TRAIN

There are express trains to Budapest (2656Ft, 2¾ hours, 216km, five daily) via Győr and Komárom. Local trains run to Szombathely (620Ft, 1¼ hours, 62km, up to 12 daily) and Wiener Neustadt in Austria (1900Ft, 40 minutes, 34km, five daily), where you change for Vienna (3850Ft, 1¼ hours, 84km, up to nine daily).

Getting Around

Bus 12, from the bus and train stations, circles the Inner Town. For the Vakáció hostel, take bus 10 from the bus station. Bus 3 goes to Ózon Camping. You can call a local taxi on ☎ 555 555, 313 313 or 06 80 626 626.

AROUND SOPRON
Lővér Hills
This range of 300m- to 400m-high foot-hills of the Austrian Alps, some 5km south and southwest of the city centre, is Sopron's playground. It's a great place for hiking and walking, but is not without bitter memories, for it was here that partisans and Jews were executed by Nazis and the fascist Hungarian Arrow Cross during WWII. You can climb to the top of **Károly Lookout** (Károly kilátótorony; ☎ 313 080; adult/child or student 250/150Ft; ☽ 9am-8pm May-Aug, 9am-7pm Sep, 9am-6pm Apr & Oct, 9am-5pm Mar, 9am-4pm Nov-Feb Tue-Sun) on the hill (394m) west of the Lővér hotel; walk to **Taródi Castle** (Csalogány köz 8; adult/student 500/300Ft; ☽ variable), a 'self-built private castle' owned by the ob-sessed Taródi family and a pack-rat's delight; or, visit the **Lővér Baths** (☎ 510 964; Lővér körút 82; adult/child day 650/375Ft, half-day 430/280Ft; ☽ covered pools 5.30am-7pm Mon-Fri, 9am-8pm Sat & Sun year-round, sauna & solarium 2-7.30pm Mon-Fri, 10am-7pm Sat & Sun year-round, outside pools 9am-8pm late May–mid-Sep).

FERTŐD
☎ 99 / pop 3400
Some 27km east of Sopron, Fertőd has been associated with the aristocratic Esterházy fam-ily since the mid-18th century when Miklós, proclaiming that 'Anything the (Habsburg) emperor can afford, I can afford too', began construction of the largest and most opu-lent summer palace in central Europe. When completed in 1766, it boasted 126 rooms, a separate opera house, a hermitage (complete with a real-live cranky old man in a sack cloth who wanted to be left alone), temples to Diana and Venus, a Chinese dance house, a puppet theatre and a 250-hectare garden laid out in the French manner. Fertőd – or Esterháza as it was known until the middle of the 20th century – was on the map.

History
Much has been written about the Esterházy Palace and many hyperbolic monikers be-stowed on it (the 'Hungarian Versailles' is the most common). But the fact remains that this baroque and rococo structure – its architects unknown except for the Austrian Melchior Hefele – is the most beautiful palace in Hungary and much of it is now under renovation. While the rooms are for the most part bare, history is very much alive here. Many of the works of composer Franz Joseph Haydn (a 30-year resident of the palace) were first performed in the Concert Hall, including the *Farewell Symphony*. In the Chinoiserie Rooms Empress Maria Theresa attended a masked ball in 1773, and in the French Garden Miklós 'the Splendour Lover' threw some of the greatest parties of all time for friends like Goethe, complete with fireworks and tens of thou-sands of Chinese lanterns.

After a century and a half of neglect (it was used as stables in the 19th century and a hospital during WWII), the palace has been partially restored to its former glory and renovations are continuing.

Orientation
The palace and its gardens on Joseph Haydn utca (formerly Béla Bartók utca) dominate the town; buses stop almost in front of the main gate. The town centre is 700m to the west. Fertőszéplak train station is 1.5km to the west, but is of little use to most travel-lers. The station at Fertőszentmiklós (on the Sopron–Győr line) is 4km to the south.

Information
OTP bank (Fő utca 7; ☽ 7.45am-noon & 12.30-3pm Mon-Thu, 7.45am-noon Fri)
Post office (Fő utca 6; ☽ 8am-4pm Mon-Fri)
Tourinform (☎ /fax 370 544; fertod@tourinform.hu; Joseph Hayden utca 3; ☽ 10am-5pm Mon-Fri, 10am-4pm Sat & Sun mid-Jun–mid-Sep, 9am-4pm Mon-Fri mid-Sep–mid-Jun) In the east wing of the Grenadier House.

Sights & Activities
About two-dozen renovated rooms at the horseshoe-shaped **Esterházy Palace** (☎ 537 640; Joseph Haydn utca 2; adult/senior or student/family 1000/600/2500Ft; ☽ 10am-6pm Tue-Sun mid-Mar–Oct, 10am-4pm Fri-Sun Nov–mid-Mar) are open to the public; the rest of the huge complex houses a hotel and a secondary school.

As you approach the main entrance to the so-called **Courtyard of Honour**, notice the ornamental wrought-iron gate, a master-piece of the rococo. You can only tour the palace with a guide, but armed with a fact sheet in English (available from the ticket office), try to lag behind and explore the rooms away from the crowds.

On the ground floor of the palace you'll pass through several rooms decorated in the pseudo-Chinese style that was all the rage in the late 18th century; the pillared **Sala Terrena**, which served as the summer dining room, with its floor of cool Carrara marble and Miklós Esterházy's monogram in floral frescoes on the ceiling; and the **Prince's Bed Chamber**, with paintings of Amor. On the 1st floor are more sumptuous baroque and rococo salons as well as the lavish **Concert Hall** and **Ceremonial Hall**, which lead on to one another. There's also an exhibit dedicated to the life and times of Haydn.

The apartment where Haydn lived, off and on, from 1761 to 1790 in the west wing of the baroque **Music House** (Muzsikaház; Madach sétány 1), southwest of the palace, now contains the **Joseph Haydn Memorial Hall** (Joseph Haydn Emlékszoba; ☎ 537 043; adult/senior or student 200/100Ft; ✆ 9am-5pm Mon-Fri May-Aug) on the 1st floor, a veritable temple to the great Austrian composer.

The area around Fertőd is great for cycling, and you can rent **bicycles** (per day 1500Ft) at Dori Hotel and Camping. Ask Tourinform for the map/brochure *Kerékpárral Nyugat-Pannóniában* (By Bicycle in Western Pannonia).

Festivals & Events

Two major musical events at the palace are the **Haydn Festival of the Budapest Strings** in July and the more established **Haydn Festival** in late August/early September. For information on both check www.artsfestivals .hu. Both are usually booked out months in advance, but you might try your luck at Tourinform.

Sleeping

Kastély (☎ 537 640; esterhazy@enternet.hu; Esterházy Palace, Joseph Haydn utca 2; d/tr/q 4900/6400/7200Ft; ℗) This 17-room hotel on the 2nd floor of the palace's east wing is one of the main reasons people come to Fertőd and the palace. You won't be sleeping in anything like the Prince's Bed Chamber, but for a palace the price is right. Book well in advance.

Bagatelle (☎ 06 30 378 5423; Lés erdő) The truly romantic should ask about the Bagatelle, a separate pavilion in the park and arboretum behind the palace with four apartments.

Újvári (☎ /fax 537 097; ujvaripanzio@freestart.hu; Kossuth Lajos utca 57/a; s 5700-5900Ft, d 7800-8200Ft,

tr 11,100-11,400Ft; ℗) This very welcoming *pension* has six rooms as well as a massage and reflexology studio downstairs. It's in Fertőd-Sarród, about 120m north of the post office.

Dori Hotel & Camping (☎ /fax 370 838; www.hotels .hu/dori; Pomogyi út 1; camp sites per tent/adult/child/car 590/690/550/590Ft, s/d/tr bungalows 6600/9800/13,200Ft, s/d/tr hotel rooms 6400/9800/13,200Ft; ℗) This large complex on the edge of a wood just 100m north of the palace has a good range of accommodation and is a great base to enjoy such activities in the area as cycling and walking.

Eating

Two very convenient restaurants for a bite to eat are both located in Grenadier House, the former living quarters of the grenadier guards opposite the palace.

Gránátos (☎ 370 944; Joseph Haydn utca 1; starters 490-850Ft, mains 990-1790Ft; ✆ 9am-10pm) Rather dark interior and very popular with Austrian groups.

Kastélykert (☎ 349 418; Joseph Haydn utca 1; mains 1190-1790Ft; ✆ 10am-10pm) The more relaxed option, with a good-value set menu (1030Ft) available throughout the day.

Coop (Fő utca 5; ✆ 6am-5pm Mon, 6am-6pm Tue-Fri, 6am-1pm Sat) A branch of the ubiquitous supermarket chain, next to the OTP bank.

Getting There & Away

Frequent bus services serve Sopron (363Ft, 45 minutes, 28km, half-hourly), as well as Győr (846Ft, 1½ hours, 67km, two to four daily) and Kapuvár (302Ft, 30 minutes, 21km, half-hourly).

Trains link Fertőszentmiklós to the south of Fertőd with Sopron (248Ft, 20 minutes, 24km, up to 12 daily) and Győr (620Ft, one hour, 61km, up to 10 daily).

NAGYCENK

☎ 99 / pop 1700
Only 14km west of Fertőd and the Esterházy Palace, but light years away in spirit, lies Nagycenk, site of the ancestral mansion of the Széchenyi clan. No two houses – or families – could have been more different than these. While the privileged, often frivolous Esterházys held court in their imperial palace, the Széchenyis – democrats and reformers all – went about their work in a sombre neoclassical manor house that

aptly reflected their temperament and sense of purpose. The mansion has been completely renovated and part of it has been turned into a superb museum dedicated to the family. It's a must for those who want to understand Hungarian history and put things in perspective.

History

The Széchenyi family's public-spiritedness started with patriarch Ferenc, who donated his entire collection of books and *objets d'art* to the state in 1802, laying the foundations for the National Library now named in his honour. But it was his son, István (1791–1860), who made the greatest impact of any Hungarian on the economic and cultural development of the nation. For more information, see boxed text below.

Orientation

The train station is near the centre of town, southwest of the Széchenyi mansion, not far from the neo-Romanesque St Stephen's Church, designed by Miklós Ybl in 1864, and the Széchenyi family's mausoleum. The bus from Sopron stops close to the mansion's main gate.

Sights

The entrance to the **Széchenyi Memorial Museum** (Széchenyi Emlékmúzeum; ☎ 360 023; www .nagycenk.hu; Kiscenki utca 3; adult/senior or student 500/250Ft; ☯ 10am-6pm Tue-Sun Apr-Oct, 10am-5pm Tue-Sun Nov-Mar) is in the mansion through the Sala Terrena – it's almost austere compared with the similarly named hall at the Esterházy Palace in Fertőd. There's a taped commentary in several languages (including English) in each room; just press the button.

The rooms on the museum's ground floor, furnished with period pieces, trace the Széchenyi family and their political development, from typical baroque aristocrats in the 18th century to key players in the 1848 War of Independence and István's involvement in the ill-fated government of Lajos Batthyány. A sweeping baroque staircase leads to the exhibits on the 1st floor – a veritable temple to István's many accomplishments – from Budapest's Chain Bridge and the Danube and Tisza Rivers' engineering works, to steamboat and rail transport. There's also an interesting exhibition on Hungarian coinage.

THE GREATEST HUNGARIAN

The contributions of Count István Széchenyi were enormous and extremely varied. In his seminal 1830 work *Hitel* (meaning 'credit' and based on *hit* or 'trust'), he advocated sweeping economic reforms and the abolition of serfdom (he himself had distributed the bulk of his property to landless peasants two years earlier).

The Chain Bridge, the design of which Széchenyi helped push through Parliament, was the first link between Buda and Pest, and for the first time everyone, nobles included, had to pay a toll to use it.

Széchenyi was instrumental in straightening the serpentine Tisza River, which rescued half of Hungary's arable land from flooding and erosion, and his work made the Danube navigable as far as the Iron Gates in Romania.

He arranged the financing for Hungary's first train lines (from Budapest to Vác in the north and Szolnok in the east, and west to what is now Wiener Neustadt in Austria), and launched the first steam transport on the Danube and Lake Balaton.

A lover of all things English, Széchenyi got the upper classes interested in horse racing with the express purpose of improving breeding stock for farming.

A large financial contribution made by Széchenyi led to the establishment of the nation's prestigious Academy of Science.

Széchenyi became part of Lajos Batthyány's revolutionary government in 1848, but political squabbling and open conflict with Vienna caused him to lose control and he suffered a nervous breakdown. Despite a decade of convalescence in an asylum, Széchenyi never fully recovered and tragically took his own life in 1860.

For all his accomplishments, Széchenyi's contemporary and fellow reformer, Lajos Kossuth, called him 'the greatest Hungarian'. This dynamic but troubled visionary retains that accolade to this day.

It is fitting that the mansion of a railway developer like István Széchenyi is near an open-air **Locomotive Outdoor Museum** (Mozdony Skanzen; admission free; ☿ 24hr), with steam engines that were still in use on main lines as late as 1950. You can actually ride a **narrow-gauge train** for 5.5km to Fertőboz and back (steam/diesel-powered one way adult 310/240Ft, child 155/120Ft). Departures between April and early October from the Kastély train station at Nagycenk are at 9.50am and 11.15am and 2pm, 3.35pm and 5.35pm on Saturday and Sunday only. All except the last turn around at Fertőboz in less than half an hour for the return trip to Kastély. There are also shorter trips to Barátság (3.3km, departures at 1.15pm and 5.05pm), which cost the same.

A 2.6km **row of linden trees** opposite the mansion's main gate, planted by István's grandmother in 1754, leads to a **hermitage**. Like the Esterházys, the Széchenyi family had a resident loner who, in this case, was expected to earn his keep by ringing the chapel bell and tending the garden.

The **Széchenyi Mausoleum** (☎ 360 059; Széchenyi tér; adult/senior or student 200/100Ft; ☿ 10am-6pm Tue-Sun May-Oct), the final resting place of István and other family members and a great place of pilgrimage for Hungarians, is in the village cemetery across the road from St Stephen's Church.

Sleeping & Eating

Kastély (☎ /fax 360 061; www.kastelyszallo.try.hu; Kiscenki utca 3; s €35-75, d €56-87, tr €68-100, ste for 2 €84-125; P ✕) In the west wing of the mansion, this beautifully appointed 19-room inn has recently got a facelift and rates vary wildly depending on the season and the room type. If you can afford it opt for room No 106 or 107, which are large suites with period furniture and restful views of the 6-hectare garden. Rates include entrance to the museum. The splendid dining room (starters 750Ft to 900Ft, mains 1650Ft to 3500Ft; open 7am to 10pm) at the Kastély is the place for lunch in these parts, and there are outdoor tables in the hotel's splendid courtyard in summer.

Getting There & Away

Nagycenk is accessible from Sopron (241Ft, 20 minutes, 15km, half-hourly) by frequent bus. The village is on the train line linking Sopron (170Ft, 15 minutes, 12km, up to a dozen daily) and Szombathely (404Ft, one hour, 50 minutes, up to a dozen daily).

If you time it right, you can reach Nagycenk by the narrow gauge train. Take the bus from Sopron to Fertőboz and board the train for Kastély at 10.35am or at 12.15pm, 3pm or 4.15pm.

SZOMBATHELY

☎ 94 / pop 80,200

Szombathely (German: Steinamanger) is a major crossroads in western Hungary, and most travellers in Western Transdanubia will eventually find themselves passing though it. That's not such a bad thing, as there is plenty to see and do here.

The city's name (*som*-bot-hay) translates as 'Saturday Place' and refers to the important weekend market held here in the Middle Ages. For Austrians who continue to cross the border at the end of the week in search of cheap edibles and services, it remains just that.

History

Szombathely got an earlier start than most. In AD 43 the Romans established a trade settlement called Savaria here on the lucrative Amber Route. By the start of the 2nd century it was important enough to be named the capital of Upper Pannonia. Over the next few centuries Savaria prospered and Christianity arrived; Martin of Tours, the patron saint of France, was born here in AD 316. But attacks by Huns, Longobards and Avars weakened its defences, and in 455 an earthquake reduced the town to rubble.

Szombathely began to develop again in the early Middle Ages, but the Mongols, then the Turks and the Habsburgs put a stop to that. It was not until 1777, when János Szily was appointed Szombathely's first bishop, that the city really began to flourish economically and culturally. The building of the train line to Graz brought further trade. In 1945 Allied bombers levelled much of the town, which has since been largely rebuilt.

Orientation

Szombathely is made up of narrow streets and squares, with the centre at enormous, leafy Fő tér. To the west are Berzsenyi

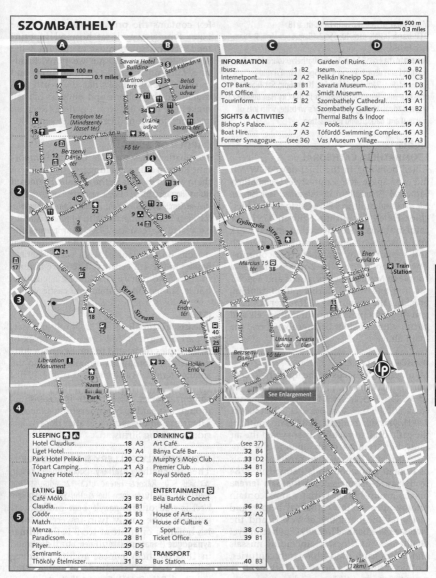

SZOMBATHELY

INFORMATION		
Ibusz	1	B2
Internetpont	2	A2
OTP Bank	3	B1
Post Office	4	A2
Tourinform	5	B2

SIGHTS & ACTIVITIES		
Bishop's Palace	6	A2
Boat Hire	7	A3
Former Synagogue	(see 36)	

Garden of Ruins	8	A1
Iseum	9	B2
Pelikán Kneipp Spa	10	C3
Savaria Museum	11	D3
Smidt Museum	12	A2
Szombathely Cathedral	13	A1
Szombathely Gallery	14	B2
Thermal Baths & Indoor Pools	15	A3
Tófürdő Swimming Complex	16	A3
Vas Museum Village	17	A3

SLEEPING		
Hotel Claudius	18	A3
Liget Hotel	19	A4
Park Hotel Pelikán	20	C2
Tópart Camping	21	A3
Wagner Hotel	22	A2

EATING		
Café Móló	23	B2
Claudia	24	B1
Gödör	25	B3
Match	26	A2
Menza	27	B1
Paradicsom	28	B1
Pityer	29	D5
Semiramis	30	B1
Thököly Ételmiszer	31	B2

DRINKING		
Art Café	(see 37)	
Bánya Café Bar	32	B4
Murphy's Mojo Club	33	D2
Premier Club	34	B1
Royal Söröző	35	B1

ENTERTAINMENT		
Béla Bartók Concert Hall	36	B2
House of Arts	37	A2
House of Culture & Sport	38	C3
Ticket Office	39	B1

TRANSPORT		
Bus Station	40	B3

Dániel tér and Templom tér (also called Mindszenty József tér), the administrative and ecclesiastical centres of the city respectively. The train station is on Éhen Gyula tér, about 1km northeast of Mártírok tere at the end of Széll Kálmán út. The bus station is on Petőfi Sándor utca, northwest of Fő tér.

Information

Ibusz (☎ 314 141; Fő tér 44; ⏱ 8am-5pm Mon-Fri, 9am-1pm Sat Jun-Aug) Good for private rooms but not general information.

Internetpont (☎ 310 161, 06 70 204 9368; Kossuth Lajos utca 19; per hr adult/student 420/360Ft; ⏱ noon-midnight Mon-Sat, 6pm-midnight Sun) Some 15 machines available southwest of Fő tér.

Main post office (Kossuth Lajos utca 18)

OTP bank (Király utca 10; ⏰ 7.45am-5pm Mon, 7.45am-3pm Tue-Fri)

Tourinform (☎ 514 451; szombathely@tourinform.hu; Kossuth Lajos utca 1-3; ⏰ 9am-5pm Mon-Fri mid-Sep–mid-Jun, 9am-6pm Mon-Fri, 10am-6pm Sat & Sun mid-Jun–mid-Sep) South of Fő tér in the City Hall building.

www.szombathely.hu The city's website, with lots of practical and background information.

Sights

SZOMBATHELY CATHEDRAL

Allied bombing in the final days of WWII did not spare the Zopf-style **Szombathely Cathedral** (Szombathelyi Székesegyház; Templom tér; free admission) built in 1797. Designed by Melchior Hefele for Bishop Szily in 1791, the cathedral was once covered in stucco work and frescoes by Franz Anton Maulbertsch and supported by grand marble columns. They're now gone, of course, though a couple of Maulbertsch originals and a glorious red-and-white marble pulpit remain, breaking the monotony of this sterile place, and there is a plaster sunburst of angels and *putti* (winged babies or cherubs) above the main altar.

BISHOP'S PALACE

Maulbertsch frescoes in the upstairs Reception Hall at the **Bishop's Palace** (Püspöki palota; ☎ 312 056; Berzsenyi Dániel tér 3; adult/senior or student 200/100Ft; ⏰ 9.30am-noon & 12.30-3pm Mon-Fri, 9.30-11.30am Sat), built in 1783 and south of the cathedral, miraculously survived the air raids, but are not usually open to the public. You can, however, admire the murals of Roman ruins and gods painted in 1784 by István Dorffmeister in the **Sala Terrena** on the ground floor. Other rooms contain photographs of the cathedral before and just after the bombing of WWII and the **Diocesan Collection and Treasury** (Egyházmegyei Gyűjtemény és Kincstár), including missals and Bibles from the 14th to 18th centuries, Gothic vestments, a beautiful 15th-century monstrance from Kőszeg and even a bejewelled replica of St Stephen's Crown made in the USA.

SMIDT MUSEUM

In a baroque mansion just south of the Bishop's Palace, the **Smidt Museum** (☎ 311 038; Hollán Ernő utca 2; adult/senior or student/family 460/250/900Ft; ⏰ 10am-5pm Tue-Sun Mar-Dec, 10am-5pm Tue-Fri Jan &

Feb) contains the private collection of one Lajos Smidt, a pack-rat hospital superintendent who spent most of his adult life squirreling away antique weapons, furniture, fans, pipes, clocks, Roman coins and so on. None of it looks like it's worth very much, but the volume and zaniness of it all makes the museum worth a visit. (Keep an eye open for Franz Liszt's pocket watch.)

GARDEN OF RUINS

Szombathely has some of the most important Roman ruins in Hungary, and many of them are on display in the so-called **Garden of Ruins** (Romkert; ☎ 313 369; Templom tér 1; adult/senior or student/family 360/180F/700Ft; ⏰ 9am-5pm Tue-Sun mid-Mar–Nov), containing a wealth of Savaria relics excavated here since 1938. Don't miss the beautiful mosaics of plants and geometrical designs on the floor of what was **St Quirinus Basilica** in the 4th century. There are also remains of Roman road markers, a customs house, shops and the medieval castle walls.

ISEUM

The **Iseum** (Rákóczi Ferenc utca 12), south of Fő tér, is part of a grand 2nd-century complex of two temples dedicated to the Egyptian goddess Isis by Roman legionnaires. When the smaller temple was excavated in the 1950s, the city decided to reconstruct it – with cement blocks. The result is grotesque, though it is said to be undergoing a facelift. The frieze on the sacrificial altar depicts Isis riding the dog Sirius.

SZOMBATHELY GALLERY & SYNAGOGUE

The **Szombathely Gallery** (Szombathelyi Képtar; ☎ 508 800; Rákóczi Ferenc utca 12; adult/student 360/180Ft; ⏰ 10am-5pm Tue & Thu-Sun, 10am-7pm Wed) is one of Hungary's best modern art galleries. The lovely twin-towered Moorish building opposite at No 3 is the former **synagogue** (zsinagóga; Rákóczi Ferenc utca 3) designed in 1881 by the Viennese architect Ludwig Schöne. Today it's a music school and the attached **Béla Bartók Concert Hall**. A plaque marks the spot from where '4228 of our Jewish brothers and sisters were deported to Auschwitz on 4 July 1944'.

SAVARIA MUSEUM

The **Savaria Museum** (☎ 500 720; Kisfaludy Sándor utca 9; adult/senior or student/family 360/230/900Ft; ⏰ 10am-5pm Tue-Sat mid-Apr–mid-Oct, 10am-5pm

Tue-Fri mid-Oct–mid-Apr), fronting a little park east of Mártírok tere, is worth a short look around. The ground floor is devoted to highly decorative but practical items carved by 19th-century shepherds to while away the hours; the cellar is full of Roman altars, stone torsos and blue-glass vials found at Savaria excavation sites. There's a local history exhibit on the 1st floor and a collection devoted to the Romanesque church at Ják.

VAS MUSEUM VILLAGE
The **Vas Museum Village** (Vasi Múzeumfalu; ☎ 311 004; Árpád út 30; adult/senior or student/family 500/250/1000Ft; ◷ 10am-5pm Tue-Sun Apr-early Nov), on the western bank of the fishing lake northwest of the city centre, is an open-air museum with some 40 18th- and 19th-century *porták* (farmhouses) moved from more than two dozen villages in the Őrség region. They're arranged around a semicircular street, as was usual on the western border. The most interesting of these are the Croatian, German and 'fenced' houses. Nettles from a strange plant called *kővirózsa* (stone rose) growing on the thatch were used to pierce little girls' ears.

Activities
The rowing and fishing lakes northwest of the city centre along Kondervei utca cover 12 hectares and make up Szombathely's playground; **boats** (◷ 9am-5.30pm Mar–mid-Sep) can be hired from the western side of the little island in the middle. The huge **Tófürdő swimming complex** (☎ 505 690; Liget utca; adult/child 790/670Ft; ◷ 9am-8pm mid-May–mid-Oct) close by has huge pools and a bunch of slides for both big and small kids. The city's **thermal baths and indoor pools** (☎ 314 336; Bartók Béla körút 41; adult/child 750/500Ft; ◷ thermal baths 4-7pm Mon-Fri, 9am-5.30pm Sat & Sun, swimming pool 2-9.30pm Mon, 6am-9.30pm Tue-Fri, 9am-6pm Sat & Sun year-round) are just to the south. Admission is cheaper the later you enter.

Sleeping
Tourinform has a list of student hostels (dorm from approximately 2000Ft), with beds available over summer. Try Ibusz for private rooms (double from 5000Ft).

Wagner Hotel (☎ /fax 322 208; www.hotelwagner .hu; Kossuth Lajos utca 15; s 10,500-14,500Ft, d 16,500Ft, ste from 20,500Ft; Ⓟ ⊠ Ⓑ) A lovely hotel, with a sunny inner courtyard and a dozen rooms,

just southwest of Fő tér. Rooms are small but comfortable, and have all the mod cons.

Park Hotel Pelikán (☎ 513 800; www.hotelpelikan .hu; Deák Ferenc utca 5; s 15,500-18,500Ft, d 21,500-24,900Ft Oct-Apr, s 20,000-21,000Ft, d 24,000-27,000Ft May-Sep; Ⓟ ⊠ Ⓑ Ⓛ Ⓑ) This stunner of a four-star hotel north of the city centre occupies a former orphanage and children's hospital, and retains many of the building's original features. Its 43 spacious rooms have everything you need, and the affiliated **Pelikán Kneipp Spa** (Markusovszky 2) a few metres to the west has an indoor pool, spa, sauna and fitness room and an encyclopaedia of various treatments available.

Hotel Claudius (☎ 313 760; www.claudiushotel.hu; Bartók Béla körút 39; s 11,900-12,900Ft, d 14,900-15,900Ft, ste from 17,900Ft; Ⓟ ⊠) This large, modern-looking hotel near the lakes has lost a few rooms (there are now 87) and gained a star (now four) after a major refurbishment. It still isn't much to look at from the outside but the rooms and public areas are fresher and brighter.

Liget Hotel (☎ 509 323; www.hotels.hu/liget_szom bathely; Szent István park 15; s/d with shower 5000/6000Ft, with bath 6999/7999Ft; Ⓟ) West of the city centre, Liget has 38 rooms that are functional at best, but it's in a quiet neighbourhood, and is convenient to the lakes and the museum village. The monstrous Liberation monument – the two concrete 'wings' on the hill to the northwest – was topped with a big red star until the mid-1990s.

Tópart Camping (☎ 509 038; fax 509 039; Liget utca 14; camp sites per tent/adult/child 500/700/350Ft, d/q bungalows 6500/10,500Ft; ◷ May-Sep; Ⓟ Ⓡ) Northwest of the city centre, near the lakes and swimming complex, this is a pleasant place to stay. From the bus stop (bus 27) on Bartók Béla körút, walk along Liget utca to the camping ground.

Eating
RESTAURANTS
Pityer (☎ 508 010; Rumi út 18; soups 350-990Ft, starters 900-1600Ft, mains 1590-2990Ft; ◷ 11am-11pm Sun-Thu, 11am-midnight Fri & Sat) One and a half kilometres southwest of Fő tér, this traditional *halászcsárda* (restaurant serving fish dishes) is worth the trip if you're in search of fish. Portions are large and the surrounds are quite atmospheric.

Gödör (☎ 510078; Hollán Ernő utca 12; soups 170-550Ft, starters 620-1550Ft, mains 860-1790Ft; ◷ 11am-11pm

Mon-Thu, 11am-midnight Fri & Sat, 11am-3pm Sun) This restaurant-cum-wine cellar is affiliated with the Jégverem in Sopron (p166) and as such caters to 'greedy-guts' types. Portions are massive, dishes relatively authentic and prices reasonable. You really can't go wrong eating here.

Café Móló (☎ 509 200; Rákóczi Ferenc utca 1-3; pizza 790-1290Ft; ☠ 10am-midnight Mon-Thu, 11am-1am Fri & Sat, 11am-midnight Sun) This modern, upbeat place opposite the less-than-appetising Iseum should be your first choice if you just want a pizza.

Paradicsom (☎ 342 012; Belsö Uránia Udvar; starters 480-990Ft, pizza 650-2000Ft) The 'Tomato' is an above-average Italian restaurant with a good vegetarian selection. The pizza and pasta (740Ft to 990Ft) are quite good. Belsö Uránia Udvar can be accessed from Mártírok tére or Fő tér 20.

CAFÉS

Claudia (☎ 313 375; Savaria tér 1; ice cream from 90Ft; ☠ 9am-10pm Mon-Sat, 2-10pm Sun) Excellent cakes and ice cream are served here, and it's a great place to relax, especially in summer when tables spill out onto the pavement.

Semiramis (Király utca 7; coffees 230-490Ft; ☠ 7am-6pm Mon-Fri, 8am-1pm Sat) Semiramis easily fits the bill of a downtown Manhattan café. It probably serves the best coffee in Szombathely, too.

QUICK EATS & SELF-CATERING

Menza (☎ 511 348; Mártírok tere 5/b; meals 190-660Ft; ☠ 9am-5pm Mon-Fri, 9am-3pm Sat) This modern take on a workers' (or student) canteen serves basic but filling meals at remarkably low prices.

Match (cnr Óperint utca & Kiskar utca; ☠ 6am-7pm Mon-Fri, 6am-2pm Sat) A huge central branch of the popular supermarket chain.

Thököly Ételmiszer (Thököly Imre utca 35; ☠ 5am-midnight Mon-Sat, 6am-midnight Sun) Grocery store with extended hours.

Drinking

Art Café (☎ 310 661; Fő tér 10; ☠ 8am-11pm Mon-Sat, 9am-11pm Sun) This sedate café-pub on the main square attracts watchers and talkers, not party people. Come here for a quiet drink.

Royal Söröző (☎ 339 727; Fő tér 16; ☠ 8.30am-midnight Sun-Thu, 8.30-1am Fri & Sat) A popular pub with sidewalk tables on the northeastern

side of Fő tér, opposite the House of Arts. What's more, it has Internet access (130Ft per half-hour).

Premier Club (☎ 330 792; Uránia Udvar; ☠ 9am-11pm Mon-Thu, 9am-6am Fri & Sat, 4-11pm Sun) A big, raucous pub with eight pool tables in the Uránia Udvar shopping arcade.

Bánya Café Bar (☎ 321 123; Szinyei Merse Pál utca; ☠ 10am-11pm Mon-Wed, 10am-midnight Thu & Fri, 2pm-2am Sat, 2-10pm Sun) This impressive basement (*bánya* means 'mine'), a former workers' pub, has been dragged into the 21st century and wouldn't look out of place in London. There are parties and live music on Saturday and Sunday.

Murphy's Mojo Club (☎ 315 891; Semmelweis Ignác utca 28; ☠ 4.30pm-midnight Mon-Thu, 4.30pm-1am Fri & Sat, 4.30-11pm Sun) This bar is not exactly in the centre of Szombathely, but worth the trip for the music (canned). It also serves reliable food.

Entertainment

An excellent source of information is the free biweekly entertainment guide *Szombathelyi Est*. For tickets to most events head to the **ticket office** (☎ 312 579; Király utca 11; ☠ 10am-1pm & 2-5pm Mon-Fri, 9am-noon Sat) just south of the old Savaria Hotel. Enter from Mártírok tere.

Szombathely has devoted a lot of attention to music ever since Bishop Szily engaged the services of full-time musicians to perform at church functions – not services. Important venues include the **Béla Bartók Concert Hall** (☎ 313 747; Rákóczi Ferenc utca 3), attached to the former synagogue, where the Savaria Symphony Orchestra performs throughout the year; the **House of Arts** (Művészetek Háza; ☎ 509 641; Fő tér 10); and the ugly **House of Culture & Sport** (Művelődési és Sportház; ☎ 312 666; Március 15 tér 5) dating from the 1960s.

Getting There & Away
BUS

In general the bus service isn't so good to/from Szombathely, though there are frequent departures to Ják (241Ft, 20 minutes, 21km, 15 daily), Kőszeg (302Ft, 35 minutes, 21km, hourly) and Körmend (363Ft, 30 minutes, 29km, hourly). Also three weekly buses depart for Vienna (2454Ft, 2½ hours, 165km) at 6.40am Wednesday, 7am Friday and 3.55am Saturday.

Other destinations to/from Szombathely include the following:

Destination	Price	Duration	Km	Frequency
Budapest	3150Ft	3½-4½hr	230	3 daily
Győr	1570Ft	2½hr	125	5 daily
Kaposvár	2300Ft	3½hr	188	3 daily
Keszthely via Hévíz	1090Ft	2¼hr	90	2 daily
Nagykanizsa	1330Ft	2½hr	107	6 daily
Pécs	3260Ft	5hr	261	2-3 daily
Sárvár	423Ft	1hr	35	hourly
Sopron	968Ft	1¾hr	76	up to 6 daily
Sümeg	907Ft	1½hr	73	2-3 daily
Szeged	4230Ft	7½hr	348	1 daily at 7.38am
Velem	302Ft	40min	21	up to 8 daily
Veszprém	1450Ft	2½hr	117	2-3 daily
Zalaegerszeg	725Ft	1½hr	56	2-3 daily

TRAIN

Express trains to Budapest (from 2226Ft, 3½ hours, 236km, 15 daily) go via Veszprém and Székesfehérvár. Győr (1142Ft, 1½ to two hours, 117km, eight daily) is also served by express train (via Celldömölk), as is Pécs (from 2376Ft, four hours, 250km, four daily). There are local trains to Kőszeg (170Ft, 30 minutes, 18km, up to 12 daily), Sopron (620Ft, 1¼ hours, 62km, up to 12 daily) and Körmend (248Ft, 30 minutes, 26km, up to 12 daily). There are also direct trains to/from Graz (4750Ft, three hours, 136km, three daily).

Getting Around

Szombathely is simple to negotiate on foot, but bus 27 will take you from the train station to the Vas Museum Village, lakes, camping ground and the Liget Hotel. Bus 1 or 1/c is good for the Kámon Arboretum. You can also call a taxi on ☎ 322 322 or 333 666.

AROUND SZOMBATHELY
Ják
☎ 94 / pop 2300
This sleepy village boasts the **Benedictine Abbey Church** (Bencés apátsági templom; ☎ 356 217; adult/senior or student 260/130Ft; ⏱ 8am-5pm May-Aug, 9am-5pm Sep-Apr), one of the finest examples of Romanesque architecture in Hungary. Its main feature, a magnificent portal carved in geometric patterns 12 layers deep and featuring carved stone statues of Christ and his

Apostles, on the west side, was renovated for Hungary's millennium celebrations in 1996. The decorative sculptures on the outside wall of the sanctuary and the church's interior are also worth a look.

The two-towered structure was begun as a family church in 1214 by Márton Nagy and dedicated to St George four decades later in 1256. Somehow the partially completed church escaped destruction during the Mongol invasion, but it was badly damaged during the Turkish occupation. The church has had many restorations, the most important three being in the mid-17th century, between 1896 and 1904 (when most of the statues in the portal were recut or replaced, rose stained-glass windows added and earlier baroque additions removed) and from 1992 to 1996 for Hungary's millecentenary celebrations.

Enter through the south door, once used only by the monks. The interior, with its single nave and three aisles, has a much more graceful and personal feel than most Hungarian Gothic churches. To the west and below the towers is a gallery reserved for the benefactor and his family. The rose-and-blue frescoes on the wall between the vaulting and the arches below could very well be of Márton Nagy and his progeny.

To the west of the Romanesque church is the tiny clover-leaf **Chapel of St James** (Szent Jakab-kápolna) topped with an onion dome. It was built around 1260 as a parish church, since the main church was monastic. Note the paschal lamb (symbolising Christ) over the main entrance, and the baroque altar and frescoes inside.

Buses from Szombathely (241Ft, 20 minutes, 21km, 15 daily) are frequent and will drop you off in Szabadság tér. From Ják you can return to Szombathely or continue on to Körmend (302Ft, 30 minutes, 20km, two or three daily) and make connections there.

SÁRVÁR
☎ 95 / pop 15,350
Sárvár is well known for its 44°C thermal waters, discovered in the '60s during exploratory drilling for oil. Recently the spa complex to the southeast of the town centre has seen a lot of investment, and the town of 'Mud Castle' has gone from being a haven for retired Austrians seeking a cure for whatever ails them to a modern spa centre with some of

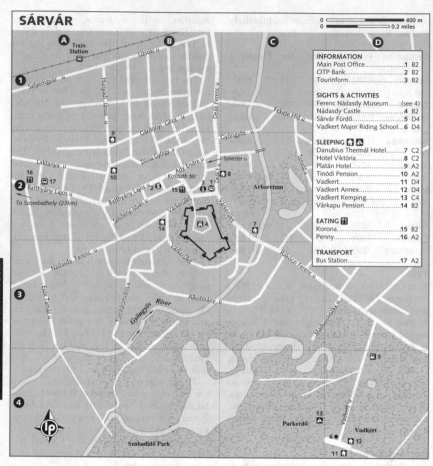

SÁRVÁR

0 ————— 400 m
0 ————— 0.2 miles

INFORMATION
Main Post Office.....................1 B2
OTP Bank...............................2 B2
Tourinform.............................3 B2

SIGHTS & ACTIVITIES
Ferenc Nádasdy Museum.......(see 4)
Nádasdy Castle.......................4 B2
Sárvár Fürdő..........................5 D4
Vadkert Major Riding School...6 D4

SLEEPING
Danubius Thermál Hotel........7 C2
Hotel Viktória.........................8 C2
Platán Hotel...........................9 A2
Tinódi Pension.......................10 A2
Vadkert..................................11 D4
Vadkert Annex.......................12 D4
Vadkert Kemping....................13 C4
Várkapu Pension....................14 B2

EATING
Korona...................................15 B2
Penny....................................16 A2

TRANSPORT
Bus Station............................17 A2

WESTERN TRANSDANUBIA

the most up-to-date facilities in Hungary. It's very clean, well managed, and overflowing with facilities and fun for the whole family.

Of course, not everyone visits Sárvár for the hot water. Some want a glimpse of the castle where a certain 18th-century countess developed a taste for blood – literally (see boxed text, opposite).

History
Some 27km east of Szombathely on the Rába River, Sárvár has experienced some good and some very bad times over the past 500 years or so. During the Reformation Sárvár's fortified castle was a centre of Calvinist culture and scholarship, and its owners, the Nádasdy family, were a respected

dynasty in statecraft and military leadership. In 1537 Tamás Nádasdy set up a press that published the first two printed books in Hungarian – a Magyar grammar in Latin and a translation of the New Testament. Ferenc Nádasdy II, dubbed the 'Black Captain', fought heroically against the Turks, and his grandson Ferenc III, a lord chief justice, created one of the greatest libraries and private art collections in central Europe.

But everything began to go pear-shaped at the start of the 17th century. It seems that while the Black Captain was away at war, his wife Erzsébet Báthory, as mad as a hatter and bloodthirsty to boot, was up to no good. Then Ferenc III's involvement in a plot led by Ferenc Wesselényi to overthrow the Habsburgs was exposed. He was beheaded in Vienna in 1671.

Orientation

Sárvár's train station is on Selyemgyár utca. To reach the town centre, walk south along Hunyadi János utca and turn east on Batthyány Lajos utca, which leads to Kossuth tér and the castle. Rákóczi Ferenc utca leads southeast to Vadkert utca and the spa complex. The bus station is at the western end of Batthyány Lajos utca.

Information

Main post office (Várkerület 32)

OTP bank (Batthyány Lajos utca 2)

Tourinform (☎ 520 178; sarvar@tourinform.hu; Várkerület 33; ☼ 9am-4pm Mon-Fri) This tourist office is almost opposite the castle entrance.

Sights

NÁDASDY CASTLE

The entrance to the **Ferenc Nádasdy Museum** (☎ 320 158; Várkerület 1; adult/senior or student/family 460/230/900Ft; ☼ 9am-5pm Tue-Sun) in pentagonal Nádasdy Castle is across a brick footbridge from Kossuth tér and through the gate of a 14th-century tower. Parts of the castle date from the 13th century, but most of it is 16th-century Renaissance and in good condition despite Erzsébet Báthory's shenanigans and all the plundering by the Habsburgs. As punishment for the Nádasdy family's involvement in the rebellion of 1670, their estate was confiscated by the Austrian crown and the castle's contents – including much of the library – were taken to Vienna. As a result, many of the furnishings, tapestries and *objets d'art* you see in the museum's three wings today were collected from other sources.

THE BLOOD COUNTESS

It was the scandal of the 17th century. On the night of 29 December 1610 the Lord Palatine of Hungary, Count György Thurzó, raided the castle at Csejta (now Čachtice in western Slovakia) and caught Countess Erzsébet Báthory literally red-handed – or so he and history would later claim. Covered in blood and screaming like a demon, the widow of the celebrated Black Captain was in the process of eating (as in chomp, chomp) one of her servant girls.

Yet another one, or so it would seem… By the time Thurzó had finished collecting evidence from household staff and the townspeople at Čachtice and Sárvár, some 300 depositions had been given, accusing the countess of torturing, mutilating, murdering and – worst of all – disposing of the bodies of more than 600 girls and young women without so much as a Christian burial.

The case of the so-called Blood Countess has continued to grab the imagination of everyone from writers (Erzsébet is believed to have been the model for Bram Stoker's *Dracula*) and musicians (remember the Goth group Bathory?) to filmmakers and fetishists over the centuries, and some pretty crazy theories as to why she did it have emerged. Some say she considered the blood of young maidens to be an *elixir vitae* and bathed in it to stay young. Others claim she suffered from acute iron deficiency and just had to have those red corpuscles. Still others point to the high incidence of lunacy in the two, much intermarried branches of the Báthory dynasty. Most likely, however, Erzsébet Báthory herself was the victim of a conspiracy.

When the Black Captain died in 1604, his widow inherited all of his estates – properties coveted by both Thurzó and Erzsébet's son-in-law Miklós Zrínyi, the poet and great-grandson of the hero of Szigetvár (see p305), who themselves were linked by marriage. Worse, the election of the countess' nephew Gábor Báthory as prince of Transylvania, a vassal state under Ottoman rule, threatened to unite the two Báthory families and strengthen the principality's position. It was in the interest of the Palatine – and the Habsburgs – to get this matriarch of the Báthory family out of the way.

Gábor was murdered in 1613 and the 'Báthory faction' in Hungary ceased to be a threat. The case against the Blood Countess never came to trial, and she remained interned 'between stones' (ie in a sealed chamber) at the castle until she died in 1614 at the age of 54.

Was Erzsébet as bloodthirsty as history has made her out to be? Did she really bite great chunks out of the girls' necks and breasts and mutilate their genitals? Much of the villagers' testimony does appear to be consistent, but to form your own conclusions read Tony Thorne's well-researched *Countess Dracula: The Life and Times of Elisabeth Bathory*.

One thing the Habsburgs could not take with them was the magnificent ceiling fresco in the **Knight's Hall**, picturing Hungarians – the Black Captain included – doing battle with the Turks at Tata, Székesfehérvár, Győr, Pápa, Kanizsa and Buda. They were painted by Hans Rudolf Miller in the mid-17th century. The biblical scenes on the walls, depicting Samson and Delilah, David and Goliath, Mordechai and Esther, and so on were painted in 1769 by István Dorffmeister. There's a particularly beautiful 16th-century cabinet of gilded wood and marble to the right of the hall as you enter.

The museum also has one of the nation's best collections of weapons and armour, and almost an entire wing is given over to the Hussars, a regiment of which was named after the Nádasdy family. The uniforms, all buttons, ribbons and fancy epaulets, would do a Gilbert and Sullivan operetta proud.

Among the exhibits about the castle and Sárvár is the printing press established here, and some of the then inflammatory Calvinist tracts it published. One work in Hungarian, entitled *The Pope Is Not the Pope – That's That* and dated 1603, was later vandalised by a Counter-Reformationist who defiantly wrote 'Lutheran scandal' across it in Latin.

A superb (and priceless) collection of some 60 antique Hungarian maps donated by a UK-based expatriate Hungarian in 1986 and called 'Carta Hungarica' is on exhibit in a room at the end of the west wing.

The 9-hectare **arboretum** (Várkerület 30/a; admission free; 9am-7pm Apr–mid-Oct, 9am-5pm mid-Oct–Mar), east of the castle and bisected by the Gyöngyös River, a tributary of the Rába River, was planted by the Nádasdys' successors, the royal Wittelsbach family of Bavaria (the castle's last royal occupant was Ludwig III, who died in exile in 1921).

Activities

A huge and very modern spa and wellness complex southeast of the castle, **Sárvár Fürdő** (523 600; www.sarvarfurdo.hu; Vadkert utca 1; adult/child 6-16yr 1600/700Ft, adult after 5/8pm 1100/700Ft; thermal baths 8am-10pm year-round, outdoor pools 9am-8pm May-Sep) has indoor and outdoor thermal and swimming pools, several types of sauna, a wellness and fitness centre, and comprehensive medical facilities with all kinds of treatments. The summer entrance to the open-air pools is just south of the main entrance.

There are **tennis courts** (per hr 400Ft) and the **Vadkert Major riding school** (320 045) at the end of Vadkert utca. Ask the staff at the Vadkert inn about **horse riding** (per 30min 1500Ft) and **coach rides** (up to 3 people 4500Ft).

Sleeping

BUDGET

Vadkert (/fax 320 045; Vadkert utca; main building s/d/tr 7500/8800/10,700Ft, annexe 6200/7500/9800Ft; P) This inn south of the spa is among the most atmospheric places to stay in Sárvár. It's a 19th-century royal hunting lodge, with 24 rooms in an old building and a newer annexe with 16 rooms. The older rooms are furnished in rustic pine, and the common sitting room with the large hearth looks to be from an Agatha Christie whodunnit novel.

Vadkert Kemping (523 600; Vadkert utca; camp sites per tent/adult/child 900/650/500Ft; P) This camping ground is just north of the Vadkert inn and within easy walking distance of the spa complex.

MIDRANGE

Várkapu Pension (/fax 326 475; www.varkapu.hu; Várkerület 5; s 6700-7000Ft, d 9300-9900Ft, tr 12,300-13,200Ft; P) As close to the castle as can get without actually staying there, the 'Castle Gate' has nine clean and accommodating rooms. It also has a sauna and a great restaurant.

Tinódi Pension (/fax 323 606; www.tinodifogado .hu; Hunyadi János utca 11; s/d/tr 7800/9900/13,500Ft) A colourful little boarding house (its term), with 15 renovated rooms and a quiet courtyard. The rustic restaurant is very popular.

Hotel Viktória (/fax 320 525; www.hotel-viktoria .hu; Deák Ferenc utca 6; s/d/ste 7500/11,000/12,000Ft; P) There's not much left to let you in on the secret that this was once the site of Sárvár's Romantic-style synagogue built in 1850. It's now a comfortable enough 20-room hotel, close to the arboretum and the castle.

TOP END

Platán Hotel (320 623; www.platanhotel.hu; Hunyadi János utca 23; d/tr 13,500/17,500Ft; P) This is a lovely smallish (20 rooms) hotel with swimming pool. Though it's close to the train station, it's a bit removed from Sárvár's action.

Danubius Thermál Hotel (888 400; www.danu biusgroup.com/sarvar; Rákóczi Ferenc utca 1; s €91-98, d €122-130; P) Sárvár's poshest established hostelry (there are a couple of new kids on the block down by the spa complex). With 136 rooms just on the edge of the arboretum, it boasts all the mod cons, indoor and outdoor thermal pools, and complete curative facilities.

Eating

Várkapu (☎/fax 320 045; Vadkert utca; soups 390-560Ft, starters 750-1390Ft, mains 1490-2390Ft; 8.30am-10pm Sun-Thu, 8.30am-11pm Fri & Sat) The pick of the crop in Sárvár, and we especially like the Hungarian and international menu that changes with the seasons and the good selection of Hungarian wines. There are restful views of the castle and surrounding park.

Tinódi (☎/fax 323 606; www.tinodifogado.hu; Hunyadi János utca 11; soups & starters 260-650Ft, mains 990-2300Ft; 8am-10pm) The cellar restaurant at this *pension* is warm and inviting in winter, but in summer try to get a table in the large and leafy internal courtyard. It's a good place for breakfast (330Ft to 490Ft) alfresco, too.

Platán (☎ 320 623; Hunyadi János utca 23; soups 250-780Ft, starters 860-1600Ft, mains 750-2300Ft) The main draw of the *csárda* at the Platán, which also has a well-stocked and popular bar, is the terrace in summer.

Korona (☎ 320 542; Kossuth tér 3; ice cream from 100Ft, cakes 80-160Ft; 9am-9pm) This café and pastry shop is a great choice for cakes and ice cream.

Penny (Batthyány Lajos utca; 7am-8pm Mon-Sat, 7am-2pm Sun) This large branch of the supermarket chain is just west of the bus station.

Getting There & Away

BUS

Buses that run to/from Sárvár:

Destination	Price	Duration	Km	Frequency
Budapest	2780Ft	3hr	221	1-2 daily
Bük	363Ft	40min	28	8-10 daily
Celldömölk	363Ft	50min	28	8 daily
Győr	1090Ft	2hr	96	2 daily
Kaposvár	1930Ft	3¼hr	159	1 daily
Keszthely	907Ft	1½-2hr	75	2 daily
Lenti	1450Ft	2¾hr	117	1 daily Mon-Fri
Pápa	605Ft	1½hr	50	2-3 daily
Pécs	2780Ft	4½hr	224	1 daily
Sitke	133Ft	15min	10	8-10 daily
Sopron	786Ft	1¼hr	62	2-3 daily
Sümeg	484Ft	1hr	40	2-3 daily
Szombathely	423Ft	1hr	35	hourly
Veszprém	907Ft	1½hr	77	2-3 daily
Zalaegerszeg	1030Ft	1¾hr	85	2-3 daily

TRAIN

Sárvár is on the train line linking Szombathely (363Ft, 40 minutes, 29km, hourly) with Veszprém (946Ft, two hours, 100km, up to six daily), Székesfehérvár (1534Ft, 2½ hours, 145km, up to six daily) and Budapest (from 2076Ft, 3½ hours, 224km, up to six daily). From Szombathely up to five daily trains continue on to Graz (5500Ft, four hours, 136km) in Austria via Szentgotthárd.

KŐSZEG

☎ 94 / pop 11,500

The tranquil town of Kőszeg (German: Güns) is sometimes called 'the nation's jewellery box', and as you pass under the pseudo-Gothic Heroes' Gate into Jurisics tér, you'll see why. What opens up before you is a treasure-trove of colourful Gothic, Renaissance and baroque buildings that together make up one of the most delightful squares in Hungary. At the same time the nearby Kőszeg Hills, which includes Mt Írottkő (882m), the highest point in Transdanubia, and the Írottkő Nature Park, offer endless possibilities for outdoor activities.

Orientation

Kőszeg's historic district, the Inner Town, is ringed by the Várkör, which follows the

FOR WHOM THE BELL TOLLS

Kőszeg has played pivotal roles in the nation's defence over the centuries. The best-known story is the storming of the town's castle by Suleiman the Magnificent's troops in August 1532, which sounds all too familiar but has a surprise ending. Miklós Jurisics' 'army' of fewer than 50 soldiers and the town militia held the fortress for 25 days against 100,000 Turks. An accord was reached when Jurisics allowed the Turks to run up their flag over the castle in a symbolic declaration of victory provided they left town immediately thereafter. The Turks kept their part of the bargain (packing their bags at 11am on 30 August), and Vienna was spared the treatment that would befall Buda nine years later. To this day church bells in Kőszeg peal an hour before noon to mark the withdrawal.

KŐSZEG

INFORMATION
Írottkő Nature Park
  Information Centre....(see 14)
Main Post Office..............1 C3
Öregcsuka........................2 D2
OTP Bank..........................3 C3
Savaria Tourist..................4 C2
Tourinform...................(see 14)

SIGHTS & ACTIVITIES
Black Moor Pharmacy
  Museum..........................5 C3
Castle Museum............(see 11)
Church of St Henry.......(see 6)
Church of St James..........6 C2
Church of the Sacred
  Heart...............................7 C3
General's House................8 C2
Golden Unicorn Pharmacy
  Museum..........................9 C2
Heroes' Gate...................10 C2
Jurisics Castle.................11 B2
Municipal Swimming Pool.12 D1
Old Tower........................13 B2
Renaissance House..........14 C2
Synagogue......................15 C1
Town Hall........................16 C2

SLEEPING
Aranystrucc Hotel............17 C3
Castle Tourist Hostel.......18 B2
Gyöngyvirág Camping......19 C1
Gyöngyvirág Panzió......(see 19)
Írottkő Hotel....................20 C3
Kóbor Macskához Inn.......21 B3
Miklós Jurisics College......22 B3
Portré Hotel.....................23 C3

EATING
Bécsikapu........................24 C2
Garabonciás...............(see 14)
Ibrahím...........................25 C2
Match..............................26 C2
Pizzéria da Rocco.............27 B3
Szenátor..........................28 C3
Taverna Flórián................29 C3

DRINKING
Poncichter.......................30 C2

TRANSPORT
Bus Station......................31 D3

Map labels: To Kálvária-hegy (1.5km); Austria (3km); Árpád tér; Inner Town; Jurisics tér; Fő tér; Várkör; To Király-völgy (1km); Írottkő Nature Park (3km); Cemetery; To Szabó-hegy (4km); Temető u; To Train Station (1.5km); Szombathely (18km); Sopron (50km); Petőfi tér; Liszt Ferenc u; Gyöngyös River; 0 300 m / 0 0.2 miles

---

old castle walls. The city's bus 'station' is a half-dozen stands on Liszt Ferenc utca, a few minutes' walk to the southeast. The train station is on Alsó körút, about 1.5km in the same direction.

Information

Írottkő Nature Park information centre (☎ 563 121; www.naturpark.hu; Jurisics tér 7; ⏱ 8am-4pm Mon-Fri) Shares space with Tourinform.

Main post office (Várkör 65) Just west of Savaria Tourist.

Öregcsuka (☎ 561 546; Kiss János utca 18; per 30min 500Ft; ⏱ 11am-midnight) The 'Old Pike' fish restaurant near the Gyöngyös River has Internet access on three machines.

OTP bank (Kossuth Lajos utca 8; ⏱ 7.45am-5pm Mon, 7.45am-3pm Tue-Thu, 7.45am-12.30 Fri) Also has a foreign currency-exchange machine.

Savaria Tourist (☎ 563 048; fax 563 049; Várkör 69; ⏱ 8am-4pm Mon-Fri, 8am-noon Sat) Just off Fő tér.

Tourinform (☎ 563 120; koszeg@tourinform.hu; 1st fl, Jurisics tér 7; ⏱ 8am-4pm Mon-Fri, 9am-1pm Sat & Sun mid-Jun–mid-Sep, 8am-4pm Mon-Fri mid-Sep–mid-Jun) On the main square, it's in the same building as Garabonciás's café.

Sights

Heroes' Gate (Hősök kapuja), leading into Jurisics tér, was erected in 1932 (when these nostalgic portals were all the rage in Hungary) to mark the 400th anniversary of Suleiman's withdrawal. The tower above is open to visitors and accessible from the **General's House** (Tábornokház; ☎ 360 240; Jurisics tér 6; adult/senior or student 360/180Ft; ⏱ 10am-5pm Tue-Fri, 10am-1pm Sat mid-Mar–Sep), which contains exhibits on folk art, trades and guilds, and the natural history of the area.

Almost all the buildings in Jurisics tér are interesting. The red-and-yellow **Town Hall** (Városháza; Jurisics tér 8), a mixture of Gothic, Renaissance, baroque and neoclassical styles, has oval paintings on its façade of worldly and heavenly worthies. The **Renaissance house** (Jurisics tér 7), built in 1668 and

---

DISCOUNT CARDS

The **Kőszeg Ticket** is a daily ticket allowing entry into all of the town's museums. It costs 600/300/1200Ft per adult/child/family.

now housing a pub, is adorned with graffiti etched into the stucco. A few doors down is the **Golden Unicorn Pharmacy Museum** (Arany Egyszarvú Patikamúzeum; ☎ 360 337; Jurisics tér 11; adult/senior or student 360/180Ft; ☺ 10am-5pm Tue-Sun Apr-Nov), one of two pharmacy museums in little Kőszeg. For those of you who can't get enough of controlled substances under glass, the other one is the **Black Moor Pharmacy Museum** (Fekete Szerecseny Patikamúzeum; ☎ 360 980; Rákóczi Ferenc utca 3; adult/senior or student 360/180Ft; ☺ 1-5pm Tue-Fri Mar-Nov).

In the centre of Jurisics tér a statue of the Virgin Mary (1739) and the town fountain (1766) adjoin two fine churches. The Gothic **Church of St James** (Szent Jakab-templom), built in 1407, is to the north and contains very faded 15th-century frescoes on the east wall (ie to the right of the main altar) of a giant St Christopher carrying the Christ Child, Mary Misericordia sheltering supplicants under a massive cloak, and the Three Magi bearing their gifts of gold, frankincense and myrrh. The altars and oaken pews are masterpieces of baroque woodcarving, and Miklós Jurisics and two of his children are buried in the crypt. The baroque **Church of St Henry** (Szent Imre-templom) with the tall steeple has two art treasures: a painting of the church's patron by István Dorffmeister above the altar, and one of Mary visiting her cousin Elizabeth by Franz Anton Maulbertsch, on the north wall (ie to the left of the main altar).

Just off Rajnis József utca to the northwest is a path leading to **Jurisics Castle** (☎ 360 113; Rajnis József utca 9; adult/child 120/80Ft; ☺ 10am-5pm Tue-Sun). Originally built in the mid-13th century, but reconstructed several times (most recently in 1962), the four-towered fortress is now a hotchpotch of Renaissance arcades, Gothic windows and baroque interiors. The **Castle Museum** (Vármúzeum; ☎ 360 240; adult/senior or child/family 460/230/900Ft; ☺ 10am-5pm Tue-Sun) on the 1st floor has exhibits on the history of Kőszeg from the 14th century (with the events of 1532 taking up most of the space; see boxed text, page 181) and on local wine production. Among the latter is the curious *Szőlő jövésnek könyve* (Arrival of the Grape Book), a kind of gardener's logbook of grape shoot and bud sketches begun in 1740 and updated annually on St George's Day (23 April). You can climb two of the towers, from where a brass ensemble entertained the townspeople in the Middle Ages.

Walking south along narrow Chernel utca, with its elegant baroque façades and saw-toothed rooftops (which allowed the defenders a better shot at the enemy), you'll pass the remains of the ancient **castle walls** and the so-called **Old Tower** (Öreg Zwinger; ☎ 360 240; Chernel utca 16; adult/senior or child 200/100Ft; ☺ 10am-1.30pm Tue-Fri & odd-numbered Sat), an 11th-century corner bastion, the oldest structure in town.

The neo-Gothic **Church of the Sacred Heart** (Jézus Szíve-templom; Fő tér), built in 1894, is unexceptional save for its refreshingly different geometric frescoes and those 'midday' bells at 11am. The circular **synagogue** (zsinagóga; Várkör 38), built in 1859, with its strange neo-Gothic towers, once served one of the oldest Jewish communities in Hungary, but now sits abandoned and in decay to the northeast of Jurisics tér.

Activities

Walking up to the baroque chapel on 394m-high **Kálvária-hegy** (Calvary Hill) northwest of the town centre, or to the vineyards of **Király-völgy** (Royal Valley) west of Jurisics Castle, is a very pleasant way to spend a few hours. You can also follow Temető utca southwest and then south up to 458m-high **Szabó-hegy** (Tailor's Hill). Tourinform has a brochure with easy walks in the area called *Kőszeg-Hegyaljai Séták* (Kőszeg Upland Paths), but a copy of Cartographia's 1:40,000-scale *Kőszeg-hegység* (Kőszeg Hills; No 13; 650Ft) map will prove more useful if you plan to do adventurous hiking or visit the **Írottkő Nature Park** to the west.

The **municipal swimming pool** (városi uszoda; adult/child 650/400Ft, Kiss János utca; ☺ 10am-6pm mid-Jun-Aug) is east of the town centre.

Sleeping

BUDGET

Savaria Tourist can arrange private rooms (2500Ft per person).

Kóbor Macskához Inn (☎ /fax 362 273; Várkör 100; d with washbasin/shower 4000/5500Ft; Ⓟ) Just west of the Inner Town, 'At the Sign of the Stray Cat' is a charming nine-room inn with relatively large rooms and a downstairs bar that can sometimes be noisy.

Gyöngyvirág Panzió (☎ 360 454; fax 364 574; Bajcsy-Zsilinszky utca 6; s/d/tr/q with washbasin 4000/5000/6200/8200Ft, s/d with shower 5500/6500Ft; Ⓟ) This spotless guesthouse next to the town's

AUTHOR'S CHOICE

Aranystrucc Hotel (☎ 360 323; www.aranystrucc
.hu; Várkör 124; s 5400Ft, d 8200-9200Ft; **P**) The
'Golden Ostrich' is a worn though wonderfully atmospheric hotel in the heart of
Kőszeg. It has 15 rooms in an 18th-century
building, near the entrance to the Inner
Town. Room No 7, on the corner with balcony views over the main square (Fő tér), is
the biggest and the best. The most expensive rooms have antique furnishings.

only camping ground is surrounded by
greenery and very quiet.

Miklós Jurisics College (☎ /fax 361 404; Hunyadi
János utca 10; dm 1900Ft; **P**) This enormous college west of the Inner Town has over 100
beds in dormitory accommodation available in July and August.

Castle Tourist Hostel (☎ 360 113, 360 227; Rajnis
József utca 9; dm approx 1500Ft) A cheap and central option, this hostel is in a small building near the entrance to Jurisics Castle. It's
very well worn, but the location makes it
attractive.

Gyöngyvirág Camping (☎ 360 454; fax 364 574;
Bajcsy-Zsilinszky utca 6; camp sites per tent/car/adult/child
400/400/700/300Ft; **P**) By the little Gyöngyös
River, the 'Lily of the Valley' is a basic camping ground with space for approximately
20 to 25 tents.

MIDRANGE
Portré Hotel (☎ 363 170; www.portre.com; Fő tér 7;
d/tr 9000/11,000Ft; 🖳) This positive stunner of
a boutique hotel offers a half-dozen wonderfully decorated rooms on the town's
main square. Try and get a room on the
1st floor, as those on the 2nd have dormer
windows.

Írottkő Hotel (☎ 360 373; www.hotelirottko.hu;
Fő tér 4; s/d/tr 9800/13,100/15,400Ft; 🖳) Kőszeg's
main hotel. It's large (48 rooms) and central
and, while the building is rather uninspiring, the renovated guestrooms and public
areas have improved tremendously in recent years.

Eating & Drinking
Taverna Flórián (☎ 563 072; Várkör 59; starters
850-1890Ft, mains 1490-2990Ft; ⏰ 11.30am-2.30pm &
7-10pm Wed-Sun) For fine dining, head here
for quality Mediterranean food in beautiful

cellar-like surroundings. Pasta dishes (650Ft
to 1590Ft) are particularly recommended.

Bécsikapu (☎ 563 122; Rajnis József utca 5; soups &
starters 210-1350Ft, mains 990-2290Ft; ⏰ 11am-10pm)
Almost opposite the Church of St James,
this is a pleasant *csárda* with a back garden looking towards the castle. It fills up at
lunch with tourists, though.

Pizzéria da Rocco (☎ 362 379; Várkör 55; pizza
500-1500Ft; ⏰ noon-10pm) With its huge garden within the old castle walls, da Rocco is
a coveted address and great for a pizza or
indeed just a drink.

Ibrahim (☎ 360 854; Fő tér 17; ice cream from 80Ft;
⏰ 8am-10pm) For ice cream don't go past this
place; what looks like half the population of
Kőszeg queuing outside can't be wrong.

Szenátor (☎ 360 320; Rákóczi Ferenc utca 6; ⏰ 3pm-
midnight) This upbeat *cukrászda* (cake shop)
and café gets the thumbs up from readers
who love its cakes.

Garabonciás (☎ 360 050; Jurisics tér 7; pizzas 350-
2290Ft; ⏰ noon-10pm Mon-Sat, 5-10pm Sun) A simple but very centrally located café in a lovely
historical building on the main square.

Ponchichter (Rajnis József utca 10; ⏰ 9am-9pm Tue-
Sun) For wine (generally common Sopron
vintages), go to this old wine cellar, which
has vaulted ceilings, high Gothic windows
and, in the warmer months, an inviting
garden.

Match (Várkör 20; ⏰ 6am-7pm Mon-Fri, 6am-4pm
Sat) A very central branch of the supermarket chain.

Getting There & Away
Departures are frequent to Sopron (665Ft,
1½ hours, 55km, up to six daily), Szombathely (302Ft, 35 minutes, 21km, hourly) and
Velem (182Ft, 20 minutes, 11km, up to six
daily), but more sporadic to Lenti (1570Ft,
three hours, 126km, Monday to Friday at
3.45pm), Nagykanizsa (1570Ft, three hours,
125km, two daily) and Körmend (605Ft,
70 minutes, 47km, one daily).

Three weekly buses head for Oberpullen-
dorf (324Ft, 40 minutes, 18km) and Vienna
(2139Ft, 2½ hours, 125km) in Austria at
7.05am on Wednesday, 8.10am on Friday
and 4.15am Saturday.

Kőszeg is at the end of an 18km railway
spur from Szombathely (302Ft, 35 minutes,
21km, hourly). The only express train – at
7.51pm – takes just 19 minutes to reach
Szombathely.

ŐRSÉG REGION

This westernmost region, where Hungary, Austria and Slovenia converge, has for centuries been the nation's 'sentry', or *őrség*, and its houses and villages, spaced unusually far apart on the crests and in the valleys of the Zala foothills, once served as the national frontier. For their service as guards, the inhabitants of the region were given special privileges by the king, which they retained until the arrival of the Batthyány family.

Much of this region forms the boundaries of the 440-sq-km **Őrség National Park**, which borders both Austria and Slovenia, and is a boon for lovers of the great outdoors. The park is crisscrossed with marked hiking trails that link many of Őrség's villages, including Őriszentpéter, Szalafő, Velemér and Pankasz. Cartographia's 1:60,000-scale map *Őrség, Göcsej* (No 21; 900Ft) is a good reference.

Information

The **Őrség National Park information centre** (☎ 548 034; www.orseginpi.hu in Hungarian; Siskaszer 26/a; 8am-4.30pm Mon-Fri year-round, 9am-5pm Sat & Sun May-Aug) is in Őriszentpéter just before the turnoff to Szalafő. Also in Őriszentpéter on the road to Szalafő, **Őrségi Teleház** (Őrség Full House; ☎ 548 038; www.orsegitelehaz.hu; Városszer 116; 8am-4.30pm Mon-Fri) can help with general information and accommodation.

Őriszentpéter

☎ 94 / pop 1200

Őriszentpéter, the centre of the Őrség region, is a pretty village of timber and thatch-roofed houses and large gardens; it's the best Őrség town in which to base yourself. Its most interesting sight, a remarkably well-preserved 13th-century **Romanesque church** (Templomszer 15), is an easy 2km walk northwest of the village centre. On the southern extension of the church is a wonderful carved portal and small fragments of 15th-century frescoes. On the north side, a set of wooden steps leads to the choir. The writings on the internal south walls, dating from the 17th century, are Bible verses in Hungarian, and the 18th-century altarpiece was painted by a student of Franz Anton Maulbertsch.

Szalafő

☎ 94 / pop 300

Energetic travellers may want to continue another 4km or so along Templomszer, past arcaded old peasant houses and abandoned crank wells to Szalafő, the oldest settlement in the Őrség. In Szalafő-Pityerszer, 2km west of the village, is the **Open-Air Ethnographical Museum** (Szabadtéri Néprajzi Múzeum; ☎ 06 30 467 7022; adult/senior or student/family 400/200/800Ft; 10am-6pm Jun-Aug, 10am-6pm Tue-Sun mid-Mar–May, Sep & Oct), the grandiose name given to a mini-*skanzen* (open-air museum displaying village architecture) of three folk compounds of 10 houses, storerooms and outbuildings unique to the Őrség. Built around a central courtyard, the houses have large overhangs, which allowed neighbours to chat when it rained – a frequent occurrence in this very wet region. The **Calvinist church** in the village centre has frescoes from the 16th century.

Sleeping & Eating

Both the national park's information centre and Őrség Full House have comprehensive lists of accommodation in the area, including several peasant houses (from 2500Ft per person) in the Csörgőszer section of Szalafő.

Centrum (☎ 428 002; www.hotels.hu/centrum panzio; Városszer 17; s/d/tr/q 3500/6500/8500/10,500Ft; P) This eight-room place in the centre of 'downtown' Őriszentpéter has a popular restaurant and two bowling alleys, which attract young bloods from miles around.

Domino (☎ 428 115, 06 30 463 9542; Siskaszer 5/a; r per person 3000-5000Ft; P) This place has five lovely little bungalows complete with kitchen and separate bathroom. It's a bit remote, though, and you should have your own transport – though it does rent bikes.

Bognár (☎ 428 027; Kovácsszer 96; mains 720-2200Ft; 7am-9pm) In Őriszentpéter, this is a reliable choice for a meal. It's about 500m up the hill, north of the bus station.

Getting There & Away

Őriszentpéter (and sometimes Szalafő) can be reached by bus from Körmend (484Ft, 70 minutes, 37km, six daily) and from Zalaegerszeg (485Ft, 1½ hours, 40km, two daily with a change at Zalalövő). Other destinations include Kőszeg (1090Ft, two hours, 87km, one daily), Szentgotthárd (302km, one hour, 25km, four daily) and Lenti (605Ft, one hour, 44km, two daily).

An infrequent bus service connects Őriszentpéter with Szalafő (133Ft, six to 10 minutes, 7.5km, up to five daily).

WESTERN TRANSDANUB 3

Lake Balaton Region

Lake Balaton, often called the 'Hungarian Sea', is the country's substitute for a coastline, a place where many locals (and Germans) escape Europe's summer heat. At 78km long, 15km across at its widest point and covering 600 sq km, it's Europe's largest body of fresh water and an aqua-playground big enough to cater to most holiday-makers.

The lake itself is a tale of two shores. Its southern coast is essentially only long resorts: from Siófok to Fonyód you'll find high-rise hotels, small sandy beaches jammed with sun worshippers, tacky stalls selling imitation wares and greasy *lángos* (deep-fried treats), and clubs attracting international DJs and night-crawlers. Here the water is shallowest and safest for kids (the lake's depth averages only 3m and the temperature is 26°C May to October).

Its northern side is as refined as its southern is brash, with pretty towns such as Keszthely, Badacsony and Balatonfüred catering to a more mature crowd looking for some quiet respite alongside splashing about in the sun. Tihany, a unique peninsula cutting the lake almost in half, is home to an important historical church and some of Balaton's deepest beaches while the thermal lake at Hévíz (Europe's largest) is a natural wonder. Hills create a backdrop to the north's reedy beaches, and vineyards, woods, castles and hiking trails all vie for their rightful land space. Easy day trips from the lake include historic towns such as Veszprém and Székesfehérvár, where seminal moments at the very beginning of Magyar settlement took place.

Balaton won't appeal to everyone's tastes with its shallow, silky waters, but when its surface appears a kaleidoscope of colours, changing shades before your very eyes, it's easy to fall under its hypnotic spell like so many artists and holiday-makers have over the centuries.

LAKE BALATON REGION

HIGHLIGHTS

- Gazing at the Church of the Ascension's wonderful frescoes and the hilltop Sümeg Castle in **Sümeg** (p203)

- Watching the setting sun change Lake Balaton's silky surface from pink to orange to dark blue. **Siófok's lakeside campgrounds** (p191) are a good spot for sunset views

- Soaking up the thermal goodness at Europe's largest thermal lake in **Hévíz** (p197)

- Meandering up Castle Hill to World's End in **Veszprém** (p215)

- Exploring Tihany's hilly peninsula and ochre-coloured **Abbey Church** (p208)

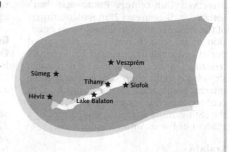

LAKE BALATON REGION

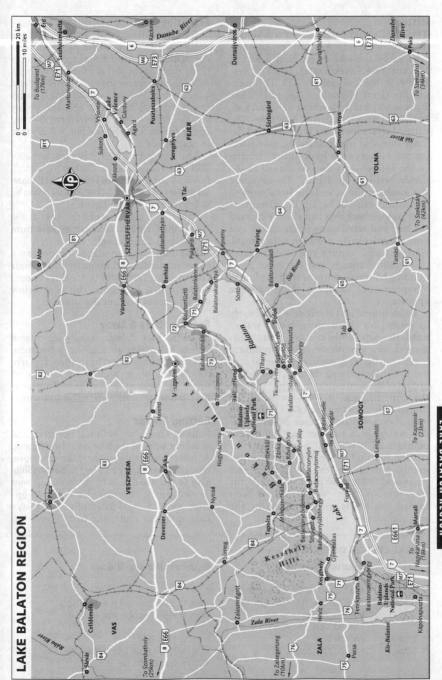

LAKE BALATON REGION

History

The area around Lake Balaton was settled as early as the Iron Age and the Romans, who called the lake Pelso, built a fort at Valcum (now Fenékpuszta), south of Keszthely, in the 2nd century AD. Throughout the Great Migrations (see p21), Lake Balaton was a reliable source of water, fish, reeds for thatch and ice in winter. The early Magyars found the lake a natural defence line, and many churches, monasteries and villages were built in the vicinity. In the 16th century the lake served as the divide between the Turks, who occupied the southern shore, and the Habsburgs to the northwest, but before the Ottomans were pushed back they had already crossed the lake and razed many of the towns and border castles in the northern hills. Croats, Germans and Slovaks resettled the area in the 18th century, and the subsequent building booms gave towns such as Sümeg, Veszprém and Keszthely their baroque appearance.

Balatonfüred and Hévíz developed early as resorts for the wealthy, but it wasn't until the late 19th century that landowners, their vines destroyed by phylloxera lice, began building summer homes to rent out to the burgeoning middle classes. The arrival of the southern railway in 1861 and the northern line in 1909 increased the tourist influx, and by the 1920s resorts on both shores welcomed some 50,000 holiday-makers each summer. Just before the outbreak of WWII that number had increased fourfold. After the war, the communist government expropriated private villas and built new holiday homes for trade unions. Many of these have been turned into hotels, greatly increasing the accommodation options.

Activities

The main pursuits for visitors at Lake Balaton – apart from swimming, of course – are **boating** (p52) and **fishing** (p52). Motorboats running on fuel are banned entirely, so 'boating' here means sailing, rowing and windsurfing. Fishing is good – the indigenous *fogas* (pike-perch) and the young version, *süllő*, being the prized catch – and edible *harcsa* (catfish) and *ponty* (carp) are in abundance.

You can get a fishing licence for 500/2000Ft per day/week from **Siotour** (opposite), in Siófok, or the **National Federation of Hungarian Anglers** (MOHOSZ; ☎ 1-248 2590; www.mohosz.hu; XII Korompai utca 17) in Budapest.

One of the big events of the year at the lake is the **Cross-Balaton Swimming Race** from Révfülöp to Balatonboglár in late July.

Lake cruises are a popular pastime over the summer months and range from one hour (adult/child 1200/600Ft) to three hours (2800/1400Ft) in length. The table below shows some of ports of departure.

Getting There & Away

Trains to Lake Balaton usually leave from Déli or Kelenföld train stations in Budapest, and buses from Népliget bus station. If you're travelling north or south from the lake to towns in Western or Southern Transdanubia, buses are usually preferable to trains.

Getting Around

Railway service on both the northern and southern sides of the lake is fairly frequent. A better way to see the lake up close, though, is on a ferry run by the **Balaton Shipping Co** (Balatoni Hajózási Rt; ☎ 84-310 050; www.balatonihajozas.hu; Krúdy sétány 2, Siófok). Ferries operate on the Siófok–Balatonfüred–Tihany–Balatonföldvár route, and from Fonyód to

LAKE CRUISES TIMETABLE		
Town	Departures Jul–Mid-Aug	Departures Mid-Aug–Mid-Sep
Badacsony	4pm Tue, Wed, Fri, Sat, Sun; 8pm Mon, Fri	
Balatonfüred	10am, 12.30pm, 2pm, 4pm, 6pm, 8pm Mon-Wed, Fri, Sun	11am, 12.30pm, 2pm, 4pm Mon, Tue, Thu, Sat
	10am, 12.30pm, 2pm, 4pm Thu & Sat	10am, 12.30pm, 2pm, 4pm Wed, Fri & Sun
Keszthely	every 2hr 11am-7pm	every 2hr 11am-5pm
Siófok	every 2hr 11am-5pm	10.30am, 2pm, 4.30pm, 6.30pm Mon & Wed-Sun
		10.30am, 2pm, 6.30pm Tue

BARGAINS GALORE

The number of visitors to Lake Balaton is dropping as Hungarians take advantage of cheap flights to sunnier climes and attack the Croatian coastline in swarms. This is of course disastrous for the local economy, but a blessing for those looking for bargains. While prices remain high in July and August, arrive in late May to early June or September and you'll more than likely land yourself a whopping discount on accommodation, particularly at the camping grounds.

If this isn't enough of an incentive to save some cash, then the newly-launched **Balaton Card** may very well be. The Standard (1499Ft; valid one season) variety offers discounts of anything between 5% to 25% on selected hotels, restaurants, special events and sports equipment rental, while the 4-Day card (6500Ft) includes, among other things, entry to museums, tickets on public transport in selected towns and even a fishing licence. A 10-Day card should also be available by the time you read this. Cards are sold at all Tourinform offices on the lake; check www.balatoncard.com for online information.

---

the Badacsony, up to four times daily in April/May and September/October, with many more frequent sailings from June to August. From late May to early September, ferries ply the lake from Balatonkenese to Keszthely and Révfülöp to Balatonboglár. There is also a regular car ferry between Tihanyi-rév and Szántódi-rév (from early March to late November). There are no passenger services on the lake in winter, ie from November to March.

Adults pay 720Ft for distances of one to 10km, 1020Ft for 11km to 20km and 1240Ft for 21km to 70km. Children pay half-price and return fares are slightly less than double the one-way fare. To transport a bicycle it costs 400/700Ft one way/return.

The car ferries charge 360/150/550/1040Ft per person/bicycle/motorcycle/car.

SIÓFOK
☎ 84 / pop 22,700
Siófok typifies the resorts of the southern shore: it's loud, brash and crowded in July and August. Dedicated pursuits here are eating, drinking, sunbathing, swimming and sleeping – and whatever comes in between. It is the largest of the lake's resorts and is jammed at the height of summer – so much so that it is officially allowed to call itself 'Hungary's summer capital'.

Orientation
Greater Siófok stretches for some 17km, as far as the resort of Balatonvilágos (once reserved exclusively for communist honchos) to the east and Balatonszéplak to the west. The dividing line between the so-called Aranypart, or Gold Coast, in the east, where

most of the big hotels are, and the less-developed Silver Coast (Ezüstpart) to the west is the lake-draining Sió Canal, which runs in a southeasterly direction to the Danube River.

Szabadság tér, the centre of Siófok, is to the east of the canal and about 500m southeast of the ferry pier. The bus and train stations are in Millennium Park just off Fő utca, the main drag.

Information
Main post office (Fő utca 186)
OTP bank (Szabadság tér 10/a) Has a currency-exchange machine and ATM.
Siotour (☎ 310 806; www.siotour.hu; Batthyány Lajos utca 2/b) A commercial agency that handles all the large camp sites along the southern shore.
Tourinform (☎ 310 117; siofok@tourinform.hu; Szabadság tér; ☒ 8am-8pm mid-Jun–mid-Aug; 9am-6pm Mon-Fri, 9am-noon Sat mid-Aug–mid-Sep; 9am-4pm Mon-Fri, 9am-noon Sat mid-Sep–mid-Jun) Has an office at the base of the old *víztorony* (water tower) which dates from 1912.
www.siofok.hu More information on the town.

Sights
There's not a whole lot to see of cultural or historical importance in a place where the baser instincts tend to rule. The shark aquarium at the **Coral Aquarium** (☎ 311 036; Batthyány Lajos utca 22; adult/child 600/400Ft, shark show extra 300Ft; ☒ 10am-6pm Apr-Oct, 10am-4pm Nov-Mar) is the largest of its kind in Hungary, but it seems out of place next to shallow Lake Balaton.

The **canal locks** system, which was partly built by the Romans in AD 292 and used extensively by the Turks in the 16th and 17th centuries, can be seen from Krúdy sétány, the walkway near the ferry pier, or Baross

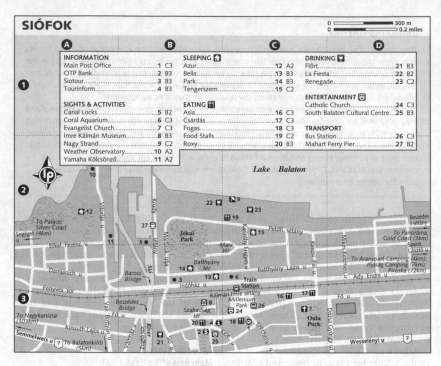

SIÓFOK

INFORMATION				SLEEPING				DRINKING		
Main Post Office	1	C3		Azur	12	A2		Flört	21	B3
OTP Bank	2	B3		Bella	13	B3		La Fiesta	22	B2
Siotour	3	B3		Park	14	B3		Renegade	23	C2
Tourinform	4	B3		Tengerszem	15	C2				
								ENTERTAINMENT		
SIGHTS & ACTIVITIES				EATING				Catholic Church	24	C3
Canal Locks	5	B2		Asia	16	C3		South Balaton Cultural Centre	25	B3
Coral Aquarium	6	C3		Csárdás	17	C3				
Evangelist Church	7	C3		Fogas	18	C3		TRANSPORT		
Imre Kálmán Museum	8	B3		Food Stalls	19	C2		Bus Station	26	C3
Nagy Strand	9	C2		Roxy	20	B3		Mahart Ferry Pier	27	B2
Weather Observatory	10	A2								
Yamaha Kölcsönző	11	A2								

Bridge to the south. Nearby are the headquarters of the Hungarian navy. The tower on the western tip of the canal entrance is the **weather observatory** of the National Meteorological Service (Országos Meteorológiai Szolgálat). Believe it or not, Lake Balaton can actually get quite rough when the wind picks up and there's a system of warning signals.

If you walk north on narrow Hock János köz, you'll reach the **Imre Kálmán Museum** (☎ 311 287; Kálmán Imre sétány 5; adult/child 250/150Ft; ☯ 9am-5pm Tue-Sun Apr-Oct, 9am-4pm Tue-Sun Nov-Mar). It is devoted to the life and works of the composer of popular operettas, Imre Kálmán, who was born in Siófok in 1882.

East of Szabadság tér in Oulu Park, Hungary's maverick architect Imre Makovecz strikes again with his winged and 'masked' **Evangelist church** (Evangélikus templom), which bears a strong resemblance to an Indonesian *garuda* (mythical bird).

Activities

Nagy Strand (adult/child 700/350Ft), Siófok's 'Big Beach', is east of the observatory and just north of Petőfi sétány; there's often free concerts here on summer evenings. There are many more 'managed' **swimming** areas along the Gold and Silver Coasts where it costs 700/350Ft per adult/child for a day pass and 3500/1750Ft for a weekly pass.

There are rowing boats and sailing **boats** for hire at various locations along the lake, including the Nagy Strand. See Activities (p188) for information on **lake cruises**. On the canal's western bank you'll find **Yamaha Kölcsönző** (Vitolás utca; ☯ mid-May–mid-Oct) where you can hire bicycles for 400/1600Ft per hour/day and mopeds for 1000/4000Ft.

Horse riding is another popular pastime in these parts; **Kersák** (☎ 322 819; Töltényi utca 2/b) in nearby Balatonkiliti has lessons for 2500Ft per hour, and accommodation.

Sleeping

Siófok is one of the few places on the lake where you might have trouble finding accommodation from late July to August – during this time, it is worth booking ahead. Also note that many small establishments only open during this time.

Tourinform and Siotour can both find you a private room (€10 to €20 per person) and an apartment for slightly more. Singles are rare and those staying only one or two nights are generally unwelcome; if you want to do it alone, check for 'Zimmer frei' signs along Erkel Ferenc utca and Damjanich utca on the Silver Coast, and Petőfi sétány and Beszédes József sétány on the Gold Coast.

BUDGET
There are over two dozen camp sites on Balaton's southern shore, and Siófok has nine, most with bungalows sleeping up to four people. They are open from May to September; the highest rates apply during most of July and August.

Tengerszem (☎ 310 146; Petőfi sétány 24; s/d 6000/8500Ft; ☻ Jun-Sep; ℗) In an old house close to the town's beach, Tengerszem has comfy rooms and a homely feel.

Aranypart Camping (☎ 353 399; aranypart@siotour .hu; Szent László utca 183-185; camp sites per tent 1140-1660Ft, person 1190-1870Ft, bungalows 3060-23,460Ft; ℗) Four kilometres east of the centre in Balatonszabadi is this camping ground with its own beach, restaurant, and bungalows which are basically small apartments.

Ifjúság Camping (☎ 352 571; ifjusag@siotour.hu; Pusztatorony tér 1; camp sites per tent 590-920Ft, person 770-1080Ft, bungalows 11,000-18,000Ft, cabins 2300-3570Ft; ℗) This place in gusto, 7km east of Siófok between tiny 'Salt Lake' and Lake Balaton, is good for fishing, swimming and generally kicking back. Choose from bungalows with bathroom and kitchen or wood cabins with shared facilities.

Piroska (☎ 584 521; cpiroska@balatontourist.hu; Aligai út 15; camp sites per tent 860-1500Ft, adult 795-1025Ft, child 625-820Ft, bungalows 9570-18,950Ft; ℗) For those who like to camp au naturel, there's a nudist site at Balatonakarattya at the northeastern end of the lake about 12km northeast of Siófok. It is within easy walking distance of the Balatonakarattya train station, which is on the line running along the lake's northern shore.

MIDRANGE
Bella (☎ 510 078; www.siofokbella.hu; Batthyány Lajos utca 14/a; r 6500-15,000Ft; ℗) This new block has modern, compact apartments with kitchen and balcony, and is on a fairly quiet street within easy walking distance of the beach.

Park (☎ 310 539; www.hotel-net.hu/Park-Siofok; Batthyány Lajos utca 7; s €25-60, d €30-70; ℗) Park is a small house not far from the lake. Its sizable rooms are done up in pastel colours with natural-wood furniture and bare-wood floors.

Panoráma (☎ 311 638; www.panoramahotel-siofok .hu; Beszédes József sétány 80; s €46-61, d €57-74; ℗ ☻) This high-rise four-star hotel is a very modern complex with large rooms overlooking the lake; unfortunately it doesn't have its own private beach, but it does have a pool.

TOP END
Ázur (☎ 501 413; www.hotelazur.hu; Vitorlás utca 11; s €64-116, d €72-135; ℗ ☻ ✖) After recently enjoying a complete makeover, Ázur is now Siófok's premier hotel. Its rooms are not only styled to create a warm and cosy atmosphere but also to bring you all the mod-cons you'll likely need, and the wellness and fitness centres are top-rate. There's also a private beach for guest use.

Eating
Quantity, not quality, is the word used to describe the eating options in Siófok. At least you won't starve…

Fogas (☎ 311 405; Fő utca 184; mains 1000-2000Ft; ☻ Mar-Oct) While the décor of Fogas is fairly standard, the same cannot be said for its fish selection, which is one of the largest, and best, in town.

Asia (☎ 312 546; Fő utca 93; mains 1000Ft) This is one of the very few places in town serving Asian food, and has a bright, open conservatory out front in which to enjoy it.

Csárdás (☎ 310 642; Fő utca 105; mains 1000-2000Ft; ☻ mid-Mar-Oct) An old-fashioned place attracting tours by the boatload with hearty Hungarian cuisine and live Gypsy music. Its garden towards the rear is a good spot to sample the regional white wine from Balatonboglár, which is usually light and not very distinctive (though the Chardonnay isn't bad).

Roxy (☎ 506 573; Szabadság tér; pizzas 570-1000Ft) This pseudo-rustic restaurant-pub on busy Szabadság tér attracts diners with a wide range of pizzas and a lively atmosphere. It may be hard to find a table after 9pm though.

For quick eats, attack one of a bunch of **food stalls** (Petőfi sétány) by the Nagy Strand.

Drinking & Entertainment

South Balaton Cultural Centre (☎ 311 855; Fő tér 2) Siófok's main cultural venue stages concerts, dance performances and plays.

Catholic church (Váradi Adolf tér) This church often hosts organ recitals over the summer months.

Siófok is the region's club central; try any of the following for a long, boozy and loud night out.

Flört (☎ 20-333 3303; www.flort.hu; Sió utca 4) Well-established club with trippy light shows, carnival girls and queues.

Palace (☎ 351295; www.palace.hu; Deák Ferenc utca 2) Hugely popular club on the Silver Coast, which has begun to attract quality international DJs; accessible by free bus from outside Tourinform between 9pm and 5am daily from May to mid-September.

La Fiesta (Petőfi sétány 3-5) A veritable drinker's den overlooking the beach; the place to end the night either on or under the table.

Renegade (Petőfi sétány 9) A thumping pub packed with young folk looking to enjoy every minute of their summer holiday.

Getting There & Away

BOAT

From late March to late October, four daily Mahart ferries run between Siófok and Balatonfüred, three of which carry on to Tihany. Up to nine ferries follow the same route in July and August. See also Getting Around (p188) for more details about other routes and frequencies for ferry services.

BUS

Buses serve a lot of destinations from Siófok, but compared with the excellent train connections, they're not very frequent. The exceptions are to Kaposvár (1030Ft, two hours, 85km), with hourly departures. Other destinations include Budapest (1330Ft, 1½-three hours, 108km, seven daily), Harkány (1930Ft, 3¾ hours, 160km, one daily), Hévíz and Keszthely (968Ft, 1½ hours, 78km, three daily), Pécs (1690Ft, 3 hours, 134km, three daily), Szekszárd (1210Ft, 2¼ hours, 96km, five daily) and Veszprém (605Ft, 1¼ hours, 48km, five daily).

TRAIN

The main railway line running through Siófok carries trains to Székesfehérvár (430Ft, 55 minutes, 48km), to Déli and Kelenföld train stations in Budapest (1212Ft, two hours, 115km), to the other resorts on the lake's southern shore and Nagykanizsa (1212Ft, two hours, 106km) up to 26 times daily in each direction. Only one daily train

---

HIGHWAY PROSTITUTION

Prostitutes lining the major thoroughfares throughout much of Eastern Europe are a fairly common sight – particularly close to border crossings – and Hungary is no exception. Take Rd 7 along the southern coast of Lake Balaton and the sight of women standing in the middle of nowhere, coyly waving as you drive by, is not uncommon.

Prostitution is legal in Hungary, but it is illegal to prostitute others (ie, pimp). However, it is illegal to prostitute yourself within a hundred metres of a number of public institutions (municipal buildings, schools, kindergartens, churches, etc) and major country roads (highways and roads with a one- or two-digit number). Therefore women lining Road No 7 are breaking the law, and whether it is just to make some extra cash or because force is being used is unfortunately not clear.

Official statistics on street prostitution and trafficking in women don't exist, but unofficial police estimates state that in summer up to 50% of sex workers in Hungary are from abroad. Once again, it is unclear whether these women are being trafficked across international borders or are just in Hungary looking for work. There is also the problem of trafficking within the country for sexual exploitation, which amounts to the lion's share of trafficked persons. The consenting age in Hungary is 14, so some women may have been involved in trafficking rings from a very early age.

The present government is in favour of further legalisation of the sex industry, resulting in more organised prostitution, such as brothels. This will provide law enforcers with more control in the area, but it remains to be seen how much this line of action will affect the trafficking in human beings.

For more information, check out **NANE** (www.nane.hu), the Hungarian Women's Rights Association.

from Budapest to Zagreb stops at Siófok. Local trains run south from Siófok to Kaposvár three times daily (1004Ft, two hours, 95km).

Getting Around
Leaving the bus station, just outside the train station buses 1 and 2 run to the Silver Coast and Gold Coast, respectively. There are also **taxis** (☎ 317 713) around town.

KESZTHELY
☎ 83 / pop 22,400
Keszthely, occupying a prime position at the western end of Balaton, is the only town on the lake not entirely dependent on tourism; in fact, it generally goes about life without an overbearing concern for its watery neighbour and its accompanying tourist forints. It's a pleasant town of grand houses, trees, cafés and enough to see and do to hold you for a spell.

History
The Romans built a fort at Valcum (now Fenékpuszta) 5km to the south, and their road north to the colonies at Sopron and Szombathely is today's Kossuth Lajos utca. The town's former fortified monastery and Franciscan church on Fő tér were strong enough to repel the Turks in the 16th century.

In the middle of the 18th century, Keszthely and its surrounds (including Hévíz) came into the possession of the Festetics family, progressives and reformers very much in the tradition of the Széchenyis. In fact, Count György Festetics (1755–1819), who founded Europe's first agricultural college, the Georgikon, here in 1797, was an uncle of István Széchenyi.

Orientation
The centre of town is Fő tér, from where Kossuth Lajos utca, lined with colourful old houses, runs to the north (pedestrian only) and south. The bus and train stations are opposite one another near the lake at the end of Mártírok útja. From the stations, follow Mártírok útja up the hill, then turn north into Kossuth Lajos utca to reach the centre. The ferry docks at a stone pier within sight of the Hullám hotel. From here, follow the path past the hotel. Erzsébet királyné utca, which flanks Helikon Park, leads to Fő tér.

Information
Keszthely Tourist (☎ 314 288; Kossuth Lajos utca 25)
Main post office (Kossuth Lajos utca 46-48)
OTP bank (Kossuth Lajos utca 38)
Stone's (Kisfaludy utca 17; per min 15Ft; ☺ 10am-midnight Mon-Sat, 5pm-midnight Sun) Small bar with Internet access.
Tourinform (☎ 314 144; keszthely@tourinform.hu; Kossuth Lajos utca 28; ☺ 9am-8pm Mon-Fri, 9am-6pm Sat mid-Jun–mid-Sep; 9am-5pm or 6pm Mon-Fri, 9am-12.30pm Sat mid-Sep–mid-Jun) An excellent source of information on Keszthely and the entire Balaton area.

Sights
FESTETICS PALACE
The **Festetics Palace** (Festetics kastély; ☎ 312 190; Kastély utca 1; adult/student 1300/700Ft; ☺ 9am-6pm Jul-Aug, 9am-5pm Tue-Sun Sep-Jun), built in 1745 and extended 150 years later, contains 100 rooms in two sprawling wings. The 19th-century northern wing houses a music school, city library and conference centre; the **Helikon Palace Museum** (Helikon Kastélymúzeum) and the palace's greatest treasure, the renowned **Helikon Library** (Helikon Könyvtár) are in the baroque south wing.

The museum's rooms (about a dozen in all, each in a different colour scheme) are full of portraits, bric-a-brac and furniture, much of it brought from England by Mary Hamilton, a duchess who married one of the Festetics men in the 1860s. The library is renowned for its 90,000-volume collection, but just as impressive is the golden oak shelving and furniture carved in 1801 by local craftsman János Kerbl. Also worth noting are the Louis XIV Salon with its stunning marquetry, the rococo music room and the private chapel (1804).

If you have time take a peek at the attached **Coach Museum** (adult/child 600/400Ft), with coaches and sleighs fit for royalty. To visit both the palace and coach museum costs 1600/800Ft per adult/child, and a one-hour guided tour of everything in one of four languages costs 'only' 6500/3500Ft.

GEORGIKON FARM MUSEUM
The **Georgikon Farm Museum** (Georgikon Majormúzeum; ☎ 311 563; Bercsényi Miklós utca 67; adult/child 400/200Ft; ☺ 10am-5pm Tue-Sat, 10am-6pm Sun May-Oct) is housed in several early-19th-century buildings of what was the Georgikon's experimental farm. It contains exhibits on the history of the college and the later

LAKE BALATON REGION

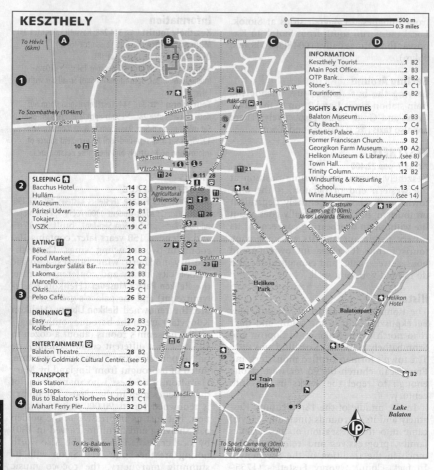

KESZTHELY

Pannon Agricultural University (now a few blocks to the southeast on the corner of Széchenyi utca and Deák Ferenc utca), viniculture in the Balaton region and traditional farm trades such as those performed by wagon builders, wheelwrights, coopers and blacksmiths.

OTHER SIGHTS

Fő tér is a colourful square with some lovely buildings, including the late-baroque **Town Hall** on the northern side, the **Trinity Column** (1770) in the centre and the former **Franciscan church** (Ferences templom) in the park to the south. The church was originally built in the Gothic style in the late 14th century for Franciscan monks, but many

alterations were made in subsequent centuries, including the addition of the steeple in 1898. The Gothic rose window above the porch remains, though, as do some faded 15th-century frescoes in the sanctuary and on the southern wall. Count György and other Festetics family members are buried in the crypt below.

The **Balaton Museum** (☎ 312 351; Múzeum utca 2; adult/child 500/200Ft; 🕙 10am-6pm Tue-Sat May-Oct, 9am-5pm Tue-Sat Nov-Apr) was purpose-built in 1928 and contains much on the Roman fort at Valcum (Fenékpuszta) and traditional life around Lake Balaton. Also of interest are exhibits depicting the history of navigation on the lake and the photos of summer frolickers at the start of the 20th century.

The **Kis-Balaton** (Little Balaton) region to the south of Keszthely falls under the protection of the **Balaton Uplands National Park** (Felvidéki Nemzeti Park; www.bfnpi.hu) and is a great place to enjoy the wildlife of the area. A bird-ringing camp run by the **Hungarian Ornithological & Nature Conservation Society** (MME; ☎ 1-275 6261 in Budapest; www.mme.hu in Hungarian; admission free) in Fenékpuszta near the delta of the Zala River has very knowledgeable staff and can fill you in on bird species on and around the lake. The camp is one stop on the train heading for Balatonszentgyörgy; if you're driving from Keszthely, the exit is at the 111km stone on Rte 71. At the southern end of Kis-Balaton is a **Buffalo Reserve** (☎ 87-555 291; adult/child 500/200Ft), which is home to some 200 water buffalo; the best time to visit is late afternoon, when the buffalo gather near the reserve headquarters. It's more than a trek to get there by public transport, so the only real option is under your own steam; the reserve is near the tiny village of Kápolnapuszta.

Activities

Keszthely has two beaches that are OK for **swimming** or **sunbathing**: City Beach (Városi Strand), which is good for kids and close to the ferry pier, and reedy Helikon Beach further south. They do, however, have a unique view of both the north and south shores of the lake. There's a **windsurfing** and **kitesurfing** school at City Beach in summer. (See Activities p188 for information on lake cruises.)

There are several **horse-riding** schools in the area, including **János Lovarda** (☎ 30-401 6691) in Sömögye-dűlő, northeast of Keszthely.

For wine tastings, try the **Wine Museum** (☎ 510 450; Erzsébet királyné utca 18; admission free; ☒ 10am-11pm) at the Bacchus hotel (right) where wine tastings are available (6/10 sorts 1500/2400Ft).

Festivals & Events

The biggest annual cultural event in Keszthely is the **Balaton Festival** (music and street theatre) held throughout May.

Sleeping

Keszthely Tourist can help find private rooms (from 2500Ft per person) whereas Tourinform will only supply you with a list. Otherwise, strike out on your own (particularly along Móra Ferenc utca) and keep an

eye out for '*szoba kiadó*' or '*Zimmer frei*' (Hungarian and German, respectively, for 'room for rent') signs.

BUDGET

Múzeum (☎ 313 182; Múzeum utca 3; s/d 3000/6000Ft) Ignore the effervescent smell of stale air and dog on entering – rooms here are well-aired and very clean, and the whole place has a homey feel; it's an easy walk to the stations.

VSZK (☎ 515 300; Mártírok útja; s/d 2500/5000Ft; ☒ Jul-Aug; ☒) This large, concrete block of a student dorm has stripped-back rooms with a bed and sink, and is within easy walking distance of transport connections.

Castrum Camping (☎ 312 120; Móra Ferenc utca 48; camp sites per adult/child/tent from €3/2.40/4.20; ☒ Apr-Oct; ☒ ☒) North of the stations, this place is more suited to caravans and the lake is across the railway tracks, but it's large and has a plethora of facilities.

Sport Camping (☎ 313 777; Csárda utca; camp sites per tent/person 990/990Ft; bungalows 6000Ft; ☒) This lush and green camping groun may look to some an unkempt jungle, but it does have its fair share of wilderness charm. Unfortunately it's a bit close to the train tracks, but the lake is only a minute away.

MIDRANGE

Bacchus (☎ 510 450; www.bacchushotel.hu; Erzsébet királyné utca 18; s €33-47, d €40-58; ☒) Bacchus wins the 'Best in Show' award with its warm and welcoming staff, immaculate rooms and more than handy location to the town centre. The cellar is given over to a wine museum (left) and there's a good restaurant.

Tokajer (☎ 319 875; www.pensiontokajer.hu; Apát utca 21; s €26-31, d €22-50; ☒ ☒) Spread over four buildings in a quiet area of town, Tokajer has rooms in excellent condition, some with balcony and kitchen. Added extras include three pools, free use of bicycles and fitness room, and a mini wellness centre. Price depends on season and room facilities.

Hullám (☎ 312 644; www.hotelhullam.hu; Balatonpart 1; s €32-52, d €43-66; ☒ Apr-Oct; ☒) Built in 1892, this old-worldly hotel still exudes plenty of charm even though it looks a bit down on its luck. Rooms are large and many look directly onto the lake, and guests can use the swimming pool and sports centre at the nearby Helikon Hotel.

Párizsi Udvar (☎ 311 202; Kastély utca 5; r from 7900Ft; ☒) A good choice near Festetics Palace is this small *pension* which takes up part of the original palace complex. Its handful of apartments are huge.

Eating & Drinking

Lakoma (☎ 313 129; Balaton utca 9; midday menu 450Ft; mains from 800Ft) With a good vegetarian selection (for Hungarian-restaurant standards), grill/roast specialities and a back garden which transforms itself into a leafy dining area in the summer months, it's hard to go wrong with Lakoma. Surprisingly, there is only a small selection of fish dishes.

Oázis (☎ 311 023; Rákóczi tér 3; mains 800-1000Ft; 🕙 11am-4pm Mon-Fri) A vegetarian restaurant near the palace. It has buckets of good energy and healthy pickings during the midweek lunch-hour rush.

Béke (☎ 318 219; Kossuth Lajos utca 50; midday menu 600-900Ft, mains from 1000Ft) This half bar, half restaurant hybrid is a colourful, lively spot with plenty of fish choices, a large inner courtyard and live music on weekends.

Bacchus (☎ 510 450; Erzsébet királyné utca 18) The imaginative selection of Hungarian dishes on the Bacchus hotel menu is complimented by game and fish dishes. Needless to say, its accompanying wine is top-rate.

Marcello (☎ 313 563; Városház utca 4; pizzas from 650Ft) This cool cellar restaurant has a summer patio and a large selection of made-to-order pizzas and salads.

Pelso Café (☎ 315 415; coffee & cake from 250Ft; 🕙 9am-9pm) This café is in a two-level modern tower-like structure in the park just south of the Catholic church, a fine spot to take cake and coffee and watch the world go by.

Hamburger Saláta Bár (Erzsébet királyné utca; burgers from 350Ft) If you're looking for a bite on the run, or a quick sit-down meal, this place will fill you up with burgers and salads.

Keszthely's lively food market combines the best and worst of Hungary's markets, with homemade honeys and jams alongside T-shirts with Indians on Harleys.

There are several interesting places for a drink south of the centre on Kossuth Lajos utca, including:

Easy (Kossuth Lajos utca 79) Attracts local young bloods.
Kolibri (Kossuth Lajos utca 81) Cocktail bar more suited to an older crowd.

Entertainment

Károly Goldmark Cultural Centre (☎ 515 251; Kossuth Lajos utca 28) This is where you can catch Hungarian folk dancing in the courtyard over the summer months.

Balaton Theatre (☎ 515 230; Fő tér 3) The latest in theatre performances can be seen at this new theatre on the main square.

Festetics Palace (Festetics kastély; ☎ 312 190; Kastély utca 1) Concerts are often held in the music room during the summer.

Getting There & Away

BUS
Destinations served by more than 10 daily buses from Keszthely are Hévíz (133Ft, 15 minutes, 8km), Sümeg (423Ft, 50 minutes, 31km), Tapolca (363Ft, 35 minutes, 28km) and Veszprém (968Ft, 1¾ hours, 77km); there are about six to Nagykanizsa (725Ft, 1½ hours, 57km). Other towns served by bus include Badacsony (363Ft, 35 minutes, 27km, seven daily), Budapest (2300Ft, three to four hours, 190km, six daily) and Pécs (3½ hours, 152km, four daily). Some of these buses – including those to Hévíz, Nagykanizsa and Sümeg – can be boarded at the bus stops in front of the Catholic church on Fő tér.

For buses to the lake's northern shore (Badacsony, Nagyvázsony and Tapolca), you can catch the bus along Tapolcai út.

TRAIN
Keszthely is on a branch line linking Tapolca and Balatonszentgyörgy, from where up to seven daily trains continue along the southern shore to Székesfehérvár (1420Ft, 2¾ hours, 125km) and to Keleti or Déli train stations in Budapest (2030Ft, three to four hours, 190km). To reach Szombathely (1420Ft, three hours, 126km), you must change at Tapolca and sometimes at Celldömölk, too; for towns along Lake Balaton's northern shore, a change at Tapolca is required.

From mid-June to late August, **MÁV Nostalgia** (☎ 318 162; www.mavnosztalgia.hu) runs a vintage steam-train from Keszthely to Badacsonytomaj (1¾ hours) at 10am from Tuesday to Sunday, returning at 2.50pm. Verify this service with MÁV Nostalgia by phone or check the website before making plans.

Getting Around
Buses run from the train and bus stations to the Catholic church on Fő tér, but unless there's one waiting on your arrival it's just as easy to walk. You can also make a booking for a **taxi** (☎ 333 333).

HÉVÍZ

☎ 83 / pop 4310

If you enjoy visiting spas and taking the waters, you'll love Hévíz, site of Gyógy-tó, Europe's largest thermal lake. The people of this town some 7km northwest of Keszthely have made use of the warm mineral water for centuries, first in a tannery in the Middle Ages and later for curative purposes. The lake was first developed as a private resort by Count György Festetics of Keszthely in 1795.

Orientation

The centre of Hévíz is Park Wood (Parkerdő) and its thermal lake. The bus station (Deák tér) is a few steps from the northern entrance to the lake; the small commercial centre lies to the west of the bus station. Kossuth Lajos utca, where most of the big hotels are located, forms the western boundary of the Park Wood.

Information

Caffe Machiato (Széchenyi utca 7; per hr 600Ft; ☾ 9am-1pm) Internet access.

OTP bank (Erzsébet királynő utca 7) Has ATM and money-exchange machine.

Post office (Kossuth Lajos utca 4)

Zalatour (☎ 341 048; Rákóczi utca 8) A source for information on the town.

Activities

Thermal Lake (Gyógy-tó; Park Wood; 3 hr/4 hr/5 hr/whole day 900/1200/1400/1600Ft, rubber-ring hire 300Ft; ☾ 8.30am-5pm in summer, 9am-4.30pm in winter) is an astonishing sight: a surface of almost 5 hectares in the Park Wood, covered for most of the year in pink and white lotuses. The source is a spring spouting from a crater some 40m below ground that disgorges up to 80 million litres of warm water a day, renewing itself every 48 hours or so. The surface temperature averages 33°C and never drops below 26°C in winter, allowing bathing throughout the year, even when there's ice on the fir trees of the Park Wood.

A covered bridge leads to the thermal lake's *fin-de-siècle* **central pavilion**, from where catwalks and piers fan out. You can swim protected beneath these or make your way to the small rafts and 'anchors' further

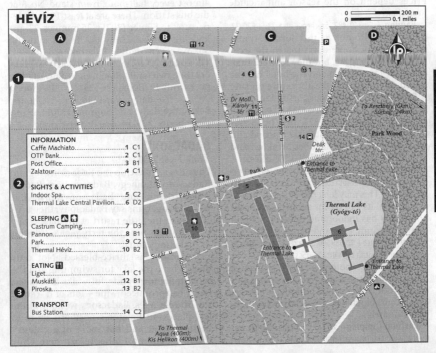

HÉVÍZ

INFORMATION	
Caffe Machiato	1 C1
OTP Bank	2 C1
Post Office	3 B1
Zalatour	4 C1

SIGHTS & ACTIVITIES	
Indoor Spa	5 C2
Thermal Lake Central Pavilion	6 D2

SLEEPING	
Castrum Camping	7 D3
Pannon	8 B1
Park	9 C2
Thermal Hévíz	10 B2

EATING	
Liget	11 C1
Muskátli	12 B1
Piroska	13 B2

| TRANSPORT | |
| Bus Station | 14 C2 |

To Keszthely (5km); Sümeg (24km)

Park Wood

Thermal Lake (Gyógy-tó)

Entrance to Thermal Lake

To Thermal Aqua (400m); Kis Helikon (400m)

out on rubber rings. There are some piers along the shore for sunbathing as well.

If you're looking for treatments, head to the **indoor spa** (adult/child 600/300Ft; ☼ 7am-5pm) which offers every kind of thermal remedy imaginable. **Zalatour** (☎ 341 048; Rákóczi utca 8) rents bikes for 800Ft per day.

Sleeping

Most hotels have specials for stays of one week or more, and the rates vary depending on the season.

Zalatour can find you a private room (€20 to €25 per double), though things could be tight in summer and you may be charged an extra fee for stays of less than three nights. You'll see a lot of signs reading 'Zimmer frei' and 'szoba kiadó' along Kossuth Lajos utca and Zrínyi utca, where you can make your own deals directly.

Kis Helikon (☎ 340 754; kishelikonhotel@axelero .hu; Kossuth Lajos utca 72; s €30-44, d €36-72; P) Kis Helikon is a small, privately-run hotel with large, modern rooms (some with balcony and separate lounge), a middle-of-the-road restaurant and its own wellness centre. Prices depend on the season and include breakfast.

Pannon (☎ 340 482; Széchenyi utca 23; s €20-22, d €34-44; P) Rooms at this former trade-union holiday home don't match the exuberance of the foyer, but they're more than adequate for sleeping and the hotel has the added advantage of a health centre on site.

Park (☎ 341 190; postmaster@betapark.axelero.net; Petőfi Sándor tér 26; s €42-62, d €58-83; P 🐾) In elegant Kató Villa (1927), this hotel has seen better days but it still has a proud and serene air. The price includes breakfast and full use of the hotel's wellness facilities.

Thermal Hévíz (☎ 889 400; thermalheviz.reservation@ danubiusgroup.com; Kossuth Lajos utca 9-11; s €61-94, d €86-148; P 🐾) This may look rather dire from the outside, but its 210 rooms are in good condition and it has indoor and outdoor pools, a sauna, solarium, gym and tennis courts.

Thermal Aqua (☎ 889 500; aqua.reservation@danubi usgroup.com; Kossuth Lajos utca 13-15; s €51-78, d €72-116; P 🐾) This is another of Hévíz's massive hotels with a fitness and wellness centre and comfy rooms; the actual building – a large, communist block – leaves a lot to be desired, unfortunately.

Castrum Camping (☎ 343 198; camping@hevizcas trum.axelero.net; Tó-part; camp sites per tent 730-10,400Ft;

adult 780-1250Ft, child 620-990Ft; pension s/d 8200/9900Ft; ☼ year-round; P) Only a short walk from the lake is this very green and very large camp site, with a range of accommodation options and Fort Knox–like security.

Eating

Muskátli (☎ 341 475; Széchenyi utca 30; mains around 1000Ft) An extensive fish selection among a heavy-laden Hungarian menu is Muskátli's most appealing aspect; its pretty terrace and relaxed ambience follow close behind.

Piroska (☎ 30-687 4348; Kossuth Lajos utca 10; mains 1000-1500Ft) If you're into shady terraces, live folk music and fish dishes, then Piroska will probably fit the bill.

Liget (Dr Moll Károly tér; pizzas & mains 1000-1200Ft) The décor here hasn't changed since Khrushchev was in power, but that doesn't seem to bother the regular patrons who enjoy its sunny terrace and standard Hungarian fare.

Getting There & Away

Hévíz isn't on a train line, but buses travel east to Keszthely (133Ft, 15 minutes, 8km) almost every half-hour from stand No 3 at the bus station. There are at least 10 daily departures to Sümeg (302Ft, 35 minutes, 23km) and less to Badacsony (423Ft, 45 minutes, 35km, seven daily), Balatonfüred (908Ft, 1½ hours, 75km, eight daily) and Veszprém (1210Ft, two hours, 96km, eight daily). Other buses run to Budapest (2540Ft, 3¼ hours, 205km, five daily), Pápa (1030Ft, 1¾ hours, 84km, five daily) and Sopron (1570Ft, 2½ to three hours, 129km, one or two daily).

BADACSONY
☎ 87 / pop 2300

Four towns make up the Badacsony region: Badacsonylábdihegy, Badacsonyörs, Badacsonytördemic and Badacsonytomaj. But when Hungarians say Badacsony, they usually mean the little resort at the Badacsony train station, near the ferry pier southwest of Badacsonytomaj.

Badacsony is thrice-blessed. Not only does it have the lake for swimming and the mountains for wonderful walks and hikes, but it has produced wine – lots of it – since the Middle Ages. Badacsony was one of the last places on Balaton's northern shore to be developed and has more of a country feel to it than most other resorts here. Only

Tihany vies for supremacy in the beauty stakes (both places are 'landscape protection reserves'), and you might stop here for a day or two to relax.

Orientation

Rte 71, the main road along the lake's northern shore, runs through Badacsony as Balatoni út; this is where the bus lets you off. The ferry pier is on the eastern side of this road; almost everything else is to the west. Above the village, several *pensions* and houses with private accommodation ring the base of the hill on Római út, which debouches into Balatoni út at Badacsonytomaj, a few kilometres to the northeast. Szegedi Róza utca branches off to the north from Római út and runs through

the vineyards to the Kisfaludy House restaurant (p201) and the base of the hill.

Information

Balatontourist (☎ 531 021; Park utca 4) Organises private rooms, fishing licences and will exchange money.
Miditourist (☎ 431 028; Egry sétány 3; ☒ 8.30am–5pm Mon-Fri, 8.30am-noon Sat May–Oct); branch office (☎ 431 028; Park utca 53; ☒ 9am-7pm May–Oct) The main office is in the centre of the village, the branch is to the northeast.
OTP ATM (Park utca 4) Beside Balatontourist.
Post office (Park utca 3)
Tourinform (☎ 431 046; badacsonytomaj@tourinform.hu; Park utca 6; ☒ 9am-6pm mid-Jun–mid-Sep, 8am-5pm Mon-Fri, 10am-2pm Sat & Sun mid-Sep–mid-Jun) Informed staff have details on the region.

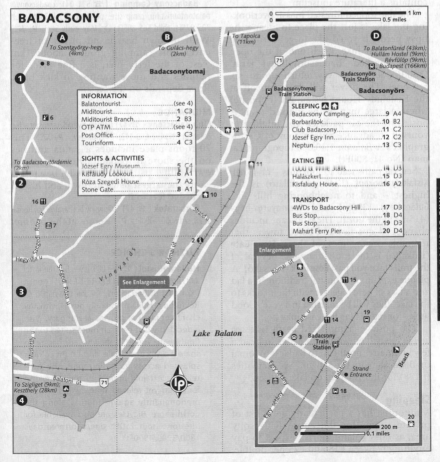

BADACSONY

0 ——————— 1 km
0 ——————— 0.5 miles

To Szentgyörgy-hegy (4km)
To Gulács-hegy (2km)
To Tapolca (11km)
To Balatonfüred (43km)
Hullám Hostel (9km)
Révfülöp (9km)
Budapest (166km)

Badacsonytomaj

Badacsonyörs Train Station

Badacsonytomaj Train Station

Badacsonyörs

To Badacsonytördemic (2km)

To Szigliget (9km)
Keszthely (28km)

Lake Balaton

Balatoni út

INFORMATION
Balatontourist...................(see 4)
Miditourist...........................1 C3
Miditourist Branch.................2 B3
OTP ATM............................(see 4)
Post Office.........................3 C3
Tourinform.........................4 C3

SIGHTS & ACTIVITIES
József Egry Museum...............5 C4
Kisfaludy Lookout.................6 A1
Róza Szegedi House...............7 A2
Stone Gate.........................8 A1

SLEEPING
Badacsony Camping................9 A4
Borbarátok........................10 B2
Club Badacsony...................11 C2
József Egry Inn...................12 C2
Neptun...........................13 C3

EATING
Food & Wine Stalls...............14 D3
Halászkert.......................15 D3
Kisfaludy House..................16 A2

TRANSPORT
4WDs to Badacsony Hill...........17 D3
Bus Stop.........................18 D4
Bus Stop.........................19 D3
Mahart Ferry Pier................20 D4

Enlargement

Római út

Badacsony Train Station

Strand Entrance

Beach

0 ——————— 200 m
0 ——————— 0.1 miles

LAKE BALATON REGION

Sights & Activities

The **József Egry Museum** (☎ 431 044; Egry sétány 12; adult/child 300/150Ft; ☺ 10am-8pm Jul-Aug, 10am-6pm Tue-Sun May-Jun & Sep-Oct) is devoted to the Balaton region's leading painter (1883–1951) and Hungary's equivalent to Kokoschka. Many of his works powerfully capture the essence of village and fishing life on the lake through the use of strong, dark colours.

The dramatic slopes and vineyards above the town centre are sprinkled with little wine-press houses and 'folk baroque' cottages. One of these is the **Róza Szegedi House** (☎ 430 906; Szegedi Róza utca; adult/child 400/200Ft; ☺ 10am-6pm Tue-Sun May-Sep), which belonged to the actress wife of the poet Sándor Kisfaludy from Sümeg. Established in 1790, it contains a literature museum.

The flat-topped forested massif overlooking the lake is just the place to escape the tipsy herds. If you'd like to get a running start on your hike, catch one of the open 4WDs marked 'Badacsony-hegyi járat' (3600/5000Ft one way/return up to six persons). The driver will drop you off at the Kisfaludy House restaurant (opposite) where a large map of the marked trails is posted by the car park. Or you might arm yourself in advance with a copy of Cartographia's *A Balaton* 1:40,000 topographical map (No 41; 800Ft).

Several paths lead to lookouts – at 437m, **Kisfaludy Lookout** (Kisfaludy kilátó) is the highest – and to neighbouring hills like **Gulács-hegy** (393m) and **Szentgyörgy-hegy** (415m) to the north. The landscape includes abandoned quarries and basalt towers that resemble organ pipes; of these, **Stone Gate** (Kőkapu) is the most dramatic. Several of the trails take you past **Rose Rock** (Rózsakő). A plaque explains an unusual tradition: 'If a lad and a lass sit here together with their backs to the lake, they will be married in a year'. Good luck – or regrets (as the case may be).

The postage-stamp-sized **beach** (admission free) is reedy; you would do better to head a few kilometres northeast to Badacsonytomaj or Badacsonyörs for a swim. See Activities (p188) for information on lake cruises.

Sleeping

Miditourist has a particularly good list of private rooms for the entire Badacsony area, as does Balatontourist; expect to pay anything between €18 and €25 per double.

Note that it generally costs more for stays of less than three nights. If you want to strike out on your own there are plenty of places along Római út and Park utca.

BUDGET

Neptun (☎ 431 293; Római út 156; dm 2000Ft, s/d 6000/7000Ft; **P**) This, the sister *pension* of Borbarátok, is a short walk to the train station and has a choice of rooms, including basic dorm-style rooms.

József Egry Inn (471 057; Római út 1; 1-5-bed r per person 1500-2500Ft; ☺ mid-Apr–mid-Oct) This simple inn is about as cheap as you can find in Badacsony, and is within walking distance of the Badacsonytomaj train station. Its rates depend on the season.

Badacsony Camping (☎ 531 041; cbadacsony@ balatontourist.hu; camp sites per tent 705-1035Ft, adult 705-975Ft, child 565-805Ft; ☺ May–early Sep; **P** ☒) With its own beach and plenty of tree-cover, this camping ground, about 1km west of the ferry pier, is a fine place for families and those wanting to kick back. Price depends on the season.

MIDRANGE

Club Badacsony (☎ 471 040; www.badacsonyhotel.hu; Balatoni út 14; r €50-112; ☺ Apr-Nov; **P** ☒) This 70-room place includes a sauna and lies on the shore in Badacsonytomaj with its own (rather pathetic and reedy) beach. It's easily the largest place in town, and has an exclusive feel to it.

Borbarátok (☎ 471 597; www.borbaratok.hu; Római út 78; s/d 6000/7000Ft; **P**) Rooms at this *pension*

AUTHOR'S CHOICE

Hullám Hostel (☎ 463 089; www.balatonhostel .hu; Füredi út 6; dm €12, s €15-18, d €30/36) About 9km east of Badacsony in the township of Révfülöp is Hullám, the only hostel with any character in all of provincial Hungary. With a decidedly laid-back air more suited to the Caribbean, young staff who are happy to share a drink and a tale, and bright colours splashed across its basic rooms, this hostel will certainly appeal to those looking for a fun yet relaxed time away from the predominantly ageing tourists along the north shore. Bicycles are also available for hire (one hour 250Ft, one/two/three days 1800/3200/4500Ft).

AUTHOR'S CHOICE

Kisfaludy House (☎ 431 016; Szegedi Róza utca 87; mains 1500-2500Ft; ☾ to midnight Apr-Nov) Perched high on the hill overlooking the vineyards and the lake is Kisfaludy House, a charming stone cottage built in 1798 that was once a press house of the Kisfaludy family. The view from its alfresco terrace easily ranks among the top five on the entire lake, and is the best place in Badacsony for a meal or a drink. To the west is lovely Szigliget Bay, and directly across to the south lie what Hungarians call the two 'breasts' of Fonyód: the Sípos and Sándor Hills.

are above its restaurant and a little on the small side but comfy enough. It's a short walk to the lake and has the advantage of an extensive wine cellar.

It's also worth striking out on your own on the road north of the train line as there are several small *pensions* among the vineyards.

Eating

Halászkert (☎ 431 054; Park utca 5; mains 1500Ft) If you can't make it up the hill to Kisfaludy and are looking for a range of fish dishes to choose from, head here. It may be crowded and touristy at times, but the food is top-rate.

Borbarátok (☎ 471 597; Római út 78; mains 1000-2000Ft) A lively bar and restaurant where the food is served on wooden plates (adds to the flavour perhaps?). It's a good place to try a glass of Badacsony's premier white wines, Kéknyelű (Blue Stalk) or Szürkebarát (Pinot Gris).

Neptun (☎ 431 293; Római út 156) Borbarátok's sister *pension*, with its simple restaurant and large terrace, is also a fine choice.

Food stalls with picnic tables dispensing sausage, fish soup, *lángos* and *gyros* (meat skewers), line the pedestrian walkway between the train station and Park utca, and are intermingled with **wine stalls** (80Ft per glass, 450Ft to 600Ft per litre) serving cheap plonk.

Getting There & Away

There are three daily buses that go to Balatonfüred (544Ft, 50 minutes, 44km) and Székesfehérvár; other buses run to Budapest (2060Ft, three hours, 170km, one daily), Hévíz (423Ft, 45 minutes, 35km, one daily),

Keszthely (363Ft, 35 minutes, 27km, one daily), Tapolca (241Ft, 30 minutes, 16km, two daily) and Veszprém (786Ft, 1½ hours, 62km, one daily).

Badacsony is on the train line linking all the towns on Lake Balaton's northern shore with Déli and Kelenföld train stations in Budapest (1828Ft, 3½ hours, 170km) and with Tapolca (182Ft, 20 minutes, 14km). To get to Keszthely (346Ft, one hour, 39km) you must change at Tapolca.

Passenger ferries between Badacsony and Fonyód run at least four times daily from late April to late October; there are eight ferries daily in June and September and nine daily in July and August. In Fonyód you can get a connection to Southern Transdanubia by taking a train direct to Kaposvár.

See Keszthely (p196) for information on the MÁV Nostalgia steam-train service between the two towns.

TAPOLCA

☎ 87 / pop 18,200

This pleasant town has a particularly fine setting wedged between the Balaton Highlands and the Southern Bakony Hills some 14km northeast of Badacsony. It's quite a gentile place and by no means touristy, so if you're looking for somewhere to take a day out from the tourist-swamped lake shore, consider heading here.

History

Tapolca has always been an important crossroads; under the Romans both the road between Rome and Aquincum and the road that linked Savaria (Szombathely) and Arrabona (Győr) passed through here. The Romans were followed by the Avars and, in turn, by the Slavs, who called the area Topulcha, from the Slavic root word for 'hot springs'. Tapolca's original source of wealth was wine – a legacy of the Romans – but it only really appeared on the map when the Bakony bauxite mining company set up its headquarters here.

Orientation

Tapolca's main thoroughfare is Deák Ferenc utca, which runs west from Hősök tere, where the bus station is located, and east to Fő tér, just north of Mill Lake. The train station is on Dózsa György út, about 1.2km southwest of the centre.

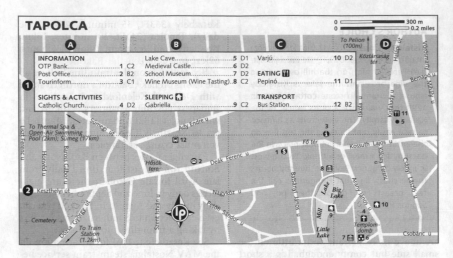

Information

OTP bank (Fő tér 2) Has an ATM and money-exchange machine.

Post office (Deák Ferenc utca 19)

Tourinform (☎ 510 777; tapolca@tourinform.hu; Fő tér 17; ☷ 9am-5pm Mon-Fri, 9am-noon Sat May-Aug; 9am-4pm Mon-Fri Sep-May) Just north of Mill Lake.

Sights

MILL LAKE

Mill Lake (Malom-tó), just south of Fő tér is reached through the gateway at No 8 or by walking south along Arany János utca. A small footbridge divides it in two: to the north is the **Big Lake** (Nagy-tó), which is about the size of a large pond, and to the south the **Little Lake** (Kis-tó). Created in the 18th century to power a water mill, the lake has been artificially fed since the nearby bauxite mine lowered the level of the karst water. But it remains a picturesque area, with pastel-coloured houses reflected in the water of the Big Lake and a church and a museum near the Little Lake. In the centre are the slowly turning blades of the mill house, which is now the Gabriella hotel (opposite).

The **Catholic church** (☷ services only) on Templom-domb has a Gothic sanctuary but the rest of it is 18th-century baroque. The ruins of Tapolca's **medieval castle**, destroyed during the Turkish occupation, can be seen to the southwest. Nearby is the small **School Museum** (Iskola Múzeum; ☎ 413 415; Templom-domb 15; adult/child 200/100Ft; ☷ 9am-4pm Mon-Fri mid-Apr–mid-Oct), which doubles as the City Museum.

LAKE CAVE

Tapolca's second big attraction, the **Lake Cave** (Tavasbarlang; ☎ 412 579; Kisfaludy utca 3; adult/child 400/200Ft; ☷ 10am-6pm Tue-Sun Jun-Aug, 10am-5pm Tue-Sun mid-Apr–May & Sep–mid-Nov) is a short distance to the northeast. You can visit about 100m of the cave and even row a boat (400Ft) on a small underground pond, which has returned since mining ended here in 1990.

Activities

There's a **thermal spa** and **open-air swimming pool** (Sümegi út; adult/child 600/400Ft; ☷ 10am-8pm Mon-Fri, 9am-8pm Sat & Sun May-Sep) northwest of the centre, but for something a little less energetic make a beeline for the **Wine Museum** (Bormúzeum; ☎ 414 186; Arany János utca 1; adult/child 400/200Ft; ☷ 9am-6pm) to sample various Bakony wines in its long, cool cellar.

Sleeping & Eating

There's no real need to overnight in Tapolca with the lake and its attractions so close, but if you find yourself stuck, check in with Tourinform for private rooms.

Pelion (☎ 513 100; reserve@hotelpelion.hunguest hotels.hu; Köztársaság tér 10; s/d from €72/102; ☐ ☒) This all-in-one wellness/thermal hotel has every possible treatment to turn back the clock (or stop it in its tracks), including its very own humidity cave. Rooms here are modern and comfy, and designed for a good night's sleep.

Varjú (☎ 510 522; kalomista.imre@kaloplastik.hu; Arany János utca 14; s/d 4000/8000Ft, mains 1000Ft; ☐)

Directly opposite the Catholic church is this sparkling new *pension* with well-kept rooms with a minimum of character, and a restaurant with a secluded inner courtyard and good wine list.

Pepinó (☎ 414 133; Kisfaludy utca 9; pizzas from 600Ft) Near the Lake Cave, this is a simple pizzeria with generous portions and street-side seating.

Getting There & Away
BUS
Tapolca is a major transport hub with buses departing almost hourly for Keszthely (363Ft, 35 minutes, 28km), Nagyvázsony (363Ft, 33 minutes, 28km), Sümeg (302Ft, 40 minutes, 22km) and Veszprém (605Ft, one to 1½ hours, 49km). Other important destinations serviced by bus include Balatonfüred (725Ft, 1½ hours, 55km, two buses daily), Badacsonytomaj (241Ft, 30 minutes, 16km, up to six daily), Budapest (1570Ft, 3½ hours, 162km, three daily), Pápa (846Ft, two hours, 67km, three daily) and Székesfehérvár (two hours, 94km, four daily).

TRAIN
Tapolca is the main terminus for the train line linking most of the towns along Lake Balaton's northern shore with Székesfehérvár (1212Ft, 2¾ hours, 117km) and Budapest (2030Ft, three-4½ hours, 184km). The train line also heads northwest to Sümeg (182Ft, 20 minutes, 20km) and Celldömölk (544Ft, one hour, 56km), from where frequent trains continue on to Szombathely (1212Ft, 2¼ hours, 100km) in western Hungary.

SÜMEG
☎ 87 / pop 6800
This small town, some 19km northwest of Tapolca between the Bakony and Keszthely Hills, has a few pleasant surprises for the traveller. The first is obvious as Sümeg swings into view – a hilltop castle with commanding views of the surrounding lands. The second, arguably the best baroque frescoes in the country, is well hidden in the town's back streets.

History
Sümeg was on the map as early as the 13th century, when an important border fortress was built by King Béla IV in the aftermath of the Mongol invasion. The castle was strengthened several times during the next three centuries, repelling the Turks but falling to the Habsburg forces, which torched it in 1713.

Sümeg's golden age came later in the 18th century when the all-powerful bishops of Veszprém took up residence here and commissioned some of the town's fine baroque buildings.

Orientation
Kossuth Lajos utca is the main street running north–south through Sümeg. The bus station is on Béke tér, a continuation of Kossuth Lajos utca south of the town centre. The train station is a 10-minute walk northwest, at the end of Darnay Kálmán utca.

Information
Balatontourist (☎ 550 259; Kossuth Lajos utca; ☺ 8am-5pm Mon-Fri)

OTP bank (Kossuth Lajos utca 17) Has a currency-exchange machine and ATM.

Post office (Kossuth Lajos utca 1)

Tourinform (☎ 550 276; sumeg@tourinform.hu; Kossuth Lajos utca 15; ☺ 9am-5pm Mon-Fri, 9am-1pm Sat Jun-Aug; 8am-4pm Mon-Fri Aug-May) Shares a building with Balatontourist.

Sights
SÜMEG CASTLE
Sitting on a 270m-high cone of limestone above the town – a rare substance in this region of basalt – is this imposing **castle** (adult/child 800/400Ft; ☺ 9am-6pm May-Sep, 9am-5pm Oct-Apr). You can reach it by climbing Vak Bottyán utca, which is lined with lovely baroque *kúriák* (mansions), from Szent István

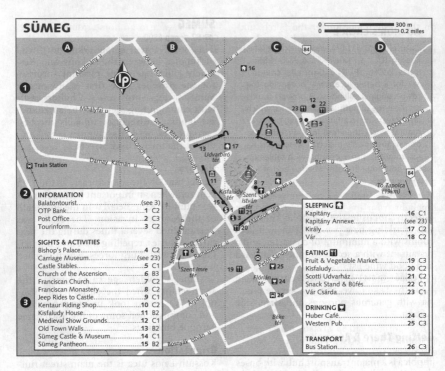

SÜMEG

tér and then following Vároldal utca past the **Castle Stables** (Váristálló; Vároldal utca 5), which now house a riding school (opposite). The castle is also accessible from the northeast via Rte 84 and by hitching a ride in a jeep (350Ft per person) from the parking lot at the end of Vároldal utca.

Sümeg Castle fell into ruin after the Austrians abandoned it early in the 18th century, but was restored in the 1960s. Today it is the largest and best preserved castle in all of Transdanubia and well worth the climb for the views east to the Bakony Hills and south to the Keszthely Hills. There's a small **Castle Museum** (Vármúzeum) of weapons, armour and castle furnishings in the 13th-century **Old Tower** (Öregtorony); pony rides and archery in the castle courtyard; a snack bar; and a restaurant. Medieval tournaments and feasts within the castle walls are organised throughout the year. You can still see bits of the **old town walls** below the castle at the northern end of Kossuth Lajos utca (Nos 13 to 33). A 16th-century tower is now the living room of the house at No 31.

CHURCH OF THE ASCENSION

The castle may dominate the town, but for many people it is not Sümeg's most important sight. For them that distinction is reserved for the **Church of the Ascension** (church office ☎ 352 003; Szent Imre tér; admission free; ☾ 9am-noon & 1-6pm Mon-Fri Apr-Sep, 9am-noon & 1-4pm Mon-Fri Oct & Nov, 9am-noon & 1-5pm Mon-Fri Mar; services only Sat & Sun year-round). You would never know it from the outside: architecturally, the building (1756) is unexceptional. But step inside and marvel at what has been called the 'Sistine Chapel of the rococo'.

That's perhaps an overstatement, but it's true that Franz Anton Maulbertsch's frescoes (1757–58) are the most beautiful baroque examples in Hungary and by far the prolific painter's best work. The frescoes, whose subjects are taken from the Old and New Testaments, are brilliant expressions of light and shadow. Pay special attention to the Crucifixion scene in Golgotha on the northern wall in the nave; the Adoration of the Three Kings, with its caricature of a Moor opposite Golgotha; the Gate of Hell, across the aisle under the organ loft on the western side under the porch; and the altarpiece of Christ ascending airily to the clouds. Maulbertsch managed to include himself in a couple of his works, most clearly among the shepherds in the first fresco on the southern wall (he's the one holding the round cheeses and hamming it up for the audience). The commissioner of the frescoes, Márton Padányi Bíró, bishop of Veszprém, is shown on the western wall near the organ. Drop a coin in the machine to illuminate the frescoes and to view them at their best.

OTHER SIGHTS
The Church of the Ascension steals the limelight from the 17th-century **Franciscan church** (Ferences templom; Szent István tér 7; admission free), which has modern frescoes, a beautifully carved baroque altar and a pietà that has attracted pilgrims for 300 years. Don't miss the ornate pulpit with the eerie dismembered hand grasping a crucifix. The baroque **Franciscan monastery** (Ferences kolostor; Szent István tér 9; admission free; 11.30am-3pm), built in 1657, is next door, but there's not a lot to see.

The former **Bishop's Palace** (Püspöki palota; Szent István tér 8-10) was a grand residence when completed in 1755, but now it needs some TLC. You can still admire the two Atlases holding up the balcony at the entrance and the copper rain-spouts in the shape of sea monsters.

Kisfaludy House (Kisfaludy szülőháza; 30-491 9719; Kisfaludy tér 4; adult/child 400/200Ft; 10am-6pm Tue-Sun) is the birthplace of Sándor Kisfaludy (1772–1844), the Romantic 'poet of the Balaton'. Together with a history of his life and work, the museum contains further exhibits on Sümeg Castle and the area's geology. Outside along a wall is the **Sümeg Pantheon** of local sons and daughters who made good.

The small **Carriage Museum** (Vároldal utca; admission free), next to the Kapitány hotel's annexe, has well-restored horse carriages and a small array of medieval weapons and armour. Ask for the key at the Vár Csárda restaurant.

Activities
There is excellent **hiking** east of Sümeg into the Bakony Hills (known as 'Hungary's Sherwood Forest'), but get yourself a copy of Cartographia's *Bakonyi-hegység – déli rész* (Bakony Hills – Southern Part) 1:40,000 map (No 3; 800Ft).

If you want to go horse riding, visit the **Castle Stables** (550 087; varistallo@axelero.hu; Vároldal utca 5) or **Kentaur riding shop** (351 836; Vároldal utca 10; 9am-6pm); both places charge around 2500Ft per hour.

Medieval shows (352 598; admission 700Ft; 11am Jul & Aug), consisting of swashbuckling antics and horsemanship prowess, are all the rage in Sümeg and take place in the show grounds of Kapitány hotel annexe.

Sleeping
Tourinform can help with private rooms (about 2500Ft per person).

Király (352 605; Udvarbíró tér 5; s/d 4000/6000Ft; P) This six-room, family-run *pension* in an old farmhouse is a cosy, flower-bedecked place with a *csárda* (Hungarian-style restaurant) and a welcome you'd usually only receive from friends and family.

Kapitány (352 598; www.hotelkapitany.hu; Tóth Tivadar utca 19; r from 10,900Ft; P) A modern, well-designed hotel north of the castle, this place has plenty of added extras, including sauna, tennis court, horses for rent, a wine cellar and a newly completed wellness centre. It also has an annexe near the Carriage Museum.

Vár (352 352; www.hotelvar.hu in Hungarian; Vak Bottyán utca 2; s/d 7000/9000Ft) Vár has modern yet sterile rooms, but if all you're looking for is a quiet spot for a good sleep then it may just fit the bill.

Eating & Drinking
Kisfaludy (352 128; Kossuth Lajos utca 13; mains 1000Ft) This restaurant at the former Kisfaludy hotel is one of the few places in the centre of town where you can have a sit-down meal, and is pleasantly bereft of kitsch Hungarian décor. The *cukrászda* here is popular for ice cream and cakes.

Vár Csárda (350 924; Vároldal utca; mains 1500-2000Ft) Closer to the castle, this caters to tourist crowds with Gypsy music and medieval banquets but it's very pleasant in warmer weather to sit under the walnut trees in full view of the hilltop fortress.

Scotti Udvarház (350 997; Szent István tér 1; pizzas from 800Ft) Scotti also accommodates busloads of tourists but with its big portions and huge, covered garden it's still an attractive bet.

For quick eats, head for the compact **fruit and vegetable market** (Árpád utca) near the bus station or pick a *büfé* (snack stand) along the access road to the castle from Rte 84.

Popular watering holes are concentrated around the bus station and include the fairly sedate **Huber Café** (Flórián tér 8) and much rowdier **Western Pub** (Petőfi Sándor utca 1), with its split-log tables and jukebox rave music.

Getting There & Away

Daily buses leave Sümeg hourly for Hévíz (302Ft, 35 minutes, 23km), Keszthely (423Ft, 50 minutes, 31km) and Tapolca (302Ft, 40 minutes, 22km); departures to Pápa (605Ft, 1¼ hours, 50km) and Veszprém (846Ft, two hours, 68km) are also frequent. Other buses go to Budapest (2300Ft, four hours, 184km, four daily), Győr (1210Ft, 2¼ hours, 99km, four daily) and Sopron (1330Ft, 2½-3½ hours, 107km, three daily).

Sümeg is on the train line linking Tapolca (182Ft, 25 minutes, 20km) and Celldömölk (346Ft, 45 minutes, 36km), from where frequent trains continue on to Szombathely (890Ft, two hours, 81km). For Budapest (2200Ft, four to five hours, 205km) and other points to the east and west along the northern shore of Lake Balaton, change at Tapolca.

NAGYVÁZSONY

☎ 88 / pop 1810

When you grow tired of the Balaton hubbub, head north to Nagyvázsony, a sleepy little market town in the southern Bakony Hills. The drive from Badacsony via Tapolca or from Tihany, 15km to the southeast, takes you through some of the prettiest countryside in the Lake Balaton region, and it's here you'll find the important 15th-century Vázsonykő Castle.

Orientation & Information

In the centre of town you'll find Nagyvázsony's three bus stops and the **post office** (Kinizsi utca 59); there's not a lot else around.

Sights

VÁZSONYKŐ CASTLE

This **castle** (☎ 264 786; Vár utca; adult/child 600/400Ft; ☼ 8am-5pm Mon-Fri, 9am-5pm Sat & Sun Apr-Oct), on a gentle slope north of the tiny town centre, was begun early in the 15th century by the Vezsenyi family, but in 1462 it was presented to General Pál Kinizsi by King Matthias Corvinus in gratitude for the brave

general's military successes against the Turks. It became an important border fortress during the occupation and was used as a prison in the 1700s.

The castle is essentially a rectangle with a horseshoe-shaped barbican. The 30m-high, six-storey keep is reached via a bridge over the dry moat. A large crack runs from the top of the tower to the bottom, but it must be secure enough: the upper rooms contain the **Kinizsi Castle Museum** (Kinizsi Vármúzeum), while the lower room displays dummies torturing one another. Part of General Kinizsi's red-marble sarcophagus sits in the centre of the restored chapel and there's a collection of archaeological finds in the crypt.

OTHER SIGHTS

The **Post Office Museum** (Postmúzeum; ☎ 264 300; Temető utca 3; adult/child 150/75Ft; ☼ 10am-6pm Tue-Sun Mar-Oct) is opposite the castle. Nagyvázsony was an important stop along the postal route between Budapest and Graz in the 19th century (horses were changed here). The museum is a lot more interesting than it sounds, particularly the section on the history of the telephone in Hungary beginning with the installation of the first switchboard in Budapest in 1890. Next to the museum is an 18th-century **Evangelist church** with a free-standing belfry.

Nearby is a small **Open-Air Folk Museum** (Szabadtéri Néprajzi Múzeum; ☎ 264 724; Bercsényi utca 21; adult/child 200/100Ft; ☼ 10am-6pm Tue-Sun May-Oct) at a farmhouse dating from 1825. It was once the home of a coppersmith and his workshop remains.

The **Church of St Stephen** (Szent István templom; Rákóczi utca) was built by General Kinizsi in 1481 on the site of an earlier chapel. Most of the interior, including the richly carved main altar, is baroque.

Sleeping & Eating

Malomkő (☎ 264 165; www.malomko.hu; Kinizsi utca 47-49; s/d 3000/6000Ft; P ☼) Malomkő is the liveliest and flashiest accommodation in town, with spacious rooms (some with kitchen) filled with natural-wood furniture and plenty of light. The ground floor is given over to a simple but satisfying restaurant which often hosts bands on weekends.

Vázsonykő (☎ 264 344; Sörház utca 2; s/d 3500/5000Ft; P) This friendly and welcoming *pension* a short walk from the castle has good-sized rooms and a peaceful setting. Its restaurant serves up good home cooking inside or on its small patio.

Vár Csárda (Temető utca 5; mains 1000Ft; ⏱ 10am-6pm Jun-Sep) This thatched place has a relaxing garden overlooking the castle and attracts most visitors to the stronghold

Getting There & Away

Some 12 buses a day link Nagyvázsony and Veszprém (302Ft, 30 minutes, 22km); and up to eight run to Tapolca daily (363Ft, 35 minutes, 28km) to the southwest.

TIHANY

☎ 87 / pop 1450

The place with the greatest historical significance on Lake Balaton is Tihany, 14km southwest of Balatonfüred. It is on a peninsula of the same name that juts 5km into the Balaton, almost linking the lake's two shores. The entire peninsula is a nature reserve of hills and marshy meadows; it has an isolated, almost wild, feel to it that is unknown around the rest of the lake. The village, on a hilltop on the eastern side of the peninsula, is one of the most charming in the Balaton region.

History

There was a Roman settlement in the area, but Tihany first appeared on the map in 1055, when King Andrew I (r 1046–60), a son of King Stephen's great nemesis, Vászoly, founded a Benedictine monastery here. The Deed of Foundation of the Abbey Church of Tihany, now in the archives of the Benedictine abbey at Pannonhalma (p161), is one of the earliest known documents bearing any Hungarian words – some 50 place names within a mostly Latin text. It's a linguistic treasure in a country where, until the 19th century, the vernacular in its written form was spurned – particularly in schools – in favour of the more 'cultured' Latin and German.

In 1267 a fortress was built around the church and was able to keep the Turks at bay when they arrived 300 years later. But the castle was demolished by Habsburg forces in 1702 and all you'll see today are ruins.

Tihany Peninsula is a popular recreational area with beaches on its eastern and western coasts and a big resort complex on its southern tip. The waters of the so-called Tihany Well, off the southern end of the peninsula, are the deepest – and coldest – in the lake, reaching an unprecedented 12m in some parts.

Orientation

Tihany village, perched on an 80m-high plateau along the peninsula's eastern coast, is accessible by two roads when you turn south off Rte 71. The Inner Harbour (Belső kikötő), where ferries to/from Balatonfüred and Siófok dock, is below the village. Tihany Port (Tihanyi-rév), to the southwest at the tip of the peninsula, is Tihany's recreational area. From here, car ferries run to Szántódi-rév and passenger ferries to Balatonföldvár.

Two inland basins on the peninsula are fed by rain and ground water. The Inner Lake (Belső-tó) is almost in the centre of the peninsula and visible from the village, while the Outer Lake (Külső-tó), to the northwest, has almost completely dried up and is now a tangle of reeds. Both basins attract bird life.

Information

Post office (Kossuth Lajos utca 37) Has an ATM and an exchange bureau.

Tihany (www.tihany.hu) More information on the town and its surrounds.

Tihany Tourist (☎ 448 481; www.tihanytourist.hu; Kossuth Lajos utca 11; ⏱ 9am-5pm Apr-Oct)

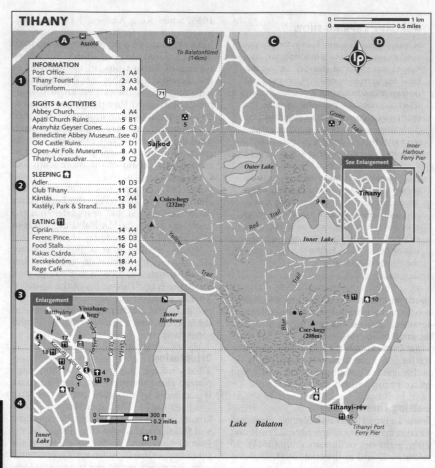

TIHANY

INFORMATION
Post Office..........................1 A4
Tihany Tourist.....................2 A3
Tourinform........................3 A4

SIGHTS & ACTIVITIES
Abbey Church.....................4 A4
Apáti Church Ruins...............5 B1
Aranyház Geyser Cones.........6 C3
Benedictine Abbey Museum..(see 4)
Old Castle Ruins.................7 D1
Open-Air Folk Museum..........8 A3
Tihany Lovasudvar..............9 C2

SLEEPING
Adler...............................10 D3
Club Tihany......................11 C4
Kántás.............................12 A4
Kastély, Park & Strand.........13 B4

EATING
Ciprián............................14 A4
Ferenc Pince.....................15 D3
Food Stalls.......................16 D4
Kakas Csárda.....................17 A3
Kecskeköröm......................18 A4
Rege Café.........................19 A4

Tourinform (☎ 448 804; tihany@tourinform.hu; Kossuth Lajos utca 20; ☿ 9am-7pm Mon-Fri, 10am-6pm Sat & Sun mid-Jun–mid-Sep; 9am-5pm Mon-Fri, 10am-4pm Sat mid-Apr–mid-Jun & early Sep, 10am-4pm Mon-Fri early Sep–mid-Apr)

Sights
ABBEY CHURCH

This twin-spired and ochre-coloured **church** (☎ 538 200; adult/child 500/250Ft; tours 8000Ft; ☿ 9am-6pm May-Sep, 10am-5pm Apr & Oct, 10am-3pm Nov-Mar) was built in 1754 on the site of King Andrew's church and contains fantastic altars, pulpits and screens carved between 1753 and 1779 by an Austrian lay brother named Sebastian Stuhlhof. They are baroque-rococo masterpieces and all are richly symbolic.

With your back to the sumptuous main altar (the saint with the broken chalice and snake is Benedict, the founder of Western monasticism) and the Abbot's throne, look right to the side altar dedicated to Mary. The large angel kneeling on the right supposedly represents Stuhlhof's fiancée, a fisherman's daughter who died in her youth. On the Altar of the Sacred Heart across the aisle, a pelican (Christ) nurtures its young (the faithful) with its own blood. The besotted figures atop the pulpit beside it are four doctors of the Roman Catholic church: Sts Ambrose, Gregory, Jerome and Augustine. The next two altars on the right- and left-hand sides are dedicated to Benedict and his twin sister, Scholastica; the last pair, a baptismal font and the Lourdes Altar, date from the 20th century.

Stuhlhof also carved the magnificent choir rail above the porch and the organ with all the cherubs. The frescoes on the ceilings by Bertalan Székely, Lajos Deák-Ébner and Károly Lotz were painted in 1889, when the church was restored.

The remains of King Andrew I lie in a limestone sarcophagus in the Romanesque **crypt**. The spiral sword-like cross on the cover is similar to ones used by 11th-century Hungarian kings.

The **Benedictine Abbey Museum** (Bencés Apátsági Múzeum), next door to the Abbey Church in the former Benedictine monastery, is entered from the crypt. It contains exhibits about Lake Balaton, liturgical vestments, religious artefacts, a handful of manuscripts, and a history of King Andrew.

OTHER SIGHTS

Pisky sétány, a promenade running along the ridge north from the church to Visszhanghegy, passes a cluster of folk houses that have now been turned into a small **Open-Air Folk Museum** (Szabadtéri Néprajzi Múzeum; ☎ 538 022; adult/child 300/150Ft; ☉ 10am-6pm Tue-Sun Easter–mid-Oct).

You'll find **Visszhang-hegy** (Echo Hill) at the end of Pisky sétány. At one time, up to 15 syllables of anything shouted in the direction of the Abbey Church would bounce back but, alas, because of building in the area (and perhaps climatic changes) you'll be lucky to get three nowadays. From Visszhang-hegy you can descend Garay utca and Váralja utca to the Inner Harbour and a small beach, or continue on to the hiking trails that pass this way.

Activities

Hiking is one of Tihany's main attractions; there's a good map outlining the trails near the front of the Abbey Church. Following the Green Trail northeast of the church for an hour will bring you to the **Russian Well** (Oroszkút) and the ruins of the **Old Castle** (Óvár) at 219m, where Russian Orthodox monks, brought to Tihany by Andrew I, hollowed out cells in the soft basalt walls.

The 232m-high **Csúcs-hegy** (Csúcs Hill), with panoramic views of Lake Balaton, is about two hours west of the church via the Red Trail. From here you can join up with the Yellow Trail originating in Tihanyi-rév,

which will lead you north to the ruins of the 13th-century **Apáti Church** (Ápáti templom) and to Rte 71. From the church, it's possible to follow the Yellow Trail south till it crosses the Blue Trail near **Aranyház**, a series of geyser cones formed by warm-water springs and resembling (somewhat) a 'Golden Horse'. From here, you can take the Blue Trail north to the **Inner Lake** and on to the town centre.

Horses are available for hire at the **Tihany Lovasudvar** (☎ 30-275 3293; Kiserdőtelepi utca 10; 1 hr riding 3000Ft) just north of the Inner Lake.

As the lake bottom drops away quicker here than in other parts of the lake, Tihany's **beaches** are an inviting option. The stretches on the eastern side are the most accessible, which also mean they're the most popular, but if you're looking to escape the crowds head to **Sajkod** at the peninsula's northwestern point. A small track leads south from this small settlement to a secluded beach; with Tihany's hills as a backdrop, it's one of the most peaceful spots to while away an afternoon, or a week.

Sleeping

Accommodation in Tihany is limited and expensive; you could consider making it a day trip from Balatonfüred by bus. Also, most of the hotels listed in this section are closed between mid-October or November and March or April.

For private rooms (from 6000Ft per double), consult Tihany Tourist. Many houses along Kossuth Lajos utca and on the little streets north of the Abbey Church have 'Zimmer frei' signs.

Kastély, Park & Strand (☎ 448 611; Fürdőtelepi út 1; s 5100-22,000Ft; d 6900-23,800Ft; ℗) On the Inner Harbour, this hotel has suitably fine rooms in a former Habsburg summer mansion (the Kastély), dated rooms in an ugly modern wing (the Park) and simple but appealing rooms in a small one-level building (the Strand). There's also a 5-hectare garden and a private beach to run amok in.

Club Tihany (☎ 538 564; www.clubtihany.hu; Rév utca 3; s €48-93, d €80-138, bungalows from €44; ℗ ⊛ ⊠) Just up from the car-ferry pier, this is a 13-hectare resort with 160 bungalows and a 330-room hotel – and every sporting, munching and quaffing possibility imaginable. It has two-person bungalows and some rooms in the high-rise hotel have lake views and balconies.

Also worth considering:

Kántás (☎ 448 072; www.hotels.hu/kantas; Csokonai út 49; r €33-41) Below tourist-central on a quiet street, with small but cosy rooms and balcony.

Adler (☎ 538 000; www.adler-tihany.hu; Felsőkopaszhegyi utca 1/a; r €35-43; P ₂ ₃) Secluded romantic getaway with natural wood and white-washed rooms; Jacuzzi, sauna and restaurant on site.

Eating

Like the hotels, most restaurants are closed between mid-October or November and March or April.

Rege Cafe (☎ 448 280; Kossuth Lajos utca 22; mains 1000-2000Ft) Rege has possibly the best panoramic view of the lake on the Balaton from its high vantage point near the Benedictine abbey; its cakes and light meals aren't bad either.

Kecskeköröm (Fossil Shell; Kossuth Lajos utca 13; mains 1500Ft) Kecskeköröm has its fair share of Hungarian kitsch but it's fortunately not done in a garish way; in fact, it compliments the solid Hungarian menu offered here.

Kakas Csárda (☎ 448 541; Batthyány utca 1; mains 1500Ft) In a rambling basalt house almost opposite Kecskeköröm is this homely restaurant with its fair share of kitsch and Hungarian specialities.

Ciprián (☎ 448 515; Kossuth Lajos utca; mains from 1500Ft) Offering an alternative to views of the lake, Ciprián looks inwards towards Tihany's interior and has a simple Hungarian menu to attract tourists and a talking cockatoo to attract kids.

Cheap food stalls greet passengers to-ing and fro-ing across the lake at Tihanyi-rév.

AUTHOR'S CHOICE

Ferenc Pince (☎ 448 575; Cser-hegy 9; mains from 1200Ft) Ferenc is both a wine- and food-lover's dream; not only does its chef cook up a Hungarian storm in the kitchen with a mixture of local and national meat and fish dishes, but some of the best wine available is served by the very people who produce the stuff. During the day, its open terrace offers expansive views of the lake, while at night the hypnotic twinkling lights of the southern shore are in full view from its cosy thatched-roof house. Ferenc Pince is just under 2km south of the abbey church.

Getting There & Away

Buses cover the 14km from Balatonfüred's train station to and from Tihany about 20 times daily (182Ft, 30 minutes). The bus stops at both ferry landings before climbing to Tihany village.

The Balaton passenger ferries from Siófok, Balatonfüred and elsewhere stop at Tihany from late April to late October. Catch them at the pier below the abbey or at Tihanyi-rév. From March to mid-October the car ferry takes 10 minutes to cross the narrow stretch of water between Tihanyi-rév and Szántódi-rév, and departs every 40 minutes to an hour.

BALATONFÜRED

☎ 87 / pop 13,000

Balatonfüred is the oldest and most popular resort on the northern shore of Lake Balaton. It has none of the frenzy or brashness of Siófok, partly because of its aristocratic origins and partly because the thermal waters of its world-famous heart hospital attract a much older crowd.

History

The thermal water here, rich in carbonic acid, have been used as a cure for stomach ailments for centuries, but its other curative properties were only discovered by scientific analysis in the late 18th century. Balatonfüred was immediately declared a spa with its own chief physician in residence.

Balatonfüred's golden age was in the 19th century, especially the first half, when political and cultural leaders of the Reform Era (roughly 1825–48) gathered here in the summer. The town became a writers' colony of sorts. Balatonfüred was also the site chosen by István Széchenyi to launch the lake's first steamship Kisfaludy in 1846.

By 1900 Balatonfüred was a popular place for increasingly wealthy middle-class families to escape Budapest's heat. Wives would base themselves here all summer along with their children while husbands would board the 'bull trains' in Budapest at the weekend. The splendid promenade and a large wooden bath were built on the lake to accommodate the increasing crowds.

Orientation

Balatonfüred has two distinct districts: the lakeside resort area and the commercial

centre in the older part of town around Szent
István tér to the northwest. Almost everything to see and do is down by the water.

The train and bus stations are on Dobó
István utca, about a kilometre northwest of
Vitorlás tér, where the ferry pier is located.
The quickest way to get to the lake from ei-
ther station is to walk east on Horváth Mi-
hály utca and then south on Jókai Mór utca.

Information

OTP bank (Petőfi Sándor utca 8) With 24-hour ATM.
Post office (Zsigmond utca 14)
Tourinform (☎ 580 480; balatonfured@tourinform.hu;
Petőfi Sándor utca 68; ☉ 9am-7pm Mon-Fri May-Oct,
9am-7pm Mon-Fri, 9am-6pm Sat, 9am-1pm Sun mid-Jun–
mid-Sep, 9am-5pm Mon-Fri, 9am-1pm Sat mid-Sep–Oct,

9am-4pm Mon-Fri Nov–mid-Jun) Inconveniently located
1km northeast of the centre.
www.balatonfured.hu Online information in a number
of languages.

Sights

The **Jókai Memorial Museum** (Jókai Emlékmúzeum;
☎ 343 426; Jókai Mór utca; adult/child 300/150Ft;
☉ 10am-6pm Tue Sun May Oct) is housed in the
summer villa of the prolific writer Mór
Jókai, just north of Vitorlás tér. In his
study here, Jókai churned out many of his
200 novels under the stern gaze of his wife,
the actress Róza Laborfalvi.

Across the street is the tiny neoclassical
Round Church (Kerek templom; ☎ 343 029; Blaha Lujza
utca 1; admission free; ☉ services only) completed in

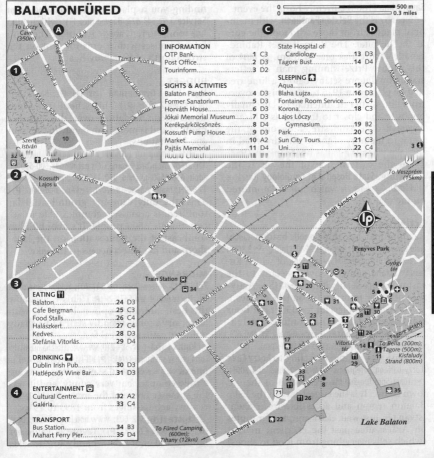

1846. The *Crucifixion* (1891) by János Vaszary sits above the altar on the western wall and is the only notable thing inside.

If you walk down Blaha Lujza utca you'll pass the villa (now a hotel) at No 4 where the 19th-century actress-singer Lujza Blaha spent her summers from 1893 to 1916. A short distance further along is Gyógy tér, the heart of the spa. In the centre of this leafy square, **Kossuth Pump House** (1853) dispenses slightly sulphuric, but drinkable, thermal water. This is as close as you'll get to the hot spring. Although Balatonfüred is a major spa, the mineral baths are reserved for patients of the State Hospital of Cardiology.

The late baroque **Horváth House** (Gyógy tér 3), for many years a hotel, was the site of the first Anna Ball in 1825 (see right), but the former **Sanatorium** (1802) currently hosts the event.

Nearby is the **Balaton Pantheon**, with memorial plaques from those who took the cure at the hospital. The Bengali poet Rabindranath Tagore was one of them. A **bust** of this Nobel Prize-winning man of letters stands on Tagore sétány before a lime tree that he planted in 1926 to mark his recovery from illness after treatment here. Diagonally opposite and closer to the lake is a bizarre **memorial** of a hand stretching out of the water in memory of those who drowned in the lake when the Pajtás boat sank in 1954.

On the eastern side of the tér is the sprawling, **State Hospital of Cardiology** (Országos Szívkórház; Gyógy tér 2), which put Balatonfüred on the map.

Activities

Balatonfüred has three **public beaches** (adult/child per day 330/190Ft, per week 1980/1140Ft; ☺ 8.30am or 9am-6pm or 7pm mid-May–mid-Sep), of which **Kisfaludy Strand** along Aranyhíd sétány to the east of Tagore sétány is the best. (See Activities p188 for information on lake cruises.)

You can rent bicycles for 350Ft per hour from several places in Balatonfüred, including **Kerékpárkölcsönzés** (bicycle rentals; ☎ 480 671; Tagore Hotel, Zákonyi Ferenc utca; ☺ 9am-7pm).

Consider walking or cycling to **Lóczy Cave** (Lóczy-barlang; Öreghegyi utca; adult/child 300/200Ft; ☺ 10am-5pm Tue-Sun May-Sep), north of the old town centre. It is the largest cave in the Lake Balaton region and accessible from Szent István tér. Just walk east a couple of minutes on Arácsi utca past the excellent market (which sells everything from food to shoes)

and then north on Öreghegyi utca. There's also good **hiking** in the three hills with the names Tamás (Thomas), Sándor (Alexander) and Péter (Peter) to the northeast.

In July the **Anna Ball** is held in the Sanatorium, near Gyógy tér; it's a prime event on the Hungarian calendar. Tickets cost from 25,000Ft. Concerts and other events accompany the ball; keep your eyes peeled if you're here during July.

Sleeping

Prices fluctuate throughout the year and usually peak between early July and late August.

As elsewhere around Lake Balaton, private room prices are rather inflated. **Sun City Tours** (☎ 481 798; Csokonai utca 1) can help with finding you a place, as can **Fontaine Room Service** (☎ 343 673; Honvéd utca 11), which also has rooms to rent above its office. There are lots of houses with rooms for rent on the streets north of Kisfaludy Beach.

BUDGET

Lajos Lóczy Gymnasium (☎ 343 428; Bartók Béla utca 4; dm 2000Ft; P) This school turns into dorm accommodation over the summer months, and is more than handy to the train and bus stations.

Füred Camping (☎ 580 241; cfured@balatontourist .hu; Széchenyi utca 24; camp sites per tent 18,600-5300Ft, adult 650-1500Ft, child 550-1100Ft, bungalows 6400-19,970Ft; motel r 5460-19,970Ft; ☺ Apr–mid-Oct; P) This, the only camping ground at Balatonfüred, is a massive complex able to accommodate 3500 people. It's about 1.5km southeast of the train station on the lakeshore and has direct access to the lake.

MIDRANGE

Zöld Tető (Green Roof; ☎ 341 701; zoldteto@netquick .hu; Huray utca 4; s/d €37/52; P) This is arguably the best midrange option in town, with large, airy rooms, friendly staff and a shady outdoor patio for breakfast.

Blaha Lujza (☎ 581 210; www.hotelblaha.hu; Blaha Lujza utca 4; s/d from €32/41; P) This small hotel is one of the loveliest to stay in. Its rooms are a little compact but very comfy, and it was the summer home of the much loved 19th-century actress-singer from 1893 to 1916.

Tagore (☎ 342 603; www.hoteltagore.com; Deák Ferenc utca 56; r €24-28; P) Tagore is value for money and more than handy to the lake;

its rooms aren't modern but they're certainly comfy enough.

Park (☎ 343 203; www.parkhotel.hu; Jókai Mór utca 24; s 6000-12,500Ft; d 12,000-15,000Ft; P 🐕) This is a rather posh old-world hotel, with huge rooms (some with balcony) and a private garden. The rate includes half-board.

Uni (☎ 581 360; www.hotels.hu/uni; Széchenyi utca 10; s/d 9700/13,000Ft; P) Big and impersonal, this large square block of a hotel is a hangover from the busy communist days. It does however have its own beach, rooms come with balcony, and there is something appealing about reliving the bad old days...

A huddle of attractive *pensions* can be found close to the bus and train stations:

Korona (☎ 343 278; www.koronapanzio.hu; Vörösmarty utca 4; s €26.50-37, d €31.50-46; P) Homely décor bordering on kitsch; big, bright rooms.

Aqua (☎ 342 813; www.balaton.hu/aquahaz; Garay utca 2; r €28-41; P) Spotless rooms in a thoroughly modern, albeit slightly clinical, pension.

Eating & Drinking

Halászkert (☎ 343 039; Zákonyi Ferenc utca 3; mains 1000-1500Ft) This place serves some of the best *korhely halászlé* (drunkard's fish soup) in Hungary on its large, shaded terrace. If that's not your style, there's plenty of other fish dishes to choose from.

Balaton (☎ 481 319; Kisfaludy utca 5; mains 1000-2000Ft) This cool, leafy oasis amid all the hubbub is set back from the lake in a shaded park area. It serves huge portions and, like so many restaurants in town, has an extensive fish selection.

Bella (☎ 481 815; Tagore sétány; pizzas 800Ft) Bella has good pizzas, Hungarian staples and the wonderful panorama terrace facing the lake. It's also quite touristy, but it's hard to find a place in these parts that isn't.

Stefánia Vitorlás (Tagore sétány 1; mains 1500Ft) It's hard to find a more central location right on the lake's edge than Vitorlás. This does mean it's often crowded with diners, so a quiet, intimate dinner is not always an option here.

Cafe Bergman (☎ 341 087; Zsigmond utca 3; 🕙 10am-7.30pm) Escape the crowds down by the lake and head to popular Bergman, an elegant café with the town's best selection of cake and ice cream.

Kedves (Blaha Lujza utca 7) Like Bergman, Kedves will appeal to those looking for a break from madding crowds; this chilled café was also where Lujza Blaha herself took tea.

Dublin Irish Pub (Blaha Lujza utca 9) This pseudo-Irish pub with Guinness on tap is a popular stop for thirsty folk who've been enjoying the lake's attractions all day.

Hatlépcsős (Six Steps; Jókai Mór utca 30) A cheap wine bar that attracts students and dipsomaniacs. Its huge patio isn't a bad place to try one of Balatonfüred's famous Rieslings.

For cheap eats, head west along the lake and Zákonyi Ferenc utca where you'll come across a plethora of food stalls.

Entertainment

Cultural centre (☎ 481 187; Kossuth Lajos utca 3) The staff at this centre near Szent István tér can tell you what's on, such as musical performances and theatre productions.

Galéria (Zákonyi Ferenc utca; 🕙 Fri & Sat) There are clubs all over town in summer, including this disco.

Getting There & Away
BOAT

From April to late October, up to seven daily Mahart ferries link Balatonfüred with Siófok and Tihany. Up to eight daily ferries serve these ports from late May to mid-September.

BUS

Buses for Tihany (182Ft, 30 minutes, 14km) and Veszprém (302Ft, 40 minutes, 20km) leave throughout the day. Other departures are to Budapest (1690Ft, 2½ hours, 136km, four daily), Győr (1210Ft, 2½ hours, 100km, seven daily), Hévíz (907Ft, 1½ hours, 75km, six daily), Kecskemét (2660Ft, five hours, 214km, one daily), Nagykanizsa (1570Ft, 2¾ hours, 26km, one daily) and Székesfehérvár (846Ft, 1½ hours, 69km, seven daily).

TRAIN

Frequent express and local trains travel northeast to Székesfehérvár (658Ft, 1½ hours, 65km) and to Déli and Kelenföld stations in Budapest (1420Ft, 2½ hours, 132km); and southwest to Tapolca (544Ft, 1¼ hours, 52km) and lakeside towns as far as Badacsony (346Ft, one hour, 38km).

Getting Around

You can reach Vitorlás tér and the lake from the train and bus stations on buses 1, 1/a and 2; bus 1 continues on to Füred Camping.

You can also book a local **taxi** (☎ 444 444).

VESZPRÉM

☎ 88 / pop 62,900

Spreading over five hills between the northern and southern ranges of the Bakony Hills, Veszprém has one of the most dramatic locations in the Lake Balaton region. The walled castle district, atop a plateau, is a living museum of baroque art and architecture. It's a delight to stroll through the windy Castle Hill district's single street, admiring the embarrassment of fine churches. As the townspeople say, 'Either the wind is blowing or the bells are ringing in Veszprém'.

History

The Romans did not settle in what is now Veszprém but 8km to the southeast at Balácapuszta, where important archaeological finds have been made. Prince Géza, King Stephen's father, founded a bishopric in Veszprém late in the 10th century, and the city grew as a religious, administrative and educational centre (the university was established in the 13th century). It also became a favourite residence of Hungary's queens.

The castle at Veszprém was blown up by the Habsburgs in 1702, and lost most of its medieval buildings during the Rákóczi War of Independence (1703–11) shortly thereafter. But this cleared the way for Veszprém's golden age, when the city's bishops and rich landlords built most of what you see today. The church's iron grip on Veszprém prevented it from developing commercially,

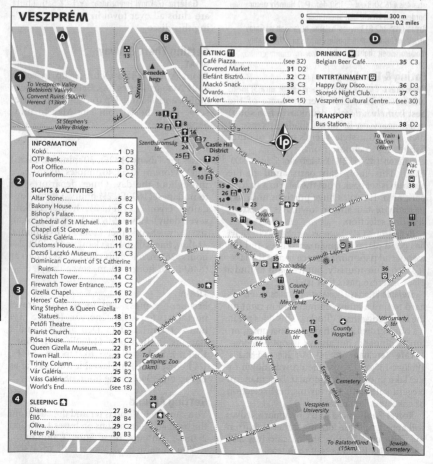

VESZPRÉM

0 — 300 m
0 — 0.2 miles

EATING 🍴
Café Piazza...........................(see 32)
Covered Market........................**31** D2
Elefánt Bisztró........................**32** C2
Mackó Snack.........................**33** C3
Óváros.............................**34** C3
Várkert............................(see 15)

DRINKING 🍸
Belgian Beer Café....................**35** C3

ENTERTAINMENT 🎭
Happy Day Disco.....................**36** D3
Skorpió Night Club...................**37** C3
Veszprém Cultural Centre....(see 30)

TRANSPORT
Bus Station.........................**38** D2

INFORMATION
Kokó.................................**1** D3
OTP Bank.............................**2** C2
Post Office............................**3** D3
Tourinform...........................**4** C2

SIGHTS & ACTIVITIES
Altar Stone...........................**5** B2
Bakony House........................**6** C3
Bishop's Palace......................**7** B2
Cathedral of St Michael.............**8** B1
Chapel of St George.................**9** B1
Csikász Galéria......................**10** B2
Customs House.....................**11** C2
Dezső Laczkó Museum.........**12** C3
Dominican Convent of St Catherine
  Ruins...............................**13** B1
Firewatch Tower....................**14** C2
Firewatch Tower Entrance......**15** C2
Gizella Chapel.......................**16** B2
Heroes' Gate........................**17** C2
King Stephen & Queen Gizella
  Statues.............................**18** B1
Petőfi Theatre.......................**19** C3
Piarist Church........................**20** B2
Pósa House..........................**21** C2
Queen Gizella Museum..........**22** B1
Town Hall.............................**23** C2
Trinity Column.......................**24** B2
Vár Galéria...........................**25** B2
Váss Galéria.........................**26** C2
World's End.........................(see 18)

SLEEPING 🛏
Diana................................**27** B4
Élló..................................**28** B4
Oliva................................**29** C2
Péter Pál.............................**30** B3

To Veszprém Valley
(Betekints Valley);
Convent Ruins (500m);
Herend (13km)

St Stephen's
Valley Bridge

Benedek-
hegy

Castle Hill
District

To Train
Station
(4km)

To Érdei
Camping; Zoo
(3km)

County
Hall

County
Hospital

Veszprém
University

To Balatonfüred
(15km)

Jewish
Cemetery

however, and it was bypassed by the main railway line in the 19th century.

Orientation

The bus station (Piac tér) is a few minutes' walk northeast from Kossuth Lajos utca, a pedestrian street of shops and travel agencies. If you turn north at the end of Kossuth Lajos utca at Szabadság tér, and walk along Rákóczi utca you'll soon reach the entrance to Castle Hill (Vár-hegy) at Óváros tér.

The train station is 3km north of the bus station at the end of Jutasi út.

Information

Kokó (Kossuth Lajos utca; per hr 500Ft; 9am-10pm Mon-Thu, 9am-midnight Fri & Sat, 2-10pm Sun) A cake shop on the 1st floor of the Cserhát shopping complex with Internet access.

OTP bank (Óváros tér 25) With ATM.

Post office (Kossuth Lajos utca 19)

Tourinform (404 548; veszprem@tourinform.hu; Vár utca 4; 9am-6pm Mon-Fri, 10am-4pm Sat, 10am-4pm Sun Jun-Aug, 9am-5pm Mon-Fri Sep-May) Has lots of information on the city and the surrounding villages and also free Internet access.

Veszprem (www.veszprem.hu) Find out more about Veszprém by logging on here.

Sights

CASTLE HILL

You should begin any tour of Veszprém in Óváros tér, the medieval market place at the foot of Castle Hill. Of the many fine 18th-century buildings in the square, the most interesting is the late baroque **Pósa House** (Óváros tér 3), built in 1793 and now a bank. There are also the former **customs house** (Óváros tér 7), also a bank, and the **town hall** (Óváros tér 9).

As you begin to ascend Castle Hill and its sole street, Vár utca, you'll pass through **Heroes' Gate** (Hősök kapuja), an entrance built in 1936 from the stones of a 15th-century castle gate.

To your left is the **firewatch tower** (tűztorony; 425 204; Vár utca 9; adult/child 300/200Ft; 10am-6pm May-Oct, 10am-5pm mid-Mar–Apr), which, like the one in Sopron, is an architectural hybrid of Gothic, baroque and neoclassical styles. You can climb to the top for excellent views of the rocky hill and the Bakony Hills.

The extremely rich **Piarist church** (Piarista templom; 426 088; Vár utca 12; admission free; 10am-6pm May-Aug, 10am-5pm Tue-Sun Sep–mid-Oct) was built in 1836 in the neoclassical

style. The red marble **altar stone** (1467) diagonally opposite outside the parish office at No 27 is the oldest piece of Renaissance stonework in Hungary.

The U-shaped **Bishop's Palace** (Püspöki palota; 426 088; Vár utca 16; adult/child 500/250Ft; 10am-6pm May-Aug, 10am-5pm Tue-Sun Sep–mid-Oct), designed by Jakab Fellner of Tata in the mid-18th century, is where the queen's residence stood in the Middle Ages. It faces Szentháromság tér, named for the **Trinity Column** (1751) in the centre.

Next to the Bishop's Palace is the early Gothic **Gizella Chapel** (Gizella-kápolna; 426 088; Vár utca 18; adult/child 100/70Ft; 10am-6pm May-Aug, 10am-5pm Tue-Sun Sep–mid-Oct), named after Gizella, the wife of King Stephen, who was crowned near here early in the 11th century. The chapel was discovered when the Bishop's Palace was being built in the mid-18th century. Inside the chapel are Byzantine-influenced 13th-century frescoes of the Apostles. The **Queen Gizella Museum** (426 088; Vár utca 35; adult/child 300/150Ft; 10am-6pm May-Aug, 10am-5pm Sep–mid-Oct) of religious art is opposite the chapel.

Parts of the dark and austere **Cathedral of St Michael** (székesegyház; 328 038; Vár utca 18-20; admission free; 10am-6pm May-Aug, 10am-5pm Sep–mid-Oct), which is the site of the first bishop's palace, dates from the beginning of the 11th century, but the cathedral has been rebuilt many times since then – the early Gothic crypt is original, though. Beside the cathedral, the octagonal foundation of the 13th-century **Chapel of St George** (Szent György kápolna; 426 088; adult/child 100/70Ft; 10am-6pm May-Aug, 10am-5pm Tue-Sun Sep–mid-Oct) sits under a glass dome.

From the rampart known as **World's End**, at the end of Vár utca, you can gaze north to craggy Benedek-hegy (Benedict Hill) and the Séd Stream, and west to the concrete viaduct (now St Stephen's Valley Bridge) over the Betekints Valley. In Margit tér, below the bridge, are the ruins of the medieval **Dominican Convent of St Catherine** and to the west is what little remains of the 11th-century **Veszprém Valley Convent**, whose erstwhile cloistered residents are said to have stitched Gizella's crimson silk coronation robe in 1031. The **statues of King Stephen and Queen Gizella** at World's End were erected in 1938 to mark the 900th anniversary of King Stephen's death (see boxed text, p216).

LAKE BALATON REGION

REACH OUT & TOUCH

It could have been a chapter from a Mills & Boon novel for the macabre. It was 1996. Millecentenary celebrations honouring the arrival of the Magyars in the Carpathian Basin in 896 were under way in Hungary. People were in the mood to mark dates and one of those people was the archbishop of Veszprém.

He knew that it had been in Veszprém that the future king, Stephen, and a Bavarian princess, Gizella, were married in 996. Just suppose, he thought, that the bishop of the Bavarian city of Passau, where Gizella's remains had been resting these nine centuries, agreed to send her hand to Hungary. The Holy Dexter, St Stephen's revered right hand, could be brought down from the Basilica in Budapest and they could... Well, the mind boggled.

All parties agreed (the bishop of Passau even threw in Gizella's arm bone) and the date was set. In the square in front of the Cathedral of St Michael in Veszprém, the hands were laid together and – 1000 years to the day of the wedding – coyly touched in marital bliss once again.

The world did not change as we know it that fine spring morning – tram 2 raced along the Danube in Budapest; Mr Kovács dished out steaming *lángos* from his stall somewhere along Lake Balaton; schoolchildren in Sárospatak recited their *ábécé*. But all true Magyars knew, deep in their hearts, that all was right with the world.

Vár utca is home to a number of **art galleries**, including the **Váss Galéria** (☎ 561 310; Vár utca 7; adult/child 400/200Ft; ☼ 10am-6pm May-Oct, 10am-5pm Tue-Sun Nov-Apr), the **Csikász Galéria** (☎ 425 204; Vár utca 17; adult/child 250/150Ft; ☼ 10am-6pm May-Oct, 10am-5pm Nov-Apr) and the **Vár Galéria** (☎ 425 204; Vár utca 29; adult/child 250/150Ft; ☼ 10am-6pm May-Oct, 10am-5pm Nov-Apr), which exhibit everything from religious paintings to postmodernist sculpture.

DEZSŐ LACZKÓ MUSEUM

The **Dezső Laczkó Museum** (Bakony Museum; ☎ 564 310; Erzsébet sétány 1; adult/child 300/150Ft; includes entrance to Bakony House; ☼ 10am-6pm Tue-Sun mid-Mar–mid-Oct; noon-4pm Tue-Sun mid-Oct–mid-Mar) is south of Megyeház tér. It has archaeological exhibits (the emphasis is on the Roman settlement at Balácapuszta), a large collection of Hungarian, German and Slovak folk costumes and superb wooden carvings, including objects made by the famed outlaws of the Bakony Hills in the 18th and 19th centuries. Next to the main museum is **Bakony House** (Bakonyi ház; ☎ 564 330; adult/child 200/100Ft; ☼ 10am-6pm Tue-Sun May-Sep), a copy of an 18th-century thatched peasant dwelling in the village of Öcs, southwest of Veszprém. It has the usual three rooms found in Hungarian peasant homes, and the complete *kamra* (workshop) of a flask-maker has been set up.

PETŐFI THEATRE

Take a peek inside this **theatre** (☎ 564 220; Óváry Ferenc utca 2; ☼ 9am-5pm) even if you're

not attending a performance. It's a pink, grey and burgundy gem of Hungarian Art-Nouveau architecture and its decoration was designed by István Medgyaszay in 1908. It's also important structurally, as the theatre was the first building in Hungary to be made entirely of reinforced concrete. The large round stained-glass window entitled *The Magic of Folk Art* by Sándor Nagy is exceptional. For information on performances, see the Entertainment section.

Tours

From June to August **Tourinform** (☎ 404 548; Vár utca 4) offers free tours of the city, leaving at 10am Wednesday and Saturday from a temporary booth on Kossuth Lajos utca.

Festivals & Events

The **Veszprém Festival**, held at the beginning of August, attracts some big international names in the field of jazz and classical music.

Sleeping

Oliva (☎ 403 875; www.oliva.hu; Buhim utca 14-16; s/d 14,100/16,000Ft; P ⬜) This exquisite little *pension* has stylish and modern rooms with enough space to be comfortable and is only a short stroll to the Castle Hill.

Péter Pál (☎ 567 790; info@peterpal.hu; Dózsa György utca 3; s/d 6600/8900Ft; P) Only a short walk to the centre, Péter Pál is another fine choice with simple yet stylish rooms, a lovely garden and above-average restaurant, and very friendly and helpful staff.

Diana (☎ 421061; József Attila utca 22; s/d 6800/9200Ft; **P**) Quiet, clean and value-for-money, this is an excellent bet for those looking for a bed for the night and a minimum of fuss. There's also a decent restaurant here.

Éllő (☎ 420 097; József Attila utca 25; s/d 10,500/12,000Ft; **P**) Éllő occupies an alpine-style house more commonly found in Austria. Rooms arc outdated but on the large size, and come with bathroom.

Erdei Camping (☎ 326 751; Kittenberger utca 14; camp sites per adult/child/tent 850/425/800Ft, bungalows 9300Ft; motel s/d 3500/6800Ft; ☼ mid-Apr–mid-Oct; **P**) This small camping ground is a fair way west of town, which is great if you're looking for some peace and quiet, but you'll need your own transport. It's surrounded by fields and woods, and is next to the zoo. Motel rooms have shared facilities.

Eating & Drinking

Oliva (☎ 403 875; Buhim utca 14-16; mains 1800-2500Ft) Oliva compliments its *pension* with an upmarket eatery, featuring in-season Hungarian specialities, a substantial wine selection and a huge outdoor patio.

Várkert (☎ 442 992; Vár utca 17) Várkert was receiving a serious overhaul at the time of writing, but expect to find a restaurant with a bustling atmosphere, a huge patio and plenty of choices in the heart of the Castle Hill district.

Óváros (☎ 326 790; Szabadság tér 14; mains 6500-1500Ft) This restaurant attracts diners throughout the day with its baroque setting, an extensive menu including fish dishes, and reliable cuisine.

Belgian Beer Café (☎ 444 900; Szabadság tér 5) Why Belgian beer is such a hit in Hungary when the amber liquid north of the border is a far better option is anyone's guess, but no matter, this place attracts punters by the dozen with its convivial, relaxed atmosphere.

The large **covered market** (Piac tér), where you can buy food among other things, is south of the bus station.

Mackó Snack (Szabadság tér; burgers & pizza slices from 260Ft) Join students and workers on the run at lunchtime for Mackó's quick snacks of burgers and pizzas.

The following two places at the foot of Castle Hill are both pleasant spots:

Elefánt Bisztró (☎ 329 695; Óváros tér 6; mains from 1000Ft) From steaks to salads, Elefánt has a go at most Hungarian dishes and has outdoor seating.

Café Piazza (☎ 444 445; Óváros tér 4; pizzas 800Ft; ☼ 8.30am-10pm) Simple pizzeria with big pizzas and seating on the square.

Entertainment

Veszprém Cultural Centre (☎ 429 111; Dózsa György utca 2) This is where the city's symphony orchestra is based.

Petőfi Theatre (☎ 564 220; Óváry Ferenc utca 2; ☼ 9am-5pm) This theatre is magnificent and stages both plays and concerts; tickets are available from the box office (open 9am to 1pm and 2pm to 5pm weekdays) in the theatre. See also opposite.

Happy Day Disco (Budapest út 7; ☼ to 4am Fri-Sun) A popular club with an unfortunate name, Happy Day pumps till the wee-small hours on weekends.

Skorpió Night Club (Virág Benedek utca 1; ☼ to 2am Mon-Thu, to 4am Fri & Sat, to 1am Sun) If you're looking for a fun, rowdy and boozy evening, look no further than the Skorpió.

Getting There & Away

BUS

Connections with Veszprém are excellent, with between half-hourly and hourly departures to Budapest (1450Ft, 2¼ hours, 112km), Herend (302Ft, 20 minutes, 21km), Nagyvázsony (302Ft, 30 minutes, 22km), Keszthely (1090Ft, two hours, 88km), Pápa (665Ft, 1¼ hours, 52km) and Tapolca (725Ft, 1¼ hours, 59km).

Other destinations from Veszprém:

Destination	Price	Duration	Km	Frequency
Győr	968Ft	2hr	79	9 daily
Kecskemét	2300Ft	4hr	184	3 daily
Pécs	2300Ft	4hr	181	2 daily
Siófok	605Ft	1¼hr	48	8 daily
Sümeg	846Ft	2hr	68	5 daily

TRAIN

Three railway lines meet at Veszprém. The first connects Veszprém with Szombathely (1420Ft, two hours, 124km) and Budapest's stations (1212Ft, two hours, 112km) via Székesfehérvár (up to seven/14 daily to Budapest/Szombathely). The second line carries up to six trains daily north to Pannonhalma (544Ft, 1¾ hours, 58km) and Győr (774Ft, 2¼ hours, 80km), where you can transfer for Vienna (see p382). The third, southeast to Lepsény, links Veszprém with the railway lines on the northern and southern shores of Lake Balaton up to six times daily.

Getting Around

Buses 1 and 2 run from the train and bus stations to Szabadság tér. You can also book a local taxi (☎ 444 444).

AROUND VESZPRÉM
Herend

☎ 88 / pop 3330

The porcelain factory at **Herend** (www.herend.hu), 13km west of Veszprém, has been producing Hungary's finest handpainted chinaware for over 150 years. There's not a lot to see in this dusty one-horse village, and prices at the outlet don't seem any cheaper than elsewhere in Hungary, but the **Porcelánium** (☎ 523 262; www.porcelanium.com; Kossuth Lajos utca 140; adult/child factory & museum 1500/500Ft; ☒ 9am-6pm Apr-Oct, 9am-4.30pm Tue-Sat Nov-Mar) is worth the trip. It consists of a museum which displays the most prized pieces of the rich Herend collection, and a mini-factory, where you can witness first-hand how ugly clumps of clay become delicate porcelain. It's a five-minute walk northeast from the bus station. Labels are in four languages, including English, which makes it easy to follow the developments and changes in patterns and tastes (see boxed text, below), and there's a short film tracing the history of Herend porcelain.

The complex has a **shop** (☒ 9.30am-6pm Mon-Fri, 9.30am-5pm Sat, 9.30am-4.30pm Sun) selling antique pieces; otherwise scout around the

few shops close to the Porcelánium for new pieces.

Should you feel hungry, Porcelánium has an upmarket restaurant called **Apicius** (menu 400Ft). **Lila Akác** (Kossuth Lajos utca 122; mains from 800Ft) is a more down-to-earth place west of the museum and across Vasút utca, with a hearty selection of Hungarian dishes.

GETTING THERE & AWAY

You can reach the town of Herend by bus from Veszprém at least every 30 minutes (302Ft, 20 minutes, 21km); other destinations include Sümeg (665Ft, 1½ hours, 52km, three daily) and Balatonfüred (484Ft, one hour, 37km, two daily). Six trains run through Herend daily on their way to Ajka (264Ft, 20 minutes, 22km). Change there for Szombathely.

PÁPA

☎ 89 / pop 33,500

This attractive and peaceful town some 50km northwest of Veszprém has been called the 'Athens of Transdanubia' largely because of its Calvinist school. It was attended by such literary greats as the poet Sándor Petőfi and the novelist Mór Jókai in the 19th century. Religious tolerance has been a hallmark of Pápa for centuries.

History

Protestantism gained ground swiftly in the area in the 16th century and the first Hungarian translation of the Heidelberg Catechism was published here in 1577. During the late Middle Ages, Pápa was the third

---

HEREND PORCELAIN

A terracotta factory, set up at Herend in 1826, began producing porcelain 13 years later under Mór Farkasházi Fischer of Tata in Western Transdanubia.

Initially it specialised in copying and replacing the nobles' broken chinaware settings imported from Asia. You'll see some pretty kooky 19th-century interpretations of Japanese art and Chinese faces on display in the Porcelánium museum here. But the factory soon began producing its own patterns; many, like the *Rothschild bird* and *petites roses,* were inspired by Meissen and Sèvres designs from Germany and France. The Victoria pattern of butterflies and wild flowers of the Bakony was designed for Queen Victoria after she admired a display of Herend pieces at the Great Exhibition in London in 1851.

To avoid bankruptcy in the 1870s, the Herend factory began mass production; tastes ran from kitschy pastoral and hunting scenes to the ever-popular animal sculptures with the distinctive scale-like triangle patterns. In 1993, three quarters of the factory was purchased by its 1500 workers and became one of the first companies in Hungary privatised through an employee stock-ownership plan. The state owns the other quarter.

most important Protestant stronghold in Transdanubia after Sopron and Sárvár.

Pápa flourished after liberation from the Turks, with Bishop Károly Esterházy overseeing the construction of many of its fine baroque buildings; his family effectively owned the town from 1648 to after WWII (1939–45). His brother Ferenc encouraged trade by allowing Jews to settle in Pápa. Pottery, broad cloth and paper-making industries were mainly run by Jews and by the end of the 19th century Pápa had one of the largest Jewish populations in Hungary.

Orientation

Pápa's main drags are Fő tér and Fő utca, which run southeast from Kastély-park to Március 15 tér. Pedestrian Kossuth Lajos utca runs southward from the large parish church on Fő tér. The bus station (Szabadság utca) is a short distance east of the church. The train station (Béke tér) is north of the centre at the end of Esterházy Károly utca.

Information

K&H bank (Kossuth Lajos utca 27) With ATM.
Main post office (Kossuth Lajos utca 29)
OTP bank (Fő utca 5) Also with ATM.
Tourinform (☎ 311 535; papa@tourinform.hu; Fő utca 5; ◷ 9am-5pm Mon-Fri) Small office near the main square.

Sights

The enormous U-shaped yellow building at the entrance to Kastély-park is the former **Esterházy Palace** (Esterházy kastély; ☎ 313 584; admission free; ◷ 9am-5pm Tue-Sun) built in 1784 on the foundations of an older castle. Russian soldiers were billeted here as late as 1990. The palace contains a small regional museum, a music school and a library, but don't be surprised to find the doors locked due to sporadic renovation.

South of the palace is the **Great Church** (Nagytemplom; Fő tér; admission free; ◷ 9am-4pm) built by Jacob Fellner in 1786 and dedicated to St Stephen. It contains wonderful frescoes (1781–82) of St Stephen's life and martyrdom by Franz Anton Maulbertsch (the same artist who did the frescoes in Sümeg) and Hubert Mauer, but its bland, grey walls are rather depressing.

The **Calvinist Church History Museum** (Református Egyháztörténeti Múzeum; ☎ 342 240; Fő utca 6; adult/child 150Ft/free; ◷ 9am-5pm Tue-Sun May-Oct) may not sound like a crowd-pleaser but it

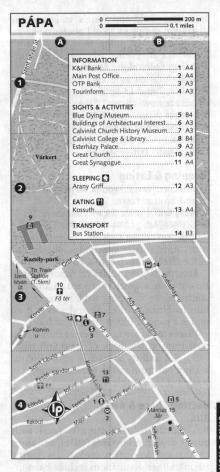

has a lovely collection of simple wooden altars and puts in perspective Protestantism and the role of the **Calvinist College** (Református Kollégium; ☎ 324 420; Március 15 tér 9; admission free; ◷ 8am-4pm Tue-Fri, 9am-5pm Sat & Sun). The college is a little further south and its **library**, with 75,000 valuable tomes, can be visited.

Arguably the most popular museum in Pápa is the **Blue Dyeing Museum** (Kékfestő Múzeum; ☎ 324 390; Március 15 tér 12; adult/child 400/200Ft; ◷ 9am-5pm Tue-Sun Apr-Oct, 9am-4pm Tue-Sat Nov-Mar), which showcases a method of colouring cotton fabric deep blue that was a famous Pápa export throughout Hungary. The museum is housed in a factory that stopped operating in 1956, but the machines remain in perfect working order, demonstrations are

LAKE BALATON REGION

sometimes held and there's an interesting display of samples and old photographs.

The streets running west off Kossuth Lajos utca are particularly rich architecturally, especially along **Korvin utca**; check out the Gothic, baroque and rococo gems at Nos 4, 9, 7 and 13 on Korvin utca, most of which are now offices. To the south the **Great Synagogue** (Nagyzsinagóga; Petőfi Sándor utca 24-26), a romantic structure built in 1846 with some 100,000 bricks donated by the Esterházy family, sadly barely stands.

Sleeping & Eating

Tourinform can fill you in on private rooms in and around town.

Arany Griff (☎ 312 000; www.hotelaranygriff.hu; Fő tér 15; s 5984-7480Ft, d 8704-11,790Ft; **P**) This is the only decent option aside from private rooms, with comfy, dated rooms and excellent views of the Great Church across Fő tér.

Kossuth (Kossuth Lajos utca 22; mains 600-1000Ft) Kossuth, in a quiet courtyard in the Kossuth Udvar shopping mall, mixes pizzas into its Hungarian menu and serves it all under a pagoda-like structure outdoors.

Places to eat are rather scarce though the restaurant at the back of **Arany Griff** (mains 1000-2000Ft) and its *cukrászda*, with outdoor seating out front in the warmer months, is a safe bet for reliable food.

Getting There & Away

BUS

Bus service to/from Pápa is good with hourly departures to Győr (605Ft, one hour, 48km) and Veszprém (665Ft, 1¼ hours, 50km). Other destinations include Balatonfüred (786Ft, 1¾ hours, 63km, two daily), Budapest (2060Ft, four hours, 170km, three daily), Keszthely (968Ft, 2¼ hours, 80km, eight daily), Sümeg (665Ft, 1¼ hours, 51km, five daily) and Tapolca (725Ft, 1½ to two hours, 59km, four daily).

There is a bus to Vienna at 6.55am on Monday, Thursday and Friday.

TRAIN

Pápa is on the rail line linking Győr (430Ft, one hour, 47km) with Celldömölk, from where you can carry on to Szombathely (658Ft, one to two hours, 70km) up to 19 times daily. The only other place you can reach by rail from Pápa is Csorna, which is on the main line between Győr and Sopron.

SZÉKESFEHÉRVÁR

☎ 22 / pop 106,300

Székesfehérvár (*sake*-kesh-fehair-vahr) may look like just another big city off the M7 between Budapest and Lake Balaton. But this city is traditionally known as the place where the Magyar chieftain Árpád first set up camp, making it the oldest town in Hungary. But that doesn't make it the hottest tourist destination in the country; quite to the contrary, Székesfehérvár is often overlooked by tourists. This is a pity because its pretty centre and handful of attractions are worth a detour and even warrant an overnight stay.

History

As early as the 1st century, the Romans had a settlement at Gorsium near Tác. When Árpád arrived late in the 9th century, the surrounding marshes and the Sárvíz River offered protection – the same reason Prince Géza built his castle here less than 100 years later. But it was King Stephen I who raised the status of Székesfehérvár by building a fortified basilica in what he called Alba Regia. Hungary's kings (and some of its queens) would be crowned and buried here for the next 500 years. In fact, the city's name means 'Seat of the White Castle', as it was the royal capital and white was the king's colour.

With Visegrád, Esztergom and Buda, Székesfehérvár served as an alternative royal capital for centuries, and it was here in 1222 that King Andrew II was forced by his mercenaries to sign the Golden Bull, an early bill of rights. The Turks captured Székesfehérvár in 1543 and used the basilica to store gunpowder. It exploded during a siege in 1601; when the Turks left in 1688, the town, the basilica and the royal tombs were in ruins.

Stephen, and much less Árpád, would hardly recognise today's Székesfehérvár. The stones from his basilica were used to construct the Bishop's Palace in 1801; several decades later, the marshland was drained and the Sárvíz was diverted. The city had been at a crossroads since the 11th century, when crusaders (on a budget) from Western Europe passed through on their way to the Adriatic Sea. The arrival of the railway in the 1860s turned the city into a transport hub.

In March 1945 the Germans launched the last big counteroffensive of WWII near Székesfehérvár. Though the fighting razed the city's outskirts (the historic centre was left more or less intact), it opened the way for postwar industrial development.

Orientation

Városház tér and Koronázó tér form the core of the old town. Pedestrian Fő utca – what the Romans called Vicus Magnus – runs north from here. The train station is a 15-minute walk southeast and can be reached via József Attila utca and its continuation, Deák Ferenc utca. The bus station is near the market, just outside the old town's western wall.

Information

Ibusz (☎ 348 316; Táncsics Mihály utca 5; ☼ 8am-5pm Mon-Fri) Will exchange money.

Library (Bartók Béla tér 7; per hr 200Ft; ☼ 10am-6pm Mon-Fri, 10am-5pm Sat) Internet access.

Main post office (Kossuth Lajos utca 16)

OTP bank (Fő utca 6) With ATM.

Tourinform (☎ 537 261; tourinform@pmhiv.szekesfe hervar.hu; Városház tér 1; ☼ 9am-7pm mid-May–mid-Sep, 9am-4pm Mon-Fri mid-Sep–mid-May) Has an office next to the town hall and sells theatre tickets.

www.szekesfehervar.hu Has more information about this city.

Sights
ST STEPHEN'S CATHEDRAL

St Stephen's Cathedral (Szent István székesegyház; Géza nagyfejedelem tér; admission free; ☼ services only), just off Arany János utca, was constructed in 1470 and originally dedicated to Sts Peter and

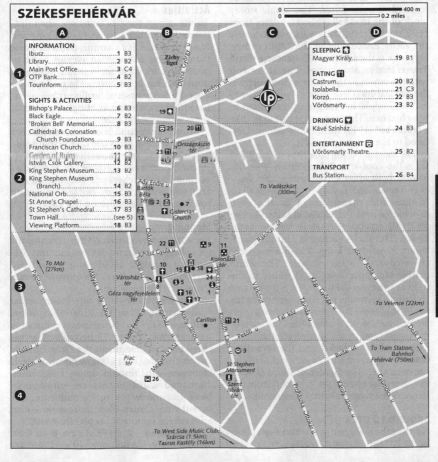

SZÉKESFEHÉRVÁR

0   400 m
0   0.2 miles

INFORMATION
Ibusz..................................1 B3
Library................................2 B2
Main Post Office................3 C4
OTP Bank...........................4 B3
Tourinform........................5 B3

SIGHTS & ACTIVITIES
Bishop's Palace..................6 B3
Black Eagle........................7 B2
'Broken Bell' Memorial......8 B3
Cathedral & Coronation
   Church Foundations.......9 B3
Franciscan Church............10 B3
Garden of Ruins................11
István Csók Gallery...........12 B2
King Stephen Museum......13 B2
King Stephen Museum
   (Branch)........................14 B2
National Orb.....................15 B3
St Anne's Chapel...............16 B3
St Stephen's Cathedral.....17 B3
Town Hall.....................(see 5)
Viewing Platform.............18 B3

SLEEPING 🛏
Magyar Király....................19 B1

EATING 🍽
Castrum............................20 B2
Isolabella..........................21 C3
Korzó................................22 B3
Vörösmarty.......................23 B2

DRINKING 🍷
Kávé Színház.....................24 B3

ENTERTAINMENT 🎭
Vörösmarty Theatre..........25 B2

TRANSPORT
Bus Station.......................26 B4

Zichy liget

Dózsa György u

Berényi út

To Vadászkürt
(300m)

Dr Koch László u

Országzászló tér

Ady Endre u
Bartók Béla tér

Cistercian Church

To Mór
(27km)

Mátyás Király körút

Pálca út

Juhász Gyula u

Oskola

Jókai

Várkörút

Rákóczi út

Kégl György u

Távirda u

József Attila u

Városház tér

Megyeház

Arany János u

Géza nagyfejedelem tér

Koronázó tér

Fal köz

Kálmán u

Petőfi u

To Velence (22km)

Carillon

Halász u

Sélyem u

Piac tér

Megyeház körút

Liszt Ferenc u

St Stephen Monument

Szent István tér

Budai út

Károly János u

To Train Station;
Bahnhof
Fehérvár (750m)

Deák Fu

Gyümölcs u

Prohászka Ottokár u

To West Side Music Club;
Szárcsa (1.5km);
Taurus Kastély (16km)

Paul, but what you see today is essentially an 18th-century baroque church. The ceiling frescoes inside were done by Johannes Cymbal in 1768. On the paving stones in front of the cathedral are foundation outlines of an earlier (perhaps 10th century) church. The wooden crucifix on the northern wall is dedicated to the victims of the 1956 Uprising.

Just north of the cathedral is **St Anne's Chapel** (Szent Anna kápolna; Arany János utca; admission free; ☉ services only) built around the same time, with additions (the tower, for example) made some centuries later. The Turks used the chapel as a place of worship; you can still see the remains of a painting from that era.

AROUND VÁROSHÁZ TÉR & KORONÁZÓ TÉR

Arany János utca debouches into Városház tér and Koronázó tér. The single-storey block of the **town hall** (Városház tér) dates from 1690; the larger northern wing was formerly the Zichy Palace built in the 18th century. Opposite is the austere 1745 **Franciscan church** (Ferences templom; admission free). The stone ball with the crown in the centre of the square is the **National Orb** (Országalma – which means 'national apple' in Hungarian) dedicated to King Stephen. The monument that looks like a **broken bell** (1995) lying on its side is dedicated to the victims of WWII.

The most imposing building on Koronázó tér is the Zopf-style **Bishop's Palace** (Püspöki palota), built with the rubble from the medieval basilica and royal burial chapels. The basilica and chapels stood to the east, in what is now the **Garden of Ruins** (Romkert; ☎ 315 583; adult/child 290/130Ft; ☉ 9am-5pm Tue-Sun Apr-Oct). The site is sacred to Hungarians – about 30 of their kings and queens were crowned and 15 buried here. The white marble sarcophagus in the chamber to the right as you enter the main gate is thought to contain the remains of Géza, Stephen or his young son, Imre. Decorative stonework from the basilica and royal tombs lines the walls of the loggia, and in the garden are the foundations of the **cathedral** and the **Coronation Church**. A small amount of excavation of the site continues. The Garden of Ruins is open to visitors but you can see most of it from the street or the **viewing platform** (Koronázó tér).

AROUND FŐ UTCA

North of the town centre, the **Black Eagle** (Fekete Sas; ☎ 315 583; Fő utca 5; adult/child 290/130Ft; ☉ 10am-6pm Tue-Sun) is a pharmacy set up by the Jesuits in 1758, with beautiful rococo furnishings. Just to the west, on Oskola utca, the **István Csók Gallery** (☎ 314 106; Bartók Béla tér 1; adult/child 290/130Ft; ☉ 10am-7pm Mon-Fri, 10am-6pm Sat & Sun) has a good collection of 19th- and 20th-century Hungarian art. Note that the gallery is closed on the first Monday of each month.

The **King Stephen Museum** (István Király Múzeum; ☎ 315 583; Fő utca 16; adult/child 290/130Ft; ☉ 10am-4pm Tue-Sun May-Sep, 10am-2pm Tue-Sun Oct-Apr) has a large collection of Roman pottery (some of it from Gorsium), an interesting folk-carving display and an exhibit covering 1000 years of Székesfehérvár history. The **museum branch** (☉ 2-6pm Tue-Sun May-Sep, 2-4pm Tue-Sun Oct-Apr) on Országzászló tér has temporary exhibits.

Activities

To the east of the city is **Velence**, the third-largest lake in Hungary at 10.5km long and 26sq km in size. It's a far more subdued lake than Balaton, and with an average depth of under 2m, it's ideal for families. Almost a third of its surface is covered in reeds, so it's a good place to observe birdlife; other activities include swimming, boating, windsurfing, water skiing and fishing.

Most of the action is concentrated in the towns of **Gárdony** and **Agárd** on the south side of the lake, and **Velence** to the east, including 10 camp sites and a plethora of hotels and *pensions*. Székesfehérvár's Tourinform can arm you with a handy booklet outlining much of what's on offer on the lake.

Sleeping

For cheap options, check with Tourinform for college accommodation in July and August for between 2000Ft and 4000Ft per person. Ibusz can arrange private rooms (from 4500Ft per person).

Taurus Kastély (☎ 447 030; castlehotel@inbound.hu; Kastély utca 1; s/d €75/81, ste €138; P ☎) Some 16km southeast of town at Seregélyes is this stately home, surrounded by 22 hectares of manicured parkland. Originally the Zichy family's country manor (1821), it now houses a hotel, complete with frescoed dining hall, tennis court and sauna; rooms are surprisingly basic, but you're paying for ambience, not over-the-top luxury. You can rent the entire joint (sleeps up to 104 people) for €4400.

Magyar Király (☎ 311 262; Fő utca 10; s/d 9300/11,000Ft; P) So old fashioned (it's a 150-year-old hotel) it doesn't even have an email address. And while it's fading, it still exudes a semblance of grandeur, with a regal banquet hall, elaborate staircase and dated rooms.

Szárcsa (☎ 325 700; www.szarcsa.com; Szárcsa utca 1; s/d 12,000/17,500Ft; P) This is a fair distance south from the town centre but it's worth the trip. Each of its nine rooms are individually decorated with antique furniture and the entire effect is one of a giant doll's house. There's a quality restaurant here, too.

Vadászkürt (☎ 507 515; www.jagerhorn.hu; Berényi út 1; s/d 5900/9000Ft; P) This *pension* caters to business travellers and has lifeless rooms, but they're modern, clean and cheap and the centre is only 15 minutes' walk away.

Eating & Drinking

The restaurants at Taurus Kastély, Magyar Király and Szárcsa are all worth dining at. The wine to try in these parts is Ezerjó from Mór, 27km to the northwest in the Vértes Hills. It's an acidic, greenish-white tipple that is light and fairly pleasant. Tourinform has a list of wine cellars to visit in Mór.

Korzó (☎ 312 674; Fő utca 2; mains 900-1500Ft) With a pole position allowing views the length of Fő utca, Korzó is the pick of the restaurants in the very heart of Székesfehérvár. Its menu is filled with hefty Hungarian cuisine and its terrace is perfect for enjoying a sunny day.

Castrum (☎ 505 720; Várkörút 3; midday menu 700Ft, mains 1300-3000Ft) Show your chivalry and head to this medieval-themed cellar restaurant for above-average Hungarian fare; in the summer months, tree-shaded outdoor seating on Országzászló tér is thankfully an option.

Vörösmarty (Fő utca 6; ice cream 90Ft; 9am-9pm) This is an ice cream and cake shop that keeps the crowds satisfied with sweet delights throughout the year.

Isolabella (☎ 328 318; Kossuth Lajos utca 12; pizzas 1000Ft) Head to Isolabella if you're in the mood for pizza and people-watching; this restaurant attracts a regular following and shares a courtyard with a couple of bars.

Kávé Színház (Coffee Theatre; ☎ 310 923; Táncsics Mihály utca 1) This little spot is great for a quiet drink, day or night. Its huge terrace overlooks Koronázó tér and the Garden of Ruins.

Entertainment

For more information on what's on, check the free bi-weekly *Fehérvári Est* magazine.

Vörösmarty Theatre (☎ 515 350; Fő utca 8) This theatre, near the Magyar Király hotel, has recently experienced a complete overhaul, so expect cultural performances here to enjoy a grand backdrop.

Bahnhof Fehérvár (Takaródó utca 1) This club, east of the train station, revs (and raves) up at the weekend. It's easy to spot – a locomotive is parked into the side of the building.

West Side Music Club (☎ 507 633; Vörösmarty tér 1) Southeast of the bus station, this is another club that attracts large crowds, and has bowling and billiards if you're not up for drinking and dancing.

Getting There & Away

BUS

Buses depart for Budapest (846Ft, 1¼ hours, 68km), Veszprém (544Ft, 50 minutes, 45km) and the vineyards near Mór (302Ft, 35 minutes, 22km) about once every half hour, and you can reach Lake Velence towns like Velence and Gárdony (via Agárd) throughout the day (241Ft, around 30 minutes, 20km).

Other destinations from Székesfehérvár:

Destination	Price	Duration	Km	Frequency
Balatonfüred	786Ft	1¾hr	61	6 daily
Keszthely	1690Ft	3hr	132	5 daily
Pápa	1210Ft	2¼hr	97	2 daily
Siófok	544Ft	50min	44	6 daily
Sümeg	1450Ft	3hr	116	3 daily
Szekszárd	1330Ft	2hr	104	5 daily
Tapolca	1150Ft	2¼hr	94	3 daily

TRAIN

The town is a main train junction and you can reach most destinations in Transdanubia from here. One line splits at Szabadbattyán (10km to the south), leading to Lake Balaton's northern shore and Tapolca on one side of the lake, and to the southern shore and Nagykanizsa on the other.

Trains every half-hour link Székesfehérvár with Kelenföld and Déli train stations in Budapest (658Ft, 1¼ hours, 65km); frequent trains run daily to Szombathely (1828Ft, 2½ to four hours, 170km) via Veszprém (430Ft, one hour, 45km). A local train runs north to Mór (264Ft, 35 minutes, 30km, six daily).

Getting Around

Bus 12/a runs close to Szárcsa Hotel. You can also book local **taxis** (☎ 222 222).

Great Plain

The nationalist poet Sándor Petőfi, in describing the Great Plain as 'My world and home...The Alföld, the open sea', accurately summed up the nostalgic fervour Hungarians have for their beloved 'Midwest'. Like Australians and their Outback, many Magyars view it romantically: shepherds fight the elements in winter and try not to go stir-crazy in summer when the notorious mirages rise off the baking soil, leading them, their mop-like puli dogs and flocks astray.

The Great Plain, covering some 45,000 sq km east and southeast of Budapest, makes up half the nation's territory but only about a third of the population lives there. At times numbingly flat and monotonous, at others captivating and enthralling, there's no arguing that it has a spell-binding quality that only comes from big skies and endless, uninterrupted prairies.

But the Plain is not a one-dimensional attraction; it is also home to cities of graceful architecture and easy-going recreational areas. Szeged, the unofficial capital of the Plain, is a centre for art and contains Art-Nouveau gems, while its neighbour Kecskemét is a small city packing a big punch with *fin de siècle* elegance. Debrecen, Hungary's second-largest city, commands the east with a vibrant mix of bars, clubs and engaging museums, while the spas of the Hajdúság region and the resort towns on Lake Tisza ensure your stay can be as lazy as you like.

While Hungarians generally divide the Great Plain into 'between the Danube and the Tisza Rivers' and the land 'beyond the Tisza', this does not really reflect the lie of the land, the routes that travellers usually take or, frankly, what's of interest. Instead, it can be divided into the Central Plain, the Eastern Plain and the Southern Plain.

HIGHLIGHTS

- Applauding the astounding 'five-in-hand' horsemanship at Bugac's **horse show** (p247)

- Enjoying the best Szeged has to offer: **Ferenc Móra Museum** (p263), **Art Nouveau New Synagogue** (p263) and *szegedi halászlé* (spicy fish soup)

- Kicking back with nature in **Hortobágy** (p238), the epitome of the *puszta* ('deserted' or 'uninhabited' lands)

- Wondering how such fine Art-Nouveau and Secessionist architecture ever arrived in **Kecskemét** (p243)

- Taking in the museums and nightlife of **Debrecen** (p233), the capital of the east

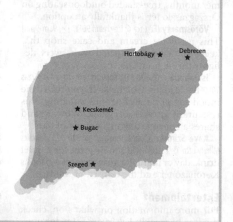

GREAT PLAIN

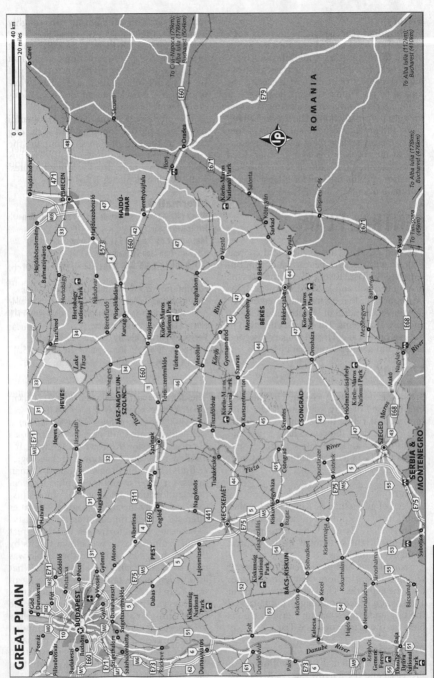

GREAT PLAIN

History

Five hundred years ago the region was not a steppe but forest land at the constant mercy of the flooding Tisza and Danube Rivers. The Turks felled most of the trees, destroying the protective cover and releasing the topsoil to the winds; villagers fled north or to the market towns and *khas* (towns under the sultan's jurisdiction). The region had become the *puszta*, home to shepherds, fisher folk, runaway serfs and outlaws. The regulation of the rivers in the 19th century dried up the marshes and allowed for methodical irrigation, paving the way for intensive agriculture, particularly on the Southern Plain.

CENTRAL PLAIN

The Central Plain, the smallest of the Great Plain's divisions, stretches eastward from Budapest to the Tisza River and encompasses the likes of Szolnok and Jászberény, towns of little importance to most travellers even though they have a handful of architectural delights and historical gems. The biggest attraction in the region is Lake Tisza, Hungary's second largest and a water-lover's paradise.

SZOLNOK

☎ 56 / pop 77,600

Szolnok is not a pretty city; much of its skyline consists of ugly concrete blocks built for practical, rather than aesthetic, purposes. The centre does, however, have a few old monuments, and the city's thermal spas across the Tisza lend it a calm, almost laid-back feel.

History

A 'deed of gift' issued by King Géza I makes mention of Szolnok, then called Zounok, as early as 1075, and it has remained the most important settlement in the Central Plain ever since.

Szolnok has had its share of troubles: it was laid to waste more than a dozen times over the centuries. The last disaster came in 1944, when Allied bombing all but flattened the city and the retreating German troops blew up the bridge over the Tisza.

Orientation

Szolnok is situated on the confluence of the Tisza and the narrow Zagyva Rivers. Its main street, Kossuth Lajos út, runs roughly east–west a few blocks north of the Tisza. Across the Tisza Bridge (Tisza híd), rebuilt in 1963, is the city's recreational area Tisza Park (Tisza-liget), which has the majority of the city's accommodation, as well as swimming pools. A backwater of the Tisza, Alcsi-Holt-Tisza, lies southeast of the park.

The city's busy train station (Jubileumi tér) is a couple of kilometres west of the city centre at the end of Baross Gábor út (the continuation of Kossuth Lajos út). The bus station (Ady Endre utca) is a few minutes' walk north of Kossuth Lajos út.

Information

Ibusz (☎ 423 602; Szapáry út 24; ☼ 8am-5pm Mon-Fri) Travel agent.

Main post office (☎ 341 301; Baross Gábor út 14; ☼ 7am-7pm Mon-Fri, 8am-1pm Sat)

OTP bank (☎ 420 033; Szapáry út 31) Has a 24-hour ATM.

Tourinform (☎ 424 704; szolnok-m@tourinform.hu; Ságvári körút 4; ☼ 8am-5pm Mon-Fri, 9am-2pm Sat mid-Jun–mid-Sep, 8am-4pm Mon-Fri mid-Sep–mid-Jun) Small office just south of the bus station.

Verseghy Ferenc library (☎ 510 110; Kossuth tér 2; per hr 100Ft; ☼ 10am-6pm Tue-Fri, 8am-1pm Sat) Internet access.

Sights

The **János Damjanich Museum** (☎ 421 602; Kossuth tér 4; one exhibition 200Ft, all exhibitions 700Ft, guided tours 1500Ft, Tue admission free; ☼ 9am-5pm Tue-Sun), a well-laid out museum devoted to Szolnok's history, is easily the town's highlight. It's divided into three sections: archaeological finds from the Bronze Age and Roman times; an extensive ethnographical collection; and exhibits relating to Szolnok's history, especially the artists' colony. The latter often showcases contemporary local artists.

Like so many fortresses on the Great Plain, Szolnok Castle was blown to bits by the Habsburgs in 1710, and the rubble was later used to rebuild the city centre. What little is left of the **castle ruins** – just a bit of wall – can be seen near Gutenberg tér, across the Zagyva River. Gutenberg tér is also the site of Hungary's most famous **artists' colony** (művésztelep; ☎ 425 549; Gutenberg tér 4), founded in 1902 and once counting among its members the realist painters Adolf Fényes, István Nagy and László Mednyánszky. Fronting the Zagyva northeast of Szabadság tér is the

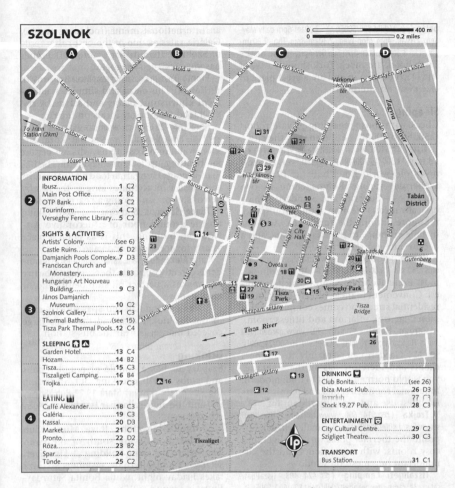

SZOLNOK

0 ————— 400 m
0 ————— 0.2 miles

INFORMATION
Ibusz	1 C2
Main Post Office	2 B2
OTP Bank	3 C2
Tourinform	4 C2
Verseghy Ferenc Library	5 C2

SIGHTS & ACTIVITIES
Artists' Colony	(see 6)
Castle Ruins	6 D2
Damjanich Pools Complex	7 D3
Franciscan Church and Monastery	8 B3
Hungarian Art Nouveau Building	9 C3
János Damjanich Museum	10 C2
Szolnok Gallery	11 C3
Thermal Baths	(see 15)
Tisza Park Thermal Pools	12 C4

SLEEPING
Garden Hotel	13 C4
Hozam	14 B2
Tisza	15 C3
Tiszaligeti Camping	16 B4
Trojka	17 C3

EATING
Caffé Alexander	18 C3
Galéria	19 C3
Kassai	20 D3
Market	21 C1
Pronto	22 D2
Róza	23 B2
Spar	24 C2
Tünde	25 C2

DRINKING
Club Bonita	(see 26)
Ibiza Music Klub	26 D3
Jazzclub	27 C3
Stock 19.27 Pub	28 C3

ENTERTAINMENT
City Cultural Centre	29 C2
Szigliget Theatre	30 C3

TRANSPORT
Bus Station	31 C1

Tabán district, with the last remaining peasant houses in Szolnok.

The **Szolnok Gallery** (☎ 378 023; Templom utca 2; adult/child 100/50Ft; 🕑 9am-5pm Tue-Sun May-Oct, 10am-4pm Tue-Sun Nov-Apr) shows works by contemporary artists from the region. The primary reason for visiting the gallery is to see the building itself – a Romantic-style **synagogue** that was designed by Lipót Baumhorn in 1898. (Baumhorn also did the glorious temples in Szeged and Gyöngyös.) West of the gallery are the baroque **Franciscan church and monastery** (Ferences templom és kolostor; Templom utca 8) completed in 1757 – the city's oldest buildings.

Architecture buffs should walk up Szapáry út from the Szolnok Gallery for a look

at a fine example of a **Hungarian Art Nouveau building** (Szapáry út 19); today it houses a few small businesses.

Activities

Szolnok is a spa town and has several places where you can 'take the waters'. The **Tisza Park thermal pools** (Tiszaligeti sétány; adult/child 750/550Ft; 🕑 9am-8pm mid-May–Aug), across the river, is the town's largest swimming complex and comes complete with slides.

Closer to town, just before the Tisza Bridge, is the **Damjanich indoor and outdoor thermal pool** (Damjanich utca 3; adult/child 550/400Ft; 🕑 6am-7pm Mon-Fri, 7am-7pm Sat & Sun May-Sep; 6am-6.30pm Mon-Sat, 7am-1pm Sun Oct-Apr) and a large sunbathing area. The more serious **thermal**

baths (adult/child 800/500Ft; ☽ 7.30am-6pm daily May-Sep, 7.30am-4pm Mon-Wed, 7.30am-8pm Thu, 7.30am-10pm Fri & Sat, 7.30am-1pm Sun Oct-Apr), those at the Tisza hotel, are mock Turkish with a bit of Art Deco thrown in and are a great place to laze away an afternoon.

Sleeping

Check with Ibusz regarding private rooms (2500Ft to 4000Ft per person) in the city.

Tisza (☎ 510 850; www.hoteltisza.hu; Verseghy park 2; s/d from 11,300/15,700Ft; P ⍺) Tisza is Szolnok's old-world hotel built in 1928 over a thermal spring. Rooms come in two categories – Superior and Standard (which basically means the more money you spend, the more antique the furniture). Add-ons include entrance to the attached spa, and a decent pub and restaurant.

Hozam (☎ 510 530; www.hozamhotel.hu; Mária utca 25; s/d 16,000/22,000Ft; P ⍺) Szolnok's most exclusive hotel and one of its smallest. Convenient to the centre, it is on a quiet residential street and comes complete with a sauna, Jacuzzi, solarium and fitness room.

Garden Hotel (☎ 520 530; www.gardenhotel .hu in Hungarian; Tiszaligeti sétány; s/d 16,500/21,500Ft; P ✹) Garden caters mainly to business clients and therefore has all the amenities you would normally expect to find: modern, functional rooms, a sauna and tennis courts for guest use and a quality restaurant.

Trojka (☎ 514 600; www.trojka.hu; Tiszaligeti sétány 5; s/d 4000/8000Ft) This small *pension*, opposite the thermal pools on Tiszaliget, has cosy rooms, with wood floors and the all-important bug mesh on windows.

Tiszaligeti Camping (☎ 424 403; Tiszaligeti sétány 34; camp sites per adult/child/tent 800/600/500Ft, 2-person bungalows 6700Ft; motel dm/s/d 2100/5600/6500Ft; camping ☽ May-Sep; P) This large camping site occupies a quiet corner of the Tiszaliget. Its motel complex looks more like an army barracks than anything else, but its small bungalows are cosy in a rustic way.

Eating

Kassai (☎ 426 603; Damjanich utca 5; mains 1000Ft) Kassai is very much a no-frills restaurant that has top-rate food, service and atmosphere. The menu is packed with Hungarian favourites and, with the Tisza so close, plenty of fish dishes.

Galéria (☎ 378 358; Szapáry út 1; mains 1600-2500Ft) With a cool interior, prompt service and an international menu (including curry!), Galéria rates as one of the best restaurants in Szolnok. Its outdoor seating in summer has views of the synagogue.

Pronto (Kossuth Lajos út 6; pizzas & salads under 600Ft; ☽ Mon-Sat) This clean and simple establishment churns out pizzas and salads by the truckload for hungry locals on the run.

Róza (☎ 426 630; Konstantin utca 36; mains 1000Ft; ☽ 11am-10pm Mon-Sat, 11am-4pm Sun) Róza is a short walk from Kossuth tér, which is perfect for building up an appetite for the better-than-average Hungarian food served here. Its courtyard is peaceful, as long as the nearby petrol station isn't doing a roaring trade.

Tünde (Szapáry út 28; ice cream from 100Ft) Taking up the ground floor of a decorative Art-Nouveau building, this is as good a place as any for ice cream and cake.

Caffé Alexander (Táncsics Mihály utca 15) Alexander is directly opposite the Szigliget Theatre and makes a perfect pit stop before and/or after a show.

There's a food hall and Spar supermarket in the Szolnok Plaza while the city's large covered market is near the bus station.

Drinking

Szapáry út has a couple of popular pubs and clubs worth checking out, including the strangely named **Stock 19.27 Pub** (Szapáry út 7) and the dark cellar bar **Jazzclub** (cnr Szapáry út & Sóház utca).

Szolnok's big clubs, Ibiza Music Klub and Club Bonita, are south of the river. They share the same building at Tiszaligeti sétány 1, and alternate evenings – Ibiza takes Friday night, while Bonita Saturday. Entry is around 500Ft.

Entertainment

For up-to-date entertainment information, check the listings in the freebie biweekly *Szolnoki Est*.

City Cultural Centre (☎ 514 575; Hild János tér 1) This centre near Tourinform can tell you when there are concerts on at the Franciscan church and whether Szolnok's celebrated symphony orchestra or Béla Bartók Chamber Choir are performing.

Szigliget Theatre (Szigligeti színház; ☎ 342 633; Tisza park 1) Across from the Tisza hotel, it is one of the most attractive theatres in provincial Hungary. At the forefront of drama in Hungary in the 1970s and '80s, the

Szigliget was the first theatre in Eastern Europe to stage *Dr Zhivago* (1988) – pretty daring stuff at the time.

Getting There & Away

Buses go to towns around Hungary, including Jászberény (725Ft, 1¼ hours, 55km, eight daily), Kecskemét (846Ft, 1¾ hours, 65km, seven daily), Budapest (1150Ft, 1¾ hours, 95km, two daily), Szeged (1690Ft, three hours, 135km, seven daily) and Tiszafüred (907Ft, two hours, 70km, three daily).

Szolnok has excellent train services: you can travel to/from Budapest (1004Ft, 1¾ hours, 100km), Debrecen (1420Ft, 1¾ hours, 120km), Nyíregyháza (1828Ft, two hours, 170km), Békéscsaba (1004Ft, 1½ hours, 95km) and dozens of points in between without changing. For Miskolc (2030Ft, 3¾ hours, 185km), change at Hatvan; Cegléd is where you transfer for Kecskemét (544Ft, one hour, 60km) and Szeged (1624Ft, 2¾ hours, 145km).

Getting Around

From the train station, buses 7 or 8 will take you to Kossuth tér. If heading for the accommodation in Tisza Park, take bus 15.

You can also take a **taxi** (☎ 444 444).

JÁSZBERÉNY

🆔 *57 / pop 20,200*

Today Jászberény is a sleepy town of tree-lined streets and quiet squares, but as early as the 13th century it was the main political, administrative and economic centre of the Jazygians, an obscure pastoral people of Persian origin brought in by King Béla IV (r 1235–70) to strengthen his position. Its biggest (if only) drawcard has always been the Lehel Horn, an ancient, almost magical ivory piece, for centuries the Jazygians chief's symbol of power.

Orientation

The main street is a long 'square' (Lehel vezér tér), which runs almost parallel to the narrow 'city branch' of the Zagyva River. The bus station (Petőfi tér) is two blocks to the west across the Zagyva River, while the train station is 1.5km southwest at the end of Rákóczi út.

Information

Ibusz (☎ 412 143; Szövetkezet utca 7/a) To the southwest of Tourinform.

OTP bank (Lehel vezér tér 28) With ATM.
Post office (Lehel vezér tér 8)
Tourinform (☎ 406 439; jaszbereny@tourinform.hu; Lehel vezér tér 33; ☾ 8am-5pm Mon-Fri, 9am-1pm Sat mid-Jun–mid-Sep, 8am-4.30pm Mon-Fri mid-Sep–mid-Jun) In the Déryné Cultural Centre.

Sights & Activities

The **Jász Museum** (☎ 412 753; Táncsics Mihály utca 5; adult/child 200/100Ft; ☾ 9am-5pm Tue-Sun Apr-Oct), housed in what was once the Jazygian military headquarters, runs the gamut of Jász culture and life – from costumes and woodcarving to language. But all aisles lead to the **Lehel Horn**, an 8th-century Byzantine work. Legend has it that a Magyar leader called Lehel (or Lél) was taken captive in the Battle of Augsburg (AD 955) against the united German armies and, just before he was executed, killed the king by hitting him on the head with the ivory horn. The alleged murder weapon, richly carved with birds, battle scenes and anatomically correct satyrs, doesn't seem to have suffered any serious damage from the blow to the royal noggin.

The museum also spotlights local sons and daughters who made good, including the watercolourist András Sáros and the 19th-century actress Róza Széppataki Déryné. You've seen Mrs Déry before, though you may not know it. She is forever immortalised in that irritating Herend porcelain figurine seen in antique shops everywhere of a woman in a wide organza skirt playing her *lant* (lute) and kissing the air.

Have a look at the fading ceiling frescoes inside the Roman Catholic **parish church** (plébániatemplom; Szentháromság tér 4; admission free) north of Tourinform; the nave was designed in 1774 by András Mayerhoffer and József Jung, two masters of baroque architecture.

For swimming all year round, there's a **thermal spa & pools** (☎ 412 108; Hatvani út 5; spa adult/child 500/350Ft; ☾ 9am-8pm Tue & Thu, 9am-6pm Wed, Fri & Sat, 9am-5pm Sun, pools adult/child 500/350Ft; ☾ 9am-6pm May-Aug) west of the Zagyva.

Sleeping & Eating

Ibusz can arrange private rooms (2500Ft per person).

Kakukkfészek (Cuckoo's Nest; ☎ 412 345; Táncsics Mihály utca 8; s/d 2000/4000Ft) The owners of Kakukkfészek may be a little cuckoo themselves, but they're supremely friendly and have created a homely atmosphere. Rooms

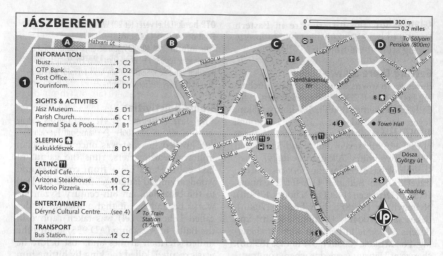

JÁSZBERÉNY

INFORMATION		
Ibusz	1	C2
OTP Bank	2	D2
Post Office	3	C1
Tourinform	4	D1

SIGHTS & ACTIVITIES		
Jász Museum	5	D1
Parish Church	6	C1
Thermal Spa & Pools	7	B1

SLEEPING		
Kakukkfészek	8	D1

EATING		
Apostol Cafe	9	C2
Arizona Steakhouse	10	C1
Viktorio Pizzeria	11	C2

ENTERTAINMENT		
Déryné Cultural Centre	(see 4)	

TRANSPORT		
Bus Station	12	C2

are filled with mismatching furniture and bedding and there are no *en suite* options.

Sólyom Pension (☎ 401 267; www.hotels.hu /solyom; Sólyom út 8; r from 6000Ft; lunch menu 600Ft, mains 1200Ft; Ⓟ) The facilities at this *pension* may be more modern and comfortable than at Kakukkfészek but its often unfriendly service and location, 800m northeast of the centre, are less appealing. Its restaurant packs in the locals at midday with its hearty Hungarian cuisine.

Arizona Steakhouse (cnr Rákóczi út & Serház utca; mains 1500-2500Ft) A rare breed in these parts, with an international menu and American-style steaks, Arizona Steakhouse is decked out in wild-west gear and has picnic tables in the middle of the square.

Viktorio Pizzeria (☎ 411 053; Holló András utca; pizzas 400-1000Ft, mains 500-1000Ft) On a peaceful street just around the corner from the cultural centre, this simple pizzeria has an incredible selection (40 varieties) of pizza.

Apostol Cafe (Hold utca 4; ice cream 100Ft; ☷ 9am-9pm) Apostol is for those who worship that lovely substance – ice cream. Its large terrace is perfect for watching the comings and goings in the town's bus station.

Entertainment

Déryné Cultural Centre (☎ 406 439; Lehel vezér tér 33) This central cultural centre is your first and best source of information for what's on; otherwise, consult the free bi-weekly *Szolnoki Est* for slim listings on Jászberény.

Getting There & Away

Frequent bus departures include those to Budapest (1030Ft, 1¾ hours, 80km, nine daily), Szolnok (725Ft, 1¼ hours, 55km, six daily) and Kecskemét (1090Ft, two hours, 85km, seven daily). There are also daily buses to Szeged (2540Ft, 4¼ hours, 200km, three daily) and Tiszafüred (1330Ft, 2½ hours, 105km, one daily).

Jászberény lies approximately halfway between Hatvan and Szolnok on the train line. These two cities are on Hungary's two main trunk lines, and virtually all main cities in the east are accessible from one or the other. Both Hatvan and Szolnok have direct links to Budapest.

Getting Around

Bus 4 connects the train station with the bus terminus, from where you can walk to the centre of town.

TISZAFÜRED

☎ 59 / pop 13,700

Tiszafüred was a rather sleepy town on the Tisza River until the early 1980s when the river was dammed and a reservoir opened up more than 125 sq km of lakes to holiday-makers. While hardly the 'Lake Balaton of the Great Plain' as the tourist brochures say, Lake Tisza (Tisza-tó) and its primary resort Tiszafüred offer swimmers and boating enthusiasts a break before continuing on to the country's attractions to the east.

Orientation

Tiszafüred lies at the northeast end of Lake Tisza. From the bus and train stations, opposite one another on Vasút utca, walk 10 or 15 minutes west and then southwest to the beach and camp sites. To reach the centre of town, follow Baross Gábor utca and then Fő út south for about a kilometre.

Information

E-Punkt (Örvényi út 5; per hr 125Ft; 🕑 8am-4pm Mon-Thu, 8am-noon Fri) Internet access.
OTP bank (Piac út 3) Behind Fő út.
Post office (Fő út 14) On the main artery running through the centre.
Tourinform (☎ 511 123; tiszafured@tourinform.hu; Fürdő út 21; 🕑 8am-6pm Mon-Fri, 10am-6pm Sat & Sun mid-Jun–mid-Sep, 8am-4pm Mon-Fri mid-Sep–mid-Jun) A helpful office between the lake and the town's thermal spa.

Sights

Tiszafüred is essentially a resort town, but there are a couple of sights worth stopping for, including the **Pál Kiss Museum** (☎ 352 106; Tariczky sétány 6; adult/child 200/100Ft; 🕑 9am-noon, 1-5pm Tue-Sun). Housed in a beautiful old manor (1840) south of the city's thermal baths, its collection is given over to the everyday lives of Tisza fisher folk and the work of local potters.

The area east of Szőlősi út is a veritable patchwork of traditional houses, with thatched roofs and orderly little flower and vegetable gardens – a nice respite from the hubbub of the beach. One of them, the **Gáspár Nyúzó House** (Nyúzó Gáspár Fazekas Tájház; Malom utca 12; adult/child 150/100Ft; 🕑 9am-noon, 2-5pm Tue-Sun May-Oct), is a former potter's residence and contains antique potting wheels, drying racks, furniture and plates in pale primary colours and patterns of stars, and birds and flowers unique to the region. Just southeast of the village house is the working pottery workshop of **Imre Szücs** (☎ 351 483; Belsőkertsor út 4/a). His pottery, with its highly decorative and colourful markings, is in stark contrast to the dark and sombre creations from Mohács or Nádudvar.

Activities

Activities on the lake include fishing, boating, swimming and baking in the sun. **Fortuna Camping** (☎ 511 304; Holt-Tisza part) and **Hableány** (☎ 353 333; Hunyadi utca 2) rent canoes/paddle boats/motorboats for 1000/1000/4000Ft a day. There's an extra charge of around 2000Ft for fuel with motorboat rentals. If you prefer to let someone else do the driving, contact **Kormorán boat harbour** (☎ 350 350; Tiszaörvény), **Szabics boat harbour** (☎ 06 30 954 8620; Tiszaörvény) or **Városi Kikötő** (☎ 06 20 916 2589; www.varosikikoto.hu; Gát sétány 1), all of whom offer fishing and sightseeing packages starting around 7500Ft.

If the lake is too cold for you, Tiszafüred's **thermal spa** (☎ 352 366; Poroszlói út; adult/child 450/350Ft; 🕑 pools 7.30am-7pm May-Sep, sauna 8am-7pm mid-Mar–mid-Nov) has four open-air pools, as well as a sauna and a wide range of medical services.

Those looking for exercise away from water can try their hand at horse riding at **Gulyás farm** (☎ 351 814; per hr 2500-3500Ft) in Tiszaörvény near the Hableány hotel, or rent a bicycle (200/1000Ft per hour/day) from **Angler Camping** (☎ 351 220; Holt-Tisza part), **Fortuna Camping** (☎ 511 304; Holt-Tisza part) or **Hableány** (☎ 353 333; Hunyadi utca 2).

Sleeping

Tourinform can supply you with a long list of private accommodation (rooms from 2500Ft) in and around Tiszafüred.

Füzes (☎ 351 854; Húszöles út 31b; s/d 3500/6600Ft; Ⓟ ❄) Füzes is a friendly 10-room *pension* with cosy and functional rooms, many of which overlook the Molnár restaurant next door. It's also fairly quiet, considering its proximity to busy Húszöles út.

Aurum (☎ 351 338; Ady Endre utca 29; r 7600Ft; Ⓟ) Aurum is for those looking for a more homely feel than Füzes offers; room décor dates from when Kádár still held the country's reins (but bathrooms are modern) and the owners are welcoming.

Thermál Camping (☎ 352 911; Húszöles út 2; camp sites per person/tent 820/670Ft, bungalows 8900-9700Ft; 🕑 Apr–mid-Nov; Ⓟ) Of the 11 camp sites in Tiszafüred's immediate vicinity, Thermál is the best organised and laid out. Its tree-lined avenues are generally crammed with holiday makers over the summer, however, it's a bit of a walk to the lake's public beaches.

Angler Camping (☎ 351 220; horg.camp@dpg.hu; Holt-Tisza part; camp sites per adult/child/tent/car 650/400/500/250Ft, d/tr/q 4900/5900/6900Ft, bungalows 6000-9900Ft; 🕑 Apr-Oct; Ⓟ) This lakeside place has plenty of amenities, such as snack stalls, a restaurant, recreational facilities (including tennis) and holiday homes accommodating

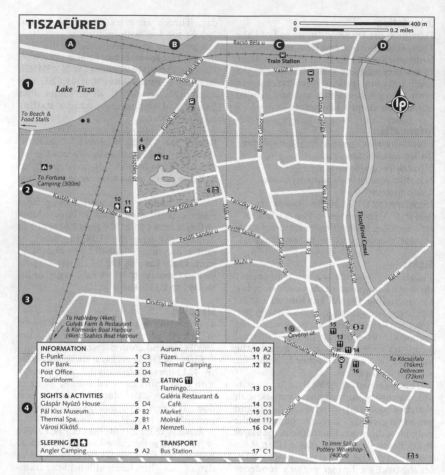

TISZAFÜRED

Map of Tiszafüred

INFORMATION
E-Punkt..........................1 C3
OTP Bank........................2 D3
Post Office......................3 D4
Tourinform......................4 B2

SIGHTS & ACTIVITIES
Gáspár Nyúzó House..............5 D4
Pál Kiss Museum.................6 B2
Thermal Spa....................7 B1
Városi Kikötő...................8 A1

SLEEPING
Angler Camping..................9 A2

Aurum..........................10 A2
Füzes..........................11 B2
Thermál Camping................12 B2

EATING
Flamingo.......................13 D3
Galéria Restaurant &
  Café.........................14 D3
Market.........................15 D3
Molnár.....................(see 11)
Nemzeti........................16 D4

TRANSPORT
Bus Station....................17 C1

two/three/four people with shared showers. Bungalows come with or without bathrooms.

Fortuna Camping (☎ 511 304; Holt-Tisza part; camp sites per adult/child/tent 600/450/650Ft, bungalows from 5200Ft; ☯ May-Sep; Ⓟ) Fortuna occupies its own corner of the town and is surrounded by trees, making it a very secluded camp site. There are sports fields, a volley ball court and bike hire, and the lake is within easy walking distance.

Eating

Galéria Restaurant & Café (☎ 350 512; Fő utca 15; mains under 1000Ft) The terracotta patio on the first floor of this inviting restaurant is by far the best place to enjoy a meal in town. The

menu is loaded with fish dishes and folk art is sprinkled around the interior.

Hableány (☎ 353 333; Hunyadi utca 2; mains 1000-2000Ft) According to the locals, this is the best restaurant for fish in the Tiszafüred area, but you'll need to have your own wheels: it's in the Hotel Tiszaörvény, about 4km to the southwest.

Nemzeti (☎ 352 349; Fő út 8; lunch menu 530Ft, mains 1000Ft) The bright yellow exterior of this restaurant in the centre of town hides a rather plain interior and the occasional band of Gypsy musicians; its midday meal is excellent value, but Galéria is a better deal in the evenings.

Molnár (☎ 352 705; Húszöles út 31/b; mains 1000-2000Ft) This restaurant has a good fish selection, as well as a handful of game and vegetarian dishes. Its breezy terrace (protected from mosquitos by netting) is a welcome respite on sticky summer days.

Flamingo (Fő út; ice cream 90Ft; ☺ 8am-8pm) This combination of *cukrászda* (cake shop) and *bronzárium* (tanning studio) does some excellent baking and scoops up some fine ice cream.

The town's **market** (Piac tér) is postage-stamp sized but has fresh fruits and vegetables; otherwise, for a quick bite, try the food stalls serving gyros, pizza and *lángos* (deep-fried dough with toppings) at the public beach and the camp sites.

Getting There & Away
Other destinations served daily by bus include Budapest (2300Ft, four hours, 185km, four daily), Szolnok (907Ft, two hours, 70km, three to five daily), Eger (725Ft, 1¼ hours, 55km, 10 daily), Jászberény (1330Ft, 2½ hours, 105km, two daily) and Debrecen (846Ft, 1¼ hours, 70km, six daily).

Tiszafüred is on the train line linking Füzesabony – from where you can carry on to Eger (430Ft, 1¼ hours, 45km) or Miskolc (890Ft, two hours, 85km) – and Debrecen (774Ft, 1½ hours, 75km), which passes through the Hortobágy region.

EASTERN PLAIN

When people imagine the *puszta,* it's the Eastern Plain (Kelet-Alföld) they see. This is where the myth of the lonely *pásztor* (shepherd) in billowy trousers, the wayside *csárdák* (inns) and Gypsy violinists was born – to be kept alive in literature, fine art and the imagination of the Hungarian people.

But it's not all open plain and big-sky country. Debrecen, Hungary's second-largest city, located on the eastern fringes of the plain, brings balance via a healthy restaurant and bar scene.

DEBRECEN
☎ 52 / pop 211,000
Debrecen is a vibrant metropolis rich in history. Its centre is surprisingly pretty, especially after the unsightly mess surrounding the bus and train stations, and is dominated by the country's largest Protestant church. Bars and restaurants are dotted

around its heart, creating a lively scene for night crawlers, while an array of museums keep most visitors busy for a day or two. It also makes a good base for forays into the *puszta* and the northeast.

History
The area around Debrecen has been settled since the earliest times. When the Magyars arrived late in the 9th century, they found a colony of Slovaks here who called the region Dobre Zliem for its 'good soil'. Debrecen's wealth, based on salt, the fur trade and cattle-raising, grew steadily through the Middle Ages and increased during the Turkish occupation; the city kept all sides happy by paying tribute to the Ottomans, the Habsburgs and Transylvanian princes at the same time.

By the mid-16th century much of the population had converted to Protestantism and churches were being erected with gusto, earning the city the nickname 'Calvinist Rome'. Debrecen played a pivotal role in the 1848–49 War of Independence, and it experienced a major building boom in the late 19th and early 20th centuries.

Orientation
Debrecen is an easy city to negotiate. A ring road, built on the city's original earthen walls, encloses the Belváros, or Inner Town. This is bisected by Piac utca, which runs northward from the train station (Petőfi tér) to Kálvin tér, site of the Great Church and Debrecen's centre. With the exception of Nagyerdei Park, the recreational 'Big Forest Park' some 3km north, almost all of Debrecen's attractions are within easy walking distance of Kálvin tér.

The bus station (Külső-Vásártér) is on the 'outer marketplace' at the western end of Széchenyi utca.

Information
Csokonai Bookshop (☎ 535 786; Piac utca 45) Has good foreign language and map sections.
Data Net Cafe (☎ 536 724; Kossuth utca 8; per hr 420Ft; ☺ 8am-midnight) Also has cheap international calls.
Ibusz (☎ 415 555; Révész tér 2) Near the Little Church.
Kenézy Gyula Hospital (☎ 413 555; Bartók Béla út 2-25)
Main post office (Hatvan utca 5-9)
Maróthi György College Library (☎ 502 780; Blaháné utca 15; ☺ 9am-4pm Mon-Thu, 9am-2pm Fri) First hour is free.

DEBRECEN

0 — 500 m
0 — 0.3 miles

INFORMATION
Csokonai Bookshop..................1 C3
Data Net Café.........................2 C2
Ibusz....................................3 C3
Main Post Office......................4 B2
OTP Bank...............................5 C2
OTP Bank...............................6 C3
Tourinform.............................7 C2
Tourinform Booth.....................8 C2
Tourinform Hajdú-Bihar.............9 C2

SIGHTS & ACTIVITIES
Bicycle Shop..........................10 C2
Déri Museum..........................11 B2
Great Church..........................12 C3
Little Church..........................13 C3
Medgyessy Museum..................14 C1
Orthodox Synagogue................15 B2
Reformed College....................16 C1
Status Que Conservative
  Synagogue...........................17 B2
Tímárház...............................18 D3

SLEEPING
Aranybika..............................19 C2
Fönix....................................20 C4
Kálvin...................................21 C1
Maróthi György College.............22 D2
Rákóczi Pension......................23 C1

EATING
Büfé Falatozó......................(see 28)
Carpe Diem............................24 C3
Chinese Takeaway...................25 C2
Csokonai...............................26 C3
Flaska...................................27 C3
Fruit & Vegetable Market...........28 C2
Gara....................................29 C2
Grocery Shop.........................30 C3
Hajdúsági..............................31 C2
Klári Salátabár.......................32 C2
Lucullus................................33 C3
Morik Caffé............................34 C3
Pompeji................................35 C2

DRINKING
Bakelit Music Café...............(see 26)
Belgian Beer Café....................36 C2
Genius..................................37 C2
Play Pub House.......................38 D3
Saxophone.............................39 C2

ENTERTAINMENT
Babalu Restaurant and Music Club..40 C3
Csokonai Theatre.....................41 C2
Mezon Youth Information Office.....42 C2

SHOPPING
Mestermű Kincs és Galéria.............43 C2

TRANSPORT
Bus Station............................44 B3

To Péterfia & Centrum (100m);
Aquila Nature Tours (150m);
Nagyerdei Park &
Leveles (1.5km); Nagyerdő
& Aquaticum (3km)

To Kenézy Gyula
Hospital (300m)

To Fönix
Hall (200m)

To Flea Market (1.5km);
Puszta Forest (10.5km)

Train
Station

OTP bank (Piac utca 16 & 45) Both have 24-hour ATMs.

Tourinform (☎ 412 250; debrecen@tourinform.hu);
town hall office (Piac utca 20; ☺ 8am-8pm mid-Jun–mid-Sep, 9am-5pm Mon-Fri mid-Sep–mid-Jun); summer booth
(Kossuth tér; ☺ 10am-6pm Mon-Fri mid-Jun–mid-Sep)
The very helpful town hall office has more information
than you can carry away; it can also provide contacts for
city guides.

Tourinform Hajdú-Bihar (☎ 534 544; hajdu-m@tour
inform.hu; Kálvin tér 2/a; ☺ 9am-6pm Mon-Fri, 9am-
1pm Sat) Information on the entire region.

www.debrecen.hu Covers a range of subjects in
Hungarian, English and German.

Sights

Many of the town's big sights are at the
northern end of Piac utca, including the

yellow neoclassical **Great Church** (Nagytemplom;
☎ 412 694; Kálvin tér; adult/child 200/100Ft; ☺ 9am-4pm
Mon-Fri, 9am-1pm Sat, noon-4pm Sun Apr-Oct, 10am-1pm
Mon-Sat, 11.30am-1pm Sun Nov-Mar). Built in 1821, it
has become so synonymous with Debrecen
that mirages of its twin clock towers were
reportedly seen on the Great Plain early
last century. Accommodating some 3000
people, the Great Church is Hungary's largest Protestant church, and it was here that
Lajos Kossuth read the Declaration of Independence from Austria on 14 April 1849.
The nave is rather plain and austere aside
from the magnificent organ in the loft behind the pulpit. Climb the 210 steps to the
top of the west clock tower for grand views
over the city.

North of the church stands the **Reformed College** (Református Kollégium; ☎ 414 744; Kálvin tér 16; adult/child 300/150Ft; guided tours 2000Ft; ✆ 9am-5pm Tue-Sat, 9am-1pm Sun), built in 1816, the site of a prestigious secondary school and theological college since the Middle Ages. Downstairs, there are exhibits on religious art and sacred objects (including a 17th-century chalice made from a coconut) and on the school's history, where 'early to bed, early to rise' was the motto. Upstairs is the relatively bland 650,000-volume library and the bright, white oratory, where the breakaway National Assembly met in 1849 and Hungary's postwar provisional government was declared in 1944.

Folklore exhibits at the **Déri Museum** (☎ 322 207; Déri tér 1; adult/child 650/325Ft; ✆ 10am-6pm Tue-Sun Apr-Oct, 10am-4pm Tue-Sun Nov-Mar), a short walk west of the Reformed College, offer excellent insights into life on the *puszta* and the bourgeois citizens of Debrecen up to the 19th century. Mihály Munkácsy's mythical interpretations of the Hortobágy and his *Christ's Passion* take pride of place in a separate art gallery. The museum's entrance is flanked by four superb bronzes by sculptor Ferenc Medgyessy, a local boy who merits his own **Medgyessy Museum** (☎ 413 572; Péterfia utca 28; adult/child 200/100Ft; ✆ 10am-4pm Tue-Sun) in an old burgher house to the northeast.

Just walking along Piac utca and down some of the side streets, with their array of neoclassical, baroque and Art Nouveau buildings, is a treat. Kossuth utca and its continuation Széchenyi utca, where the baroque Calvinist **Little Church** (Kistemplom; ☎ 342 872; Révész tér 2; admission free; ✆ 9am-noon Mon-Fri & Sun), completed in 1726, stands with its bastion-like tower, are especially interesting. The **Status Que Conservative Synagogue** (Kápolnási utca), just south of Bajcsy-Zsilinszky utca, dates from 1909 and is once again falling apart, while the façade of the nearby **Orthodox synagogue** (Pászti utca 6) has enjoyed a lick of paint but its interior is still waiting for some much-needed TLC.

Away from the centre, the **Tímárház** (☎ 321 260; Nagy Gál István utca 6; ✆ 10am-5pm Tue-Fri, 10am-2pm Sat) is a folk-craft centre and workshop, where embroiderers, basket weavers, carvers and so on do their stuff in rotation, while the colourful **flea market** (Vágóhíd utca; ✆ daily) attracts a motley group of Ukrainians, Poles, Romanians, Roma and Hungarians from Transylvania who hawk everything from socks to live animals. It's served by buses 9, 15, 30 and 30/a from the train station.

Activities

The city's **Nagyerdei Park** offers boating and walks along leafy trails, but the main attraction here is the **Aquaticum** (☎ 514 100; www.aquaticum.hu; adult/child 1799/1299Ft; ✆ 10am-10pm), a complex offering all manner of slides and waterfalls alongside a half-dozen indoor and open-air pools of brownish mineral and fresh water, and every type of therapy imaginable.

If you want to see more of the great outdoors, head for the **Puszta Forest** (Erdőspuszta), a protected area of pine and acacia forests, lakes and trails a few kilometres to the east and southeast of Debrecen. Bánk, the centre, has a splendid **arboretum** (Fancsika utca 93a) and there are **boats for rent** on Vekeri Lake (Vekeri-tó).

Bikes are for rent from the **bicycle shop** (☎ 456 220; Csapó utca 19; ✆ 9am-6pm Mon-Fri, 9am-1pm Sat) for 700Ft a day.

Festivals & Events

Annual events to watch out for include the **Masquerade Carnival** in February, the **Spring Festival** of performing arts in March, the famous **Floral Carnival** held in mid-August and **Jazz Days** in September.

Sleeping

BUDGET

Ibusz can arrange private rooms (from 2500Ft per person), while Tourinform can provide a list of dormitory accommodation in summer; most are located 3km north of the centre.

Maróthi György College (☎ 502 780; Blaháné utca 15; s/d 2200/4400Ft; P) Right in the heart of town, this is one central place with dormitory accommodation. Rooms are fairly basic, facilities are shared, and there are kitchens, a courtyard and a basketball court for guest use.

Rákóczi Pension (☎ 416 638; Rákóczi utca 39; s/d 6000/84000Ft; P) Rákóczi has an excellent location on a peaceful, leafy street within easy striking distance of the centre. Its rooms, which are arranged around an inner courtyard, are big, bright with *en suite* facilities, and the modern furniture rests on cool tiled floors.

Főnix (☎ 413 054; Barna utca 17; s/d 3000/4900Ft; **P**) This communist-style block, with dark corridors and simple rooms, is run by friendly staff and is just off the main drag. Ask for a room with a balcony.

MIDRANGE
Péterfia (☎ 418 246; peterfiapanzio@axelero.hu; Péterfia utca 37/b; s/d 7000/8000Ft; **P**) Péterfia is a 20-room *pension* not far north of the centre, with good-sized *en-suite* rooms filled with natural-wood furniture. Staff are friendly and its back garden is for guest use.

Centrum (☎ 416 193; centrumpanzio@axelero.hu; Péterfia utca 37/a; s/d 6900/7500-8000Ft; **P**) A bit like your grandmother's apartment if she collected tacky paraphernalia; knick-knacks and flowery odds and ends line the reception walls and public areas. Rooms are far less cluttered and the furniture is quite modern. There's a private garden out back.

Nagyerdő (☎ 410 588; reserve@hotelnagyerdo.hun guesthotels.hu; Pallagi út 5; s €46-55, d €62-76; **P** 🖫) This well-organised spa hotel is a tall block in the centre of Nagyerdei Park. Rooms are comfy but fairly plain, and there's a restaurant with grilling facilities on site.

Kálvin (☎ 418 522; kalvin@civishotels.hu; Kálvin tér 4; s 9750-12,800Ft, d 10,450-14,650Ft; **P**) A large hotel on top of the Udvarház Shopping Centre, Kálvin offers a range of rooms with either pseudo-antique or bulky dark-wood furniture. Space is no problem here, and lower-priced rooms face busy Kálvin tér.

TOP END
Aranybika (☎ 508 600; aranybika@civishotels.hu; Piac utca 11-15; s €49-79, d €60-96; **P** 🍴 🖫) This is a landmark Art-Nouveau hotel, with 200 very different rooms, and is still *the* place to stay in Debrecen. Rates vary depending on whether you stay in the charming old wing or garish new building.

Aquaticum (☎ 514 111; www.aquaticum.hu; Nagyerdei park 1; r 18,500-19,500Ft; **P** 🍴 🖳 🖫) Aquaticum is Debrecen's answer to those wishing to enjoy the town's thermal pleasures without having to wander far. It has everything a good four-star hotel should have, plus wellness features.

Eating
RESTAURANTS
Csokonai (☎ 410 802; Kossuth utca 21; mains 1200-1800Ft) This quality cellar-restaurant may be

a pub to some but it's a far better restaurant to most. Medieval décor, sharp service and excellent Hungarian specialities all help to create one of Debrecen's top eating experiences.

Lucullus (☎ 418 513; Piac utca 41; mains 1200-1800Ft) Lucullus is a favourite with locals who enjoy the restaurant's throne-like seating, convivial air and slow but attentive service. The menu is a varied selection of Hungarian dishes, including a couple of vegetarian options.

Flaska (☎ 414 582; Miklós utca 4; mains 1500Ft) Flaska is easily spotted on Miklós utca; the giant terracotta-red flask jutting out from the wall is a dead give-away. This basement restaurant comes locally recommended and serves up a storm of good Hungarian cuisine.

Leveles (☎ 532 982; Medgyessy sétány; mains 1000-2000Ft) This eatery is close to the thermal pools in a quiet park. Its German/Hungarian menu just keeps tallying up local recommendations, as does its large outdoor patio.

Pompeji (☎ 416 988; Batthyány utca 4; pizzas 900Ft) A flashy restaurant with its very own jungle, Pompeji serves fine Italian dishes and is a good spot for a drink on a warm summer evening.

Hajdúsági (cnr Liszt Ferenc utca & Kossuth utca; lunch set menu 400Ft; ⊙ 11am-3pm & 4-10pm Mon-Fri, 4-10pm Sat) This is a simple restaurant, but its ever-changing set menu is a magnet to what appears to be half of Debrecen's city workers.

CAFÉS
Carpe Diem (☎ 319 007; Batthyány utca 8; teas & snacks 400Ft) With its hammock seats, greenery and serene atmosphere, this small teahouse is an oasis on a pedestrian street dominated by concrete eyesores. It stocks teas from around the world for instant consumption or later enjoyment.

Morik Caffé (☎ 413 808; Miklós utca 1; coffee 200Ft) This mock-18th-century café has its waitresses running around in blue frocks and frilly white bonnets, which is either quaint or ridiculous depending on your taste. Either way, the coffee is great.

Gara (Kálvin tér 6; ice cream from 100Ft; ⊙ 9am-6pm) Gara has some of the best cakes and ice cream (made with real fruit and loads of it) outside Budapest and has lines of eager ice-cream lovers to prove it.

QUICK EATS

Büfé Falatozó (Csapó utca; 100g sausages 200Ft; 5am-3pm Mon-Sat, 5-11am Sun) In the fruit and vegetable market, this has more sausage varieties than you can shake a long roll of meat at. Try the 'inviting' liver and blood sausage; as they say, 'When in Rome...'

Chinese takeaway (☎ 588 479; Arany János utca 28; mains 550Ft) This hole in the wall is a genuine Chinese takeaway and good for a quick, cheap meal.

Klári Salátabár (☎ 412 203; Bajcsy-Zsilinszky utca 3; 100g salad 100-300Ft; 9am-7pm Mon-Fri) Catering to vegetarians only, this simple salad bar is a rare breed indeed in provincial Hungary; salads are served by the 100g.

SELF-CATERING

There's a **grocery shop** (Piac utca 75; 24hr) within walking distance of the train station and the bustling covered **fruit & vegetable market** (Csapó utca; 5am-3pm Mon-Sat, 5-11am Sun) has plenty on offer.

Drinking

Bakelit Music Café (Kossuth utca 19; 9am-11pm Mon-Thu, 9am-2am Fri, 6pm-2am Sat) A student pub of sorts near the centre, Bakelit attracts a boisterous and friendly crowd with its loud music, dark corners and orange-and-brown booths. This is certainly not a place for a quiet chat over a glass of chilled white wine.

Belgian Beer Café (☎ 536 373; Piac utca 29) Why locals drink Belgian beer when neighbouring Slovakia and Czech Republic make such great beverages is anyone's guess. But there's no denying the popularity of this street-side café with its beer hall atmosphere.

Saxophone (Piac utca 18) Pretty people gravitate to Saxophone, and since Hungary is filled with pretty folk, it's often bursting at the seams. Its fine cocktails may also have something to do with it.

AUTHOR'S CHOICE

Genius (☎ 508 644; Piac utca 11-15; 11am-7pm Mon & Thu, 11am-3am Tue & Fri, 11am-11pm Wed, 7pm-5am Sat) Genius, in the Aranybika hotel, is arguably the best bar outside Budapest. Its dark red interior, lounge chairs, sexy sounds and excellent cocktails combine to create a decadent air, all of which is topped off by the occasional live music act.

Play Pub House (Batthyány utca 24-26) On a pedestrian-only street, this place is as close to an English-style pub as you'll find in town, and has outside tables made for warm weather.

Entertainment

Debrecen prides itself on its cultural life but at present has no cultural centre; for information check with the staff at **Tourinform** (☎ 412 250; Piac utca 20), the delightful **Csokonai Theatre** (☎ 455 075; Kossuth utca 10) or the **Mezon youth information office** (☎ 415 498; Batthyány utca 2b; 10am-6pm). The latter specialises in the popular music scene and has Internet access. Otherwise, pick up a copy of the biweekly entertainment freebie *Debreceni Est* and scan the listings.

Babalu Restaurant and Music Club (☎ 536 414; Piac utca 26a; noon-midnight) With its cane chairs and tropical plants, Babalu exudes a safari feel and attracts a more mature crowd. It's also one of the better spots to catch some live jazz.

Főnix Hall (☎ 518 400; Kassai utca 28) 'Phoenix' Hall is Debrecen's main venue for large events, whether they be cultural or sporting.

Shopping

You can't leave the city without buying – or at least trying – some of the famous Debrecen sausage available at butcher shops and grocery stores everywhere; the market is also a good place to procure some. While on the way to the market, why not stop in at the lovely antique-cum-curio shop **Mestermű Kincs és Galéria** (Csapó utca 24) nearby.

Getting There & Away

BUS

From Debrecen you can catch a direct bus to any of the following destinations:

Destination	Price	Duration	Km	Frequency
Békéscsaba	1690Ft	3hr	135	10 daily
Eger	1690Ft	2½hr	130	8 daily
Hajdúszoboszló	302Ft	30min	20	half-hourly
Miskolc	1210Ft	2½hr	100	hourly
Nádudvar	544Ft	1hr	40	7 daily
Nyíregyháza	907Ft	1½hr	70	4 daily
Szarvas	1930Ft	3¼hr	155	2 daily
Szeged	2910Ft	5hr	230	3 daily
Tokaj	1030Ft	2hr	85	2 daily

Foreign destinations served by bus include Košice (Kassa) in Slovakia at 7am Monday to Thursday and, in Romania, Oradea (Nagyvárad) at 6.30am on Tuesday and Thursday and at 5am on Saturday March to October.

TRAIN
Debrecen is served by around 20 trains daily from Nyugati (and sometimes Keleti) station in Budapest (2360Ft, 220km) via Szolnok (1420Ft, 1¾ hours, 120km), including nine 2½-hour expresses daily. Cities to the north and northwest – Nyíregyháza (430Ft, 45 minutes, 50km), Tokaj (890Ft, 1½ hours, 80km) and Miskolc (1420Ft, 2½ hours, 135km) – can best be reached by train. For Eger (1212Ft, three hours, 120km), take the train to Füzesabony and change. For points south, use the bus or a bus/train combination.

Daily international departures from Debrecen to Valea lui Mihai in Romania leave at 7.15am and 2.40pm.

Getting Around
Tram 1 – the only line in town – is ideal both for transport and sightseeing. From the train station, it runs north along Piac utca to Kálvin tér and then carries on to Nagyerdei Park, where it loops around for the same trip southward.

Most other city transport can be caught at the southern end of Petőfi tér. Trolleybuses 2 and 3 link the train and bus stations.

You can also ring for a local **taxi** (☎ 444 444, 444 555).

HORTOBÁGY
☎ 52 / pop 1770
This village, some 40km west of Debrecen, is the centre of the Hortobágy region, once celebrated for its sturdy cowboys, inns and Gypsy bands. But you'll want to come here to explore the 810-sq-km Hortobágy National Park and wildlife preserve – home to hundreds of birds, as well as plant species that are usually found only by the sea. Its importance as a cultural landscape has not just been noted in Hungary – in 1999 Unesco promoted the park to world heritage status.

It's true that the Hortobágy has been milked by the Hungarian tourism industry for everything its worth, and the

stage-managed horse shows, costumed *csikósok* (cowboys) and tacky gewgaws on sale are all over the top. Still, dark clouds appearing out of nowhere to cover a blazing sun and the possibility of spotting a mirage may have you dreaming of a different Hortobágy – the mythical one that only ever existed in paintings, poems and active imaginations.

Orientation & Information
Buses – as few as there are – stop on the main road (Rte 33) near the village centre or on Petőfi tér near the shopping centre; the train station is to the northeast at the end of Kossuth utca.

Hortobágy National Park Information Centre (☎ 529 935; Kossuth utca; www.hnp.hu; ☼ 8am-5pm Mon-Fri) Housed in the new Visitors Centre.

OTP ATM In the shopping complex.

Post office (Kossuth utca 2; ☼ 8am-4pm Mon-Fri)

Tourinform (☎ 589 321; hortobagy@tourinform.hu; Kossuth utca; ☼ 8am-5pm Mon-Fri, 9am-4pm Sat) In the new Visitors Centre.

Sights
HORTOBÁGY NATIONAL PARK
With its varied terrain and water sources, the park has some of the best bird-watching in Europe. Indeed, some 344 species (of the continent's estimated 400) have been spotted here in the past 20 years, including many types of grebes, herons, shrikes, egrets, spoonbills, storks, kites, warblers and eagles. The great bustard, one of the world's largest birds, standing a metre high and weighing in at 20kg, has its own reserve with limited access to two-legged mammals.

Visitor passes, available from the **national park's head office** (☎ 529 935; Kossuth utca; admission 900Ft), allow entry to four restricted areas of the park. To see the best parts of the park, though – the closed areas north of Rte 33 and the saline swamplands south of it – you must have a guide and travel by horse, carriage or special 4WD; the national park's head office offers infrequent tours of the park. A taster of the park's flora and fauna through interactive displays is available at the new **Visitors Centre** (under construction at the time of research), along with traditional crafts, such as woodcarving, leather work, pottery, and the like.

Aquila Nature Tours (☎ 30-326 3426; Péterfia utca 46, Debrecen), a Debrecen-based travel

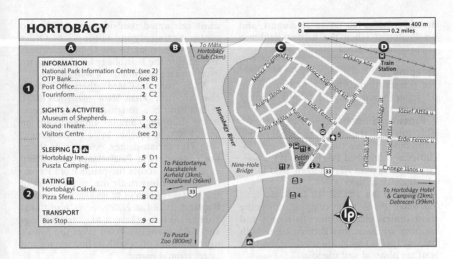

HORTOBÁGY

INFORMATION
National Park Information Centre..(see 2)
OTP Bank.................................(see 8)
Post Office.....................................1 C1
Tourinform.....................................2 C2

SIGHTS & ACTIVITIES
Museum of Shepherds................3 C2
Round Theatre..............................4 C2
Visitors Centre.............................(see 2)

SLEEPING
Hortobágyi Inn...............................5 D1
Puszta Camping............................6 C2

EATING
Hortobágyi Csárda........................7 C2
Pizza Sfera.....................................8 C2

TRANSPORT
Bus Stop..9 C2

agency with specialised bird-watching and nature tours, also offers guiding services.

OTHER SIGHTS

The **Nine-Hole Bridge** (Kilenc-lyukú híd), built in 1833 and spanning the marshy Hortobágy River, is the longest stone bridge (and certainly the most sketched, painted and photographed) in Hungary. Just before it stands the **Hortobágyi Csárda**, one of the original eating houses (1781) used by salt traders on their way from the Tisza River to Debrecen. The inns provided itinerant Roma fiddlers with employment, though they did not originally live in this part of Hungary. Gypsy music and *csárdas* have been synonymous ever since.

The **Puszta Zoo** (☎ 589 110; adult/child 300/150Ft, horse show 1000/500Ft; ☼ 9am-6pm Mar-Nov), with its weird and wonderful animals of the *puszta*, is a fun place for kids of all ages. You'll find God's acid experimentations here, too; the heavy-set Hungarian grey cattle, the curly-haired *mangalica* pig, the Rasta-like *kuvasz* dog, and the *racka* sheep, whose corkscrew-like horns are particularly devilish.

The **Museum of Shepherds** (Petőfi tér 1), in an 18th-century carriage house across from the *csárda*, was closed at the time of research for restoration. When it reopens expect to find displays on pastoral life at the turn of last century, and web-cams of the *puszta* and other such hi-tech installations.

Like the Museum of Shepherds next door, the **Round Theatre** (Körszín) was having a change of heart during research (like the entire village it seems) and will reopen primarily as an exhibition space for crafts produced at the workshops housed in the new visitors centre.

Activities

At Máta, about 2km north of Hortobágy village, is Hungary's largest riding centre, the **Hortobágy Club** (☎ 369 020; www.hortobagyhotel.hu). Here you can take riding lessons for beginners (4800Ft per hour) and intermediates (3000Ft per hour), or ride off into the sunset across the *puszta* (advanced riders only; 3000Ft per hour); two-hour carriage rides (2000Ft per person) of the *puszta* are available too. The club also offers bird-watching tours (per person 16,000Ft), fishing (gear hire 500Ft per day) and boating trips (2000Ft per person), and hot-air ballooning (33,000Ft per person).

The national park office organises scenic **flights** (☎ 06 30 565 7959) over the region, but they're not cheap – 1500Ft per minute for up to three people. Planes take off from the airfield at Macskatelek, about 3km west of the village at the 70km stone.

Bicycles are available for rent from **Puszta Camping** (☎ 369 300; baranyais@freemail.hu) for 1000Ft per day and Hortobágy Club for 2000Ft per day.

Festivals & Events

The area is busiest in July when Máta hosts the **International Equestrian Day**, during the

Hortobágy Bridge Fair on 19-20 August, and on Pentecost when the **National Herdsmen Competition & Shepherd's Meeting** is held.

Sleeping

For private rooms, check with Tourinform or scour Arany János utca and Czinege János utca.

Pásztortanya (☎ 369 127; s/d 2500/5000Ft; **P**) This inn is a traditional Hortobágy-style farmhouse of four rooms with shared facilities and attached restaurant. It's a solitary building 3km west of town, next to the Macskatelek airfield.

Hortobágy Inn (☎ 369 137; Kossuth utca 1; s/d 3500/6000Ft; **P**) Without camping, this is the most central place to stay. Its rooms and facilities are basic, but they do come with balcony (perfect for storm watching) and the staff are pleasant and friendly.

Puszta Camping (☎ 369 300; baranyais@freemail .hu; camp sites per adult/child/tent 700/550/650Ft, bungalows per person 1600Ft; Ⓨ May-Sep; **P** 🐾) Occupying a quiet spot away from busy Rte 33 and close to the river, Puszta offers basic facilities and a tiny thermal pool.

Hortobágy Hotel & Camping (☎ 369 071; camp sites per person/tent 500/750Ft, s/d/tr 2900/5800/7800Ft; **P**) Hortobágy is another basic hotel, this time 2km east of the town centre. Rooms have bathrooms and windows are guarded by the all-important insect netting; camping consists of pitching your tent on the front lawn and using the hotel's facilities.

Eating

Hortobágyi Csárda (☎ 589 399; Petőfi tér 2; mains 1000-2000Ft; Ⓨ 8am-10pm) This is Hungary's

---

AUTHOR'S CHOICE

Hortobágy Club (☎ 369 020; www.hortobagy hotel.hu; s 14,000-16,800Ft, d 18,000-21,600Ft, ste 22,000-26,400Ft, house 22,000-26,400Ft; **P** 🐾) Hortobágy Club offers a taste of the *puszta* without having to rough it like the shepherds of old. This four-star hotel has excellent amenities – swimming pool, sauna, fitness centre, sports fields and two restaurants – and alongside its deluxe rooms and suites, individual houses complete with private stables. Thankfully the complex isn't multistorey, so doesn't impact on its surroundings.

---

most celebrated roadside inn, which also means it's touristy and a little pricey. Order a duck dish, relax to the Gypsy standards and admire the Hortobágy kitsch taking up every square centimetre of wall space.

Aside from the Csárda, there ain't much else around: **Pizza Sfera** (pizzas 600-1000Ft; Ⓨ 5am-10pm) is a rough-and-ready pizzeria in the shopping complex and **Hortobágy Inn** (mains 1000Ft) is another basic establishment with Hungarian dishes. Away from town, the restaurant at **Pásztortanya** (mains 1000Ft) enjoys views across the plains from its terrace, but for less rustic dining try either of the **Hortobágy Club's** (☎ 369 020) restaurants; **Magyaros** (mains 1000-2000Ft) serves traditional Hungarian fare in tavern-like surroundings and **Hajdú** (mains 1500-3000Ft) takes the town's top restaurant prize with its fine service and international menu.

Getting There & Away

Up to eight daily buses between Debrecen (via Hajdúszoboszló; 484Ft, 35 minutes, 40km) and Eger (1150Ft, two hours, 95km) stop in Petőfi tér. Hortobágy is on the train line linking Debrecen (430Ft, 50 minutes, 40km) and Füzesabony (658Ft, 1¼ hours, 60km) and is served by up to seven trains daily, with the last train leaving for Debrecen about 8.30pm. Trains headed for Füzesabony (last one at 8.32pm) also stop at Tiszafüred (346Ft, 35 minutes, 30km).

HAJDÚSZOBOSZLÓ
☎ 52 / pop 23,400
Hajdúszoboszló, 20km southwest of Debrecen, is Hungary's largest bathing centre. Thousands flock here to take advantage of the thermal spa's medicinal benefits, or simply to relax in its temperate waters.

Orientation

Almost everything you'll want or need can be found on the broad street (Rte 4) running through town and changing names four times: Debreceni útfél, Szilfákalja út, Hősök tere and Dózsa György utca. The thermal baths and park, lumped together as the Holiday Area (Üdülőterület), occupy the northeastern portion of Hajdúszoboszló. Hősök tere – the town centre – lies to the southwest.

The bus station (Fürdő utca) is just north of Debreceni útfél. The train station (Déli sor) lies about 3km south. Reach Hősök tere by walking northwest along Rákóczi utca.

Information

Main post office (Kálvin tér 1)
OTP bank (Szilfákalja út 10) With an ATM next to the ABC supermarket.
Tourinform (☎ 558 929; hajduszoboszlo@tourinform.hu; Szent István Park 1-3; ❍ 8am-6pm Mon-Fri, 8am-2pm Sat Jun–mid-Sep, 9am-5pm Mon-Fri, 9am-2pm Sat mid-Sep–May) At the main thermal baths entrance.

Sights & Activities

The striking **Forest of Bells Monument**, honouring the dead of wars throughout Hungarian history, stands near the entrance to the **thermal baths** (☎ 558 558; Szent István 1-3; baths adult/child 900/800Ft, after 4pm 700/600Ft, week-pass 5400/4800Ft, including entrance to open-air pools; ❍ baths 7am-7pm, open-air pools 8am-8pm Jul-Aug, 8am-7pm Jun, 8am-6pm May & Sep), a complex comprising a dozen mineral and freshwater pools, a wave pool, saunas, solarium and treatment centre. Rowing boats are available for 1000Ft per hour. Towards the back of the baths is the **Aquapark** (adult/child 2000/1000Ft; ❍ 10am-6pm),

a water park with nine adventurous slides and plenty of hyped kids.

Near the **Calvinist church** (Kálvin tér 9; admission free), built in 1717, is a 20m stretch of wall and a small tower – all that remains of a 15th-century Gothic **fortress** destroyed by the Turks in 1660. Across Hősök tere a **statue of István Bocskai** stands not so proud – a pint-sized prince out of all proportion to his snorting stallion and great deeds.

Down Bocskai utca, past the 18th-century baroque **Catholic church** (Bocskai utca 6) with its invariably locked doors, where Pope John Paul II prayed as Karol Wojtyla, Bishop of Kraków, in the early 1970s, is the **Bocskai Museum** (☎ 362 165; Bocskai utca 12; adult/child 400/200Ft; ❍ 9am-1pm & 2-4pm Tue-Sun), a temple to the memory of Prince István and his *hajdúk* (Heyduck) helpers. Among the saddles, pistols and swords hangs Bocskai's banner – the standard of the Heyduck cavalry, picturing the prince doing battle with a leopard (which mysteriously changes into a lion in later versions).

A lovely thatched cottage houses the **István Fazekas Pottery House** (☎ 361 358; Ady Endre

HAJDÚSZOBOSZLÓ

0 — 500 m
0 — 0.3 miles

To Airport; Thermal Camping (1km); Aquapark (1km)

To Debrecen (20km)

To Train Station (3km)

To Train Station (3km)

GREAT PLAIN

utca 2; 🕙 8am-4pm Mon), featuring the distinctive black pottery produced by the Fazekas family in neighbouring Nádudvar.

Sleeping

The choice of accommodation in this tourist-oriented town is enormous (Mátyás király sétány is particularly loaded down with high-rise hotels), so you shouldn't have trouble tracking something appropriate down. If you're looking for a private room, consult the list provided by Tourinform or hunt around for *szoba kiadó* (room for rent) signs that in the high season sprout like mushrooms after a rain.

Négy Évszak (☎ 273 140; www.hotelnegyevszak .net; Jókai sor 12; s/d €38/45; **P**)) This newly built hotel puts most of Hajdúszoboszló's contemporaries to shame, with spacious rooms and colourful, modern furniture and décor. It's an easy stroll away to the spa.

Muskátli (☎ 363 744; muskatlihajduszoboszlo@mat avnet.hu; Daru zug 5a; s €40-42, d €55-60; **P** 🕭) This upmarket hotel moonlights as a wellness centre, offering all manner of beauty, spa and medical therapies. Rooms are suitably large, with bare-wood or tiled floors and surprisingly basic furniture.

Délibáb (☎ 360 366; delibab@civishotels.hu; József Attila utca 4; s €28-50, d €40-63; **P** 🕭) With a massive 250 rooms, Délibáb is one of the larger spa hotels. It has its own wellness centre and rooms are old fashioned but comfy enough. Rates vary depending on the facilities.

Thermal Camping (☎ 558 552; Böszörményi út 35a; camp sites per person/tent 800/800Ft; **P**) Thermal Camping is part of the thermal spa but is located on the northern side of the complex. It's a flat, basic site with some tree cover, overlooking farmers' fields and the town's airport.

Eating

Invariably your hotel or *pension* will have an attached restaurant, so you won't have to wander far for food. There are also plenty of sausage, *lángos* and ice-cream stalls along Szilfákalja út and in the park.

Arany Oroszlán (☎ 273 094; Bessenyei utca 14; lunch menu 510Ft; mains 1000Ft) This quiet restaurant offers a relaxed meal away from the kitsch of the main street. The menu is solidly Hungarian, with specialities like grilled trout.

Kemencés (☎ 362 221; Szilfákalja út 40/a; mains 1000Ft; 🕙 8am-9pm) With its pseudo-rustic

trappings and traditionally clad waitresses, Kemencés is cashing in on the *puszta* in a big way but it does have good daily specials and conscientious staff.

Nelson (☎ 270 226; cnr Hősök tere & Kossuth utca; mains 1200-2000Ft) With an expansive menu, quality cuisine, attentive staff and streetside seating, Nelson is a popular choice with locals and tourists alike.

Szilfa (József Attila utca 2; mains 800-1500Ft) This pleasant and simple eatery is handy to the thermal baths and has a covered terrace for escaping the summer heat.

The partially covered **market** (Bethlen Gábor utca) deals mainly in fresh produce, flowers and plenty of gossip.

Entertainment

Hajdúszoboszló is a family town so don't expect hip bars and pumping clubs.

City Cultural Centre (☎ 557 693; Szilfákalja út 2) This centre offers tips on what's on in town, including organ and choral concerts in the Calvinist church.

Al Hambra Eastern Bar (Mátyás király sétány 8) A suitable place to rehydrate after a long day soaking in steamy brown mineral water.

Getting There & Away

Buses from Hajdúszoboszló depart for Miskolc five times daily (1450Ft, three hours, 120km) and up to two dozen head to Debrecen daily (302Ft, 30 minutes, 20km). International destinations served by bus include Oradea (6am Tuesday and Thursday) in Romania and Košice (6.20am Monday to Thursday) in Slovakia.

Trains headed for Szolnok (1212Ft, 1½ hours, 100km) and Budapest (2200Ft, 2½ hours, 200km) from Debrecen (182Ft, 15 minutes, 20km) stop at Hajdúszoboszló a couple of times an hour throughout the day.

SOUTHERN PLAIN

The Southern Plain (Dél-Alföld), spanning the lower regions of the Danube and Tisza Rivers, holds the lion's share of the Great Plain's more intriguing towns and cities. Kecskemét and Szeged, for example, are two centres for fine arts and culture, with attractive architecture, absorbing museums and an above-average (for the plain) bar and restaurant scene. But the *puszta* is not far away; Bugac, one of Hungary's better hubs depicting life on the plain, is easily reached from many of the area's western towns.

KECSKEMÉT

☎ 76 / pop 103,300

Halfway between the Danube and the Tisza Rivers in the heart of the Southern Plain is Kecskemét, a city ringed with vineyards and orchards that don't seem to stop at the limits of this 'garden city'. Colourful architecture, fine museums, apricot groves and the region's excellent *barackpálinka* (apricot brandy) beckon, and the Kiskunság National Park, the *puszta* of the Southern Plain, is right at the back door.

History

Kecskemét's agricultural wealth was used wisely – it was able to redeem all its debts in cash in 1832 – and today the city can boast some of the most spectacular architecture in the country. It was also – and still is – an important cultural centre, home to an artists' colony and the world-famous Institute of Music Education.

Orientation

Kecskemét is a city of multiple squares that run into one another without warning and can be a little confusing at first. The bus and main train stations are opposite one another near József Katona Park. A 10-minute walk southwest along Nagykőrösi utca will bring

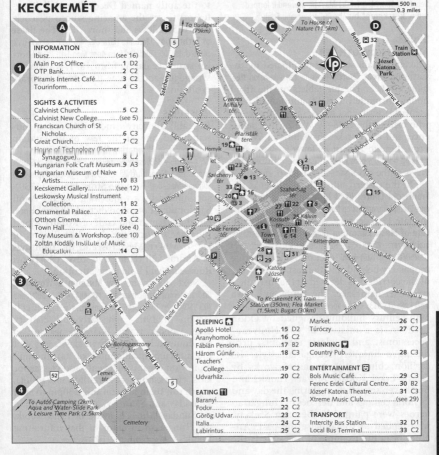

KECSKEMÉT

	0	500 m
	0	0.3 miles

INFORMATION
Ibusz.....................................(see 16)
Main Post Office.....................1 D2
OTP Bank................................2 C2
Piramis Internet Café.............3 C2
Tourinform.............................4 C3

SIGHTS & ACTIVITIES
Calvinist Church......................5 C2
Calvinist New College.........(see 5)
Franciscan Church of St
  Nicholas..............................6 C3
Great Church...........................7 C2
House of Technology (Former
  Synagogue)..........................8 C2
Hungarian Folk Craft Museum..9 A3
Hungarian Museum of Naive
  Artists.................................10 B3
Kecskemét Gallery.............(see 12)
Leskowsky Musical Instrument
  Collection...........................11 B2
Ornamental Palace................12 C2
Otthon Cinema.....................13 C2
Town Hall..........................(see 4)
Toy Museum & Workshop...(see 10)
Zoltán Kodály Institute of Music
  Education............................14 C3

SLEEPING
Apolló Hotel.........................15 D2
Aranyhomok.........................16 C2
Fábián Pension.....................17 B2
Három Gúnár........................18 C3
Teachers'
  College...............................19 C2
Udvarház..............................20 C2

EATING
Baranyi.................................21 C1
Fodor....................................22 C2
Görög Udvar.........................23 C2
Italia.....................................24 C2
Labirintus.............................25 C2

Market..................................26 C1
Túróczy.................................27 C2

DRINKING
Country Pub..........................28 C3

ENTERTAINMENT
Bols Music Café....................29 C3
Ferenc Erdei Cultural Centre...30 B2
József Katona Theatre...........31 C3
Xtreme Music Club............(see 29)

TRANSPORT
Intercity Bus Station.............32 D1
Local Bus Terminal................33 C2

To Autós Camping (2km);
Aqua and Water-Slide Park
& Leisure Time Park (2.5km)

To Kecskemét KK Train
Station (350m); Flea Market
(1.5km); Bugac (30km)

GREAT PLAIN

you to the first of the squares, Szabadság tér. The city's other train station, Kecskemét KK (Halasi út), from where narrow-gauge trains head for Bugac, is on the southern continuation of Batthyány utca.

Information

Ibusz (☎ 486 955; Kossuth tér 3) In Aranyhomok hotel.
Main post office (Kálvin tér 10-12) Near the centre of town.
OTP bank (Szabadság tér 1/a) Has foreign exchange and ATM.
Piramis Internet Café (Csányi utca 1-3; per hr 300Ft; ⏰ 10am-8pm Mon-Fri, noon-8pm Sat & Sun) Upstairs in a small shopping mall.
Tourinform (☎ 481 065; kecskemet@tourinform.hu; Kossuth Lajos tér 1; ⏰ 8am-6pm Mon-Fri, 9am-1pm Sat & Sun Jul-Aug, 8am-6pm Mon-Fri, 9am-1pm Sat Jun & Sep, 8am-5pm Mon-Fri Oct-May) Helpful and informed.
www.kecskemet.hu Also in German and English.

Sights

AROUND KOSSUTH TÉR

The city's main square is dominated by the Catholic **Great Church** (Kossuth tér; admission free) built in 1806. The big tablets on the front honour (from left to right) a mounted regiment of Hussars that served in WWI; citizens who died in the 1848–49 War of Independence; and the Kecskemét victims of WWII. From June to August its **tower** (admission 300Ft; ⏰ 9am-noon & 3-6pm Tue-Sun) can be climbed for views of the city's sun-bleached rooftops.

On the eastern side of Kossuth tér is the **Franciscan Church of St Nicholas** (Szent Miklós ferences templom; admission free), dating in part from the late 13th century; the **Zoltán Kodály Institute of Music Education** (Kodály Zoltán Zenepedagógiai Intézet; ☎ 481 518; Kéttemplom köz 1; adult/child 120/60Ft; ⏰ 10am-6pm) occupies the baroque monastery behind it to the east. Inside, one of the corridors is devoted to the institute's composer-namesake. The sandy-pink **town hall** (☎ 513 513; ⏰ by appointment), a lovely late-19th-century building designed by Ödön Lechner, is a mixture of Art Nouveau/Secessionist and folkloric elements, producing a uniquely Hungarian style. Its carillon chimes out strains of works by Ferenc Erkel, Kodály, Mozart, Handel and Beethoven several times during the day and its floral ceilings and frescoes of Hungarian heroes were painted by Bertalan Székely, who tended to romanticise the past. Another beautiful example of this style is the

restored **Otthon Cinema** (Széchenyi tér 4), on the corner of pedestrian Görögtemplom utca.

SZABADSÁG TÉR

Walking northeast into Szabadság tér, you'll pass the 17th-century **Calvinist church** and the **Calvinist New College** (Református újkollégium) from 1912, a later version of the Hungarian Romantic style that looks like a Transylvanian castle and is now a music school. Two other buildings in the square are among the city's finest. The Art Nouveau **Ornamental Palace** (Cifrapalota), which dates from 1902 and is covered in multicoloured majolica tiles, now contains the **Kecskemét Gallery** (Kecskeméti Képtár; ☎ 480 776; Rákóczi út 1; adult/child 260/130Ft; ⏰ 10am-5pm Tue-Sun). Don't go in so much for the art; climb the steps to the aptly named Decorative Hall (Díszterem) to see the amazing stucco peacock, bizarre windows and more tiles. The **House of Technology** (Technika Háza; ☎ 487 611; Rákóczi út 2; adult/child 100/50Ft; ⏰ 8am-4pm Mon-Fri), a Moorish structure dating from 1871, was once a synagogue and is now used for temporary exhibitions.

MUSEUMS

Arguably the city's most interesting museum and one of the few of its kind in Europe, the **Hungarian Museum of Naive Artists** (Magyar Naiv Müvészek Múzeuma; ☎ 324 767; Gáspár András utca 11; adult/child 150/50Ft; ⏰ 10am-5pm Tue-Sun mid-Mar–Oct) is in the Stork House (1730), surrounded by a white wall, just off Petőfi Sándor utca. Lots of predictable themes here, but the warmth and craft of Rozália Albert Juhászné's work, the drug-like visions of Dezső Mokry-Mészáros and the paintings of András Süli (Hungary's answer to Henri Rousseau) will hold your attention.

Next door, the **Toy Museum & Workshop** (Szórakaténusz Játékmúzeum; ☎ 481 469; adult/child 300/150Ft; ⏰ 10am-5pm Tue-Sun) has a small collection of 19th- and early-20th-century dolls, wooden trains, board games and so on, dumped haphazardly in glass cases. But the museum spends most of its time and money on organising events and classes for kids (workshops adult/child 300/150Ft), which run 10am to noon and 2.30pm to 5pm Thursday and Saturday, and 10am to noon on Sunday. Much is made of Ernő Rubik, the Hungarian inventor of that infuriating Rubik's Cube from the 1970s.

The **Hungarian Folk Craft Museum** (Magyar Népi Iparművészet Múzeuma; ☎ 327 203; Serfőző utca 19a; adult/child 200/100Ft; ⏰ 10am-5pm Tue-Sat), the granddaddy of all museums in Kecskemét, is further southwest and a block in from Dózsa György út. Some 10 rooms of an old farm complex are crammed with embroidery, woodcarving, furniture, agricultural tools and textiles, so don't try to see everything at once.

The **Leskowsky Musical Instrument Collection** (Leskowsky Hangszergyűjtemény; ☎ 486 616; Zimay László utca 6/a; admission free; ⏰ by appointment) traces the development of music-making over the centuries and has a decent collection of instruments from five continents.

MARKET
Kecskemét's lively **flea market** (Kulső Szegedi út) is southeast of the city.

Activities
Kecskeméts main summer attraction is its **Aqua and Water-Slide Park** (☎ 481 724; Csabay Géza körút 2; adult/child 1000/800Ft; ⏰ 9am-7pm mid-May–Aug) which, as the name suggests, is a swimming complex loaded with fun things for the kids, but it's also equipped with three spas to soothe any aches and pains. Otherwise, join local frolickers at the lake in **Leisure Time Park** (Szabadidőpark) just north of the swimming complex.

Festivals & Events
Special events in Kecskemét's calendar include the cultural **Spring Festival** in March and the **Hirős Week Festival** in late August which pays homage to the richness of Kecskemét agricultural produce, notably the golden *sárgabarack* (apricot). June is a changeable month: every even year sees the **International Children's Festival** hit town, and every odd year accommodates the **Kodály International Music Festival**.

Sleeping
BUDGET
Tourinform has an extensive list of college accommodation in town and Ibusz can arrange private rooms (from 3000Ft).

Teachers' College (☎ 486 977; Piaristák tere 4; s/d 2000/4000Ft; ⏰ mid-Jun–Aug; P) This is the most central of Kecskemét's college accommodation; rooms are typically basic yet functional, with single beds and shared bathrooms.

Autós Camping (☎ 329 398; Csabay Géza körút 5; camp sites per person/tent 750/660Ft, bungalows 4500-7150Ft; ⏰ Apr-Oct; P) Autós is 3km southwest of the centre, next to the Aqua Park. Its neat rows of tents and bungalows (with kitchen and bath, but no hot water) have minimal shade.

MIDRANGE
Aranyhomok (☎ 503 730; aranyhomok@axelero.hu; Kossuth tér 3; s/d 9200/13,700Ft; P ✷) This is the city's ugliest hotel from the outside, but inside it's surprisingly modern. Many rooms overlook the town's pretty main square, and the hotel's wellness centre is included in the price.

Három Gúnár (☎ 483 611; Batthyány utca 1-7; s/d 9,100/11,300Ft; P) This charming and friendly small hotel, formed by cobbling four old townhouses together, has 46 smallish rooms (the best are Nos 306 to 308). From here it's an easy walk to the centre.

Apolló Hotel (☎ 412 620; apollo.hotel@matavnet .hu; Tatay András utca 1/b; s/d €30/42; P ✷) Rooms (some of which come with a balcony) at the Apolló are big, airy and comfy, even though the furnishings are dated. The staff can be somewhat chaotic but friendly all the same.

Udvarház (☎ 413 912; Csányi utca 1-3; s/d 11,900/14,500Ft; P ✷) Tucked away in a courtyard with 17 rooms, this place is small, quiet, central and almost falls in the shadow of the Great Church.

Eating & Drinking
Görög Udvar (☎ 492 513; Széchenyi tér 9; mains 950-1500Ft) Görög Udvar looks grubby from the outside but inside it's another story; excellent Greek food is served either in its quiet inner courtyard or open restaurant rooms.

Labirintus (Kéttemplom köz 2; pizzas from 400Ft) A cellar restaurant with a smattering of charm close to the centre; its vast array of pizza and pastas is popular with the locals.

Túróczy (☎ 509 175; Szabadság tér 2; set menu 2600Ft) Túróczy is Kecskemét's silver service restaurant, with set menus of Hungarian and international cuisine, and a terrace overlooking the main square.

Fodor (Szabadság tér 2; ☼ 9am-9pm) This pink ice-cream and cake shop not only serves some of the finest confections in Kecskemét, but – with its position right on the main square – also has one of the best spots in which to consume them.

Baranyi (Nagykőrösi utca 15; ☼ 9am-9pm) On Kecskemét's very own yellow brick road, Baranyi is another popular ice-cream shop that produces particularly tasty cakes.

Italia (☎ 484 627; Hornyik János körút 4; pizzas from 500Ft) Italia is a less atmospheric pizzeria than Labirintus but it does a roaring trade with students from the nearby teacher's college, serving sizable pizzas at bargain prices.

Market (Jókai utca) Kecskemét's large market, with both a covered and an open-air section, is located north of Szabadság tér behind the Piarist church.

Like so many Hungarian towns, Kecskemét has a plethora of 'Wild West' themed pubs. One convivial example is **Country Pub** (Lestár tér 1), west of the József Katona Theatre.

Entertainment

Kecskemét is a city of music and theatre.

Ferenc Erdei Cultural Centre (☎ 503 880; Deák Ferenc tér 1) This centre, which sponsors some events, is a good source of information and should be the first place you head to. Otherwise pick up a free copy of biweekly *Kecskeméti Est* for more information on clubs, films, events and parties.

József Katona Theatre (Katona József tér 5; ticket office ☎ 483 283; ☼ 10am-1pm & 3-6pm Tue-Fri) A 19th-century theatre that stages dramatic works, as well as operettas and concerts by the Kecskemét Symphony Orchestra; check with the ticket office for details.

Bols Music Café (Kisfaludy utca 4; ☼ 11am-11pm) is a convenient drinking spot before moving on to the underground **Xtreme Music Club** (☼ 10pm-4am) next door.

Getting There & Away
BUS

Kecskemét is well served by buses, with frequent departures for the most far-flung

destinations. Buses depart hourly to Budapest (1030Ft, 1½ hours, 85km), every two hours to Szeged (1090Ft, 1¾ hours, 85km) and twice daily to Pécs (2410Ft, 4½ hours, 200km). Other destinations include Baja (2410Ft, 2½ hours, 120km, four daily), Békéscsaba (1570Ft, three hours, 125km, five daily), Debrecen (2910Ft, 5½ hours, 235km, one daily), Eger (1829Ft, four hours, 145km, two daily), Gyula (1690Ft, 3¼ hours, 140km, two daily) and Szolnok (968Ft, 1¾ hours, 75km, seven daily).

TRAIN

Kecskemét is on the train line linking Nyugati station in Budapest (1212Ft, 1½ hours, 105km) with Szeged (890Ft, 1¼ hours, 85km). To get to Debrecen (2030Ft, three hours, 180km) and other towns on the Eastern Plain, you must change at Cegléd. A very slow narrow-gauge train leaves Kecskemét KK train station, south of the city centre, up to three times daily for Kiskőrös (544Ft, three hours, 55km). Transfer there for Kalocsa (1420Ft, 2¾ hours, 130km). Kecskemét KK is also the station from which trains leave for Bugac for Kiskunság National Park.

Getting Around

Buses 1, 5 and 15 link the bus and train stations with the local bus terminus behind the Aranyhomok hotel and buses 2 and 2/a connect Kecskemét KK station and the centre. For the pools and camping ground bus 22 is the best, while bus 13 serves the flea market.

Taxis (☎ 480 762) can also be ordered.

KISKUNSÁG NATIONAL PARK
☎ 76

Kiskunság National Park (adult/child including museum & horse show 1100/550Ft) consists of half a dozen 'islands' of land totalling more than 760 sq km. Much of the park's alkaline ponds, dunes and grassy 'deserts' are off-limits to casual visitors, but you can get a close look at this environmentally fragile area – and see the famous horse herds go through their paces – at **Bugac** on a sandy steppe 30km southwest of Kecskemét.

The best source of information on attractions at the park, transport possibilities and the park in general is **Bugac Tours** (☎ 372 827; bugactours.kft@axelero.hu; Szabadság tér 4/a,

Bugac; ☺ 9am-noon & 1-4pm Mon-Fri); it also has a small office at the park entrance that can only help with prices. The **House of Nature** (☎ 482 611; www.knp.hu in Hungarian; Liszt Ferenc utca 19, Kecskemét; ☺ 9am-4pm Tue-Fri, 10am-2pm Sat), the park's official office in Kecskemét, is another good source of information.

At the park's entrance you can board a **horse-driven carriage** (adult/child including museum & horse show 2200/1100Ft; ☺ 12.15pm May-Sep, extra carriage 2.15pm Jun-Aug) or walk 1.5km along the sandy track to the **Herder Museum** (☺ 10am-5pm May-Oct), a circular structure designed to look like a horse-driven dry mill. It's filled with stuffed fauna and pressed flora of the Kiskunság, as well as branding irons, carved wooden pipes, embroidered fur coats and a tobacco pouch made from a gnarled old ram's scrotum.

The **horse show** (☺ 1.15pm May-Sep, extra show 3.15pm Jun-Aug) is the park's highlight. Outside, you may come across a couple of noble Nonius steeds being made to perform tricks that most dogs would be disinclined to do, but the real reason for coming is to see the *csikósok* (cowboys) crack their whips, race one another bareback and ride 'five-in-hand'. This is a breathtaking performance in which one *csikós* gallops five horses around the field at full tilt, while standing on the backs of the last two.

sleeping and dining in control around **Bugaci Karikás Csárda** (☎ 575 112; Nagybugac 135; mains 1500Ft) at the entrance to the park. It's overly kitsch (and the decaying bulls head inside the door is a little off-putting) but the food is hearty and the accompanying folk-music ensemble will get your foot tapping. Next door, **Bugac Tours** (☎ 575 122; camp sites per person 800Ft, bungalows per person 4500Ft; ℗) has a basic camp site and rustic bungalows.

The bus (423Ft, one hour, 35km) is your best option for getting from Kecskemét to the park; the 11am departure will plonk you at the entrance around noon. The return journey leaves at 4pm Monday to Friday and 6.25pm on Saturday and Sunday (a change at Jakabszállás is required on weekends), but a better (and more fun) option on weekends is the narrow-gauge train (326Ft) between the two centres. It leaves Bugac-felső station (a 15-minute walk south of the park entrance) at 5.34pm, arriving at Kecskemét KK train station around 6.50pm. The train from Kecskemét

to Bugac leaves at 7.30am, so you'll be twiddling your thumbs for quite some time until the horse show starts.

KALOCSA
☎ 78 / pop 18,200

Kalocsa is a quintessential small Hungarian town – rich in history, but as quiet as a cemetery on a weekday. Its past has certainly left its mark though (with Esztergom, Kalocsa was one of the two episcopal seats founded by King Stephen in 1009 from the country's 10 dioceses), and a couple of sights are worthy of a detour.

Orientation & Information
The streets of Kalocsa fan out from Szentháromság tér, site of Kalocsa Cathedral and the Archbishop's Palace. The bus station lies at the southern end of the main avenue, tree-lined Szent István király út. The train station (Mártírok tere) is to the northeast, a 20-minute walk from Szentháromság tér along Kossuth Lajos utca.

Kávészü Net (Városház utca 1; per hr 240Ft; ☺ 10am-10pm) Internet access.

Korona Tours (☎ 561 201; Szentháromság tér 4; ☺ 8am-5pm Mon-Fri) This office in hotel Kalocsa is the only source of information in town.

OTP bank (Szent István király út 43-45)

Post office (Szent István király út 44) Along the main street.

Sights
KALOCSA CATHEDRAL
Almost everything of interest in Kalocsa is on or near Szent István király út, beginning at Szentháromság tér, where the **Trinity Column** (1786) is corroding into sand. **Kalocsa Cathedral** (☎ 462 641; admission free), the fourth church to stand on the site, was completed in 1754 by András Mayerhoffer and is a baroque masterpiece, with a dazzling pink-and-gold interior full of stucco, reliefs and tracery. Some believe that the sepulchre in the crypt is that of the first archbishop of Kalocsa, Asztrik, who brought King Stephen the gift of a crown from Pope Sylvester II, thereby legitimising the Christian convert's control over Hungary. A plaque on the south side outside memorialises this event. Franz Liszt was the first to play the cathedral's magnificent 3560-pipe organ.

The **Cathedral Treasury** (Főszékesegyházi kincstár; ☎ 462 641; Hunyadi János utca 2; adult/child 400/200Ft; ☺ 9am-5pm May-Oct), just east of the

KALOCSA

0 — 300 m
0 — 0.2 miles

INFORMATION
Kávészü Net.................................1 C2
Korona Tours.........................(see 13)
OTP Bank...................................2 C2
Post Office.................................3 D2

SIGHTS & ACTIVITIES
Archbishop's Palace.....................4 B1
Cathedral Treasury Entrance........5 B1
City Gallery..................................6 C1
Episcopal Library.....................(see 4)
Kalocsa Cathedral.......................7 B1
Károly Viski Museum....................8 C2
Kinematic Light Tower Chronos 8.....9 D3
Paprika Museum........................10 B1
Schöffer Collection.....................11 D3
Trinity Column............................12 B1

SLEEPING
Kalocsa.....................................13 B1
Pirosarany.................................14 C2

EATING
Market.......................................15 C2
Trófea.......................................16 B1

DRINKING
Barokk......................................17 B1
Club No 502 S&M......................18 D3

ENTERTAINMENT
Kalocsa Cultural & Youth Centre.....19 B1

TRANSPORT
Bus Station................................20 D3

To House of
Folk Arts (1km);
Train Station (2km)

To Aunt Judy's
Csárda (5km);
Baja (45km)

---

cathedral across Kossuth Lajos utca, is a trove of gold and bejewelled objects and vestments. In case you were wondering, the large bust of St Stephen was cast for the Millenary Exhibition in 1896 and contains 48kg of silver and 2kg of gold. Among the other valuable objects is a 16th-century reliquary of St Anne and a gold and crystal baroque monstrance.

ARCHBISHOP'S PALACE

The Great Hall and the chapel of the **Archbishop's Palace** (Érseki palota; ☎ 462 166; Szentháromság tér 1) (1766) contain magnificent frescoes by Franz Anton Maulbertsch, but you won't get to see these unless there's a concert on. The **Episcopal Library** (Érseki könyvtár; adult/child 500/300Ft; ☯ 9am-noon & 2-5pm Tue-Sun Apr-Oct), however, is open to visitors and is one of the most impressive in Hungary. It contains more than 100,000 volumes, including 13th-century codices, a Bible belonging to Martin Luther that is annotated in the reformer's hand, illuminated manuscripts, and verses cut into palm fronds from Sri Lanka.

MUSEUMS

The **Károly Viski Museum** (☎ 462 351; Szent István király út 25; adult/child 350/200Ft; ☯ 9am-5pm Wed-Sun mid-May–mid-Sep, 9am-5pm Tue-Sat mid-Mar–mid-May & mid-Sep–Oct) is rich in folklore and art, and highlights the life and ways of the Swabian (Sváb), Slovak (Tót), Serbian (Rác) and Hungarian peoples of the area. It's surprising to see how colourful interiors of peasant houses became as wealth increased; walls, furniture, doors – virtually nothing was left undecorated by the famous 'painting women' of Kalocsa. The museum also has a large collection of coins dating from Roman times to today. The **City Gallery** (Városi Képtár; Szent István király út 12-14; admission free; ☯ 10am-5pm Tue-Sun Apr-Oct) is diagonally opposite.

Other places to see examples of wall and furniture painting include the **House of Folk Arts** (Népművészeti tájház; ☎ 461 560; Tompa Mihály utca 5-7; adult/child 500/300Ft; ☯ 10am-5pm Tue-Sun mid-Apr–mid-Oct) and **Aunt Judy's Csárda** (Juca Néni Csárdája; ☎ 461 469), a touristy restaurant near the Danube ferry crossing. Some people find

(Continued on page 257)

GREAT PLAIN

Nyugati train station, Budapest (p123)

A stand at Nagycsarnok market, Budapest (p114)

Café scene near the Oktogon, Budapest (p92)

Locals waiting at a bus stop, Budapest

DAVID GREEDY

The Independence Bridge which spans the Danube, Budapest (p71)

The huge Széchenyi Baths in City Park, Budapest (p97)

MARTIN MOOS

JONATHAN SMITH

Margaret Island looking towards the water tower, Budapest (p75)

The striking Parliament building, Budapest (p91)

MARTIN M

MARTIN MOOS

The 100-roomed Festetics Palace, Keszthely (p193)

View from the Bishop's Palace, Sümeg (p205)

WAYNE WALTON

EMMA MILLER

A sailboat on Lake Balaton (p188)

252

Art-Nouveau building on Fő tér, Szombathely (p172)

Buildings with baroque façades dwarfed by the 60m-high firewatch tower, Sopron (p164)

The pseudo-Gothic Heroes' Gate, Kőszeg (p182)

MARTIN MOOS

Poncichter wine cellar, Kőszeg (p184)

MARTIN MOOS

Picking grapes in a vineyard near Villány (p292)

Pouring Egri Bikavér (Bull's Blood), Eger (p331)

DAVID GREEDY

DAVID GREEDY

Statue Park, a well-manicured trash heap of history near Budapest (p127)

The Hungarian National Gallery courtyard, Budapest (p70)

JONATHAN SMITH

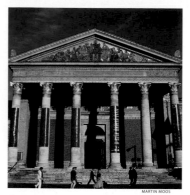

MARTIN MOOS

The Palace of Art, Budapest (p96)

The Palace of Education which houses the Ferenc Móra Museum, Szeged (p263)

MARTIN M

MARTIN MOOS

Jurisics Castle, a hotchpotch of architectural styles, Kőszeg (p183)

MARTIN MOOS

A poppy field in rural Tihany (p207)

The four-towered Diósgyőr Castle, Miskolc (p339)

MARTIN MOOS

256

VERONICA GARBUTT

A man wearing a traditional folk costume from the area around Szentendre (p133)

The Calvinist church bell tower, Nyírbátor (p360)

MARTIN MOOS

Women performing a traditional dance, Debrecen (p233)

MARTIN M

(Continued from page 248)

today's flower and paprika motifs twee and even garish; compare the new work with that in the museums and see what you think.

An exhibition of the futuristic work of the Paris-based artist Nicholas Schöffer, who was from Kalocsa, can be seen at the **Schöffer Collection** (☎ 462 253; Szent István király út 76; adult/child 300/150Ft; 10am-noon & 2-5pm Tue-Sun). The collection would be more impressive if it was cleaned more often, but you can see some of his work near the bus station; his **kinematic light tower Chronos 8** (1982) is a Meccano-set creation of steel beams and spinning reflecting mirrors that two decades ago was supposed to portend the art of the new century.

Festivals & Events

The **International Danube Folklore Festival** is held in mid-July, and the **Kalocsa Paprika Days** in September celebrate the harvest of the town's 'red gold'.

Sleeping

Kalocsa is lacking in quality sleeping options, so you might be inclined to visit the town as a day-trip. Private rooms are quite rare; try your luck along Kossuth Lajos utca.

Kalocsa (☎ 561 200; www.hotelkalocsa.hu; Szentháromság tér 1; s/d €10/60;) This hotel housed in beautifully restored episcopal offices built in 1780, is the best in town. At the time of writing, it was undergoing major renovations.

Pirosarany (☎ 462 220; Szent István király út 37; r from 5400Ft) This dusky-pink hotel is an option if Kalocsa is full or too expensive; rooms are spartan but adequate.

RED GOLD

Along with Szeged, Kalocsa is the largest producer of paprika, the *piros arany* ('red gold') so important to Hungarian cuisine. You can learn all about its development (it was first mentioned in documents way back in the 16th century), production and beneficial qualities (it's higher in vitamin C than citrus fruits) at the **Paprika Museum** (☎ 461 819; Szent István király út 6; adult/child 500/300Ft; 10am-5pm Mar-Nov). If you happen to be in Kalocsa in September, visit any of the nearby villages to see the green fields transformed into red carpets.

Eating & Drinking

Trófea (☎ 167 001; Szilháč utca; mains 1000Ft) This traditional Hungarian restaurant, on the banks of the Vajas stream or Vajas-fok, has a peaceful ambience and serves hearty goulash and the like; insect repellent is mandatory for the terrace in summer.

Kalocsa (☎ 561 200; Szentháromság tér 4; mains 1500Ft) In the hotel of the same name, Kalocsa is the town's upmarket option, with Hungarian specialities and a fine selection of vegetarian dishes.

Aunt Judy's Csárda (Juca Néni Csárdája; ☎ 461 469; mains 700-1500Ft) If you happen to be heading for the Danube ferry crossing over to Gerjen southwest of Kalocsa, call in at this traditional/touristy place for a taste of a rural tavern from early last century.

Kalocsa's **market** (Búzapiac tér) has a lot more than just grain.

This may be a garrison town, but the bar scene is pretty dire. **Barokk** (Kossuth Lajos utca), a café opposite the cathedral, attracts many locals with its location and relaxed atmosphere. **Club No 502 S&M** (Szent István király út 64) is a more boisterous option for those looking to have more than their fair share.

Entertainment

Kalocsa Cultural & Youth Centre (☎ 462 200; Szent István király út 2-1) This centre is housed in an 18th-century baroque seminary; inquire about any concerts scheduled in the Great Hall (Nagy Terem) of the Archbishop's Palace or the cathedral.

Getting There & Away

There are very frequent buses to/from Budapest (1450Ft, 2½ hours, 120km), Baja (544Ft, one hour, 45km) and Solt (425Ft, 45 minutes, 35km), a horse-breeding centre with many riding and carriage-driving opportunities. There are also buses to Szeged (1450Ft, three hours, 115km, four daily), Kecskemét (1450Ft, 2½ hours, 115km, three daily) and Székesfehérvár (2780Ft, 2¾ hours, 120km, two daily).

Kalocsa is at the end of a rail spur to Kiskőrös (346Ft, 50 minutes, 30km, four daily). From Kiskőrös you can make connections to Budapest (1420Ft, three hours, 140km). A very slow (2¼-hour) narrow-gauge train links Kiskőrös with the smaller of Kecskemét's two train stations, Kecskemét KK (p246).

HAJÓS CELLARS

The village of Hajós, 21km southwest of Kalocsa, is – or should be – a magnet for wine lovers. Around 1300 wine cellars (Europe's largest concentration) are squashed into its winding streets and alleys, creating seemingly endless rows of sharply-pointed *pincék* (cellars). Centuries ago, a healthy Swabian population settled the region and began fermenting and storing wine; the conditions were seemingly perfect for such activities and the result is what you see today. Full-bodied reds are the mainstay of wine production in the area, and the best odds for tastings are over the summer, when most visitors are expected. Hajós can be reached by four daily buses from Kalocsa.

BAJA

☎ 79 / pop 37,200

About 45km south of Kalocsa on the banks of the Danube is Baja, a town best known as a holiday and sports centre. It's a perfect place to wind down during summer; beaches and flood-bank forests abound, and the city itself strikes a nice balance between repose and activity. It's also famous for its fish soup, a local concoction of carp, pike-perch, catfish and the ubiquitous paprika spice.

Orientation

Vörösmarty utca and the pedestrian-only Eötvös utca connect Baja's three main squares: Vörösmarty tér, Szent Imre tér and Szentháromság tér. The last one lies on the Kamarás-Duna (or Sugovica as it is known locally), a branch of the Danube River that cuts Petőfi and Nagy Pandúr Islands off from the mainland before emptying into the main river downstream. The bus station (Csermák Mihály tér) is northeast of the centre; the train station is a few minutes to the north across Vonat kert (Train Garden).

Information

Internet Kávézó (Tóth Kálmán tér 7; per hr 500Ft; ☼ noon-1pm & 5-9pm Mon-Fri, 9am-1pm Sat)
K&H bank (Szentháromság tér 10) With a currency-exchange machine and ATM.
OTP bank (cnr Szentháromság tér & Deák Ferenc utca)

Post office (Oroszlán utca 5)
Tourinform (☎ 420 792; baja@tourinform.hu; Szentháromság tér 5; ☼ 9am-5pm Mon-Fri) Has an office overlooking the main square.

Sights

The enormous **Szentháromság tér**, a colourful square of baroque and neoclassical buildings marred only by the multitude of parked cars, is dominated on the east side by the city's **town hall** and its 'widow's walk' looking out towards the Danube.

South of the town hall stands the **István Türr Museum** (☎ 324 173; Deák Ferenc utca 1, enter from Roosevelt tér; adult/child 350/250Ft; ☼ 10am-4pm Wed-Sat mid-Mar–mid-Dec), named after a local hero who fought in the 1848–49 War of Independence and alongside Garibaldi in southern Italy in 1860. The museum's prime exhibit, entitled 'Life on the Danube', covers wildlife, fishing methods and boat building. Another deals with the folk groups of Baja and its surrounds: the Magyars, Germans, South Slavs (Bunyevác, Sokac) and – surprisingly for Hungary – Roma; all have lived together in this region for several centuries. The rarely seen Roma woodcarving is superb, and don't miss the exquisite South Slav black lace, the gold work for which Baja was once nationally famous, or the weavings from Nagybaracska to the south.

The **István Nagy Gallery** (☎ 325 649; Arany János utca 1; adult/child 350/250Ft; ☼ 10am-4pm Sat mid-Mar–mid-Dec), built in 1820, was once the mansion of the Vojnich family and an artists' colony after WWII. It is named after the leading painter of what is known as the Alföld School. Other members are featured, including Gyula Rudnay, as well as 'outsiders' such as the cubist Béla Kádár and sculptor Ferenc Medgyessy.

Buildings of architectural note include the **Franciscan church** (Ferences templom; Bartók Béla utca; admission free) behind the town hall, which was built in 1728 and has a fantastic baroque organ; and the late baroque **Serbian Orthodox church** (☎ 423 199; Táncsics Mihály utca 21; admission free; ☼ 9am-noon Wed & Thu) in a quiet square. The iconostasis is definitely worth a detour.

However, the neoclassical **synagogue** (☎ 322 741; Munkácsy Mihály utca 7-9; admission free; ☼ 1-6pm Mon-Thu, 10am-6pm Fri, 8am-noon Sat), from 1845, beats them both. On the right as you enter the gate, you'll pass a sheltered memorial to

BAJA

0   300 m
0   0.2 miles

the victims of fascism. Above the columns on the synagogue's tympanum (the façade below the roof) on the west side, the Hebrew inscription reads: 'This is none other than the house of God and the gate to heaven'. The tabernacle inside, with its Corinthian pilasters, is topped with two lions holding a crown while four doves pull back a blue and burgundy curtain. Now a public library, it holds a massive 180,000 volumes, including a first full edition of the 18th-century French *Diderot & D'Alembert's Encyclopaedia*.

One of the liveliest **flea markets** in Hungary, full of Serbs, Romanians and Hungarians from Transylvania, takes place on Wednesdays and Saturdays north of Árpád tér, just beyond the bridge to Petőfi Island.

Activities

The **Sugovica** (☎ 321 755; Petőfi-Sziget 32) resort on Petőfi Island has fishing, boating, mini-golf and tennis for those willing to pay, and there's a covered pool – the **Sports Pool** (☎ 326 773; adult/child 450/300Ft; ⊙ 7am-7pm Thu-Tue) – across the walkway on Petőfi Bridge (Petőfi hid).

Avoid the **public beaches** on Petőfi Island in favour of the less crowded ones on the mainland in Szentjános, east of Halász-part, or on Nagy Pandúr Island. But be prepared to swim to the latter or face a long walk to the southern suburb of Homokváros, across the bridge to Nagy Pandúr Island and then north to the beach.

The **Gemenc Forest**, bordering the west side of the Danube, is a unique reserve famed for its incredible beauty and narrow-gauge train trips; a good way to see it up close is via a **boat and rail trip** (☎ 425 356; per person 2700-3300Ft; ☼ 9.45am Wed, Sat & Sun Jul-Aug, 9.45am Sat May-Oct) available through **Tourinform** (☎ 420 792; Szentháromság tér 5). For more information on the forest see p283.

Festivals & Events

The big event of the year is the **Baja Folk Festival** held on the second Saturday in July. It's more a celebration of the town's famous fish soup; 2000 stew pots of the stuff (a Guinness record) are served on the day.

Sleeping

Vizafogó (☎ 326 585; vizafogo@citromail.hu; Petőfi-Sziget 27; s/d 5000/6000Ft; P) Vizafogó occupies a quiet spot on Petőfi Island, across from the popular mainland beaches. Rooms are fitted with modern furnishings and come with balconies overlooking the Sugovica River.

Duna (☎ 323 224; www.hotelduna.hu in Hungarian; Szentháromság tér 6; s/d from 4700/5500Ft; P ▨) This is a wonderful old place right by the Danube, where rooms either overlook the Sugovica or Szentháromság tér. It may not look like much from the outside but the hotel has recently undergone some renovations, including the installation of an indoor pool and wellness centre.

Sugovica (☎ 321 755; www.hotelsugovica.hu; Petőfi-Sziget 32; s/d from 6000/7500Ft, camp sites per person/tent/car from 440/590/300Ft, bungalows 3900-16,500Ft; camping ☼ May-Aug; P ▨) Sugovica was once Baja's prime hotel, but its standards have fallen somewhat. Rooms are still spotless and spacious, but dated, while its camp site is secluded and shady. Some bungalows can sleep up to five.

Also recommended:

Kolibri (☎ 321 628; Batthyány utca 18; P) Undergoing a complete renovation at the time of research, Kolibri should be a thoroughly modern *pension* at a reasonable price.

József Eötvös College (☎ 321 655; Szegedi út; s/d 2000/4000Ft; ☼ Jul-Aug; P) Near the bus station, with basic and clean student accommodation.

Eating & Drinking

Vizafogó (☎ 326 585; Petőfi-Sziget 27; mains 750-1400Ft) At the *pension* of the same name, this is a fine destination for Baja's famous fish soup while eyeing the river for more delectable morsels.

Véndió (☎ 326 585; Martinovics utca 8/b; mains from 800Ft) Véndió's reputation for consistent quality and an excellent location down by the water keeps diners coming back for more. If the waiters moved faster than sloths, it would be a top-class restaurant all-round.

Pizzeria La Piovra (Halász-part; pizzas from 800Ft) Squeezed in among a line of bars is this simple pizzeria, with unexceptional if not filling pizzas. The view makes up for any shortcomings the pizzas may have

There's a stretch of lively but nondescript pubs and bars facing the water at Halász-part, including the Calypso Drink Bar, the Riverside Pub and the Serrano Saloon.

Entertainment

József Attila Cultural Centre (☎ 326 633; Árpád tér 1) This is your source for information about what's going on in Baja. Ask about concerts in the old Serbian church (now a music school and hall) on Batthyány utca.

Getting There & Away

BUS

Buses to Kalocsa (544Ft, one hour, 45km) and Szeged (1330Ft, 2½ hours, 105km) depart at least once an hour; there are five to 10 daily departures to Mohács (605Ft, 1¼ hours, 50km), Szekszárd (544Ft, one hour, 40km), Kecskemét (1330Ft, 2½ hours, 110km) and Budapest (2060Ft, 3¾ hours, 160km) as well.

TRAIN

The train line here links Bátaszék and Kiskunhalas; you must change at the former for Budapest (2030Ft, four hours, 190km), Szekszárd (346Ft, one hour, 40km), Pécs (1624Ft, 2¾ hours, 150km) and other points in Southern Transdanubia. From Kiskunhalas, it's impossible to get anywhere of importance without at least another change (the one exception is the fast train to Budapest).

SZEGED

☎ 62 / pop 156,400

Szeged – a corruption of the Hungarian word *sziget*, or 'island' – is the largest and most important city on the Southern Plain, yet tourist-wise it would rank among Hungary's most under-rated. This is a crying shame, because it has so much to offer the traveller. Theatre, opera and all types of classical and popular music performances abound year-round, and architectural delights are scattered throughout its surprisingly pretty centre. If this isn't enough then perhaps the city's famed edibles will win you over: Szeged paprika, which combines so well with fish from the Tisza River in *szegedi halászlé* (spicy fish soup), and Pick, Hungary's finest salami.

History

Remnants of the Körös culture suggest that these goddess-worshipping people lived in the Szeged area 4000 or 5000 years ago, and one of the earliest Magyar settlements in Hungary was at Ópusztaszer to the north. By the 13th century, the city was an important trading centre, helped along by the royal monopoly it held on the salt being shipped in via the Maros River from Transylvania. Under the Turks, Szeged was afforded some protection since the sultan's estates lay in the area, and it continued to prosper in the 18th and 19th centuries as a royal free town.

The watery fingers of the Tisza almost wiped Szeged off the map in 1879 (see boxed text, p263) but the town bounced back with a vengeance and an eye for uniform architecture. Since WWII, Szeged has been an important university town – students marched here in 1956 before their classmates in Budapest (see p32) did – and a cultural centre.

Orientation

The Tisza River, joined by the Maros, flows west and then turns abruptly south through the centre of Szeged, splitting the city in two as cleanly as the Danube bisects Budapest. But comparison of the two cities and their rivers stops there. The Tisza is a rather undignified muddy channel here, and the other side of Szeged is not the city's throbbing commercial heart as Pest is to Budapest but a large park given over to sunbathing, swimming and other hedonistic pursuits.

Szeged's many squares and inner and outer ring roads make the city confusing for some, but virtually every square in the city has a large signpost with detailed plans and a legend in several languages. The main train station (Indóház tér) is south of the city centre; tram 1 connects the station with the town. The bus station (Mars tér), to the west of the centre, is within easy walking distance via pedestrian-only Mikszáth Kálmán utca.

Information

Cyber Arena (Deák Ferenc 26; per hr 360Ft; ☺ 24hr) Also has cheap Internet calls.

Libri (☎ 541 126; Jókai utca; ☺ 9am-7pm Mon-Fri, 9am-2pm Sat) Small foreign-language section that's big on Hungarian writers, historians and famous figures.

Main hospital (☎ 484 184; Kossuth Lajos Sugárút 42)

Main post office (Széchenyi tér 1)

Map shop (☎ 424 667; Attila utca 9) An excellent source of maps, not only for Hungary but the world.

Tourinform (☎ 488 699; szeged@tourinform.hu; Dugonics tér 2; ☺ 9am-5pm Mon-Fri, 9am-1pm Sat) Tucked away in a quiet courtyard.

Tourinform Booth (Széchenyi tér; ☺ 9am-9pm May-Sep) A separate pavilion.

www.szegedportal.hu Not the city's official site, but loaded with useful information and in English.

Sights

CITY CENTRE

Begin an easy walking tour of Szeged in Széchenyi tér, a square so large it's a park. The neobaroque **town hall**, with its graceful tower and colourful tiled roof, dominates the square, while statues of Lajos Tisza, István Széchenyi and the *kubikosok* (navvies) who helped regulate the Tisza River take pride of place under the chestnut trees. Take a quick detour north of the square to the **Gróf Palace** (Arany Jáns utca), a fantastical office building completed in 1913 in Secessionist style.

Pedestrian Kárász utca leads south through Klauzál tér. Turn west on Kölcsey utca and walk for about 100m to the **Reök Palace** (Reök-palota; Tisza Lajos körút), a mind-blowing green and lilac Art Nouveau structure built in 1907 that looks like an aquarium decoration. Sadly, it's been left to the elements and is coming off second-best.

Further south, Kárász utca meets Dugonics tér, site of the **Attila József Science University** (abbreviated JATE in Hungarian), named after its most famous alumnus. József (1905–37), a much loved poet, was actually expelled from here in 1924 for writing the verse 'I have no father and I have no mother/I have no God and I have no country' during the ultraconservative rule of Admiral Miklós Horthy. A **music fountain** in the square plays at irregular intervals throughout the day.

From the southeast corner of Dugonics tér, walk along Jókai utca into Aradi vértanúk tere. **Heroes' Gate** (Hősök kapuja) to the south was erected in 1936 in honour of Horthy's White Guards, who were responsible for 'cleansing' the nation of 'Reds' after the ill-fated Republic of Councils in 1919. The fascistic murals have disappeared

(replaced with some 'nice' but amateurish ones), but the brutish sculptures are still a sight to behold.

DÓM TÉR

Dóm tér, a few paces northeast of Heroes' Gate, contains Szeged's most important monuments and is the centre of events

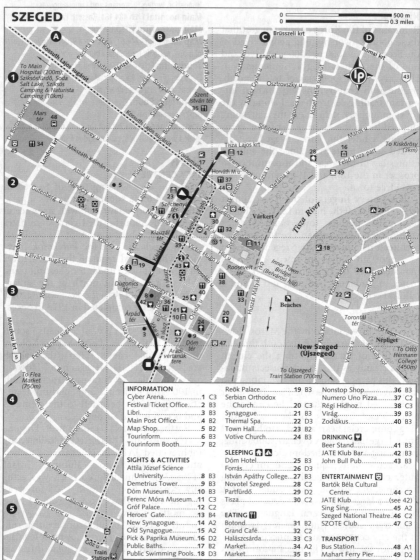

during the annual summer festival. The **National Pantheon** – statues and reliefs of 80 notables running along an arcade around three sides of the square – is a crash course in Hungarian art, literature, culture and history. Even the Scotsman Adam Clark, who supervised the building of Budapest's Chain Bridge, wins accolades, but you'll look forever for any sign of a woman.

The Romanesque **Demetrius Tower** (Dömötörtorony; 600Ft; ☺ 9am-5pm Mon-Wed & Fri, noon-5pm Thu, 9am-5pm Sat, 1-5pm Sun), the city's oldest structure, is all that remains of a church erected here in the 12th century. In its place stands the twin-towered **Votive Church** (Fogadalmi templom; ☎ 429 379; 400Ft, Sunday free, crypt 150Ft; ☺ 9am-5pm Mon-Wed & Fri, noon-5pm Thu, 9am-5pm Sat, 1-5pm Sun), a disproportionate brown brick monstrosity that was pledged after the flood but not completed until 1930. The interior borders on gaudy but it's still an impressive achievement; the huge nave and gigantic organ (11,500 pipes in all) dominate the entire scene. The nearby **Serbian Orthodox church** (☎ 325 278; adult/child 150/100Ft), dating from 1778, is far more rewarding. Take a peek inside at the fantastic iconostasis: a central gold 'tree', with 60 icons hanging from its 'branches'. You'll find the key at Somogyi utca 3 (flat 1/5). Back on Dóm tér, duck into the **Dóm Museum** (Dóm tér 5; adult/child 60/30Ft; ☺ 10am-6pm Tue-Sun) and pick through the small collection of monstrances, crosses and goblets from across the plains.

FERENC MÓRA MUSEUM

Oskola utca, one of the city's oldest streets, leads from Dóm tér to Roosevelt tér and the Palace of Education (1896) at No 1-3, which now houses the **Ferenc Móra Museum** (☎ 549 040; Várkert; adult/child 400/250Ft; ☺ 10am-5pm Tue-Sun). The museum's strength lies in its colourful collection of folk art from Csongrád County, bearing intelligent descriptions in several languages. The unique exhibit of 7th-century Avar finds of gold work and other art pieces showcases the sophistication and art appreciation of these often forgotten people while another room is given over to an even more obscure group, the Sarmatians. Originating in present-day Iran, these people moved to the plain as allies of the Romans; construction of the new M5 motorway has unearthed a 1st-century village, along with pottery, jewellery and graves.

SYNAGOGUES

For many people, Szeged's most compelling sight is the Hungarian Art Nouveau **New Synagogue** (Új zsinagóga; ☎ 423 849; Gutenberg utca 13; adult/child 250/100Ft; ☺ 10am-noon & 1-5pm Sun-Fri Apr-Sep, 10am-2pm Sun-Fri Oct-Mar), which was designed by Lipót Baumhorn in 1903. It is the most beautiful Jewish house of worship in Hungary and still very much in use. If the grace and enormous size of the exterior don't impress you, the blue-and-gold interior will. The cupola, decorated with stars and flowers (representing Infinity

---

THE FLOODING TISZA

Snaking its way some 800km across the Great Plain is the Tisza, Hungary's second-longest river. Once described by Daniel Defoe as 'three parts water and two parts fish', this wonderful natural resource has a habit of flooding on an all-too-regular basis, despite the government's best efforts to keep it from breaching its banks.

The first major flood to wash through Szeged occurred in the spring of 1838, destroying thousands of houses, but worse was yet to come; in March 1879 the river burst its banks again, this time leaving only 300 houses, out of an estimated 6300, standing. Flood protection was quickly built, and things went swimmingly (at least flood damage was kept to a minimum) for almost a hundred years until May 1970 when the river reached its highest recorded level and gave the city another bath. A string of floods hit the city around the millennium – in March 1999, April 2000 and March 2001 – and even as recently as 2005, restaurants, camping grounds and swimming pools along the river were closed due to flood damage.

Upgrade work on flood-control barriers has been underway over the past few decades, and currently about 60% are complete. All the human endeavour in the world will probably never stop the Tisza washing over its banks, but at least the current efforts will minimise the risks. Of course the best solution would be to move to higher ground, but that's not much of an option on the Great Plain...

and Faith), appears to float skyward, and the tabernacle of carved acacia wood and metal fittings is a masterpiece. There are a few other buildings of interest in this area, the former Jewish quarter, including the neoclassical **Old Synagogue** (Ózsinagóga; Hajnóczy utca 12), built in 1843, and just south of Széchenyi tér, the remains of another old **synagogue** (Nádor utca 3), now a private house.

OTHER SIGHTS

If you'd like to know more about the making of Szeged's famed salami – from hoof to shrink-wrap – the **Pick & Paprika Museum** (☎ 20-980 8000; Felső Tisza-part 10; adult/child 320/240Ft; 🕑 3-6pm Tue-Sat) can oblige, and if that doesn't satisfy your taste buds, there's plenty of paprika to burn them into submission. Pick salami can be purchased from the Pick shop next to the museum.

Szeged's ramshackle **flea market** is near Vám tér at the start of Szabadkai út southwest of the centre.

Activities

Just north of Széchenyi tér you'll find the newly renovated **public baths** (☎ 487 711; Tisza Lajos körút 24; adult/child 600/450Ft; 🕑 6am-8pm Mon-Fri, 8am-8pm Sat & Sun), with its very own wellness centre. Across the Tisza River, the parkland of New Szeged (Újszeged) has **swimming pools** as well as **beaches** along the river, but at the time of research everything was closed due to flood damage. The nearby **thermal spa** (☎ 431 133; Fürdő utca 1; adult/child 700/550Ft; 🕑 6am-8pm) is still open for business however. About 10km west of town in the suburb of Sziksósfürdő is the thermal **Soda Salt Lake** (adult/child 600/300Ft; 🕑 10am-6pm Mon-Fri, 8am-6pm Sat & Sun May-Sep). Alongside a conventional *strand*, swimming pool and rowing boats, it also has a nudist beach and camp site.

Tourinform (☎ 488 699; Dugonics tér 2) will rent you bicycles for 900/2500/7000Ft per hour/day/week.

Festivals & Events

The **Szeged Open-Air Festival** unfolds on Dóm tér from mid-July to late August, with the two towers of the Votive Church as a backdrop. The outdoor theatre here seats some 6000 people. Main events include an opera, an operetta, a play, folk dancing, classical music, ballet and a rock opera. Festival tickets and information are available from the **festival ticket office** (☎ 554 713; ticket@szinhaz.szeged.hu; Kelemen utca 7; 🕑 1-5pm Mon, 10am-5pm Tue-Fri, 10am-noon Sat). But Szeged isn't all highbrow; others might prefer the annual **Beer Festival** at the beginning of June or the one-week **Wine Festival** at the end of May.

Sleeping

BUDGET

Szeged's *pension* situation is surprisingly poor; there are plenty around but none truly stand out. Most are either concentrated northwest of town near the bus station or to the west of the train station. Tourinform can supply you with a comprehensive list, and can also organise private rooms (3000Ft).

István Apáthy College (☎ 545 896; Eötvös utca 4; r 5000Ft) Plenty of student dormitories in Szeged open their doors to travellers in July and August, and this college is a rundown but supremely central option.

Ottó Hermann College (☎ 544 309; Temesvári körút 52; s/d 2500/5000Ft; P) On a quiet residential street, Ottó Hermann is the best of the bunch over in New Szeged.

Partfürdő (☎ 430 843, fax 425 559; Közép-kikötő sor; camp sites per adult/child/tent 600/430/600Ft, bungalows from 6000Ft) In New Szeged, it was closed at the time of research due to flood damage. Fortunately its bungalows escaped the worst of it.

Sziksós Camping (☎ 463 029; Sziksósi út; camp sites per person/tent 1200/200Ft, bungalows from 3800Ft; P 🏊) Further out in the suburb of Sziksósfürdő is this friendly camping ground, with cabin-style bungalows and plenty of shade.

Naturista Camping (☎ 463 988; Vereshomok dűlő 1; camp sites per person/tent/car 300/780/400Ft, bungalows from 4500Ft; P 🏊) A nudist site, with simple bungalows and a small lake to splash about in.

MIDRANGE

Tisza (☎ 478 278; www.tiszahotel.hu; Wesselényi utca 1; s/d from 8900/12,900Ft; P) Built in 1885, Tisza is Szeged's old-world hotel, with chandeliers, wrought-iron stair railings, and an air of class. Unfortunately rooms don't match the extravagance of the rest of the hotel but they're bright and airy and quite comfortable.

Forrás (☎ 430 130; www.hotelforras.szeged.hu; Szent-Györgyi Albert utca 16-24; s/d from €36/49; P ✖ 🏊) In New Szeged, this spa hotel looks rather ugly from the outside but its facilities (which include thermal treatments and massages) and large rooms are in good nick and the staff are professional and helpful. Bike rental is available for 200Ft per hour.

TOP END
Dóm Hotel (☎ 423 750; www.domhotel.hu; Bajza utca 6; s/d 12,600/15,200Ft; P ⬛ ✕) This small and modern hotel is in the heart of the city. Sizable rooms are contemporarily styled in pastel hues and there's a sauna (800Ft) for guest use.

Novotel Szeged (☎ 562 200; h2996@accor.com; Maros utca 1; s/d €80/90; P ✕ ⬛) This is a modern 136-room hotel near a noisy stretch of road but with good views of the river, and rooms with all the trimmings.

Eating
RESTAURANTS
Halászcsárda (☎ 555 980; Roosevelt tér 14; mains 1500-2000Ft) Halászcsárda is a Szeged institution that knows how to prepare the best fish in town, including *szegedi halászlé*. On hot summer days its large terrace near the Tisza is thankfully tree-shaded.

Régi Hídhoz (☎ 420 910; Oskola utca 4; mains 1000Ft) Some believe Hídhoz serves comparable fish dishes to its neighbour Halászcsárda, which is saying something. The atmosphere here is, however, more relaxed and family-orientated.

Kiskőrösy (☎ 495 698; Felső Tisza-part 336; mains 1000-2000Ft) Housed in a traditional fisherman's cottage on the banks of the Tisza a few kilometres east of the centre, this excellent fish restaurant is an atmospheric place to dine. Unfortunately it was affected by the latest flood, so check with Tourinform on its opening times.

Zodiákus (☎ 420 914; Oskola utca 13; mains 1000-2000Ft) Zodiákus wins over diners with its unusual astrological theme and international menu.

Numero Uno Pizza (☎ 424 745; Széchenyi tér 5; pizzas from 390Ft) We can't guarantee that this simple pizzeria is number one in the city but it's certainly up there with the best. Its inner-courtyard garden is also fine for a quiet drink.

Botond (☎ 420 435; Széchenyi tér 13; mains 1000-2000Ft) Botond serves better-than-average Hungarian food. Its pleasant outside seating overlooks Széchenyi tér.

CAFÉS
Grand Café (☎ 420 578; Deák Ferenc utca 18; ✕ 3pm-midnight Mon-Fri, 5pm-midnight Sat & Sun) For coffee, cake and a bit of peace and quiet (except when it's hosting film nights), head to this light-hearted café on the 2nd floor of an office block.

Virág (☎ 541 360; Klauzál tér 1; ✕ 8am-10pm) A café since 1922, Virág serves possibly the best ice cream in town, and its cakes aren't bad either. Take a seat in its traditional booths outside on large Klauzál tér, or directly opposite in its modern counterpart, Kis Virág.

SELF-CATERING
Szeged has two big **fruit & vegetable markets**, one on Mars tér, site of the notorious Star Prison for political prisoners early in the 1950s, and the other northwest of Széchenyi tér on Szent István tér. There's also a **non-stop shop** (Zrínyi utca 1).

Drinking
There's a vast array of bars, clubs and other night spots in this student town, especially between Dugonics tér and Dom tér.

JATE Klub bar (Toldy utca 2; ✕ noon-midnight) A reasonably laid-back spot, attracting students with its cheap drinks and terrace.

Beer stand (Somogyi utca; ✕ May-Sep) A very popular spot further east that appeals more to city workers.

John Bull Pub (☎ 484 217; Oroszlán utca 6) This pub does a grand job of 'English Pub' imitation (minus the 11 o'clock closing!!), with carpets, proper pints and bar stools. Its garden is a welcome respite from the centre.

Both **Numero Uno** (☎ 424 745; Széchenyi tér 5) and **Grand Café** (☎ 420 578; Deák Ferenc utca 18) are worth stopping in for a drink even if you're not having a meal.

Entertainment
Your best sources of entertainment information in this culturally active city are Tourinform, the **Bartók Béla Cultural Centre** (☎ 479 566; Vörösmarty utca 3), or the free biweekly entertainment guide *Szegedi Est*.

Szeged National Theatre (Szegedi Nemzeti Színház; ☎ 479 279; Deák Ferenc utca 12-14) Built in 1886, it has always been the centre of cultural life in Szeged, and usually stages operas and ballet.

New Synagogue (Új zsinagóga; ☎ 423 849; Gutenberg utca 13) There are free organ concerts here from late March to mid-September;

it's a good chance to take in the splendour of the building without having to pay.

Sing Sing (☎ 420 314; Mars tér C pavilon; ☺ 10am-5am Wed & Sat) Sing Sing occupies a huge pavilion near the bus station and hosts rave parties twice a week.

JATE Klub (☎ 420 445; Toldy utca 1; ☺ 9.30am-4am Mon-Fri, 10am-5am Sat) and **SZOTE Club** (Dom tér 13; ☺ 10-5am Wed, Fri & Sat) are two student haunts without compare in Szeged; both are fairly grungy, host a mix of DJs and live acts, and are packed to the gunnels with students.

Getting There & Away

BUS

The bus service is good from Szeged, with frequent departures to Kecskemét (1090Ft, 1¾ hours, 85km), Békéscsaba (1150Ft, two hours, 95km), Gyula (1820Ft, 3½ hours, 145km), Csongrád (725Ft, 1½ hours, 60km), Ópusztaszer (363Ft, 45 minutes, 30km) and Hódmezővásárhely (363Ft, 35 minutes, 30km).

Other destinations from Szeged:

Destination	Price	Duration	Km	Frequency
Debrecen	2910Ft	5hr	230	2 daily
Mohács	1450Ft	3¼hr	155	6 daily
Népliget station	2170Ft	3hr	175	8 daily
Pécs	2410Ft	4¼hr	195	7 daily
Tiszafüred	2660Ft	5hr	220	2 daily
Veszprém	2910Ft	5hr	235	3 daily

Buses also head for Arad, across the Romanian border, daily at 6.30am Monday to Saturday. Buses run to Novi Sad in Serbia and Montenegro at 4pm daily and to Subotica up to four times daily. A 9.30pm bus on Friday departs for Vienna.

TRAIN

Szeged is on a main train line to Budapest's Nyugati station (2030Ft, 2¾ hours, 190km). Another line connects the city with Hódmezővásárhely (346Ft, 35 minutes, 30km) and Békéscsaba (1004Ft, two hours, 95km), where you can change trains for Gyula (1212Ft, three hours, 115km) or Romania. Southbound local trains leave Szeged for Subotica in Serbia and Montenegro twice daily at 6.20am and 4.25pm.

Getting Around

Tram 1 from the train station will take you north to Széchenyi tér. The tram turns west

on Kossuth Lajos sugárút and goes as far as Izabella Bridge, where it turns around. To get to Szentmihály and the flea market, take bus 76 or tram 4. From the main bus station catch bus 7/f for Sziksósfürdő and bus 2 for student accommodation in New Szeged.

Local **taxis** (☎ 444 444, 555 555) can also be ordered.

ÓPUSZTASZER

☎ 62 / pop 2300

About 28km north of Szeged, the **Ópusztaszer National Historical Memorial Park** (Ópusztaszeri Nemzeti Történeti Emlékpark; ☎ 275 133; www.opusztaszer.hu; admission park only 800Ft, park & panorama painting adult/student or child 1800/1200Ft; ☺ 9am-6pm Apr-Oct, 9am-4pm Nov-Mar) in Ópusztaszer commemorates the single most important event in Hungarian history: the *honfoglalás*, or 'conquest', of the Carpathian Basin by the Magyars in 896 (see p22).

Contrary to what many people think (Hungarians included), the park does not mark the spot where Árpád, mounted on his white charger, first entered 'Hungary'. That was actually the Munkács Valley, Hungarian territory until after WWI and now Ukrainian territory. But according to the 12th-century chronicler known as Anonymous, it was at this place called Szer that Árpád and the six clan chieftains, who had sworn a blood oath of fidelity to him, held their first assembly, and so it was decided that a **Millennium Monument** would be erected here in 1896. (Scholars had actually determined the date of the conquest to be between 893 and 895, but the government was not ready to mark the 1000-year anniversary until 1896.)

Situated on top of a slight rise in the Great Plain about 1km from the Szeged road, the park is an attractive though sombre place. Besides the neoclassical monument with Árpád taking pride of place, there are ruins of an 11th-century **Romanesque church** and **monastery** (still being excavated) and an excellent **open-air museum** (skanzen; ☺ Apr-Oct), with a farmhouse, windmills, an old post office, a schoolhouse and cottages moved from villages around southeast Hungary. In one, the home of a rather prosperous and smug onion-grower from Makó, a sampler admonishes potential gossips: 'Neighbour lady, away you go/If it's gossip that you want to know' (or words to that effect).

To the west of the park beside the little lake, a museum reminiscent of a Magyar chieftain's tent houses a huge **panorama painting** entitled *The Arrival of the Hungarians*. Completed by Árpád Feszty for the Millenary Exhibition in Budapest in 1896, the enormous work, which measures 15m x 120m, was badly damaged during WWII and was restored by a Polish team in time for the 1100th anniversary of the conquest in 1996. Two **galleries** (1 gallery adult/child 500/300Ft, 2 galleries adult/child 700/600Ft) above the painting are devoted to art and history of the area. Of particular interest are photos of rough-and-ready tribal Magyars dressed in their traditional 19th-century garb.

There are also **horse shows** (adult/child 500/400Ft; 11.30am & 2.30pm Apr-Oct) celebrating the life of the nomadic Magyars of yesteryear, bows to be shot (150Ft) and horses to be ridden (300Ft).

Ópusztaszer must be done as a day-trip; there is no accommodation within walking distance of the entrance and the only food option is within the park. Up to 12 buses daily travel between Szeged (363Ft,

45 minutes, 30km) and Ópusztaszer, the last leaving for Szeged at 8.30pm.

HÓDMEZŐVÁSÁRHELY

☎ 62 / pop 47,900

Folk art, particularly pottery, has a rich tradition in Hódmezővásárhely (Beaver Meadow Marketplace); some 400 independent artisans working here in the mid-19th century made it the largest pottery centre in Hungary. Today you won't see much more pottery outside the town's museums than you would elsewhere, but the influence of the dynamic artists' colony here is felt well beyond Kohán György utca – from the galleries and **Autumn Weeks** art festival in October to the ceramic and bronze street signs by eminent artists.

Orientation

The bus station (Bocskai utca) is just off Andrássy utca, about a 10-minute walk east from Kossuth tér, the city centre. There are two train stations in town: the main one and Hódmezővásárhelyi-Népkert. The first is east of the city centre at the end of Mérleg

HÓDMEZŐVÁSÁRHELY

0 ——————— 500 m
0 ——————— 0.3 miles

INFORMATION		Folk Art House...............8 B2	Öszöm-Iszom.................14 B2
Main Post Office.............1 B2		János Tornyai	
OTP Bank.......................2 B2		Museum......................9 B2	**DRINKING**
Petőfi Cultural		Thermal Spa.................10 A3	Fekete Sas...................15 A2
Centre........................3 B2			Sarokház.....................16 B2
Tourinform....................4 B2		**SLEEPING**	
		Fáma...........................11 C1	**ENTERTAINMENT**
SIGHTS & ACTIVITIES		Thermál Camping........12 B3	Hordó........................17 A2
Alföld Gallery..............5 B2			
Artists' Colony..............6 A2		**EATING**	**TRANSPORT**
Entrance to Spa............7 A2		Bandula......................13 B1	Bus Station.................18 C2

utca, the second southwest at the end of Ady Endre utca.

Information

Main post office (Kossuth tér 8) On the south side of Kossuth tér.

OTP bank (Andrássy utca 1) This bank is on the east side of Kossuth tér and has an ATM.

Petőfi Cultural Centre (☎ 241 710; Szántó Kovács János utca 7; per hr 50Ft; 9am-8pm Mon-Fri)

Tourinform (☎ 249 350; hodmezovasarhely@tourinform .hu; Szőnyi utca 1; 7.30am-4pm Mon-Fri) Just to the southeast of the main square.

Sights

The **János Tornyai Museum** (☎ 344 424; Szántó Kovács János utca 16-18; adult/child 200/100Ft; 10am-4pm Tue & Wed, 10am-5pm Thu-Sun), named after a leading member of the Alföld School of alfresco painting, displays some early archaeological finds, but its *raison d'être* is to show off the folk art of Hódmezővásárhely – the painted furniture, 'hairy' embroidery done with yarn-like thread, and pottery unique to the region. The collection of jugs, pitchers and plates, most of them made as wedding gifts, is the finest of all and represents the many types once made here and named after city districts, including Csúcs (white and blue), Tabán (brown) and Újváros (yellow and green).

More pottery is on display at the **Csúcs Pottery House** (Csúcsi Fazekasház; ☎ 242 224; Rákóczi utca 101; admission free; 1-5pm Tue-Sun), once the home of master potter Sándor Vékony, and at the **Folk Art House** (Népművészeti tájház; ☎ 20-444 0560; Árpád utca 21, entry from Kaszap utca; admission free; 10am-4pm Tue-Sun), two old thatched farmhouses standing self-consciously in the middle of a housing estate.

Outsiders are not allowed into the **artists' colony** (művésztelep; Kohán György utca 2), founded in the early part of last century, but you can view selected members' work at the **Alföld Gallery** (☎ 242 247; Kossuth tér 8, enter from Szönyi utca; adult/child 200/100Ft; 10am-4pm Tue & Wed, 10am-5pm Thu-Sun) housed in a neoclassical former Calvinist school. Naturally the Alföld School dominates; you might go a little crazy looking at horses and *shahoof* (seep wells) and cowboys on the Great Plain in every season through the eyes of Tornyai, István Nagy and József Koszta, but there are other things to enjoy such as the work of Menyhért Tóth and the impressionist János Vaszary.

Activities

The **thermal spa** (☎ 244 238; Ady Endre utca 1; adult/child 650/480Ft; 8am-8pm) in the Népkert, south of Kossuth tér, has eight hot and cold pools where you can immerse yourself, but Mártély, about 10km to the northwest on a backwater of the Tisza, is the city's real recreational centre, with **boating**, **fishing** and **swimming** available.

The **Aranyági Stud Farm** (☎ 30-218 3354; Serháztér út 2), 4km northeast of the centre, has horse shows, horse riding and horse tours on request.

Sleeping

Fáma (☎ 222 231; faama@vnet.hu; Szeremlei utca 7; s/d from 6490/7520Ft; P) This quiet hotel offers a touch of serenity just behind the city's synagogue. Rooms are spacious yet simple (only those on the 1st floor have air-con), and there's a restaurant and a private grassy courtyard for guest use.

Kenguru (☎ 534 841; kenguru@vasarhely.hu; Szánto Kovás János utca 78; r from 7250Ft; P) Even though it isn't centrally located, Kenguru is a fine option. Big, bright rooms with natural wood furniture and floors surround an inner courtyard used for secure parking; guests can use the pool, sauna and solarium.

Vándorsólyom (☎ 535 150; Kutasi út; s/d 6250/7000Ft; P) This nine-room inn has a peaceful, rural setting 4km east of town. The entire place could do with a makeover but it's the perfect place to combine accommodation with horse-riding (stables are next door).

Also recommended:

Tisza-part Camping (☎ 228 057; martelycamping@freemail.hu; camp sites per adult/child/tent 650/400/650Ft; bungalows per person 1350Ft; May-Sep; P) Camp site in Mártély near plenty of recreational activities.

Thermál Camping (☎ 245 033; Ady Endre utca 1; camp sites per adult/child/tent 720/360/850Ft; bungalows 6050-6600Ft; P) Small site handy to the spa.

Eating & Drinking

Bandula (☎ 244 234; Pálffy utca 2; mains 1000-2000Ft) With an international menu, quick service and cosy surroundings, Bandula is the best option for food in town.

Fekete Sas (☎ 249 326; Kossuth tér 5; drinks 300Ft) On the ground floor of the grand old Fekete Sas Hotel (currently under renovation), Fekete Sas is the town's 'mature' bar, with a more relaxed crowd and colourful interior.

Sarokház (Kossuth tér 7; coffee 100Ft; ☺ 9am-9pm Sun-Thu, 9am-10pm Fri & Sat) The 'Corner House' is a quiet café filled with locals gossiping about the days' events or whiling away the time people-watching and reading.

Öszöm-Iszom (☎ 239 341; Szent Antal utca 8; mains 600-1200Ft; ☺ 9am-midnight Sun-Thu, 9am-2am Fri, 9am-3am Sat) That's 'I Eat-I Drink' in Szeged dialect – and it's OK for a quick meal and a pint.

Entertainment

Petőfi (☎ 241 710; Szántó Kovács János utca 7) It can advise you on what's on in town.

Hordó (☎ 20-924 7381; Városház utca; ☺ 5pm-4am Fri & Sat) This cellar bar is a meeting point on Friday and Saturday nights for those wishing to drink and play up large.

Getting There & Away

Buses to Szeged (363Ft, 35 minutes, 30km), Békéscsaba (846Ft, 1½ hours, 70km), Csongrád (544Ft, one hour, 40km) and the resort area of Mártély (182Ft, 20 minutes, 12km) are frequent; there is a minimum of three daily departures to Kecskemét (1210Ft, two hours, 95km) and Budapest (2300Ft, 3½ hours, 185km).

Two train lines pass through Hódmező-vásárhely, and all trains serve both train stations which are 2km apart. The more important of the two lines connects Szeged (346Ft, 35 minutes, 30km) with Békéscsaba (658Ft, 1¼ hours, 65km).

CSONGRÁD

☎ 63 / pop 18,500

Csongrád's sleepy charm lies in its Öregvár (Old Castle) district – a quiet fishing village of thatched cottages and narrow streets on the bank of the Tisza – which hasn't changed much since the 17th century. However, back in the 13th century Csongrád was a place of importance, gaining the title of royal capital of Csongrád County. The invading Mongols put paid to that, all but destroying the town; it wasn't until the 1920s that it once again became known as a town.

Orientation

Csongrád lies on the right bank of the Tisza, close to where it is joined by the Körös River, some 58km north of Szeged. A backwater (Holt-Tisza) south of town is used for recreation. The bus station (Hunyadi tér) is five minutes from the main street, Fő utca. The train station lies to the southwest at the end of Vasút utca.

Information

Main post office (Dózsa György tér 1) Northeast of the bus station.

OTP bank branch (Szentháromság tér 8) Has an ATM.

Tourinform (☎ 570 325; csongrad@tourinform.hu; Szentháromság tér 8; ☺ 9am-5pm mid-Jun–mid-Sep, 8am-4pm Mon-Fri mid-Sep–mid-Jun) In the cultural centre.

Sights & Activities

The town's big museum, the **László Tari Museum** (☎ 481 103; Iskola utca 2; adult/child 200/100Ft; ☺ 1-5pm Tue-Fri, 8am-noon Sat, 8am-noon & 1-5pm Sun), examines the history of Csongrád, starting with tribes that settled the region as far back as the Bronze Age.

Walking eastward from the museum to the Öregvár district, you'll pass the baroque **Church of Our Lady** (Nagyboldogasszony temploma), built in 1769, and the beautiful Secessionist **János Batsányi College** (Kossuth tér). A bit further on is **St Rókus Church**, built in 1722 on the site of a Turkish mosque.

The cobblestone streets of the protected **Old Castle** district begin at a little roundabout three blocks east of the church. Most of the district is made up of private homes or holiday houses, but the **Village Museum** (Tájház; Gyökér utca 1; admission free; ☺ 1-5pm Tue-Sun May-Oct) gives a good idea of how the simple fisher folk of Csongrád lived until not so long ago. It's housed in two old cottages connected by a long thatched roof and contains period furniture, household items and lots of fish nets and traps.

The town's **thermal spa** (Dob utca 3-5; adult/child 550/430Ft; ☺ 7am-8pm Mon-Thu, 7am-10pm Fri, 8am-10pm Sat, 8am-8pm Sun), fed by a spring with water that reaches 46°C, is in a large park and there are also **outdoor pools** and a **strand** (☺ 7am-8pm). **Tourinform** (☎ 570 325; Szentháromság tér 8) can point you in the right direction for horse riding and fishing in the area.

Sleeping

Fishing cottages (☎ 483 631; idegenforgalom@cson grad.hu; information Fő utca 3; houses 5000-16,000Ft; Ⓟ) The most atmospheric places to stay in town are these cottages in the Old Castle district. The 200-year-old houses are squat dwellings with thick whitewashed walls, clay

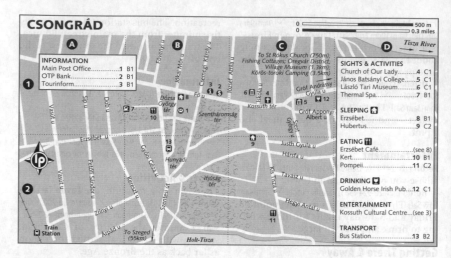

CSONGRÁD

0 / 500 m
0 / 0.3 miles

Tisza River

INFORMATION
Main Post Office..............1 B1
OTP Bank.........................2 B1
Tourinform......................3 B1

To St Rókus Church (750m);
Fishing Cottages; Öregvár District;
Village Museum (1.3km);
Körös-toroki Camping (3.5km)

SIGHTS & ACTIVITIES
Church of Our Lady.........4 C1
János Batsányi College......5 C1
László Tari Museum.........6 C1
Thermal Spa....................7 B1

SLEEPING
Erzsébet...........................8 B1
Hubertus.........................9 C2

EATING
Erzsébet Café.................(see 8)
Kert................................10 B1
Pompeii..........................11 C2

DRINKING
Golden Horse Irish Pub...12 C1

ENTERTAINMENT
Kossuth Cultural Centre...(see 3)

TRANSPORT
Bus Station....................13 B2

Train Station

To Szeged (55km)

Holt-Tisza

ovens, polished wood floors, and oodles of character. Each comes with a fully equipped kitchen and often two bedrooms.

Hubertus (☎ 484 997; vi-ma@csongrad.hu; Justh Gyula utca 5; r 7200Ft; P) Csongrád's newest *pension* is a bright yellow collaboration with spotless *en-suite* rooms and a private courtyard for parking and relaxing in.

Erzsébet (☎ 483 960; Fő utca 3; s/d 5500 7500Ft) This old hotel is minutes from the bus station and has considerably large rooms filled with so-so wood furniture. Rates include entry to the thermal spa.

Körös-toroki Camping (☎ 481 185; 3-person camp sites 3000Ft; bungalows 6000-8000Ft; ☼ mid-May–mid-Sep; P ☢) Körös-toroki sits at the confluence of the Tisza and Körös Rivers and has the added bonus of direct access to a beach and bungalows on stilts – the area floods in heavy rain and the mosquitoes can be unbearable.

Eating & Drinking

Kert (☎ 483 199; Dózsa György tér 6; mains 1000-2000Ft) This garden inn, set back in a small park, has an excellent array of Hungarian dishes to whet most appetites and an atmosphere to get most tongues wagging.

Erzsébet Café (☎ 483 106; Fő utca 3; coffee 200Ft) Recently given a complete overhaul, Erzsébet is now the town's finest café, serving inviting cakes and coffee in smart surroundings.

Pompeii (☎ 470 160; Kis Tisza utca 6; mains 1000Ft) Hidden behind drooping willow trees in a

renovated old house, this restaurant serves decent pizza and South Slav specialities.

Golden Horse Irish Pub (Gróf Andrássy Gyula utca 17/a) This is about the only decent place in town for a drink, and is east of the centre on the way to the Öregvár.

Entertainment

Kossuth Cultural Centre (☎ 483 414; Szentháromság tér 8; ☼ noon-8pm Mon-Fri) Information on Csongrád's cultural activities, along with Internet access (100Ft per hour), is available here.

Getting There & Away

From Csongrád buses run to Békéscsaba (1090Ft, two hours, 90km, three daily), Budapest (1690Ft, 2½ hours, 140km, eight daily), Hódmezővásárhely (544Ft, one hour, 40km, nine daily) and Kecskemét (665Ft, one hour, 55km, 13 daily). The 15 daily buses to Szeged (725Ft, 1½ hours, 60km) go via Ópusztaszer.

Csongrád is on the 40km secondary train line linking Szentes (182Ft, 15 minutes, 15km) to the east with Kiskunfélegyháza (264Ft, 35 minutes, 25km) to the west. You can't get very far from Szentes but Kiskunfélegyháza is a stop on the Budapest–Szeged express-train line.

BÉKÉSCSABA

☎ 66 / pop 66,500

Békéscsaba is a sprightly town of leafy avenues and church spires, and a handful of sights. Mention the place to most

Hungarians however, and they usually think of two very disparate things: fatty sausage and bloody riots. *Csabai*, a sausage not dissimilar to Portuguese *chorizo*, is manufactured here, and Békéscsaba was the centre of the Vihar Sarok, the 'Stormy Corner' of the Great Plain, where violent riots broke out among day labourers and harvesters in 1890.

History

Békéscsaba was an important fortified settlement as early as the 14th century, but it was razed and its population scattered under Turkish rule. Early in the 18th century, a Habsburg emissary named János György Harruckern invited Rhinelanders and Slovaks to resettle the area, and it soon became a Lutheran stronghold.

Development began to reach Békéscsaba in the 19th century when the railway passed through the city (1858) and by 1950, Békéscsaba had surpassed nearby Gyula in importance and the county seat was moved here – something for which Gyula has yet to forgive her sister city.

Orientation

Békéscsaba's train and bus stations stand side by side at the southwestern end of Andrássy út, the main drag. A long stretch of this street, from Petőfi utca and Jókai utca to Szent István tér, is a pedestrian walkway, and just beyond it lies the Élővíz-csatorna, the 'Living Water Canal' that links Békéscsaba with Békés to the north, Gyula to the east, and the Körös River. To the east of the canal lies the Parkerdő, the city's cool and leafy playground.

Information

Main post office (Irány utca)
OTP bank (Szent István tér 3; Andrássy út 4)
Tourinform (☎ 441 261; bekescsaba@tourinform.hu; Szent István tér 9; ♥ 9am-5pm Mon-Fri, 9am-2pm Sat) Happy to supply truckloads of information on the town and county.
www.bekescsaba.hu The city's website.

Sights & Activities

The splendid **town hall** (városháza; Szent István tér 7) on the main street has a façade (1873) designed by the overworked Budapest architect Miklós Ybl. Walk east on József Attila utca to the canal and Árpád sor, which

is lined with busts of Hungarian literary, artistic and musical greats and some wonderful late-19th-century mansions. Within sight is the **István Mill** (István Malom; Gőzmalom tér), a grey-brick colossus from the early 20th century. It closed in 2005, with the unfortunate loss of hundreds of jobs.

Across the canal from the mill is the **Mihály Munkácsy Museum** (☎ 323 377; Széchenyi utca 9; adult/child 300/150Ft; ♥ 10am-6pm Tue-Sun Apr-Sep, 10am-4pm Tue-Sun Oct-Mar), which has exhibits devoted to the wildlife and ecology of the Great Plain, as well as to the folk culture of the region. Essentially, though, it's a temple to the painter Munkácsy (1844–1900). Some may find his depictions of the Great Plain and its denizens a little sugar-coated, but as a chronicler of that place and time (real or imagined) he is unsurpassed in Hungarian fine art. An ethnographic exhibit traces the history of the Romanian, Slovak, German and Hungarian ethnic groups of the region.

The Lutheran **Great Church** (Nagytemplom; Kossuth tér; admission free), completed in 1824, and the 18th-century **Small Church** (Kistemplom; Kossuth tér; admission free), facing each other across Kossuth tér, attest to the city's deeply rooted Protestantism. The baroque **Greek Orthodox church** (Bartók Béla utca 51-53; admission free), dating from 1838, could easily be mistaken for yet another Lutheran church from the outside.

Present or future farmers would no doubt be interested in the **Grain Museum** (Gabonamúzeum; ☎ 441 026; Gyulai út 65; adult/child 150/80Ft; ♥ 10am-5pm Tue-Sun May-Sep), housed in several old thatched barns and crammed with traditional tools and implements. The bladeless 19th-century windmill nearby is one of the best examples surviving in Hungary.

The **Slovakian Village House** (Szlovák tájház; ☎ 327 038; Garay utca 21; adult/child 100/50Ft; ♥ 10am-noon & 2-6pm Tue-Sun Apr-Sep, 10am-noon & 2-4pm Thu-Sun Oct-Mar), is a wonderful Slovakian farmhouse built in 1865 and full of folk furniture and ornamentation. A lot of other typical peasant houses can be found in the neighbourhood, especially on Szigetvári utca and Sarkantyú utca.

The **Árpád thermal baths** (☎ 549 800; Árpád sor 2; adult/child 900/600Ft; ♥ 6am-8pm Nov-Sep) has both indoor and outdoor pools but not a whole lot of fun slides for kids.

BÉKÉSCSABA

INFORMATION
Main Post Office...............1 C3
OTP Bank...........................2 C3
OTP Bank...........................3 C2
Tourinform.........................4 C2

SIGHTS & ACTIVITIES
Árpád Thermal Baths........5 D3
Great Church......................6 C2
Greek Orthodox Church....7 B3
István Mill...........................8 D2
Mihály Munkácsy Museum.9 C2
Peasant Houses.................10 B1
Peasant Houses.................11 B2
Slovakian Village House...12 C1
Small Church.....................13 C2
Town Hall..........................14 C2

SLEEPING
Déak Ferenc College.........15 A4
Fiume.................................16 C2

EATING
Halászcsárda.....................17 D3
Holsten..............................18 C2
Market...............................19 B3
Márvány.............................20 B3
Speedy Pizzeria.................21 C2

DRINKING
Bacchus.............................22 C3

ENTERTAINMENT
Club Narancs....................23 C2
County Cultural Centre....24 C2
Jókai Theatre....................25 C2

TRANSPORT
Bus Station.......................26 A4

Sleeping

Garzon Fenyves (☎ 457 377; www.fenyveshotel
.hu; s/d 8300/10,300Ft; P 🐾) This retreat-like
hotel occupies a cool, leafy oasis in the

AUTHOR'S CHOICE

Fiume (☎ 443 243; Szent István tér 2; s/d
8750/11,750Ft; P) Fiume bears the old
name of the Adriatic port of Rijeka (now in
Croatia) and is Békéscsaba's premier hotel
and one of the nicest in Hungary. Rooms
are bedecked in period furniture and range
from tiny to spacious, and corridors seem to
go on forever, much like the Overlook in *The
Shining*. But don't let that put you off.

Ifjúsági-tábor and has huge, modern rooms
and friendly staff.

Déak Ferenc College (☎ 325 620; e-deak@freeweb
.hu; Andrássy út 56; dm 1100Ft, s/d 1200/2400Ft; ☼ Jul-
Aug; P) This college accommodation is
handy to both the bus and train stations and
has simple but comfy rooms with shared
facilities.

Eating & Drinking

Fiume (mains around 1200Ft) At the hotel of the
same name, this fine diner has a menu
weighed down with heavy Hungarian meat
dishes; choose from tables under chandeliers or seating with tree-shade.

Halászcsárda (☎ 446 625; Árpád sor 1; mains 1500-
2000Ft) Halászcsárda is the place of choice

for those in the mood for fish. Many of its tables overlook the canal.

Holsten (☎ 441 827; Irányi utca 12; mains 850Ft) This basic eatery has simple Hungarian fare and a lively atmosphere that fills tables quickly on most nights of the week.

Márvány (Andrássy út 21; ice cream from 60Ft; ☒ to 9pm) Those with a sweet tooth can satisfy their urges at this popular café, with outside seating on a pretty square southeast of the main street.

Bacchus (Andrássy út 10; ☒ 7am-10pm) Bacchus is one of the few places on pedestrian Andrássy út where you can procure a late night drink *and* sit outside.

For those looking for a quick bite to eat, Békéscsaba's big food **market** (Szabó Dezső utca; ☒ Wed & Sat) has a few food stalls and **Speedy Pizzeria** (Justh Gyula utca; pizzas 400-1000Ft) churns out tasty morsels.

Entertainment

Club Narancs (☎ 453 032; Szent István tér 3; ☒ 4.30-10pm Mon-Wed, 4.30pm-4am Thu-Sat) A true student haunt with minimal décor, cheap drinks, loud music and a raucous vibe, Narancs is the place to go for a bit of a booze-up. Thursday thru Saturday sees various themed clubbing events.

The **Jókai Theatre** (☎ 441 527; Andrássy út 1), the Great Church and the Town Hall are the main cultural venues in Békéscsaba. Ask at Tourinform or the **County Cultural Centre** (☎ 527 660; Luther utca 6) for dates and times. Check the listings in *Békési Est*, a biweekly entertainment guide distributed free.

Getting There & Away

Buses leave for Gyula (241Ft, 30 minutes, 15km) every half-hour and for Szarvas (605Ft, one hour, 45km) once an hour. Twelve buses daily go to Szeged (1150Ft, two hours, 95km) and two to Budapest (2660Ft, four hours, 210km). Other destinations include Kecskemét (1820Ft, three hours, 145km, five daily) and Vésztő (484Ft, 1¼ hours, 35km, five to nine daily – direct, via Gyula or via Mezőberény).

Up to 10 daily trains – most of them expresses – link Békéscsaba with Szolnok (1004Ft, 1½ hours, 95km) and Budapest's Keleti station (2030Ft, 2½ hours, 195km). Trains are frequent (up to 17 daily) to Gyula (182Ft, 15 minutes, 15km), and six continue on to Vésztő (658Ft, 1½ hours, 65km, a

change at Kötegyán may be required). Up to 11 trains daily depart from Békéscsaba for Szeged (1004Ft, two hours, 95km).

Getting Around

From the bus and train stations you can reach Szent István tér on foot via Andrássy út in about 20 minutes or wait for bus 5 to Szabadság tér. Bus 9 passes through the same square on its way past the stadium and Grain Museum. Board Bus 7 for the college, Fényves hotel and Parkerdő.

You can also order a **taxi** (☎ 444 444).

VÉSZTŐ

☎ 66 / pop 7900

The **Vésztő-Mágor National Historical Monument** (☎ 477 148; adult/child 300/100Ft; ☒ 9am-6pm May-Sep; 10am-4pm Apr & Oct), 4km northwest of Vésztő, contains two burial mounds of a type found throughout Hungary (see, for example, p128) and as far east as Korea. Such mounds are not all that rare on the Great Plain, but these are particularly rich in archaeological finds. The first is a veritable layer cake of cult and everyday objects, shrines and graves dating from the 4th century BC onward. The second contains the 10th-century **Csolt monastery** and church which is partially restored, but a lot of imagination is required to piece it all together. It is in the centre of the patchwork 520-sq-km **Körös-Maros National Park**, which is very rich in aquatic vegetation and wildlife. For information contact the **park visitors centre** (☎ 313 855; Anna-liget 1, Szarvas; adult/child 300/200Ft; ☒ 9am-5pm Tue-Sun Apr-Oct).

The national monument is 4km from Vésztő and is connected by four buses Monday to Saturday; the last leaves at 7.39pm. At least five daily buses run between Vésztő and Gyula (484Ft, 1¼ hours, 35km) and Békéscsaba (484Ft, 1¼ hours, 35km). Up to six daily trains leave Békéscsaba for Vésztő (658Ft, 1½ hours, 65km; a change at Kötegyán may be required) by way of Gyula (430Ft, 1¼ hours, 50km).

SZARVAS

☎ 66 / pop 18,000

Szarvas is a pretty green town 45km northwest of Békéscsaba on a backwater of the Körös River (Holt-Körös). Its biggest drawcard is the arboretum, easily the best in Hungary, but the best thing to ever happen to Szarvas was the arrival of Sámuel Tessedik, a Lutheran minister and pioneering scientist who established one of Europe's first agricultural institutes here in 1770.

Orientation

Szabadság út, the main street, bisects the town and leads westward to the Holt-Körös and arboretum. On either side of Szabadság út are dozens of small squares organised in chessboard-like fashion by Tessedik, full of flower gardens and even small orchards.

The train station is in the eastern part of town at the end of Vasút utca, while the bus station (Szabadság út) is in the centre at the corner of Bocskai István utca.

Information

K&H bank (Szabadság út)
Main post office (Szabadság út 9)
Panorama (☎ 312 760; Kossuth tér 3/2; per hour 180Ft) In the pizzeria; has Internet access.
Tourinform (☎ 311 140; szarvas@tourinform.hu; Kossuth tér 3; ⏲ 9am-6pm Mon-Fri, 9am-1pm Sat mid-Jun–mid-Aug, 9am-5pm Mon-Fri May–mid-Jun, 9am-4pm Mon-Fri Sep-Apr) In the cultural centre.

Sights & Activities

The **Szarvas Arboretum** (☎ 312 344; adult/child 500/300Ft; ⏲ 8am-6pm mid-Mar–mid-Nov, 8am-3pm mid-Nov–mid-Mar), with some 30,000 individual plants not native to the Great Plain, is Hungary's finest. On 82 hectares it contains around 1600 species of rare trees, bushes and grasses, including mammoth pines, ginkgo

trees, swamp cedars, Spanish pines and pampas grass. The arboretum is about 2km northwest of the centre across the Holt-Körös.

The **Sámuel Tessedik Museum** (☎ 216 608; Vajda Péter utca 1; adult/child 200/100Ft; ⏲ 10am-6pm Tue-Sun Apr-Oct, 10am-4pm Tue-Sun Nov-Mar) has some interesting Neolithic exhibits from the goddess-worshipping Körös culture taken from burial mounds on the Great Plain, and while the section devoted to Tessedik is intriguing, it's only in Hungarian. The **birthplace of Endre Bajcsy-Zsilinszky** (Vajda Péter utca), the resistance leader murdered by Hungarian fascists in 1944, is on the same street four blocks to the north.

The neoclassical **Bolza Mansion** (Bolza-kastély; Szabadság út 2), facing the Holt-Körös, was built in 1819 as the homestead of a land-owning family of that name who also founded the arboretum. Today the mansion is part of the Tessedik Agricultural College but the grounds can be visited. Splitting Holt-Körös' current in two in front of the mansion is the **Millennium Monument**, a statue of St Stephen's Crown flanked by two angels on top of a pole.

Just north of Tourinform in the town's dusty back alleys is Hungary's best-preserved horse-driven **dry mill** (szárazmalom; ☎ 216 609; Ady Endre utca 1; adult/child 300/150Ft; ⏲ 1-5pm Tue-Sun Apr-Oct), built in the early 19th century, and a **Slovakian Village House** (Szlovák tájház; ☎ 312 492; Hoffmann utca 1; adult/child 200/100Ft; ⏲ 1-5pm Tue-Sun Apr-Oct) filled with hand-woven textiles and articles from everyday life.

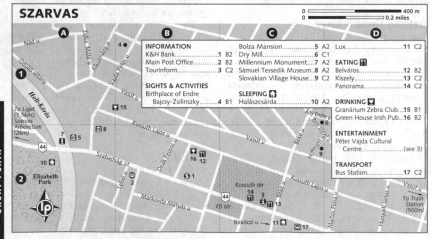

SZARVAS			
	0 ————— 400 m		
	0 ————— 0.2 miles		
INFORMATION	Bolza Mansion..............5 A2	Lux...............11 C2	
K&H Bank..................1 B2	Dry Mill.......................6 C1		
Main Post Office............2 B2	Millennium Monument.....7 A2	**EATING** 🍴	
Tourinform..................3 C2	Sámuel Tessedik Museum..8 A2	Belváros..............12 B2	
	Slovakian Village House....9 C2	Kiszely...............13 C2	
SIGHTS & ACTIVITIES		Panorama..............14 C2	
Birthplace of Endre	**SLEEPING** 🛏		
Bajcsy-Zsilinszky.........4 B1	Halászcsárda...............10 A2	**DRINKING** 🍸	
		Gránárium Zebra Club...15 B1	
		Green House Irish Pub...16 B2	
		ENTERTAINMENT	
		Péter Vajda Cultural	
		Centre....................(see 3)	
		TRANSPORT	
		Bus Station...............17 C2	

Sleeping

Lux (☎ 313 417; lux@szarvas.hu; Szabadság út 35; r from 8500Ft; P ☒) Lux is only a stone's throw from the bus station and has large rooms with dated furniture, a restaurant and fitness centre, sauna and solarium.

Halászcsárda (☎ 311 164; l ker 6; r 8500Ft; P ☒) This more rustic option has small attic rooms and is located on the edge of Elizabeth Park, creating a secluded, retreat feel.

Liget (☎ 311 954; www.ligetpanzio.hu; camp sites per adult/child/tent 800/600/650Ft, 4-person bungalows 10,500, r from 9900Ft; P ☒) This all-in-one accommodation option is a family-orientated place, with a wellness centre, pool and lake swimming. Camping, bungalows and modern *en-suite* rooms are available.

Eating & Drinking

Halászcsárda (mains 1000-2000Ft) In the *pension* of the same name is this fish restaurant, with a relaxed atmosphere and tables on a terrace overlooking the river.

Kiszely (cnr Szabadság út & Béke utca; ice cream from 80Ft; ⏰ 9am-9pm) Kiszely is a cute *cukrászda*, small in size but big on ice cream and cake selections.

Green House Irish Pub (Kossuth Lajos utca 25) Next to Belváros is this large pub that's far more green than Irish, and has the potential to get rather rowdy on weekends.

For a quick, cheap pizza, try **Panoráma** (☎ 312 760; Kossuth tér 3/2; pizzas from 500Ft), next to Tourinform, which has the advantage of outdoor seating, or **Belváros** (☎ 312 525; Kossuth Lajos utca 23; pizzas 500-1000Ft), an appealing option on a quiet back street.

Entertainment

Péter Vajda Cultural Centre (☎ 311 181, Kossuth tér 3) This centre should have updates on what might be on in Szarvas.

Granárium Zebra Club (☎ 311 946; Kossuth Lajos utca 2) This is the town's mainstay for loud live acts; otherwise, pick up a free copy of biweekly *Békési Est* for more information.

Getting There & Away

Szarvas can be reached by bus from Békéscsaba (605Ft, one hour, 45km, at least hourly), Debrecen (1930Ft, three to four hours, 155km, two daily), Gyula (786Ft, 1¾ hours, 65km, one daily), Kecskemét (968Ft, 1¾ hours, 80km, six daily) and Szeged (907Ft, two hours, 75km, six daily).

Szarvas is on the train line linking Mezőhegyes and Orosháza with Mezőtúr and has services six times daily. From Békéscsaba (774Ft, 1½ to two hours, 75km), it's faster to take an express train to Mezőtúr and change for Szarvas there.

GYULA
☎ 66 / pop 32,000

A town of spas with the last remaining medieval brick castle on the Great Plain, Gyula is a wonderful place to recharge your batteries before crossing into Romania, just 4km to the east. It also has a couple of rewarding museums worth poking around in while your skin de-prunes.

History

Gyula refused to allow the Arad-bound railway to cross through the town in 1858 – a development welcomed by Békéscsaba, 20km to the west. As a result, Gyula was stuck at the end of a spur and developed at a much slower pace. In 1950 the county seat was moved from here (after 500 years, Gyulans like to point out) to its sister city, Békéscsaba. Gyula is still seething and a strong rivalry persists between the two: from who should be allocated more county money, to whose football team and sausage is better.

Orientation

Gyula is actually two towns: the commercial centre on Városház utca to the west and the Várfürdő (Castle Bath) in a big park to the east. The areas are within walking distance of each other. The Élővíz Canal runs east–west through the centre of Gyula, from a branch of the Körös River to Békéscsaba and beyond.

Gyula's bus station (Vásárhelyi Pál utca) is south of Kossuth Lajos tér. Walk north through the park to the square and over the canal bridge to reach the town centre. The train station is at the northern end of Béke sugárút.

Information

Erste bank (Városház utca) Has ATM.
Post office (Eszperantó tér) South of the canal.
Tourinform (☎ 561 681; bekes-m@tourinform.hu; Kossuth Lajos utca 7; ⏰ 9am-7pm Mon-Fri, 9am-7pm Sat & Sun mid-Jun–mid-Sep, 9am-5pm Mon-Fri mid-Sep–mid-Jun) Very helpful office located in a gallery.
www.gyula.hu The town's website, in Hungarian and German.

Sights

Gothic **Gyula Castle** (☎ 464 117; Várfürdő utca 1; adult/child 800/400Ft; ☺ 9am-7pm mid-Jun–Aug, 9am-5pm Tue-Sun Sep–mid-Jun), overlooking a picturesque moat near the Castle Baths, was originally built in the mid-15th century but has been expanded and renovated many times over the centuries, most recently in May 2004. Its 24 rooms now showcase the castle's history, focusing in particular on its medieval days when the Ottoman Turks were in town, and the weapons used to finally fend them off. Like any self-respecting castle, there's a thick wall to wander along, a tower to climb and a dungeon to explore, but the latter is only open during breaks in Castle Theatre performances. Close by is the **Ferenc Erkel Museum** (☎ 361 236; Kossuth Lajos utca 17; adult/child 400/200Ft; ☺ 1-5pm Tue, 9am-5pm Wed-Sat, 9am-1pm Sun). It has a **Dürer Room** devoted to archaeological finds – pottery, jewellery and weapons – from the region.

The **György Kohán Museum** (☎ 361 795; Béke sugárút 35; adult/child 400/200Ft; ☺ 1-5pm Tue, 9am-5pm Wed-Sat, 9am-1pm Sun), in quiet Göndöcs-Népkert, is Gyula's most important art

museum, with more than 3000 paintings and graphics bequeathed to the city by the artist upon his death in 1966. The large canvases of horses and women in dark blues and greens, and the relentless summer sun of the Great Plain, are quite striking and well worth a look.

The baroque **Inner City Church** (Belvárosi templom; Harruckern tér 1; admission free; ☺ 10am-6pm), from 1777, has interesting contemporary ceiling frescoes highlighting events in Hungarian and world history – including an astronaut in space! The Zopf **Romanian Orthodox church** (Gróza Park; admission free), from 1812, has a beautiful iconostasis (you can try and get the key from the house just south of the church entrance), but for contemporary icons at their kitschy best, no place compares with the **Mary Museum** (Apor tér 11; adult/child 400/200Ft; ☺ 9am-noon & 12.30-3pm Tue-Sat, 9am-noon Sun Mar-Nov, 9am-noon Tue-Sun Dec-Feb). You've never seen the Virgin in so many guises. On the same square is the **Ferenc Erkel House** (☎ 463 552; Apor tér 7; adult/child 400/200Ft; ☺ 1-5pm Tue, 9am-5pm Wed-Sat, 9am-1pm Sun), birthplace of the man who composed

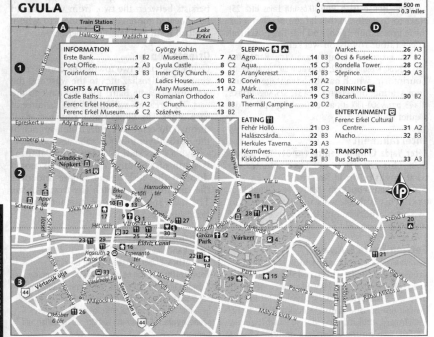

GYULA

0 — 500 m
0 — 0.3 miles

INFORMATION
Erste Bank...............................1 B2
Post Office..............................2 A3
Tourinform..............................3 B3

SIGHTS & ACTIVITIES
Castle Baths............................4 C3
Ferenc Erkel House...............5 A2
Ferenc Erkel Museum.........6 C2

György Kohán
Museum..................................7 A2
Gyula Castle...........................8 C2
Inner City Church................9 B2
Ladics House.......................10 B2
Mary Museum......................11 A2
Romanian Orthodox
Church................................12 B3
Százéves..............................13 B2

SLEEPING
Agro..14 B3
Aqua......................................15 C3
Aranykereszt........................16 B3
Corvin...................................17 A2
Márk......................................18 C2
Park.......................................19 C3
Thermál Camping...............20 D2

EATING
Fehér Holló...........................21 D3
Halászcsárda........................22 B3
Herkules Taverna................23 A3
Kézműves..............................24 B2
Kisködmön............................25 B3

Market...................................26 A3
Öcsi & Fusek.........................27 B2
Rondella Tower...................28 C2
Sörpince................................29 A3

DRINKING
Bacardi..................................30 B2

ENTERTAINMENT
Ferenc Erkel Cultural
Centre.................................31 A2
Macho...................................32 B3

TRANSPORT
Bus Station...........................33 A3

operas and the music for the Hungarian national anthem. The house contains memorabilia about his life and music.

An interesting – and, for Hungary, very unusual – museum is **Ladics House** (☎ 463 940; Jókai Mór utca 4; adult/child 400/200Ft; ☺ 1-5pm Tue, 9am-5pm Wed-Sat, 9am-1pm Sun), the perfectly preserved and beautifully furnished mid-19th century residence of a prosperous bourgeois family. Next door, the **Százéves** (☎ 362 045; Erkel tér 1; ☺ 10am-8pm) cake shop and museum is a visual and culinary delight. Established around 1840 (no doubt Mrs Ladics bought her *petits-fours* here), the Regency-blue interior is filled with Biedermeier furniture and mirrors in gilt frames. It is one of the most beautiful *cukrászdák* in Hungary.

Activities

The **Castle Baths** (Várfürdő; Várkert utca 2; adult/child mid-Jun–Aug 1300/1050Ft, Sep–mid-Jun 950/800Ft; ☺ indoor pools 8am-6pm, outdoor pools 8am-8pm mid-Jun–Aug) are in the 30-hectare Castle Garden (Várkert) east of the city centre and include 19 pools both indoors and out and a thoroughly modern wellness complex of the highest standards.

Festivals & Events

The biggest event of the year is the **Gyula Theatre Festival**, with performances in the castle courtyard from July to mid-August. There's also an **All-Hungarian Folkdance Festival** around the 20th August.

Sleeping

BUDGET

There is a plethora of private rooms (from 2500Ft) and *pensions* south of Part utca; Tourinform can provide you with a list for both, and also for student-dorm accommodation over the summer months. All can be found on the town's website.

Márk (☎ 463 380; Vár utca 5; 2-person camp sites 2600Ft; ☺ year-round) Of Gyula's camping grounds, this is the friendliest, most central and charming, but it's very small and only for caravans and tents.

Thermál Camping (☎ 463 704; www.gyulacamping.hu; Szélső utca 16; camp sites per adult/child/tent from €3/2/2.50, s/d €17/24; ℗) Some 700m from the town's action, Thermál Camping is a bit out of the way but it does have good camp facilities, such as a restaurant, café and kitchens.

MIDRANGE

There are plenty of hotels in or around the Várfürdő, most of them sprawling, modern affairs with everything you could possibly need. Room rates vary widely depending on the season, but generally the most expensive times are from June to September and over the Christmas and New Year holidays.

Aranykereszt (☎ 463 194; www.hotels.hu/arany kereszt; Eszperantó tér 2; s/d from 5000/7000Ft; ℗) Away from Várfürdő but alongside the canal, this hotel has simple rooms with old-fashioned furniture but overall has the most charm of any in Gyula. Rooms overlooking the canal exude a rustic yet retreat-like feel.

Aqua (☎ 463 146; aqua-hotel@axelero.hu; Part utca 7/c; s/d from €24/36; ℗ ☻) Recently renovated rooms at the Aqua are modern and spacious, and staff are exceedingly friendly. Bicycles are available for guest use and pick-ups from the bus and train stations can be arranged.

Corvin (☎ 362 044; www.corvin-hotel.hu; Jókai utca 9-11; s/d from €42/51; ℗ ☻) Located in the town centre away from any water, Corvin is the odd hotel out in Gyula. Rooms are quite plush, with unusual window designs, an array of pastel shades and solid wooden floors.

Also recommended:

Park (☎ 463 711; parkgyula@civishotels.hu; Part utca 15; s/d from 6000/9500Ft; ℗ ☻) Alpine-style hotel on the edge of the baths.

Agro (☎ 463 522; www.hotels.hu/agrogyula; Part utca 5; s/d from €31/44; ℗) Adequate rooms and a bunch of wellness facilities.

Eating & Drinking

Kisködmön (☎ 463 934; Városház utca 15; mains 1200-2000Ft) Hidden away down an uninviting alley is this wonderful restaurant, with décor that looks as though it belongs in the early 1800s. Food is traditionally prepared, with organic products as much as possible.

Herkules Taverna (☎ 30-430 7730; Bodoky utca; mains 1000-1200Ft) This typically blue-and-white Greek restaurant has a secluded spot with tables overlooking the canal.

Halászcsárda (☎ 466 303; Part utca 3; mains 900-1500Ft) Facing the canal, this place offers the usual fishy dishes in pleasant surroundings and is only a short walk from most hotels and the centre.

Sörpince (☎ 362 382; Kossuth tér 2; mains 1000Ft) Sörpince is a dark drinker's den with a surprisingly good menu of Hungarian dishes (with a few veggie options thrown in for fun) and comes locally recommended.

Öcsi & Fusek (☎ 468 495; Kossuth Lajos utca 6; mains 800-1600Ft) This is not only popular for its great back courtyard but also for its hearty lunch-time set menu (6000Ft). It's also fashionable with workers needing a drink after work.

Fehér Holló (☎ 457 835; Tiborc utca 49; mains 800-1500Ft) This place has a nice quiet spot near the canal and is a good choice for *csárda*-style Hungarian meals, especially if you're staying at Thermál Camping.

Bacardi (Kossuth Lajos utca 3; ☾ 10am-midnight Sun-Thu, 10am-3am Fri, 10am-4am Sat) A magnet for Gyula's 20- to 30-somethings, who make the most of a night out on the town.

For coffee and cake, Gyula does itself proud; take your pick from the squat 16th-century Rondella tower with a delightful terrace in summer near the castle, the original caféhouse **Százéves** (☎ 362 045; Erkel tér 1) or **Kézműves** (Városház utca 21; ice cream from 85Ft; ☾ 7am-10pm Mon-Fri, 10am-10pm Sat & Sun), a modern establishment that sates many locals of their ice-cream cravings.

Gyula's main **market** (Október 6 tér) for fruit, vegetables and other produce is southwest of the bus station.

Entertainment

Ferenc Erkel Cultural Centre (☎ 463 806; Béke sugárút 35) This centre in Göndöcs-Népkert has staff that can tell you what cultural events are on offer in Gyula. Organ concerts are sometimes held at the Inner City Church, especially around Christmas.

Macho (Városház utca 1; ☾ to 4am Sun-Thu, to 6am Fri & Sat) This is the town's badly named main club; check the free biweekly *Békési Est* for more information on bars in Gyula.

Getting There & Away

With Gyula lying on an unimportant rail spur, buses are the preferred mode of transport. There are dozens each day departing for Békéscsaba (241Ft, 30 minutes, 15km) and three go to Debrecen (1690Ft, three hours, 130km). Other destinations include Budapest (2780Ft, four to six hours, 230km, two daily), Kecskemét (1820Ft, 3¼ hours, 145km, two daily), Szeged (1820Ft, 3½ hours, 145km, seven daily), and Vésztő (484Ft, 1¼ hours, 35km, three daily).

Some 17 trains daily run west on line 128, Gyula's link to the Békéscsaba–Szolnok–Budapest train line. Travelling most on this poky line will get you to Vésztő (430Ft, 1¼ hours, 50km), Szeghalom and eventually to Püspökladány, where you can change trains for Debrecen (1624Ft, 3½ hours, 150km).

Southern Transdanubia

With its mild climate, gently undulating hills, minimal industry and rural ambience, Southern Transdanubia is a region of calm, a place to enjoy life at a slow, almost Mediterranean, pace. Aside from a few centres, it's only marginally touched by tourism, and could be just the answer for those looking to get off the beaten track in a country that's been crisscrossed by travellers since time immemorial.

The region is thickly settled with villages, and agriculture is still the mainstay of most people's lives: fruit orchards dot the landscape in the north, almond trees surround Pécs in its heart and vineyards stretch for miles around Szekszárd and Villány-Siklós in its easterly reaches. Late summer/early autumn, when harvesting is in full swing, is a gorgeous time of year in these parts.

Easily the highlight of the region – and arguably all of provincial Hungary – is Pécs, Southern Transdanubia's capital city. Art museums and theatres abound, and history is also alive and well within its borders. Both the Romans and Turks thought much of the place, leaving their mark for all to gape at; more Roman tombs than you can shake an archaeologist's shovel at have been uncovered near (or under) the city's Basilica, and a handful of Turkish monuments have survived in a country where almost all were put to the torch.

While Pécs steals the limelight, a number of other towns are worth visiting. Imposing castles dominate Siklós and Szigetvár, and in Harkány you can take advantage of curative thermal waters (which we know is a hard task). And any excursion to the south would be incomplete without a glass of some of the country's best wines from Szekszárd and Villány.

HIGHLIGHTS

- Wandering the picturesque streets from one impressive sight to the next in **Pécs** (p294)

- Sampling and – of course – buying the big, bold reds of **Villány** (p292) and **Szekszárd** (p280)

- Exploring the rural **Ormánság region** (p293), Southern Transdanubia's quiet 'back corner'

- Riding the **narrow-gauge train** (p284) through the Gemenc Forest in the Sárköz region

- Taking a dip in the cure-all **thermal baths** (p291) at Harkány, especially in winter

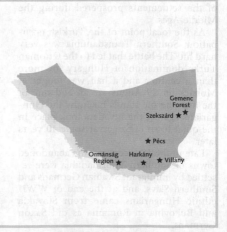

Gemenc Forest
Szekszárd ★ ★
★ Pécs
Ormánság   Harkány
Region ★   ★   ★ Villány

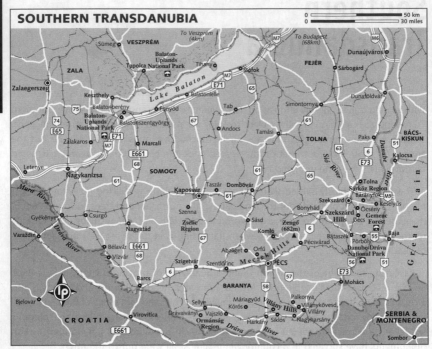

SOUTHERN TRANSDANUBIA

History

Southern Transdanubia was settled by the Celts and then by the Romans, who established important towns at Alisca (Szekszárd) and Sophianae (Pécs) and introduced grape-growing. The north–south trade route passed through here and many of the settlements prospered during the Middle Ages.

As the focal point of the Turkish occupation, Southern Transdanubia was very hard hit. The battle that led to the Ottoman Turks domination of Hungary for more than a century and a half was fought at Mohács on 29 August 1526, and one of the most heroic stands taken by the Hungarians against the invaders took place in the quiet town of Szigetvár some 40 years later.

Late in the 17th century, the abandoned towns of Southern Transdanubia were resettled by immigrant Swabian Germans and Southern Slavs, and at the end of WWII ethnic Hungarians came from Slovakia and Bukovina in Romania as did Saxon Germans.

SZEKSZÁRD
☎ 74 / pop 36,200

The more-than-attractive town of Szekszárd lies south of the Sió River, which links Lake Balaton with the Danube River, among seven of the Szekszárd Hills. It is the capital of Tolna County and the centre of the Sárköz folk region, but more than anything else Szekszárd is the gateway to Southern Transdanubia. In fact, you can see the Sárköz region start in the town's main square (Garay tér), where the Great Plain, having crossed the Danube, rises slowly, transforming into the Szekszárd Hills.

History

Szekszárd was a Celtic and later a Roman settlement called Alisca. The sixth Hungarian king, Béla I, conferred royal status on the town and founded an important Benedictine abbey here in 1061.

The Turkish occupation decimated Szekszárd; however, the area was repopulated late in the 17th century by Swabian Germans, and the cultivation of wheat and viticulture in the 18th century revitalised the economy.

Orientation

The bus and train stations are opposite one another on Pollack Mihály utca. From here, follow pedestrian Bajcsy-Zsilinszky utca west through the park to the town centre. Garay tér ascends to the old castle district, today's Béla tér. Munkácsy Mihály utca runs southwest from Béla tér to Kálvária utca and Calvary Hill.

Information

Main post office (Széchenyi utca 11-13)
OTP bank (Szent István tér 5-7) With ATM.
Tourinform (☎ 511 263; szekszard@tourinform.hu; Garay tér 18; ☼ 9am-5pm Mon-Fri, 9am-5pm Sat & Sun Jun-Aug; 9am-5pm Mon-Fri Sep-May) The straight-faced but helpful staff have loads of information on the town and Tolna County.

Sights

All museums and exhibitions cost 200/100Ft per adult/child and are free on Saturdays.

You can get a good idea of Szekszárd by following Kálvária utca from just south of the catholic church and up the grassy steps to **Kálvária-hegy** (Calvary Hill; 205m). The hill's name recalls the Crucifixion, and there is an 18th-century chapel erected here by grief-stricken parents who lost their child (still remembered thanks to a famous poem by Mihály Babits, a native son of Szekszárd). The Danube and the Great Plain are visible to the east, the Sárköz region beyond the hills to the south and the Szekszárd Hills to the west; on a clear day, you can just see Hungary's sole nuclear power station at Paks, 30km to the north.

The little village – the so-called Upper Town (Felsőváros) – in the valley to the northwest is full of vineyards and private cellars. Walk along Bartina utca, which becomes Remete utca, to **Remete Chapel** (Remete kápolna; 1778), an important pilgrimage site; return via Bocskai utca to the north of Szekszárd Stream.

NOTABLE BUILDINGS

The neoclassical **county hall** (vármegyeháza; ☎ 419 667; Béla tér 1; ☼ 9am-5pm Tue-Sun Apr-Sep, 9am-3pm Tue-Sun Oct-Mar), designed by Mihály Pollack in 1828, sits on the site of Béla's abbey and an earlier Christian chapel; you can see the excavated foundations in the central courtyard. On the upper floor of the building, there is the **Franz Liszt Exhibition** and across the hall the **Eszter Mattioni Gallery**, whose works in striking mosaics of marble, glass and mother-of-pearl invoke peasant themes with a twist. The square's yellow baroque **Inner City Catholic Church** (Belvárosi templom; 1805), is the largest single-nave church in Hungary. Franz Liszt performed several times at the pink neo-Gothic **Augusz House** (Széchenyi utca 36-40); today it houses a music school.

MUSEUMS

Szekszárd produced two of Hungary's most celebrated poets: Mihály Babits (1883–1941) and the lesser-known János Garay (1812–53). The **Mihály Babits' Birthplace** (szülőháza; ☎ 312 154; Babits Mihály utca 13; ☼ 9am-5pm Tue-Sun Apr-Sep, 9am-3pm Tue-Sat Oct-Mar) has been turned into a memorial museum. Although the poet's avant-garde, deeply philosophical verse may be obscure, even in Hungarian, it's a good place to see how a middle-class family lived in 19th-century provincial Hungary.

The **Mór Wosinszky Museum** (☎ 316 222; Szent István tér 26; ☼ 10am-6pm Tue-Sun Apr-Sep, 10am-4pm Tue-Sun Oct-Mar) was purpose-built in 1895. It is now named after a local priest and archaeologist who discovered the remains of a Neo-lithic culture in the town of Lengyel to the northwest. The finds, objects left by various peoples who passed through the Danube Basin ahead of the Magyars, are among the best anywhere (don't miss the fine Celtic and Avar jewellery), as is the large folk collection of Serbian, Swabian and Sárköz artefacts. Three period rooms – that of a well-to-do Sárköz farming family, another from the estate of the aristocratic Apponyi family of Lengyel and a poor gooseherd's hut – illustrate very clearly the different economic brackets that existed side by side in the region a century ago.

The Middle Eastern flourishes of the **House of Arts** (Művészetek Háza; ☎ 511 247; Szent István tér 28; ☼ 10am-6pm Tue-Fri), behind the museum, reveal its former life as a synagogue. It is now used as a gallery and concert hall. Four of its original iron pillars have been placed outside and enclosed in an arch, suggesting the tablets of the 10 Commandments. A short distance south of the museum is a striking 'tree of life' monument to 'Szekszárd's heroes and victims of WWII'.

Activities

Try the covered **thermal baths** and **outdoor pools** (☎ 412 035; Toldi utca 6; adult/child 500/250Ft;

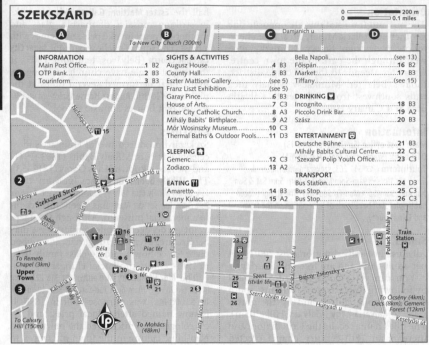

SZEKSZÁRD

0   200 m
0   0.1 miles

INFORMATION
Main Post Office.............................1 B2
OTP Bank..2 B3
Tourinform.....................................3 B3

SIGHTS & ACTIVITIES
Augusz House..................................4 B3
County Hall......................................5 B3
Eszter Mattioni Gallery...............(see 5)
Franz Liszt Exhibition...................(see 5)
Garay Pince.....................................6 B3
House of Arts...................................7 C3
Inner City Catholic Church.............8 A3
Mihály Babits' Birthplace................9 A2
Mór Wosinszky Museum................10 C3
Thermal Baths & Outdoor Pools......11 D3

SLEEPING
Gemenc..12 C3
Zodiaco..13 A2

EATING
Amaretto..14 B3
Arany Kulacs...................................15 A2

Bella Napoli.................................(see 13)
Főispán...16 B2
Market..17 B3
Tiffany..(see 15)

DRINKING
Incognito...18 B3
Piccolo Drink Bar............................19 A2
Szász..20 B3

ENTERTAINMENT
Deutsche Bühne...............................21 B3
Mihály Babits Cultural Centre...........22 C3
'Szexard' Polip Youth Office.............23 C3

TRANSPORT
Bus Station......................................24 D3
Bus Stop..25 C3
Bus Stop..26 C3

To New City Church (300m)
Damjanich u

baths 2-8pm Mon, 6am-8pm Tue-Sun year-round, pools 9am-6pm mid-May–Aug), near the train and bus stations.

There are several places dotted around Szekszárd where you can sample the local vintage. One of the best venues is the **Garay Pince** (412 828; Garay tér 19; 10am-5pm Mon-Thu, 9am-6pm Fri & Sat, 10am-2pm Sun), with some of Szekszárd's best wines for tasting and purchasing. Tourinform has a full list of wine cellars in town and a Wine Road Map of the surrounding area.

Festivals & Events
Among the big events staged annually in Szekszárd are the **Feast of Szekszárd Stew and Wine** in late June, the **International Danube Folklore Festival** jointly sponsored with Kalocsa and Baja in mid-July, and the **Szekszárd Wine Days** in late September.

Sleeping
For a town with such a pleasant atmosphere, Szekszárd has a surprising lack of accommodation. Tourinform has a few private rooms (from 3000Ft per person), on its

books, which are usually in the high-rise blocks near the cultural centre.

Zodiaco (511 150; www.hotelzodiaco.hu; Szent László utca 19; s/d 9700/13,100Ft) There are no prizes for guessing that this hotel sports an astrological theme. It's by far the best place in town, with large, modern 2nd-floor rooms 'parading' themselves around an inner courtyard.

Gemenc (311 722; Mészáros Lázár utca 1; s 5550-7700Ft, d 7500-10,700Ft;) This may be an ugly hotel, but it's centrally located and has all the usual amenities – restaurant, coffee shop, nightclub etc. More expensive rooms come with mini-bar.

Eating
Arany Kulacs (413 369; Nefelejcs köz 7; mains 1500Ft) For fine dining and even finer wine, head for the 'Golden Flask'. Once there, choose from picnic tables on a fairly barren terrace (with partial views of the town) or the cellar-like surroundings inside.

Tiffany (311 079; Nefelejcs köz 3-5; mains 1000-1500Ft) Next door to Arany Kulacs is this small place, with an even smaller terrace.

Its simple Hungarian fare and generous sprinklings of paprika attract diners from all walks of life.

Főispán (☎ 312 139; Béla tér 1; mains 1200Ft) Housed in a renovated wine cellar, Főispán is a solid option in the centre of town. It also has a small but interesting collection of assorted wine-making implements, which purports to be a wine museum.

Bella Napoli (Szent László utca; mains from 700Ft; ☺ Mon-Sat) In the courtyard of the Zodiaco hotel, Bella Napoli is a small pizzeria with extra large pizzas and fast service.

Amaretto (Garay tér 6; ice cream from 90Ft; ☺ 9am-6pm) Amaretto is small in size but big on ice cream, and doesn't do a bad job with cakes either. There's also a terrace to enjoy your purchase on.

Food supplies can be bought at the big market in Piac tér along Vár köz, just down the steps from Béla tér.

Drinking & Entertainment

Szász (Garay tér 20) For a drink on the town, try the central 'Saxon' pub, which attracts a relaxed crowd of all ages.

Piccolo Drink Bar (Fürdőház utca 3) With its younger devotees, this is a more rowdy and boisterous bar than the Szász.

Incognito (Garay tér; ☺ 8pm-4am Thu-Sat) This is the most central place for a night out clubbing.

Mihály Babits Cultural Centre (☎ 529 610; Szent István tér 10) This is a modern place and has information about concerts and other cultural events taking place in the County Hall courtyard, the New City Church (Újváros templom) on Pázmány tér and the House of Arts.

Deutsche Bühne (Német Színház; ☎ 316 533; Garay tér 4) A Romantic-style German theatre from the early 20th century, still staging performances.

'Szexard' Polip youth office (☎ 411 475; ☺ 1-6pm Mon-Sat) For alternative culture, visit the 'Szexard' office to the rear of the cultural centre. Otherwise consult the free biweekly *Szekszárdi Est* magazine.

Getting There & Away
BUS
There are between nine and 14 daily departures to Budapest (1820Ft, three hours, 150km) and Pécs (786Ft, 1½ hours, 62km), and at least five buses leave daily for Baja

(484Ft, one hour, 40km) and Mohács (605Ft, one hour, 49km). From Szekszárd you can reach Harkány (via Pécs; 968Ft, 2¼ hours, 80km, three daily), Balatonfüred (1820Ft, three hours, 150km, one daily), Kaposvár (1210Ft, 2¼ hours, 99km, two daily), Szeged (1820Ft, 3½ hours, 146km, three daily) and Veszprém (2060Ft, 3½ hours, 163km, one daily). Some of these buses are boarded on Szent István tér south of the cultural centre.

Buses bound for Keselyűs (between two and five daily) will drop you off near the Gemenc Excursion Centre in Bárányfok.

TRAIN
Only two direct trains leave Budapest's Déli train station every day for Szekszárd (1624Ft, 2¾ hours, 149km). Otherwise, take the Pécs-bound train from Budapest's Déli, Kelenföldi or Keleti station and change at Sárbogárd. To travel east (to Baja), west (to Kaposvár) or south (to Pécs) you must change trains at Bátaszék, 20km to the south. Öcsény (100Ft, seven minutes, 4km) and Decs (100Ft, 15 minutes, 8km) are on the train line to Bátaszék.

Getting Around
Bus 1 goes from the stations through the centre of town to Béla tér, and then on to the Upper Town as far as Remete Chapel. Local taxis can be ordered on ☎ 555 555.

AROUND SZEKSZÁRD
Gemenc Forest
The Gemenc, a 180-sq-km flood forest of poplars, oxbow lakes and dikes 12km from Szekszárd, is part of the Danube-Dráva National Park. Until engineers removed some 60 curves in the Danube in the mid-19th century, the Gemenc would flood to such a degree that the women of the Sárköz region were forced to go to Szekszárd's market by boat. Under the old regime, it was the favourite hunting ground of communist leaders, who came here to shoot its famous red deer.

Today the backwaters, lakes and ponds beyond the earthen dams, which were built by wealthy landowners to protect their farms, offer sanctuary to red deer, boar, black storks, herons and woodpeckers. Hunting is restricted to certain areas and you can visit the forest all year.

For information about hunting, contact the **Hungarian National Hunting Protection Association** (OMVV; ☎ 1-355 6180; www.vadaszativedegylet.hu; II Medve utca 34-40) in Budapest.

Sights & Activities

The main entrance is at the **Gemenc Excursion Centre** (☎ 74-312 552; ✆ 9.30am-5pm year-round) in Bárányfok, about halfway down Keselyűsi út between Szekszárd and the forest. It offers activities such as coach rides for 1300Ft and can supply you with a map of walking and cycling trails through the forest. (Keselyűsi út was once the longest stretch of covered highway in the Austro-Hungarian Empire, when in the late 19th century mulberry trees were planted along it to feed the worms at the silk factory in Szekszárd.)

Near the centre is a wooden hall, built without nails for Archduke Franz Ferdinand to keep his hunting trophies. It now houses the **Forest Museum** (adult/child 600/300Ft; ✆ 10am-6pm Tue-Sun mid-Mar–Oct). The hall was exhibited at the 1896 Millenary Exhibition in Budapest and is now in its fourth location, most recently reassembled from Szent István tér in Szekszárd by Polish labourers who – this is not a Polish joke – used nails.

LIVING TRADITIONS

The isolation of areas like the Sárköz region and the Ormánság region south of Szigetvár – places 'somewhere behind the back of God', as the Hungarians call them – helped preserve folk customs and crafts found nowhere else in Hungary.

In the Sárköz, lookout for local pottery decorated with birds, the distinctive black-and-red striped woven fabric so common that it was once used as mosquito netting in this bug-infested region, and the unique *írókázás fazékok* (inscribed pots), usually made as wedding gifts.

In the Ormánság, shepherds are famous for the everyday items they carve from horn or wood, including crooks, pocket mirror frames and shaving kits. The oaken trousseau chests, decorated with geometrical shapes and made to hold the distinctive Ormánság bridal brocaded skirts and 'butterfly' headdresses, are unique and superior to the *tulipán ládák* (tulip chests) found in prosperous peasant houses elsewhere in Hungary.

NARROW-GAUGE TRAIN

A **narrow-gauge train**, which once carried wood out of the Gemenc Forest, is a fun – but difficult – way to go. The train runs from Bárányfok to Pörböly (one way/return adult 650/950Ft, child 450/700Ft, two hours), some 30km to the south, once a day at 3.35pm from May to October. Two other trains – at 10.40am and 1.35pm – go only as far as the Gemenc-Dunapart (adult/child 750/550Ft, 11km), where you'll need to change trains for Pörböly.

From Pörböly, a train leaves at 8.30am to Bárányfok (one way/return adult 650/950Ft, child 450/700Ft, two hours). Two other trains leave at 10am and 1.15pm, but they go only as far as the Gemenc Delta (one way/return adult 450/750Ft, child 550/350Ft, 1¼ hours, 19km).

The abridged trip in itself is worthwhile, weaving and looping around the Danube's remaining bends, but it's a good idea to double-check the times with Tourinform in Szekszárd, or with the train station at **Pörböly** (☎ 74-491 483; www.gemencrt.hu; Bajai út 100) before you set out. You wouldn't want to be marooned in the Gemenc with a lot of hunters running wild.

Sleeping & Eating

It's possible to stay at the excursion centre in **wooden bungalows** (☎ 74-410 151; 2/3 people 8000/9000Ft), which have all the amenities of a hotel. The **Trófea** (☎ 74-712 552; mains from 1000Ft) is a *csárda* (Hungarian-style restaurant), near the entrance to the centre and opens daily till 10pm. See p283 for information on buses from Szekszárd to the centre.

Sárköz Region

The folkloric region of Sárköz, consisting of five towns southeast of Szekszárd between Rte 56 and the Danube, is the centre of folk weaving in Hungary. **Öcsény** is the largest town, but for the visitor the most interesting is **Decs**, with its high-walled cottages, late Gothic Calvinist church and folk houses.

The Sárköz became a very rich area after flooding was brought under control in the mid-19th century. In a bid to protect their wealth and land, most families had only one child. And, judging from the displays at the **Regional Museum** (Tájház; Kossuth utca 34-36; adult/child 150/75Ft; ✆ 9am-1pm Tue-Sun), located in a peasant house in Decs, these families spent a lot of their money on lavish interior decoration and some of the most ornate (and Balkan-looking) embroidered folk clothing in Hungary. The house was built in 1836 from earth and woven twigs, so that when the floods came only the mud had to be replaced; check out the ingenious porcelain 'stove with eyes' (concave circles radiate more heat).

MOHÁCS

☎ 69 / pop 19,200

Mohács is a sleepy little port on the Danube that comes to life during the annual **Busójárás festival**, a pre-Lent free-for-all late in February or March when 'devils' come out to play. The town is also a convenient gateway to Croatia and the beaches of the Adriatic, with the border crossing at Udvar some 12km to the south.

The defeat of the Hungarian army by the Turks here on 29 August 1526 was a watershed in the nation's history. With it came partition and foreign domination that would last almost five centuries. It is not an exaggeration to say that the effects of the battle at Mohács can still be felt in Hungary today.

Orientation

The centre of Mohács is located on the west bank of the Danube; residential New Mohács, or Újmohács, is on the opposite side of the river. Szabadság utca, the main street, runs west from the Danube, beginning and ending with large war memorials now in decay.

The bus station is on Rákóczi utca, only a few minutes' walk south of leafy Deák tér. The port's train station is situated approximately 1.5km north of the city centre, near the Strandfürdő, at the far end of Bajcsy-Zsilinszky utca.

Information

K&H bank (Szabadság utca 23) With ATM.

OTP bank (Jókai Mór utca 1) Also with ATM.

Post office (Széchenyi tér 2) In the southern wing of the Town Hall.

Tourinform (☎ 505 515; mohacs@tourinform.hu; Széchenyi tér 1; ☺ 7.30am-4pm Mon-Fri, 9am-noon Sat mid-Jun–mid-Sep; 7.30am-4pm Mon-Thu, 7.30am-1pm Fri mid-Sep–mid-Jun) Housed in the Moorish Town Hall.

www.mohacs.hu In Hungarian, with a small amount of information in English.

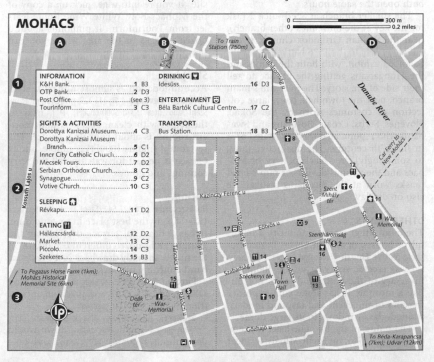

MOHÁCS

0 ———— 300 m
0 ———— 0.2 miles

INFORMATION
K&H Bank.................................1 B3
OTP Bank.................................2 D3
Post Office...........................(see 3)
Tourinform..............................3 B3

SIGHTS & ACTIVITIES
Dorottya Kanizsai Museum.........4 C3
Dorottya Kanizsai Museum
  Branch..................................5 C1
Inner City Catholic Church.........6 D2
Mecsek Tours.........................7 D2
Serbian Orthodox Church..........8 C2
Synagogue..............................9 C2
Votive Church........................10 C3

SLEEPING
Révkapu................................11 D2

EATING
Halászcsárda.........................12 D2
Market..................................13 C3
Piccolo.................................14 C3
Szekeres..............................15 B3

DRINKING
Idesüss................................16 D3

ENTERTAINMENT
Béla Bartók Cultural Centre......17 C2

TRANSPORT
Bus Station...........................18 B3

To Train
Station (750m)

Danube River

Car Ferry to
New Mohács

Szent
Mihály
tér

War
Memorial

Szentháromság
tér

To Pegazus Horse Farm (1km);
Mohács Historical
Memorial Site (6km)

Deák
tér

War
Memorial

Town
Hall

Kossuth Lajos u

Kazinczy Ferenc u

Eötvös u

Szabadság u

Széchenyi u

Dózsa György u

Gőzhajó u

To Béda-Karapancsa
(7km); Udvar (12km)

Sights

MOHÁCS HISTORICAL MEMORIAL SITE

This historical **Memorial Site** (Mohácsi Történelmi Emlékhely; ☎ 382 130; adult/child 550/350Ft; ☯ 9am-6pm Tue-Sun May-Sep, 10am-4pm Wed-Sun Apr & Oct), west of Rte 56 at Sátorhely (literally 'encampment') about 6km southwest of Mohács, was opened in 1976 to mark the 450th anniversary of the battle. It's a fitting memorial to the dead: over 100 carved wooden markers in the shape of bows, arrows, lances and heads lean this way and that over a common grave that was only discovered in the early 1970s. Above the entrance, a carved sign poignantly announces: 'Here began the deterioration of a strong Hungary.' Explanations of the battle are in Hungarian, but free audio guides in English and German are available.

DOROTTYA KANIZSAI MUSEUM

This **museum** (☎ 311 536; Városház utca 1; adult/child 250/120Ft; ☯ 10am-4pm Tue-Sat Apr-Oct), named after the heroic noblewoman from Siklós who presided over the burial of the dead after the battle at Mohács, has two branches, both open the same hours.

The smaller branch at Szerb utca 2 (ask for the key at the museum's other branch), near the Serbian Orthodox church, is devoted entirely to the 1526 battle. It's a well-balanced exhibit, with both the Turks and the Hungarians getting the chance to tell their side of the story. The museum's main branch, near the town hall, has a large collection of costumes worn by the Sokác, Slovenes, Serbs, Croats, Bosnians and Swabians who repopulated this devastated area in the 17th century. The distinctive (and, to some, ugly) grey-black pottery of Mohács and the various devil's- or ram's-head masks worn at the Busójárás festival are also on display.

OTHER SIGHTS

The city's other sights amount to a handful of houses of worship. The Byzantine-style **Votive Church** (Fogadalmi templom; Széchenyi tér) was erected in 1926 for the 400th anniversary of the battle and looks not unlike a mosque. It has some contemporary frescoes of the event and inspired modern stained-glass windows in its large dome.

The pulpit in the baroque **Inner City Catholic Church** (1776), on Szent Mihály tér near the Csele hotel, is interesting. From here it's a short walk north to the **Serbian Orthodox church** (Szentháromság utca 33), which was built in 1732 and until WWI served a very large local congregation of Serbs. The church's icons and ceiling frescoes date from the 18th century.

In the courtyard of the old **synagogue** (Eötvös utca 1), a large monument featuring stars of David, menorahs, tablets and inscriptions in Hungarian and Hebrew honours the Jewish victims of fascism.

Activities

The **Béda-Karapancsa**, a 100-sq-km woodland some 7km southeast of Mohács, is where locals head to fish, hike and bike. Like the Gemenc Forest, it's part of the Danube-Dráva National Park. Purchase a good map of the area, such as Béda-Karapancsai tájegység (Béda-Karapancsa Region; 800Ft), from Tourinform; unfortunately there is nowhere in town to hire bicycles.

You can rent horses at the **Pegazus Horse Farm** (☎ 301 244; Eszéki út 2), south of the city centre on the road to the Mohács battle site. If you're into **wine**, pick up a copy of the Mohács-Bóly White Wine Route leaflet from Tourinform. It pinpoints about a dozen villages in the area where you can sample the local drop.

Sleeping

Accommodation is almost nonexistent in Mohács. **Révkapu** (☎ 311 129; mvgv@dravanet.hu; Szent János utca 1; s/d 5000/6000Ft; ☐), next to the ferry, with clean, spacious and modern rooms, is about your only choice. The restaurant (mains 1000Ft) is simple, but its terrace is perfect for watching all the ferry comings and goings.

Eating

Halászcsárda (☎ 322 542; Szent Mihály tér 5; mains 1500Ft) Easily the best place in town to dine. It has a beautiful terrace overlooking the Danube and a dozen different fish dishes on the menu; the only drawback is the resident band churning out tacky folk music.

Piccolo (☎ 322 097; Szabadság utca 24; pizzas under 800Ft) In a small courtyard, this is an upbeat, friendly and popular pizzeria.

Szekeres (Dózsa György utca 2; ice cream 100Ft; ☯ 9am-6pm) No self-respecting town would do without a quality ice-cream and cake shop, and Mohács is no exception. Szekeres fits the bill here, with delectable cakes and rich ice cream.

Fresh produce, food stalls and tacky knick-knacks are all available at the town's market, just west of Jókai Mór utca.

Drinking & Entertainment

Idesüss (Jókai Mór utca 2) The makeshift pavilion of Idesüss is as good a place as any to enjoy a *korsó* (pint) or two during the evening.

Béla Bartók Cultural Centre (☎ 510 357; Vörösmarty utca 3), north of Széchenyi tér, has staff who can fill you in on what's happening in Mohács.

Getting There & Away

BUS

Bus services from Mohács aren't as frequent as other towns, but to Pécs (544Ft, 1¼hours, 44km) and Baja (605Ft, one hour, 47km) they leave almost hourly. Other destinations include Budapest (2410Ft, four hours, 200km, six daily), Villány (423Ft, one hour, 30km, three daily), Siklós (544Ft; 1½ hours, 44km, three daily), Harkány (846Ft, 1½ hours, 66km, five daily), Kalocsa (544Ft, one hour, 43km, one daily Monday to Saturday), Szeged (1930Ft, 3¼ hours, 152km, seven daily) and Szekszárd (605Ft, one hour, 49km, five daily).

TRAIN

Mohács is linked by rail with Villány (264Ft, 25 minutes, 24km) and Pécs (544Ft, 1¼ hours, 60km) and there are up to seven trains a day to these places. To get anywhere else, the bus is the best – indeed, often the only – option.

Getting Around

Buses for any of the following towns will let you off at the Mohács battle site: Nagynyárád, Majs, Lippó, Bezedek and Magyarbóly (133Ft). A year-round car ferry (130/660Ft per person/car) links Szent Mihály tér with residential New Mohács – and the start of the Great Plain – across the Danube to the east.

SIKLÓS

☎ 72 / pop 10,300

Protected from the north, east and west by the Villány Hills, Siklós, Hungary's southernmost town, has been making wine

(mostly whites) since the Romans settled here at a place they called Seres. These days the town itself doesn't have much aside from its hilltop castle, but it's certainly worth dropping in on your journey between the spa at Harkány and the wine cellars of Villány.

Orientation

The town centre of Siklós runs from the bus station (Szent István tér) along Felszabadulás utca to Kossuth tér. Siklós Castle stands watch over the town from the hill to the west. The main train station is northeast of Kossuth tér at the end of Táncsics Mihály utca. The town's other train station, Siklósiszőlők, northwest of the centre on the road to Máriagyűd, is more convenient to the bus station.

Information

OTP bank (Felszabadulás utca 60-62)

Post office (Flórián tér 1)

Tett-Hely (Kossuth tér 3; per hr 100Ft; ☼ 2-5pm Mon-Fri) Internet access is available here.

Tourinform (☎ 579 090; siklos@tourinform.hu; Felszabadulás utca 3; ☼ 8am-4pm Mon-Fri) It has information on wine makers in the area, and plans are afoot to offer wine tours.

Sights

SIKLÓS CASTLE

Though the original foundations of **Siklós Castle** (Vár körút; adult/child 660/330Ft; ☼ 9am-6pm Tue-Sun Apr-Oct, 9am-4pm Tue-Sun Nov-Mar) date from the mid-13th century, what you see when you look up from the town is an 18th-century baroque palace, girdled by 15th-century walls and bastions. The castle has changed hands many times since it was built by the Siklósi family and, until very recently, it was the longest continuously inhabited castle in the country. Its most famous occupant was the reformer Count Kázmér Batthyány (1807–54), among the first of the nobility to free his serfs. He joined the independence struggle of 1848 and was made prime minister of Hungary's new parliamentary government.

Walk to the castle either from Kossuth tér via Batthyány Kázmér utca, or up Váralja utca from Szent István tér, near the bus station. The drawbridge leads to the entrance at the **barbican**, which is topped with loopholes and a circular lookout.

SIKLÓS, MÁRIAGYŰD & HARKÁNY

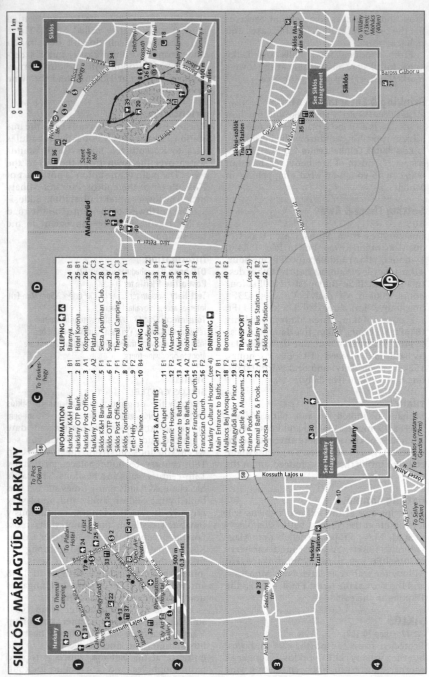

INFORMATION
Harkány K&H Bank	**1** B1
Harkány OTP Bank	**2** B1
Harkány Post Office	**3** A1
Harkány Tourinform	**4** A2
Siklós K&H Bank	**5** F1
Siklós OTP Bank	**6** F1
Siklós Post Office	**7** F1
Siklós Tourinform	**8** F2
Tett-Hely	**9** F2
Tour Chance	**10** B4

SIGHTS & ACTIVITIES
Calvary Chapel	**11** E1
Ceramic House	**12** F2
Entrance to Baths	**13** A1
Entrance to Baths	**14** A2
Former Franciscan Church	**15** E1
Franciscan Church	**16** F2
Harkány Cultural House	(see 4)
Main Entrance to Baths	**17** B1
Malkocs Bej Mosque	**18** F2
Máriagyűdi Bajor Pince	**19** F2
Siklós Castle & Museums	**20** F2
Strand Pools	**21** F4
Thermal Baths & Pools	**22** A1
Vadrózsa	**23** A3

SLEEPING
Baranya	**24** B1
Hotel Korona	**25** B1
Központi	**26** F2
Platán	**27** C3
Siesta Apartman Club	**28** A1
Suzi	**29** A1
Thermál Camping	**30** C3
Xavin	**31** A1

EATING
Amadeus	**32** A2
Food Stalls	**33** B1
Hamburger	**34** F1
Maestro	**35** E3
Market	**36** A1
Robinson	**37** A1
Tenkes	**38** F3

DRINKING
Borozó	**39** F2
Borozó	**40** E2

TRANSPORT
Bike Rental	(see 25)
Harkány Bus Station	**41** B2
Siklós Bus Station	**42** E1

You can also explore the castle and enjoy some fine views of the Villány Hills from along the promenade, linking the four mostly derelict towers.

The castle's main attraction, the **Castle Museum** (Vármúzeum), is in the south wing. To the right as you enter the main door is an unusual exhibit devoted to the manufacture and changing styles of gloves, fans and umbrellas since the Middle Ages. The exhibit's emphasis is very much on the Hamerli and Hunor factories at Pécs, which produced some of Europe's finest kid gloves in the 19th century. The **cellar** contains barely recognisable stone fragments from Roman, Gothic and Renaissance times. Most of the 1st floor is now a modern art gallery, and don't miss the wonderful **Sigismund Hall** (Zsigmond-terem) with its Renaissance fireplace and star-vaulted, enclosed balcony.

To the right of the museum entrance, two doors lead to the dark and spooky **cells** – a real dungeon if ever there was one. The walls here are several metres thick, and up to five grilles on the window slits discouraged any would-be escapers. Woodcuts on the walls of the upper dungeon explain how various torture devices were used. After this, the Gothic **chapel** (☎ 579 262; admission free; appointment needed) is a vision of heaven itself, with its brilliant arched windows behind the altar, web vaulting on the ceiling and 15th-century frescoed niches.

Other Sights & Activities

The 15th-century Gothic **Franciscan church** on Vajda János tér is south of the castle but still within its walls; its cloister is now the **Ceramic House** (Kerámia Alkotóház; Vajda János tér 4; admission 100Ft; ✆ 10am-5pm mid-Apr–Sep).

If you walk down Batthyány Kázmér utca past the little statue of the heroic Dorottya Kanizsai, you'll come to the 16th-century **Malkocs Bej Mosque** (Malkocs bej dzsámija; ☎ 579 279; Vörösmarty utca 14; adult/child 200/100Ft; ✆ 9am-5pm Tue-Sun Apr-Sep; ✆ appointment needed Oct-Mar). Now beautifully restored, the mosque houses temporary exhibits.

If the sticky summer days become too much, join the locals at the **Strand Pools** (☎ 579 840; Baross Gábor utca; adult/child 500/350Ft; ✆ 10am-7pm Sun-Thu, 10am-8pm Fri & Sat Jun-Aug) south of the centre.

Sleeping & Eating

Accommodation and eating options are slim on the ground; Tourinform has a small list of private rooms in town.

Központi (☎ 352 513; www.kozponti.hu; Kossuth tér 5; s/d from 6800/8800Ft, **P** ✖) Finally, after years of renovation, Központi is open for business, and Siklós is once again the proud owner of a hotel. Its rooms are in tip-top shape but lack warmth. There's a sauna, Jacuzzi and fitness room for guest use, and a restaurant (mains 1000-1500Ft) with an exclusively Hungarian menu.

Hamburger (Felszabadulás utca 22; ✆ 9am-6pm) Despite its savoury name, this cake shop is still going strong, with its delicious selection of sweet things.

The **market**, with everything from knock-off jeans and trainers to *čevapčiči* (spicy meatballs) is just west of the bus station.

For something close to the bus station and Siklósi-szőlők train station, try either of the following:

Tenkes (☎ 352 900; Felszabadulás utca 65/a; mains 900-1500Ft) Pleasant restaurant that specialises in fish.

Maestro (☎ 579 206; Felszabadulás utca 69; pizzas & pasta from 500Ft) A more basic eatery, serving mainly Italian fast food.

Drinking

You should really save the wine tasting for Villány and the cellars at Villánykövesd, but if you want to sample a glass here, try the little *borozó* (wine bar) in the castle courtyard. It also serves snacks.

Getting There & Away

Generally you won't wait more than 30 minutes for buses to Pécs (363Ft, 45 minutes, 29km) or Harkány (133Ft, 10 minutes, 8km); hourly buses leave for Máriagyűd and Villány (182Ft, 20 minutes, 14km). For Mohács (544Ft, 1½ hours, 44km), count on between five and 10 buses a day. Other destinations include Szigetvár (907Ft, 2¼ hours, 71km, one to three daily) and Sellye (544Ft, 1¼ hours, 40km, Monday to Friday three daily, Saturday and Sunday two daily).

Up to seven trains a day connect Siklós with Villány (182Ft, 21 minutes, 19km; change here for Mohács or Pécs), Máriagyűd (100Ft, four minutes, 2km), Harkány (100Ft, 10 minutes, 7km) and Sellye (346Ft, 1¼ hours, 39km). All trains heading east or west pass through both of Siklós' stations.

AROUND SIKLÓS
Máriagyűd
☎ 72

The former **Franciscan church** (☎ 579 000; Vujicsics Tihamér utca 66; admission free; ☻ 8am-7pm Mon-Sat, 7.30am-7pm Sun mid-Apr–mid-Oct, 9am-5pm Mon-Sat, 7am-3pm Sun mid-Oct–mid-Apr) at the top of this small village to the northwest of Siklós has been a place of pilgrimage for 800 years. You can make your own way to it from Siklós by walking for about 3km along Gyűdi út and Pécs út before turning north on Járó Péter utca when the church's two towers come into view (or hopping on a Máriagyűd- or Harkány-bound bus).

Máriagyűd was on the old trade route between Pécs and Eszék (now Osijek in Croatia) and a church has stood here since the mid-12th century. Today's church is a large 18th-century affair with modern frescoes on the ceiling, baroque painted altars, some beautifully carved pews and the main object of devotion, Mary and the Christ Child in gold and silver over the main altar. The most interesting time to visit is on Sunday or on a *búcsú* (a patron's festival – the Virgin Mary has lots of them) when merchants set up their stalls beside the church (see boxed text, below).

Mass is conducted in Hungarian at the Calvary Chapel, but at the outdoor altar on the hill above it, just as many people attend German-language services, often with accompanying oompah band music.

Máriagyűdi Bajor Pince (☎ 351 143; Tenkes utca 14; ☻ noon-3.30pm), in an old cellar in the square just below the church, is a good place to sample some of Siklós' white wines. If it's closed and your thirst is getting the better of you, the simple *borozó*, just to the south, should suffice. From here, you can start a 6km hike up and around the 408m-high Tenkes-hegy (Mt Tenkes).

Harkány
☎ 72 / pop 3300

There is no denying that Harkány is a spa town; literally everything centres on the 62°C spring (which has the richest sulphuric content in Hungary and accounts for the occasionally strong whiff of 'rotten eggs') that bubbles up from the ground. Of course, all that means crowds (well over 100,000 Hungarian, German, Croatian and Serbian visitors in the high season: June to September), *lángos* (deep-fried dough with toppings) and *gyros* (meat skewers) stalls in spades. But you might like it. People come to Harkány to socialise, and the town is on the western edge of the Villány-Siklós region, so there is plenty of wine about.

It's a wonder however that no statue stands in honour of János Pogány, a poor

---

FAREWELL TO ALL THAT

The word *búcsú* (church patronal festival) derives from the ancient Turkish for 'absolution', or 'the forgiveness of sins'. From medieval times it has taken on the additional meaning of 'pilgrimage' in Hungarian.

Búcsúk were usually linked with an icon or statue in a particular church, such as the Black Madonnas at Andocs, north of Kaposvár, and Máriapócs (p361), near Nyírbátor in the Northeast. They could also honour the name of a church's patron saint. People would march, often for days, to the holy place carrying banners and singing. Local people would accommodate and feed the pilgrims for little, or nothing. Often the faithful would spend the night in the church itself, believing that the absolution – or the cure – was more likely to occur in sleep.

Over the centuries *búcsúk* took on a more secular tone. Merchants would set up their stalls around the church, selling not only relics and religious articles but clothing, food and drinks as well. Showmen, buskers and musicians entertained the crowds and, in some places, there was even a 'bride market' with hopeful young women appearing with their full dowries. While the old and infirm congregated in the church to touch and venerate the holy picture or statue, the young remained outside for the entertainment.

As it happens, *búcsú* has yet another meaning in Hungarian: 'farewell'. Thus the Budapesti Búcsú (Budapest Goodbye) every June marking the departure of the last Soviet soldier from Hungarian soil in 1991 has a double meaning: it is both a raging party paying homage to hedonism and a 'goodbye' to the last of the much-despised occupiers.

peasant from Máriagyűd who cured himself of swollen joints by soaking in a hot spring he had discovered here. The Batthyány family recognised the potential almost immediately, erecting bathing huts in 1824 near the source of the spring, and since then the town has never looked back.

ORIENTATION

Harkány is essentially the Gyógyfürdő, a 12-hectare green square filled with pools, fountains and walkways, and bordered by hotels and holiday homes of every description. The four streets defining the thermal complex are Bartók Béla utca to the north, Ady Endre utca to the south, Bajcsy-Zsilinszky utca (with most of the hotels) to the east, and Kossuth Lajos utca, with several restaurants, to the west.

The bus station (Bajcsy-Zsilinszky utca) is at the southeast corner of the park. The train station is to the northwest on Petőfi utca, which branches off from Kossuth Lajos utca.

INFORMATION

Harkány Cultural House (Harkányi Művelődési Ház; ☎ 480 459; Kossuth Lajos utca 2/a; ☑ 9.45am-5.45pm Mon-Thu, 10am-2pm Fri; Internet access per hr 200Ft)
K&H bank (Bajcsy-Zsilinszky utca) Has a bureau de change at the main entrance to the spa.
OTP bank (Bajcsy-Zsilinszky utca)
Post office (Kossuth Lajos utca 57)
Tourinform (☎ 479 624; harkany@tourinform.hu; Kossuth Lajos utca 2/a; ☑ 9am-6pm Mon-Fri, 10am-1pm Sat mid-Jun–mid-Sep, 9am-4pm Mon-Fri mid-Sep–mid-Jun) Has an office at the Harkány Cultural House.
www.harkany.hu Information about the spa in Hungarian and German.

ACTIVITIES
Thermal Spa

The main entrance to Harkány's **thermal baths** (Gyógyfürdő; ☎ 480 251; day ticket adult/child from 1790/1090Ft, week ticket 10,740/6540Ft; ☑ 9am-6pm year-round) and **outside pools** (adult/child 550/400Ft; ☑ 9am-10pm mid-Jun–Aug, 9am-6pm Sun-Thu, 9am-8pm Fri & Sat Sep–mid-Jun), which are meant to cure just about every ailment under the sun, is on Bajcsy-Zsilinszky utca. The services here range from drinking cures and mud massages to an enticing 'wine foam bath', but it's just as enjoyable to swim in the 38°C outdoor pool, especially in cool weather.

Other Activities

You can ride horses (3500Ft per hr) or hire a coach (6000Ft per hr) at **Vadrózsa** (☎ 479 141; Széchenyi tér 30/c) northwest of the centre, off Petőfi utca, and at **Lantos Lovastanya** (☎ 480 077) near the village of Gordisa, 7km south of Harkány. **Bike rental** (400/1600Ft per hour/day) is available from the Korona Hotel during summer, and **cruises** (adult/child 1200/900Ft) on the Dráva River running along the border to Croatia can be organised through Tourinform or **Tour Chance** (☎ 480 272; www.tourchance.hu; Táncsics Mihály utca 54/a).

SLEEPING

Even though Harkány has an incredible array of hotels and *pensions* to suit all budgets, it pays to book over holiday periods as places can fill up quickly.

Budget

Tourinform has a comprehensive list of private rooms and apartments from 3000Ft and will make bookings.
Thermál Camping (☎ 480 117; Bajcsy-Zsilinszky utca 6; camp sites per person/tent 700/700Ft, bungalows for up to 4 people 8000Ft, pension d 3500Ft, hotel d 5000Ft; ☑ mid-Mar–mid-Oct) This lush, green camping ground is an easy walk to the pools and a jack-of-all-trades, with tent sites, bungalows, pension rooms with kitchens and standard hotel rooms.

Midrange

Suzi (☎ 70-205 53 56; www.harkanyapartman.hu; Kossuth Lajos utca 55/20; d €25-27, tr €32-35; **P**) This newly built apartment complex has stylish and immaculate rooms, with wood floors and warm, bright colours. A fully equipped kitchen comes with each apartment.
Xavin (☎ 479 399; www.xavin.hu; Kossuth Lajos utca 43; s/d 8200/12,200Ft; **P** ☑) Away from most of the hustle and bustle, this three-star hotel has cosy, open rooms and its own indoor pool with stress-relieving sauna.
Hotel Korona (☎ 580 830; www.hotels.hu/korona; Bajcsy-Zsilinszky utca 3; r 10,000-14,000Ft; **P**) There may have been a name change but this hotel housed in an Art-Deco sanatorium once used by Communist Party honchos is still one of the best options in town. It has a certain charm and lovely grounds, but most clientele aren't the sprightliest.
Baranya (☎ 480 160; www.hotelbaranya.hu; Bajcsy-Zsilinszky utca 5; s/d 5300/8100Ft; **P**) Spreading

itself across three buildings – each with its own distinct character – is Baranya. A solid bet, with homely rooms directly opposite the baths' main entrance.

Siesta Apartman Club (☎ 480 611; siesta.chotel@ hsch-szallodalanc.hu; Kossuth Lajos utca 17; s 5000-6800Ft; d 6700-8900Ft; **P**) Siesta is more than handy to the spa's Kossuth Lajos entrance, and while the place has seen better days, its rooms are close to spotless and still in good condition.

Platán (☎ 480 507; www.hotelplatan.hu; Bartók Béla utca 15; s/d from €20/29; **P**) This is a quiet, 60-room hotel in two former trade union holiday houses to the east of town. Rates depend on the season, the building and whether the room has a balcony.

EATING

Most visitors eat at their hotel's or *pension's* restaurant, of which there are more than enough. Unfortunately the quality is not always up to scratch but you're certainly not going to starve.

Xavin (☎ 479 399; Kossuth Lajos utca 43; mains 1200-2000Ft) The well-established restaurant of the Xavin hotel, it has silver service and an extensive wine list.

Robinson (☎ 580 090; Kossuth Lajos utca 7; mains 1000-1500Ft) For a decent sit-down meal, try this place, with its Caribbean-themed décor and mixed menu of Hungarian dishes and Italian cuisine.

Amadeus (Kossuth Lajos utca 12; ice cream from 90Ft; ⏰ 9am-7pm) For something sweet on a hot day, head to Amadeus, an ice-cream and cake store near Tourinform.

GETTING THERE & AWAY
Bus

While buses depart once or twice an hour for Siklós (133Ft, 10 minutes, 8km) and Pécs (484Ft, one hour, 37km), other destinations are not so well served. There is only one bus a day to Baja (1450Ft, 2¾hours, 116km), Sellye (423Ft, one hour, 34km, weekdays), Szekszárd (1150Ft, 2¼ hours, 95km) and Mohács (846Ft, 1½ hours, 69km).

In summer, buses to Stuttgart via Munich leave Harkány on Thursday at 1.30pm and Sunday at 2.30pm. They arrive in the German city at 6.30am on Friday and 7.30am on Monday, respectively. Buses also go to Frankfurt via Pécs and Nuremberg at 1.30pm on Sunday, arriving there at 8am on

Monday. There are also services to Munich and Stuttgart at 1.30pm on Thursday and 2.30pm on Sunday.

Train

By rail from Harkány, you can reach Sellye (346Ft, 1¼ hours, 32km, up to four times daily) to the west. There are also up to six trains daily to Siklós (100Ft, 10 minutes, 7km) and Villány (264Ft, 32 minutes, 26km) to the east. Change at Villány for Mohács or Pécs.

VILLÁNY
☎ 72 / pop 2750

Some 13km northeast of Siklós and dominated by Szársomlyó-hegy (422m) to the west, Villány is a village of vineyards; in fact it's one of Hungary's principal producers of wine. And by the looks of the buildings in the village centre, it's surviving very nicely on plonk, thank you very much.

Villány also has its place in the annals of Hungarian history. In 1687 it was the site of what is known as the 'second battle of Mohács', a ferocious confrontation in which the Turks got their comeuppance: they were driven southward by the Hungarians and slaughtered in the Dráva marshes. Serbs and Swabians moved in after the Turkish occupation and viticulture resumed.

Orientation

Villány is essentially just one main street, Baross Gábor utca. The bus stops in the centre of the village, near the ABC supermarket and the Town Hall. The train station is about 1200m to the north on Ady Endre fasor, en route to Villánykövesd.

Information
OTP bank (Baross Gábor utca 27) With ATM.
Post office (Vörösmarty utca 2) Next to the Oportó restaurant in the centre.
Villány-Siklós Wine Route Association (☎ 492 181; www.borut.hu; Deák Ferenc utca 22; ⏰ 8am-4pm Mon-Fri) Just north of the bus station, it produces the handy *Villány-Siklós Wine-Route* booklet covering places to buy and sample local wines in the region. It also organises wine tours.

Sights & Activities
The **Wine Museum** (Bormúzeum; ☎ 492 130; Bem József utca 8; admission free, wine tastings for groups only;

⊗ 9am-5pm Tue-Sun), housed in a 200-year-old tithe cellar, has a collection of 19th-century wine-producing equipment, such as barrels and hand corkers. Downstairs in the cellars, Villány's celebrated wines age in enormous casks, and vintage bottles dating from 1895 to 1971 are kept in safes. There's a small shop at the entrance selling Villány and Siklós wines, some of them vintage and among the best labels available in Hungary.

You can sample wines in many of the family **cellars** that line Baross Gábor utca, including Pólya at No 58, Szende at No 87 and Fritsch at No 97. They're normally open 9am to 6pm daily; expect to pay around 1100/2200Ft to sample four/eight wines. The best time to visit is during the September harvest, when the town is a hive of activity. Human chains pass buckets of grapes from trucks to big machines that chew off the vines, reduce the fruit to a soggy mass and pump the must – the unfermented grape juice – into enormous casks.

Sleeping & Eating

There are plenty of signs advertising private rooms in Villány.

Gere (☎ 492 195; www.gere.hu; Diófás tér 4; s/d 8000/10,600Ft; P) You shouldn't miss the chance to stay at this eight-room *pension*, near the main road. Rooms are big and cosy, there's a peaceful garden to laze around in, and its fine restaurant serves some of the best wine in these parts.

Kövári (☎ 492 117; Rákóczi utca 25; s/d 3000/6000Ft; P) This small *pension* is more like Grandma's big, rambling house in the countryside, with oil heating-stoves and old, mismatched furniture, where guests are assured of a warm, hearty welcome. Everything is spotlessly clean and there's a huge garden out back.

Cabernet (☎ 493 200; www.hotelcabernet.hu; Petőfi utca 29; s/d from 9000/11,000Ft; P) Cabernet, in Villánykövesd, is worth considering if you really want to stay in the centre of the wine area. It has 25 rooms, a restaurant and does wine tasting.

Oportó (Baross Gábor utca 33; mains 1500Ft) Oportó is the town's large, central restaurant, with a vine-covered terrace. A huge choice of wines accompanies its selective Hungarian menu.

Fülemüle Csárda (☎ 492 939; Ady Endre fasor; mains 1200-2000Ft) This lovely old farm house,

WINE TOWNS APLENTY

Villány may win the prize for most wine cellars per square kilometre, but it by no means has a monopoly in the region. Harkány and Siklós have their fair share, but both towns lack atmosphere; if you're heading east from either town, you'd be better off stopping in at the cellars of **Nagytótfalu**, **Kisharsány** or **Nagyharsány**, around 7km east of Siklós.

Arguably the best place for tastings is in the cellars cut into the loess soil at **Villánykövesd**, about 3.5km northwest of Villány along the road to Pécs. Cellars line the main street (Petőfi út) and the narrow lane (Pincesor) above it. Along Petőfi út, try the deep Polgár cellar at No 51 or Baschta at No 63. On Pincesor, No 14-15 is the cellar of master vintner Imre Tiffán, while Schwarzwalter is at No 16 and Blum at No 24. The cellars keep odd hours, so it's a hit-or-miss proposition.

Another 5km further on from Villánykövesd is the tiny village of **Palkonya** with its two cellars and rural vibe.

a couple of hundred metres past the train station, is a good place to stop for a bite on your way to/from Villánykövesd.

Júlia (☎ 702 610; Baross Gábor utca 73b; mains 1000-2000Ft) An intimate little restaurant that serves excellent veal *pörkölt* (stew), has wine tasting and plans to open rooms for accommodation on the top floor.

Getting There & Away

There are only two buses a day to Pécs, and seven to Siklós, Harkány and the villages in between. Villánykövesd can be reached five times daily on weekdays but only twice daily on Saturday. Trains run east to Mohács (264Ft, 25 minutes, 24km), west to Siklós (182Ft, 21 minutes, 19km) and Harkány (264Ft, 32 minutes, 26km), north to Pécs (346Ft, 45 minutes, 36km) and south to Sarajevo.

ORMÁNSÁG REGION

About 30km west of Harkány, this plain was prone to flooding by the Dráva River for centuries. That and the area's isolation are reflected in its unusual architecture, folk ways and distinct dialect. Couples usually had just one child since, under the land-tenure system here, peasants were not allowed to enlarge their holdings. That's not the only reason why the area's *talpás házak* are so small; these 'footed houses' were built on rollers so that they could be dragged to dry land in the event of flooding.

Sellye
☎ 73 / pop 3200

In Sellye, the 'capital' of the Ormánság region, a representative 'footed house' constructed of mortar, lime and a wooden frame sits behind the **Géza Kiss Ormánság Museum** (☎ 480 201; Köztársaság tér 6; admission 150Ft; ☽ 10am-4pm Tue-Sun Apr-Oct, 10am-2pm Nov-Mar). The house has the typical three rooms but includes some big differences not normally associated with traditional dwellings: the parlour was actually lived in; the front room was a 'smoke kitchen' – without a chimney; and, to keep mosquitoes at bay, what few windows the house had were kept very small. The museum's rich collection contains Ormánság costumes and artefacts.

There's an **arboretum** with rare trees and plants surrounding the Draskovich family mansion (now a school), behind the museum.

Mátyás király utca, the main drag, is southwest of the bus station, and the train station is to the southeast on Vasút utca.

Other Ormánság Villages
The **Calvinist church** (Dózsa utca 1/b; admission free) at **Drávaiványi**, with its colourful panelled ceiling and choir loft dating from the late 18th century, is 5km southwest of Sellye and can be reached by bus; the key is available from Kossuth Lajos 4. **Vajszló**, an Ormánság village 11km southeast of Sellye with several 'footed houses', is on the same train line as Sellye. Buses travel eastward from Vajszló to **Kórós**, whose folk-decorated **Calvinist church** (Kossuth Lajos utca 40; admission 60Ft) is among the most beautiful in the region. Its key is kept at Kossuth Lajos 31.

Getting There & Away
Harkány is the easiest starting point for any excursion into the Ormánság (423Ft, one hour, 34km, one weekdays to Sellye), but the area is also accessible by public transport from Szigetvár (423Ft, 50 minutes,

31km, one daily); however, if you catch the train, you must change at Szentlörinc. The train from Harkány to Vajszló and Sellye (346Ft, 1¼ hours, 32km, up to four daily) involves no change. See the Harkány section for more information.

PÉCS
☎ 72 / pop 162,500

Blessed with a mild climate, an illustrious past and a number of fine museums and monuments, Pécs is the jewel of Southern Transdanubia, if not all provincial Hungary. For these reasons and more, many travellers put it second to Budapest on their 'must-see' list.

Lying equidistant from the Danube and Dráva Rivers on a plain sheltered from northern winds by the Mecsek Hills, Pécs enjoys an extended summer and is an ideal place for viticulture and fruit and nut growing, especially almonds. But for the visitor, the capital of Baranya County, Pécs, is more than anything else a 'town of art', beating Szentendre on the Danube Bend hands down.

History
The Romans may have settled in Pécs for the region's weather, fertile soil and abundant water, but more likely they were sold by the protection offered by the Mecsek Hills. Calling their settlement Sophianae, it quickly grew into the commercial and administrative centre of Lower Pannonia (see p21). The Romans brought Christianity with them, and reminders of it can be seen in the early clover-shaped chapels unearthed at several locations here.

Pécs' importance grew in the Middle Ages, when it was known as Quinque Ecclesiae after its five churches (it is still called Fünfkirchen in German). King Stephen founded a bishopric here in 1009, and the town was a major stop along the trade route to Byzantium. Pécs developed as an intellectual and humanist centre with the founding of a university – Hungary's first – in 1367. The 15th-century bishop Janus Pannonius, who wrote some of Europe's most celebrated Renaissance poetry in Latin, was based in Pécs.

The city was fortified with walls after the Mongol invasion of the early 13th century, but they were in such poor condition three

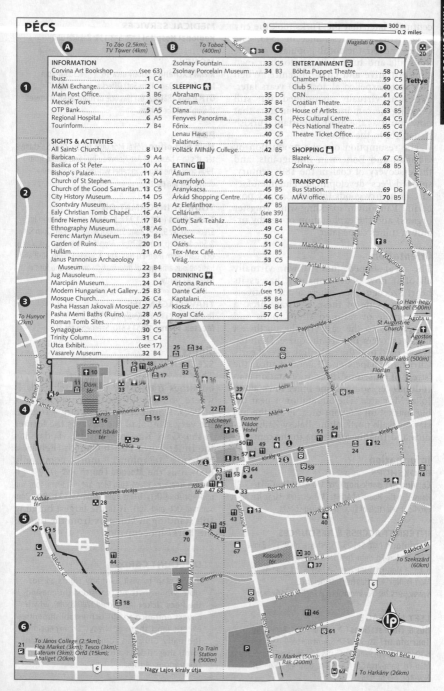

PÉCS

0   300 m
0   0.2 miles

INFORMATION
Corvina Art Bookshop..............(see 63)
Ibusz...1 C4
M&M Exchange.............................2 C4
Main Post Office...........................3 B6
Mecsek Tours................................4 C5
OTP Bank......................................5 A5
Regional Hospital.........................6 A5
Tourinform...................................7 B4

SIGHTS & ACTIVITIES
All Saints' Church.........................8 D2
Barbican.......................................9 A4
Basilica of St Peter......................10 A4
Bishop's Palace...........................11 A4
Church of St Stephen..................12 D4
Church of the Good Samaritan...13 C5
City History Museum...................14 D5
Csontváry Museum......................15 B4
Ealy Christian Tomb Chapel......16 A4
Endre Nemes Museum................17 B4
Ethnography Museum.................18 A6
Ferenc Martyn Museum..............19 B4
Garden of Ruins..........................20 D1
Hullám...21 A6
Janus Pannonius Archaeology
  Museum.....................................22 B4
Jug Mausoleum............................23 B4
Marcipán Museum.......................24 D4
Modern Hungarian Art Gallery...25 B3
Mosque Church............................26 C4
Pasha Hassan Jakovali Mosque...27 A5
Pasha Memi Baths (Ruins)..........28 A5
Roman Tomb Sites.......................29 B4
Synagogue...................................30 C5
Trinity Column.............................31 C4
Utca Exhibit...........................(see 17)
Vasarely Museum........................32 B4

Zsolnay Fountain........................33 C5
Zsolnay Porcelain Museum........34 B3

SLEEPING
Abraham......................................35 D5
Centrum.......................................36 B4
Diana...37 D5
Fenyves Panoráma......................38 C1
Fönix...39 C4
Lenau Haus..................................40 B4
Palatinus......................................41 C4
Pollack Mihály College................42 B5

EATING
Áfium..43 C5
Aranyfolyó...................................44 A5
Aranykacsa..................................45 B5
Árkád Shopping Centre...............46 C6
Az Elefánthoz..............................47 B5
Cellárium...............................(see 39)
Cutty Sark Teaház.......................48 B4
Dóm..49 C4
Mecsek..50 C4
Oázis...51 C4
Tex-Mex Café..............................52 B5
Virág..53 C5

DRINKING
Arizona Ranch.............................54 D4
Dante Café.............................(see 15)
Kaptalani.....................................55 B4
Kioszk..56 B4
Royal Café...................................57 C4

ENTERTAINMENT
Bóbita Puppet Theatre................58 D4
Chamber Theatre........................59 C5
Club 5..60 C6
CRN...61 C6
Croatian Theatre.........................62 C3
House of Artists...........................63 B5
Pécs Cultural Centre....................64 C5
Pécs National Theatre.................65 C4
Theatre Ticket Office...................66 C5

SHOPPING
Blazek..67 C5
Zsolnay..68 B5

TRANSPORT
Bus Station..................................69 D6
MÁV office...................................70 B5

To Zóo (2.5km);
TV Tower (4km)

To Toboz
(400m)

Magaslati út

Tettye

To Hunyor
(2km)

To Havi-hegy
Chapel (500m)

To Budaivárös (500m)

St Augustine
Church

To János College (2.5km);
Flea Market (3km); Tesco (3km);
Laterum (3km); Orfü (15km);
Abaliget (20km)

To Train
Station
(500m)

To Market (50m);
Rák (200m)

To Szekszárd
(60km)

To Harkány (26km)

Nagy Lajos király útja

centuries later that the Turks took the city with virtually no resistance in 1543. The Turks moved the local populace outside the walls and turned Pécs into their own administrative and cultural centre. When they were expelled almost 150 years later, Pécs was virtually abandoned, but still standing were monumental souvenirs that now count as the most important Turkish structures in the nation.

The resumption of wine production by German and Bohemian immigrants, and the discovery of coal in the 18th century, spurred Pécs' development. The manufacture of luxury goods (gloves, Zsolnay porcelain, Pannonvin sparkling wine, Angster organs) and the exploitation of nearby uranium mines came later.

Orientation

The oval-shaped inner town, virtually all of it now pedestrian-only, has as its heart Széchenyi tér, where a dozen streets converge. One of these is Király utca, a promenade of restored shops, pubs and restaurants to the east. To the northwest lies Pécs' other important square, Dóm tér. Here you'll find the cathedral, several early Christian chapels and Káptalan utca, the 'street of museums'. Pécs' train station is in Indóház tér, south of the inner town along Jókai Mór utca. The bus station is near the big market on Zólyom utca. From the bus station walk north along Bajcsy-Zsilinszky utca and Irgalmasok utcája to the centre.

Information

BOOKSHOPS

Corvina Art Bookshop (☎ 310 427; Széchenyi tér 7-8) Housed in the House of Artists (Művészetek Háza); has an excellent selection of English-language books.

INTERNET ACCESS & RESOURCES

Tourinform (☎ 511 232; Széchenyi tér 9; ⏰ 8am-5.30pm Mon-Fri, 9am-2pm Sat & Sun Jun-Sep, 8am-5.30pm Mon-Fri, 9am-2pm Sat May & Oct, 8am-4pm Mon-Fri Nov-Apr) Has free Internet access. **www.pecs.hu/** For information in English and German.

LEFT LUGGAGE

Bus & Train stations (⏰ per hr 150Ft; 8am-6pm) **Tourinform** (☎ 511 232; Széchenyi tér 9; ⏰ 8am-5.30pm Mon-Fri, 9am-2pm Sat & Sun Jun-Sep, 8am-5.30pm Mon-Fri, 9am-2pm Sat May & Oct, 8am-4pm Mon-Fri Nov-Apr; per hr 100Ft)

MEDICAL SERVICES

Regional Hospital (☎ 533 133; Rákóczi út 2)

MONEY

M&M Exchange (Király utca 16; ⏰ 8.30am-5pm Mon-Fri, 8.30am-1pm Sat) Offers a decent rate. **OTP bank** (Rákóczi út) Has one a many ATMs scattered throughout the centre.

POST

Main post office (Jókai Mór utca 10) South of Széchenyi tér, it's in a beautiful Art-Nouveau building dating from 1904 (note the angels in relief writing, mailing and delivering the post).

TOURIST INFORMATION

Tourinform (☎ 511 232; baranya-m@tourinform.hu; Széchenyi tér 9; ⏰ 8am-5.30pm Mon-Fri, 9am-2pm Sat & Sun Jun-Sep, 8am-5.30pm Mon-Fri, 9am-2pm Sat May & Oct, 8am-4pm Mon-Fri Nov-Apr) Knowledgeable staff and has copious amounts of information on Pécs and for the Baranya County.

TRAVEL AGENCIES

Ibusz (☎ 211 011; Király utca 11) **Mecsek Tours** (☎ 513 370; Széchenyi tér 1)

Sights

SZÉCHENYI TÉR

This lovely square of mostly baroque buildings framed by the Mecsek Hills is where you should start any walking tour of Pécs. Dominating the square – indeed, the very symbol of the city – is the former Pasha Gazi Kassim Mosque. Today it's the Inner Town Parish Church (Belvárosi plébánia templom), more commonly known as the **Mosque Church** (☎ 321 976; admission free; ⏰ 10am-4pm Mon-Sat, 11.30am-4pm Sun mid-Apr–mid-Oct, 10am-noon Mon-Sat, 11.30am-2pm Sun mid-Oct–mid-Apr). It is the largest building still standing in Hungary from the time of the Turkish occupation.

DISCOUNT CARDS

If you plan to visit as many sights as possible while in town, consider purchasing the **Pécs Ticket** (adult/child 1700/850Ft), which covers entrance to all such establishments except (and there is always an exception) the early Christian tomb and the Roman tomb sites. Tickets are available direct from the various sights.

The square mosque with its green copper dome was built with the stones of the ruined medieval church of St Bertalan in the mid-16th century; after the expulsion of the Turks, the Catholic Church repossessed it. The northern semicircular part was added in the 20th century. The Islamic elements on the south side are easy to spot: windows with distinctive Turkish ogee arches; the prayer niche (mihrab) carved into the interior southeast wall; faded verses from the Koran to the southwest; lovely geometric frescoes on the corners. The mosque's minaret was pulled down in 1753 and replaced with a tower.

The **Janus Pannonius Archaeology Museum** (Janus Pannonius Régészeti Múzeum; ☎ 312 719; Széchenyi tér 12; adult/child 200/100Ft; ☼ 10am-4pm Tue-Sun Apr-Oct, 10am-2pm Tue-Sat Nov-Mar), behind the Mosque Church in the 17th-century home of a janissary commander, traces the history of Baranya County up to the time of Árpád. It also contains many examples of Roman stonework from Pannonia, a model of St Bertalan's Church and medieval porcelain.

The **Trinity Column** in the lower part of Széchenyi tér is the third one to grace the spot and dates from 1908. The porcelain **Zsolnay Fountain**, with a lustrous glaze and pagan bull's head to the southeast in front of the rather gloomy **Church of the Good Samaritan**, was donated to the city by the Zsolnay factory in 1892.

KOSSUTH TÉR

This square southeast of Széchenyi tér has two important buildings: the Eclectic **town hall** (1891) to the north and the **synagogue** (adult/child 300/200Ft; ☼ 10am-5pm Sun-Thu May-Oct) to the east. The synagogue was built in the Romantic style in 1869, and a fact sheet, available in 11 languages, explains the history of the building and the city's Jewish population. Shortly after the fascist Hungarian government established a ghetto in Pécs in May 1944, most of the city's 3000 Jews were deported to the Nazi death camps; only 150 Jews now live in the city.

AROUND DÓM TÉR

The foundations of the four-towered **Basilica of St Peter** (☎ 513 030; Dóm tér; adult/child 1000/500Ft, includes entry to Jug Mausoleum, cathedral only 700/350Ft; ☼ 9am-5pm Mon-Sat, 1-5pm Sun Apr-Oct; 10am-4pm Mon-Sat, 1-4pm Sun Nov-Mar) – or simply

székesegyház (cathedral) – date from the 11th century and the side chapels are from the 1300s. But most of what you see today of the neo-Romanesque structure is the result of renovations carried out in 1881. Guided tours are conducted in Hungarian and German and cost 2000Ft.

The basilica is very ornate inside; the elevated central altar is a copy of a medieval one. The most interesting parts of the basilica are the four chapels under the towers and the crypt, the oldest part of the structure. The **Chapel of Mary** on the northwest side and the **Chapel of the Sacred Heart** to the northeast contain works by the 19th-century painters Bertalan Székely and Károly Lotz. The **Mór Chapel** to the southeast has more works by Székely as well as magnificent pews. The **Corpus Christi Chapel** on the southwest side (enter from the outside) boasts a 16th-century red marble tabernacle, one of the best examples of Renaissance stonework in the country.

The **Bishop's Palace** (Püspöki palota; 1770) to the southwest is only open to groups (and even then, rarely), but have a look at the curious **statue of Franz Liszt** (Imre Varga; 1983), peering over from a balcony. On the southern side of the baroque **Ecclesiastical Archives** (Egyházi levéltár) is the entrance to the **Jug Mausoleum** (Korsós sírkamra; adult/child 300/150Ft; ☼ 10am-6pm Tue-Sun), a 4th-century Roman tomb whose name comes from a painting of a large drinking vessel with vines found here. The **early Christian tomb chapel** (Ókeresztény sírkápolna; ☎ 312 719; Szent István tér 12; adult/child 350/200Ft; ☼ 10am-6pm Tue-Sun Apr-Oct, 10am-4pm Tue-Sun Nov-Mar), across Janus Pannonius utca, dates from about AD 350 and has frescoes of Adam and Eve, and Daniel in the lion's den. Two **Roman tomb sites** (Apáca utca 8 & 14; adult/child 350/200Ft; ☼ 10am-6pm Tue-Sun Apr-Oct) containing 110 graves, are a little further south. The entire area, which so far consists of 16 burial chambers and several hundred graves, is now a designated Unesco site.

The **Csontváry Museum** (☎ 310 544; Janus Pannonius utca 11; adult/child 600/300Ft; ☼ 10am-6pm Tue-Sun Apr-Oct, 10am-4pm Tue-Sun Nov-Mar) exhibits the major works of Tivadar Kosztka Csontváry (1853–1919), a unique symbolist painter whose tragic life is sometimes compared with that of Vincent van Gogh, who was born in the same year. Many of

Csontváry's oversized canvases are masterpieces, especially Storm on the Great Hortobágy (1903), Solitary Cedar (1907) and Baalbeck (1906), an artistic search for a larger identity through religious and historical themes.

To the west and north of Dóm tér is a long stretch of the **old city wall** that enclosed an area far too large to defend properly. The circular **barbican** (Esze Tamás utca 2), the only stone bastion to survive in Pécs, dates from the late 15th century and was restored in the 1970s.

KÁPTALAN UTCA

Káptalan utca, running east from Dóm tér to Hunyadi János út, contains a plethora of museums, all of them in listed buildings.

The **Ferenc Martyn Museum** (☎ 324 822; Káptalan utca 6; adult/child 400/200Ft; ❧ 10am-2pm Tue-Sun Apr-Oct) displays works by the Pécs-born painter and sculptor (1899–1986) and sponsors special exhibits of local interest.

The entry fee to the museum includes entry to the **Endre Nemes Museum** (☎ 310 172; Káptalan utca 5; ❧ 10am-2pm Tue-Sun Apr-Oct), which is devoted to paintings by the surrealist Endre Nemes (1908–85). In a separate pavilion behind it is Erzsébet Schaár's Utca (also included in the Martyn Museum ticket), a complete artistic environment in which the sculptor set her whole life in stone.

The **Modern Hungarian Art Gallery** (Modern Magyar Képtár; ☎ 324 822; Káptalan utca 4; adult/child 400/200Ft; ❧ 10am-6pm Tue-Sun Apr-Oct, 10am-4pm Tue-Sun Nov-Mar) is the best place to get an overview of art in Hungary between 1850 and today. For art up to 1950 pay special attention to the works of Simon Hollósy, József Rippl-Rónai and Ödön Márffy. For more abstract and constructionist art, watch out for the names András Mengyár, Tamás Hencze, Béla Uitz and Gábor Dienes. The **Péter Székely Gallery** behind the museum has large stone and wood sculptures.

The two most interesting museums are at the eastern end of the street: the **Vasarely Museum** (☎ 324 822; adult/child 600/300Ft; ❧ 10am-6pm Tue-Sun Apr-Oct, 10am-4pm Tue-Sun Nov-Mar) at No 3 and the **Zsolnay Porcelain Museum** (☎ 507 604; adult/child 700/350Ft; ❧ 10am-6pm Tue-Sun Apr-Oct, 10am-4pm Tue-Sun Nov-Mar) at No 2. Victor Vasarely was the father of Op Art and, although some of the works on exhibit by him and his disciples are dated, most are

evocative, very tactile and just plain fun. The Zsolnay porcelain factory was established in Pécs in 1853 and was at the forefront of art and design in Europe for more than half a century. Many of its majolica tiles were used to decorate buildings throughout the country and contributed to establishing a new pan-Hungarian style of architecture. Zsolnay's darkest period came when the postwar communist government turned it into a plant for making ceramic electrical insulators. It's producing art again (in very limited quantities), but contemporary Zsolnay can't hold a candle to the chinoiserie pieces from the late 19th century and the later Art-Nouveau and Art-Deco designs done in the lustrous eosin glaze. The museum, housed in a residence dating from the Middle Ages, was the home of the Zsolnay family and contains many of their furnishings and personal effects. Also in the museum is an exhibition of sculptures by Amerigo Tot (1909–84).

OTHER SIGHTS

Southwest of the inner town and opposite the Pátria hotel is the **Pasha Hassan Jakovali Mosque** (Jakováli Hasszán Pasa dzsámija; ☎ 313 853; Rákóczi út 2; adult/child 240/100Ft; ❧ 10am-1pm & 2-6pm Thu-Tue Apr-Sep), wedged between a trade school and a hospital. The 16th-century mosque – complete with minaret – is the most intact of any Turkish structure in Hungary and contains a small museum of Ottoman *objets d'art*. The **Ethnography Museum** (Néprajzi Múzeum; ☎ 315 629; Rákóczi út 15; adult/child 300/150Ft; ❧ 10am-6pm Tue-Sun Apr-Oct, 10am-4pm Tue-Sun Nov-Mar) to the southeast, showcases ethnic Hungarian, German and South Slav folk art in the region.

One of Pécs' most enjoyable pedestrian streets, Ferencesek utcája, runs east from Rákóczi út to Széchenyi tér, where Király utca also becomes pedestrian. You'll pass the ruins of the 16th-century **Pasha Memi Baths** (Memi pasa fürdője; Ferencesek utcája 35), three beautiful old churches and, on Király utca, the neo-rococo **Pécs National Theatre**. Just past the theatre you'll run into the **Marcipán Museum** (☎ 225 453; Király utca 36; adult/child 300/200Ft; ❧ 11am-8pm), where you can make your own delectable delight or buy one from the museum shop. After passing the **Church of St Stephen** (Szent István-templom; Király utca 44/a), turn south (right), where you'll find the excellent

City History Museum (Várostörténeti Múzeum; ☎ 310 165; Felsőmalom utca 9; adult/child 300/150Ft; ☻ 10am-4pm Tue-Sat May-Oct, 10am-2pm Tue-Sat Nov-Apr).

The suburb of Budaiváros to the northeast of the town centre is where most Hungarians settled after the Turks banned them from living within the city walls. The centre of this community was the **All Saints' Church** (Mindenszentek temploma; ☎ 324 937; Tettye utca 14; admission free). Originally built in the 12th century, it was reconstructed in Gothic style 200 years later. All Saints was the only Christian church allowed in Pécs during the occupation and was shared by three sects – who fought bitterly for every square centimetre. Apparently it was the Muslim Turks who had to keep the peace among the Christians.

To the northeast up on a hill is **Havi-hegy Chapel** (☎ 314 715; Havihegyi utca 7; admission free), built in 1691 by the faithful after the town was spared the plague. The church is an important city landmark, and offers wonderful views of the inner town and the narrow streets and old houses of the Tettye Valley.

To get a taste of the Mecsek Hills, walk northeast from the centre of Pécs to Tettye and the **Garden of Ruins** (Romkert), what's left of a bishop's summer residence built early in the 16th century and later used by Turkish dervishes as a monastery. To the northwest, up Fenyves sor and past the **zoo** (állatkert; ☎ 312 788; adult/child/student 600/450/500Ft; ☻ 9am-6pm Apr-Oct), a winding road leads to **Misina Peak** (535m) and a **TV tower** (☎ 336 900; adult/student/child 450/350/300Ft; ☻ 9am-9pm Sun-Thu, 9am-11pm Fri & Sat Jun-Aug; 9am-6pm Sep-May), an impressive 194m structure with a viewing platform and café-bar. But these are just the foothills: from here, trails lead to the lovely towns of **Orfű** and **Abaliget**, on a plateau 15km and 20km to the northwest, respectively; and to Southern Transdanubia's highest peak, **Zengő-hegy** (682m).

The Sunday flea market (Vásár tér), about 3km southwest of the inner town on Megyeri út, attracts people from the countryside, especially on the first Sunday of the month.

Activities

The closest swimming complex to the centre is **Hullám** (☎ 512 935; Szendrey Júlia utca 7; adult/child 700/350Ft; ☻ indoor pool 6am-10pm, outdoor pool 9am-7pm in summer).

Festivals & Events

Among the big annual events in this party town are **International Culture Week** (www.icwip.hu) in late July that focuses on theatrical performances; **Pécs Days** in late September, a 10-day festival of dance and music with a couple of alcohol-related events; and the **European Wine Song Festival** (www.winesongfestival.hu) also in late September, and Europe's only festival exclusively for male singers.

Sleeping

BUDGET

Both Mecsek Tours and Ibusz can arrange private rooms (from 2500Ft per person) and while Tourinform has a list of such places, it will only book hotels. Many of Pécs' *pensions* are sprinkled in the surrounding hills and rather difficult to get to without your own transport.

Centrum (☎ 311 707; www.hotels.hu/centrum_kishotel; Szepessy Ignác utca 4; s/d 4500/5600Ft) Centrum believes in old-fashion hospitality – homely, welcoming and slightly left of centre. Rooms are a collection of mismatching furniture but its central position is unbeatable.

Laterum (☎ 252 113; www.laterum.hu; Hajnóczy utca 37-39; s/d 5200/8400Ft; ℗) The institutional air of this large hotel, 3km west of town, is offset by exceptionally large and clean rooms, reasonable prices, and a bar and restaurant on site.

Főnix (☎ 311 682; www.fonixhotel.hu; Hunyadi János út 2; s/d 5990/9990Ft; ℗) Főnix appears to be a hotel too large for the land it's built on; not an inch is left over for an outdoor area. Some rooms are not even big enough to swing a cat in, while others sport balconies. It is however only a stone's throw from the Mosque Church.

In July and August many of the city's colleges (1600Ft to 2000Ft per person) open up their doors to travellers, including central **Pollack Mihály College** (☎ 315 846; Jókai utca 8) and **János College** (☎ 251 234; Szánto Kovács János utca 1/c) further to the west; both have dormitories with two to five beds. Tourinform has a list of more places if you require.

MIDRANGE

Lenau Haus (☎ 332 515; lenauhaus@mail.datanet.hu; Munkácsy Mihály utca 8; s/d 6800/8800Ft; ℗) Rooms on the top floor of the house where the composer Nikolaus Lenau resided are among the best options in Pécs.

Expect to find large rooms with spotless en suite bathrooms.

Diana (☎ 328 594; www.hoteldiana.hu; Tímár 4/a; s/d 7000/10,000Ft; P) With eight excellent hotel-style rooms, this *pension* has plenty of home comforts and a warm welcome. A great choice just south of the synagogue.

Abraham (☎ 510 422; Munkácsy Mihály utca 8; s/d 7500/10,500Ft; P) This excellent little *pension*, with sparkling blue rooms, a well-tended, peaceful garden and friendly welcome, has a distinct Mediterranean feel. Note that it is a religious establishment, so raucous behaviour isn't welcome.

Toboz (☎ 510 555; www.tobozpanzio.hu; Fenyves sor 5; s/d 8600/11,600Ft; P) Just south of the zoo on a tree-lined street high above the city, Toboz has a retreat feel and old, uncomfortable rooms.

Palatinus (☎ 889 400; palatinus.reservation@danubiusgroup.hu; Király utca 5; s €58-86, d €66-94; P) Palatinus is Pécs' old-world hotel. Its reception is quite exceptional, featuring plenty of marble and Moorish flourishes, but unfortunately the rooms leave a little to be desired. All in all, though, it's a grand old dame.

Hunyor (☎ 512 640; postmaster@ptehunyor.axelero.net; Jurisics Miklós utca 16; s/d 9200/12,400Ft; P) Hunyor is in the Mecsek foothills and a bit out of the way, but it has excellent views of the city and a laid-back air. There's a pleasant restaurant attached, so it's not far to wander for a meal.

Fenyves Panoráma (☎ 315 996; www.hotelfenyves.hu; Szőlő utca 64; s/d 8900/11,100Ft; P) Fenyves is another hotel in the foothills to the north, with a balcony looking down onto the city below. Its rooms are big but bland.

Eating

RESTAURANTS

Tex-Mex Café (☎ 215 427; Teréz utca 10; mains 1000-1500Ft) For a welcome change of pace from Hungarian music and cuisine, duck into this colourful cellar restaurant, serving tacos, enchiladas and a shot of tequila to wash it all down with.

Aranykacsa (☎ 518 860; Teréz utca 4; mains 2000Ft) This eatery may have dropped its pretentiousness a couple of notches, but it still takes pride in its silver service and sports a menu with the likes of duck liver with caviar, and pheasant roast accompanied by green salad.

Dóm (☎ 210 088; Király utca 3; mains 1000-1500Ft, steaks 3000Ft) This loft restaurant has wonderful *fin-de-siècle* paintings and stained-glass windows, not to mention steaks.

Az Elefánthoz (☎ 216 055; Jókai tér 6; mains 1500Ft) With its enormous terrace and quality Italian cuisine, Elefánthoz is a sure bet for first-rate food in the centre of town.

Aranyfolyó (☎ 212 269; Váradi Antal utca 9; mains 1000Ft) The two Chinese dragons guarding the door of this restaurant are a dead giveaway to the cuisine on offer, which includes all the standards from the land many miles to the east.

Cellárium (☎ 314 453; Hunyadi János út 2; mains 1000-1500Ft) Just below the Főnix hotel, this is a more than reliable choice for a meal close to the centre.

CAFÉS

There's an ongoing debate in Pécs over which *cukrászda* (cake shop) serves better cakes and ice cream: the **Mecsek** (☎ 315 444; Széchenyi tér 16), near the old Nádor hotel, or the **Virág** (☎ 313 793; Irgalmasok utcája). The best bet is to try them both.

Cutty Sark Teaház (☎ 513 082; Káptalan utca 6; tea from 100Ft; ☉ 10am-10pm) For a quality cuppa and a sandwich (hopefully cucumber), drop into this little 'slice of England' tucked away among the museums along Káptalan utca.

QUICK EATS

Oázis (Király utca 17; kebabs & dishes 500-800Ft) A cheap little kebab house serving a mix of Turkish and Middle Eastern dishes. This is a great spot for a meal on the run.

Árkád Shopping Centre (Bajcsy-Zsilinszky utca 11/1; ☉ 9am-8pm Mon-Sat, 10am-6pm Sun) This big, bold and new shopping centre has a food court, which is a safe bet for quick food.

AUTHOR'S CHOICE

Áfium (☎ 511 434; Irgalmasok utca 2; mains 1000-1500Ft) With Croatia and Serbia so close, it's a wonder that more restaurants don't concentrate, as Áfium does, on cuisine from south of the border. But no matter, this restaurant will fulfil most diners searching for such tastes. The food is better than average and the atmosphere decidedly relaxed, while the décor could easily double as the set for Steptoe & Son. If you've eaten elsewhere, Áfium is just as good for a quiet drink.

SELF-CATERING

Pécs' fruit and vegetable market (Zólyom utca) is near the bus station, and a 24-hour **Tesco** (Makay István út) is to the west.

Drinking

Dante Café (☎ 210 361; Janus Pannonius 11) Occupying the ground floor of the Csontváry Museum, this is a good place to meet local students, and has a huge garden and occasionally live music.

Kaptalani (Janus Pannonius utca) A lovely little *borozó*, with outdoor seating near the cathedral. Kaptalani is also a great spot to try the local wine – white Cirfandli, a speciality of the Mecsek Hills.

While visiting the cathedral or the museums along Káptalan utca, stop in for a drink or a coffee at the **Kioszk** in the little park between Káptalan utca and Janus Pannonius utca. It's probably the only chance you'll ever have to drink in what was once a baptistry.

Pubs and bars line the entire length of Király utca, so you should have no problem finding one that suits. Reliable choices include the **Royal Café** at No 1 and **Arizona Ranch** at No 29.

Entertainment

MUSIC & THEATRE

Pécs is a city of culture. The list of theatres and concert venues is extensive for a place of its size, and most times of the year you can find something going on. For tickets and information visit the **Pécs Cultural Centre** (☎ 336 622; Széchenyi tér 1), or pick up the biweekly freebie Pécsi Est.

House of Artists (☎ 522 834; Széchenyi tér 7-8; ☷ noon-5pm Mon-Fri) It advertises its many cultural programmes outside, including classical music concerts.

Lenau Haus (☎ 332 515; Munkácsy Mihály utca 8; s/d 6800/8800Ft; Ⓟ) This one-time residence of composer Nikolaus Lenau hosts classical concerts throughout the year.

Pécs National Theatre (www.pnsz.hu/; ☎ 512 660; Király utca) Pécs is also renowned for its opera company and the Sophianae Ballet, which perform here. If you're told that tickets are sold out, try for a cancellation at the box office an hour before the performance. Advance tickets can be purchased from the theatre office (☎ 512 675; Perczel Mór 17; ☷ 10am-7pm Tue-Fri, 1hr before performances Sat & Sun).

Other venues:

Chamber Theatre Next door to the National Theatre.
Croatian Theatre (☎ 210 197; Anna utca 17)
Bóbita Puppet Theatre (☎ 210 301; Mária utca 18) Somewhere John Malkovich would be proud to perform.

CLUBS & DISCOS

Pécs, a big university town, has a good nightlife. Some of the city's most popular discos and music clubs:

Club 5 (☎ 212 621; Irgalmasok utca 24) This basement bar transforms itself into a small club on Saturday and Sunday, and invites punters in with funky sounds and late-nite drinks.

CRN (☎ 30-650 7021; Czindery utca 6) A big club, popular with the 'In' crowd.

Rák (☎ 502 557; Ipar utca 7) Beyond the fruit and vegetable market, this is the place to go for rock and heavy beats.

Shopping

Pécs has been renowned for its leatherwork since Turkish times and you can pick up a few bargains in several shops around the city; try one called **Blázek** (Teréz utca 1), which deals mainly in handbags and wallets. **Zsolnay** (☎ 507 609; Jókai tér 2) porcelain also has an outlet just north of here.

Getting There & Away

BUS

Departures are frequent (once an hour) to Siklós (363Ft, 45 minutes, 29km), Mohács (544Ft, 1¼ hours, 44km), Harkány (484Ft, one hour, 37km), Kaposvár (786Ft, 1½ hours, 65km), Szigetvár (423Ft, 50 minutes, 35km) and Szekszárd (786Ft, 1½ hours, 62km). There are four buses a day to Abaliget (241Ft, one hour, 20km) and three to Orfű (302Ft, 40 minutes, 22km) in the Mecsek Hills throughout the year, but far more in summer.

You can also reach the following:

Destination	Price	Duration	Km	Frequency
Budapest	2540Ft	4½hr	208	5 daily
Győr	2660Ft	4½hr	217	2 daily
Kecskemét	2780Ft	4¼hr	226	2 daily
Sellye	725Ft	1½hr	57	2 daily
Siófok	1690Ft	3hr	133	3 daily
Szeged	2410Ft	4¼hr	196	8 daily
Székesfehérvár	1930Ft	3hr	157	3 daily
Veszprém	2300Ft	4¼hr	181	2 daily
Villány	423Ft	1¼hr	34	1-2 daily

TRAIN

Up to nine direct trains a day connect Pécs with Budapest (2360Ft, 2½ to four hours, 228km). You can reach Nagykanizsa (1624Ft, three hours) and other points northwest via a rather circuitous but scenic 148km journey along the Dráva River. From Nagykanizsa, up to eight trains a day continue on to Szombathely (2510Ft, four to 5½ hours, 250km). One early morning express (5.21am) follows this route from Pécs all the way to Szombathely. Three daily trains run from Pécs (4.58am, 2.45pm and 8.42pm) to Osijek (Hungarian: Eszék), the last of which continues onto Sarajevo.

The **MÁV office** (Jókai Mór utca 4; 9am-3.30pm Mon & Fri, 9am-4.30pm Tue-Thu) has more information on train arrivals and departures.

Getting Around

To get to the Hunyor hotel, take bus 32 from the train station, or from opposite the Mosque Church. Buses 34 and 35 run direct to the Fenyves hotels from the train station, with bus 35 continuing onto the TV tower. For the Laterum hotel, take bus 4 from the train station or the market near the bus station to the end of the line at Uránváros. Buses 3 and 50 from the train station are good for the flea market on Vásár tér.

You can order a local taxi by calling ☎ 333 333.

MECSEK HILLS

The Mecsek Hills, a string of hills and valleys dotted with villages and the occasional lake to the north of Pécs, is the city's playground. There's good hiking to be had here, but before setting out on any big excursions, pick up a copy of Cartographia's 1:40,000 *A Mecsek* map (No 15; 800Ft).

For transport information, see Pécs Getting There and Away.

Orfű

☎ 72 / pop 700

The most accessible of the Mecsek Hills resorts and the one with the most recreational facilities is Orfű – a series of settlements on four artificial lakes, where you can swim, row, canoe and fish. There's a riding school at the **Tekeresi Lovaspanzió** (Tekeres Horse Pension; ☎ 06 30 227 1401; Petőfi utca 3) at Tekeres to the northwest. From Széchenyi tér you can walk south along tiny Lake Orfű to the

Mill Museum (Malommúzeum; ☎ 498 440; adult/child 300/200Ft; 10am-5pm May-Sep), a series of old pump houses.

SLEEPING & EATING

Tekeresi Lovaspanzió (☎ 06 30 227 1401; fleisch mane@freemail.hi; Petőfi utca 3; r 600Ft, apt 11,000Ft; P) At the horse-riding centre of the same name, this is a kid-friendly and welcoming place; you will of course have to put up with the whiff of horse every now and then. It has well-kept rooms and apartments, which feel more like home than anything else.

Panoráma Camping (☎ 378 501; www.panorama camping.hu; Dollár utca 1; camp sites per adult/child/tent €2.50-3/1.50-1.70/2.50-5.50, bungalows €21.50-28; May-mid-Sep; P) Above the large public beach in the lake's southwestern corner, this place has dinghies, sailboards and bicycles for rent. The campground itself is green and secluded, and the staff is exceptionally friendly.

Also worth noting:

Atrium (☎ 498 288; www.hotels.hu/atriumpanzio; Széchenyi tér 17; r from 10,200Ft; P) It has a kid's playground and front garden. There is a good restaurant and the rooms are spotless.

Molnár Pension (☎ 378 563; Széchenyi tér 18/a; s/d from 4500/9000Ft; P) A small *pension* five minutes' walk to the lake, with homely rooms.

Muskátli (Széchenyi tér; mains 1000Ft) A pleasant little restaurant near Molnár Pension.

Abaliget

☎ 72 / pop 660

Abaliget, about 3km north of Orfű and accessible by bus or on foot via a trail up and over the hill behind Panoráma Camping, is quieter but not as attractive. Aside from a relaxed air, the town's main attraction is the **Abaliget Cave** (☎ 498 766; adult/child 750/550Ft; 9am-6pm Apr-Sep, 10am-3pm Oct-Mar), which, at 1.3km, is the longest cave open to the public in Southern Transdanubia. However, only 450m of the caves can be visited.

There are some private rooms and *pensions* along Kossuth Lajos utca, the main street, or try **Barlang Camping** (☎ 515 700; camp sites per adult/child/tent 800/400/1000Ft, pension r 5400Ft, bungalows 6600Ft; P) on the town's tiny lake. The camping ground is OK, but the *pension* rooms will only do at a pinch.

The last bus for Pécs leaves at 8.18pm daily from outside the caves.

KAPOSVÁR

☎ 82 / pop 68,700

Considering the ugly suburbs encapsulating Kaposvár, it comes as a pleasant surprise to find the city's main street so full of charm, with pastel coloured two-storey houses and buckets of cultural heritage. The city is associated with three famous Hungarian painters – the postimpressionists József Rippl-Rónai and János Vaszary, as well as Aurél Bernáth – and the Gergely Csiky theatre is among the best in provincial Hungary. It's also the capital of Somogy County, which is usually associated with the Balaton and rightly so; it controls the entire money-spinning southern shore of the lake from Siófok to Balatonberény, some 55km to the north.

Orientation

The train and bus stations are a block apart on Budai Nagy Antal utca, south of the city centre. From here, walk up Teleki utca to Kossuth tér and Fő utca, a lovely pedestrian street where most of the action is.

Information

Main post office (Bajcsy-Zsilinszky utca 15) West of Széchenyi tér.

OTP bank (Széchenyi tér 2) Has several ATMs.

Tourinform (☎ 512 921; kaposvar@tourinform.hu; Fő utca 8; ☆ 9am-6pm Mon-Fri, 9am-5pm Sat, 9am-2pm Sun mid-Jun–mid-Sep, 9am-5pm Mon-Fri, 9am-2pm Sat mid-Sep–mid-Jun) Has Internet access free of charge.

www.kaposvar.hu Check for online information on the town.

Sights

In among the pretty, pastel-coloured buildings lining Fő utca is the former county hall (1820) at No 10, which now houses two museums: the **Somogy County & Rippl-Rónai Museums** (☎ 314 114; adult/child 600/300Ft; ☆ 10am-4pm Tue-Sun Apr-Oct, 10am-3pm Tue-Sun Nov-Mar). Inside the Somogy County Museum, you'll find a large ethnographical collection and a gallery of contemporary art on the ground floor. There is a grand collection of paintings on the 1st floor, which include works by Vaszary, Bernáth and Béla Kádár.

The folk collection is noteworthy for its wood and horn carvings (at which the

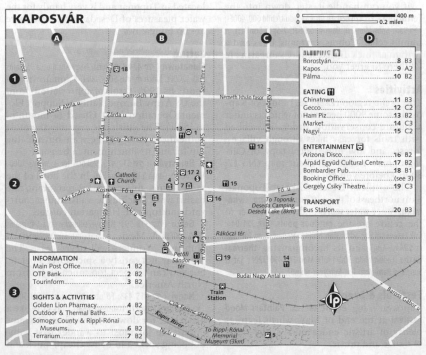

KAPOSVÁR

0 ——————— 400 m
0 ——————— 0.2 miles

SLEEPING
Borostyán..................................8 B3
Kapos.......................................9 A2
Pálma.....................................10 B2

EATING
Chinatown..............................11 B3
Gecco....................................12 C2
Ham Piz.................................13 B2
Market...................................14 C3
Nagyi....................................15 C2

ENTERTAINMENT
Arizona Disco.........................16 B2
Árpád Együd Cultural Centre...17 B2
Bombardier Pub......................18 B1
Booking Office.....................(see 3)
Gergely Csiky Theatre.............19 C3

TRANSPORT
Bus Station............................20 B3

INFORMATION
Main Post Office...........................1 B2
OTP Bank.....................................2 B2
Tourinform...................................3 B2

SIGHTS & ACTIVITIES
Golden Lion Pharmacy...................4 B2
Outdoor & Thermal Baths.............5 C3
Somogy County & Rippl-Rónai
  Museums.................................6 B2
Terrarium.....................................7 B2

swineherds of Somogy County excelled); examples of famous *kékfestő* (indigo-dyed cotton fabrics); an exhibition on the county's infamous outlaws (including the paprika-tempered 'Horseshoe Steve'); and costumes of the Croatian minority, who dressed and decorated their houses in white fabric during mourning periods as the Chinese do. The top floor is full of paintings by Ödön Rippl-Rónai, the brother of Kaposvár's most celebrated – and arguably Hungary's best – painter, József Rippl-Rónai (1861–1927).

József Rippl-Rónai was born at Fő 19, above the lovely **Golden Lion Pharmacy** (Aranyoroszlán Patika; admission free; ☉ 7.30am-6pm Mon-Fri), built in 1774 and now a museum. Most of his work is exhibited in the **Rippl-Rónai Memorial Museum** (Rippl-Rónai Emlékmúzeum; ☎ 422 144; Rómahegy 88; adult/child 400/200Ft; ☉ 10am-6pm Tue-Sun Apr-Oct, 10am-4pm Nov-Mar), a graceful 19th-century villa about 3km southeast of the city centre.

Built in 1911, the cream and lemon-coloured Secessionist **Gergely Csiky Theatre** (Rákóczi tér 2), with its hundreds of arched windows, is worth a look even if you are not attending a performance.

If you can handle it, step down into the **Terrarium** (☎ 424 460; Fő utca 31; adult/child 600/400Ft; ☉ 9am-5pm Mon-Fri, 9am-noon Sat, 2-5pm Sun) in a humid cellar. Cobras, caymans, boas and a python as thick as a stevedore's forearm are all there to greet you.

Activities

The Zselic region (Zselicség) south of Kaposvár, some 9000 hectares of which is under a nature-conservation order, is webbed with trails for easy **hikes** through villages, forests and low hills. Get a copy of Cartographia's 1:60,000 *A Zselic* map (No 17; 800Ft) before you go.

The artificial Deseda Lake at Toponár, 8km northeast of the city, offers **cycling**, **swimming**, other **water sports** and **tennis**. Closer to the centre are the **outdoor pools** (☎ 321 044; Csík Ferenc sétány; admission 220Ft; ☉ 9am-7pm Tue-Sun mid-May–Aug) and its accompanying **thermal baths** (adult/child 300/170Ft Mon-Fri, 490/220Ft Sat & Sun; ☉ 9am-7pm Tue-Sun year-round).

Festivals & Events

Kaposvár's big event is the **Painters Mood Festival** at the end of May, which features plenty of artistic endeavours in the fields of dance and music.

Sleeping

Tourinform has information on private rooms (from 3000Ft), but it won't help you with making bookings.

Borostyán (☎ 512 475; Rákóczi tér 3; s/d from 7900/8900Ft; P) An upmarket six-room Art-Nouveau extravaganza, this is one of provincial Hungary's most interesting caravanserais. Rooms are more than spacious and tastefully decorated, and bathrooms come with tubs.

Pálma (☎ 420 227; Széchenyi tér 6; r 6800Ft; P) Considering its location so close to the centre, Pálma is a surprisingly quiet and peaceful *pension*, with big rooms filled with comfy, if mismatched, furniture. Breakfast can be taken on the covered terrace towards the rear.

Kapos (☎ 316 022; www.kaposhotel.hu; Kossuth tér; s/d from 5900/8000Ft; P ☐) Kapos was once probably the town's luxury establishment, but these days it's a fairly unattractive block with little character. It is, however, very central and the staff is happy to see you.

Deseda Camping (☎ 312 020; ☉ mid-Jun–late Aug) Deseda is the closest campsite to the city. It's located in Toponár and is very handy for the water pleasures of Deseda Lake. Note there are no bungalows.

Eating

Chinatown (☎ 424 828; Budai Nagy Antal utca 9; mains 700-1200Ft, lunch menus 500-700Ft) Chinatown still sports its 1998 'scroll of appreciation' from the US Army Europe National Support Element Operation Joint Guard (a mouthful in itself). The cuisine is arguably the most authentic Chinese-American outside the capital and its lunch menu a bargain.

Borostyán (☎ 512 475; Rákóczi tér 3; mains 1000-1800Ft; ☉ until 11pm Mon-Sat) In the hotel of the same name, this colourful restaurant/café has art work gracing the walls, a quiet courtyard and top-rate Hungarian cuisine.

Gecco (☎ 312 993; Bajcsy-Zsilinszky utca 54; mains 1500-200Ft) A Mexican eatery in provincial Hungary! Wonders will never cease. The food may not satisfy a spice-lover's palate, but you can't expect too much so far from North America.

Nagyi (☎ 315 433; Fő utca 35; lunch meals 500Ft; ☉ 7am-8pm Mon-Fri, 10am-4pm Sat) Nagyi is like a black hole for downtown workers; it seems impossible for most to wander past without being sucked in by its cheap, quick and good lunch meals. You'll probably find the gravity pull too much to resist as well.

Ham Piz (Bajcsy-Zsilinszky utca 13; burgers & pizzas from 350Ft) Next to the main post office, this place attracts groups of gabbling students and those looking for a cheap bite to eat, with quick service and filling fast food.

The fruit and vegetable **market** is east of Rákóczi tér.

Entertainment

Árpád Együd Cultural Centre (☎ 512 228; Csokonai utca 1) Has information on cultural events in Kaposvár, as does the free biweekly magazine *Kapo Est*.

Gergely Csiky Theatre (☎ 528 458; Rákóczi tér 2) At the forefront of Hungarian artistic innovation in the 1970s, the theatre is a masterpiece of Art-Nouveau (or Secessionist) architecture and is now in need of repair. Its plays have a great reputation around the country. The **booking office** (☎ 511 208; Fő utca 8; ☯ 8.30am-12.30pm & 1-5pm Mon-Fri, 8.30am-noon Sat) is at Tourinform.

Kaposvár is known for its choral groups, and concerts are given in venues around the city, including the Catholic church on Kossuth tér.

Kaposvár has two clubs competing for custom; at present, **Arizona Disco** (☎ 411 443; Fő utca 14), in the heart of town, is pipping **Bombardier Pub** (☎ 423 721; Honvéd utca 8) at the popularity post.

Getting There & Away

BUS

Twelve daily buses go to Pécs (786Ft, 1½ hours, 65km). Other destinations include Hévíz (1150Ft, 2¼ hours, 95km, two daily), Nagykanizsa (968Ft, 1¾ hours, 77km, two daily), Szekszárd (1210Ft, 2½ hours, 99km, one daily), Szigetvár (544Ft, 1¼ hours, 40km, two daily), Szombathely (2300Ft, 3½ hours, 188km, three daily) and Zalaegerszeg (1570Ft, 2½ hours, 128km, four daily).

TRAIN

You can reach Kaposvár by train from both the eastern (Siófok) and western (Fonyód) ends of Lake Balaton's southern shore. Another line links Kaposvár with Budapest (2030Ft, 3½ hours, 195km; via Dombóvár) to the northeast up to twice a day and, to the west, with Gyékényes (658Ft, 1½ hours, 70km, two daily).

Getting Around

Buses 8 and 18 terminate near the lake and the campsite in Toponár. For the Rippl-Rónai Memorial Museum in Róma-hegy, take bus 15.

Local taxis are available by calling ☎ 555 555.

SZIGETVÁR

☎ 73 / pop 11,350

Szigetvár, a quiet town 33km west of Pécs and 40km south of Kaposvár, is home to the remains of one of Hungary's most celebrated castles and a handful of Turkish-era monuments. Also close by is the Park of Turkish–Hungarian Friendship, which has helped to cement the friendly ties between the two former enemies.

The town began life as a Celtic settlement before the Romans moved in and renamed it Limosa. After the Magyar conquest its strategic importance was recognised and in 1420 a fortress was built on a small island – Szigetvár means 'island castle' – in the marshy areas of the Almás. But Szigetvár would be indistinguishable today from other Southern Transdanubian towns had the events of September 1566 not taken place (see boxed text, p307).

Orientation

The bus and train stations are close to one another, a short distance south of the town centre at the end of Rákóczi utca. To reach the centre follow this road north into lovely Zrínyi tér. Vár utca on the northern side of the square leads to the castle.

Information

Main post office (József Attila utca 27-31)

OTP bank (Vár utca 4) On the way to the castle, with an ATM.

Tájoló Agency (☎ 312 654; Zrínyi tér 3; ☯ 9am-4pm Mon-Thu, 9am-3pm Fri) Can supply you with a small amount of information on the town.

Vigadó (József Attila utca; per hr 200Ft; ☯ 9am-5pm Mon, Tue & Fri, 9am-3pm Wed & Thu) Internet access is available here.

Zrínyi Castle

Our hero Miklós Zrínyi would probably not recognise the four-cornered **castle** (Vár utca; adult/child 400/250Ft; ☯ 9am-5pm Tue-Sun May-Sep, 9am-3pm Tue-Sun Apr & Oct) he so valiantly fought to save more than 400 years ago.

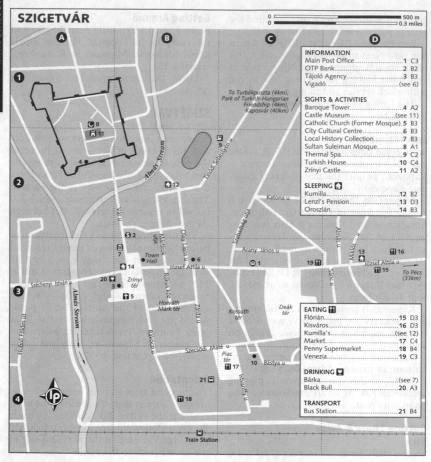

SZIGETVÁR

The Turks strengthened the bastions and added buildings; the Hungarians rebuilt much of the castle again in the 18th century. Today there are only a few elements of historical interest left: walls from 3m to 6m thick linked by the four bastions; the **Baroque Tower** crowning the southern wall; the 16th-century **Sultan Suleiman Mosque** (Szulejmán pasa dzsámija), with its truncated minaret; and a summer mansion built by Count Andrássy in 1930, which now houses the **Castle Museum**.

Naturally, the museum's exhibits focus on the siege and its key players: Zrínyi's praises are sung throughout; there's a detailed account of how Suleiman built a bridge over the Dráva River in 16 days to attack Szigetvár; and miniatures of Hungarian soldiers being captured, chopped up and burned are still quite horrifying. Sebestyén Tinódi, the beloved 16th-century poet and wandering minstrel who was born in Szigetvár, also rates an altar of worship. The mosque next door, completed in the year of the siege, contains an art gallery; the arches, prayer niches and Arabic inscriptions on the walls are worth a look. There's also a small *büfé* (snack bar) north of the mosque.

OTHER SIGHTS

The tiny **Local History Collection** (Helytörténeti Gyűjtemény; Vár utca 1; adult/child 200/100Ft; 9am-4pm Tue-Sat) is a hotchpotch of folk carvings, embroidery and valuables from local churches, but it also displays a great collection of 18th- and 19th-century shop signs as well as locks and keys from the castle.

The ogee (called 'donkey's back' arches in Hungarian) windows and hexagonal roof of the baroque **Catholic church** (Zrínyi tér 9; admission free) are the only exterior signs that this was once the Pasha Ali Mosque, built in 1589. The altarpiece of the Crucifixion and the ceiling frescoes depicting the deaths of Zrínyi and Suleiman were painted by István Dorffmeister in 1789.

Not far from the bus station, the 16th-century **Turkish House** (Török-ház; Bástya utca 3; adult/child 200/100Ft; ☒ 10am-noon & 1-3pm Tue-Sun Jun-Sep) was a caravanserai during the occupation and contains an exhibit of Turkish miniatures.

The Catholic church at Turbékpuszta, about 4km northeast of Szigetvár, was originally built as a **tomb for Suleiman**. But according to local tradition, only the sultan's heart lies within; his son and successor, Selim II, had the body exhumed and returned to Turkey.

Some 4km north of Szigetvár on Rte 67 to Kaposvár, a Turkish-era battlefield has been turned into the **Park of Turkish–Hungarian Friendship** (Török-Magyar barátság parkja; ☒ dawn-dusk), with interesting stone memorials in the shape of domes and turbans, and statues commemorating both Suleiman and Zrínyi.

You can't miss the flamboyant **City Cultural Centre** (Városi Művelődési Ház; József Attila utca), which was designed – surprise, surprise – by maverick architect Imre Makovecz (using his own 'organic' style).

Activities

Szigetvár's **thermal spa** (☎ 312 840; Tinódi Sebestyén utca 23) was closed for renovation at the time of research but expect it to be open between the hours of 9am and 5pm or 7pm daily.

Sleeping

The Tájoló Agency may be able to help you find a private room.

Kumilla (☎ 514 015; szik.kft@axelero.hu; Olay Lajos utca 6; s/d from 5200/7000Ft; P) Kumilla is starting to look a little run-down but with its peaceful location backing onto a small stream, views of the castle, welcoming staff and cosy rooms, it's still the best option in Szigetvár.

Lenzl's Pension (☎ 413 045; lenzls@dravanet.hu; József Attila utca 63; s/d from 4000/4500Ft; P) This very friendly *pension* has small but attractive rooms (some of which come with a balcony), free parking and a restaurant on the ground floor.

Oroszlán (☎ 310 116; mexbor@axelero.hu; Zrínyi tér 2; s/d 7300/9600Ft; P) With its purely functional rooms and drab décor, Oroszlán is a last resort if the above options are full.

Eating & Drinking

Flórián (☎ 311 939; József Attila utca 58; mains 1000Ft) This simple restaurant has a rather appealing garden at the rear, away from the busy

---

BIG SALLY OF SZIGETVÁR

For more than a month at Szigetvár in late 1566, Captain Miklós Zrínyi and the 2500 Hungarian and Croatian soldiers under his command held out against Turkish forces numbering up to 80,000. The leader of the Turks was Sultan Suleiman I, who was making his seventh attempt to march on Vienna and was determined to take what he derisively called 'this molehill'. When the defenders' water and food supplies were exhausted – and reinforcements from Győr under Habsburg Emperor Maximilian II were refused – Zrínyi could see no other solution but a suicidal sally. As the moated castle went up in flames, the opponents fought hand to hand, and most of the soldiers on the Hungarian side, including Zrínyi himself, were killed. An estimated one-quarter of the Turkish forces died in the siege; Suleiman died of a heart attack and his corpse was propped up on a chair during the fighting to inspire his troops and avoid a power struggle until his son could take command.

More than any other heroes in Hungarian history, Zrínyi and his soldiers are remembered for their self-sacrifice in the cause of the nation and for saving Vienna – and thereby Europe – from Turkish domination. *Peril at Sziget*, a 17th-century epic poem by Zrínyi's great-grandson and namesake, Miklós Zrínyi (1620–64), immortalises the siege and is still widely read in Hungary.

main road, and has made room for a few vegetarian dishes on its meat-heavy menu.

Kumilla's (☎ 514 015; Olay Lajos utca 6; mains 800-1500Ft) In the hotel of the same name, this quiet and pleasant restaurant serves solid Hungarian fare and a large terrace.

Venezia (József Attila utca 41; pizzas from 500Ft) Venezia's outdoor tables may face busy József Attila utca but it's still the best spot in town for pizzas.

Kisváros (☎ 312 514; József Attila utca 81; mains 800Ft) Directly opposite Flórián, this basic restaurant serving Hungarian food is quite dingy indoors; its outdoor seating area out the back is a far better option.

Szigetvár's market, near the bus and train stations, is the usual motley assortment of tacky goods, food stalls and fresh fruit and vegetables.

Szigetvár is not known for its nightlife, but there are a couple of places for a quiet drink during the evening. **Black Bull** (Széchenyi utca 2) serves average pizza but it's a popular place for a beer, while **Bárka** (Vár utca 1), a small coffee shop/bar in the Local History Collection, is a more sedate option.

Getting There & Away
BUS
Nine daily buses depart for Pécs (423Ft, 50 minutes, 35km), and two run to Kaposvár (544Ft, 1¼ hours, 40km). There are also buses to Hévíz (1930Ft, 3½ hours, 154km, one daily), Nagykanizsa (1330Ft, 2½ hours, 107km, four daily), Sellye (423Ft, 50 minutes, 31km, one daily) and Siklós (907Ft, two hours, 72km, three daily).

TRAIN
Szigetvár is on the train line linking Pécs (346Ft, 45 minutes, 34km) and Nagykanizsa (1212Ft, two hours, 114km). The 84km stretch from Barcs to Nagykanizsa follows the course of the Dráva River and is very scenic, especially around Vízvár and Bélavár. If you're trying to leave Hungary from here, get off at Murakeresztúr (two stops before Nagykanizsa), through which trains pass en route to Zagreb and Ljubljana.

NAGYKANIZSA
☎ 93 / pop 52,100
Nagykanizsa is not especially noted for its sights; the town is almost totally focused on drilling for oil, making light bulbs and furniture, and brewing beer. But if you think of it as a convenient stepping stone, you'll (quite literally) be on the right track. From Nagykanizsa you can easily reach Western Transdanubia, both the northern and southern shores of Lake Balaton, Italy, Slovenia, Croatia and the beaches of the Adriatic.

Orientation
The train station (Ady Endre utca) is south of the city centre. To reach the centre walk north along this road for about 1200m, and you'll be on Fő út, the main street. The bus station is in the centre to the west of Erzsébet tér.

Information
Main post office (Ady Endre utca 10)
OTP bank (15 Deák Ferenc tér)
OTP bank (6 Ady Endre utca)
Tourinform (☎ 313 285; nagykanizsa@tourinform.hu; Csengery út 1-3; ☽ 9am-5pm Mon-Fri, 9am-1pm Sat) Is helpful, well-informed and has Internet access free of charge.

Sights
The **György Thury Museum** (☎ 317 233; Fő út 5) was in the process of refurbishment when we called, but expect to find exhibitions on folk art from the area and displays on the daily life of peasant workers during the first decades of last century. Check with Tourinform for prices and opening times.

The Franciscan **Lower Town Church** (Alsóvárosi templom; cnr Szent Imre utca & Nagyváthy utca; admission free), begun in 1702 but not completed for 100 years, has ornate stucco work and a rococo pulpit. You can't miss the holy-water font, carved from the burial stone of the Turkish general Pasha Mustafa.

Activities
The so-called Lower Town Forest (Alsóvárosi erdő), 6km east of the town centre, has a large rowing lake with **boats** available in summer.

There are **outdoor pools** (adult/child 340/170Ft; ☽ 9.30am-6.30pm mid-Jun–early-Sep) and an **indoor pool** (adult/child 340/170Ft; ☽ 11am-7pm Mon, 6am-8pm Tue-Thu, 6am-7pm Fri, 9am-6pm Sat & Sun year-round) at Csengery út 49. But if you want to take the (thermal) waters, you'll have to go to the spa at **Zalakaros**, 18km to the northeast near the Little Balaton (Kis-Balaton). The Zalakaros

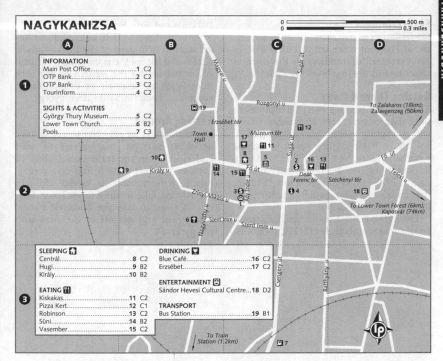

NAGYKANIZSA

0   500 m
0   0.3 miles

INFORMATION
Main Post Office.........................1 C2
OTP Bank.................................2 C2
OTP Bank.................................3 C2
Tourinform..............................4 C2

SIGHTS & ACTIVITIES
György Thury Museum...............5 C2
Lower Town Church...................6 B2
Pools....................................7 C3

SLEEPING 🏠
Centrál....................................8 C2
Hugi.......................................9 B2
Király....................................10 B2

EATING 🍴
Kiskakas.................................11 C2
Pizza Kert..............................12 C1
Robinson................................13 C2
Süni......................................14 B2
Vasember...............................15 C2

DRINKING 🍷
Blue Café...............................16 C2
Erzsébet................................17 C2

ENTERTAINMENT 🎭
Sándor Hevesi Cultural Centre...18 D2

TRANSPORT
Bus Station............................19 B1

spring, which gushes out of the ground at an incredible 92°C, was discovered by workers drilling for oil in the early 1960s.

Sleeping

Hugi (☎ 336 100; Király utca 7; s/d 5000/7500Ft; P) Within walking distance of the centre is this solid *pension*, with secure parking, large rooms and surprisingly little road noise considering its location.

Király (☎ 325 480; Király utca 29; s/d 5400/8200Ft) This is a pleasant *pension* on the 1st floor of a small shopping and office complex, with nine large, bright modern rooms.

Centrál (☎ 314 000; hotelcentral@chello.hu; Erzsébet tér 23; s/d 11,000/13,000Ft; P) Central, a hotel built in 1912, tries to corner the business market, making it overpriced for what is on offer. The rooms, however, are modern and quite comfortable.

Eating & Drinking

Vasember (☎ 314 555; Erzsébet tér 1; mains 1000Ft) With consistently good Hungarian cuisine, this cellar restaurant in the 'Iron Man House' is the town's best restaurant.

Kiskakas (☎ 321 600; Múzeum tér 6; mains 1000-2000Ft) Tucked away in a quiet courtyard/parking lot is Kiskakas, an upmarket spot with a Hungarian menu and covered outdoor seating area.

Süni (Erzsébet tér 2; ice cream from 90Ft) Süni is one of the better ice cream shops in the centre, with an extensive array of the creamy stuff.

Robinson (Deák Ferenc tér 9; pizzas from 800Ft) A rather dark but fashionable pizzeria popular with Nagykanizsa's young bloods and open till late.

Pizza Kert (Sugár út 5; pizzas 800Ft) With its large terrace facing a peaceful park, Pizza Kert serves big pizzas in a relaxed atmosphere.

The local Kanizsai beer flows as freely throughout the year as it does at the Kanizsai Days Festival at the beginning of October, and there are a lot of decent pubs and bars, including **Blue Café** (Deák Ferenc tér 13; 🕙 11am-10pm Sun-Thu, 11-2am Fri & Sat), with its retro glass-brick bar and neon lighting; and **Erzsébet** (Erzsébet tér 21; 🕙 9am-midnight Mon-Sun), a more refined café/bar, with street-side seating suitable for coffee during the day and drinks at night.

Entertainment

Sándor Hevesi Cultural Centre (☎ 311 468; Széchenyi tér 5-9) The centre can tell you what's on in Nagykanizsa; information on the town is also listed in the free biweekly *Zalai Est*.

Getting There & Away

There's a bus running every 30 minutes to the Zalakaros spa (241Ft, 25 minutes, 18km) and also hourly ones to Zalaegerszeg (665Ft, 1¼ hours, 51km). Other services include Keszthely (725Ft, 1½ hours, 59km, six daily), Kaposvár (1330Ft, 2½ hours, 107km, four daily), Pécs (1820Ft, three hours, 142km, five daily) and Szombathely (1330Ft, 2½ hours, 107km, six daily).

From Nagykanizsa, up to eight daily trains go north to Szombathely (1212Ft, 2¼ hours, 102km) and one heads south to Zagreb. Trains run direct to Déli, Kelenföld and Keleti stations in Budapest (2360Ft, four hours, 221Ft) and the southern shore resorts, but if you're headed for the western or northern sides (such as Keszthely or Balatonfüred), you must change at Balatonszentgyörgy.

Getting Around

Nagykanizsa is an easy city to get around on foot, but you may prefer to wait and ride. From the train station, bus 18 goes to the bus station and city centre. Bus 17/b terminates its service close to the rowing lake in the Lower Town Forest, or you can take the Budapest-bound local train and get off at the first stop (Nagyrécse).

Northern Uplands

If the Great Plain is the 'Midwest' of Hungary, then the Northern Uplands (Északi Felföld) are the Rockies. But before your imagination runs wild with dreams of soaring, snow-tipped peaks and hiking trails through untamed wilderness, take a deep breath and note that the highest peak here – the Kékes in the Mátra Hills – 'soars' to just over 1000m. But in a country as flat as a tone-deaf soprano, these foothills of the Carpathians stand head and shoulders above most of Hungary in the environmental and recreational stakes.

For starters, several hills are heavily forested and have minimal human habitation (although accommodation is readily available), creating hiking opportunities. A large part of the lower slopes are given over to grape growing, and some of Hungary's best wines – particularly in the Tokaj region – are made here. In the northern reaches of the Uplands at Aggtelek are the Baradla-Domica caves, Europe's largest stalactite system with 25km of interlinking caves.

But it's not all about nature. This is a land where far too many battles were won and lost, and their reminders – aging castles and evocative ruins – sprinkle the landscape like hundreds-and-thousands on a birthday cake. Eger, a city in constant battle with Pécs for provincial Hungary's 'Best in Show' ribbon, will wow even the most hardened traveller with its Bull's Blood wine, baroque architecture and laid-back feel. The last vestiges of traditional folk life are found here, especially among the Palóc people of the Cserhát Hills and the Matyó of Mezőkövesd.

The Northern Uplands include five ranges: the Cserhát, the Mátra, the Bükk, the Aggtelek (in reality, an adjunct to the eastern Cserhát region) and the Zemplén.

HIGHLIGHTS

- Visiting castles, castles, and more castles – from Füzérs' lonely edifice, **Füzér Castle** (p353), to Boldogkőváralja's strong defender, **Boldogkő Castle** (p344)

- Exploring **Eger** (p327), a town of legendary wine, baroque architecture and easy-going temperament

- Hiking through the lush green forests of the **Zemplén** (p344), **Mátra** (p322) and **Bükk Hills** (p327)

- Wandering through **Hollókő** (p317), a tiny village where folk tradition is very much alive and still kicking up its heels

- Spelunking in **Aggtelek National Park** (p342), home to Europe's largest stalactite caves

NORTHERN UPLANDS

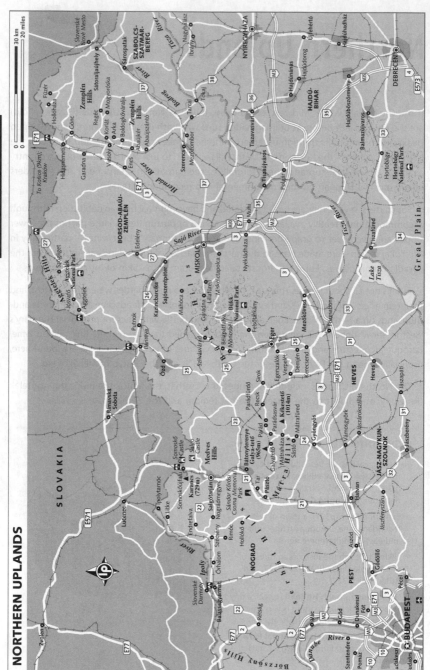

CSERHÁT HILLS

The Cserhát Hills are a rather unimpressive entry to the Northern Uplands; none of them are higher than 650m, much of the area is cultivated and densely populated, and Hungary's serious hiking options are further to the east. But while they may not be graced with soaring peaks and dense forests, they are cloaked in a rich folk-culture tapestry belonging to the Palóc people. Hollókő, a tiny village snuggled into a remote valley, may for some be Hungary's folk 'Disneyland', but there's no denying the beauty of its quaint cottages and old ways. To the west is Balassagyarmat (a mouthful in its own right), home to the best museum of Palóc culture the country has to offer.

BALASSAGYARMAT

☎ 35 / pop 18,500

As the centre of the Cserhát region, Balassagyarmat bills itself as the 'capital of the Palóc' and, while other places may look more folksy, the town's excellent Palóc Museum gives it the leading edge. Lying just south of the Ipoly River and the Slovakian border, Balassagyarmat suffered more than most towns in the region during the Turkish occupation. Its castle was reduced to rubble and its houses were abandoned for decades. It regained stature late in the 18th century as the main seat of Nógrád County, but even that was taken away after WWII in favour of the 'new town' of Salgótarján. Today Balassagyarmat's few baroque and neoclassical buildings and the odd monument don't pull in the crowds; it's the town's link with Palóc culture that beckons.

Orientation

The train station is about 600m south of the town centre at the end of Bajcsy-Zsilinszky utca. The bus station is behind the town hall on Köztársaság tér, which splits Rákóczi fejedelem útja, the main drag, in two.

Information

Library (☎ 300 622; Rákóczi fejedelem útja 50; per hr 100Ft; ⏱ 7.30am-7pm Mon-Fri, 1-5pm Sat) Has Internet access.

OTP bank (Rákóczi fejedelem útja 44) Has a secure 24-hour ATM.

Post office (Rákóczi fejedelem útja 24) On the main drag, near the Roman Catholic church.

Tourinform (☎ 500 640; balassagyarmat@tourinform .hu; Köztársaság tér 6; ⏱ 9am-5pm Mon-Fri, 9am-noon Sat mid-Jun–mid-Sep, 9am-4.30pm Mon-Fri mid-Sep–mid-Jun) Housed in the old county hall.

Sights

The **Palóc Museum** (☎ 300 168; Palóc liget 1; adult/child 500/250Ft; ⏱ 10am-4pm Tue-Sun May-Sep, 10am-4pm Tue-Sat Oct-Apr) in Palóc Park (a lovely green space of mature trees and grassy corners, and perfect for a picnic) was purpose-built in 1914 to house Hungary's richest collection of Palóc artefacts and is a must for anyone planning to visit traditional villages in the Cserhát Hills.

The standing exhibit 'From Cradle to Grave' on the 1st floor takes you through the important stages in the life of the Palóc people, and includes pottery, superb carvings, mock-ups of a birth scene, a classroom and a wedding. There are also votive objects used for the all-important *búcsúk* (church patronal festivals; see p290). But the Palóc women's needlework – from the distinctive floral embroidery in blues and reds to the almost microscopic white-on-white stitching – leaves everything else in the dust.

An **open-air museum** (adult/child 300/150Ft; ⏱ 10am-1pm Tue-Sun May-Sep) including an 18th-century Palóc-style house, stable and church, stands in the garden behind the main museum.

THE GOOD PALÓC PEOPLE

The Palóc people are a distinct Hungarian group living in the fertile hills and valleys of the Cserhát Hills (Cserhátalja). Ethnologists are still debating whether they were a separate people who later mixed with the Magyars, or a Hungarian ethnic group that, through isolation and Slovakian influence, developed its own ways. What's certain is that the Palóc continue to speak a distinct dialect of Hungarian (unusual in a country where language differences are virtually nonexistent) and, until recently, clung to their traditional folk dress, particularly in such towns as Hollókő, Bugac, Rimóc and Őrhalom. Today, with the Matyó people of Mezőkövesd, they are considered the guardians of living folk traditions in Hungary.

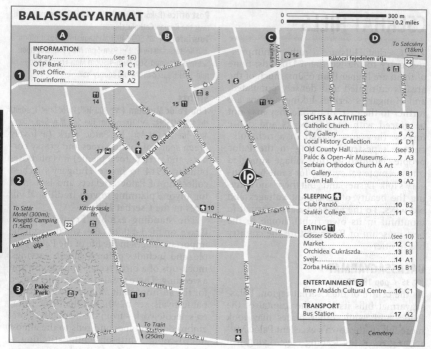

BALASSAGYARMAT

INFORMATION
Library.................................(see 16)
OTP Bank...............................1 C1
Post Office.............................2 B2
Tourinform.............................3 A2

SIGHTS & ACTIVITIES
Catholic Church.......................4 B2
City Gallery.............................5 A2
Local History Collection............6 D1
Old County Hall...................(see 3)
Paléc & Open-Air Museums........7 A3
Serbian Orthodox Church & Art
  Gallery.................................8 B1
Town Hall...............................9 A2

SLEEPING
Club Panzió.............................10 B2
Szalézi College........................11 C3

EATING
Gösser Söröző.....................(see 10)
Market...................................12 C1
Orchidea Cukrászda.................13 B3
Svejk.....................................14 A1
Zorba Háza.............................15 B1

ENTERTAINMENT
Imre Madách Cultural Centre.....16 C1

TRANSPORT
Bus Station............................17 A2

OTHER SIGHTS

The **City Gallery** (Városi Képtár; ☎ 300 186; Köztársaság tér 5; adult/child 150/100Ft; ☟ 10am-noon & 12.30-5pm Tue-Sun), housed in a very run-down building opposite the old county hall, is devoted to contemporary Nógrád painters, sculptors and graphic artists from the 1960s onward, and is worth a look around.

The **Local History Collection** (Helytörténeti Gyűjtemény; ☎ 300 663; Rákóczi fejedelem útja 107; admission free; ☟ 8am-4.30pm), in an 18th-century noble's mansion called Csillagház (Star House), honours more locals, including the artist Endre Horváth, who lived here and designed some of the forint notes in circulation.

The cute and amazingly tiny **Serbian Orthodox church** (Szerb templom; ☎ 300 622; Szerb utca 5; admission free; ☟ 2-6pm Tue-Sun), which you can enter through an archway at Rákóczi fejedelem útja 30, features temporary exhibitions from local artists.

Sleeping

Club Panzió (☎ 301 824; nyirjes@axelero.hu; Teleki László utca 14; r 10,000Ft, apt for 4 people with kitchen 20,000Ft; P) Of Balassagyarmat's meagre

accommodation options, Club is the best and most central. Rooms are in OK condition, but could do with a spruce up.

Sztár Motel (☎ 301 152; Kővári út 12; r 5500Ft; P) Sztár is a mediocre place to the west of the town centre, but it does have the added advantage of a restaurant on the premises.

Szalézi College (☎ 301 765; szalezikollegium@free mail.hu; Ady Endre utca 1; dm 2000Ft; P) With 50 rooms and not a lot going on over the summer break in town, you'll be guaranteed of a bed at this basic student dorm between mid-June and August.

Kisegítő Camping (☎ 300 404; Kővári út 13; camp sites per adult/child/tent 700/350/700Ft, cabins 3000Ft; ☟ mid-Jun–Aug; P) This small and simple camp site, with tent sites and three small cabins, is on the main road leading west out of town.

Eating

Svejk (☎ 300 999; Szabó Lőrinc utca 16; mains around 1000Ft) With the Slovakian border so close, it's surprising there aren't more restaurants like Svejk serving Czech and Slovakian dishes. The large covered inner courtyard is made for sampling a proper Budvar.

Zorba Háza (☎ 315 976; Rákóczi fejedelem útja 28; mains 600-1000Ft; ☺ 10am-midnight Mon-Sat, 2-11pm Sun) Housed in a small shopping centre away from loud Rákóczi fejedelem útja, Zorba serves a mix of Greek and Italian food in blue-and-white surroundings.

Orchidea Cukrászda (☎ 311 450; Bajcsy-Zsilinszky utca 12; ice cream 90Ft; ☺ 9am-7pm Mon-Fri, 8am-7pm Sat & Sun) Opposite Palóc Park, this place makes such excellent ice cream and cakes that locals cross town to pick up the goodies.

Gösser Söröző (lunch menu 500Ft, mains around 1000Ft) This place at Club Panzió is not overly inviting, but it does serve solid Hungarian fare.

Market (Thököly utca) The town's large market has plenty of food stalls and stand-up places to eat.

Entertainment

Imre Madách Cultural Centre (☎ 300 622; Rákóczi fejedelem útja 50; ☺ 8am-8pm Mon-Fri, 1-8pm Sat & Sun) This is the place to find out what's on.

Also check out the free biweekly *Nógrádi Est* magazine, which includes coverage of Balassagyarmat.

Getting There & Away

Some 12 daily buses link Budapest with Balassagyarmat via Vác (968Ft, 1¾ hours, 76km). There is one daily bus to Gyöngyös (907Ft, 2¼ hours, 72km), and plenty to Salgótarján via Litke or Endrefalva (665Ft, 1¼ hours, 52km). Nine buses go daily to Szécsény on Monday to Friday and three or four daily on the weekend (241Ft, 25 minutes, 18km); Szécsény is the place to change for Hollókő. There are three buses daily Monday to Saturday to Hont (363Ft, 50 minutes, 28km) on the Slovakian border at 6am, 11.50am and 4.50pm.

Balassagyarmat can be reached throughout the day via a snaking train line from Vác (658Ft). The trip takes over two hours; the bus will cut that time in half. If coming from Budapest (1212Ft, 2½ hours, 110km) or the east by train, change at Aszód.

SZÉCSÉNY

☎ 32 / pop 6600

Just 18km east of Balassagyarmat in the picturesque Ipoly Valley, Szécsény is a town bordering on comatose and usually given a miss by travellers headed for its tiny, but much better-known, neighbour to the

southeast, Hollókő. But while Hollókő has folklore, Szécsény has history. In 1705, in a camp behind where Forgách Manor now stands, the ruling diet made Ferenc Rákóczi II of Transylvania the prince of Hungary and the commander in chief of the *kuruc* (anti-Habsburg mercenaries) fighting for independence from the Austrians.

Orientation

The train station is about 1.5km north of the town centre just off Rákóczi út en route to Litke. The bus station is on Király utca, east of the firewatch tower on Fő tér.

Information

Tourinform (☎ 370 777; szecseny@tourinform.hu; Ady Endre utca 12; ☺ 8am-6pm Mon-Fri Jun-Sep, 8am-4pm Mon-Fri Oct-May) has an office in the same building as the cultural centre. The **OTP bank** (Rákóczi út 86) is northwest of the town hall, and the **post office** (Dugonics utca 1) is to the south of the OTP bank.

Sights

FORGÁCH MANOR & MUSEUMS

Forgách Manor (Ady Endre utca 7) was constructed around 1760 from the remains of a medieval border fortress. In the mid-19th century it passed into the hands of the aristocratic Forgách family who made further additions, and today it houses a motley assortment of exhibits, such as the **Ferenc Kubinyi Museum** (☎ 370 143; adult/child 300/150Ft; ☺ 10am-4pm Tue-Sun).

On the ground floor there's a pharmaceutical exhibit, as well as a few rooms done up much the way the Forgách family would have liked to see them. Upstairs, beyond the Stone Age bones and chips, the reconstructed Neolithic house and the Bronze Age jewellery, is a ghastly hunting exhibit, with any number of 'useful' items (napkin rings, cups, pistol butts, umbrella handles) carved and whittled from the carcasses and coats of our furred and feathered friends.

Only a little less frightening is the **Bastion Museum** (Bástya Múzeum) located in the northeast tower, from where part of the original 16th-century castle wall is seen to the west and south. Exhibits include an all-too-complete collection of torture implements: racks, yokes, stocks and a flogging bench.

Those of a nervous disposition will seek refuge in the **Sándor Kőrösi Csoma Memorial**

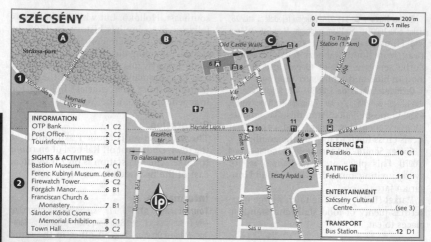

Exhibition (Kőrösi Csoma Sándor Emlék-kiállítás) in the manor's gate house. Kőrösi Csoma (1784–1842) was a Hungarian Franciscan monk who travelled to Tibet and wrote the first Tibetan-English dictionary.

FRANCISCAN CHURCH & MONASTERY

Parts of the Gothic **Franciscan church and monastery** (Ferences templom és kolostor; ☎ 370 076; Haynald Lajos utca 7-9; adult/child 300/150Ft) date from the 14th century, and the latter has been restored to its former glory after years of neglect. In the church sanctuary (the oldest section) a guide will point out the 500-year-old carvings of saints, flowers and fruits on the vaulted ceiling (the carvings on the pillars were destroyed by the Turks when they occupied Szécsény in 1552). You can also see where Muslims carved out a mihrab (prayer niche) in the south wall.

In the baroque monastery (essentially dating from the 17th century, with parts of the Gothic church incorporated into it), you'll see the monks' cells and, depending on what's open, the library, dining hall, Gothic oratory overlooking the church's interior, and/or the Rákóczi Room, where the newly appointed prince and military commander met with his war cabinet in 1705. Tours of the church and monastery depart at 10am, 11am, 1pm, 2pm, 3pm and 4pm Tuesday to Saturday.

FIREWATCH TOWER

You may think you're seeing things but, yes, the 19th-century **firewatch tower** (tűztorony;

Rákóczi út 86; adult/child 200/100Ft; ☯ 10am-4pm Tue-Sun May-Sep, 10am-4pm Mon-Fri Oct-Apr), on Fő tér in the centre of town, is leaning (by three degrees) – the result of shelling and bombing in 1944, and clay subsidence. You can climb to the top for views of the town.

Sleeping & Eating

Paradiso (☎ 372 427; Ady Endre utca 14; s/d 5500/8300Ft; mains 900-1800Ft; ☯ restaurant Mon-Sat; **P**)) Paradiso, with its welcoming staff and comfortable and spacious – if uninspiring – rooms, is the best bet in town. Its restaurant is quite good, serves local specialities and has outside seating in a lovely courtyard with a fountain. The complex is the former servants' quarters of Forgách Manor.

Frédi (☎ 370 372; Rákóczi út 85; pizza & mains 500-1100Ft) This is a decent restaurant and *cukrászda* (cake shop); specialities are all meat-based, and its attractive garden overlooks Fő tér.

Entertainment

The staff at the **Szécsény Cultural Centre** (Szécsényi Művelődési Központ; ☎ 370 494; Ady Endre utca 12) may have information on what's on in Szécsény; otherwise, consult the free biweekly *Nógrádi Est* magazine which includes Szécsény.

Getting There & Away

Some seven buses depart daily for Hollókő on Monday to Friday (241Ft, 30 minutes, 17km), with up to nine on Saturday and five on Sunday. You shouldn't have to wait more than a half-hour for buses to Balassagyarmat (241Ft, 25 minutes, 18km) or Salgótarján (with a possible change for the latter at Litke, Endrefalva or Nógrádmegyer; 423Ft, one hour, 34km). There are seven daily buses to Budapest (1150Ft, two hours, 94km).

Szécsény is on a minor train line linking it with Balassagyarmat (182Ft, 30 minutes, 19km) and Aszód to the west and southwest, and Ipolytarnóc to the north on the Slovakian border, where you can board trains for Lučenec. To get to Vác (890Ft, three to four hours, 89km) from Szécsény by train, you must change at Balassagyarmat.

HOLLÓKŐ

☎ 32 / pop 375

People either love Hollókő (Raven Rock) or they hate it. To some, the two-street village nestling in a valley 16km southeast of Szécsény is Hungary's most beautiful, and deserves kudos for holding on to its traditional architecture and a few old customs. Others see it as a staged tourist trap run by Budapest entrepreneurs with paid 'performers'. Unesco agreed with the former view in 1987 when it put Hollókő on its World Heritage List of cultural sites – the first village in the world to receive such an honour. What sets Hollókő apart is its restored 13th-century castle and the architecture of the so-called Old Village (Ófalu), where some 60 houses and outbuildings have been listed as historic monuments.

The village has burned to the ground many times since the 13th century (most recently in 1909), but the villagers have always rebuilt their houses exactly to plan

with wattle and daub – interwoven twigs plastered with clay and water.

Today few women wear the traditional Palóc dress – wide, red-and-blue, pleated and embroidered skirts, and ornate headpieces. Still, on Sunday mornings, important feast days, such as Easter and Assumption Day (15 August), or during a wedding, you may get lucky and catch some in fancy garb.

Orientation

The bus will stop on Dózsa György utca at the top of Kossuth Lajos utca; from there walk down the hill to the Old Village.

Information

The **post office** (Kossuth Lajos utca 72; ☻ 8am-4pm Mon-Fri) will provide cash advances on credit cards, and **Tourinform** (☎ 579 011; holloko@tourinform.hu; Kossuth Lajos utca 68; ☻ 8am-8pm Mon-Fri, 10am-4pm Sat & Sun May-Sep, 8am-6pm Mon-Fri, 8am-4pm Sat & Sun Sep-May) can supply as much information as you need about Hollókő. For general information on the town, see www.holloko.hu/.

Sights

The Old Village's **folk architecture** is its main attraction. Stroll along the two cobblestone streets, past the whitewashed houses with carved wooden gables and porches and red-tiled roofs. Wine is stored in the small cellars that open onto the streets.

VILLAGE CHURCH

A little wooden **church** (Kossuth Lajos utca), the focus of the village's spiritual and social life, is on the corner where Petőfi utca, the Old Village's 'other' street, branches off from Kossuth Lajos utca. Built as a granary in the

---

IPOLYTARNÓC PRESERVE

Squeezed between the Ipoly River and the Slovakian border, some 25km northwest of Salgótarján, is the town of Ipolytarnóc and its unusual **preserve** (☎ 32-454 113; adult/child 500/350Ft; ☻ 9am-4pm Apr-Oct, 9am-3pm Nov-Mar). Graciously nicknamed 'ancient Pompeii' by all and sundry, the preserve is home to prehistoric finds dating back 20 million years. It seems that around this time a volcano decided to blow its top, and the subsequent lava flows and ash fall sealed for all prosperity animal footprints, subtropical trees and leaves, and even shark teeth. While many other such fossilised remains are located across the continent, Ipolytarnóc is particularly celebrated for its diversity of flora and fauna; there are an impressive 5000 leaf prints and 2000 animal footprints (including those of an ancient rhinoceros). It is widely believed that the area was once the site of a river flowing into a tropical sea. Tours of the preserve depart every hour on the half-hour.

Ipolytarnóc is best reached by train from Balassagyarmat (430Ft, 1¼ hours, 41km) or Szécsény (264Ft, 39 minutes, 22km, up to 10 daily).

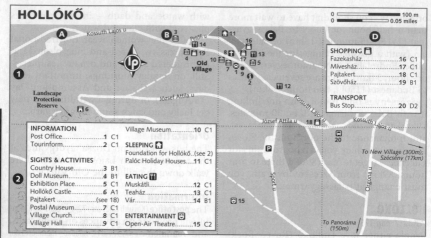

HOLLÓKŐ

16th century and sanctified in 1889, it is a fairly austere affair both inside and out, and like most churches throughout the country, a locked gate bars entry to the main nave.

MUSEUMS

Five small museums in traditional houses line Kossuth Lajos utca. The **Postal Museum** (Postamúzeum; ☎ 379 288; Kossuth Lajos utca 80; adult/child 200/100Ft; ☻ 10am-6pm Apr-Oct) is a branch of the one in Budapest. Next door, the **Village Museum** (Falumúzeum; ☎ 379 258; Kossuth Lajos utca 82; adult/child 150/100Ft; ☻ 10am-4pm Apr-Oct) is the usual three-room Hungarian setup, with folk pottery, painted furniture, embroidered pillows and, in the back yard, an interesting carved wine press dating from 1872. A nature exhibition at the **Country House** (Tájház; ☎ 06 30 529 6439; Kossuth Lajos utca 99-100; adult/child 250/150Ft; ☻ 10am-4pm) deals with the flora, fauna and human inhabitants of the Eastern Cserhát Landscape Protection Reserve, part of which surrounds the village.

The **Exhibition Place** (Kiállítóhely; ☎ 370 547; Kossuth Lajos utca 79; adult/child 200/100Ft; ☻ 10am-5pm Apr-Oct) spotlights the work of a local master woodcarver and a photographer. The **Doll Museum** (Babamúzeum; ☎ 379 088; Kossuth Lajos utca 96; adult/child 150/100Ft; ☻ 10am-5pm Apr-Oct) exhibits some 200 porcelain dolls in traditional dress.

HOLLÓKŐ CASTLE

On Szár-hegy (Stalk Hill), **Hollókő Castle** (Hollókői Vár; ☎ 06 30 968 1739; adult/child 400/200Ft;

☻ 10am-5.30pm Apr-Oct) can be reached by following the trail up the hill across from the Country House or from the bus stop by walking up to József Attila utca and then following the west-bound trail from the car park. At 365m, the castle has a commanding view of the surrounding hills.

The castle was built at the end of the 13th century and strengthened 200 years later. It was captured by the Turks and not liberated until 1683 by the Polish king Jan Sobieski (r 1674–96). It was partially destroyed after the War of Independence early in the 18th century but is, in fact, one of northern Hungary's most intact fortresses. The views from the top of the pentagonal keep, across fields and forested hills without a trace of human occupation, are stunning.

Activities

Pajtakert (☎ 379 273; www.hollokotourism.hu; Kossuth Lajos utca 46; ☻ 9am-4pm Apr-Sep, 9am-4pm Mon-Fri Oct-Mar), based in the shop and gallery of the same name, can organise **folk-craft lessons**, such as weaving, woodcarving, pottery and egg painting; while lessons are for groups only, you may be able to tag along if you're at the right place at the right time. There are some gentle **walks** into the hills and valleys of the 140-hectare landscape protection reserve to the west and south of the castle. A Cserhát, the 1:60,000 Cserhát map (No 8; 800Ft) from Cartographia, will help you plan your route.

NORTHERN UPLANDS

Festivals & Events

Hollókő marks its calendar red for the annual **Easter Festival** in late March or April, the **Nógrád Folklore Festival** and **Palóc Homespun Festival** held at the open-air theatre in July, and the **Castle Days**, a touristy medieval tournament at the castle in late June, August and September.

Sleeping

Hollókő is a day-trippers village, and after the last tour bus leaves you'll have the place to yourself. This, of course, has its advantages and disadvantages; you'll have a supremely restful night, but don't count on food being served after 8pm.

Tourinform can organise private rooms (from 3000Ft per person), but it's not the norm.

Panoráma (☎ 378 077; Orgona utca 31; camp sites per person/tent/car 500/450/200Ft; r 5000Ft; bungalows 6000Ft; Ⓟ) On the hill off Sport utca south of the village, this holiday complex has a small *pension*, four-bed bungalows and a camp site. There is a campfire area set up for outdoor feasts, and good views of the village.

Eating

Vár (☎ 379 029; Kossuth Lajos utca 93-95; mains 1500-2000Ft; Ⓨ 11am-8pm) This is one of the few places to eat in Hollókő (remember it closes early). It serves venison specialities in season, and has a shady courtyard.

Muskátli (☎ 379 262; Kossuth Lajos utca 61; mains 1000-2000Ft; Ⓨ 11am-5pm Wed-Fri & Sun, 11am-6pm Sat) Housed in a traditional cottage, Muskátli

---

AUTHOR'S CHOICE

Palóc Holiday Houses (☎ 579 010; holokozal@ mail.datanet.hu; houses around 8000Ft; Ⓟ) Throughout the village some 17 traditional houses (the largest concentration is along Petőfi utca), which could easily double as folk museums, are available for rent throughout the year. They're basically squat cottages, with whitewashed walls, traditional furniture with beds wide enough to lose your partner in, wood-beamed ceilings and small gardens.

Rental can be arranged through the Foundation for Hollókő (book ahead in the high season), which shares the same building and opening hours as Tourinform.

---

is more like a coffee shop that serves full meals. It frequently caters to groups.

Teaház (Teahouse; ☎ 380 016; Petőfi utca 4; cakes 400Ft) This little place tucked away off Petőfi utca is good for snacks during the daytime, and has a small wine bar in its cellar.

Shopping

Hollókő is a shopper's paradise for Hungarian folk art. Shops generally only open from 10am to 5pm unless there is a bus load of tourists expected.

Szövőház (Loom House; ☎ 379 273; Kossuth Lajos utca 94) This is a good place for hand-woven and embroidered goods. It's interesting to watch the women demonstrate how their enormous loom works, and you can give it a go yourself (adult/child 150/100Ft).

Míveshaz (Craft House; ☎ 380 016; Petőfi utca 4) This artisans' workshop is an excellent place to admire and buy Palóc folk dress and costumes.

Fazekasház (Pottery House; ☎ 379 252; Petőfi utca 6) Folk-art pottery – and colourful nontraditional pieces – in the shape of hand-thrown vases, jugs, candlesticks and decorative items are all available here.

Pajtakert (☎ 379 273; www.hollokotourism.hu; Kossuth Lajos utca 46; Ⓨ 9am-4pm Apr-Sep, 9am-4pm Mon-Fri Oct-Mar) The decorated *mézeskalács* (honey cakes) on sale make great gifts.

Getting There & Away

Szécsény is the gateway to Hollókő, with some buses heading there twice an hour (241Ft, 30 minutes, 17km, up to 20 daily) Monday to Friday; there are 17 buses on Saturday and nine on Sunday. You can also catch one of about six weekday buses (five on Saturday, four on Sunday) to Salgótarján via Pásztó (605Ft, 1½ hours, 50km).

SALGÓTARJÁN

☎ 32 / pop 45,000

After an idyllic day in Hollókő or any of the rural villages of the Cserhát, arriving in the modern city of Salgótarján, 25km east of Szécsény, is like stepping into a cold shower. This is a town where the communist's idealism of architecture lives on, and a place to see its sharp corners and strong lines first hand. Ravaged by fire in 1821 and by serious flooding 70 years later, Salgótarján can boast almost no buildings that predate last century.

The surrounding Medves Hills have been mined for coal since the 19th century, and it's on this that Salgótarján's success is based. As in Miskolc, the Communists found the coal miners and steelworkers here sympathetic to their cause, and were supported both during the Republic of Councils and after WWII (though this didn't stop the dreaded ÁVH secret police from shooting over 100 citizens here during the 1956 Uprising). For its support, Salgótarján was made the county seat in 1950 and rebuilt throughout the 1960s.

Orientation

Because it has virtually swallowed the village of Somoskőújfalu some 10km to the north, Salgótarján feels like a large city. The train and bus stations are a short distance apart to the southwest of the city centre.

Information

Ibusz (☎ 421 200; Fő tér 6)

OTP bank (Rákóczi út 12) Below the Catholic church. The second branch is on Rákóczi út 22.

Post office (Fő tér 1) Located closer to the end of Klapka György tér, despite its official address.

Tourinform (☎ 512 315; salgotarjan@tourinform.hu; Fő tér 5; ☒ 9am-6pm mid-Jun–Sep, 9am-5pm Mon-Fri, 10am-1pm Sat & Sun Oct–mid-Jun) In the same building as the Attila József Cultural Centre, the staff are helpful and friendly, and can provide information on the surrounding area.

Sights

The **Mining Museum** (Bányászati Múzeum; ☎ 420 258; Zemlinszky Rezső utca 1; adult/child 400/200Ft;

☒ 9am-3pm Tue-Sun Apr-Sep, 9am-2pm Tue-Sun Oct-Mar), the city's only real sight, is a short walk southwest of the train and bus stations. Filled with geological maps and samples, old uniforms and a statue of St Barbara (the patron of miners) standing proudly next to old communist banners calling for the nationalisation of the mines, the museum's style is somewhat outdated and is not particularly interesting. Across the street a 280m-long **mine** continues to be 'worked' by performers in unrealistically clean overalls; you can wander through the pits.

Aside from the museum, the city's attractions amount to a plethora of communist architecture, if you can call that an attraction. The **Town Hall** is a particular marvel, which closely resembles a Spam can, but at least it has curves. Salgótarján is also one of the few cities in Hungary that still has **socialist monuments** prominently displayed, and both of these monuments are in Fő tér; Budapest put its own collection in the 'zoo' that is Statue Park (p127) years ago. The monument to the west of the square depicts a supporter of Béla Kun's 1919 Republic of Councils running with a rifle in hand; the other, to the east, in front of the cultural centre, shows a couple of socialist youths looking rather guilty as they set doves free.

Festivals & Events

Dixie jams resound off Salgótarján's communist façades during the **International Dixieland Festival** held in May.

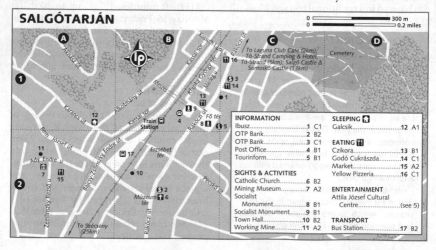

SALGÓTARJÁN

0 _____ 300 m
0 _____ 0.2 miles

To Laguna Club Cafe (2km);
Tó-Strand Camping & Hotel,
Tó-Strand (5km); Salgó Castle &
Somoskő Castle (13km)

Cemetery

To Szécsény
(25km)

INFORMATION	
Ibusz	1 C1
OTP Bank	2 B2
OTP Bank	3 C1
Post Office	4 B1
Tourinform	5 B1

SIGHTS & ACTIVITIES	
Catholic Church	6 B2
Mining Museum	7 A2
Socialist Monument	8 B1
Socialist Monument	9 B1
Town Hall	10 B2
Working Mine	11 A2

SLEEPING	
Galcsik	12 A1

EATING	
Czikora	13 B1
Godó Cukrászda	14 C1
Market	15 A2
Yellow Pizzeria	16 C1

ENTERTAINMENT	
Attila József Cultural Centre	(see 5)

TRANSPORT	
Bus Station	17 B2

Sleeping

There's no real need to overnight in Salgótarján unless you're stuck without any options. Aside from the hotels listed here, Tourinform has a list of rural accommodation that may be more appealing. For private rooms (from 5000Ft) in one of the city's many high-rises, contact Ibusz.

Galcsik (☎ 422 660; www.galcsikhotel.hu; Alkotmány út 2; s 3380-7900Ft, d 5280-10,900Ft; P) Galcsik is a well-maintained *pension*, with bright rooms and sparkling bathrooms. Near the bus station, it's the best deal in the city centre.

Hotel Tó-Strand (☎ 432 400; tó-strand; s/d 5480/7990Ft; P) Next to a small fishing pond north of the city is this modern hotel, with comfortable if not spartan rooms, a restaurant and sauna (1300Ft) for guest use.

Tó-Strand Camping (☎ 430 168; Kemping út; camp sites per person/tent 600/750Ft, bungalows per person 1200Ft, heated motel r 4300Ft, unheated motel r 3200Ft; P) About 5km northeast of the city centre, off the road to Somoskő, is this green oasis in a sea of characterless buildings. Aside from the shaded tent sites, there are two year-round motels, and bungalows that are available from April to September. Pools, tennis courts and a boating lake are nearby. You can reach Tó-Strand on bus 46 or 63 from Rákóczi út.

Eating

Galcsik (☎ 422 660; Alkotmány út 2; mains around 1000Ft; ☺ 7am-9pm Mon-Sat, 7am-8pm Sun) At the *pension* of the same name, this small restaurant has a solid Hungarian menu and a terrace for warm summer days.

Czikora (CZZ; ☎ 311 384; Fő tér 1; mains 690-980Ft; ☺ 7.30am-9pm Mon-Sat) Almost directly opposite the cultural centre is CZZ, a simple eatery with outdoor seating in a shady spot.

Godó Cukrászda (☎ 416 068; Rákóczi út 12; ☺ 10am-9pm Mon-Sat, 9am-9pm Sun) For cake and ice cream just north of Fő tér, join the queues at Godó and then plonk yourself down on its terrace to enjoy the summer treat.

Yellow (☎ 310 480; Rákóczi út 11; pizza 380-700Ft; ☺ 8.30am-midnight Mon-Fri, 9.30am-midnight Sat) An unimaginative pizzeria in an ugly square block, but if you don't fancy Hungarian, there isn't any other choice.

Entertainment

Attila József Cultural Centre (☎ 310 503; Fő tér 5; ☺ 8am-7.45pm Mon-Fri, 10am-6pm Sat & Sun) Salgótarján's premier cultural venue.

Laguna Club Café (☎ 06 20 936 7072; Füleki út 56; ☺ 9am-5am Wed-Sat) A popular club to the north of the city centre.

Other entertainment spots can be found in the free biweekly *Nógrádi Est*.

Getting There & Away

Buses leave Salgótarján hourly for Balassagyarmat (665Ft, 1¼ hours, 52km) and Szécsény via Endrefalva (423Ft, one hour, 34km). You can also get to Budapest (1330Ft, 1¾ hours, 109km, half-hourly; some via route No M3), Eger (846Ft, two hours, 66km, 11 daily Monday to Friday, seven on Saturday, five on Sunday), Gyöngyös (786Ft, 1¾ hours, 62km, twice daily) and Parádfürdő (544Ft, 1¼ hours, 44km, twice daily).

A train line links Salgótarján with Hatvan (544Ft, 1½ hours, 59km) and the main Budapest–Miskolc trunk line to the south and, to the north, Somoskőújfalu (100Ft, 10 minutes, 6km), and Lučenec, in Slovakia.

AROUND SALGÓTARJÁN
Salgó & Somoskő Castles

Eight kilometres northeast of the city centre is **Salgó Castle** (admission free; ☺ dawn-dusk), built in the 13th century atop a basalt cone some 623m up in the Medves Hills. After Buda Castle fell to the Turks in 1541, Salgó served as an important border fortress but it, too, was taken 23 years later and fell into ruin after the Turks abandoned it in the late 16th century. The castle is best remembered for the visit made by Sándor Petőfi in 1845, which inspired him to write *Salgó*, one of his best loved poems. Today you can make out the inner courtyard, tower and bastion from the ruins, but views of Somoskő and into Slovakia are excellent from this peaceful spot.

To visit the interior of **Somoskő Castle** (admission 160Ft; ☺ 8am-8pm Apr-Oct, 8am-4pm Nov-Mar), which is in Slovakian territory, you must cross the border at Somoskőújfalu – don't forget your passport – and follow a path east on foot for about 3km to the castle. Built in the 14th century from basalt blocks, Somoskő was able to hold off the Turkish onslaught longer than Salgó Castle, not falling until 1576. Ferenc Rákóczi used it during the independence war in 1706, and for that reason it was partially destroyed by the Austrians, although, with its semi-complete walls and turrets, it remains a more solid edifice than Salgó.

Adventurous souls who have time on their hands might want to follow the marked trail westward from Somoskőújfalu along the Slovakian border for 4km to **Mt Karancs** (729m); you'll see the High Tátra from the lookout tower on top of what's known locally as the 'Palóc Olympus'. Cartographia's 1:60,000 *A Karancs, a Medves és a Heves-Borsodi-dombság* map (No 11; 800Ft) covers these hills.

To get to Salgó Castle, catch bus 11/b (at least 12 daily) anywhere along Rákóczi út in Salgótarján to the Eresztvény recreational area; the castle is up the hill to the southwest. An easier way to reach it, though, is to stay on the same bus to the terminus in Salgóbánya, the city's old mining district, and follow the path leading off Vár út to the west. Bus 11/a (at least three daily) also goes to Eresztvény and then heads for Somoskő.

Buddhist Stupa

Travelling along Rte 21 towards Pásztó, some 22km south of Salgótarján, you might think you've driven through a black hole and arrived in Southeast Asia. There, on a hillside to the north of the village of **Tar**, is a full-sized Buddhist stupa (the largest of its kind in Europe), its little chimes tinkling and coloured pendants fluttering in the gentle breeze. It's all part of **Sándor Kőrösi Csoma Memorial Park**, consecrated in 1992 by the Dalai Lama in memory of the early 19th-century Hungarian Franciscan monk who became a Hungarian Bodhisattva (Buddhist saint). The stupa, with a revolving prayer wheel containing sacred texts, has become something of a local tourist attraction, and there's a gift shop selling Indian crafts and a **snack bar** (☉ 9am-7pm Tue-Sun Apr-Sep, 10am-4pm Tue-Sun Oct-Mar). Buses to Tar, a couple of kilometres to the south, and to Pásztó stop along the highway just below the stupa.

MÁTRA HILLS

The Mátra Hills, which boast Hungary's highest peaks, are the most developed and easily accessible of the Northern Uplands ranges. And with all the recreational options – from hiking and picking wild mushrooms in the autumn to hunting and skiing in winter – there's enough here to satisfy all tastes.

The Mátra Hills can easily be reached from Eger, but Gyöngyös is its real springboard. It is also the centre of the Mátraalja wine-growing region, noted especially for Hárslevelű (Linden Leaf), a green-tinted white wine that is spicy and slightly sweet at the same time.

For general information on the Mátra Hills, see www.matrahegy.hu.

GYÖNGYÖS

☎ 37 / pop 33,500

A colourful, small city at the base of the Mátras, Gyöngyös, from the Hungarian word meaning 'pearl', is the gateway to the hills. With its museum, abundance of churches (the largest Gothic church in Hungary is here) and rich medieval library, it's easy to let the delights of the hills wait while exploring the city's nooks and crannies, or simply kicking back on its pastel-shaded square and sampling a glass or two of the region's finest wines.

Orientation

The bus station is on Koháry út, a 10-minute walk southeast of Fő tér, the main square. The main train station is on Vasút utca, near the eastern end of Kossuth Lajos utca. The Előre station, from where the narrow-gauge trains depart (p324), is next to the Mátra Museum at the start of Dobó István utca.

Information

Ibusz (☎ 311 861; Kossuth Lajos utca 6) The town's best travel agency.

OTP bank (Fő tér 1)

Post office (Páter Kiss Szaléz utca 9-11) Accessed from Mátyás király utca.

Tourinform (☎ 311 155; gyongyos@tourinform.hu; Fő tér 10; ☉ 7.30am-4pm Mon-Thu, 7.30am-1pm Fri) Opposite the Town Hall.

Vachott Sándor Library (☎ 311 883; Fő tér 10; per hr 100Ft; ☉ 9am-6pm Mon-Wed, 9am-6pm Fri, 9am-1pm Sat) Offers Internet access.

www.gyongyos.hu This website should be in English and German, but don't be surprised if it isn't.

Sights

The **Mátra Museum** (☎ 311 447; Kossuth Lajos utca 40), in an old manor house in Orczy Garden, was closed at the time of research for major renovations. Expect to find spruced-up exhibitions on the history of Gyöngyös,

GYÖNGYÖS

0 _____ 300 m
0 _____ 0.2 miles

INFORMATION
Ibusz.....................................1 B2
OTP Bank.............................2 A2
Post Office..........................3 B3
Tourinform..........................4 A3
Vachott Sándor Library......(see 4)

SIGHTS & ACTIVITIES
Előre Narrow-Gauge Train
    Station............................5 C2
Former Franciscan Monastery &
    Hungarian Franciscan Memorial
    Library............................6 B3
Franciscan Church...............7 B3
House of Mátra Wines.........8 A2
House of the Holy Crown &
    Ecclesiastical Treasury.....9 A2

Mátra Museum &
    Mikroárium....................10 C2
Memorial Synagogue..........11 A3
New Synagogue.................12 A3
St Bartholomew's Church....13 A2
Town Hall..........................14 A2

SLEEPING
Opál...................................15 C3
Vincellér............................16 D1

EATING
Café Liezler.......................17 A3
Cukrászda..........................18 C2
Giardinetto d'Italia.............19 A3
Il Camineto........................20 B2
Kékes.................................21 A2

Sissi Kávézó.....................(see 17)

ENTERTAINMENT
Mátra Cultural Centre.........22 B3

TRANSPORT
Bus Station........................23 C3

To Mátrafüred
(6km)

To Farkasmály-
Borpincék;
Lajosháza (11km)
Gyöngyös
felső

To Király-völgy
Kemping (11km)

NORTHERN UPLANDS

---

with much emphasis on Benevár – a 14th-century castle northeast of Mátrafüred and now in ruins – and the natural history of the Mátra region, including a 'baby' mammoth. City lore has it that the wrought-iron railings enclosing the garden were made from gun barrels taken during the *kuruc* uprising. The downstairs section originally housed the **Mikroárium**, an aquarium-terrarium full of snakes, lizards and tropical fish, but this may change with the renovations.

St Bartholomew's Church (Szent Bertalan templom; Szent Bertalan út 1; admission free; services only) is on the east side of Hanisz Imre tér. It was built in the 14th century and is the largest Gothic church in Hungary. You'd hardly know it though, with the baroque restoration (including an unusual upper-storey gallery inside) that was carried out 400 years later. To the southeast the so-called **House of the Holy Crown** (Szent Koronaház), which served as a safe house for the St Stephen's Crown three times from 1806 to 1809 during the Napoleonic Wars, contains the city's **Ecclesiastical Treasury** (Egyházi Kincstár; ☎ 311 143; adult/child 300/150Ft; 10am-noon &

2-5pm Tue-Sun), a rich collection of liturgical objects and church plate.

The **Franciscan church** (Ferences templom; Bárátok tere 1; admission free; services only) was built around the same time as St Bartholomew's but it, too, has undergone some major changes, with the light frescoes and baroque tower added in the 18th century. The church's most celebrated occupant – well, second-most famous to the faithful – is János Vak (Blind) Bottyán, a heroic but sight-challenged commander who served under Ferenc Rákóczi II during the War of Independence. The former **Franciscan monastery** (built 1730), which is attached to the church, contains the **Hungarian Franciscan Memorial Library** (Magyar Ferencesek Műemlék Könyvtára; ☎ 311 361; Bárátok tere 2; admission free; 2-6pm Tue-Fri, 10am-1pm & 3-6pm Sat, 9am-noon & 3-6pm Sun), the only historical archive in Hungary to have survived the Turkish occupation intact. Among its 14,000 volumes are some of the rarest books written in Hungarian.

Gyöngyös was home to a relatively large Jewish community from the 15th century to WWII, and two splendid synagogues bear witness to this. The older of the two, the neoclassical **Memorial Synagogue** (Műemlék zsinagóga; Vármegye utca), built in 1820, faces Gyöngyös Stream and now houses the city's TV studios. The Moorish-Secessionist **New Synagogue** (Új zsinagóga; Kőrösi Csoma Sándor utca), on the corner with Gárdonyi Géza utca, was designed by Lipót Baumhorn in 1930, two decades after he completed his masterpiece in Szeged. Unfortunately it is now a warehouse and in need of some repair.

Activities

The **House of Mátra Wines** (Mátrai Borok Háza; ☎ 302 226; Fő tér 10; ☺ 9am-5pm Tue-Fri, 9am-1pm Sat), in a courtyard by Tourinform, showcases local and regional wines and offers tastings. If you're interested in trying the region's Rieslings, Leányka and Hárslevelű, ask Tourinform for a copy of *A Mátraaljai Borút* (The Mátraalja Wine road) map and a list of cellars offering tastings.

Two **narrow-gauge trains** (☎ 302 025) depart from Előre station just beyond the Mátra Museum. One heads 7km northeast to Mátrafüred and the other goes to Lajosháza, 11km north of Gyöngyös; these are easily the most enjoyable way to enter the Mátra Hills. The latter offers no real destination, except a place to begin hiking, but the slow ride gives you a good feel for what's on offer further into the hills. A fine hiking excursion, for example, leads east along the Nagy-völgy (Big Valley) past a series of water catchments or north as far as Galyatető, at 965m Hungary's second-highest peak. If you take the little train back from Mátrafüred, get off at Farkasmály-Borpincék, where there's a row of wine cellars. To return, you can wait for the train (6.37pm May to September, 4.23pm October to April) or jump onto a bus coming down Rte 24, but it's an easy 4km walk (or crawl) back to Gyöngyös.

Be advised that trains to Lajosháza (adult/child one way 260/130Ft, return 500/250Ft) run only on the weekend and holidays from May to September (maximum four trains daily in each direction, five from June to August). Up to 10 trains daily make the run to Mátrafüred (adult/child one way 260/130Ft, return 500/250Ft) from April to October. During the rest of the year, count on five trains daily on Monday to Friday and seven daily on the weekend.

Sleeping

For such a pretty town, there's a surprising lack of accommodation in the centre. Both Tourinform and Ibusz can book you a private room (from 2500Ft per person) in Gyöngyös or the Mátra Hills.

Vincellér (☎ 311 691; Erzsébet királyné út 22; s/d 6800/7600Ft, apt 11,000-13,000Ft; P ✕) Away from the town centre on the road to Mátrafüred is this quiet *pension*, with an attractive and secluded courtyard-restaurant, large rooms and accommodating staff.

Opál (☎ 505 400; www.hotelopal.hu; Könyves Kálmán tér 12; s/d 8000/11,000Ft; P ⌨) Housed in a former college, this small hotel has a slightly clinical feel to it, but staff are friendly, rooms are basic and clean, and added extras, such as a fitness room, sauna and bar, add to Opál's overall good value.

Király-völgy Kemping (☎ 364 185; www.kiraly volgykemping.hu; Táncsics Mihály út 40; camp sites per adult/child/tent €2.50/1.50/3.50; ☺ May-Sep) The closest camp site to town is in Sástó (p326), but this fine option lies 11km northwest in Gyöngyöspata. It's a small site on the southern edge of the hills, with two dozen sites and its very own babbling brook.

Eating & Drinking

Kékes (☎ 311 915; Fő tér 7; mains 1000-2000Ft) Kékes is the town's top restaurant, with a big soup selection, plenty of game, fish and regional specialities, and a lovely terrace looking onto the main square.

Giardinetto d'Italia (☎ 300 709; Rózsa utca 8; pasta & pizza 1000Ft) With a terrace in a little park south of Fő tér, a healthy range of Italian cuisine and statues of the Blues Brothers guarding the entrance, Giardinetto is good for both drinks and food.

Il Camineto (☎ 312 652; Kossuth Lajos utca 19; pizza from 300Ft) This small pizzeria, tucked away in a quiet corner, serves pizza from its clay oven on its shaded terrace. Take away is also available.

A nameless *cukrászda* (cake shop) and **ice-cream parlour** (Mátrai út; ice cream 100Ft; ☺ 10am-7pm Mon, Wed & Thu, 9am-7pm Fri-Sun) in Orczy Garden, north of the Mátra Museum, is worth going out of your way for; its terrace is normally swamped with locals in summer.

Also worth a look:

Café Liezter (☎ 304 591; Móricz Zsigmond utca 5; mains around 800Ft) Convivial spot serving snack food, such as pizzas and hamburgers; doubles as a popular bar on weekends.

Sissi Kávézó (Móricz Zsigmond utca 7; ☺ 7.30am-10pm Sun-Thu, 7.30-1am Fri & Sat) Café devoted to Sissi, Austria's former Habsburg empress, with a relaxed air and plenty of beer.

Entertainment

Mátra Cultural Centre (Mátra Művelődési Központ; ☎ 312 281; Barátok tere 3; ☺ 8am-9pm Mon-Sat) Described as a 'Finnish functionalist-style building', with huge colourful stained-glass windows, this is where Gyöngyös entertains itself.

For entertainment listings, pick up a copy of the free biweekly *Gyöngyösi Est* magazine.

Getting There & Around
BUS

You won't wait for more than 20 minutes for buses to Budapest (968Ft, 1½ hours, 79km), Eger (665Ft, one hour, 52km, three daily via Parádfürdő), Mátrafüred (133km, 10 minutes, 6km) and Mátraháza (182Ft, 15 minutes, 15km).

Further destinations from Gyöngyös:

Destination	Price	Duration	Km	Frequency
Parád & Parádfürdő	363Ft	1¼hr	30	9 daily
Recsk	423Ft	1½hr	31	8 daily
Sirok	544Ft	1¾hr	42	5 daily
Szolnok	1210Ft	2hr	98	5 daily
Salgótarján	786Ft	1¾hr	62	3 daily
Tiszafüred	1330Ft	2½hr	106	2 daily

TAXI
You can book a taxi on ☎ 312 222.

TRAIN
Gyöngyös is on a dead-end spur some 13km from the Vámosgyörk stop on the Budapest–Miskolc trunk line. Nine trains a day connect the city with Vámosgyörk (182km, 14 minutes, 13km), six of which carry on to Keleti train station in Budapest (1004Ft, 1½ hours to two hours, 100km).

GYÖNGYÖS TO EGER

Rte 24 wends its way through the Mátra Hills north of Gyöngyös to Parádsasvár and then cuts eastward onto Eger (60km); if you're travelling under your own steam, it's one of the prettiest routes in the country. The section to Mátraháza is popular with

bikers, who constantly attack the road and its hairpin corners with wanton abandon, especially on weekends. Excellent if you're into bikes, but annoying (and loud) if you're not.

Buses to Mátrafüred, Mátraháza, Parád and Parádfürdő are frequent, but the best approach is by the narrow-gauge train that terminates in Mátrafüred.

Mátrafüred
☎ 37

Mátrafüred is a pleasant little resort at 340m. Though there is a small **Palóc ethnographic private collection** (Palóc néprajzi magángyűjtemény; ☎ 320 137; Pálosvörösmarti út 2; adult/child 200/100Ft; ☺ 9am-5pm May-Sep, 9am-4pm Oct-Apr) of dolls, textiles and carvings not far south of the narrow-gauge train, the many easy **walks** in the area are the main attraction. Buy a copy of Cartographia's 1:40,000 *A Mátra* map (No 14; 800Ft) before setting out.

You can change money at the **post office** (Béke utca 5; ☺ 8am-noon & 12.30-3.30pm Mon-Fri) or use the ATM on the same road nearby. For general information on Mátrafüred, see www.matrainfo.hu (in Hungarian).

SLEEPING & EATING
There are lots of signs advertising private rooms (per person from 2000Ft) along most streets in Mátrafüred, but Béke utca has the bulk of them.

Gyöngyvirág (☎ 520 001; zsapek@axelero.hu; Béke utca 8; s/d 6500/8500Ft, apt 12,000Ft; P 🐾) Wheelchair access, a heated pool, mini golf, a playground for kids and an outside grill in summer help make this the best accommodation choice in Mátrafüred. Rooms are suitably modern and tastefully furnished.

Diana (☎ 06 30 565 8320; Turista utca 1; s/d/tr 6000/9000/10,000Ft, apt 15,000Ft; P) A basic but comfortable 12-room hotel on a quiet street just off Béke utca. Its apartment has cooking facilities.

There are plenty of food stalls and the like on Parádi utca opposite the train station, but for something more substantial, try Gyöngyvirág or **Fekete Rigó** (Blackbird; ☎ 320 052; Avar utca 2; mains 800-1200Ft, apt per 1/2/3/4 people 2500/3600/4800/5400Ft), a relaxed choice with a lovely beer garden nestled in among trees; its upstairs apartment sleeps eight and is an absolute bargain for groups who want to cook for themselves.

Sástó

☎ 37

Three kilometres north of Mátrafüred, **Sástó Camping** (☎ 374 025; www.sasto.elpak.hu; camp sites per adult/child/tent 1300/700/1000Ft, r from 4500Ft, comfortable/uncomfortable houses from 8200/3450Ft, bungalows from 5200Ft; ☺ mid-Apr–mid-Oct) is the highest camp site in Hungary (520m). Centred on a small lake with rowing boats, fishing and a 54m-high lookout tower, the complex offers a wide range of accommodation, including bungalows that sleep up to four people and motel rooms for two people. Its 'comfortable' houses come with bathrooms, while the 'uncomfortable' (as they put it) variety have shared facilities; both sleep up to three people. The site would improve greatly if the tacky stalls and snack bars on the lake were relocated. There is also the **Sásto Vendéglő** (☎ 374 061; mains 1000Ft), quite a decent restaurant, and a small grocery shop here.

Mátraháza

☎ 37

Mátraháza is built on a slight incline 715m above sea level and is about 5km north of Sástó. It has an alpine feel and is an attractive spot to base yourself for short walks in the immediate area or more adventurous hiking further afield. The **post office** (☺ 8am-3.30pm Mon-Fri) is at the start of the road to Kékestető, the country's highest point and centre for winter sport, and there's an OTP bank ATM at the bus station along the main road through the village.

SLEEPING & EATING

Pagoda Pihenő Panzió (☎ 374 023; www.hotels.hu /pagoda; s/d from 5700/9200Ft; ℗) This is an old hotel with a pagoda-like roof in the centre of Mátraháza village. Situated among pine trees, it exudes an alpine feel and its rooms come with a balcony. Breakfast is served in Borostyán.

Bérc (☎ 374 102; berchotel@axelero.hu; s/d from 7000/10,000Ft; ℗ ▣) About halfway between Sástó and Mátraháza is this communist eyesore, an imposing edifice of odd angles. It does, however, have loads of sports facilities, extensive views of the Kékes Hills (top-floor rooms with balcony are the best) and simple yet functional rooms.

Borostyán (☎ 374 090; mains 1200Ft; ☺ 9am-10pm in summer, 9am-10pm Tue-Sun winter) Opposite the car park at the start of the ascent to Kékestető, this place has very good food and service, and a lovely pavilion with seating for watching the bikes zip up and down.

Kékestető

☎ 37

Next to the Pagoda pension in Mátraháza, you'll see the end of a ski trail that runs down from Kékestető and Mt Kékes. In the absence of a lift, skiers wanting another go hop on the bus, which continuously covers the 4km to the top. The modern nine-storey **TV tower** (☎ 367 086; adult/child 400/200Ft; ☺ 9am-6pm May-Sep, 9am-5pm Oct-Apr) at the top is open to view-seekers; the old tower in front of it houses the **Hegycsúcs** (☎ 567 004; www.hotels.hu /hegycsucs; r from 6000Ft; ℗), a down-on-its-luck hotel, with sauna and gym. Choose one of the two rooms on the 7th floor (No 13 is a twin, No 14 a double), and you'll be sleeping at the highest point in Hungary.

You won't exactly be on top of the world, but the nearby **Kékes Fogadó** (☎ 0670 217 9954; s/d with shared bathroom 2500/5000Ft, apt 10,000Ft; ℗) is still very high; it is, however, not in good shape and is a last resort for overnighting.

Parádsasvár

☎ 36 / pop 586

Parádsasvár is where the country's most effective – and most odoriferous – *gyógyvíz* (medicinal drinking water) is bottled. Stop for a glass if you can stand the stench of this sulphuric brew. The **Parád Crystal Factory** (Parád Kristály Manufaktura; ☎ 06 30 290 9584; Rákóczi utca 46-48; including entry to gallery 7 adult/child 500/300Ft), which produces Hungary's highest-quality crystal and glassware, can be visited on a guided tour. Get in quick, though; it's soon to be sold or closed down. Some of the factory's arty creations are on display in its **Sasvár Gallery** (Sasvár Galéria; ☺ 9.45am-12.30pm & 1.30-2.30pm Mon-Fri), while more run-of-the mill pieces are for sale at the **factory shop** (☎ 20-358 7991; ☺ 9am-5pm Mon-Fri, 9am-3pm Sat & Sun).

The 58-room hotel **Sasvár Kastélyszálloda** (Sasvár Castle Hotel; ☎ 444 444; www.sasvar.hu; Kossuth Lajos utca 1; r 56,200-216,200Ft; ℗ ▨ ▣), in a restored Renaissance-style hunting lodge, was built in 1882 by Miklós Ybl, the same man responsible for the Hungarian State Opera House in Budapest. It has every mod con and facility you could possibly wish for (including Secret Service–style security), and is surrounded by 2.5 hectares of parkland.

Across the road from the grand Sasvár is the small *pension*, **St Hubertus** (☎ 544 060; Rákóczi út 2; s/d 7100/9700Ft; **P**)), with attic rooms featuring plenty of natural wood. Its downstairs restaurant features a very Hungarian menu and often caters to tour groups.

Parád & Parádfürdő
☎ 36 / pop 2200

Parád and Parádfürdő run into one another and effectively make up one long town. You can't miss the **Coach Museum** (Kocsimúzeum; ☎ 364 387; Kossuth Lajos utca 217; adult/child 380/250Ft; ☼ 9am-5pm Tue-Sun Apr-Oct, 10am-4pm Tue-Sun Nov-May), housed in the red marble Cifra Istálló (Ornamental Stables) of Count Károlyi, one of the most interesting small museums in Hungary. (For the record, the word 'coach' comes from Kocs, a small village in Transdanubia, where these lighter horse-drawn vehicles were first used in place of the more cumbersome wagons.) Inspect the interiors of the diplomatic and state coaches, which are richly decorated with silk brocade, especially the closed coach used by 19th-century philanderers on the go, and the bridles containing as much as 5kg of silver. There are **horse riding** possibilities here as well.

The lovely **Erzsébet Királyné Park Hotel** (Queen Elizabeth Park Hotel; ☎ 444 044; www.erzsebetpark hotel.hu; Kossuth Lajos utca 372; s/d from 15,000/17,800Ft; **P** 🐾 🖥)) at the eastern end of Parádfürdő was designed by Miklós Ybl in 1893 and still exudes an air of grace. Rooms are surprisingly modern and tasteful, the best of which face away from the road towards the woods.

Recsk
☎ 36 / pop 3000

From Parádfürdő the road continues on for 2km to Recsk, a place that lives on in infamy as the site of Hungary's most brutal forced-labour camp, set up by Mátyás Rákosi in 1950 and closed down by the reformer Imre Nagy in 1953. In honour of those who slaved and died here, the **Recsk Forced-Labour Death Camp** (Recski Kényszermunka Haláltábor; ☎ in Budapest 1-312 6105; admission 200Ft; ☼ 9am-5pm May-Sep, 9am-3pm Sat & Sun Oct-Apr) has been partially reconstructed near the quarry, about 5km south of the village. It's now a peaceful spot, which makes it all that more poignant.

Sirok
☎ 36 / pop 2070

Sirok, 8km to the east of Recsk, is effectively the last town in the Mátra Hills. The ruins of an early-14th-century **castle** (admission free; ☼ dawn-dusk) perched on a mountain top due north of the village provide superb views of the Mátra and Bükk Hills and the mountains of Slovakia. **Vár Camping** (☎ 361 558; Dobó István utca 30; camp sites per person/tent/car 650/600/350Ft; ☼ mid-May–Sep; **P**) is a laid-back, quiet and basic camping ground at the foot of the castle ruins.

BÜKK HILLS

The Bükk Hills, which take their name from the many 'beech trees' growing here, are a green lung, buffering baroque Eger and industrial Miskolc. Although much of the area has been mined for ore for the ironworks of Miskolc and other towns of the scarred Sajó Valley to the east, a large tract – over 430 sq km, in fact – is a national park. The Bükk teems with wildlife, and is popular with cyclists and hikers. If you're looking to do either – or both – check out Cartographia's three 1:40,000 maps (800Ft each) of the region: *A Bükk-fennsík* (Bükk Plateau; No 33); *A Bükk – északi rész* (Bükk – northern section; No 29) and *A Bükk – déli rész* (Bükk – southern section; No 30). For information contact the **Bükk National Park Directorate** (Bükki Nemzeti Park Igazgatósága; ☎ 36-411 581; Sánc utca 6) in Eger.

EGER
☎ 36 / pop 58,300

Everyone loves Eger, and it's immediately apparent why: the beautifully preserved baroque architecture gives the town a relaxed, almost Mediterranean, feel; it is the home of the celebrated Egri Bikavér (Eger Bull's Blood) wine known the world over; and it is flanked by two of the Northern Uplands most inviting ranges. But these aren't the only reasons Hungarians visit Eger: it was here that their forebears fended off the Turks for the first time during the 170 years of occupation in 1552 (see boxed text, p330).

History
The Turks came back to Eger in 1596 and this time captured the city, turning it into

EGER

0 — 500 m
0 — 0.3 miles

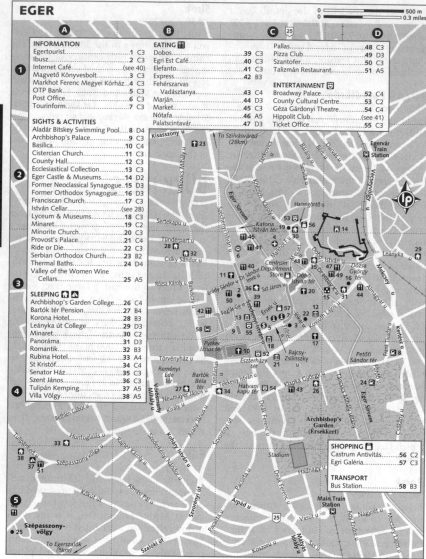

a provincial capital, and erecting several mosques and other buildings until they were driven out at the end of the 17th century. All that remains of this architectural legacy is a lonely little minaret pointing its long finger towards the heavens in indignation.

Eger played a central role in Ferenc Rákóczi II's attempt to overthrow the Habsburgs early in the 18th century, and it was then that a large part of the castle was razed by the Austrians. Having enjoyed the status of an episcopate since the time of King Stephen in the 11th century, Eger flourished in the 18th and 19th centuries, when the city acquired most of its wonderful baroque architecture.

Orientation

Dobó István tér, the centre of Eger, is just a couple of minutes on foot to the east of the renovated bus station on Pyrker János tér. To reach the city centre from the main train station on Vasút utca, walk north on Deák Ferenc utca and then head along pedestrian Széchenyi István utca, Eger's main drag. The Egervár train station, which serves Szilvásvárad and other points north, is on Vécseyvölgy utca, and about a five-minute walk north of Eger Castle.

Information

BOOKSHOPS
Magvető Könyvesbolt (☎ 517 757; Bajcsy-Zsilinszky utca 4; ☺ 9am-5pm Mon-Fri, 9am-1pm Sat) Small selection of English titles, and maps.

INTERNET ACCESS
Tourinform has Internet access for 400Ft per hour.
Egri Est Café (☎ 411 105; Széchenyi utca 16; per hr 300Ft; ☺ 11am-midnight Sun-Thu, 11am-4am Fri & Sat) A café-bar that offers Internet access.

INTERNET RESOURCES
For general information on Eger, consult www.eger.hu (in Hungarian) or www.eger city.hu (in English and Hungarian).

MEDICAL SERVICES
Markhot Ferenc Megyei Kórház (☎ 411 444; Markhót Ferenc utca 1/3; ☺ 24hr)

MONEY
OTP bank (Széchenyi István utca 2)

POST
Post office (Széchenyi István utca 20-22; ☺ 8am-8pm Mon-Fri, 8am-1pm Sat)

TOURIST INFORMATION
Tourinform (☎ 517 715; eger@tourinform.hu; Bajcsy-Zsilinszky utca 9; ☺ 9am-5pm Mon-Fri, 9am-1pm Sat & Sun mid-Jun–mid-Sep, 9am-5pm Mon-Fri, 9am-1pm Sat mid-Sep–mid-Jun) Has more than enough information on the town and its surrounds, including the handy *Insight to Eger* magazine in a number of languages.

TRAVEL AGENCIES
Egertourist (☎ 510 270; Bajcsy-Zsilinszky utca 9; ☺ 9am-5pm Mon-Fri)
Ibusz (☎ 311 451; Széchenyi István utca 9)

Sights

EGER CASTLE
The best view of the city can be had by climbing up the cobblestone lane from Dózsa György tér to **Eger Castle** (Egri Vár; ☎ 312 744; Vár 1; adult/child combined ticket 900/450Ft, grounds only 400/200Ft; ☺ 8am-8pm Apr-Aug, 8am-7pm Sep, 8am-5pm Oct-Mar), erected in the 13th century after the Mongol invasion. Much of the castle is of modern construction, but you can still see the foundations of 12th-century **St John's Cathedral**. Models and drawings in the **István Dobó Museum** (☺ 9am-5pm Tue-Sun Apr-Oct, 9am-3pm Tue-Sun Nov-Mar), housed in the former Bishop's Palace (1470), show how it once looked. On the ground floor, a statue of Dobó takes pride of place in the **Heroes' Hall**. The 19th-century building on the northwestern side of the courtyard houses the **Eger Art Gallery**, with several works by Mihály Munkácsy.

Beneath the castle are **casemates** (☺ 9am-5pm) hewn from solid rock, which you may tour with a Hungarian-speaking guide included in the admission price (English-language guide 600Ft extra). Other exhibits, including the **Waxworks** (adult/child 350/250Ft) and **Minting Exhibit** (adult/child 240/120Ft) cost extra. You can tour the castle grounds, Heroes' Hall and casemates on Monday, when all the other exhibits are closed.

ESZTERHÁZY TÉR
Begin a walking tour of the city at the **Basilica** (Bazilika; Pyrker János tér 1; admission free; ☺ 9am-4pm Mon-Fri), a neoclassical monolith completed in 1836 and designed by József Hild, the same architect who later worked on the cathedral at Esztergom. Despite the cathedral's size and ornate altars, the interior is surprisingly light and airy. Northeast of the cathedral in the **Archbishop's Palace** (Érseki Palota; Széchenyi István utca 5) is the **Ecclesiastical Collection** (Egyházi Gyűjtemény; ☎ 421 332; adult/child 300/200Ft; ☺ 9am-5pm Tue-Sat Apr-Oct, 8am-4pm Mon-Fri Nov-Mar), with priceless vestments, church plate and liturgical objects.

Directly opposite the Basilica is the sprawling Zopf-style **Lyceum** (Líceum; ☎ 520 400; Eszterházy tér 1; ☺ 9.30am-3.30pm Tue-Sun Apr-Sep, 9.30am-1pm Sat & Sun Oct-Mar), dating from 1765. The 20,000-volume **library** (adult/student 500/350Ft), on the 1st floor of the south wing, contains hundreds of priceless manuscripts and codices. The **ceiling fresco** (1778) here is a *trompe l'oeuil* masterpiece depicting the

THE SIEGE OF EGER

The story of the Turkish attempt to take Eger Castle is the stuff of legend. Under the command of István Dobó, a mixed bag of 2000 soldiers held out against more than 100,000 Turks for a month in 1552. As every Hungarian kid in short trousers can tell you, the women of Eger played a crucial role in the battle, pouring boiling oil and pitch on the invaders from the ramparts. A painting by Bertalan Székely called *The Women of Eger* in the castle's art gallery pays tribute to these brave ladies.

Also significant was Eger's wine, if we're to believe the tale. It seems that Dobó sustained his soldiers with the ruby-red vintage. When they fought on with increased vigour – and stained beards – rumours began to circulate among the Turks that the defenders were gaining strength by drinking the blood of bulls. The name Bikavér (Bull's Blood) was born.

Géza Gárdonyi's *Eclipse of the Crescent Moon* (1901), which describes the siege and is required reading for many young Hungarians, can be found in English translation (published by Corvina) in bookshops throughout the land.

Counter-Reformation's Council of Trent (1545–63) and a lightning bolt setting heretical manuscripts ablaze.

The **Astronomy Museum** (adult/student 500/350Ft), on the 6th floor of the east wing, contains 18th-century astronomical equipment and an **observatory**; climb three more floors up to the observation deck for a great view of the city and to try out the **camera obscura**, the 'eye of Eger', designed in 1776 to spy on the town and to entertain townspeople.

OTHER SIGHTS
Walk north along Széchenyi utca to the **Cistercian church** (Ciszterek temploma; Széchenyi István utca 15) built in 1743. The theatrical baroque altar sculpture of St Francis Borgia in gilt and white stucco is well worth a look. The **Serbian Orthodox church** (Ráctemplom; ☎ 320 129; Vitkovics Mihály utca 30; admission 300Ft; ⏰ 10am-4pm Tue-Sun) and its enormous iconostasis of gold leaf and braid is further north; enter from Széchenyi utca 59.

Retrace your steps to the Cistercian church and turn east onto Dr Sándor Imre utca and Markhót Ferenc utca to the **minaret** (☎ 410 233; Knézich Károly utca; admission 200Ft; ⏰ 9.30am-6pm Apr-Oct), topped with a cross. Only nonclaustrophobes will brave the 97 narrow spiral steps to the top.

Mecset utca south of the minaret leads to central Dobó István tér, site of the town's market in medieval times. On the southern side of the square stands the **Minorite church** (Minorita templom; ☎ 312 744; Dobó István tér 6; admission free; ⏰ 9am-5pm Tue-Sun), built in 1771 and one of the most glorious baroque buildings in Hungary. The altarpiece of the Virgin

Mary and St Anthony of Padua is by Johann Kracker, the Bohemian painter who also did the fire-and-brimstone ceiling fresco in the Lyceum library. Statues of István Dobó and his comrades-in-arms routing the Turks in 1552 fill the square in front of the church.

From Dobó István tér cross the little Eger Stream to Dózsa György tér and turn southwest onto Kossuth Lajos utca, a fine, treelined street with dozens of architectural gems. The first of interest is the former **Orthodox synagogue** (Ortodox zsinagóga; 17 Kossuth Lajos utca), built in 1893 and now a furniture store backing onto a shopping mall. (A **neoclassical synagogue** (Dr Hibay Károly utca 7) dating from 1845 and now partly renovated is around the corner.) You'll pass several outstanding baroque and Eclectic buildings, including the **county hall** (megyeháza; 9 Kossuth Lajos utca), with a wrought-iron grid above the main door of Faith, Hope and Charity by Henrik Fazola, a Rhinelander who settled in Eger in the mid-18th century. Walk down the passageway, and you'll see two more of his magnificent works: baroque wrought-iron gates decorated on both sides that have superseded the minaret as the symbol of Eger. The gate on the right shows the seal of Heves County and has a comical figure on its handle. The more graceful gate on the left is decorated with grapes. The **Franciscan church** (Ferences templom; 14 Kossuth Lajos utca) was completed in 1755 on the site of a mosque. The wrought-iron balcony and window grids of the rococo **Provost's Palace** (Kisprépostí palota; 4 Kossuth Lajos utca) were also done by Fazola.

Activities

WINE TASTING

You can sample Eger's famous wines at many places around town, including a couple at the base of the castle, and in the **István Cellar** (☎ 313 670; Tündérpart 5; ☻ 1-10pm Tue-Sun Apr-Oct, 2-9pm Tue-Sun Oct-Mar) below the Korona hotel; Tourinform has an extensive list.

But why bother drinking in town when you can do the same in the wine cellars of the evocatively named **Valley of the Beautiful Women** (Szépasszony-völgy) so close by? The best time to visit the valley on a warm day is the late afternoon.

From the western end of the Basilica, walk south on Trinitárius utca to Bartók Béla tér and then west along Király utca to Szépasszonyvölgy utca. Veer to the left as you descend the hill past the large Talizmán restaurant into the valley, and you'll see dozens of cellars. Alternatively take the train on wheels from Dobó tér to the valley's entrance-way (one way 450Ft; running from 10am to 6pm April to October).

This is the place to sample Bull's Blood – one of very few reds produced in Eger – or any of the whites: Leányka, Olaszrizling and Hárslevelű from nearby Debrő. The choice of wine cellars can be a bit daunting and their characters can change, so walk around and have a look yourself. Cellar Nos 16, 17, 29 and 48 are always popular; for schmaltzy Gypsy music, try No 32 or 42. But if you're interested in good wine, visit cellar Nos 5, 18 and 31. Be careful, though; those glasses (about 50Ft to 80Ft) go down easily. Hours are erratic, but a few cellars are sure to be open till the early evening. The taxi fare back to the city centre is about 1000Ft.

OTHER ACTIVITIES

After sightseeing in the **Archbishop's Garden** (Érsek-kert; enter from Petőfi Sándor tér 2), once the private reserve of papal princes, unwind in the nearby **thermal baths** (☎ 413 356; Fürdő utca 1-3; adult/child 900/650Ft; ☻ women noon-6pm Wed & Fri, men noon-6pm Tue, Thu & 10am-2pm Sat), which date from Turkish times.

The stunning **Aladár Bitskey Swimming Pool** (☎ 511 810; Frank Tivadar utca; adult/senior or student 700/400Ft; ☻ 6am-9pm Mon, Wed & Fri, 6am-10pm Tue & Thu, 8am-8pm Sat, 8am-6pm Sun) nearby was designed by maverick Hungarian architect Imre Makovecz.

Bicycles can be rented from **Ride or Die** (☎ 413 903; Jókai utca 6; per hr/day 300/3000Ft; ☻ 10am-6pm Mon-Fri, 9am-1pm Sat), but requires a 25,000Ft deposit.

Tours

Tourinform organises walking tours (adult/child 700/350Ft) of the city in both English and German from July to September.

Festivals & Events

Annual events include the **Spring Festival** in late March/April, the **Border Fortress Merrymaking Festival and Games** at the castle at the end of July, **Baroque Weeks** in late July/August, the **Agria International Folkdance Meeting** in August and the **Feast of Eger** in mid-September.

Sleeping

Tourinform has a booklet of accommodation available not only in the city, but also in the surrounding area.

BUDGET

Egertourist and Ibusz can all organise private rooms (2500Ft to 4000Ft per night per person). You might also look for a room along Almagyar utca or clumped together on Mekcsey István utca (Nos 10/a, 13, 14, 14/a and 14/b). You'll also see *szoba kiadó* (room for rent) signs to the northeast of the castle along Vécseyvölgy utca.

Tulipán Kemping (☎ 410 580; Szépasszonyvölgy utca 71; camp sites per person/tent/car 600/500/300Ft, 4-/5-bed bungalows 6000/10,000Ft; ☻ year round; **P**) Tulipán occupies a quiet spot with its back

---

AUTHOR'S CHOICE

Senator Ház (☎ 320 466; www.senatorhaz.hu; Dobó István tér 11; s/d €52/72; **P** ⚡) András Cseh, the owner and manager of Senator Ház, has created what we consider to be the finest small hotel in provincial Hungary. Its warm and cosy rooms fill the upper floors of this delightful 18th-century inn on Eger's main square, while its ground floor is shared between a quality restaurant and a reception that could easily moonlight as a history museum (Cseh has been collecting – and displaying – all sorts of bric-a-brac for the past 15 years). With only 11 rooms, it's advisable to book ahead.

to the cellars and vineyards of the Valley of the Beautiful Women; there's not a lot of shade for those tenting, but the five-bed bungalows come with plenty of comforts.

A number of colleges offer accommodation for around 2500Ft per person from mid-June/July to August. We recommend: **Leányka út College** (Leányka úti Kollégium; ☎ 520 430; Leányka utca 2; P) East of the castle, with 300 beds. **Archbishop's Garden College** (Érsekkerti Kollégium; ☎ 520 432; Klapka György utca 12) An even more central option in a house full of character, with 132 beds.

MIDRANGE

Villa Völgy (☎ 321 664; www.hotels.hu/villavolgy; Tulipánkert utca 5; s/d 8200/13,600Ft; P 🏊) This immaculate hotel in a modern villa is an excellent place to stay near the Valley of the Beautiful Women. Its bright rooms are tastefully designed and feature plenty of wood, and there's a sauna, solarium, fitness room and restaurant on site.

Bartók tér Pension (☎ 515 556; ca7566@axelero.hu; Bartók Béla tér; s/d 7000/9000Ft; P) This colourful *pension* between the Valley of the Beautiful Women and the city centre has big rooms, a quiet location and a friendly welcome.

St Kristóf (Arany János utca 1; s/d 7000/9000Ft) Affiliated with Bartók tér Pension, this place is of the same standard and within eyeshot of Bartók.

Rubina Hotel (☎ 410 580; Honfoglalás utca 31/a; s/d €25/40; P 🏊) Rubina occupies a quiet spot high above the wine valley in Szépasszony-völgy. It has a few wellness extras, like a sauna and steam room.

Minaret (☎ 410 233; Knézich Károly utca 4; s/d €35/45; P 🏊) In the shadow of the minaret, this family-run hotel has good-sized rooms, a fine restaurant and is centrally located.

TOP END

Romantik (☎ 310 456; www.romantikhotel.hu; Csíky Sándor utca 26; s/d 12,000/15,500Ft; P) This very friendly and cosy 16-room hotel, with a pretty back garden, is an easy walk to the city centre, but far enough away to escape any noise in the summer months.

Korona (☎ 313 670; www.koronahotel.hu; Tündérpart utca 5; s/d from €60/75; P 🏊) On a quiet side street off Csíky Sándor utca, this place has a wellness centre, as well as a 'wine museum' in its 200-year-old wine cellar called István Cellar (p331), where you can sample wines from all regions.

Panoráma (☎ 412 886; panhotel@lelender.hu; Dr Hibay Károly utca 2; s/d from 15,000/17,500Ft; P 🏊) Panoráma aims its services at business clientele, with conference rooms, fitness areas, and a bar and restaurant on site.

Szent János (☎ 510 350; www.hotelszentjanos.hu; Szent János utca 3; s/d 12,000/15,300Ft; P 🐾) This supremely central hotel in a baroque townhouse has all the added extras of a top-of-the-line establishment, but lacks a bit of warmth.

Eating & Drinking
RESTAURANTS

Szántófer (☎ 517 298; Bródy utca 3; mains 1000Ft; 🕗 8am-10pm) With farming equipment and cooking utensils hanging like prize kills on its walls and hearty peasant cuisine filling its menu, Szántófer oozes in rustic charm. The covered courtyard out back is perfect for escaping the summer heat.

Elefanto (☎ 411 031; Katona István tér 2; mains 1000-2000Ft) Perched high above the market, this is a great place, with a nonsmoking interior and covered balcony for alfresco dining.

Senator Ház (☎ 320 466; www.senatorhaz.hu; Dobó István tér 11; entrées 350-500Ft, mains 1000-2000Ft) The café-restaurant at the Senator is a delightful place for a meal or just a snack of *palacsinta* (pancakes).

Fehérszarvas Vadásztanya (☎ 411 129; Klapka György utca 8; mains 1500-3000Ft) This is the city's silver-service restaurant. But the 'White-Deer Hunters' Farm', as its name literally translates, with its game specialities and cellar setting, is really a place to enjoy in autumn and winter.

There are several *csárdák* (Hungarian-style inns) amongst the wine cellars in

Szépasszony-völgy, which at the end of the day are much of a muchness, but if you sit down to a meal here you'll most certainly be serenaded by Imré, an old, round chap who churns out Gypsy ballads on his whiny violin. We recommend **Nótafa** (☎ 313 484; Szépasszony-völgy; mains 1000-2000Ft) because it pays homage to the man, Imre; his photo takes pride of place over the dining area.

CAFÉS

Café Mirador (☎ 333 301; Frank Tivadar utca 5) More of a cocktail bar than a café, this is a fine place to kick back after a hard day's sightseeing with a beer or cocktail and very smooth tunes.

Egri Est Café (☎ 411 105; Széchenyi István utca 16; ☯ 11am-midnight Sun-Thu, 11am-4am Fri & Sat) This decent café-bar is a colourful and lively place, with parties on weekends.

Marján (☎ 312 784; Kossuth Lajos utca 28; ☯ 9am-10pm May-Sep, 9am-8pm Oct-Apr) The big terrace of this cake shop south of Dózsa György tér is the place to try something sweet.

Other options:

Pallas (☎ 318 614; Dobó István utca 20; ☯ 9.30am-9pm) Coffeeshop in a small courtyard, with a classical motif.

Dobos (☎ 413 335; Széchenyi István utca 6; ☯ 9.30am-7pm) Pleasant café on Eger's main pedestrian street.

QUICK EATS

Express (☎ 517 920; Barkóczy utca 4; dishes under 800Ft; ☯ 7am-8pm Mon-Sat, 7am-3pm Sun) Northeast of the bus station, this large self-service restaurant is the place for a quick, cheap meal.

Pizza Club (☎ 322 914; Dr Hibay Károly utca 8; pizza 560-1000Ft) This small pizzeria is tucked away just off Dobó István tér and is good for an inexpensive bite to eat.

SELF-CATERING

Market (Katona István tér; ☯ 6am-6pm Mon-Fri, 6am-1pm Sat, 6am-10am Sun) Eger's large covered market has more fruit and vegies than you could possibly carry away.

Entertainment

Tourinform, the **County Cultural Centre** (☎ 510 020; Knézich Károly utca 8), opposite the minaret, or the city **ticket office** (☎ 518 347; Széchenyi István utca 5; ☯ 10am-1pm, 2-6pm Mon-Fri) can tell you what's on in Eger. The city's venues are the **Géza Gárdonyi Theatre** (☎ 310 026; Hatvani kapu tér 4; ☯ box office 2-7pm Mon-Fri), the Lyceum and the Basilica, where there are half-hour

organ concerts at 11.30am Monday to Saturday and at 12.45pm Sunday from mid-May to mid-October.

Broadway Palace (Pyrker János tér 3; ☯ 10pm-6am Wed, Fri & Sat) This bizarre cave-like place beneath the cathedral steps parties into the wee hours on weekends.

Hippolit Club (☎ 411 031; Katona István tér 2; ☯ 10pm-5am Fri & Sat) Eger's classic club is downstairs at the Elefanto restaurant, where the dance floor heaves until the small hours.

Eger is included in the free biweekly *Egri Est* listings magazine.

Shopping

Egri Galéria (☎ 517 518; Érsek utca 8; ☯ 10am-1pm & 2-6pm Mon-Fri, 10am-2pm Sat) This has lovely jewellery, fine art, pottery and other collectibles for sale.

Castrum Antikvitás (☎ 311 613; Harangöntő utca 2; ☯ 9am-5pm Mon-Fri) This small shop is the place to go for antiques.

Getting There & Away

Bus services are good, with buses every 30 to 40 minutes to Gyöngyös (usually via Kerecsend; 665Ft, one hour, 52km), Mezőkövesd, Szilvásvárad and Bélapátfalva. Other destinations include Aggtelek (1210Ft, 2½ hours, 100km, once daily), Budapest (1570Ft, 2½ hours, 130km, hourly via the M3), Kecskemét (2060Ft, 4½ hours, 166km, three daily), Debrecen (1690Ft, 2½ hours, 131km, seven daily), Miskolc (846Ft, 1½ hours, 68km, eight daily) and Szeged (2910Ft, 5¾ hours, 237km, twice daily) via Csongrád. The bus to Miskolc only goes through the Bükk Hills via Felsőtárkány on Sunday at 8.30am and 3.35pm from mid-April to mid-October.

Eger is on a minor train line linking Putnok and Füzesabony; you usually have to change at the latter for Budapest (1624Ft, two hours, 142km), Miskolc (774Ft, 1½ hours, 74km) or Debrecen (1212Ft, three hours, 120km). There are up to seven direct trains a day to/from Budapest's Keleti train station (2½ hours) that don't require a change.

Getting Around

From the main train station, Bus 11, 12 or 14 will drop you off at the bus station or city centre.

You can book a taxi by calling ☎ 411 222 or 555 555.

AROUND EGER

Egerszalók

☎ 36 / pop 1975

By this book's publication, this quiet rural open-air **hot spring** (hőforrás; ☎ 515 300; per 15min visit 100Ft, 7am-6pm adult/child 550/400Ft, 6pm-1am adult or child 700Ft), 8km southwest of Eger, is set to become Hungary's biggest and boldest thermal resort-hotel. Set back into the hills, the multilevel hotel will dominate a tiny valley completely transformed into parkland dotted with thermal pools of all shapes and sizes. Fortunately the original spring – cascades of *very* hot water running down from what look like steaming icebergs but are in fact mounds of salt and other minerals – will remain untouched, but how aesthetically pleasing the entire complex will be is anyone's guess.

If you're looking for a cheap alternative to the resort, try **Kelemen Vendégház** (☎ 474 559; webgast@freemail.hu; Sarló út 24; per person 2500-4000Ft; P) close to the centre of Egerszalók. Run by the friendly Judit and András, this small guesthouse offers hearty meals, local tours, and is good value for groups of up to 10 people.

The bus to Kerecsend via Demjén will drop you off 250m north of the entrance.

Mezőkövesd

☎ 49 / pop 17,800

Some 18km southeast of Eger, Mezőkövesd (www.mezokovesd.hu) is not much of a town, but it is the centre of the Matyó, a Magyar people famous for their fine embroidery and other folk art.

From the Mezőkövesd bus station on Rákóczi utca, walk south for 50m and then east along Mátyás király út for 600m to Szent László tér, where you'll find **Tourinform** (☎ 500 285; mezokovesd@tourinform.hu; Szent László tér 23; 9am-5pm Mon-Fri, 10am-2pm Sat mid-Jun–Aug, 10am-4pm Mon-Fri Sep–mid-Jun). There's an **OTP bank** (Mátyás király út 149) at the bus station end of town and the **post office** (Alkomány utca 1) is behind Tourinform.

SIGHTS

Opposite Tourinform is the **Matyó Museum** (☎ 311 824; Szent László tér 8; adult/child 400/200Ft), with displays explaining the regional differences and historical development of Matyó needlework: from white-on-white stitching and patterns of blue-and-red roses, to

the metallic fringe that was banned in the early 1920s because the high cost was ruining some families. The museum was being moved at the time of research, so check with Tourinform for opening times.

From Hősök tere, a short distance southwest of Szent László tér, enter any of the small streets running southward to find the **Hadas** district, a completely different world of thatched and whitewashed cottages. Interesting lanes to stroll along are Patkó köz, Kökény köz and Mogyoró köz, but the centre of activity is Kis Jankó Bori utca, named after Hungary's own 'Grandma Moses', who lived and stitched her famous '100 roses' patterns here for almost 80 years. Her 200-year-old cottage is now the **Bori Kis Jankó Memorial House** (Kis Jankó Bori Emlékház; ☎ 411 873; Kis Jankó Bori utca 22; adult/child 200/100Ft; 9am-7pm Jul–mid-Aug, 9am-4pm mid-Mar–Jun & mid-Aug–Oct), filled with needlework and brightly painted furniture. Other houses on Kis Jankó Bori utca that you can visit and watch the women at work are the **Folk-Art Association** (☎ 411 686; 5 Kis Jankó Bori utca), **'dance barn'** (táncpajta; 7 Kis Jankó Bori utca), Nos 9 and 38. Also poke your head into Nos 1, 4, 6 and 12 of Mogyoró köz. Most of the work is for sale directly from the embroiderers; you can also buy it at the Matyó Museum.

SLEEPING & EATING

With Eger so close, there's no point in staying overnight in Mezőkövesd. But if you miss the last bus or you want to catch an early-morning one to Miskolc, **Borsod Tourist** (☎ 412 614; Mátyás király út 153; 9am-4.30pm Mon-Thu, 9am-2pm Fri), en route to/from the bus station, can organise private rooms (around 2500Ft per person around); Tourinform also has a list. Otherwise, you can overnight at the following:

Tulipános Guesthouse (☎ 06 30 228 7119; Mogyoró köz 1; d 4000Ft; P) In the heart of the Hadas district, this holiday home has enough room to sleep eight people, and comes with kitchen and garden.

For something to eat, your best bet are these eateries:

Hungária (☎ 416 800; Alkotmány út 2; mains 700-1000Ft) Next to Tourinform, Hungária's international food and hearty lunch menu (around 550Ft) attracts locals like bees to honey.

Pizza Néró (☎ 415 676; Eötvös utca 9; pizza 600-1000Ft; ☿ 10am-11pm Sun-Thu, 10am-2pm Fri & Sat) South of Hősök tere, this pizzeria is a simpler affair.

GETTING THERE & AWAY
Buses run to/from Eger (241Ft, 30 minutes, 20km) and Miskolc (605Ft, one hour, 48km) at least every half-hour.

SZILVÁSVÁRAD
☎ 36 / pop 1900

The peaceful town of Szilvásvárad, some 28km north of Eger, is an excellent gateway for inroads into the western Bükk region, particularly for hiking into the Szalajka Valley. It's also the centre for breeding

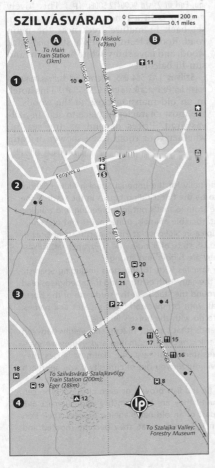

Lipizzaners (see boxed text, p336), and is the place to ride on one of Hungary's most delightful narrow-gauge trains.

Orientation
Get off the train at the first of Szilvásvárad's two stations, Szilvásvárad-Szalajkavölgy, and walk along Egri út northeast for about 10 minutes to the centre of town. The town's main train station is 3km to the north.

Information
There's an **OTP bank** (Egri út 30/a; ☿ 8am-4pm Mon-Fri) for changing money (an OTP ATM is next to the supermarket) and a **post office** (Egri út 12; ☿ 8am-4pm Mon-Fri) close by.

Sights & Activities
The open-air **narrow-gauge train** (☎ 564 004; Szalajka-völgy 6; adult/child one way 300/150Ft) chugs its way for 5km into the Szalajka Valley seven times daily from May to September (10 times daily on the weekend), with departures in April and October leaving when enough people gather.

The little open-air train stops at **Szalajka-Fátyolvízesés**. From there, you can walk for 15 minutes to **Istállóskő Cave**, where Stone Age pottery shards were discovered in 1912, or climb 958m **Mt Istállóskő**, the highest peak in the Bükk Hills. To return to Szilvásvárad, either stay on the train for the return trip or walk back for 1½ hours along shady paths, taking in trout-filled streams and the **Forestry Museum** (Erdészeti Múzeum; ☎ 355 112; adult/child 210/120Ft; 8.30am-4.30pm Tue-Sun mid-Apr–Sep, 8.30am-3pm Tue-Sun Oct, 8.30am-2pm Nov–mid-Apr), which deals with everything the forest surrenders.

The covered and the open **racecourses** (adult/child 300/150Ft) in Szilvásvárad put on Lipizzaner parades and coach races on weekends throughout summer, but times are not fixed. Learn more about these intelligent horses by visiting the whiffy **Horse Museum** (Lovas Múzeum; ☎ 355 135; Park utca 8; adult/child 350/250Ft; 9am-noon & 1-4pm Sun-Wed), in an 18th-century stable. The **Lipizzaner Stud Farm** (Lipicai Állami Ménesgazdaság; ☎ 564 400; Fenyves utca; adult/child 300/200Ft; 10am-noon & 2-4pm Thu-Sun) can also be visited. It rents out horses (1800/2500Ft per hour in the paddock/further afield) and offers coach rides (two-/four-horse coach seating three people from 4300/7400Ft). Coach driving instruction costs 5100/9000Ft an hour for two-/four- horse coaches.

The Protestant **Round Church** (Kerektemplom; Aradi vértanúk útja 33; admission free; 9-11am & 2-5pm Mon-Sat), with its Doric columns and dramatic dome raised in 1841, looks to some like a provincial attempt to duplicate the basilica at Eger. Displays in a 17th-century farmhouse called **Orbán House** (☎ 355 133; Miskolci utca 58-60; adult/child 200/150Ft; 9am-5pm Tue-Sun mid-Apr–Oct) are devoted to the flora, fauna and geology of Bükk National Park.

Mountain Bike Rentals (☎ 06 30 335 2695; Szalajka-völgy; 9am-6pm Sat-Wed, 9am-1pm Thu & Fri) has a stand opposite the narrow-gauge train station in Szalajka-völgy. Bike rentals per one/two/three/four/five hours cost 800/1000/1200/1400/1600Ft and per day 2000Ft.

Sleeping & Eating

Szalajka Fogadó (☎ 564 020; szalajka.fogado@axelero .hu; Egri út 2; s/d 9000/12,500Ft; P) This lovely *pension* is in a renovated house/mansion, set back in mature trees near the main road. Rooms feature loads of stripped-back wood, and have shiny-white bathrooms and sun-lit balconies.

Szilvás (☎ 564 065; reserve@hotelszilvas.hunguest hotels.hu; Park utca 6; s/d from €25/35; P) This hotel, in an old mansion close to the woods, is the most characterful place to stay in Szilvásvárad. Prices depend on the season, whether your room has a shower or bath,

---

THE MAGNIFICENT WHITE STALLIONS

Lipizzaners, the celebrated white horses bred originally for the imperial Spanish Riding School in Vienna under the Habsburgs, are considered to be the finest riding horses in the world – the *haute école* of dressage equines. And with all the trouble that's put into breeding and training them, it's not surprising. They are very intelligent, sociable animals, quite robust and graceful.

Lipizzaners are bred for riding and show at Lipica in Slovenia; at Piber, northeast of Graz in Austria, for the Spanish Riding School; and in the US state of Illinois. The Lipizzaners at Szilvásvárad are raised as carriage horses; as a result they are bigger and stronger.

Breeding, as they say, is paramount. Some six families with 16 ancestors (including Spanish, Arabian and Berber breeds) can be traced back to the early 18th century, and their pedigrees read like those of medieval nobility. When you walk around the stables at the stud farm or the Horse Museum, you'll notice charts on each horse's stall with complicated figures, dates and names, like 'Maestoso', 'Neapolitano' and 'Pluto'. It's all to do with the horse's lineage.

A fully mature Lipizzaner measures about 15 hands (that's about 152cm) and weighs between 500kg and 600kg. They have long backs, short thick necks, silky manes and expressive eyes. They live for 25 to 30 years and are particularly resistant to disease. But, like most horses, they are somewhat short-sighted (near-sighted) and will nuzzle you out of curiosity if you approach them while they graze.

Lipizzaners are not born white but grey, bay (ie reddish brown) or even chestnut. The celebrated 'imperial white' does not come about until they are between five and 10 years old, when their hair loses its pigment; think of it as part of an old nag's ageing process. Their skin remains grey, however, so when they are ridden hard and sweat, they become mottled and aren't so attractive.

and drop the longer you linger; note that there is a minimum stay of two nights.

Hegyi Camping (☎ 355 207; www.hegyicamping .com; Egri út 36/a; camp site per tent & 2 people 1800Ft, 2-/3-/ 4-bed cabins 4400/5400/6200Ft; ☒ mid-Apr–mid-Oct; ℗) A small, quiet camping ground close to walks, with a variety of accommodation.

A string of food stalls and restaurants line Szalajka-völgy. Many of them serve trout (40Ft to 60Ft per kilogram), the speciality of the area, and have wine tastings. We recommend the following:

Lovas (☎ 355 555; mains 900-2500Ft; ☒ 10am-8pm) With a covered terrace facing the racecourse.

Fenyő (☎ 564 015; mains 800-1500Ft; ☒ 8am-10pm) Simpler, with its back to the car park and forest.

For something more upmarket, head to the quality restaurant at Szalajaka Fogadó.

Getting There & Away
Buses to/from Eger (363Ft, 45 minutes, 30km) run often and, though they stop at Bélapátfalva (133Ft, 10 minutes, 7km) and sometimes Mónosbél, they're faster than the train. Buses also go to Budapest (1930Ft, three hours, 152km, three to four daily) and Miskolc (665Ft, 1½ hours, 55km, once daily).

Up to six trains daily link Eger (346Ft, one hour, 34km) with Szilvásvárad. If heading for Szilvásvárad from the centre of Eger, board the train at the Egervár train station. Three of these trains carry on to Putnok, from where you can enter Slovakia via Bánréve or head southeast for Miskolc.

AROUND SZILVÁSVÁRAD
Bélapátfalva
☎ 36 / pop 3500
On the train or bus to/from Szilvásvárad, you'll pass through the town of Bélapátfalva, which seems to stand out for no other reason than that the giant cement factory covers everything in fine white powder.

In fact, one of Hungary's most perfectly preserved Romanesque monuments is just a few minutes away. It's the **Bélháromkút Abbey Church** (☎ 354 784; adult/child 150/100Ft; ☒ 10am-4pm Tue-Sun mid-Mar–Oct), built by French Cistercian monks in 1232 and reached by walking east from the village centre for 1.5km (follow the 'Apátság Múzeum' signs) along Apátság utca. Along the way you'll see another sign giving the address for the key (*templom kulcsa*), which is at Rozsa Ferenc utca 42. The church, built in the shape of a

cross, is set in a peaceful dell just below Mt Bélkő. Don't miss the 19th-century painted **Calvary scene** nearby.

Most of the buses and trains linking Eger and Szilvásvárad stop at Bélapátfalva.

MISKOLC
☎ 46 / pop 184,100
Miskolc, Hungary's third-largest city, is a sprawling metropolis ringed by refineries, abandoned factories and cardboard-quality housing blocks. So why come to this 'capital of the rust belt'? For one thing, its location at the foot of the Bükk Hills makes it an ideal place to start a trek or walk into the national park. The thermal waters of nearby Miskolctapolca are among the most effective in Hungary, and the western suburb of Diósgyőr boasts a well-preserved castle.

A relatively affluent mining and steel-making town under the socialist regime, Miskolc was hit harder than most by the collapse of heavy industry here in the early 1990s.

Orientation
Miskolc is a long and narrow city, stretching from the unlovely Sajó Valley in the east to the Bükk foothills in the west. The main drag, Széchenyi István út, is lined with some surprisingly interesting old buildings, especially those around the so-called Dark Gate (Sötétkapu), an 18th-century vaulted passageway.

Miskolc's main train station, called Tiszai pályaudvar, lies to the southeast on Kandó Kálmán tér, a 15-minute tram ride from the city centre. The huge bus station is on Búza tér, a short distance northeast of Széchenyi út.

Information
Borsod Tourist (☎ 312 542; Széchenyi István út 35; ☒ 9am-5pm Mon-Fri)

Géniusz (☎ 412 932; Széchenyi István út 107) Stocks novels and travel guides on Hungary in English.

Ibusz (☎ 324 411; Széchenyi István út 14)

Main post office (Kazinczy Ferenc út 16) Located on the eastern side of Hősök tere.

OTP bank (Széchenyi István út 15) Opposite the Dark Gate.

Planet Café (Bajcsy-Zsilinsky utca; per hr 360Ft; ☒ 10am-10.30pm) Internet access in the Szinvapark mall.

Post office (Széchenyi István út 3-9; ☒ 8am-7pm Mon-Fri) This branch has a convenient location on the 1st floor of a shopping block above Plus supermarket.

NORTHERN UPLANDS

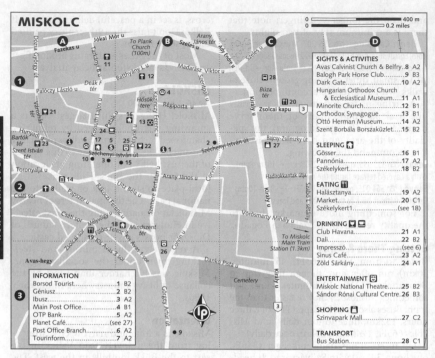

MISKOLC

0 ——— 400 m
0 ——— 0.2 miles

SIGHTS & ACTIVITIES
Avas Calvinist Church & Belfry..8 A2
Balogh Park Horse Club...........9 B3
Dark Gate.............................10 A2
Hungarian Orthodox Church
& Ecclesiastical Museum.....11 A1
Minorite Church....................12 B1
Orthodox Synagogue............13 B1
Ottó Herman Museum...........14 A2
Szent Borbála Borszaküzlet....15 B2

SLEEPING
Gösser.................................16 B1
Pannónia.............................17 A2
Székelykert..........................18 B2

EATING
Halásztanya.........................19 A2
Market................................20 C1
Székelykert1.....................(see 18)

DRINKING
Club Havana........................21 A1
Dali....................................22 B2
Impresszó........................(see 6)
Sinus Café...........................23 A2
Zöld Sárkány.......................24 A1

ENTERTAINMENT
Miskolc National Theatre.......25 B2
Sándor Rónai Cultural Centre.26 B3

SHOPPING
Szinvapark Mall....................27 C2

TRANSPORT
Bus Station..........................28 C1

INFORMATION
Borsod Tourist.......................1 B2
Géniusz.................................2 B2
Ibusz....................................3 A2
Main Post Office.....................4 B1
OTP Bank..............................5 A2
Planet Café.......................(see 27)
Post Office Branch..................6 A2
Tourinform............................7 A2

Tourinform (☎ 350 425; miskolc@tourinform.hu; Városház tér 13; 9am-6pm Mon-Sat, 9am-1pm Sun Jun-Sep,
9am-5pm Mon-Fri, 9am-1pm Sat Oct-May) Very helpful,
with bundles of information on the city and its surrounds.
www.miskolc.hu This website is available in a number
of languages.

Sights

Two houses of worship attest to the large
communities of Greeks and Jews who once
called Miskolc their home. The **Hungarian
Orthodox church** (Magyar ortodox templom; Deák Ferenc
tér 7), a splendid late-baroque structure, has
an iconostasis (1793) that is 16m high with
88 icons. A guide will escort you to the **Orthodox Ecclesiastical Museum** (Ortodox Egyházi Múzeum;
☎ 415 441; adult/child 150/100Ft; 10am-6pm Tue-
Sun Apr-Sep, 10am-4pm Tue-Sat Oct-Mar) near the
main gate. Look out for the Black Madonna
of Kazan, presented to the church by Catherine the Great, and the jewel-encrusted
Mt Athos Cross, brought to Miskolc by
Greek settlers in the 18th century. To the
southeast stands the large and, as per the
norm, crumbling **Orthodox synagogue** (Ortodox
zsinagóga; Kazinczy Ferenc utca 7), designed in 1861

by Ludwig Förster, architect of the Great
Synagogue in Budapest.

The Calvinist **Plank Church** (Deszkatemplom;
Petőfi tér) is a 1938 replica of a 17th-century
Transylvanian-style wooden church. It has
been completely rebuilt and renovated after
being badly damaged by fire in 1997.

The **Ottó Herman Museum** (☎ 346 875; Papszer
utca 1; adult/child 400/200Ft; 10am-4pm Tue-Sun),
south of the city centre, has one of Hungary's richest collections of Neolithic finds
(many from the Bükk region), good ethnographical and mineral collections, and an
exhibit of fine art. From here, take a stroll
up leafy **Avas Hill**; the best approach is via
Mélyvölgy utca, off Papszer utca, or Földes
Ferenc utca, off Mindszent tér. Veer to the
right along the narrow lane past some of
the more than 800 wine cellars cut into the
limestone.

In a cemetery below the hill is the large
Gothic **Avas Calvinist church** (Avasi református
templom; Avas-hegy), with a painted wooden interior (1410). The bell tower dates from the
mid-16th century. The key is in the parish
office at Papszer utca 14.

A must-see but a bit of a journey from the city centre is the four-towered **Diósgyőr Castle** (Map p341; ☎ 533 355; Vár utca 24; adult/child 600/300Ft; ☺ 9am-6pm), in a suburb of the same name some 7km west of Miskolc. Begun in the 13th century, the castle was heavily damaged early in the 18th century and was only restored – very insensitively in some parts – in the 1950s. Tours (included in admission price), which take you through the castle's history display, wax museum and medieval weapon stash, leave at 15 and 45 minutes past the hour, and are in Hungarian and German only.

Activities

The **Balogh Park Horse Club** (☎ 712 899; Görgey Artúr utca 12) hires out horses for riding and runs a riding school south of Mindszent tér. Further afield, there's a horse-riding school at **Kováts** (Map p341; ☎ 341 656), a riding hotel in Görömböly, south of Miskolc on Rte 3 (Pesti út). Take bus 4 from the bus station.

Sample a few of the choice local wines at **Szent Borbála Borszaküzlet** (☎ 411 188; Széchenyi István út 14; ☺ 9am-5pm Mon-Fri, 9am-1pm Sat) in a courtyard off the main street.

One of the most enjoyable forest train trips in Hungary connects Miskolc and the resort town of Lillafüred (p341). This little **narrow-gauge train** (Map p341; ☎ 530 593) departs from Kilián-Észak train station (off Kiss tábornok út in western Miskolc), almost in Diósgyőr. There is only one departure daily year-round (one way adult/child 340/220Ft), at 9.15am mid-March to mid-October, and 9am the rest of the year. Check the schedules at Tourinform in Miskolc or call for information. From Lillafüred, the train carries on another 6km to Garadna.

Another line of the narrow-gauge train branches off at Papírgyár – the paper factory that polluted the Szinva Stream – and covers the 20km between Kilián-Észak train station and Mahóca. It only runs at 9.30am on Saturday from June to August.

Festivals & Events

Several special events and festivals are held at Diósgyőr Castle, including the **Castle Games** in May, the open-air **Kaláka International Folk Festival** in mid-July, and **Medieval Castle Days** in mid-August.

Sleeping

Miskolc is bereft of any quality accommodation, so you're better off choosing a place to stay in either Miskolctapolca (p340) or Lillafüred (p342). Tourinform has a list of private rooms (approximately 2500Ft per person), whereas Ibusz or Borsod Tourist can do bookings; the rooms will probably be in one of the housing projects ringing the city.

Székelykert (☎ 411 222; Földes Ferenc utca 4; r 8000Ft) On the corner with Kisavas Alsó sor, this popular *pension* has a homey feel, an owner mad on ice hockey, an unusual restaurant and easy access to Avas Hill.

Gösser (☎ 505 045; gosser.panzio@axelero.hu; Déryné utca 7; s/d 8000/9500Ft) Gösser's main selling point is its central location; rooms are fairly ordinary, but staff are friendly and accommodating.

Pannónia (☎ 504 980; www.hotelpannonia-miskolc .hu; Kossuth Lajos utca 2; s/d 16,100/18,000Ft; ℗) Pannónia is Miskolc's most central option, and aims itself at business clientele, with particularly unstylish rooms and conference facilities.

Eating & Drinking

Székelykert (☎ 411222; Földes Ferenc utca 4; mains 1000-2000Ft) This restaurant at the *pension* of the same name serves Transylvanian specialities, dishes rarely found on restaurant menus in Hungary, in a pleasant inner courtyard.

Halásztanya (☎ 411 203; Mélyvölgy út 15; mains 1000-2000Ft; ☺ 11am-11pm Mon-Sat) At the foot of Avas Hill, this relaxed place specialises in fish dishes and has a larger than normal terrace.

Talizmán (Map p341; ☎ 378 627; Vár utca 14; mains around 1200Ft) This place, in Diósgyőr, can be recommended for its menu and pleasant location on a pedestrian street lined with chestnuts tree, just up from the castle.

Market (Zsolcai kapu) Miskolc's large market is east of Búza tér.

While the city centre has surprisingly few restaurants deserving of a review, the same cannot be said for its cafés and bars. The following are all worth popping into:

Zöld Sárkány (☎ 428 134; Széchenyi István út 19; ☺ 10am-8.45pm Mon-Fri, noon-10pm Sat) A rather earnest teahouse and café in a stunning courtyard.

Dali (Déryné utca 10) With big couches, a funky décor and chilled tunes, Dali is perfect for lolling around sipping coffee or cocktails.

Impresszó (Kossuth Lajos utca; ⊗ 9am-midnight Tue-Thu, 9am-to late Fri & Sat) Popular for its coffee, alcoholic and non-alcoholic cocktails, and shady terrace.

Sinus Café (Hunyadi utca 3) More of a cocktail bar than a café, with a heaving terrace in summer.

Club Havana (Városház tér 3; ⊗ 8am-2am) A lovely terraced café-bar, with canned Latino music.

Entertainment

Miskolc National Theatre (Miskolci Nemzeti Színház; ☎ 516 735; Széchenyi István út 23; ⊗ box office 10am-7pm Mon-Fri, 3-7pm Sat & Sun) Stages plays and other performances in a new purpose-built theatre behind the original theatre (built 1857), where the beloved 19th-century actress Róza Széppataki Déryné once walked the floorboards.

There are also performances at the **Sándor Rónai Cultural Centre** (Rónai Sándor Művelődési Központ; ☎ 342 408; Mindszent tér 3). The Hungarian Orthodox church and Orthodox synagogue are sometimes used for opera concerts.

For more listings, see the free biweekly *Miskolci Est* magazine.

Getting There & Away

Buses depart for Debrecen (1210Ft, 2¼ hours, 100km) every 30 minutes to an hour. If you're heading south, it's best to take the bus, though departures are infrequent. There are nine buses daily to Eger (846Ft, 1½ hours, 68km).

Miskolc is served by hourly trains from Keleti train station in Budapest (2030Ft, 2½ hours, 182km); about 12 trains depart daily for Nyíregyháza (890Ft, 1½ to two hours, 88km) via Tokaj (544Ft, one hour, 56km). Two of these trains carry on to Debrecen (1420Ft, 2¼ to three hours, 137km), but generally you'll have to change at Nyíregyháza. About 12 trains leave Miskolc each day for Sárospatak (774Ft, 1½ hours, 74km) and Sátoraljaújhely (890Ft, 1¼ hours, 84km).

International trains from Miskolc include those departing for Košice in Slovakia (five daily) and Kraków (one daily).

Getting Around

Tram 1 begins at the train station and travels the length of the city before turning around in Diósgyőr; Tram 2 also starts at the train station, cuts through the centre of the city, but ends up in the industrial quarter of Diósgyőr-Kóház.

Order a taxi on ☎ 333 333.

AROUND MISKOLC
Miskolctapolca
☎ 46

The curative waters of the thermal spa in this southwestern recreational suburb, 7km from the centre of Miskolc, have been attracting bathers since the Middle Ages, though the gimmicky **Cave Bath** (Barlangfürdő; ☎ 561 361; Pazár István sétány 1; adult/child/student 1600/900/1100Ft; ⊗ 9am-7pm mid-Jul–Aug, 9am-6pm Sep–mid-Jul), with its earth walls, 'mildly radioactive waters' and thrashing shower at the end, is a relatively new arrival (1959). The pretty **Strand Bath** (Strandfürdő; ☎ 368 127; Miskolctapolcai út 1), in the centre of the town's large park, also has **outside pools** (adult/child 700/550Ft; ⊗ 9am-6pm May-Sep).

SLEEPING & EATING

Unless you arrive on a weekend at peak holiday times, you should have no problem finding accommodation; aside from hotels, private rooms are almost everywhere you look, and are particularly prolific to the west of the Cave Bath. **Tourist Service** (☎ 363 970; Csabai utca 14; ⊗ 9am-7.30pm) can help with booking such places.

Zenit (☎ 561 560; zenitpanzio@axelero.hu; Egyetem út; r 9800Ft; P) This *pension* within walking distance of the pools has cute rooms with homey touches (some with balcony) and warm staff. Cars are also available for rent.

Anna (☎ 422 212; annahotel2@chello.hu; Miskolctapolcai út 7; r 10,000Ft; P) Close to the pool entrance is this modern *pension*, with friendly management and large, if not spartan, rooms. Book ahead as it is often full.

Tapolca Fogadó (☎ 562 215; www.tapolcafogado.hu; Csabai utca 36; d/t from 8000/10,000Ft; P) If you like a natural-wood finish, you'll love this place; almost every inch of this *pension* is built from the material. Rooms are simple but more than comfortable, and the structure features a turret or two.

Park (☎ 422 605; parkhotel@axelero.hu; Csabai utca 35; r 8800Ft; P) Park is not much to look at from the outside, but its rooms are bright and fresh, and some have the added bonus of a balcony. There's a sauna available for guest use.

Hungária Club (☎ 432 884; Csabai utca; mains 800-1500Ft) Set back from Csabai utca, this eatery has a menu packed with Hungarian dishes and a terrace to the rear.

There are numerous food stalls and snack bars to choose from on Aradi sétány,

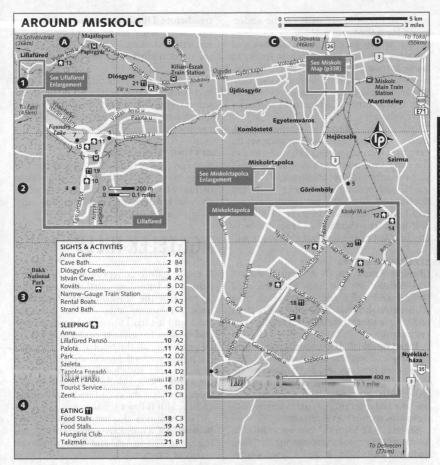

AROUND MISKOLC

SIGHTS & ACTIVITIES
Anna Cave....................................	**1** A2
Cave Bath....................................	**2** B4
Diósgyőr Castle............................	**3** B1
István Cave.................................	**4** A2
Kováts...	**5** D2
Narrow-Gauge Train Station..........	**6** A2
Rental Boats................................	**7** A2
Strand Bath..................................	**8** C3

SLEEPING
Anna...	**9** C3
Lillafüred Panzió...........................	**10** A2
Palota...	**11** A2
Park..	**12** D2
Szeleta.......................................	**13** A1
Tapolca Fogadó............................	**14** D2
Tókert Panzió...............................	**15** A2
Tourist Service.............................	**16** D3
Zenit...	**17** C3

EATING
Food Stalls...................................	**18** C3
Food Stalls...................................	**19** A2
Hungária Club...............................	**20** D3
Talizmán.....................................	**21** B1

and both Anna and Tapolca Fogadó have restaurants.

GETTING THERE & AWAY

Bus 2 serves Miskolctapolca and the Cave Bath from Búza tér in Miskolc.

Lillafüred

☎ 46

The alpine feel of Lillafüred, a tiny resort at the junction of two valleys formed by the Garadna and Szinva Streams, is in stark contrast to the urban sprawl of Miskolc only 12km to the east. While there are no major sights to drag you here, it's a nice spot to enjoy some fresh air, and a good springboard for walks and hikes into the eastern Bükk Hills.

ACTIVITIES

Sometimes called Petőfi Cave, **Anna Cave** (☎ 334 130; adult/child 650/450Ft, minimum 10 people) is below the Palota hotel and next to a cooling waterfall; on a 25-minute tour of the cave's labyrinth of tunnels, you'll come across fossilised leaves, branches, and even entire trees. Tours depart on the hour from 10am to 3pm from mid-April to mid-October.

István Cave (☎ 334 130; adult/child 650/450Ft, minimum 10 people; ☽ 9am-5pm mid-Apr–mid-Oct, 9am-4pm mid-Oct–mid-Apr) is about 500m up the mountain road leading to Eger; it offers one-hour tours on the hour, taking in stalagmites, stalactites, sinkholes and large chambers.

A number of lovely **walks** can be undertaken from the terminuses of the two lines of the narrow-gauge train at **Garadna** and **Taksalápa**, but accommodation is sparse in these parts and hikers had better be prepared to camp rough if they miss the train. Be sure to have a copy of the northern Bükk map (No 29) from Cartographia and carry extra water.

Jade-coloured **Hámori-tó** (Foundry Lake), named after the proto-blast furnace set up here by a German named Frigyes Fazola in the early 19th century to exploit the area's iron ore, offers **fishing** (☎ in Miskolc 324 702; Corvin utca 15) and boating. **Row boats** (☻ 10am-6pm May-Sep) cost 400/200Ft per adult/child per half-hour, while paddle boats cost 600Ft per half-hour. The Palota hotel rents out bicycles for 500Ft per hour, but only to guests.

SLEEPING & EATING

Lillafüred Panzió (☎ 379 299; Erzsébet sétány 7; s/d 4300/6600Ft; **P**) Just back from the road to Eger and well hidden among lush trees is this straightforward *pension*, with clean and simple rooms, friendly staff and a basic restaurant.

Tókert Panzió (☎ 533 560; tokert@tokert.hu; Erzsébet sétány 3; s/d from 8700/10,500Ft; mains 800-1200Ft; ☻ restaurant 7am-11pm; **P**) In the shadow (in every sense) of the Palota hotel, this place has good-sized rooms with great views of the lake and a decent restaurant serving fish dishes on its multilevel terrace.

Szeleta (☎ 530 130; www.hamorholiday.hu; Szeleta utca 12-14; camp site per person/tent 800/1500Ft; s/d from 11,500/15,000Ft; **P** 🔊) A few kilome-

---

AUTHOR'S CHOICE

Palota (☎ 331 411; reserve@hotelpalota.hunguesthotels.hu; Erzsébet sétány 1; s/d from €77/93, ste from €119; **P** 🔊 🖳) Dominating Lillafüred is Palota, a mock-Gothic structure that's a hotel again after a 40-year stint as a trade-union holiday home. With its regal air, sumptuous lounge and bar, and fully renovated rooms with views of the lake or forest, it's a piece of old-fashioned luxury in the Northern Uplands. Of its two restaurants, posh Mátyás, with stained-glass windows, an enormous fireplace and waiters who look like they're dressed to say Mass, is easily top dog.

---

tres before Lillafüred proper is this camp site/hotel, with brand-spanking-new (if not a little soulless) rooms, tent sites backing onto the forest, and its own sauna and cave.

For food, take your pick from the hotel and *pension* restaurants, or sidle up to the several food stalls serving *lángos* (deep-fried dough with toppings) and sausage near the narrow-gauge train station.

GETTING THERE & AWAY

You can reach Lillafüred by bus or narrow-gauge train (p339). From the end station of Tram 1 at Diósgyőr, transfer to bus 5 or 15, which leaves for Lillafüred every half-hour or so.

AGGTELEK HILLS

It can be a little unnerving leaving Miskolc behind and heading northwest along Rte 26 towards the Slovak border. One giant chemical factory after another lines the road, and it's hard to resist turning around and looking for greener pastures. But don't be put off by all the twisted steel and rusting pipes; just to the north are the Aggtelek Hills, an area with hardly a hint of urban intrusion. Here, rolling forested hills and meadows hide the occasional rural village, and life still follows the seasons.

This region is also home to the **Aggtelek National Park**, a hilly karst region encompassing some 200 sq km, and Europe's largest stalactite caves.

AGGTELEK

☎ 48 / pop 647

The tiny town of Aggtelek is the main gateway to the Baradla-Domica caves, a network of some 25km of passageways (6km of them in Slovakia). The network was declared a dual-nation Unesco World Heritage Site in 1995, and a trip underground to see the array of red-and-black stalactite drip stones, stalagmite pyramids and enormous chambers is a highlight on most people's itineraries.

Orientation

There are three entrances to the Baradla Cave system: at Aggtelek village; at Jósvafő, 6km to the east; and at Vörös-tó (Red Lake), just

---

NORTHERN UPLANDS' TOP FIVE CASTLES

- Hollókő (p318) – intact fortress with far-reaching views
- Eger (p329) – modern construction with a monumental history
- Füzér (p353) – lonely structure high above villages and pastures
- Boldogkő (p344) – classic edifice rising from solid rock
- Sárospatak (p348) – romantic stronghold in superb condition

---

before Jósvafő. Guided tours of the Baradla Cave system depart from these points, but the most popular short and long tours can be joined at the Aggtelek entrance.

Information

Tourinform (☎ 503 000; aggtelek@tourinform.hu; Baradla oldal 3; ☺ 8am-6pm Apr-Sep, 8am-4pm Oct-Mar) can supply you with information and sell you a copy of Cartographia's *Aggteleki-karszt és környéke* (Aggtelek Karst and Surrounds; No 1; 720Ft), an excellent 1:40,000 hiking map. For more detailed information, contact the **Aggtelek National Park Directorate** (Aggteleki Nemzeti Park Igazgatósága; ☎ 506 000; www.anp.hu; Tengerszem oldal 1) in Jósvafő.

The **post office** (☎ 343 156; Kossuth utca 37; ☺ 8.30am-noon & 1-4pm Mon-Fri) in Aggtelek has an ATM. Cseppkő hotel will exchange money.

Activities

CAVING

Baradla Cave (Baradla-barlang; ☺ 8am-6pm Apr-Sep, 8am-4pm Oct-Mar) has tours that depart year-round. The temperature at this level is usually about 10°C with humidity over 95%, so be sure to bring a sweater along. Tours usually include a short organ recital or some other form of music in the Concert or Giants' Halls and, if the water is high enough, a boat ride on the Styx, an underground stream.

Short tours lasting about one hour (adult/child April to September 1900/1100Ft, October to March 1700/1000Ft; 1km) start at the Aggtelek entrance at 10am, 1pm and 3pm, with additional tours at noon and 5pm from April to September. A one-hour

tour (April to September 1900/1100Ft, October to March 1700/1000Ft; 1km) that covers a different section is available from the Jósvafő entrance near the Tengerszem hotel at 9am and 4pm from April to September, and at 11.30am the rest of the year.

A two-hour 'middle tour' of the Jósvafő section (April to September 2500/1500Ft, October to March 2300/1400Ft; 2.3km) departs at 9am, 11am, noon, 1.30pm, 3pm and 4.30pm from April to September, and at 10am, noon and 2pm the rest of the year from the Vörös-tó entrance; it ends at the one in Jósvafő. You can also buy reduced-price tickets that combine the Aggtelek short and the Jósvafő middle tours (April to September 3600/2200Ft, October to March 3400/2100Ft; 2.5km) over two consecutive days.

If that doesn't fulfil your spelunking urges, try one of these; the three-hour Keresztély Raisz tour (5000/2400Ft; 3.6km), which includes an unpaved section without illumination (torches are provided); the Long tour (6000/3600Ft; 7km), which takes five hours and combines sections of the Aggtelek, middle and Keresztély Raisz tours; and the Special tour (7000/4200Ft; 8.3km), which consists of the Long tour plus a side trip to the Hall of Wonders. The first two leave at 9.30am on Saturday April to September, while the Special tour departs at 8.30am. From October to March advanced bookings are required; a minimum of 10 people are needed for tours to go ahead.

OTHER ACTIVITIES

You can join up with some excellent **hiking trails** above the Tourinform office in Aggtelek, affording superb views of the rolling hills and valleys. A relatively easy three-hour (7km) walk along the **Baradla Trail**, tagged yellow, will take you from Aggtelek to Jósvafő. There are other treks lasting five to six hours, and these can be used for **cycling** and **horse riding**. A 20km **bicycle route** links Aggtelek and Szögliget to the northeast, but unfortunately you'll have to bring your own bike. The **Hucul Stud Farm** in Jósvafő has horses for hire (1200Ft per hour) and offers hour-long carriage and, in winter, sledge (sleigh) rides for 2000Ft.

The park directorate organises a number of programs, including three-hour **guided walks** in Aggtelek and Jósvafő (adult/child

1000/600Ft), as well as **themed tours** of the national park lasting three to six hours – from ecology (600Ft to 1500Ft) to zoology and botany (1000Ft to 3000Ft). Note that some walks can be combined with cave tours.

Festivals & Events

Main events in Aggtelek and its vicinity are the **International Opera Festival** in Baradla Cave in June, the **Gömör-Torna Festival of folk and world music** in July and **Mountaineering Day** in early September, which attracts climbers from all over Hungary.

Sleeping & Eating

Baradla Hostel (Baradla oldal 2; dm adult/student mid-Apr–mid-Oct 1800/1500Ft, mid-Oct–mid-Apr 1500/1200Ft) Offers dorm rooms with two, three and six beds.

Cseppkő (☎ 343 075; Gyömrői út 2; s/d 5500/9000Ft; P) On a scenic hill above the cave entrance, this is the only hotel in Aggtelek. It has a restaurant, bar, a terrace with splendid views, and a bowling alley, tennis court and sauna/solarium.

Tengerszem (☎ 506 005; tengerszem_szallo@t-online.hu; Tengerszem oldal 2; d/tr/q mid-Apr–mid-Oct 13,000/15,000/17,000Ft, mid-Oct–mid-Apr 11,000/12,900/15,000Ft) At the Jósvafő end of the cave system is this renovated hotel, which is convenient if you intend on joining cave tours at both the Aggtelek and Jósvafő entrances.

Baradla Camping (☎ 503 005; hcseppko@axelero.hu; Baradla oldal 2; camp sites per person/tent/caravan 1000/1000/1400Ft, 4-person/6-person bungalows 5300/15,000Ft; ☺ mid-Apr–mid-Oct; P) Baradla Camping, next to the Aggtelek cave entrance, has a peaceful setting, and cute A-frame bungalows.

All sleeping possibilities have restaurants, and there are food stalls in the car park near the Aggtelek cave entrance.

Getting There & Away

Direct buses link Aggtelek with Budapest (2410Ft, four to five hours, 195km) and Miskolc (665Ft, 1½ hours, 52km). They leave Jósvafő (stopping at Aggtelek about 10 minutes later) for Budapest twice daily at 5.30am and 2.45pm (with an additional bus at 4.10pm Friday to Sunday), and for Miskolc at 4.30am and 11.30am Monday to Friday, at 5.45am Saturday and at 11.30am Sunday.

Aggtelek can also be reached from Miskolc (430Ft, 1¼ hours, 49km, five daily) by train – you want the one heading for Tornanádaska. The Jósvafő–Aggtelek train station is some 14km east of Jósvafő (and 20km from Aggtelek village); a local bus meets each of the trains to take you to either town.

Getting Around

Five buses a day link Aggtelek (stopping outside the Cseppkő hotel) and Jósvafő (stopping at the cave entrance) via Vörös-tó.

ZEMPLÉN HILLS

Wine, castles, hiking – these are three of the Zemplén Hill's most attractive possessions. Its southern and eastern slopes are dotted with market towns and vineyards of the Tokaj-Hegyalja region, where the world-renowned Tokaj wine, which attracted merchants from Greece, Serbia, Slovakia, Poland, Germany and Russia, is produced. The northern Zemplén on the border with Slovakia is the nation's 'wildest' region, full of hiking opportunities and romantic castle ruins.

BOLDOGKŐVÁRALJA
☎ 46 / pop 1185

The picturesque Hernád Valley, which basically runs from Szerencs to Hidasnémeti, near the Slovakian border, is dotted with quaint wine-producing towns, perfect for sampling the region's fine vintages. Boldogkőváralja would be just another of these charming places if it weren't for its impressive castle, seamlessly grafted to a rocky outcrop above the valley.

Orientation

Heading north from Szerencs, make sure you sit on the right-hand side of the train to see Boldogkőváralja's dramatic castle as it comes into view. The train stops on the other side of the highway about 2.5km west of the castle.

Sights & Activities

Perched atop a basalt mountain, **Boldogkő Castle** (adult/child 500/300Ft; ☺ 9am-6pm mid-Apr–mid-Oct), literally 'Happy Rock' Castle, is exactly what most people imagine a castle to be – impossibly perched on solid rock, its strong walls and turrets command 360-degree views of the southern Zemplén Hills, the Hernád Valley and nearby vineyards. Originally built in the 13th century, the castle was strengthened 200 years later, but gradually fell into ruin after the *kuruc* revolt late in the 17th century.

There's a tiny **museum** here with exhibits on notable occupants and medieval weaponry, but walking through the uneven courtyard up onto the ramparts and looking out over the surrounding countryside in the late afternoon is much more satisfying. It's easy to see how the swashbuckling lyric poet Bálint Balassi (1554–94) produced some of his finest work here.

REGIONAL HISTORY EXHIBIT

The little **Regional History exhibit** (Tajtör-téneti kiállítás; ☎ 06 30 579 0290; Kossuth Lajos utca 32; adult/child 300/200Ft; ☺ 10am-4pm Fri, Sat & Sun May-Sep) has some interesting items devoted to Balassi and local sons and daughters who made it good overseas (one set up the first Hungarian-language newspaper in the USA), as well as a display of folk dress, a fully equipped smithy, and exhibits on the flora and fauna of the Zemplén.

HIKING

Marked trails lead from the castle's northern side to **Regéc**, about 15km to the northeast via Arka and Mogyoróska, skirting mountains and 14th-century castle ruins along the way. From here you can either retrace your steps to Boldogkőváralja or follow the road westward to the Fony train stop (some six trains a day in each direction), which is about 10km to the west. The hardy and/or prepared may want to carry on another 8km north to **Gönc**, a pretty town where the wooden barrels used to age traditional Tokaj wine have been made for centuries; it's on the main train line back to Szerencs. Depending on which way you're hiking, make sure you're armed with the northern (No 22) or southern (No 23) section of Cartographia's *Zempléni-hegység* (Zemplén Hills) 1:40,000 map (800Ft each).

Sleeping & Eating

Boldogkőváralja is not a place to linger overnight but if you're stuck, head to **Bodóvár** (☎ 306 065; www.castles.hu/bodovar; Kossuth Lajos utca 61; s/d 6500/8500Ft, mains 1200Ft; P) at the bottom of the road to the castle. Its rooms are basic but adequate, with views of the castle, and the restaurant serves solid Hungarian fare.

Getting There & Away

Boldogkőváralja is on the train line connecting Szerencs (264Ft, one hour, 28km) with Hidasnémeti (264Ft, 38 minutes, 23km), and some six trains per day in each direction stop at the town. Only one of these is direct; the rest require a change (no wait) at Abaújszántó.

TOKAJ

☎ 47 / pop 5000

The wines of Tokaj, a picturesque little town of vineyards and nesting storks, have been celebrated for centuries; in fact, the town is so beloved for its amber liquid that it receives a mention in the national anthem. But Tokaj is just one of 28 towns and villages of the Tokaj-Hegyalja, a 66 sq km vine-growing region that produces wine along the southern and eastern edges of the Zemplén Hills and was declared a World Heritage Site in 2002.

Orientation

Tokaj's centre lies west of where the Bodrog and Tisza rivers meet. The train station is 1200m south of the town centre; walk north for 15 minutes along Baross Gábor utca and Bajcsy-Zsilinszky utca to Rákóczi Ferenc út, the main thoroughfare. Buses arrive and depart from along Serház utca east of Kossuth tér.

Information

OTP bank (Rákóczi Ferenc út 35; ☺ 8am-4pm Mon-Fri)
Post office (Rákóczi Ferenc út 24) In the centre of town.
Tourinform (☎ 552 070; tokaj@tourinform.hu; Serház utca 1; ☺ 10.30am-6pm Mon, 9am-7pm Tue-Sat, 10.30am-3.30pm Sun mid-Apr–mid-Oct, 9am-4pm Mon-Fri mid-Oct–mid-Apr) Just off Rákóczi Ferenc út.
www.tokaj.hu Check this website for general information on the town.

Sights

The **Tokaj Museum** (☎ 352 636; Bethlen Gábor utca 13; adult/child 400/200Ft; ☺ 10am-4pm Tue-Sun May-Nov), in the 18th-century Greek Trading House, leaves nothing unsaid about the history of Tokaj, the Tokaj-Hegyalja region and the production of its wines.

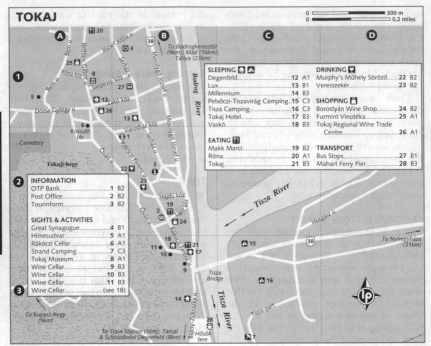

TOKAJ

There's also a superb collection of Christian liturgical art, including icons, medieval crucifixes and triptychs, and Judaica from the nearby Great Synagogue, and temporary exhibits by local artists.

East of the gallery, the 19th-century Eclectic **Great Synagogue** (Nagy zsinagóga; Serház utca 55), which was used as a German barracks during WWII, is once again boarded up and falling into ruin after partial renovations over a decade ago. There's a large **Orthodox Jewish cemetery** in Bodrogkeresztúr, 6km northwest of Tokaj.

Activities
WINE TASTING
Start with 100mL glasses; you may swallow more than you think you can drink. The correct order for sampling a half-dozen Tokaj wines is Furmint, dry Szamorodni, sweet Szamorodni and then the Aszú wines – from three to five or four to six *puttony* (a measure of Aszú essence added to base wines in making Tokaj; for more information, see p55). Private wine cellars offering tastings (usually 4pm to 9pm) are scat-

tered throughout town, including those at Rákóczi Ferenc út 2, Óvári utca Nos 3, 6, and 8, and Bem József utca Nos 2 and 16.

For the ultimate in tasting venues head for the 600-year-old **Rákóczi Cellar** (Rákóczi Pince; ☎ 352 408; Kossuth tér 15; ⏰ 10am-7pm mid-Mar–Oct, shop year-round), where bottles of wine mature in long corridors (one measures 28m by 10m). Tastings of six Tokaj wines cost around 2100Ft; individual tastings cost 230Ft, plus a 500Ft serving fee. **Hímesudvar** (Decorative Court; ☎ 352 416; www.himesudvar.hu; Bem utca 2; ⏰ 9am-9pm May-Sep, 9am-7pm Oct-Apr), a 16th-century wine cellar with shop northwest of the town centre, is another option. Tastings of six wines costs 2000Ft.

Tokaj is not the only town in the region with wine cellars; nearby Tarcal has almost as many, and Mád, Tállya and Bodrogkeresztúr all have a handful. Pick up a winemap from Tourinform for more options.

OTHER ACTIVITIES
In summer **water tours** of the Bodrog and Tisza Rivers are available from the **Mahart ferry pier** (☎ 352 937; minimum 15 people), just off

Hősök tere. Contact the **Union Federation** (Unió Alapítvány; ☎ 352 927; Bodrogkeresztúri út 5) or Tisza Camping about **canoe** and **kayak** rentals (around 250Ft per hour). There's **swimming** at **Strand Camping** (☎ 06 30 239 6300; admission 250Ft; ☼ 9am-6pm Jun-Aug) from the grassy riverfront beach across the Tisza Bridge.

Kopasz-hegy (Bald Mountain) and its TV tower west of the town centre offer a stunning panorama of Tokaj and the surrounding patchwork of vineyards.

Festivals & Events

The **Tokaj Wine Festival**, held in late May, attracts oenophiles from far and wide, as does the **Vintage Days** on the first weekend of October.

Sleeping

For private rooms (double 2800Ft to 5000Ft) pick up a list from Tourinform, or take a gander at your own leisure down Óvári utca, Bethlen Gábor utca, Serház utca or Bem József utca. Rooms on offer along Hegyalja utca are convenient to the train station and are surrounded by vineyards.

Degenfeld (☎ 552 173; www.degenfeldpalota.hu; Kossuth tér 1; s/d 7300/9000Ft; P) This very central *pension* has bright and tasteful rooms, with polished wood floors and kitchenettes; there are only four, so book ahead. It also has an excellent restaurant.

Millennium (☎ 352 247; www.tokajmillennium .hu; Bajcsy-Zsilinszky utca 34; s/d 8800/10,200Ft; P 🖳) One of the better central accommodation options, Millennium has large rooms with standard furniture and a restaurant in its turret. The only drawback is its location on a busy road.

Lux (☎ 352 145; Serház utca 14; s/d 2700/5400Ft; ☼ mid-Apr–Dec) This friendly and accommodating six-room *pension* has its own wine cellar, so there's not far to wander to bed after a few glasses.

Vaskó (☎ 352 107, 352 689; Rákóczi út 12; d 6000Ft) The supremely central Vaskó has eight cute rooms, with window sills bedecked with flower pots. It's above a *pince* (wine cellar).

Tokaj Hotel (☎ 352 344; Rákóczi út 5; s/d from 4600/5000Ft; P) Tokaj looks as though it was brought from a 1950s sci-fi movie set, but unfortunately its rooms are by no means out of this world. However, some do have a balcony looking onto the river.

Schlosshotel Degenfeld (☎ 580 400; www.hotel grofdegenfeld.hu; Terézia kert 9; standard s/d from 23,400/25,800Ft; superior from 25,800/28,200Ft, ste s/d from 31,200/33,600Ft; P 🖳 🞣 🖳) This 'palace' hotel in the nearby village of Tarcal is a beautifully restored mansion with vineyards and parklands as a backdrop. Rooms are of the finest quality, with period furniture, a smattering of antique pieces and all the mod cons deserving of such a place. The owners are ranked among the top vintners in the region so there's plenty of excellent wine at hand.

Pelsőczi-Tiszavirág Camping (☎ 352 626; Horgász út 11; camp site per adult/child/tent 450/300/450Ft; bungalows from 4500Ft; ☼ Apr-Oct; P) This secluded camping ground is near the confluence of the Bodrog and Tisza Rivers and has quiet camp sites and unfortunately, like Tisza Camping, plenty of mosquitoes.

Tisza Camping (☎ 352 012; rakamaz2@enternet .hu; Tisza-part; camp site 800Ft, bungalows per person 1500Ft; ☼ Apr-Oct; P) Across the river and just south of the bridge, this friendly place offers shady tent sites and basic bungalows, as well as its own restaurant, boat rentals and beach.

Eating & Drinking

Degenfeld (☎ 553 050; Kossuth tér 1; mains 2000Ft) Taking as much pride as it has with its accommodation, Degenfeld has created one of provincial Hungary's finest restaurants. Housed in a lovely 19th-century townhouse, it has inventive New Magyar cuisine, an excellent wine list and beautiful décor.

Róna (☎ 352 116; Bethlen Gábor utca 19; mains 800-1500Ft; ☼ 11am-9pm) Róna has more than enough fish dishes to satisfy Poseidon and a smattering of more common fare as an afterthought.

Makk Marci (☎ 352 336; Liget köz 1; pizza 500-1000Ft; ☼ 8am-8pm) This cheap and friendly pizzeria is good for a basic meal.

Tokaj (☎ 352 344; Rákóczi út 3; mains 1000-2000Ft) Next door to the hotel of the same name, Tokaj is a simple restaurant with a good fish selection and open terrace; it may be the only place open if you're dining after 9pm.

Should you get tired of all that wine, there are a couple of pubs to turn your head – or lips – to:

Veresszekér (Red Cart; Rákóczi út 30-32; ☼ 2pm-4am) A congenial pub in a little courtyard.

Murphy's Műhely Söröző (☎ 06 20 945 8562; Rákóczi út 42; ☼ 2-10pm) The first (and we assume only) Irish 'workshop pub' in the Zemplén.

Shopping

Wine, wine and more wine – from a 10L plastic jug of new Furmint to a bottle of six-*puttony* Aszú – is available in shops and cellars throughout Tokaj. For a choice of vintage wines, head to the shop at the Rákóczi cellar; the **Borostyán wine shop** (☎ 352 313; Rákóczi út 11; 🕐 10am-9pm Mon-Fri, 10am-10pm Sat & Sun); the **Furmint Vinotéka** (☎ 353 340; Bethlen Gábor utca 14; 🕐 8.30am-6.30pm), with both wine and folk art for sale; and the **Tokaj Regional Wine Trade Centre** (☎ 552 173; Kossuth tér 1; 🕐 10am-8pm), next to Degenfeld restaurant.

Getting There & Away

Five daily buses go to Szerencs (484Ft, one hour, 36km), the chocolate capital of Hungary, but it's just as easy to get there by train. There's two buses daily to Debrecen (1030Ft, two hours, 85km) and Nyíregyháza (423Ft, 45 minutes, 31km).

Up to 16 trains a day connect Tokaj with Nyíregyháza (346Ft, 30 minutes, 32km) and some 16 with Miskolc (544Ft, one hour, 56km); you'll need to change trains at the former for Debrecen (890Ft, two hours, 81km). If you want to travel north to Sárospatak (430Ft, one to two hours, 44km) and Sátoraljaújhely (544Ft, two hours, 54km), catch the Miskolc-bound train and change at Mezőzombor.

SÁROSPATAK

☎ 47 / pop 14,700

The town of Sárospatak (Muddy Stream) is renowned for its college and castle, the finest example of a Renaissance fort extant in Hungary. It is also a convenient stop en route to Slovakia.

History

A wealthy (and free) royal wine-producing town since the early 15th century, Sárospatak soon became a centre of Calvinist power and scholarship; two centuries later it was the focal point for Hungarian resistance to the Habsburgs. The list of alumni of the town's illustrious Calvinist College, which helped earn Sárospatak the nickname 'Athens on the Bodrog', reads like a who's who of Hungarian literary and political history, and includes the patriot Lajos Kossuth, the poet Mihály Csokonai Vitéz and the novelist Géza Gárdonyi.

Orientation

Sárospatak is a compact town lying on the snaking Bodrog River and its attractive backwaters. The bus and train stations are cheek-by-jowl at the end of Táncsics Mihály utca, northwest of the city centre. Walk southeast through shady Iskola-kert to join up with Rákóczi út, the main drag.

Information

Main post office (Rákóczi út 45) Opposite the Bodrog department store.

OTP bank (Eötvös utca 3) Near the Sárospatak Cultural Centre.

Tourinform (☎ 315 316; sarospatak@tourinform.hu; Eötvös utca 6; 🕐 9am-6pm Mon-Fri, 9am-5pm Sat mid-Jun–mid-Sep, 9am-5pm Mon-Fri mid-Sep–mid-Jun) In the western wing of the Sárospatak Cultural Centre.

www.sarospatak.hu For general information about the town (partly in English).

Sights

The **Rákóczi Castle** (☎ 311 083; Szent Erzsébet utca 19-21; 🕐 10am-6pm Tue-Sun Mar-Oct, 10am-5pm Tue-Sun Nov-Feb) should be your first port of call. The oldest part of the castle, the renovated five-storey **Red Tower** (Vörös-torony), dates from the late 15th century – inside you'll find rooms from this period in almost immaculate condition. Note that this can only be visited by guided tour (1000Ft).

The **Renaissance palace wing** (palotaszárny), connected to the Red Tower by a 17th-century loggia known as the **Lorántffy Gallery**, was built in the 16th century and later enlarged by its most famous owners, the Rákóczi family of Transylvania. Today, along with some 19th-century additions, it contains the **Rákóczi Museum**, devoted to the uprising and the castle's later occupants, with bedrooms and dining halls overflowing with period furniture, tapestries, porcelain and glass. Of special interest is the small five-windowed bay room on the 1st floor near the **Knights' Hall**, with its stucco rose in the middle of a vaulted ceiling. It was here that nobles put their names *sub rosa* (literally 'under the rose' in Latin) to the *kuruc* uprising against the Habsburg emperor in 1670. The expression, which means 'in secret', is thought to have originated here. The museum can be visited free of charge but you need to pick up a ticket from the ticket desk.

An exhibit in the cellars of the east wing is devoted to the **history of wine and winemaking** in the surrounding Tokaj-Hegyalja

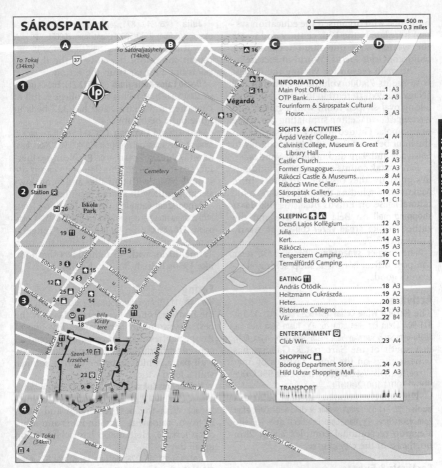

SÁROSPATAK

region. There's also a mock up of a Renaissance kitchen.

The **Castle Church** (Vártemplom; ☎ 311 183; Szent Erzsébet utca 7; adult/child 200/100Ft; ☷ 9am-4pm Tue-Sat, 11.30am-4pm Sun May-Oct), north of the castle, is one of Hungary's largest Gothic hall churches (those within castle walls), and has flip-flopped from serving Catholics to Protestants and back many times since the 14th century. The enormous baroque altar was moved here from the Carmelite church in Buda Castle late in the 18th century; the 200-year-old organ from Kassa (now Košice in Slovakia) is still used for concerts throughout the year. The statue by Imre Varga outside the church depicts the Sárospatak-born and much revered St Elizabeth, a 13th-century queen of Hungary, riding side-saddle, and her husband Louis IV on foot.

To the southwest of the church is the **Sárospatak Gallery** (☎ 511 012; Szent Erzsébet utca 4; adult/child 400/200Ft; ☷ 10am-4pm Tue-Sun), which displays the work of the sculptor János Kurta Andrássy along with some temporary exhibits.

The history of the celebrated **Calvinist College** (Református Kollégium; ☎ 311 057; Rákóczi út 1; adult/child 400/200Ft; ☷ 9am-5pm Mon-Sat, 9am-1pm Sun) is told in words and displays at the **Comenius Memorial Museum** in the last of the college's original buildings, an 18th-century physics classroom. The collection is named after János Amos Comenius, a Moravian humanist who organised the education system here late in the 17th century and wrote the world's first illustrated textbook for children, *Orbis Pictus* (World in Pictures).

The main reason for visiting the college is to see its 75,000-volume **Great Library Hall** (Nagy Könyvtárterem) in the main building, a long oval-shaped room with a gallery and a *trompe l'oeuil* ceiling simulating the inside of a cupola. Guided library tours leave on the hour between 9am and 4pm Monday to Saturday and 9am and noon on Sunday.

Sárospatak counts a number of buildings designed by the 'organic' architect Imre Makovecz, including the anthropomorphic **cultural house** on Eötvös utca, the **Hild Udvar shopping mall** on Béla Király tere and the cathedral-like **Árpád Vezér College** at Arany János utca 3-7.

The former **synagogue** (Rákóczi út 43), near the post office, is now a shop selling electronics goods.

Activities

The **Rákóczi Wine Cellar** (Rákóczi Pince; ☎ 312 310, 311 902; Szent Erzsébet utca 26; ☼ 10am-5pm Mon-Fri, 10am-6pm Sat & Sun May-Sep, 10am-5pm Mon-Fri Oct-Apr), just south of the Sárospatak Gallery, has wine tastings on the hour. Tastings of one/three/four/five/six/eight wines cost 550/700/900/1200/1400/2000Ft.

The hugely popular **thermal baths and pools** (☎ 311 639; adult/senior or child 650/400Ft, after 2pm 450Ft/free; ☼ 8am-6pm Feb-Dec) are in the Végardó recreational complex about 2km northeast of the city centre.

Festivals & Events

In early June **Saint Elizabeth Days** is a popular weekend festival in the castle quarter. Sárospatak hosts some of the events of the **Zemplén Arts Days** in mid-August along with other Zemplén towns, including Sátoraljaújhely and Füzér.

Sleeping

Kert (☎ 311 559; Rákóczi utca 31; s/d 4000/5000Ft; P) A small family-run *pension* with a homey feel, cute rooms and an attractive little garden.

Rákóczi (☎ 511 423; www.hotels.hu/rakoczipanzio; Rákóczi utca 30; s/d 4500/7500Ft; P) The town's upmarket establishment, with modern, spacious rooms centred on a quiet courtyard, as well as a sauna, solarium, fitness room and restaurant.

Júlia (☎ 312 871; enaomi@freemail.hu; Határ utca 6; s/d from 2500/5000Ft, apt from 6000Ft; P) A very friendly guesthouse with rooms in excellent condition. It's close to the thermal pools but a bit far from the action.

Dezső Lajos Kollégium (☎ 312 211; Eötvös utca 7; s/d 3000/5000Ft; P) This regal college is full of character and charm, and has 337 beds in quite basic bedrooms.

Termálfürdő Camping (☎ 311 510; Határ utca 2; camp sites per adult/child/tent/car 750/400/900/200Ft, bungalows 5500-7000Ft; ☼ Jun-Aug; P) Near the thermal spa in Végardó, this flat, open camp site is quite basic, with tent sites and bungalows sleeping four with shared facilities.

Tengerszem Camping (☎ 312 744; Herceg Ferenc utca 2; camp sites per person/tent/car 850/750/150Ft, bungalows 5200-8900Ft; ☼ Apr-Oct; P 🞂) Tengerszem is a more established camp site than Termálfürdő, with 45 bungalows that look like 1950s British holiday homes.

Eating

Vár (☎ 311 370; Árpád utca 35; mains 750-2000Ft) Across the Bodrog from the castle, this is easily the best restaurant in Sárospatak. Try one of its specialities, like *harcsapaprikás* (catfish cooked with sour cream and paprika) served with pasta, which is better than it sounds, with a local wine.

Heitzmann Cukrászda (☎ 311 567; Táncsis Mihály utca; ice cream 100Ft; ☼ 10am-7pm Mon-Thu, 10am-8pm Fri-Sun) With the best ice cream and cakes in town, colourful surroundings and a big open terrace, Heitzmann has lickers lining up all day.

Hetes (☎ 311 228; Kossuth Lajos utca 57; mains 400-600Ft; ☼ 10am-3pm Mon-Fri) Hetes is a very cheap self-service restaurant, with good old-fashioned portions and service.

András Ötödik (Andrew V; ☎ 312 415; Béla Király tere 3; mains around 1000Ft) With its inner courtyard, quick service and healthy range of Hungarian cuisine, Ötödik is popular with both locals and visitors.

Ristorante Collegno (☎ 314 494; Szent Erzsébet utca 10; pizza 600-1600Ft) This eatery named after Sárospatak's sister town in Italy has tables both in a cellar and, in warmer months, the back courtyard.

Entertainment

The **Sárospatak Cultural House** (Sárospataki Művelődés Háza; ☎ 311 811; Eötvös utca 6; ☼ 8am-8pm Mon-Fri, 9am-7pm Sat, 9am-1pm Sun) will fill you in on what's on in town; be sure to ask about organ concerts at the Castle Church. Sárospatak is included in the free biweekly *Miskolci Est* magazine.

Club Win (Szent Erzsébet utca 22; ⏰ 11am-midnight) This hole-in-the-wall is popular with students after dark.

Getting There & Away

BUS

Most of the southern Zemplén region is not easily accessible by bus from Sárospatak, but buses do travel to Debrecen (1450Ft, 2¾ hours, 119km, twice daily), Miskolc (1210Ft, 2¼ hours, 100km, one daily), Nyíregyháza (786Ft, 1½ hours, 65km, twice daily), Sátoraljaújhely (182Ft, 25 minutes, 15km, at least hourly) and Tokaj (423Ft, one hour, 34km, twice daily). Buses to Debrecen, Nyíregyháza and Miskolc can be boarded just outside the Bodrog department store on Rákóczi út; catch the bus to Sátoraljaújhely on the other side of the street in front of Rákóczi út 40.

TRAIN

To explore the southern Zemplén, you'd do better to take one of six daily trains up the Hernád Valley from Szerencs and use one of the towns along that line, such as Abaújkér, Boldogkőváralja or Korlát-Vizsoly, as your base. For the northern Zemplén, take a train or bus to Sátoraljaújhely.

Up to 12 daily trains connect Sárospatak with Sátoraljaújhely (100Ft, nine minutes, 10km) and Miskolc (774Ft, 1¼ hours to two hours, 74km), and one train (10.03am) continues on to Slovenské Nové Mesto in Slovakia, from where you can board a train to Košice. If you are coming from Debrecen, Nyíregyháza or Tokaj, change trains at Mezőzombor.

Getting Around

Hourly buses link the bus and train stations and the Bodrog department store on Rákóczi út with the Végardó recreational centre to the north.

SÁTORALJAÚJHELY

☎ 47 / pop 18,300

Sátoraljaújhely (roughly translated as 'tent camp new place' and pronounced *shah-toor-all-ya-oy-hay*) is a sleepy frontier town surrounded by forests and vineyards, and dominated by 514m **Magas-hegy** (Tall

Mountain). It unfortunately doesn't live up to its historical heritage, and though perhaps not worth a visit in its own right, it does make a good base for trekking into the northern Zemplén Hills and for crossing the border into Slovakia.

The town fell into the hands of the Rákóczi family in the 17th century and, like the family's base, Sárospatak, played an important role in the struggle for independence from Austria. It was not the last time the city would be a battleground. In 1919 fighting took place in the nearby hills and ravines between communist partisans and Slovaks, and broke out once again in the final days of WWII.

Orientation

The bus and train stations sit side by side 1km south of the city centre. From there, follow Fasor utca north past the old Jewish cemetery to Kossuth Lajos utca. This will lead you to Hősök tere and then Széchenyi tér. Two more squares follow – Kossuth tér and Táncsics Mihály tér – and then Kazinczy Ferenc utca. Slovakia comes next.

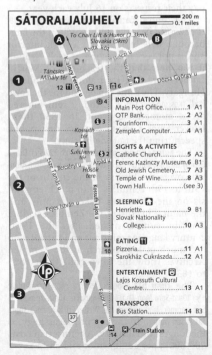

SÁTORALJAÚJHELY

0 ————— 200 m
0 ————— 0.1 miles

To Chair Lift & Húnor (1.3km);
Slovakia (5km)

INFORMATION
Main Post Office..............1 A1
OTP Bank........................2 A2
Tourinform....................3 A1
Zemplén Computer.........4 A1

SIGHTS & ACTIVITIES
Catholic Church..............5 A2
Ferenc Kazinczy Museum.6 B1
Old Jewish Cemetery.......7 A3
Temple of Wine.............8 A3
Town Hall...................(see 3)

SLEEPING
Henriette....................9 B1
Slovak Nationality
  College...................10 A3

EATING
Pizzeria......................11 A1
Sarokház Cukrászda......12 A1

ENTERTAINMENT
Lajos Kossuth Cultural
  Centre.....................13 A1

TRANSPORT
Bus Station.................14 B3

Train Station

NORTHERN UPLANDS (vertical side tab)

Information

Main post office (Kazinczy Ferenc utca 10) North of Tourinform.

OTP bank (Széchenyi tér 13) Almost opposite the Catholic church.

Tourinform (☎ 321 458; satoraljaujhely@tourinform. hu; Kossuth tér 5; ⏰ 9am-5pm Mon-Fri, 9am-1pm Sat mid-Jun–mid-Sep, 7.30am-4pm Mon-Thu, 7.30-1.30pm Fri mid-Sep–mid-Jun) Located in the town hall.

Zemplén Computer (Dózsa György utca 2; per hr 300Ft; ⏰ 8.30am-12.30pm & 1.30-5pm Mon-Fri) Offers Internet access.

Sights & Activities

The decrepit neo-Gothic former **Temple of Wine** (Bortemplom), built in 1911 and decorated with seals of the Tokaj-Hegyalja towns in Zsolnay porcelain, greets you upon arrival at the bus or train station. Don't expect much from this Frankenstein's castle; it's now just used to store wine in the cellars below and has more broken than complete windows. Due north, at the top of Fasor utca, is the **old Jewish cemetery**, where the *zaddik* (miracle-working rabbi) Moses Teitelbaum (1759–1841) is buried and pilgrims pay their respects on 16 July each year.

The central **Catholic church** (Széchenyi tér 10; admission free; ⏰ services only), rebuilt in the late-baroque style in 1792, has a stark interior and is not very interesting in itself, though it was here that the teachings of Martin Luther were first read aloud in public in Hungary. The same can be said for the **Town Hall** (Kossuth tér 5) but it, too, is remembered for a momentous event. In 1830 then-lawyer Lajos Kossuth gave his first public speech from the outside balcony.

The **Ferenc Kazinczy Museum** (☎ 322 351; Dózsa György utca 11; adult/child 400/200Ft; ⏰ 8am-4pm Mon-Sat) covers the history of the city from the 13th to 19th centuries, with much emphasis on the illustrious Rákóczi family and the natural history of the Zemplén region. The museum is named after the 19th-century language reformer and patriot who did much of his research at the Zemplén Archives (now the town hall) from 1815 to 1831.

The **chair lift** (libegő; ☎ 322 346; Torzás utca; ⏰ 10am-5pm Mon-Thu, 10am-6pm Fri, 10am-7pm Sat & Sun summer, 1.30-3.30pm Tue, Wed & Fri, 8.30am-3.30pm Sat & Sun winter), to the top of Magas-hegy, is the longest in Hungary. A return trip costs 900/600Ft per adult/senior and child.

Sleeping & Eating

Tourinform has a list of private rooms (from 2000Ft per person).

Hunor (☎ 521 521; www.hotelhunor.hu; Torzsás utca 1; s/d 9800/13,500Ft, mains around 1500Ft; P ⓡ) The stone-and-wood Hunor is the town's luxury establishment, located next to the chair lift. Rooms are thoroughly modern affairs, there's fine dining to be had on the premises and excellent Tokaj wine is served in abundance.

Henriette (☎ 323 118; ignacz@enternet.hu; Vasvári Pál utca 16; r 7000Ft; P) Henriette looks grubby from the outside but rooms are in better condition, and it's only a short walk to the city centre.

Slovak Nationality College (☎ 322 568; Kossuth Lajos utca 31; dm 1500ft; P) Accommodation is also available here in summer and on weekends throughout the year; it's within easy walking distance of the train and bus stations.

Restaurant pickings are very slim in the city centre, so you're probably better off eating at one of the hotels.

Pizzeria (Táncsics Mihály tér 4; pizza from 500Ft; ⏰ 9.30am-9pm) This jack-of-all-trades pizzeria combines a large selection of pizza and ice-cream offerings.

Sarokház Cukrászda (☎ 322 742; Táncsics Mihály tér 2; cakes 100-200Ft; ⏰ 7.30am-6pm Mon-Fri, 7.30am-4pm Sat & Sun) The right place for something sweet.

Entertainment

Consult with the staff or the listings posted at the **Lajos Kossuth Cultural Centre** (Kossuth Lajos Művelődési Központ; ☎ 321 727; Táncsics Mihály tér 3) for what's on in Sátoraljaújhely.

For more listings, check out the free bi-weekly *Miskolci Est* magazine.

Getting There & Away

There are frequent buses to the towns and villages of the northern Zemplén Hills, including three daily Monday to Friday (four daily on the weekend) to Füzér (302Ft, one hour, 25km) and up to nine daily Monday to Friday (10 daily on the weekend) to Hollóháza (363Ft, one hour, 29km).

Up to 12 daily trains connect Sátoraljaújhely with Sárospatak (100Ft, nine minutes, 10km) and Miskolc (774Ft, 1¼ hours to two hours, 74km); for trains to Slovakia, see Getting There & Away (p351). If you're approaching Sátoraljaújhely from the south

NORTHERN UPLANDS

or east (Debrecen, say, or Nyíregyháza or Tokaj), you must change at Mezőzombor.

AROUND SÁTORALJAÚJHELY
Füzér & Hollóháza

☎ 47 / pop Füzér 580, Hollóháza1020

An easy excursion, about 25km northwest of Sátoraljaújhely into the Zemplén Hills, can be made to Füzér, an idyllic little village where life is still ruled by the seasons. Aside from the chance to experience rural Hungary, the highlight here is the remains of the hill-top **Füzér Castle** (admission free; ✆ 9am-6pm), dating from the 13th century. Its position, high above the village and sticking out like a sore – but proud – thumb among lush green pastures, is arguably the most dramatic in all Hungary. To reach what's left of the castle from the village bus stop, follow the steep, marked trail and you'll soon come to the ruins sitting 370m up on a rocky crag. The castle's claim to fame is that it was chosen as a 'safe house' by Péter Perényi for the Hungarian coronation regalia from Visegrád for a year or so after the disastrous defeat at Mohács in 1526. Like most castles in the area, it was heavily damaged by the Austrians after the unsuccessful *kuruc* revolt in the late 17th century, but parts of the chapel, a tower and the outer walls remain.

Down in the village centre, the medieval **Calvinist church** (admission free; ✆ services only) has a 19th-century painted ceiling similar to those found in the Tiszahát and Erdőhát regions of Northeast Hungary. The 50 panels were decorated with geometric patterns and flowers by a local artist in 1832.

The **Koronaőr** (Crown Guardian; ☎ 340 020; www .koronaor.hu; Dózsa György utca 2/a; s/d 2300/4600Ft; P), in an old and attractive peasant house, has three modern rooms and a small restaurant serving hearty meals.

From Füzér you can return to Sátoraljaújhely or catch one of several daily buses for the 9km trip to sleepy Hollóháza, Hungary's northernmost town and in third place after Herend and Zsolnay for its porcelain. The **Porcelain Museum** (Porcelánmúzeum; ☎ 505 400; Károlyi út 11; adult/child 600/300Ft; ✆ 9am-4.30 Apr-Nov) tells the whole story. Accommodation is available at **Éva** (☎ 305 038; Szent László utca 4; r 7000Ft; P), a three-room *pension* backing onto woods near the centre of town.

Füzér and Hollóháza are excellent springboards for beginning a hike into the Zemplén Hills; several well-marked trails start here, including one that runs northeast to **Nagy Milic**, an 893m hill on the Slovakian border. Just make sure you're armed with drinking water and *A Zempléni-hegység – északi rész*, Cartographia's 1:40,000 map (No 22; 800Ft) of the Zemplén's northern section.

For transport details, see Getting There & Away (opposite).

Northeast

Some may think the Northeast a cultural void: Hungary's backward corner populated by hicks more capable of shoeing a horse than changing a car tyre. True enough, independent cinema and theatre are thin on the ground – and horse-drawn carts are not uncommon – but the region is by no means a wasteland. Instead it is steeped in folk culture, where women eke out a living embroidering patchwork pillowcases and dresses in patterns handed down over centuries, and men work the land, sharing a drink after a day toiling in the fields.

The classic example of folk culture in the Northeast is its rural churches. Small with wood-carvings and distinctive frescoes, these structures have been lovingly preserved for generations; exceptional examples can be seen in Tákos and Csaroda. Not to be outdone by such religious devotion is Szatmárcseke's cemetery, a 'shipyard' of upturned boat-shaped grave stones.

Not everything in this region of rolling hills and green pastures is related to folk art. Its capital, Nyíregyháza, is at first glance a typical communist architectural cock-up, but stroll through the city centre and you'll find Art-Nouveau and baroque gems. Nyírbátor is but a speck on the map today but its architecture reveals a rich past; two cathedrals, equally magnificent in style, vie for attention in the town centre. In Máriapócs, near Nyírbátor, is another example of religious extravagance, this time in the shape of a sumptuous Greek Catholic cathedral.

So if you want to see real Hungarian village life – replete with dirt roads, horse-drawn carts laden with hay, thatched roofs and ancient churches – this is the place to come.

HIGHLIGHTS

- Gazing at the rich tapestry of the painted wooden ceiling at Tákos' **Calvinist church** (p362)
- Picking your favourite place of worship in Nyírbátor; the **Gothic Calvinist church and bell tower** (p360) or the **Minorite church** (p360)
- Walking between the bizarre boat-shaped grave markers in Szatmárcseke's peaceful **cemetery** (p363)
- Feeling humble beneath the gorgeous iconostasis at the **Greek Catholic cathedral** (p361) in Máriapócs
- Exploring the nooks and crannies of one of Hungary's least-explored (and often-forgotten) corners, such as **Túristvándi** (p363) and **Csaroda** (p362)

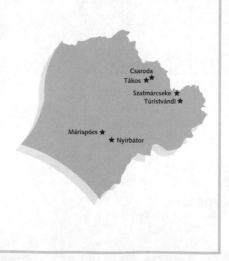

Csaroda
Tákos ★★
Szatmárcseke ★
Túristvándi ★
Máriapócs ★
★ Nyírbátor

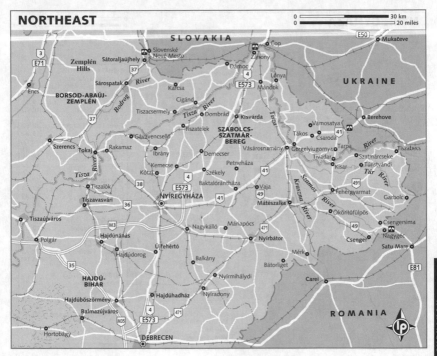

Getting There & Around

Frequent trains link the main towns of the Northeast with Debrecen and, to a lesser extent, Budapest. Smaller villages are generally only accessible by bus, and services can be slow and infrequent. Therefore the best way to see the region is under your own steam, be it by car, motorbike or bicycle.

NYÍRSÉG REGION

The Nyírség (Birch Region) contains the lion's share of the Northeast's large towns, and therefore the majority of museums and city-bound attractions. It's also the largest of three distinct areas that make up the Northeast. Grassy steppes and hills stretch from Nyíregyháza, the region's capital, to Nyírbátor, a town rich in history.

NYÍREGYHÁZA

☎ 42 / pop 118,800

At first glance, Nyíregyháza (roughly 'Birch Church'), the commercial and administrative centre of the Nyírség, looks like a blotch on the landscape, dotted with ugly high-rises and lacklustre shopping centres. But a second glance is most certainly required; its centre is a checker-board of well-tended squares and gardens, with a handful of wonderfully restored buildings. Nyíregyháza also makes an excellent springboard for visiting other Northeast towns, as well as northern Romania and Ukraine.

History

For centuries Nyíregyháza was the private domain of Transylvanian princes; then, in the 18th century, it was resettled by Slovaks from Szarvas on the southern Great Plain. Under Soviet rule the town prospered due to the establishment of a food-processing industry in the area, but recently Nyíregyháza has fallen on hard times.

Orientation

Nyíregyháza's centre is made up of a handful of interconnecting squares, including Országzászló tér, Kálvin tér, Kossuth tér and Hősök tere, and is surrounded by both

NYÍREGYHÁZA

SIGHTS & ACTIVITIES	
András Jósa Museum......................**6** B2	
Art Nouveau Building...................**7** B2	
Catholic Cathedral.......................**8** C2	
County Hall...................................**9** B1	
Evangelist Church.......................**10** C2	
Fruit & Vegetable Market...........**11** A1	
Greek Catholic Church...............**12** B2	
Julia Baths.................................**13** A2	
Liturgical Collection...............(see 12)	
Lovers' Lock Gate.......................**14** B1	
Synagogue.................................**15** B1	
Town Hall...................................**16** B2	

SLEEPING	
Európa......................................**17** C1	
Ilona Zrinyi College..................**18** A3	
Korona......................................**19** C1	

EATING	
Mozzarella Pizzéria....................**20** B3	

DRINKING	
Colorado Western Pub...............**21** A1	
John Bull..............................(see 19)	

ENTERTAINMENT	
Club Kom Ombo.......................**22** B1	
Golden Age...............................**23** A2	
Mihály Váci Cultural Centre......**24** C1	
Theatre Ticket Office.............(see 3)	
Zsigmond Móricz Theatre.........**25** B2	

TRANSPORT	
Bus Station..............................**26** A3	

INFORMATION	
Ibusz...**1** B2	
ILS...(see 3)	
Main Post Office...........................**2** B2	
Main Tourinform Office...............**3** B2	
OTP Bank......................................**4** C1	
Városi Internet Klub.....................**5** B2	

an inner and an outer ring road. Streets running north lead to Sóstófürdő, the city's sprawling 600-hectare recreational area consisting of woods, parkland, little Salt Lake (Sóstó) and a large spa complex.

The main train station, on Állomás tér, is about 1.5km southwest of the centre at the end of Arany János utca. The bus station is on Petőfi tér, just north of the train station, at the western end of Széchenyi utca.

Information

Hospital (☎ 465 666; Szent Istvan út 68) The town's main hospital.

Ibusz (☎ 311 817; Ország-zászló tér 4) Next door to the main Tourinform branch.

ILS (☎ 310 143; Ország-zászló tér 6) Language school with bookshop stocking foreign-language books.

Main post office (Bethlen Gábor utca 4) South of the town hall.

Main Tourinform branch (☎ 504 647; szabolcs-m@ tourinform.hu; Országzászló tér 6; 🕑 9am-5pm Mon-Fri, 9am-1pm Sat Jun–mid-Aug, 9am-5pm Mon-Fri Oct-May) Friendly, helpful and stocked with brochures on the city and the Northeast.

OTP bank (Dózsa György utca 2) Has an ATM.

Tourinform Water Tower (Víztorony; ☎ 411 193; sostofurdo@tourinform.hu; Sóstófürdő; 🕑 8.30am-4.30pm mid-Jun–mid-Aug) A seasonal branch of Tourinform, 5km north of the centre in the Sóstófürdő area.

Városi Internet Klub (☎ 507 281; Országzászló tér 8; 🕑 8am-7pm Mon-Fri) Internet access 300Ft per hour.

Sights

There are many houses of worship in the inner city, including the late baroque (1786) **Evangelist church** (☎ 508 770; Luther tér 14; admission free; 🕑 9am-5pm Mon-Fri) and, dominating Kossuth tér, the 1904 neo-Romanesque **Catholic cathedral** (☎ 409 691; Kossuth tér 4; admission free; 🕑 6.30am-6pm Mon-Fri, 6.30-10.30am Sun), which has arabesque pastel-coloured tiles inside. The **Greek Catholic church** (☎ 415 901; Bethlen Gábor utca 5; admission free; 🕑 8am-4pm Mon-Fri), built in 1895, contains a rich **liturgical collection** of vestments and plate. The **synagogue** (☎ 417 939; Mártírok tere 6; admission free; 🕑 8am-2pm Mon-Thu) still functions as a house of worship and has a small collection of Jewish artefacts.

It is worth taking the time to check out the architecture in the centre. If you can, visit the eclectic (1892) **County Hall** on

Hősök tere, with its splendid Ceremonial Hall (Nagy Terem); the blue-and-white Art-Nouveau building on Országzászló tér, which houses a bank and offices; or the restored **Korona hotel**.

Benczúr Gyula tér is another treasure-trove of Art Nouveau and Secessionist architecture and a modern must-see is the bizarre **Mihály Váci Cultural Centre**; built in 1981, this wobbly-looking, bridge-like structure was inspired by 'the principles of Japanese metabolism', so we're told.

The huge **András Jósa Museum** (☎ 315 722; Benczúr Gyula tér 21; adult/child 200/100Ft; ☒ 9am-4pm Tue-Sat, 9am-2pm Sun), just south of the main city centre, has exhibits devoted to Nyíregyháza's history since the Middle Ages.

Nyíregyháza's most interesting sight, however, is the open-air **Sóstó Museum Village** (Sóstói Múzeumfalu; ☎ 500 552; Tölgyes utca 1; adult/child 200/100Ft; ☒ 9am-6pm Tue-Sun mid-Jun–Aug, 9am-5pm Tue-Sun Apr–mid-Jun & Sep-Oct) in Sóstófürdő, 5km north of the city centre. Its reconstructed three-room cottages, school, wells, fire station and general store offer an easy introduction to the traditional architecture and way of life in the Northeast. All the nationalities that make up this ethnically diverse region are represented, including the Tirpák, Slovakians who lived in isolated 'bush farms known as *bokor tanyák*.

The large, covered **fruit and vegetable market** (Búza tér) is one of the more colourful in provincial Hungary, but the **Nagybani flea market** on Tokaji út, the northwest extension of Rákóczi út, is even more vibrant. Attracting a motley crowd of Hungarians, Romanians, Poles, Ukrainians and Roma selling the usual diamonds-to-rust mixture of goods, the best times to visit are weekends and weekday afternoons.

LOVERS' LOCK GATE

Since 2004 Hősök tere has been home to an unusual display of love, the so-called 'Lovers' Lock Gate'. This shrine to love consists of two park benches enclosed with jungle bars – plus a lot of padlocks. The idea is for partners to declare their love by engraving their names on a padlock, then locking it to the gate. Both partners then keep a copy of the lock's key, just in case things turn sour.

Activities

The **Park Baths** (Parkfürdő; ☎ 475 736; adult/child 600/300Ft; ☒ 9am-8pm mid-May–mid-Sep) in Sóstófürdő are just the place to while away a hot summer's afternoon, with a half-dozen large pools of fresh and thermal water, a sauna and a solarium. The **Lake Baths** (Tófürdő; ☎ 479 701; adult/child 600/300Ft) are open the same times as the Park Baths and have lake views and direct access to the lake. A more central, less crowded option is the **Julia Baths** (Julia Fürdő; ☎ 315 800; Malom utca 19; adult/child 700/550Ft; ☒ 10am-8pm Mon-Fri, 9am-8pm Sat & Sun), an indoor thermal spa with three pools.

The **Sóstó Riding Club** (☎ 475 202; Állomás utca 2; per hr 2500Ft), next to the Sóstó Museum Village, hires out horses, as does the excellent **Nyíregyháza Horse Club** (☎ 728 826; lovi.szabolcs .net; Bem József utca 22-24; per hr 2500Ft), southwest of the centre.

Sleeping

Ibusz can arrange private rooms (3000Ft to 4000Ft per person), while Tourinform has college accommodation on the books over the summer months. The closest to the centre is **Ilona Zrínyi College** (☎ 318 091; Széchenyi utca 35-39; s/d 3000/6000Ft; P), a large block not far from the bus station.

Korona (☎ 409 300; www.korona.cs.hu; Dózsa György utca 1-3; s/d 10,000/11,900Ft; P ☷ ▢) The Korona, which first opened its doors in 1895, has well-groomed rooms and is the place to splurge on accommodation. Its 35 rooms, scattered along seemingly endless corridors, come with all the mod cons.

Ózon (☎ 402 001; www.ozonpanzio.hu; Csaló köz 2; r 9200Ft; P ☷) This former communist summer retreat, near Sóstófürdő, is surrounded by woods and is the most serene place to stay in Nyíregyháza. Some rooms have balconies.

Európa (☎ 508 670; www.europahotel.hu; Hunyadi utca 2; s/d 6000/7500Ft; P ☷ ▢) This nondescript hotel faces the busy outer ring road and is very handy to the centre. There is a restaurant attached and secure parking is an extra 800Ft.

Sóstó (☎ 500 692; hotelsosto@axeleor.hu; Sóstói út 76; camp sites per person/tent 700/600Ft, dm 1300Ft, s/d 7000/8900Ft; P) Sóstó is the perfect place for families – book the kids into a hostel-style bungalow and have a night to yourselves in the hotel next door. There's a restaurant on site and plenty of open green space.

NORTHEAST

Igrice (☎ 06 30 953 6721; Blaha Lujza sétány 8; camp sites per person/car/tent 600/200/600Ft; bungalows sleeping up to 4 7900Ft, r 2800Ft; **P**) Igrice is a large camping ground right on the edge of the lake, with a rather reedy beach. Bungalows have shared facilities and motel rooms are fairly basic.

Eating & Drinking

Krúdy (☎ 596 187; Sóstói út 75; mains 1500Ft) Krúdy is in an old villa only a stone's throw from the lake and serves fine Hungarian cuisine on its open terrace.

Mozzarella Pizzéria (☎ 424 008; Kiss Ernő utca 10; pizza from 310Ft; ☽ 11am-9pm Mon-Sat, 4-9pm Sun) For simple, quick and hearty pasta and pizza, this is your best bet in town. The only drawback is it's a bit of a walk from the centre.

Tölgyes (☎ 410 590; Sóstói út 40; mains 800-1500Ft) This popular restaurant serving Hungarian food is about halfway between the centre and Sóstófürdő; the smells wafting up from the open grill on its terrace are particularly inviting.

424 Irish Pub (☎ 726 222; Blaha Lujza utca 1; mains 1000Ft) The only thing Irish about this place is the Guinness sign hanging out front, but that takes nothing away from this cute pavilion restaurant with views of the lake.

Colorado Western Pub (Búza tér 15; ☽ 11am-2am Mon-Thu, 11am-4am Fri & Sat) In most European cities you're guaranteed to find an Irish-themed pub; in Hungary it's the Wild West locals go crazy for. Colorado ticks Nyíregyháza's 'Wild West' box and has plenty of drunken revelry and a terrace for warm summer evenings.

John Bull (Dózsa György utca 1-3; ☽ 11am-midnight Sun-Thu, 11am-2am Fri & Sat) This pub-restaurant in the Korona hotel is a little bit of ersatz England in northeastern Hungary; it has live music most weekends.

Entertainment

Check with staff at the **Zsigmond Móricz Theatre** (☎ 400 375; www.moriczszinhaz.hu; Bessenyei tér 13) or the **Mihály Váci Cultural Centre** (☎ 411 822; Szabadság tér 9) for current listings. If there's a concert on at the Evangelist church on Luther tér, jump at the chance. The **theatre ticket office** (☎ 507 007; Országzászló tér 6; ☽ 9am-5pm Mon-Fri) is at the main Tourinform office.

For clubs, try the following:

Club Kom Ombo (Rákóczi utca 8; ☽ 4pm-2am Sun-Thu, 4pm-4am Fri & Sat) A trendy club in a shopping centre, with DJs and live bands.

Golden Age (Bethlen Gábor utca 24; ☽ 1pm-2am Sun-Thu, 1pm-4am Fri & Sat) A large club with pool tables.

Getting There & Away
BUS

Generally, buses serve towns near Nyíregyháza or those not on a train line. There are up to four departures an hour to Nagykálló (241Ft, 30 minutes, 16km) and buses run

---

THE ROMA

The origins of the Gypsies (Hungarian: *cigány*), who call themselves the Roma (singular Rom) and speak Romany, a language closely related to several still spoken in northern India, remain a mystery. It is generally accepted, however, that they began migrating to Persia from India sometime in the 10th century and had reached the Balkans by the 14th century. They have been in Hungary for at least 500 years, and they officially number around 190,000, although that figure could easily be higher.

Though traditionally a travelling people, in modern times the Roma have by and large settled down in Hungary and worked as smiths and tinkers, livestock and horse traders, and as musicians (see p42). As a group, however, they are chronically underemployed and have been the hardest hit by economic recession (statistically, Roma families are twice the size of *gadje*, or 'non-Roma' ones).

Unsettled people have always been persecuted in one form or another by those who stay put, and Hungarian Roma are no exception. They are widely despised and remain the scapegoats for everything that goes wrong in certain parts of the country, from the rise in petty theft and prostitution to the loss of jobs. Though their rights are inscribed in the 1989 constitution, along with other ethnic minorities, their housing ranks among the worst in the nation, police are regularly accused of harassing them and, more than any other group, they fear a revival of right-wing nationalism. You will probably be shocked at what even educated, cosmopolitan Hungarians say about Roma and their way of life.

frequently to Máriapócs (363Ft, 45 minutes, 30km), Mátészalka (725Ft, 1½ hours, 60km) and Nyírbátor (484Ft, one hour, 40km). Destinations further afield include: Debrecen (907Ft, two hours, 72km, four daily), Eger (1690Ft, 2½ hours, 132km, two daily), Kisvárda (605Ft, 1½ hours, 50km, four daily on Monday to Saturday, one on Sunday) and Vásárosnamény (725Ft, 1¼ hours, 58km, seven daily).

TRAIN

Up to 15 daily express trains link Nyíregyháza with Debrecen (560Ft, 30 minutes, 49km) and Budapest's Nyugati or Keleti station (2670Ft, three to four hours, 270km). There is at least one *személyvonat* (passenger train) an hour to Debrecen (430Ft, 45 minutes, 49km) and up up to 15 a day to Miskolc (890Ft, 1½ hours, 88km). Up to nine trains depart Nyíregyháza each day for Vásárosnamény (544Ft, two hours, 59km) and eight head for Mátészalka (544Ft, 2¼ hours, 58km), stopping at Nagykálló (182Ft, 27 minutes, 14km), Máriapócs (264Ft, 1¼ hours, 30km) and Nyírbátor (346Ft, 1¾ hours, 38km) en route (a change at Nyírbátor may be required). The Tisza Express train to Lviv, Kyiv and Moscow also stops here every day at 9.50pm; the Latorca, crossing the Ukrainian border to Čŏp, departs at 6.20pm.

Getting Around

Almost everything in the city – with the exception of Sóstófürdő – can be easily reached on foot. Take buses 7 or 8 from the train or bus station to reach the centre of town; the No 8 carries on to Sóstófürdő. For Nagybani flea market, catch bus 1/a. You can order a taxi on ☎ 555 555.

AROUND NYÍREGYHÁZA
Nagykálló
☎ 42 / pop 10,600

This town, 14km southeast of Nyíregyháza, boasts some listed buildings on its central square (Szabadság tér) – a baroque **Calvinist church** (☎ 263 171; admission free; ☿ appointment needed), on the south side, with a free-standing Gothic bell tower originally built in the 15th century; and the splendid former **County Hall** (☎ 263 128; Szabadság tér 13; ☿ appointment needed) to the northeast at No 13, which was built in the Zopf style in 1749 and later turned into a notorious asylum for the insane.

Most visitors to Nagykálló, however, are Orthodox Jewish pilgrims who come to pay their respects at the **tomb of Isaac Taub** (☎ 06 30 248 6379; Nagybalkányi út; ☿ appointment needed), especially on the anniversary of his death (February/March). Known as the 'Wonder Rabbi of Kálló' (a *zaddik* in Yiddish), Isaac Taub was an 18th-century philosopher who advocated a more humanistic approach to prayer and study. You can visit his small tomb in the old Jewish cemetery, less than 1km due south of Szabadság tér. Note that unless you've arranged a tomb visit, the cemetery gates will be locked.

Óbester restaurant (Kossuth Lajos utca; mains 800-1500Ft), in the centre of Nagykálló, is your best bet for a meal; its outside tables on the main square are popular on summer evenings. If Óbester is full, **Belvárosi Eszpresszó** (Kossuth Lajos utca; snacks 400Ft; ☿ 9am-7pm), to the northeast of the square, should suffice for a quick hunger fix.

In late July, Nagykálló hosts the popular **Téka Tábor**, a week-long folk festival 'camp' held in a bizarre structure designed by Imre Makovecz at Harangodi-tó, some 2km north of town. Contact the **Rákóczi Cultural Centre** (☎ 263 141; Báthory utca 1) for more information.

Up to eight trains a day linking Nyíregyháza (182Ft, 27 minutes, 14km) and Mátészalka stop at Nagykálló. A bus meets each incoming train and goes as far as Szabadság tér. Buses run throughout the day from Nyíregyháza to Nagykálló (241Ft, 30 minutes, 16km) and many of these carry on to Máriapócs and Nyírbátor on weekdays. They drop to four a day at the weekend.

NYÍRBÁTOR
☎ 42 / pop 13,400

Nyírbátor is quite a sleepy town, but for anyone with a love (or even a mild interest) of Gothic churches, it should be on the itinerary. The town's two Gothic churches, built in the latter part of the 15th century by István Báthory, the ruthless Transylvanian prince whose family is synonymous with the town, are some of the best preserved in the country.

Orientation

Nyírbátor is compact and everything of interest can be easily reached on foot. The train and bus stations are on Ady Endre

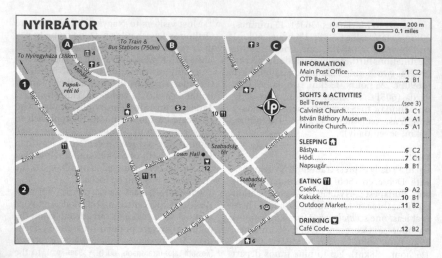

NYÍRBÁTOR

INFORMATION	
Main Post Office	1 C2
OTP Bank	2 B1

SIGHTS & ACTIVITIES	
Bell Tower	(see 3)
Calvinist Church	3 C1
István Báthory Museum	4 A1
Minorite Church	5 A1

SLEEPING	
Bástya	6 C2
Hódi	7 C1
Napsugár	8 B1

EATING	
Csekő	9 A2
Kakukk	10 B1
Outdoor Market	11 B2

DRINKING	
Café Code	12 B2

utca which is in the northern part of town, less than 1km from the centre (Szabadság tér) via Kossuth Lajos utca.

Information
Main post office (Szabadság tér) At the south end of the square.
OTP bank (Zrínyi utca 1) Across the road from Szabadság tér, is equipped with an ATM.

Sights
Walking into the **Calvinist church** (☎ 281 749; adult/child 60/30Ft; 9am-5pm Mon-Sat, 8-10am & 1-5pm Sun), on a small hill just off Báthory István utca, is like drawing a breath of crispy mountain air. Its refreshingly plain interior and long lancet windows, which flood the nave with light, allow the church's masterpiece – the ribbed vault – to gain your undivided attention. István Báthory's remains lie in a marble tomb at the back of the church; the family's coat of arms embellished with wyverns (dragon-like creatures) is on top of the tomb. The 17th-century wooden **bell tower**, standing apart from the church (as was once required of Calvinists in this overwhelmingly Catholic country) has a Gothic roof with four little turrets. You can climb the 20m to the top – its rickety wooden stairs make both the ascent and descent a little hairy, but the views (and experience) are worth it.

The **Minorite church** (☎ 281 770; Károlyi Mihály utca 19; admission free; 9am-6pm Mon-Sat, 8am-6pm Sun May-Oct, 9-11am & 4-5pm Mon-Sat, 8-11am Sun Nov-

Apr) was originally late Gothic, but, like so many Hungarian churches, it was ravaged by the Turks in 1587 and rebuilt in the baroque style 130 years later. Five spectacular altars carved in Presov (now eastern Slovakia) in the mid-18th century fill the nave and chancel. The most interesting is the first on the left, the **Krucsay Altar of the Passion** (1737), with its diverse portrayals of fear, longing, devotion and faith.

The **István Báthory Museum** (☎ 510 218; Károlyi Mihály utca 21; adult/child 200/100Ft; 9am-5pm Tue-Sun Apr-Sep, 9-11am Mon-Sat Oct-Mar), in the 18th-century monastery next to the church, focuses on the town's history. It has a very good ethnographic collection, and some medieval pieces connected with the Báthory family and the churches they built.

Early July sees the streets of Nyírbátor come alive during the **Week of the Winged Dragon International Street Theatre Festival**; expect to see actors, puppeteers and musicians trying to out-perform each other.

Sleeping
Bástya (☎ 281 657; www.hotels.hu/bastya_nyirbator; Hunyadi utca 10; s/d 5520/7820Ft;) The owners of this small hotel seem to have a penchant for garish furniture and clashing colours, but the rooms are clean and comfy and the staff are eager to please.

Napsugár (☎ 283 878; Zrínyi utca 15; s/d 6000/8000Ft;) This *pension* has eight fairly modern rooms, a small fitness centre and an average bar out front. Breakfast costs an extra 800Ft.

Eating & Drinking

Csekő (☎ 381 289; Bajcsy-Zsilinszky utca 62; pizzas 400-900Ft; ⏱ 11.30am-9.30pm) This cake shop became so popular that it took over the pizzeria next door and claimed the space for itself. Fortunately it had the sense to keep the pizzas on the menu and add a long list of salads. The cakes remain as heavenly as ever.

Kakukk (☎ 281 050; Szabadság tér 21; mains 800-1500Ft) Kakukk is the only true restaurant in the heart of the town; its daily menu (around 550Ft) of Hungarian dishes packs 'em in at midday.

Café Code (Szabadság tér 7; ⏱ 4pm-midnight Mon-Fri, 4pm-late Sat & Sun) In the centre of town, it is a small, dark but cosy place and the only bar open late daily.

Nyírbátor's outdoor market can be found at the junction of Váci Mihály utca and Radnóti utca.

Entertainment

Organ concerts and recitals can be heard throughout the year at the **Calvinist church**. Aside from that, not much raises the roof in Nyírbátor.

Getting There & Away

There are seven buses a day to Nyíregyháza via Nagykálló (484Ft, one hour, 40km) and up to six daily buses go to Máriapócs (182Ft, 15 minutes, 10km).

There are up to eight daily trains from Nyíregyháza (346Ft, 1¾ hours, 38km) that call at Nyírbátor on their way to Mátészalka; as many as 13 trains heading for Mátészalka (182Ft, 30 minutes, 20km) from Debrecen (544Ft, 1¾ hours, 58km) also stop here.

You can catch one of up to six daily trains at Mátészalka heading north for Záhony on the border of Ukraine, or three going south to Carei in Romania.

AROUND NYÍRBÁTOR
Máriapócs

☎ 42 / pop 2,200

Like Nyírbátor, Máriapócs contains one of the country's most beautiful churches. Its **Greek Catholic cathedral** (☎ 385 142; Kossuth tér 25; admission free; ⏱ 8am-5pm May-Sep, 8am-6pm Oct-Apr) takes centre stage in the heart of town. The cathedral has been an important pilgrimage site from at least 1696, when the **Black Madonna** icon, which now stands angelically above the altar on the north side of the building, first shed tears (she wept again in 1715 and 1905). Unfortunately, this is not the original icon but a 19th-century copy; the real one is now in St Stephen's Cathedral in Vienna. The Madonna is not the only highlight – the ornate gold iconostasis soars some 15m up to the vaulted ceiling. The cathedral, which was built on the site of a small wooden church, dates from the mid-18th century.

If you need to stay overnight, try the nondescript **Fekete Bárány** (Black Sheep; ☎ 385 722; Állomás tér; s/d 3000/6000Ft; ℗), an inn opposite the train station on the road linking Nyírbátor and Nagykálló.

Between two and eight daily buses from Nagykálló (133Ft, 20 minutes, 8km), Nyírbátor (182Ft, 15 minutes, 10km) and Nyíregyháza (363Ft, 45 minutes, 30km) will drop you off by the cathedral. All trains between Nyírbátor and Nyíregyháza stop at Máriapócs train station, which is 4km south of the town centre. Buses run between the centre and the station, but they are not very reliable.

TISZAHÁT & ERDŐHÁT REGIONS

If you're looking for Hungary's most far-flung regions – both geographically and culturally – then your search will bring you here. Tiszahát, which translates as 'Behind the Tisza', and Erdőhát, meaning 'Behind the Woods' (of Transylvania), were for centuries isolated outposts, regularly cut off from the rest of Hungary by the flood waters of the Tisza and Szamos rivers.

Because of these regions' isolation, folk traditions have lived on. Some of the finest examples of Hungarian popular architecture and interior church painting are found here. It is also the site of Hungary's most unusual cemetery.

VÁSÁROSNAMÉNY
☎ 45 / pop 9075

Vásárosnamény is a sleepy town (although, for the region, quite a live wire), but it was once an important trading post on the lucrative Salt Road, which ran from the forests of Transylvania, via the Tisza River and then across the Great Plain to Debrecen. With handy transport links and good facilities, such as an **OTP bank** (Szabadság tér 28-31; ☺ 7.45am-12.30pm & 1-5pm Mon, 7.45am-12.30pm & 1-3pm Tue-Thu, 7.45am-12.30pm Fri), with ATM, and a **Tourinform** (☎ 570 206; vasarosnameny@tourinform .hu; Szabadság tér 33; ☺ 8am-4pm Mon-Fri, 9am-1pm Sat), Vásárosnamény is an excellent base for exploring the region's scattered villages.

The town's **Bereg Museum** (☎ 470 638; Rákóczi utca 13; adult/child 200/100Ft; ☺ 10am-6pm Tue-Sun mid-Mar–Oct, 8.30am-4.30pm Mon-Fri Nov–mid-Mar) has a small, though interesting, collection of local embroidery, weaving, pottery, iron stoves and painted Easter eggs – a popular Central European pastime. Be sure to see the famous Bereg cross-stitching, a blend of many different styles.

Sleeping & Eating

Winkler (☎ 470 945; winklerh@hu.inter.net; Rákóczi utca 5; s/d 6000/8000Ft; ℗ ✖) Near the museum is this *pension*, which features colourful embroidery from the region and spacious rooms. Added extras include a quality restaurant (mains 1000Ft, lunch menu 550Ft) serving regional specialities, a cute patio laden with pot-plants and a sauna.

Hotel Fehér (☎ 470 854; www.hotels.hu/feherhotel; Bereg-köz 1; r €40; ℗ ✖) Fehér has less character than Winkler, with white-washed walls and '70s décor, but it's a decent option if the latter is full. The hotel also runs a restaurant (pizza from 550Ft, lunch menu 500Ft) across the road.

Diófa Camping (☎ 712 298; Gulácsi út 71; camp sites per person/tent 800/700Ft; bungalows 8000Ft; ℗) This small, open camp site is across the Tisza River from Vásárosnamény in Gergelyiugornya. Bungalows sleep up to four people and the local pool is directly opposite.

TÁKOS
☎ 45 / pop 445

A must for anyone interested in folk art is the 18th-century wattle-and-daub **Calvinist church** (☎ 701 718; Bajcsy-Zsilinszky utca 25; admission 120Ft; ☺ 7am-7pm) in Tákos, 8km northeast of Vásárosnamény on Rte 41. It has a spectacularly painted coffered ceiling of blue and red flowers, a beaten earth floor and an ornately carved 'folk baroque' pulpit sitting on a large millstone. Outside the church, which villagers call the 'barefoot Notre Dame of Hungary', stands a perfectly preserved **bell tower** (1767). The keeper of the keys, who is almost as old as the church, lives in a house just north of the church at Bajcsy-Zsilinszky utca 29.

The town's **provincial house** (tájház; Bajcsy-Zsilinszky utca 53; admission free; ☺ 7am-10pm), opposite the church, sells works by local weavers, which are very colourful and richly patterned. Snacks are also available.

CSARODA
☎ 45 / pop 655

A lovely **Romanesque church** (☎ 484 905; Kossuth utca 2; admission 100Ft; ☺ 10am-6pm Mon-Fri Mar-Oct) from the 13th century stands in this village, which is some 3km east of Tákos. The church is thought to have been founded by King Stephen, following his plan to have at least one church for every 10 villages in his domain. The building is a wonderful hybrid of a place with both Western- and Eastern-style frescoes (some from the 14th century), as well as some fairly crude folk murals dated 9 July 1647. On the walk from the car park or bus stop, you'll pass two wooden **bell towers** of a much more recent vintage which still work.

As rural settings go, Csaroda has one of the nicest. Accommodation is limited to **Székely** (☎ 484 830; www.julusi.hu/szekely; József Attila utca 54; s/d 2300/4600Ft; ℗), a traditional peasant house, with thick white-washed walls and rustic appeal. Finding food after 8pm is a problem but you may be able to arrange a meal through the house owners.

TARPA
☎ 45 / pop 2400

Some 6km further east on Rte 41 will take you to the turn-off for Fehérgyarmat. Another 10km south of the turn-off is Tarpa, a town boasting one of Hungary's last examples of a horse-driven **dry mill** (szárazmalom; ☎ 488 331; Árpád utca 36; admission 30Ft; ☺ appointment needed). The mill, which is still in working order and turns with exceptional ease, went through many incarnations – as a bar, a cinema and dance hall – before its renovation in the late 1970s and early 1980s. Nearby is a decorated **Calvinist church** (Kossuth utca 13; admission free; ☼ 8am-noon Mon-Fri).

Kuruc (☎ 488 121; tarpakurucpanzio@freemail.hu; Kossuth út 25; s/d 3500/6000Ft; **P**)) occupies a dark-pink building in the heart of Tarpa and has large rooms. There's a terrace and sauna for guest use and a fine, if loud, restaurant (mains 1000Ft) on the ground floor.

Tivadar, 5km south of Tarpa, is on a quiet bend of the Tisza. It's a more inviting place to stay, with a restaurant or two and a popular beach. Tiny **Katica Camping** (☎ 06 20 926 5803; Petőfi út 11; camp sites per person/car/tent 550/300/300Ft; ☼ mid-Jun–Aug; **P**)) is near the river, and has minimal facilities and some shade. Directly opposite is **Kunyhó Vendéglő** (Petőfi út 16; mains under 1000Ft; ☼ 11am-8pm), a pseudo-rustic eatery with an extensive fish selection and far too many stuffed animals lining the walls.

SZATMÁRCSEKE
☎ 44 / pop 1500

To get to this village, site of a cemetery with intriguing boat-shaped **grave markers** (kopjafák; Tánrsics utca; admission free), cross the river at Tivadar, turn east then carry on another 7km northeast. The 600 carved wooden markers in the cemetery are unique in Hungary, and the notches and grooves cut into them represent a complicated language all of its own: they detail marital status, social position and so on. One of the few stone markers in the cemetery is that of native son Ferenc

Kölcsey (1790–1838), who wrote the words to *Himnusz*, the Hungarian national anthem. Nearby is a small **museum** (☎ 712 095; Kölcsey utca 44; admission 100Ft; ☼ 10am-5pm) devoted to Kölcsey.

TÚRISTVÁNDI
☎ 44 / pop 772

About 4km due south of Szatmárcseke is the village of Túristvándi and its pride and joy, a wonderfully restored 18th-century **water mill** (vízimalom; ☎ 434 110; Zrínyi út 4; adult/child 100/70Ft; ☼ 8am-6pm Apr-Sep, 8am-4pm Oct-Mar). After inspecting the mill's mechanics, head next door to **Vízimalon** (☎ 721 082; www .turvizimaln.hu; Malom utca 3; camp sites per person/tent 1000/1000Ft, s/d 4000/8000Ft; camping ☼ Mar-Oct; **P**), which has food and accommodation. There's also a swimming hole on the doorstep, a kids playground and canoe hire for 1000Ft per hour.

GETTING THERE & AWAY
The ideal way to see this part of Hungary is by car or bicycle, but you'll have to bring your own. Otherwise you can visit most of the places by bus from Vásárosnamény, Mátészalka or Fehérgyarmat. Departures are infrequent, averaging only two or three daily. Carefully check return schedules from your destination before setting out. For train information, see Nyíregyháza (p359).

GETTING AROUND
If you don't have transport, the best idea is to take the train or bus from Nyíregyháza or Nyírbátor to Vásárosnamény and use that town as your springboard.

ERDŐHÁT'S FORGOTTEN VILLAGE

Nagygéc, a small village in the far reaches of Erdőhát, is a classic example of the former communist rulers' scant regard for the Hungarian way of life. On 13 May 1970 the village suffered severe flooding and residents were evacuated. Once the waters resided the communist government ruled that the threat of future floods was too great to allow people to rebuild their homes, even though the village had successfully dealt with floods since the Middle Ages (Nagygéc was first mentioned in a charter dating from 1280). Instead, villagers were dispersed and Nagygéc left to the elements.

Today, not a whole lot remains; the scattered houses are boarded up and the only visitors are the occasional farmer and a bevy of birds. The former centrepiece, a Protestant church with 13th-century Romanesque and 15th-century Gothic features, lies in ruin, ready to topple over. At its entrance stands a sign with the words: 'National memorial place. A memento for the deliberate destruction of villages, and a symbol of the will to preserve and restore'. Nagygéc can be found along an unmarked road only a few kilometres from the Satu Mare Romanian border crossing.

RÉTKÖZ REGION

Squeezed between Slovakia, Ukraine and the Tiszahát region is Rétköz, an area most people race through heading to and from Ukraine. It is, however, worth spending a day exploring this remote border region, a place once rich in folk tales and myths. Somewhat lower than the rest of Northeast Hungary, Rétköz was prone to flooding and agriculture was possible only on the larger of the islands in this mosquito-infested swampland. This isolation spurred the development of strong clan ties and a wealth of folk traditions, but aside from the once-celebrated Rétköz homespun cloth, they are not easy to find today.

KISVÁRDA

☎ 45 / pop 17,900

Kisvárda, 45km northeast of Nyíregyháza and the centre of the Rétköz region, is a good base for exploring the area and a better place to overnight than the town of Záhony if you're continuing on to Ukraine.

Orientation

The bus and train stations are about 2km southwest of Flórián tér, the town centre. Local buses await arriving trains, but it's an easy walk north along Bocskai utca, Rákóczi Ferenc utca and Szent László utca to town. Some buses also go as far as Flórián tér.

Information

Cultural centre (☎ 500 451; Flórián tér 20; ☾ 1-7pm Mon-Fri) Has Internet access for 100Ft per hour.
Main post office (Somogyi Rezső utca 4)
OTP bank (cnr Mártírok útja & Szent László utca) Has an ATM.

Sights & Activities

Flórián tér has the usual Gothic-cum-baroque **Catholic church** painted yellow, and a late-19th-century dusky pink **Calvinist church** sitting uncomfortably close by. Sadly both churches are only open during mass. Far more interesting is the Zopf-style **town library** (☾ 9.30am-12.30pm & 1-6pm Mon-Fri, 8am-noon Sat), which takes pride of place on the square.

A short distance to the east of the square is the **Rétköz Museum** (☎ 405 154; Csillag utca 5; adult/child 100/50Ft; ☾ 10am-noon & 1-6pm Tue-Sun Apr-Oct), the town's only true sight. Housed in a disused synagogue built in 1900, the building itself is as interesting as the exhibits, with its geometric ceiling patterns, blue and yellow stained glass, and wrought-iron gates in the shape of menorahs. Lots of 'typical' Rétköz village rooms and workshops (a smithy, loom etc) are set up on the ground floor of the museum, and the 1st floor has some interesting art. Just inside the west entrance is a memorial tablet, with the names of more than 1000 Kisvárda Jews who died in Auschwitz.

The ruins of **Kisvárda Castle** (☎ 405 239; Várkert; admission free; ☾ appointment needed) are about 10 minutes on foot, at the end of the street northwest of Flórián tér. Though part of one wall dates from the 15th century, most of the castle has been heavily restored.

The **Várfürdő** (Városmajor utca; adult/child 800/500Ft; ☾ 9am-7pm Mon-Sun May-Sep), beside the castle ruins, has freshwater and thermal pools, with sauna and sunbathing areas.

Sleeping & Eating

Bástya (☎ 421 100; Krucsay Márton utca 2; d with/without shower 4500/4000Ft) Rooms at Bástya are miniscule and sparsely furnished, but they're the best the town has to offer. You'll find the *pension* on the 1st floor of a shopping arcade overlooking the main square.

Amadeus (Szent László utca 27; mains 1100Ft) This cellar restaurant has exceedingly friendly staff, a menu loaded with Hungarian specialities and bizarre, throne-like seating.

Poncsák (Mártírok útja 2; ice cream 100Ft; ☾ 8am-8pm) This traditional *cukrászda* (cake shop) has the best cakes and ice cream in town.

Entertainment

Plays are sometimes put on at the **Castle Stage** (Várszínpad) at Kisvárda castle in summer; check with the staff at the modern **cultural centre** (☎ 500 451; Flórián tér 20; ☾ 1-7pm Mon-Fri).

For a quiet drink try the simple **Belvárosi Kávézó** (Szent László utca 22; ☾ 10am-11pm), which is more a pub than a café and has outdoor tables.

Getting There & Away

Only a few destinations are accessible by bus from Kisvárda including Nyíregyháza (605Ft, 1½ hours, 50km, three daily) and Vásárosnamény (363Ft, one hour, 29km, seven on weekdays, one on weekends).

The town is on the train line connecting Nyíregyháza (430Ft, 43 minutes, 43km) with Záhony, and there are up to 18 daily trains, 11 of which originate in Budapest.

Directory

ACCOMMODATION

Except during the peak summer season (ie July and most of August) in Budapest, most of Lake Balaton, the Danube Bend and the Mátra Hills, you should have no problem finding accommodation to fit your budget in Hungary. Camp sites are plentiful, university and college dormitories open their doors to guests during summer and other holiday periods, former trade-union holiday homes have been converted into hostels and cheap hotels, and family-run *pensions* have sprung up everywhere. Paying-guest services (p367) are available everywhere, too.

In this book budget accommodation – camp sites, hostels, *pensions* and cheap hotels – is anything under 7500Ft (€30) a night in the provinces and under 12,000Ft (€49) in Budapest; midrange (usually *pen-*

sions and hotels) is between 8000Ft and 15,500Ft (€31 and €63) in the counties and 12,500Ft to 25,000Ft (€50 to €102) in the capital; and top end is anything over 16,000Ft (€64) outside Budapest and over 25,500Ft (€104) in the city.

The price quoted should be the price you pay, but it's not as cut and dried. Tourist offices and travel agencies usually charge a small fee for booking a private room or other accommodation, and there's usually a surcharge on the first night if you stay for less than three nights. Most cities and towns now levy a local tourist tax of 160Ft to 300Ft per person per night (3% in Budapest for those aged 18 to 70), though sometimes only after the first night or two. People under 18 and over 70 years of age are usually exempt. Some top-end hotels in Budapest do not include the 15% Value Added Tax (VAT) in their rack rates; make sure you read the fine print. In the past, all hotels and *pensions* included breakfast in their rates, but this is not always true today.

Inflation is running at about 7% at the time of writing, so prices will almost certainly be higher than those quoted in this book, although they shouldn't change much when quoted in euros, and the relative differences between various establishments in forint should stay the same. The room rate usually increases in April for the summer season – sometimes by as much as 30%. High-season prices have been listed throughout this book.

Camping

The handy *Hungary Camping Map* published by the Hungarian National Tourist Office (HNTO; p376) lists some 425 camp sites of various sizes across the country, and these are the cheapest places to stay. Small, private camp sites accommodating as few as a dozen tents are usually preferable to the large and very noisy 'official' sites. Prices for two adults plus tent vary from as low as 1800Ft off the beaten track in Western Transdanubia to five times that amount on Lake Balaton in the height of summer.

Most camp sites open from April or May to September or October, and also rent

DIRECTORY

PRACTICALITIES

■ Budapest counts three English-language weekly newspapers: the long-established tabloid *Budapest Sun* (www.budapestsun.com; 399Ft), appearing on Thursday, with a useful classified section and *Style* arts and entertainment supplement; the *Budapest Business Journal* (www.bbj .hu; 575Ft), an almost archival publication of financial news and business, appearing on Monday; and the *Budapest Times* (www.budapesttimes.hu; 420Ft), the new kid on the block, with good reviews and opinion pieces, including 'The Weekly Stink' by local gadfly Erik D'Amato, also appearing on Monday.

■ Radio broadcasts are available with Hungarian Radio/Radio Budapest (www.english.radio. hu) in English daily from 1pm to 1.30pm on 9590 kHz, from 2.30am to 3am on 9795 kHz, and from 7pm to 7.30pm on 3975 kHz and 6025 kHz. On Sunday it broadcasts from 1am to 1.30am on 9560 kHz, and from 3 to 3.30pm on 6025 kHz and 9655 kHz.

■ Plug your hairdryer or travel kettle into a standard European adaptor with two round pins before connecting to electricity supply (220V, 50Hz AC).

■ Hungary uses the metric system for weights and measures (see the conversion table under Quick Reference on the inside front cover).

üdölőházak or *faházak* (small bungalows) from 1000/2000Ft per person without/with shower. In midsummer the bungalows may all be booked, so it pays to check with the local Tourinform office before making the trip. A Camping Card International will sometimes get you a discount of up to 10%. Camping 'wild' is prohibited in Hungary.

For more information, contact the **Hungarian Camping and Caravanning Club** (MCCC; Map p84; ☎ 1-267 5255; mccc@mccc.hu; VIII Mária utca 34, 2nd fl) in Budapest. A useful website is www .camping.hu.

Farmhouses

'Village tourism', which means staying at a farmhouse, can be even cheaper than a private room in a town or city, but most of the places are truly remote and you'll usually need your own transport. For information contact Tourinform, the **National Federation of Rural & Agrotourism** (FATOSZ; Map p84; ☎ /fax 1-352 9804; www.fatosz.hu; VII Király utca 93) or the **Centre of Rural Tourism** (Map pp80-1; ☎ 1-321 2426; www.falutur.hu; VII Dohány utca 86) in Budapest.

Hostels

Despite all the places listed in the handbook of the Budapest-based **Hungarian Youth Hostel Association** (MISZSZ; Map p86; ☎ 1-411 2392; www .youthhostels.hu; V Molnár utca 3), a Hostelling International (HI) card (or equivalent) doesn't get you very far in Hungary. With the exception of those in Budapest, most of

the *ifjúsági szállók* (youth hostels) are in places well off the beaten track. Generally, the only official year-round hostels are in Budapest. A useful website is www.youth hostels.hu.

Dormitory beds in a hostel cost 2000Ft to 5000Ft per person and doubles 6000Ft to 12,000Ft in Budapest; the prices drop considerably in the countryside. An HI card is not required, although holders will sometimes get 10% off the price or not be required to pay the tourist tax. There's no age limit at hostels, which usually remain open all day. The hostels almost always have cooking and laundry facilities, as well as free or very cheap Internet access.

Hotels

Hotels, called *szállók* or *szállodák*, run the gamut from luxurious five-star palaces to the run-down old socialist-era hovels that still survive in some towns. Breakfast is usually included.

A cheap hotel will often be more expensive than a private room, but it may be the answer if you're only staying one night or if you arrive too late to get a private room through an agency. Two-star hotels usually have rooms with a private bathroom; it's always down the hall in a one-star place. Three- and four-star hotels – many of which are new or newly renovated old villas – can be excellent value compared with those in other European countries.

For the big splurge, or if you're romantically inclined, check out Hungary's network of *kastély szállók* (castle hotels) or *kúria szállók* (mansion hotels).

Pensions

Privately run *panziók (pensions)*, which have formed the biggest growth area in the Hungarian hospitality trade over the past decade, are really just little hotels of up to a dozen or so rooms, charging from an average 8500Ft for a double with shower. They are usually new and very clean, and often have an attached restaurant. As they are often outside the centre, *pensions* are usually best for those travelling under their own steam, and visitors from Austria and Germany seem to favour them. A useful website (in Hungarian only) is www.panzio.lap.hu.

Private Rooms

Hungary's *fizetővendég szolgálat* ('paying-guest service') offers a great deal and is still relatively cheap, but with the advent of *pensions* it's not as widespread as it once was. For a single/double expect to pay from 2000Ft to 4200Ft (from 4500Ft to 6500Ft in Budapest) depending on the class and location of the room. Private rooms at Lake Balaton are always more expensive, even in the shoulder seasons. Single rooms are often hard to come by, and you'll usually have to pay a 30% supplement on the first night if you stay less than three or four days.

Private rooms are usually assigned by travel agencies. There are often several agencies offering rooms, so ask around if the price seems higher than usual or the location inconvenient. In resort areas look for houses with signs reading '*szoba kiadó*' or '*Zimmer frei*', advertising private rooms in Hungarian or German.

If you decide to take a private room, you'll share a house or flat with a Hungarian widow, couple or family. The toilet facilities are usually communal, but otherwise you can close your door and enjoy as much privacy as you please. All 1st- and some 2nd- and 3rd-class rooms have shared kitchen facilities. In Budapest you may have to take a room far from the city centre. Some agencies also have entire flats or holiday homes for rent without the owner in residence. These can be a good deal if there are four or more of you travelling together.

BOOK ACCOMMODATION ONLINE

For more accommodation reviews and recommendations by Lonely Planet authors, check out the online booking service at www.lonelyplanet.com. You'll find the true, insider lowdown on the best places to stay. Reviews are thorough and independent. Best of all, you can book online.

University Accommodation

From 1 July to 20 August (or later) and sometimes during the Easter holidays Hungary's cheapest rooms are available at vacant student dormitories, known as a *kollégium* or *diákszálló*, where beds in double, triple and quadruple rooms start as low as 1200Ft per person. There's no need to show a student or hostel card, and it usually won't get you a discount anyway. Facilities are usually – but not always – shared.

ACTIVITIES

Hungary offers an extensive range of activities, from cycling and canoeing to bird-watching and 'taking the waters' at one of the nation's many thermal spas. For details, see p48.

BUSINESS HOURS

With rare exceptions, the opening hours, or *nyitvatartás*, of any concern are posted on the front door; *nyitva* means 'open' and *zárva* 'closed'.

Grocery stores and supermarkets open from about 7am to 6pm or 7pm on Monday to Friday, and department stores generally from 10am to 6pm. Most shops stay open until 8pm on Thursday, but on Saturday they usually close at 1pm. That's changing, however, and some food shops even open for several hours now on Sunday. Many private retail shops close early on Friday and throughout most of August.

Restaurant opening hours vary tremendously across the country but are essentially from 10am or 11am to 11pm or midnight daily. Bars are equally variable but are usually open from 11am to midnight Sunday to Thursday and until 1am or 2am on Friday and Saturday. Nightclubs usually open from 4pm to 2am Sunday to Thursday and until 4am on Friday and Saturday.

DIRECTORY

Banking hours change from institution to location but banks usually operate from 7.45am to 5pm or 6pm Monday, 7.45am to 4pm or 5pm Tuesday to Thursday and from 7.45am to 4pm on Friday. The main post office in any town or city opens from 8am to 6pm weekdays, and until noon on Saturday. Branch offices close much earlier – usually at 4pm – and are almost never open on weekends.

Almost all towns and cities have at least one 'nonstop' – a convenience store, open round-the-clock (or very early/late), and selling basic food items, drinks and tobacco. Most of the hyper-supermarkets outside the big cities, such as Tesco, open on Sunday.

CHILDREN

Successful travel with young children requires planning and effort. Don't try to overdo things; even for adults, packing too much into the time available can cause problems. And make sure the activities include the kids as well – balance that morning at Budapest's Museum of Fine Arts, with an afternoon at the nearby Municipal Great Circus, a performance at the Budapest Puppet Theatre or even a stroll through the West End City Centre mall, which has lots of things to distract children. Include children in the trip planning; if they've helped to work out where you will be going, they'll be much more interested when they get there. Lonely Planet's *Travel with Children* is a good source of information.

All car-rental firms in Hungary have children's safety seats for hire for about €20 per rental; make sure you book them in advance. The same goes for highchairs and cots (cribs).

CLIMATE CHARTS

In general, winters in Hungary are cold, cloudy and damp or windy, and summers are warm – sometimes very hot (see Getting Started for more information, p12). July and August are the hottest months (average temperature 26°C) and January the coldest (-4°C). The number of hours of sunshine averages between 1900 and 2500 a year – among the highest in Europe. The average annual precipitation is about 650mm.

The climate charts in this chapter show you what to expect and when to expect it. For information on specific weather conditions

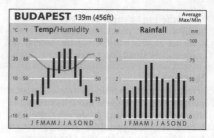

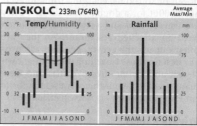

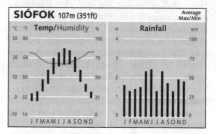

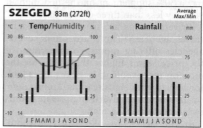

nationwide, contact the **national weather forecast service** (☎ 1-346 4600, 06 90 504 001; www.met .hu in Hungarian).

COURSES
Language

The granddaddy of all Hungarian language schools is the **Debrecen Summer University** (Debreceni Nyári Egyetem; ☎ 52-532 594; www.nyariegyetem .hu; Egyetem tér 1) in Debrecen. It organises intensive two- and four-week courses in July and August, 80-hour, two-week intensive courses in January and a super-intensive two-week course in May/June. The two-/four-week (60-/120-hour) summer courses cost €390/760; board and lodging in a triple room costs €90/180 (singles and doubles are available at extra cost). There's also now a Budapest branch (p101).

For details on reliable schools teaching Hungarian to foreigners in Budapest, see p101.

CUSTOMS
Duty-free shopping within the EU was abolished in 1999 and Hungary, as an EU member, now adheres to the rules. You cannot, for example, buy tax-free goods in, say, Poland or France and take them to Hungary. However, you can still enter an EU country with duty-free items from countries outside the EU.

The usual allowances apply to duty-free goods purchased at airports or on ferries originating outside the EU: 200 cigarettes, 50 cigars or 250g of loose tobacco; 2L of still wine and 1L of spirits; 100mL of perfume; 250cc of eau de toilette. You must declare the import/export of any amount of cash, cheques, securities etc exceeding the sum of 1,000,000Ft.

When leaving the country, you are not supposed to take out valuable antiques without a 'museum certificate', which should be available from the place of purchase.

DANGERS & ANNOYANCES
As a traveller, you are most vulnerable to pickpockets, dishonest waiters, car thieves and the scams of the capital's so-called *konzumlányok*, attractive 'consume girls' in collusion with rip-off bars and clubs who will see you relieved of a serious chunk of money (p69).

Pick pocketing is most common at popular tourist sights, near major hotels, in flea markets and on certain forms of public transport in Budapest (p69). The usual method on the street is for someone to distract you by running into you and then apologising profusely – as an accomplice takes off with the goods.

It is not unknown for waiters to try to rip you off once they see/hear that you are a foreigner. They may try to bring you an unordered dish or make a 'mistake' when

---

EMERGENCY NUMBERS

- Ambulance ☎ 104
- Central emergency number (English spoken) ☎ 112
- English-language crime hotline ☎ 1-438 8080 (8am-8pm), 06 80 660 044 (8pm-8am)
- Fire ☎ 105
- Police ☎ 107
- 24-hour car assistance ☎ 188

---

tallying the bill. If you think there's a discrepancy, ask for the menu and check the bill carefully. If you've been taken for more than 15% or 20% of the bill, call for the manager. Otherwise just don't leave a tip (p374).

Most Hungarian car thieves are not after fancy Western models because of the difficulty in getting rid of them. But Volkswagens, Audis and the like are very popular, and are easy to dismantle and ship abroad. Don't leave anything of value, including luggage, inside the car.

For important telephone numbers to know in an emergency anywhere in Hungary, see boxed text above.

DISABLED TRAVELLERS
Hungary has made great strides in recent years in making public areas and facilities more accessible to the disabled. Wheelchair ramps, toilets fitted for the disabled and inward opening doors, though not as common as they are in Western Europe, do exist and audible traffic signals for the blind are becoming commonplace in the cities.

For more information, contact the **Hungarian Federation of Disabled Persons' Associations** (MEOSZ; Map pp78-9; ☎ 1-250 9013, 388 2387; www .meoszinfo.hu; III San Marco utca 76) in Budapest.

DISCOUNT CARDS
Hostel Cards
The Hungarian Youth Hostel Association (p366) and branches of the Express travel agency chain issue HYHA cards valid for a year to Hungarian citizens and residents for 2300Ft, which includes a 300Ft NeoPhone phonecard.

DIRECTORY

Hungary Card

Those planning on travelling extensively in the country might consider buying a **Hungary Card** (☎ 1-266 3741, 267-0896; www.hungary card.hu), which gives free admission to many museums nationwide; 50% discounts on a half-dozen return train fares and some bus and boat travel, as well as other museums and attractions; up to 20% off selected accommodation; and 50% off the price of the Budapest Card (p67). The card, available at Tourinform offices nationwide, costs 8395Ft and is valid for 13 months.

Student, Youth & Teacher Cards

The **International Student Identity Card** (ISIC; www.isic.org), a plastic ID-style card with your photograph, provides bona fide students many discounts on certain forms of transport, and cheap admission to museums and other sights. If you're aged under 26 but not a student, you can apply for ISIC's International Youth Travel Card (IYTC; 1300Ft) or the Euro<26 card (1600Ft valid for summer break, 2200FT for year) issued by the European Youth Card Association (EYCA), both of which offer the same discounts as the student card. Teachers can apply for the International Teacher Identity Card (ITIC; 1300Ft).

EMBASSIES & CONSULATES
Hungarian Embassies & Consulates

Hungarian embassies (and consulates as indicated) around the world include the following. For further information (and a longer list), see www.mfa.gov.hu.

Australia Canberra (☎ 02-6282 2555; hungcbr@ozemail .com.au; 17 Beale Cres, Deakin, ACT 2600); Sydney (☎ 02-9328 7859; info@hunconsydney.com; Ste 405, Edgecliff Centre, 203-233 New South Head Rd, Edgecliff, NSW 2027)
Austria (☎ 01-537 80 300; kom@huembvie.at; 1 Bankgasse 4-6, A-1010 Vienna)
Canada Ottawa (☎ 613-230 9614; sysadmin@huembott .org; 299 Waverley St, Ottawa, ON K2P 0V9); Toronto (☎ 416-923 8981; hungarian.consulate@bellnet.ca; Ste 1115, 121 Bloor St East, Toronto, ON M4W 3M5)
Croatia (☎ 01-489 0900; secretary@hungemb.hr; Pantovčak 255-257, 10000 Zagreb)
France (☎ 01-56 36 07 54; webmaster@amb-hongrie.fr; 7-9 square Vergennes, 75015 Paris)
Germany Berlin (☎ 030-203 100; info@ungarische -botschaft.de; Unter den Linden 76, D-10117 Berlin); Munich (☎ 089-911 032; huconmuc@t-online.de; Vollmannstrasse 2, 81927 Munich)

Ireland (☎ 01-661 2902; hungarian.embassy@eircom.net; 2 Fitzwilliam Place, Dublin 2)
Netherlands (☎ 070-350 04 04; info@hungarianembassy .nl; Hogeweg 14, 2585 JD The Hague)
Romania (☎ 01-311 0062; hunembro@ines.ro; Strada Dr Prof Dimitrie Gerota 63-65, Bucharest 70202)
Serbia & Montenegro (☎ 011-244 0472; hunemblg@eunet.yu; ul Krunska 72, Belgrade 11000)
Slovakia (☎ 02-59 20 52 00; pozsony@embhung.sk; ul Sedlárska 3, 81425 Bratislava)
Slovenia (☎ 01-512 1882; huemblju@siol.net; Konrada Babnika ulica 5, 1210 Ljubljana-Sentvid)
South Africa (☎ 012-430 3030; huembprt@mweb.co.za; 959 Arcadia St, Hatfield, 0083 Pretoria)
UK London embassy (☎ 020-7235 5218; office@huemblon .org.uk; 35 Eaton Place, London SW1X 8BY); London consulate (☎ 020-7235 2664; consulate@huemblon.org.uk; 35/b Eaton Place, London SW1X 8BY)
Ukraine (☎ 044-230 8000; hungary@kiev.farlep.net; ul Rejtarskaja 33, Kyiv 01034)
USA Washington (☎ 202-362 6730; office@huembwas.org; 3910 Shoemaker St NW, Washington, DC 20008); New York (☎ 212-752 0669; huncons@humisny.org; 223 East 52nd St, New York, NY 10022); Los Angeles (☎ 310-473 9344; huconlos@mpowercom.net; Ste 410, 11766 Wilshire Blvd, Los Angeles, CA 90025)

Embassies & Consulates in Hungary

Selected countries with representation in Budapest (where the telephone code is ☎ 1) are listed here. The opening hours indicate when consular or chancellery services are available to the public. The Roman numerals preceding the street name indicate the *kerület* (district) in the capital.

Australia (☎ 457 9777; XII Királyhágó tér 8-9, 4th fl; ☽ 9-11am Mon-Fri)
Austria (☎ 413 0240; VI Benczúr utca 16; ☽ 8-10am Mon-Fri)
Canada (☎ 392 3360; II Ganz utca 12-14; ☽ 8.30-11am & 2-3.30pm Mon-Thu)
Croatia (☎ 269 5657; VI Munkácsy Mihály utca 15; ☽ 1-3pm Mon, Tue, Thu & Fri)
France (☎ 374 1100; VI Lendvay utca 27; ☽ 9am-noon Mon-Fri)
Germany (☎ 488 3505; I Úri utca 64-66; ☽ 9am-noon Mon-Fri)
Ireland (☎ 301 4960; Bank Center, Granite Tower, 7th fl, V Szabadság tér 7; ☽ 9.30am-12.30pm & 2.30-4.30pm Mon-Fri)
Netherlands (☎ 336-6300; II Füge utca 5-7; ☽ 10am-noon Mon-Fri)
Romania (☎ 384 0271; XIV Thököly út 72; ☽ 8.30am-noon Mon, Tue, Thu & Fri) Enter from Izsó utca.

Serbia & Montenegro (☎ 322 1436; VI Dózsa György út 92/b; ⊙ 10am-1pm Mon-Fri)

Slovakia (☎ 273 3500; XIV Gervay utca 44; ⊙ 8.30am-noon Mon-Fri)

Slovenia (☎ 438 5600; II Csatárka köz 9; ⊙ 9am-noon Mon-Fri)

South Africa (☎ 392 0999; II Gárdonyi Géza út 17; ⊙ 9am-12.30pm Mon-Fri)

UK (☎ 266 2888; V Harmincad utca 6; ⊙ 9.30am-12.30pm & 2.30-4.30pm Mon-Fri)

Ukraine (☎ 422 2122; XIV Stefánia út 77; ⊙ 9am-12pm Mon-Wed & Fri by appointment only)

USA (☎ 475 4164; V Szabadság tér 12; ⊙ 1-4.30pm Mon-Thu, 9am-noon & 1-4pm Fri)

FESTIVALS & EVENTS

Hungary's most outstanding annual events include the following. For more detailed coverage, pick up a copy of the HNTO's annual *Events Calendar* available from Tourinform offices.

FEBRUARY/MARCH

Busójárás (www.mohacs.hu) Pre-Lenten carnival involving anthropomorphic costumes, held in Mohács on the weekend before Ash Wednesday.

MARCH

Budapest Spring Festival (www.festivalcity.hu) Hungary's largest cultural festival, with some 200 events staged at 60 venues throughout the capital.

MARCH/APRIL

Hollókő Easter Festival (www.holloko.hu) Traditional costumes and folk traditions welcome in spring at this World Heritage listed village.

MAY

Balaton Festival (info@goldmarkmk.hu) Pop and classical music and street theatre to usher in the summer season at Keszthely.

JUNE

Hungarian Dance Festival (www.nemzetitancszinhaz .hu/english/festivals.php) The nation's most prestigious festival of dance held biannually in Győr.

Sopron Festival Weeks (www.prokultura.hu) Theatre, quiet music, folk dancing and a handicraft fair, held in Sopron.

JULY

International Danube Folklore Festival (dunafest@freemail.hu) Authentic folk music and dance, with performers from around Hungary and Europe, held in Kalocsa, Baja and Szekszárd.

Martonvásár Days (www.filharmonikusok.hu) The National Philharmonic performs Beethoven at Brunswick Mansion in Martonvásár, where Ludwig van himself once slept.

Szeged Open-Air Festival (www.szeged.hu) The most celebrated open-air festival in Hungary, with opera, ballet, classical music and folk dancing, held in Szeged.

Winged Dragon Week International Street Theatre Festival (www.szarnyas-sarkany.hu) Some 50 music and puppet performances held in and around historical buildings in Nyírbátor in the Northeast.

AUGUST

Debrecen Flower Carnival (www.debrecen.hu) Week-long spectacular in Debrecen kicked off by parade of flower floats on St Stephen's Day (20 August).

Formula One Hungarian Grand Prix (www.hungaror ing.hu) Hungary's prime sporting event held in Magyoród, 24km northeast of Budapest.

Haydn Festival (www.artsfestivals.hu) A week of classical music performance at the Esterházy Palace in Fertőd.

Hortobágy Bridge Fair (phhort@externet.hu) This 100-year-old fair in Hortobágy has dance, street theatre, folklore performances, and the occasional horse and pony.

Jászberény Summer (www.extra.hu/dmkih) Some 10 days of folk music and dancing, including the celebrated Csángó Festival, held in Jászberény.

Sziget Music Festival (www.sziget.hu) Now one of the biggest and most popular music festivals in Europe, held on Budapest's Hajógyár Island.

Zemplén Art Days Classical music festival launched by the Ferenc Liszt Chamber Orchestra and held in venues around the region, especially Sárospatak.

SEPTEMBER

Debrecen Jazz Days (titkarsag@fonixcsarnok.hu) Held in Debrecen, this is the oldest jazz festival in the country and attracts performers from all over the world.

Vintage and grape harvest festivals These bacchanalias are held in wine-growing areas throughout Hungary. The **Sopron Harvest Days** (www.prokultura .hu), held in that Transdanubian city, are just one example.

NOVEMBER

Miskolc Autumn Cultural Days (www.miskolc.hu) Jazz, pop and rock music, literary and theatrical performances, and exhibitions of photography and of industrial art take place throughout Miskolc for a week.

FOOD

Hungary has a varied, world-class cuisine and a wine-making tradition that goes back to the time of the Romans. For details, see p53.

DIRECTORY

GAY & LESBIAN TRAVELLERS

There's not much gay life beyond Budapest (p116) unless you take it along with you, but the Budapest-biased freebie pamphlet **Na Végre!** lists a handful of venues in the *vidék* (countryside); check out **At Last!** (navegre@hotmail.com). Pick it up at gay venues in Budapest or contact them directly. Other useful websites, though primarily focused on Budapest, include: www.budapestgay visitor.hu and http://budapest.gayguide.net.

The **Háttér Gay & Lesbian Association** (☎ 1-329 3380, 06 40 200 358; www.hatter.hu; ☺ 6-11pm) has an advice and helpline operating daily. **Budapest gayguide.net** (☎ 06 30 932 3334; budapestgayguide.net; ☺ 4-8pm Mon-Fri Apr-Oct) can offer advice and/or provide information via email or, seasonally, by telephone. A lesbian website is www .labrisz.hu, but it's in Hungarian only.

HOLIDAYS
Public Holidays
Hungary celebrates 10 *ünnep* (public holidays) each year:

New Year's Day 1 January
1848 Revolution/National Day 15 March
Easter Monday March/April
International Labour Day 1 May
Whit Monday May/June
St Stephen's/Constitution Day 20 August
1956 Remembrance Day/Republic Day 23 October
All Saints' Day 1 November
Christmas holidays 25-26 December

School Holidays
Hungarian school holidays fall during autumn (first week of November), over the Christmas and New Year period (12 days from around 22 December to 2 January), over Easter (one week in March/April) and, of course, in summer (11 weeks from 15 June to 31 August).

INSURANCE
A travel insurance policy to cover theft, loss and medical problems is a good idea. There is a wide variety of policies available, so check the small print.

You may prefer a policy that pays doctors or hospitals directly rather than you having to pay on the spot and claim later. If you have to claim later, make sure you keep all documentation. Some policies ask you to call back (reverse charges) to a centre in your home country where an immediate assessment of your problem can be made. For information on vehicle insurance, see p385, and for health insurance, p391.

Worldwide cover to travellers for over 44 countries is available online at www.lonely planet.com/travel_services.

INTERNET ACCESS
The Internet has arrived in a big way in Hungary, and the blue signs announcing *'eMagyarország Pont'* are telling you that you can log on somewhere in the vicinity – be it via a free access terminal, at a commercial Internet café or at a wifi hotspot. Many libraries in Hungary have free terminals; at hotels you usually have to pay to use the service. It's hit or miss with hostels, but most now have at least one terminal available to guests either for free or for a nominal sum. Commercial Internet cafés, where rates cost 200Ft to 700Ft per hour, abound in Budapest. Their numbers are more limited elsewhere in Hungary, but you'll almost always find one. Check the Information section of cities and towns throughout this book.

If you're travelling with your own notebook or hand-held computer, remember that the power-supply voltage in Hungary may vary from that at home, risking damage to your equipment. The best investment is a universal AC adaptor for your appliance, which will enable you to plug it in anywhere. You'll also need a plug adaptor for European outlets; it's often easiest to buy these before you leave home.

For the best sites to check out before arriving in Hungary, see p15.

LEGAL MATTERS
Those violating Hungarian laws, even unknowingly, may be expelled, arrested and/or imprisoned. Penalties for possession, use or trafficking in illegal drugs in Hungary are severe, and convicted offenders can expect long jail sentences and heavy fines.

Another law that is taken very seriously here is the 100% ban on alcohol when driving. Do not think you will get away with even a few glasses of wine at lunch; police conduct routine roadside checks with breathalysers and if you are found to have even 0.001% of alcohol in your blood, you will be fined up to 30,000Ft on the spot. If the level is high, you will be arrested and your licence almost certainly taken away.

COMING OF AGE

The legal age for voting, driving an automobile and drinking alcohol is 18. In 2004 the age of consent for gays and lesbians was lowered to 14 to come into line with that of heterosexual couples.

In the event of an accident, the drinking party is automatically regarded as guilty.

MAPS

Hungary's largest map-making company, **Cartographia** (www.cartographia.hu), publishes a useful 1:450,000-scale sheet map (570Ft) of the country, and its *Magyarország autóatlasza* (Road Atlas of Hungary) is indispensable if you plan to do a lot of travelling in the countryside by car. It comes in two sizes and scales – 1:360,000 (2100Ft) and 1:250,000 (2600Ft). The former has thumbnail plans of virtually every community in the land, while the larger-scale atlas has 23 city maps. Bookshops in Hungary generally stock a wide variety of maps, or you could go directly to the **Cartographia** (☎ 312 6001; www.cartographia.hu; VI Bajcsy-Zsilinszky út 37; 🕙 10am-6pm Mon-Fri; Ⓜ M3 Arany János utca) outlet in Budapest.

Cartographia also produces national, regional and hiking maps (average scale 1: 40,000 or 1:60,000), as well as city plans (1: 10,000 to 1:20 000), as around 590Ft each). Smaller companies such as Topográf, Magyar Térképház and Nyír-Karta also publish excellent city and specialised maps.

Since 1989 many streets, parks and squares have been renamed. For more details, see the boxed text on p65.

MONEY

The Hungarian currency is the forint (Ft) and today there are coins of 1Ft, 2Ft, 5Ft, 10Ft, 20Ft, 50Ft and 100Ft. Notes come in seven denominations: 200Ft, 500Ft, 1000Ft, 2000Ft, 5000Ft, 10,000Ft and 20,000Ft.

The green 200Ft note features the 14th-century king Charles Robert and his castle at Diósgyőr near Miskolc. The hero of the independence wars, Ferenc Rákóczi II, and Sárospatak Castle are on the burgundy-coloured 500Ft note.

The 1000Ft note is blue and bears a portrait of King Matthias Corvinus, with Hercules Well at Visegrád Castle on the verso. The

17th-century prince of Transylvania Gábor Bethlen is on his own on one side of the 2000Ft bill and meeting with his advisers on the other.

The 'greatest Hungarian', Count István Széchenyi, and his family home at Nagycenk are on the purple 5000Ft note. The 10,000Ft bears a likeness of King Stephen, with a scene in Esztergom appearing on the other side. The 20,000Ft note, currently the highest denomination, has Ferenc Deák, the architect of the 1867 Compromise, on the recto and the erstwhile House of Commons in Pest (now the Italian Institute of Culture on VIII Bródy Sándor utca) on the verso.

ATMs

ATMs accepting most credit and cash cards are everywhere in Hungary, even in small villages, and all the banks listed in the Information sections in this guide have them. The best ones to use are the Euronet ATMs as they dispense sums in units of 5000Ft. Many of the ATMS at branches of Országos Takarékpénztár (OTP), the national savings bank, give out 20,000Ft notes, which are difficult to break.

Cash

Nothing beats cash for convenience – or risk. It's always prudent to carry a little foreign cash, though, preferably euros or US dollars, in case you can't find an ATM nearby or there's no bank or travel agency open to cash your travellers cheques. You can always change cash at a hotel.

Credit Cards

Credit cards, especially Visa, MasterCard and American Express, are widely accepted in Hungary, and you'll be able to use them at many restaurants, shops, hotels, car-rental firms, travel agencies and petrol stations. They are not usually accepted at museums, supermarkets, or train and bus stations.

Many banks, including K&H and Posta-Bank (represented at post offices nationwide), give cash advances on major credit cards.

International Transfers

Having money wired to Hungary through an agent of **Western Union Money Transfer** (☎ 1-235 8484; www.intercash.hu) is fast and fairly

DIRECTORY

straightforward, and the procedure generally takes less than 30 minutes. You should know the sender's full name, the exact amount and the reference number when you're picking up the cash. The sender pays the service fee (about US$40 for US$500 sent, US$60 for US$1000).

Moneychangers

It is easy to change money at banks, post offices, tourist offices, travel agencies and private exchange offices. Look for the words *valuta* (foreign currency) and *váltó* (exchange) to guide you to the correct place or window.

There's no black market in Hungary to speak of but exchange rates can vary substantially, so it pays to keep your eyes open. And while the forint is a totally convertible currency, you should avoid changing too much as it will be difficult exchanging it beyond the borders of Hungary and its immediate neighbours.

Taxes & Refunds

ÁFA, a value-added tax of between 5% and 25%, covers the purchase of all new goods in Hungary. It's usually included in the price but not always, so it pays to check. Visitors are not exempt, but non-EU residents can claim refunds for total purchases of at least 50,000Ft on one receipt, as long as they take the goods out of the country (and the EU) within 90 days. The ÁFA receipts (available from where you made the purchases) should be stamped by customs at the border, and the claim has to be made within 183 days of exporting the goods. You can then collect your refund – minus commission – from the **Global Refund** (www.globalrefund.com) desk in the departures halls of Terminal 2A and 2B at Ferihegy International Airport in Budapest, or branches of the Ibusz chain of travel agencies at some 16 border crossings. You can also have it sent by bank cheque or deposited into your credit-card account.

Tipping

Hungary is a very tip-conscious society, and virtually everyone routinely tips waiters, hairdressers and taxi drivers. Doctors and dentists accept 'gratitude money', and even petrol station attendants who pump your petrol and thermal spa attendants who walk you to your changing cabin expect something. If you were less than impressed with the service at the restaurant, the joyride in the taxi or the way your hair was cut, leave next to nothing or nothing at all. He or she will get the message – loud and clear.

The way you tip in restaurants is unusual. You never leave the money on the table – this is considered both rude and stupid in Hungary – but tell the waiter how much you're paying in total. If the bill is, say, 2700Ft, you're paying with a 5000Ft note and you think the waiter deserves a gratuity of around 10%, first ask if service is included (some restaurants in Budapest and other big cities add it to the bill automatically, which makes tipping unnecessary). If it isn't, say you're paying 3000Ft or that you want 2000Ft back.

Travellers Cheques

You can change travellers cheques – American Express, Visa, MasterCard and Thomas Cook are the most recognisable brands – at most banks and post offices. Banks and bureaux de change generally don't take a commission, but exchange rates can vary; private agencies are always the most expensive. OTP has branches everywhere and offer among the best rates; Ibusz is also a good bet. Travel agents usually take a commission of 1% to 2%. Shops never accept travellers cheques as payment in Hungary.

POST

The **Hungarian Postal Service** (Magyar Posta; www.posta.hu), whose logo is a jaunty, stylised version of St Stephen's Crown, has improved greatly in recent years, but the post offices themselves are usually fairly crowded and service can be slow. To beat the crowds, ask at kiosks, newsagents or stationery shops if they sell *bélyeg* (stamps).

Postal Rates

A letter of up to 30g sent within Hungary costs 52Ft (90Ft for priority mail) while for the rest of Europe it's 170Ft (190Ft priority). *Légiposta* (airmail letters) of up to 20/50g are 185/270Ft within Europe and 210/350Ft for the rest of the world. Postcards cost 52Ft to send within Hungary, 110Ft within the rest of Europe and 140Ft to the rest of the world.

To send a parcel, look for the sign '*Csomagfeladás*' or '*Csomagfelvétel*'. Packages sent within Hungary generally cost 690Ft for up to 5kg. Packages going abroad must not weigh more than 2kg or you'll face a Kafkaesque parade of forms and queues to fill; try to send small ones. You can send up to 2kg in one box for 3470Ft surface mail to Europe and 4390Ft to the rest of the world. Airmail rates are much higher and depend on which of five zones the destination is located. For example, a 2kg package sent by airmail to the UK/USA/Australia costs 6550/9400/11,800Ft.

Sending & Receiving Mail

To get in and out of the post office with a minimum of fuss, look for the window marked with the symbol of an envelope. Make sure the destination of your letter is written clearly, and simply hand it over to the clerk, who will apply the stamps for you, postmark it and send it on its way.

Hungarian addresses start with the name of the recipient, followed on the next line by the postal code and city or town, and then the street name and number. The postal code consists of four digits. The first one indicates the city, town or region (eg '1' is Budapest, '6' is Szeged), the second and third are the district, and the last is the neighbourhood.

Mail addressed to poste restante in any town or city will go to the *főposta* (main post office), which is generally listed under Information in the relevant section in this book. When collecting poste restante mail, look for the sign '*postán maradó küldemények*' and be sure to have identification on you. Since the family name always comes first in Hungarian usage (see boxed text, p35), have the sender underline your last name, as letters are very often misfiled under foreigners' first names.

SHOPPING

Hungarian shops are well stocked with generally high-quality products. Books and folk-music tapes and CDs are affordable, and there is an excellent selection, especially of the much-loved classical music. Traditional products include folk-art embroidery and ceramics, pottery, painted wooden toys and boxes, dolls, basketry and porcelain (especially that from Herend and Zsolnay). Feather or goose-down pillows and duvets (comforters), ranked second only to the Siberian variety, are of exceptionally high quality and very good value.

Some of Hungary's new 'boutique' wines (p55) make good, relatively inexpensive gifts; a bottle of dessert Tokaj always goes down well. *Pálinka* (fruit-flavoured brandies) are a stronger option.

Foodstuffs that are expensive or difficult to buy elsewhere – potted goose liver, saffron, dried forest mushrooms, jam (especially the apricot variety), prepared meats like Pick salami, the many types of paprika – make wonderful gifts (if you are allowed to take them home). Be aware that in supermarkets and outdoor markets, fresh food is sold by weight or by *darab* (piece). When ordering by weight, you specify by kilos or *deka* (decagrams – 50dg is equal to 0.5kg or a little more than 1lb).

TELEPHONE

You can make domestic and international calls from public telephones, which are usually in good working order. They work with both coins and phonecards, though the latter are now far more common. Telephone boxes with a black-and-white arrow and red target on the door and the word '*Visszahívható*' display a telephone number, so you can be phoned back.

Local & International Calls

All localities in Hungary have a two-digit telephone area code, except for Budapest, which has just a '1'. Local codes appear in small point type under the heading name of each city and town in this book.

To make a local call, pick up the receiver and listen for the neutral and continuous dial tone, then dial the phone number (seven digits in Budapest, six elsewhere). For an intercity landline call within Hungary and whenever ringing a mobile telephone, dial ☎ 06 and wait for the second, more melodious, tone. Then dial the area code and phone number. Cheaper or toll-free blue and green numbers start with ☎ 06 40 and 06 80 respectively.

The procedure for making an international call is the same as for a local call, except that you dial ☎ 00, wait for the second dial tone, then dial the country code, the area code and the number. The country code for Hungary is ☎ 36.

Mobile Phones

Hungary uses GSM 900, which is compatible with the rest of Europe and Australia, but not with the North American GSM 1900 or the totally different system in Japan (though some North Americans have GSM 1900/900 phones that do work here). In Hungary you must always dial ☎ 06 when ringing mobile telephones, which have specific area codes depending on the telecom company: **Pannon GSM** (☎ 06 20; www.pgsm.hu), **T-Mobile** (☎ 06 30; www.t-mobile.hu) and **Vodafone** (☎ 06 70; www.vodafone.hu).

If you have a GSM phone, check with your service provider about using it in Hungary, and beware of calls being routed internationally (very expensive for a 'local' call). If you're going to spend more than just a few days here and expect to use your phone quite a bit, consider buying a rechargeable SIM chip, which will reduce the cost of making local calls (between 19Ft and 27Ft a minute) to a fraction of what you'd pay on your own mobile. Vodafone, with outlets throughout the country, including Budapest (p68), has prepaid vouchers available for 1000/2500Ft with 500/1500Ft worth of credit. Top-up cards valid for three/six/12 months cost 3000/7000/12,000Ft.

Phonecards

Phonecards, which are available from post offices, newsagents, hotels and petrol stations, come in message units of 50/120 and cost 800/1800Ft, but these are by far the most expensive way to go. As everywhere else these days, there is a plethora of phonecards on offer. Among the most widely available are T-Com's **Barangoló** (☎ 06 80 501 255; www.t-com.hu), which comes in denominations of 400Ft, 1000Ft, 2000Ft and 5000Ft, and **NeoPhone** (☎ 06 80 188 202; www.neophone.hu), with cards valued at 300Ft, 1000Ft, 2000Ft

---

USEFUL TELEPHONE NUMBERS
■ Domestic operator/enquiries (in English) ☎ 198
■ Information Plus (any enquiry; in English) ☎ 197
■ International enquiries/operator (in English) ☎ 199
■ Time/speaking clock (in Hungarian) ☎ 180
■ Wake-up service (in Hungarian) ☎ 193

---

and 5000F. Sample per-minute costs with these cards are 25Ft to most European countries, 29Ft to Australia and New Zealand, and 50Ft to South Africa.

TIME

Hungary lies in the Central European time zone. Winter time is GMT plus one hour, while in summer it's GMT plus two hours. Clocks are advanced at 2am on the last Sunday in March and set back at the same time on the last Sunday in October.

Without taking daylight-saving times into account, when it's noon in Budapest it's 3am in San Francisco, 6am in New York, 11am in London, noon in Paris, 1pm in Bucharest, 2pm in Moscow, 8pm in Tokyo, 9pm in Sydney and 11pm in Auckland. For information about other time zones and their relation to Hungary, see the World Times Zones map (pp422-3).

An important note on the complicated way Hungarians tell time: like a few other European languages, Magyar tells the time by making reference to the next hour – not the previous one as we do in English. Thus 7.30 is *fél nyolc óra* ('half eight'; sometimes written f8) and the 24-hour system is often used in giving the times of movies, concerts and so on. So a film at 7.30pm could appear on a listing as 'f8', 'f20', '½8' or '½20'. A quarter to the hour is a ¾ in front (thus '¾8' means 7.45), while quarter past is ¼ of the next hour (eg '¼9' means 8.15).

TOURIST INFORMATION

The **Hungarian National Tourist Office** (HNTO; www.hungarytourism.hu or www.hungary.com) has a chain of almost 140 tourist information bureaus called **Tourinform** (☎ within Hungary 06 80

630 800, from abroad + 36 30 30 30 600; www.tourinform
.hu) across the country. They are usually the
best places to ask general questions and pick
up brochures – and can sometimes provide more comprehensive assistance. The
main **Tourinform office** (Map p86; ☎ 1-438 8080;
hungary@tourinform.hu; V Sütő utca 2; ⊙ 8am-8pm) is
in Budapest.

If your query is about private accommodation, flights or international train travel
or you need to change money, you could
turn to a commercial travel agency, such as
Ibusz, arguably the best for private accommodation, or Express, which issues student,
youth, teacher and hostel cards, and sells
discounted Billet International de Jeunesse
(BIJ) train and cheap air tickets. See the
Information section under the various cities and towns in this book for details.

The HNTO has offices in more than
20 countries worldwide.

Austria (☎ 01-585 20 1213; www.ungarn-tourismus.at;
Opernring 5, 2nd fl, A-1010 Vienna)

Czech Republic (☎ 283 870 742; www.madarsko.cz;
M Horákovée 81, 17006 Prague 7)

France (☎ 01 53 70 67 17; www.hongrietourisme.com;
140 Ave Victor Hugo, 75116 Paris)

Germany (☎ 030-243 1460; www.ungarn-tourismus
.de; Neue Promenade 5, D-10178 Berlin)

Ireland (☎ 01-661 2879; www.visithungary.ie;
2 Fitzwilliam Place, Dublin 2)

Netherlands (☎ 070-320 9092; hong@euronet.nl; Laan
van Nieuw Oost Indie 271, 2593 BS The Hague)

UK (☎ 020-7823 1032; www.gotohungary.co.uk;
46 Eaton Place, London SW1X 8AL)

USA (☎ 212-355 0240; www.gotohungary.com; 150 East
58th St, 33rd fl, New York, NY 10155-3398)

VISAS

Citizens of virtually all European countries
as well as Australia, Canada, Israel, Japan,
New Zealand and the USA do not require
visas to visit Hungary for stays of up to 90
days. Nationals of South Africa (among
others) still require visas. Check current visa
requirements at a consulate, any HNTO or
Malév Hungarian Airlines office or on the
website of the **Hungarian Foreign Ministry** (www
.mfa.gov.hu), as requirements often change
without notice.

Visas are issued at Hungarian consulates
or missions, Ferihegy International Airport
and the International Ferry Pier in Budapest. They are rarely issued on international
buses and never on trains. Be sure to retain
the separate entry and exit forms issued with
the visa that is stamped in your passport.

Single-entry tourist visas are issued at
Hungarian consulates or missions in the
applicants' country of residence upon receipt of US$40 (or equivalent) and three
photos (US$65 at a mission outside the
country of residence or at the border).
A double-entry tourist visa costs US$75/100,
and you must have five photos. A multiple-
entry visa is US$180/200. Single and double-
entry visas are valid for six months prior
to use. Multiple-entry visas are good for
a year. (Prices quoted are for applicants'
country of residence/mission outside country of residence or at the border.)

Be sure to get a tourist rather than a
transit visa; the latter – available for single
(US$38/50), double (US$65/90) and multiple (US$150/180) entries – is only good for
a stay of 48 hours, you must enter and leave
through different border crossings, and already hold a visa (if required) for the next
country you visit.

Tourist visas are only extended in emergencies (eg medical ones; 3000Ft) and this
must be done at the *rendőrkapitányság*
(central police station) of any city or town
15 days before the original one expires.

You are supposed to register with the
local police if staying in one place for more
than 30 days; staff at your hotel, hostel,
camp site or private room booked through
an agency will do this for you. In other
situations – if you're staying with friends
or relatives, for example – you or the head
of the household will have to take care of
this within 72 hours of moving in. Address registration forms for foreigners
(lakcímbejelentő lap külföldiek részére) are
usually available at post offices.

WOMEN TRAVELLERS

Women should not encounter any particular problems while travelling in Hungary. If
you do need assistance and/or information,
ring the **Women's Line** (Nővonal; ☎ 06 80 505 101;
⊙ 6-10pm Thu-Tue) or **Women for Women Against
Violence** (NANE; ☎ 1-267 4900; info@nane.hu).

Transport

CONTENTS

GETTING THERE & AWAY

ENTERING HUNGARY

Border formalities with Hungary's three EU neighbours – Austria, Slovenia and Slovakia – are virtually nonexistent. However, as a member state that forms part of the EU's external frontier, Hungary must implement the strict Schengen border rules so expect a somewhat closer inspection of your documents when travelling to/from Croatia, Romania, Ukraine and Serbia.

Passport

Everyone needs a valid passport or, for citizens of the EU (but *not* Denmark, Ireland, Latvia, Sweden or the UK), a national identification card to enter Hungary. It's a good idea (though not a requirement) to carry your passport or other identification at all times.

Flights, tours and rail tickets can be booked online at www.lonelyplanet.com /travel_services.

AIR

Airports & Airlines

Malév Hungarian Airlines (MA; ☎ Hungary 06 40 21 21 21, abroad 1 235 3888; www.malev.hu), the national

carrier, flies nonstop or via Prague, Madrid and Amsterdam to Budapest's **Ferihegy International Airport** (☎ 1-296 7000; www.bud.hu) from North America, the Middle East and almost 60 cities in Continental Europe and the British Isles. It also flies to Beijing, Shanghai and Guangzhou in China.

Malév flights and, for the most part, those of its 18 or so code-share partners arrive and depart from Ferihegy's Terminal 2A. Malév has a **ticketing desk** (☎ 1-296 7211; 🕙 5am-11pm) at Terminal 2A and another one at **Terminal 2B** (☎ 1-296 5767; 🕙 6am-8.30pm); at the latter you'll also find a **left-luggage office** (1/2/3/6hr 350/700/1050/1400Ft, 12/24hr 1880/2200Ft, week 6500Ft; 🕙 24hr).

Most other international airlines use Terminal 2B, which is next door to 2A and within easy walking distance. The super-discount European carriers (opposite) use Terminal 1, about 5km to the west.

Other major carriers with offices in Budapest:

Aeroflot (SU; ☎ 1-318 5955; www.aeroflot.com; hub Moscow)

Air Canada (AC; ☎ 1-266 8435; www.aircanada.com; hub Toronto)

Air France (AF; ☎ 1-483 8800; www.airfrance.com; hub Paris)

Alitalia (AZ; ☎ 1-483 2170; www.alitalia.it; hub Rome)

Austrian Airlines (OS; ☎ 1-327 9080; www.aua.com; hub Vienna)

British Airways (BA; ☎ 1-411 5555; www.ba.com; hub London)

CSA Czech Airlines (OK; ☎ 1-318 3045; www.czech-air lines.com; hub Prague)

El Al (LY; ☎ 1-266 2970; www.elal.com; hub Tel Aviv)

THINGS CHANGE

The information in this chapter is particularly vulnerable to change. Check directly with the airline or a travel agent to make sure you understand how a fare (and ticket you may buy) works and be aware of the security requirements for international travel. Shop carefully. The details given in this chapter should be regarded as pointers and are not a substitute for your own careful, up-to-date research.

EgyptAir (MS; ☎ 1-266 4300; www.egyptair.com; hub Cairo)

Finnair (AY; ☎ 1-317 4022; www.finnair.com; hub Helsinki)

KLM Royal Dutch Airlines (KL; ☎ 1-373 7737; www .klm.com; hub Amsterdam)

LOT Polish Airlines (LO; ☎ 1-317 2444; www.lot.com; hub Warsaw)

Lufthansa (LH; ☎ 1-266 4511; www.lufthansa.com; hub Frankfurt)

SAS (SK; ☎ 1-266 2633; www.scandinavian.net; hub Copenhagen)

Tarom Romanian Airlines (RO; ☎ 1-235 0809; www .tarom.ro; hub Bucharest)

Turkish Airlines (TK; ☎ 1-266 4291; www.turkishair lines.com; hub Istanbul)

Africa & the Middle East

Malév flies daily to/from Tel Aviv while El Al flies there up to four times a week, depending on the season. Return flights start from around US$290. There is a Malév service to Cairo up to four times a week and EgyptAir has several direct flights each week. Return fares cost from US$245. Malév also flies nonstop to Beirut ($270; two to four times a week return) and to Damascus (US$290; three to four times a week).

Asia

Return flights from Hong Kong (with KLM via Amsterdam, Lufthansa via Frankfurt or Finnair via Helsinki) range from US$576/782 for a ticket valid for 14/21 days to US$833/1000 for one good for two/three months. These days the best place in Asia to buy discount tickets for Eastern and Central Europe is Bangkok because of the surfeit of Eastern European flag-carriers passing through Bangkok airport.

A discounted return Budapest–Bangkok ticket should cost from 169,000Ft. Expect to pay 285,000Ft from Budapest to Hong Kong via London on British Airways.

Australia & New Zealand

Although there are no direct flights to Budapest, there are a number of options from Australia. Qantas has direct flights from Sydney or Melbourne to London's Heathrow airport, connecting with a Malév or British Airways flight to Budapest. Another option is to fly from Sydney to Frankfurt or another European capital and then with Malév to Budapest. A standard return flight to Sydney from Budapest costs 280,000Ft and to Melbourne 265,000Ft; return low season fares from Sydney are around A$1865 to A$2300 and from Melbourne A$2100 to A$2400. Look out for official discounts and special deals, which are available direct from the airline from time to time.

There are a number of flights from New Zealand to European cities, with connecting flights to Budapest. Air New Zealand flies daily from Auckland to Heathrow and connects with a nonstop Malév flight to Budapest. Return fares in the low season are from around NZ$1800 to NZ$2150.

Continental Europe & the UK

Malév flies nonstop to Budapest from many European cities, including the following: Amsterdam, Athens, Berlin, Brussels, Bucharest, Copenhagen, Dublin, Frankfurt, Geneva, Hamburg, Helsinki, Istanbul, Kyiv, Larnaca, Lisbon, London, Ljubljana, Madrid, Manchester, Milan, Moscow, Munich, Paris, Prague, Rome, Sarajevo, Skopje, Sofia, Stockholm, Stuttgart, Thessaloniki, Tirana, Vienna, Warsaw, Zagreb and Zürich.

From Budapest, most destinations in Europe on Malév cost either 19,900Ft (eg Paris, Berlin and Amsterdam) or 29,900Ft, though Moscow and a few other destinations are 39,900Ft. Special deals, regularly available, will see these fares halved. Of course flexibility – such as an open return ticket and the ability to change – will bump the average fare up to around 80,000Ft.

What Hungarians call the *fapados* (wooden bench) airlines, the super discount carriers such as **Air Berlin** (www.airberlin.com), **EasyJet** (www.easyjet.com), **SkyEurope** (www.skyeurope .com) and **Wizzair** (www.wizzair.com), have made flying between Budapest and dozens of European cities very affordable. Depending on the destination, availability and the time of the flight, fares can be as low as 15,000Ft, but count on anything from 20,000Ft upward for most flights.

USA & Canada

Malév runs a daily nonstop flight to/from New York's JFK International Airport (return fare around US$500). Another option is to fly with KLM or Northwest Airlines to Amsterdam, and then board a Malév flight to Budapest. Malév also has a nonstop service to/from Toronto four times a week (return fare just over C$800). For Montreal fly Air Canada and Malév via Paris (CDG).

From Budapest, travelling with Malév, a return fare to New York starts at 99,900Ft but can go as low as 69,900Ft.

LAND

Hungary is well connected with all seven of its neighbours by road, rail and even ferry, though most transport begins or ends its journey in Budapest.

As elsewhere in Europe, timetables for both domestic and international trains and buses use the 24-hour system. Also, Hungarian names are sometimes used for cities and towns in neighbouring countries on bus and train schedules (p404).

Border Crossings

Of the 65 or so border road crossings Hungary maintains with its neighbours, about a third (mostly in the north and northeast) are restricted to local citizens on both sides of the border (or, in the case of Austria, Slovakia and Slovenia, EU citizens).

Bus

Most international buses are run by **Eurolines** (☎ 1-219 8021; www.eurolines.com) or its Hungarian associate, **Volánbusz** (☎ 1-382 0888; www.volanbusz.hu). In Budapest, all international buses arrive at and depart from the **Népliget bus station** (Map pp88-9; ☎ 1-219 8080; IX Üllői út 131; metro Népliget) in Pest. The **ticket office** (✆ 6am-6pm Mon-Fri Sep-May, 6-8pm Mon-Fri Jun-Aug, 6am-4pm Sat & Sun year-round) is upstairs.

BUS PASSES

Eurolines has passes valid for 15/30/40 days that allow unlimited travel between 35 European cities, including Budapest. You are not allowed to travel on the same routing more than twice. Adults pay €230/320/350 in the low season (mid-September to late June) and €325/435/490 in the high season. Passes for those under 26 cost €195/260/299 or €275/355/420.

WESTERN EUROPE

From Népliget station there's a long-distance bus that runs throughout the year to Amsterdam via Frankfurt and Düsseldorf (20½ hours, 1435km, Monday, Wednesday, Friday and Saturday). The bus continues on to Rotterdam (21½ hours, 1510km) on Wednesday, Friday and Saturday. Tickets cost 23,900/40,900Ft one way/return (to both destinations), with a 10% discount for those under 26, students and seniors over 60. From early June to late September, there's an extra departure on Friday evening.

In Amsterdam tickets are sold by **Eurolines Nederland** (☎ 020-560 87 88; Rokin 10) and at **Amstel bus station** (☎ 020-560 87 88; Julianaplein 5). In Budapest you can buy them at the Népliget bus station.

Buses to London via Brussels and Lille (25¼ hours, 1755km) depart on Wednesday, Friday and Sunday and cost 29,900/42,900Ft one way/return. There are additional services over the summer on Tuesday (April to late October), Thursday (late June to August) and Saturday (early July to early September). In London contact **Eurolines UK** (☎ 0870 514 3219; 52 Grosvenor Gardens SW1).

Other Eurolines services between Budapest and Western European cities, with high-season (mid-June to mid-September) one-way/return fares quoted, include the following:

Athens (via Thessaloniki, 22,900/35,900Ft, 24½ hours, 1570km, Saturday) Even if you only go as far as Thessaloniki, the ticket price is the same.

Berlin (via Prague and Dresden, 16,900/28,900Ft, 14¾ hours, 910km, four to six days a week) If you continue on to Hamburg, the cost goes up to 21,900/36,900Ft. Buses depart Tuesday, Wednesday, Friday and Saturday year-round, as well as on Thursday and Sunday from late June to mid-August.

Paris (via Vienna, Strasbourg and Reims, 23,900/41,900Ft, 21½ hours, 1460km, three days a week) Buses run Monday, Wednesday and Friday year-round. To go only as far as Strasbourg costs 20,900/38,900Ft.

Rome (via Bologna and Florence, 23,900/37,900Ft, 20½ hours, 1250km, up to seven times a week) The ticket to Bologna is 16,900/27,900Ft and to Florence 18,900/30,900Ft. Buses run Tuesday, Wednesday, Friday and Saturday April to mid-September, with extra departures on Tuesday and Wednesday and one on Sunday from mid-September to December.

Venice (13,900/22,900Ft, 11¾ hours, 770km, up to seven times a week) Buses keep the same schedule as the Rome ones.

Vienna (via Győr, 5490/7990Ft, 3¼ hours, 254km, four buses a day)

CROATIA AND SERBIA & MONTENEGRO

From late June to September a bus leaves Népliget station for Pula (return 16,900Ft, 9¾ hours, 775km) every Friday, travelling via Rijeka (return 14,900Ft, 8¾ hours, 830km) and then carrying on to Porec (return 16,900Ft, 11½ hours, 910km). There's a daily service year-round to Belgrade (one way/return 4100/6800Ft, nine hours, 422km) and two buses a day to Subotica (in Hungarian, Szabadka; one way/return 3700/5500Ft, 5¾ hours, 224km).

SLOVAKIA & CZECH REPUBLIC

From Népliget station there are buses to Bratislava (in Hungarian, Pozsony; one way/return 3400/5400Ft, four hours, 213km) daily and to Prague (9900/16,900Ft, 8¼ hours, 640km) year-round on Tuesday to Sunday. Extra overnight buses to Prague run on Thursday and Sunday from late June to mid-August.

UKRAINE

There are buses on Monday and Friday to Kyiv (one way/return 14,900/25,900Ft, 18 hours, 1155km, twice a week) via Lviv (one way/return 12,900/20,900Ft, 11 hours, 850km).

Train

Magyar Államvasutak (www.mav.hu), which translates as Hungarian State Railways and is universally known as MÁV, links up with the European rail network in all directions. Its trains run as far as London (via Munich and Paris), Stockholm (via Hamburg and Copenhagen), Moscow, Rome and Istanbul (via Belgrade).

The international trains listed here are expresses and many – if not all – require seat reservations. On long hauls, sleepers are almost always available in both 1st and 2nd class, and couchettes are available in 2nd class. Not all express trains have dining or even buffet cars; make sure you bring along snacks and drinks as vendors can be few and far between. Most Hungarian trains are hardly what you could call luxurious but they are generally clean and punctual.

In Budapest, almost all international trains arrive and depart from **Keleti station** (Map pp80-1; Eastern train station; ☎ 1-313 6835; VIII Kerepesi út 2-6); however, some trains to certain destinations in the east (eg Romania) leave from **Nyugati station** (Map p84; Western train station; ☎ 1-349 0115; VI Teréz körút 55-57), while **Déli station** (Map p83; Southern train station; ☎ 1-375 6293; I Krisztina körút 37) handles trains to some

destinations in the south (eg Osijek in Croatia and Sarajevo in Bosnia). These are not hard and fast rules, so always make sure you check which station the train leaves from when you buy a ticket. For 24-hour information on international train services call nationwide ☎ 06 40 49 49 49 or in Budapest ☎ 1-461 5500.

To reduce confusion when requesting information or buying a ticket, specify your train by the name listed in the following sections or on the posted schedule. You can buy tickets at the three international train stations in Budapest, but it's easier at the **MÁV international information and ticket centre** (Map p84; ☎ 1-461 5500, 352 2800; www.mav.hu; VI Andrássy út 35; ⓨ 9am-6pm Mon-Fri Apr-Sep, 9am-5pm Mon-Fri Oct-Mar). It accepts credit cards. For fares, check www.elvira.hu.

TICKETS & FARES

There are big nationwide discounts for return (only) fares from Hungary to neighbouring countries: 50% to Bulgaria, the Czech Republic and Poland; 60% to Serbia and Montenegro and the Baltic countries; 50% to Belarus, Russia and Ukraine; and up to 60% to Romania, Slovakia and Slovenia. Also, there's a 40% concession on return fares from Budapest to six selected cities: Prague and Brno in the Czech Republic, and Warsaw, Kraków, Katowice and Gdynia in Poland. Some 2nd-class return fares are: Prague 17,799Ft, Moscow 35,292Ft and Warsaw 24,276Ft.

For tickets to Western Europe you'll pay the same as elsewhere, unless you're under 26 and qualify for the 30% to 60% Billet International de Jeunesse (BIJ) discounts. For that, ask at MÁV, Express or **Wasteels** (Map pp80-1; ☎ 1-210 2802; 8am-8pm Mon-Fri, ⓨ 8am-6pm Sat) in Keleti train station.

The following are sample full-price return 2nd-class fares from Budapest: Amsterdam 52,940Ft, Berlin (via Prague) 40,800Ft and (via Vienna) 45,645Ft, London 96,696Ft, Munich 25,143Ft, Rome (via Ljubljana) 61,098Ft and Vienna 11,578Ft. There's a 30% discounted return fare to Vienna/and Graz of 8823Ft and 10,710Ft respectively if you return to Budapest within four days. The 1st-class seats are around 50% more expensive than 2nd class.

InterCity (IC) and EuroCity (EC) trains charge supplements of between 200Ft and

480Ft. International seat reservation costs vary according to the destination and fines are levied on those without tickets (2000Ft, plus full single fare) or seat reservations (2000Ft, plus reservation fee of 200Ft to 350Ft) on trains where they are compulsory.

Sleeper prices depend on the destination, but a two-berth 2nd-class sleeper to Berlin/Prague/Venice/Moscow costs 5585/3570/6630/5360Ft per person per night. A 2nd-class couchette in a compartment for six people costs between 2400Ft and 3417Ft on the Transbalkan to Romania and Greece, and 4973Ft on the Kálmán Imre to Munich. Tickets are valid for 60 days from purchase and stopovers are permitted.

RAIL PASSES

Covering from one to eight 'zones', **Inter Rail** (www.interrailnet.com) passes can be purchased by nationals of European countries (or residents of at least six months) from MÁV. There are three price groups for the passes: adult, ages 12 to 26 (referred to here as 'youth') and child (four to 11). The price for any one zone is €229/156/115 per adult/youth/child for 16 days and €317/220/159 for 22 days in two zones. Hungary is in Zone D along with the Czech Republic, Slovakia, Poland, Croatia and Bosnia-Hercegovina. A Global pass, covering all eight zones, costs €437/308/219.

It's almost impossible for a standard **Eurail pass** (www.eurailnet.com) to pay for itself in Hungary. If you are a non-European resident, you may consider one of its combination tickets allowing you to travel over a fixed period for a set price. These include the **Hungary N' Slovenia/Croatia pass** and the **Romania N' Hungary pass**, offering five/10 days of travel on those countries' rail networks for adults US$200/300, youths US$140/210 and children aged five to 11 US$100/150. Buy the pass before you leave home.

For information on Eurail's **Hungary pass**, see p390.

WESTERN EUROPE

Seven trains daily link Vienna with Budapest (three hours, 273km) via Hegyeshalom and Győr. Most depart from Vienna's Westbahnhof, including the EuroCity Bartók Béla and the EuroNight Kálmán Imre, both coming from Munich (7½ hours, 742km) via Salzburg (six hours, 589km). Other trains departing from the Westbahnhof include the EC 25/24 from Cologne (11 hours, 1247km) and Frankfurt (10 hours, 1026km), the EN Wiener Walzer (11½ hours, 808km) from Zürich, the Dacia to Bucharest (13½ hours, 874km) and the IC Avala to Belgrade (10 hours, 647km). The early morning EC Lehár Ferenc departs from Vienna's Südbahnhof. None of these trains requires a reservation, though it's highly recommended in summer.

Up to four trains leave Vienna's Südbahnhof every day for Sopron (75 minutes, 76km) via Ebenfurth. As many as a dozen a day also serve Sopron from Wiener Neustadt, which is easily accessible from Vienna. Three daily milk trains make the 2½-hour, 136km-long trip from Graz to Szombathely.

The EC 171/170 travels from Berlin (Zoo and Ostbahnhof stations) to Budapest (12½ hours, 1002km) via Dresden, Prague and Bratislava. The express Spree-Donau Kurier arrives from Berlin via Nuremberg and Vienna (14 hours).

CZECH REPUBLIC, SLOVAKIA & POLAND

In addition to the EC 171/170, Budapest can be reached from Prague (seven hours, 611km) on the EC 175/174, the express Jaroslav Hašek, and the Pannónia Express, which then carries on to Bucharest. The Amicus runs directly from Bratislava (three hours, 235km) every day.

The EC Polonia and the express Báthory leave Warsaw daily for Budapest (13 hours, 901km) passing through Bratislava or Štúrovo and Katowice. The Cracóvia runs from Kraków to Budapest (10½ hours, 590km) via Košice. Another train, the Rákóczi, links Budapest with Košice.

Three daily trains cover the 90km from Košice to Miskolc (two hours). The 2km hop from Sátoraljaújhely to Slovenské Nové Mesto is only a four-minute ride on the train, which runs just once at day at 8.40am.

BULGARIA AND SERBIA & MONTENEGRO

The Transbalkan, which originates in Thessaloniki in northern Greece and travels via Bucharest, links Sofia with Budapest (25 hours, 1366km). Trains between Budapest and Belgrade (seven hours, 374km) via Subotica are the Beograd and the IC Avala.

Two daily trains make the 1¾-hour, 45km-long journey daily between Subotica and Szeged.

CROATIA, SLOVENIA AND BOSNIA & HERCEGOVINA

You can get to Budapest from Zagreb (seven hours, 395km) on two trains that pass through Siófok on Lake Balaton's southern shore: the Maestral, which originates in Split, and the EC Goldoni, which goes from Venice to Budapest via Ljubljana (10 hours, 504km). Two other trains from Ljubljana are the IC Citadella and the EN Venezia, which also comes from Venice. The IC 817/816 linking Sarajevo with Budapest (14 hours, 616km) goes via Pécs.

UKRAINE & RUSSIA

From Moscow to Budapest (42 hours, 2106km), there's only the Tisza Express, which travels via Kyiv and Lvov in Ukraine. Most nationalities require a transit visa to travel through Ukraine.

ROMANIA

From Bucharest to Budapest (14 hours, 874km) you can choose from four trains: the Dacia, the EN Ister, the Transbalkan and the Pannonia. All go via Arad (5½ hours, 253km) and some require seat reservations.

There are two daily connections from Cluj-Napoca to Budapest (eight hours, 402km) via Oradea: the Ady Endre and the Corona. The EC Traianus links Budapest with Timişoara (six hours, 310km).

RIVER

A hydrofoil service on the Danube River between Budapest and Vienna (5½ to 6½ hours, 282km) operates daily from early April to October; passengers can disembark at Bratislava with advance notice. Adult one-way/return fares for Vienna are €79/99 and for Bratislava €69/89. Students with ISIC cards pay €67/84 to Vienna and €59/76 to Bratislava, and children under six go free. Taking a bicycle costs €18 each way.

In Budapest, ferries arrive and depart from the International Ferry Pier (Nemzetközi hajóállomás) on V Belgrád rakpart, between the Elizabeth (Erzsébet híd) and Independence (Szabadság híd)

bridges on the Pest side. In Vienna, the boat docks at the Reichsbrücke pier near Mexikoplatz.

In April and from mid-September to October there is a daily sailing at 9am from both Budapest and Vienna. From May to mid-September the boats leave both cities at 8am.

For information and tickets contact **Mahart PassNave** (Map p86; ☎ 1-484 4013; www .mahartpassnave.hu; V Belgrád rakpart; 8am-6pm) in Budapest and **Mahart PassNave Wien** (☎ 01-72 92 161/2; Handelskai 265) in Vienna.

GETTING AROUND

Hungary's domestic transport system is efficient, comprehensive and inexpensive. In general, almost everything runs to schedule, and the majority of Hungary's towns and cities are easily negotiated on foot.

AIR

There are no scheduled flights within Hungary. The cost of domestic air taxis is prohibitive (eg from at least 150,000Ft for up to three people from Budapest to Szeged and back), and the trips can take almost as long as the train, when you add the time it takes to get to and from the airports.

Two air taxi companies are **Farnair Hungary** (☎ 1-347 6040; www.farnair.com), which flies to/from the airstrip next to Ferihegy Terminal 1, and **Jetstream** (☎ 06 20 399 6782; www .jetstream.hu in Hungarian), based at Tököl airport on Csepel Island opposite Százhalombatta, about 30km southwest of central Budapest.

BICYCLE

Hungary offers endless opportunities for cyclists: challenging slopes in the north, much gentler terrain in Transdanubia and flat though windy (and hot in summer) cycling on the Great Plain. The problem is bicycle rentals. They can be very hard to come by and your best bets are camping grounds, resort hotels and – very occasionally – bicycle repair shops. See Activities under the various cities and towns for guidance.

Remember when planning your itinerary that bicycles are banned from all motorways and national highways with a single digit, and bikes must be equipped with lights and reflectors. Bicycles can be taken on many trains but not on buses.

For more information, see p50.

BOAT

From April to late October the Budapest-based shipping company Mahart PassNave (p383) runs excursion boats on the Danube from Budapest to Szentendre, Vác, Visegrád and Esztergom; and hydrofoils from Budapest to Visegrád, Nagymaros and Esztergom between late May and early September. For details, see p132.

Mahart also schedules three to five excursions in summer from Budapest to places like Kalocsa and Solt on the Great Plain. Its services on certain sections of the Tisza River between April and mid-October – Sárospatak to Tokaj (2¼ hours, 36km), for example, and Szeged to Csongrád (4¼ hours, 72km) – are only available to groups of at least 40 people and cost between 19,000Ft and 29,000Ft per hour.

Other passenger ferry services are the Budapest transport company **BKV** (Budapest Transport Company; ☎ 369 1359; www.bkv.hu), which operates on the Danube in Budapest, and the **Balaton Shipping Co** (Balatoni Hajózási Rt; ☎ 84-310 050; www.balatonihajozas.hu; Krúdy sétány 2, Siófok), on Lake Balaton.

BUS

Hungary's **Volánbusz** (www.volanbusz.hu) network is a good – and sometimes necessary – alternative to the trains. In Southern Transdanubia and many parts of the Great Plain, buses are essential unless you are prepared to make several time-consuming changes on the train. For short trips around the Danube Bend or Lake Balaton areas, buses are preferable to trains.

In most cities and large towns it is usually possible to catch at least one direct bus a day to fairly far-flung areas of the country – for example, Pécs to Sopron (5½ hours, 285km) or Eger to Szeged (five hours, 240km).

National buses arrive and depart from Budapest's *távolságiautóbusz pályaudvar* (long-distance bus stations), not the local stations, which are called *helyiautóbusz pályaudvar*. Outside the capital the stations are often found side by side or in the same building. Arrive early to confirm the correct departure bay or *kocsiállás* (stand), and be sure to check the individual schedule posted at the stop itself; the times shown can be different from those shown on the *tábla* (main board).

Tickets are usually purchased directly from the driver, who gives change and will hand you a receipt as a ticket. There are sometimes queues for intercity buses (especially on Friday afternoon), so it's wise to arrive early. Smoking is not allowed on buses in Hungary, though a 10- or 20-minute rest stop is made about every two or three hours. Seats on Volánbusz are spaced far enough apart for you to be able to fit your pack or bag between your knees.

Posted bus timetables can be horribly confusing if you don't speak Hungarian. The things to remember when reading a timetable are that *indulás* means 'departures' and *érkezés* means 'arrivals'. Some timetable symbols are shown in the table, p384.

Numbers one to seven in a circle refer to the days of the week, beginning with Monday. Written footnotes you might see include: *naponta* (daily), *hétköznap* (weekdays), *munkanap* (workdays), *szabadnap* (Saturday), *munkaszünetes nap* (Sunday

BUS TIMETABLE SYMBOLS

✕	Monday to Saturday (except public holidays)
⊗	Monday to Friday (except public holidays)
⊠	Monday to Thursday (except public holidays)
☐	first working day of the week (usually Monday)
⊤	last working day of the week (usually Friday)
⊙	Saturday & public holidays
⊕	Saturday, Sunday & public holidays
+	Sunday & public holidays
⊞	day before the first working day of the week (usually Sunday but Monday when Sunday is a public holiday)
▼	school days
▽	working days during school holidays (mid-June to August; first week of November; Christmas & New Year; one week in March/April)

and holidays), *szabad és munkaszünetes nap* (Saturday, Sunday and holidays), *szabadnap kivételével naponta* (daily except Saturday), *munkaszünetes nap kivételével naponta* (daily except holidays) and *iskolai nap* (school days).

In general bus services to/from most inland destinations, but especially north and north-central Hungary, are served by **Népliget bus station** (Map pp88-9; ☎ 1-219 8080; IX Üllői út 131; Ⓜ M3 Népliget; Ⓨ ticket office 6am-6pm Mon-Fri Sep-May, 6-8pm Mon-Fri Jun-Aug, 6am-4pm Sat & Sun). Generally the **Stadionok bus station** (Map pp80-1; ☎ 1-251 0125, 252 2995; XIV Hungária körút 48-52; Ⓜ M2 Stadionok; Ⓨ ticket office 6am-6pm Mon-Fri, 6am-4pm Sat & Sun) serves cities and towns to the east of the capital while buses to south-west Hungary use **Etele tér bus station** (Map pp88-9; ☎ 1-382 4900; XI Etele tér; red bus No 7; Ⓨ 6am-6pm) in Buda.

The **Árpád Bridge bus station** (Map pp78-9; ☎ 1-329 1450; XIII Róbert Károly körút; Ⓜ M3 Árpád híd; Ⓨ ticket office 6am-8pm) on the Pest side of Árpád Bridge is the place to catch buses for the Danube Bend and some towns in the Northern Uplands (eg Balassagyarmat, Szécsény and Salgótarján). The small **Széna tér bus station** (Map pp80-1; ☎ 1-201 3688; I Széna tér 1/a; Ⓨ ticket office 6.30am-4.30pm; Ⓜ M3 Moszkva tér) in Buda handles some traffic to and from the Pilis Hills and towns northwest of the capital, with a half-dozen departures to Esztergom (from bay No 5) as an alternative to the Árpád.

A few of the larger bus stations have left-rooms, but they generally close early (around 6pm). Check your bag at the train station, which is almost always nearby; the left luggage offices there keep much longer hours.

Costs

Bus fares are between 20% and 30% more expensive than comparable 2nd-class train fares. At the time of writing Volánbusz charged:

fare	distance
97Ft	for up to 5km
133Ft	for 10km
605Ft	for 50km
1210Ft	for 100km
2410Ft	for 200km
3630Ft	for 300km

CAR & MOTORCYCLE
Automobile Associations

In the event of a breakdown, the so-called **Yellow Angels** (Sárga Angyal; ☎ nationwide 24hr 188, Budapest 1-345 1755) of the **Hungarian Automobile Club** (Map pp80-1; Magyar Autóklub; ☎ 1-212 2821, 24hr helpline ☎ 1- 345 1755; II Rómer Flóris 4/a) do basic car repairs free of charge if you belong to an affiliated organisation such as AAA in the USA, AA or RAC in the UK. Towing, however, is still very expensive even with these reciprocal memberships. The number to ring in an emergency is ☎ 188.

For 24-hour information on traffic and public road conditions around Hungary, contact **Útinform** (☎ 1-336 2400, 322 2238; www .kozut.hu). In the capital ring **Főinform** (☎ 1-317 1173).

Driving Licence

Foreign driving licences are valid for one year after entering Hungary. If you don't hold a European driving licence and plan to drive here, obtain an International Driving Permit (IDP) from your local automobile association before you leave – you'll need a passport photo and a valid local licence. It is usually inexpensive and valid for one year. Be aware that an IDP is not valid unless accompanied by your original driver's licence.

Third-party liability insurance is compulsory in Hungary. If your car is registered in the EU, it is assumed you have it. Other motorists must show a Green Card or they will have to buy insurance at the border.

Fuel

Ólommentes benzin (unleaded petrol 95/98 octane) is available everywhere. Most stations also have *gázolaj* (diesel).

Hire

In general, you must be at least 21 years old and have had your licence for a year to rent a car. Drivers under 25 sometimes have to pay a surcharge. All the big international firms have offices in Budapest, and there are scores of local companies throughout the country, but don't expect many bargains. For details, see p122.

Insurance

All accidents should be reported to the police (☎ 107) immediately. Several insurance

Road Distances (km)

	Békéscsaba	Budapest	Debrecen	Dunaújváros	Eger	Győr	Kaposvár	Kecskemét	Miskolc	Nyíregyháza	Pécs	Sopron	Szeged	Székesfehérvár	Szolnok	Szombathely	Veszprém
Budapest	203																
Debrecen	130	226															
Dunaújváros	210	67	277														
Eger	220	128	130	194													
Győr	327	123	350	142	251												
Kaposvár	314	189	381	146	317	201											
Kecskemét	124	85	191	86	158	208	190										
Miskolc	228	179	98	246	61	303	368	199									
Nyíregyháza	179	245	49	311	145	368	434	240	93								
Pécs	283	198	367	131	326	241	67	176	377	416							
Sopron	414	217	436	229	338	87	220	295	390	455	287						
Szeged	94	171	224	158	245	294	251	86	286	273	189	381					
Székesfehérvár	258	66	292	55	194	87	126	134	245	310	153	174	206				
Szolnok	107	97	129	148	121	220	252	62	162	179	238	307	130	163			
Szombathely	404	222	448	211	350	105	178	280	402	467	245	70	352	156	319		
Veszprém	292	110	336	99	238	77	127	168	289	355	166	143	240	44	207	111	
Zalaegerszeg	392	224	450	216	352	154	124	268	403	468	190	124	342	161	321	54	119

companies handle auto liability, and minor claims can be settled without complications. Any claim on insurance policies bought in Hungary can be made to **Allianz Hungária** (☎ 06 40 421 421, 01-269 0033) in Budapest. It is one of the largest insurance companies in Hungary and deals with foreigners all the time.

Road Conditions

Roads in Hungary are generally good – in some cases excellent nowadays – and there are several basic types. Motorways, preceded by an 'M' (including the curiously named M0 half-ring road around Budapest), will eventually total eight. At present they link the capital with Vienna via Győr (M1) and Croatia via the southern shore of Lake Balaton (M7). They also run along the eastern bank of the Danube Bend (M2), part of the way to Slovakia as far as Miskolc (M3) and en route to Szeged and Serbia via Kecskemét as far as Kiskunfélegyháza (M5). National highways (dual carriageways) are designated by a single digit without a prefix and fan out mostly from Budapest. Secondary/ tertiary roads have two/three digits.

Road Rules

You must drive on the right. Speed limits for cars and motorbikes are consistent throughout the country and strictly enforced: 50km/h in built-up areas (from the town sign as you enter to the same sign with a red line through it as you leave); 90km/h on secondary and tertiary roads; 110km/h on most highways/dual carriageways; and 130km/h on motorways. Exceeding the limit will earn you a fine of between 5000Ft and 30,000Ft, which must be paid by postal cheque or at any post office.

The use of seat belts in the front (and in the back – if fitted – outside built-up areas) is compulsory in Hungary, but this rule is often ignored. Using a mobile phone while driving is prohibited but again this law is universally ignored. A law that is taken very seriously is the one requiring all drivers to use their headlights throughout the day outside built-up areas. Motorcyclists must illuminate headlights too, but at all times and everywhere. They also must wear helmets – a law that is strictly enforced.

There is virtually a 100% ban on alcohol when you are driving, and this rule is taken very seriously by all (p372). It's not much fun while on holiday, but you'll have to follow the lead of Hungarians and take turns with a companion in abstaining at meal and other times. Those who don't believe this warning will learn the hard way – as one of us did.

In any case, when driving in Hungary you'll want to keep your wits about you; this can be quite a trying place for motorists. It's not that drivers don't know the highway code; everyone has to attend a driver's education course and pass an examination. (That 'T' on the roof or back of a vehicle indicates *tanuló vezető* or 'learner driver', by the way – not 'taxi'.) But overtaking on blind curves, making turns from the outside lane, running stop signs and lights, and jumping lanes in roundabouts are everyday occurrences.

Though many cities and towns have a confusing system of one-way streets, pedestrian zones and bicycle lanes, parking is not a big problem in the provinces. Most centres now require that you 'pay and display' when parking your vehicle – parking disks, coupons or stickers are available at newsstands, petrol stations and, increasingly, automated ticket machines. In smaller towns and cities a warden (usually a friendly pensioner) will approach you as soon as you emerge from the car and collect 100Ft or so for each hour you plan to park. In Budapest parking on the street now costs between 120Ft and 400Ft per hour, depending on the neighbourhood.

You must obtain a motorway pass or *matrica* (vignette) to access Hungary's motorways. Passes, which cost 1120Ft for four days (1450Ft between May and September), 2300Ft for 10 days and 3900Ft for a month, are available at petrol stations, post offices and some motorway entrances and border crossings.

HITCHING

Hitching is never entirely safe in any country and we don't recommend it. Travellers who decide to hitch are taking a small but potentially serious risk. However, many people choose to hitch, and the advice that follows should help to make their journeys as fast and safe as possible.

Hitchhiking is legal everywhere in Hungary except on motorways. Though it isn't as popular as it once was (and can be very difficult here), the road to Lake Balaton is always jammed with hitchhikers in the holiday season. There is a ride-sharing service in the capital called Kenguru (p123) that matches drivers and passengers for a fee.

LOCAL TRANSPORT
Public Transport

Urban transport is well developed in Hungary, with efficient bus and, in many cities and towns, trolleybus services. Budapest, Szeged, Miskolc and Debrecen also have trams, and there's a three-line metro (underground or subway) system and a suburban railway known as the HÉV in the capital.

You'll probably make extensive use of public transport in Budapest but little (if any) in provincial towns and cities: with very few exceptions, most places are quite manageable on foot, and bus services are not all that frequent except in the largest settlements. Generally, city buses meet incoming long-distance trains; hop onto anything waiting outside when you arrive and you'll get close to the city centre.

You must purchase transport tickets (usually from 150Ft) at newsstands or ticket windows beforehand and validate them once aboard. Travelling without a ticket (or 'riding black') is an offence; you'll be put off and fined on the spot. Don't try to argue; the inspector has heard it all before.

Taxi

Taxis are plentiful on the streets of most Hungarian cities and, if you are charged the correct fare, very reasonably priced. Flag fall varies, but a fare between 6am and 10pm is from 200Ft (in Budapest from 300Ft), with the charge per kilometre about the same, depending on whether you booked it by telephone (cheaper) or hailed it on the street. The best places to find taxis are in ranks at bus and train stations, near markets and around main squares. But you can flag down cruising taxis anywhere at any time. At night, vacant taxis have an illuminated sign on the roof.

TOURS

A number of travel agencies, including Vista and Ibusz (p68), and Cityrama and Hungary

Program Centrum (p102) offer excursions and special-interest guided tours (horse riding, cycling, bird-watching, Jewish culture etc) to every corner of Hungary.

By way of example, Cityrama has a 4½-hour tour by boat and bus to Szentendre or Gödöllő by bus (11,000Ft; children under 12 free or half-price); and an 8½-hour tour of the Danube Bend by coach and boat, with stops at Visegrád and Esztergom (14,000Ft). Cityrama also offers day trips to Lake Balaton (Balatonfüred and Tihany) and Herend (16,000Ft, nine to 10 hours), as well as to Lajosmizse on the Southern Plain (18,000Ft, eight hours). Hungary Program Centrum offers similar tours at almost the same prices, as well as an eight-hour trip to Bugac in Kiskunság National Park (19,000Ft) and a nine-hour tour of the Eger wine region (22,000Ft). Vista has a six-day tour of the country that takes in parts of the Northern Uplands, Great Plain, Southern Transdanubia and Lake Balaton region. The tour includes accommodation and half-board and costs €599/499 per person single/double-sharing.

TRAIN

MÁV (www.mav.hu) operates reliable and relatively comfortable train services on just under 8000km of track, exactly a third of which is electrified. All the main railway lines converge on Budapest, though many secondary lines link provincial cities and towns. There are three main stations in Budapest. In general, Keleti station serves destinations in the Northern Uplands and the Northeast; Nyugati station the Great Plain and the Danube Bend; and Déli station Transdanubia and Lake Balaton. But these are not hard and fast rules; confirm the departure station when you buy your ticket. The 24-hour number for domestic train information is ☎ 06 40 49 49 49 nationwide or 1-461 5400 in Budapest.

Tickets for *egy útra* (one way) and *odavissza* (return) journeys in 1st and 2nd class are available at stations, the **MÁV central ticket office** (☎ 1-461 5400, 322 8082; VI Andrássy út 35; ☺ 9am-6pm Mon-Fri Apr-Sep, 9am-5pm Mon-Fri Oct-Mar) in Budapest and certain travel agencies.

There are several types of train. Express (Ex on the timetable) trains usually require a seat reservation. The InterCity (IC) trains, the fastest and most comfortable in

Hungary, and EuroCity (EC) ones levy a supplement, which generally includes a seat. *Gyorsvonat* (fast trains), indicated on the timetable by boldface type, a thicker route line and/or an 'S', often require a seat reservation. *Személyvonat* (passenger trains) are the real milk runs and stop at every city, town, village and hamlet along the way.

Depending on the station, departures and arrivals are announced by loudspeaker/Tannoy or on an electronic board and are always on a printed timetable – yellow for *indul* (departures) and white for *érkezik* (arrivals). On these, fast trains are marked in red and local trains in black. The number (or sometimes letter) next to the word *vágány* indicates the 'platform' from which the train departs or arrives; for symbols and abbreviations used, see the table on p384.

If you plan to do a lot of travelling by train, get yourself a copy of MÁV's official timetable (*Menetrend*; 850/1550Ft in small/large format), which is available at most large stations and the MÁV office on Andrássy út in Budapest. It also has explanatory notes in several languages, including English.

All train stations have left-luggage offices, some of which stay open 24 hours. You sometimes have to pay the fee (300/600Ft per normal/large bag per day) at another office or window nearby, which is usually marked *pénztár* (cashier).

Some trains have a carriage especially for bicycles; on other trains, bicycles must be placed in the first or last cars. You are able to freight a bicycle for 25% of a full 2nd-class fare.

Tickets & Fares

Domestic 2nd-class train fares are 946/1926/2676/3100/3524Ft for 100/200/300/400/500km. To travel 1st class costs 50% more.

Passengers holding a ticket of insufficient value must pay the difference plus a fine of 2000Ft. If you buy your ticket on the train rather than at the station, there's a 500Ft surcharge. You can be fined 500Ft for travelling on a domestic IC train without having paid the supplement and the same amount for not having a seat reservation when it is compulsory.

On Hungarian domestic trains, seat reservations may be compulsory (indicated on

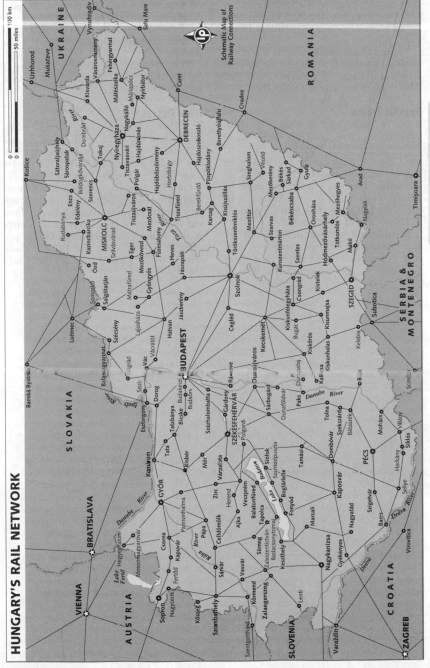

HUNGARY'S RAIL NETWORK

the timetable by an 'R' in a box), mandatory only on trains departing from Budapest (an 'R' in a circle) or simply available (just a plain 'R').

Express trains usually require a seat reservation costing 130Ft, while the IC ones levy a surcharge of between 200Ft and 480Ft, which includes the reservation.

Special Trains

Some 16 *keskenynyomközü vonat* (narrow-gauge trains) for the most part run by Állami Erdei Vasutak (ÁEV; State Forest Railways) on 220km of track can be found in many wooded and hilly areas of the country. They are usually taken as a return excursion by holiday-makers, but in some cases can be useful for getting from A to B (eg Miskolc to Lillafüred and the Bükk Hills).

An independent branch of MÁV runs vintage *nosztalgiavonat* (steam trains) in summer, generally along the northern shore of Lake Balaton (eg from Keszthely to Tapolca via Badacsonytomaj) and along the Danube Bend from Budapest to Szob or Esztergom. For information contact **MÁV Nostalgia** (☎ 1-238 0558; www.mavnosztalgia.hu) in Keleti train station.

The only other train line in Hungary is called GySEV and links Győr and Sopron with Ebenfurth in Austria.

Train Passes

The Hungary pass from Eurail, available to non-European residents only, costs US$52/82 for five/10 days of 2nd-class travel in a 15-day period and US$79/124 for 1st class. Children five to 11 pay half-price.

Euro Domino Hungary is a pass that allows European residents to travel on Hungary's entire rail network for between three and eight days of travel over a one-month period. A three-day pass costs €92/60 per adult in 1st/2nd class and €47 for those aged 12 to 25. Eight-day passes cost €203/136/100.

Health

Good travel health depends on your predeparture preparations, your daily health care while travelling and the way you handle any medical problem that develops while you are on the road. Although the potential dangers might seem frightening, in reality few travellers experience anything more than an upset stomach.

BEFORE YOU GO

A little planning before departure, particularly for pre-existing illnesses or conditions, will save trouble later. See your dentist before a long trip, carry a spare pair of contact lenses or glasses, and take your optical prescription with you. Bring medications in their original, clearly labelled containers. A signed and dated letter from your physician describing your medical conditions and medications, including their generic names, is also a good idea. If carrying syringes or needles, be sure to have a physician's letter documenting their medical necessity.

INSURANCE

If you're an EU citizen, a European Health Insurance Card (EHIC), available from health centres or, in the UK, post offices, covers you for most medical care. It will not cover you for nonemergencies or emergency repatriation. Citizens from other countries should find out if there is a reciprocal arrangement for free medical care between their country and Hungary.

In Hungary, foreigners are entitled to first-aid and ambulance services only when they have suffered an accident and require immediate medical attention; follow-up treatment and medicine must be paid for.

If you do need health insurance while travelling (p372), consider a policy that covers you for the worst possible scenario, such as an accident requiring an ambulance or an emergency flight home. Find out in advance if your insurance plan will make payments directly to providers or reimburse you later for overseas health expenditures. The former option is generally preferable, as it doesn't require you to pay out of pocket in a foreign country.

RECOMMENDED VACCINATIONS

Hungary doesn't require any vaccination of international travellers, but the World Health Organisation (WHO) recommends travellers be covered for diphtheria, tetanus, measles, mumps, rubella and polio, regardless of their destination. Since most vaccines don't produce immunity until at least two weeks after they're given, visit a physician or clinic at least six weeks before departure.

INTERNET RESOURCES

The WHO's online publication *International Travel and Health* is revised annually and is available at www.who.int/ith. Other useful websites:

www.ageconcern.org.uk Advice on travel for the elderly.
www.fitfortravel.scot.nhs.uk General travel advice for the lay person.
www.mariestopes.org.uk Information on women's health and contraception.
www.mdtravelhealth.com Travel-health recommendations for every country; updated daily.

It's usually a good idea to consult your government's travel health website before departure, if one is available:
Australia (www.dfat.gov.au/travel/)
Canada (www.travelhealth.gc.ca)
UK (www.dh.gov.uk/home/fs/en)
USA (www.cdc.gov/travel/)

HEALTH

IN TRANSIT

DEEP VEIN THROMBOSIS

Blood clots may form in the legs (deep vein thrombosis or DVT) during plane flights, chiefly because of prolonged immobility. The longer the flight, the greater the risk. The chief symptom of DVT is swelling or pain in the foot, ankle or calf – usually but not always – on just one side. When a blood clot travels to the lungs, it may cause chest pain and breathing difficulties. Travellers with any of these symptoms should seek medical attention immediately.

To prevent the development of DVT on long-haul flights, you should walk about the cabin, contract the leg muscles while sitting, drink plenty of fluids and avoid alcohol.

JET LAG & MOTION SICKNESS

To avoid jet lag, which is common when crossing more than five time zones, you should drink plenty of nonalchoholic fluids and eat light meals. Upon arrival, get exposure to natural sunlight and readjust your schedule (for meals, sleep and so on) as soon as possible.

Antihistamines such as dimenhydrinate (Dramamine) and meclizine (Antivert, Bonine) are usually the first choice for treating motion sickness. A herbal alternative is ginger.

IN HUNGARY

AVAILABILITY & COST OF HEALTH CARE

Medical care in Hungary is generally adequate and good for routine problems but not complicated conditions. Treatment at a rendelő intézet (public outpatient clinic) costs little, but doctors working privately will charge much more. Very roughly, a consultation in an orvosi rendelő (doctor's surgery) costs from 5000Ft while a home visit is from 10,000Ft.

Most large towns and all of Budapest's 23 districts have a gyógyszertár or patika (rotating 24-hour pharmacy). A sign on the door of any pharmacy will help you locate the closest one.

INFECTIOUS DISEASES

Tickborne encephalitis is spread by *kullancs* (ticks), which burrow under the skin; in recent years, it has become a common problem in parts of Central and Eastern Europe, especially eastern Austria, Germany, Hungary and the Czech Republic. Encephalitis is a serious infection of the brain, and vaccination is advised for campers and hikers, particularly in Transdanubia and the Northern Uplands between May and September. For up-to-date information log on to www.masta.org/tickalert.

Lyme disease is another tick-transmitted infection not unknown in Central and Eastern Europe. The illness usually begins with a spreading rash at the site of the tick bite and is accompanied by fever, headaches, extreme fatigue, aching joints and muscles and mild neck stiffness. If untreated, these symptoms usually resolve over several weeks, but over subsequent weeks or months disorders of the nervous system, heart and joints might develop.

Poliomyelitis is spread through contaminated food and water. It's one of the vaccines given in childhood and should be boosted every 10 years, either orally or by injection.

Typhoid and hepatitis A are spread through contaminated food (particularly shellfish) and water. Typhoid can cause septicaemia; hepatitis A causes liver inflammation and jaundice. Neither is usually fatal, but recovery can be prolonged. Typhoid vaccine (typhim Vi, typherix) will give protection for three years. In some countries, the oral vaccine Vivotif is also available. Hepatitis A vaccine (Avaxim, VAQTA, Havrix) is given as an injection; a single dose will give protection for up to a year, a booster after a year gives 10 years' protection. Hepatitis A and typhoid vaccines can also be given as a single dose vaccine, hepatyrix or viatim.

Rabies is spread through bites or licks on broken skin from an infected animal and is always fatal unless treated. Three injections are needed over a month. If you have not been vaccinated, you will need a course of five injections starting 24 hours or as soon as possible after the injury.

ENVIRONMENTAL HAZARDS
Insect Bites & Stings

Mosquitoes are a real scourge around Hungary's lakes and rivers in summer; the bloodthirsty beasties might not carry malaria but can still cause irritation and infection. Just make sure you're armed with a DEET-based insect repellent, or *rovarírtó*, and wear long-sleeved shirts and long trousers around sundown

Bees and wasps cause real problems only to those with a severe allergy (anaphylaxis). They should carry an 'epipen' or similar adrenaline injection.

Water

The WHO reports that arsenic in Hungary's drinking water has been detected at concentrations higher than the guideline level of 0.01 mg/L. Avoid drinking tap water in favour of the bottle stuff, which is available everywhere.

WOMEN'S HEALTH

If using oral contraceptives, remember that some antibiotics, diarrhoea and vomiting can stop the pill from working and lead to the risk of pregnancy. Time zones, gastro-intestinal upsets and antibiotics do not affect injectable contraception.

Travelling during pregnancy is usually possible but always consult your doctor before planning your trip. The riskiest times for travel are during the first 12 weeks of pregnancy and after 30 weeks.

SEXUAL HEALTH

The numbers of registered AIDS cases in Hungary and those who are HIV-positive are relatively low (just over 1100), though Hungarian epidemiologists estimate the actual number of those infected with HIV to be around 3000 or more. That number could multiply substantially as Budapest claims its less-than-distinctive title of 'sex industry capital of Eastern and Central Europe'. Two AIDS lines to contact in Budapest are the **Anonymous AIDS Association** (☎ 1-466-9283; ☺ 5-8pm Mon, Wed & Thu, 9am-noon Tue & Fri) and the **AIDS helpline** (☎ 1-338 2419, 266 0465; ☺ 8am-3pm Mon-Thu, 8am-1pm Fri), with some English spoken.

HEALTH

Language

Hungarian (*Magyar*) is a member of the Ugric group of the Uralic family of languages that is related very, very distantly to Finnish (with five million speakers), Estonian (one million) and about a dozen other minority languages in Russia and western Siberia (with far fewer speakers). It's not an Indo-European language, meaning that English is actually closer to French, Russian or Hindi in vocabulary and structure than it is to Hungarian. As a result you'll come across very few recognisable words – with the exception of borrowings like *disko*, *szex* or *hello*, which is the slangy way young Hungarians say 'goodbye'.

There are also a fair number of misleading homophones (words with the same sound but different meanings) in Hungarian: *test* is not a quiz but 'body'; *fog* is 'tooth'; *comb* is 'thigh'; and *part* is 'shore'. *Ifjúság*, pronounced (very roughly) 'if you shag', means 'youth'; *sajt* (pronounced 'shite'), as in every visiting Briton's favourite *sajtburger*, means 'cheese'.

For more Hungarian words and phrases than there is space for here, get a copy of Lonely Planet's *Hungarian Phrasebook*.

PRONUNCIATION

Hungarian may seem daunting with its long words and strange-looking accents, but it's surprisingly easy to pronounce. Like English, Hungarian isn't always written the way it's pronounced, but if you stick to the phonetic guides that accompany each phrase or word you can't go wrong.

The Hungarian alphabet has 44 letters and is based on the Latin alphabet. It includes accented letters and consonant combinations. The stroke over a vowel in the pronunciation guides (eg **ā**) means you say it as a long vowel sound.

The letters **ö** and **ő**, and **ü** and **ű**, are listed as separate pairs of letters in dictionaries (following **o**, **ó** and **u**, **ú** respectively). The consonant combinations **cs**, **dz**, **dzs**, **gy**, **ly**, **ny**, **sz**, **ty** and **zs** also have separate entries.

Letter	Pronunciation Guide	
a	o	as in 'hot'
á	aa	as in 'father'
e	e	as in 'bet'
é	ay	as the 'ai' in 'air"
i	i	as in 'hit'
í	ee	as in 'meet'
o	aw	as in 'law' but short
ó	āw	as in 'awl'
ö	eu	as the 'u' in 'curt' but short
ő	ēū	as the 'er' in 'her' (British)
u	u	as in 'pull'
ú	ū	as in 'rule'
ü	ew	like **i** but with rounded lips (like **u** in French *tu*)
ű	ēw	as in strewn' **ü**

Remember, always pronounce **y** as in 'yes', but without a vowel sound. We've used an apostrophe (as in **n'**, **d'**, **t'**) to show this **y** sound when it falls at the end of a syllable. You'll also see double consonants like **bb**, **dd** or **tt** – draw them out a little longer than you would in English.

Letter	Pronunciation Guide	
c	ts	as in 'rats'
cs	ch	as in 'cheese'
dz	dz	as in 'adze'
dzs	j	as in 'joke'
gy	dy/d'	as the 'du' in 'dune' (British)
j/ly	y	as in 'yes'
ny	n'	as the 'ny' in 'canyon'
r	r	as in 'run' (but rolled)

s	sh	as in 'ship'
sz	s	as in 'sit'
ty	ty/t'	as the 'tu' in 'tube' (British)
zs	zh	as the 's' in 'pleasure'

Syllables & Word Stress

In this language guide, the syllables in the pronunciation guides are separated by a dot (eg *kawn*-tsert) so you'll have no problem isolating each unit of sound. Accents don't influence word stress which always falls on the first syllable of the word. We've used italics to show stress, which should make things even easier.

ACCOMMODATION

Where's a ...?

Hol van egy ...?	hawl von ed' ...
camping ground	
kemping	kem·ping
guesthouse	
panzió	pon·zi·āw
hotel	
szálloda	saal·law·do
room in a private home	
fizető vendégszoba	fi·ze·tēū ven·dayg saw·bo
youth hostel	
ifjúsági szálló	if·yū·shaa·gi saal·lāw

What's the address?

| Mi a cím? | mi o tseem |

May I see it?

| Megnézhetem? | meg·nayz·he·tem |

I'll take it.

| Kiveszem. | ki·ve·sem |

I'd like to book a ... room, please.

Szeretnék egy ... szobát foglalni.	
se·ret·nayk ed' ... saw·baat fawg·lol·ni	
single	
egyágyas	ed'·aa·dyosh
double	
francia ágyas/	fran·tsi·o aa·dyosh/
dupla ágyas	dup·lo·aa·dyosh
twin	
kétágyas	kayt·aa·dyosh

How much is it per ...?

Mennyibe kerül egy ...?	men'·nyi·be ke·rewl ed' ...
night	
éjszakára	ay·so·kaa·ro
person	
főre	fēū·re

CONVERSATION & ESSENTIALS

Be Polite!

As in many other Western languages, verbs in Hungarian have polite and informal forms in the singular and plural. The polite address (marked as 'pol' in this section) is used with strangers, older people, officials and service staff. The informal address (marked as 'inf' in this language guide) is reserved for friends, children and sometimes foreigners, but is used much more frequently and sooner than its equivalent in, say, French. Almost all young people use it among themselves – even with strangers. In the following phrases, the polite 'you' (*Ön* and *Önök*) is given except for situations where you might wish to establish a more personal relationship.

Note that when you want to say 'Hello', 'Hi', or 'Bye', the word will change depending on whether you are speaking to one person or more than one. Look for the symbols 'sg' (singular) or 'pl' (plural) to determine which word to use.

Hello.

| Szervusz. (sg) | ser·vus |
| Szervusztok. (pl) | ser·vus·tawk |

Hi.

| Szia/Sziasztok. (sg/pl) | si·o/si·os·tawk |

Good ...

Jó ... kívánok.	yāw ... kee·vaa·nawk
morning	
reggelt	reg·gelt
afternoon/day	
napot	no·pawt
evening	
estét	esh·tayt

Goodbye.

Viszontlátásra. (pol)	vi·sawnt·laa·taash·ro
Szia. (inf sg)	si·o
Sziasztok. (inf pl)	si·os·tawk

Good night.

| Jó éjszakát. | yāw ay·y·so·kaat |

Yes.

| Igen. | i·gen |

No.

| Nem. | nem |

Please.

| Kérem. (pol) | kay·rem |
| Kérlek. (inf) | kayr·lek |

Thank you (very much).
(Nagyon) Köszönöm. (no·dyawn) keu·seu·neum
You're welcome.
Szívesen. see·ve·shen
Excuse me. (to get attention)
Elnézést kérek. el·nay·zaysht kay·rek
Excuse me. (to get past)
Bocsánat. baw·chaa·not
Sorry.
Sajnálom. shoy·naa·lawm
How are you?
Hogy van? (pol) hawd' von
Hogy vagy? (inf) hawd' vod'
Fine. And you?
Jól. És Ön/te? (pol/inf) yāwl aysh eun/te
What's your name?
Mi a neve? (pol) mi o ne·ve
Mi a neved? (inf) mi o ne·ved
My name is ...
A nevem ... o ne·vem ...
I'm pleased to meet you.
Örvendek. eur·ven·dek
Where are you from?
Ön honnan jön? (pol) eun hawn·non yeun
Te honnan jössz? (inf) te hawn·non yeuss
I'm from ...
Én ... jövök. ayn ... yeu·veuk

Local Lingo
Great!
Nagyszerű! nod'·se·rēw
Maybe.
Talán. to·laan
Just a minute.
Egy pillanat. ed' pil·lo·not
No problem.
Nem probléma. nem prawb·lay·mo
Clear. (as in 'understood')
Világos. vi·laa·gawsh

DIRECTIONS
Where's (the market)?
Hol van (a piac)? hawl von (o pi·ots)
What's the address?
Mi a cím? mi o tseem
How do I get there?
Hogyan jutok oda? haw·dyon yu·tawk aw·do
How far is it?
Milyen messze van? mi·yen mes·se von
Can you show me (on the map)?
Meg tudja mutatni meg tud'·yo mu·tot·ni
nekem (a térképen)? ne·kem (o tayr·kay·pen)
It's straight ahead.
egyenesen előttünk van. e·dye·ne·shen e·lēūt·tewnk von

SIGNS	
Bejárat	Entrance
Kijárat	Exit
Nyitva	Open
Zárva	Closed
Foglalt	Reserved/Occupied
Felvilágosítás/Információ	Information
Belépni Tilos	No Entry
Tilos	Prohibited
Tilos a Dohányzás	No Smoking
Toalett/WC	Toilets
Férfiak	Men
Nők	Women

Turn ...
Forduljon ... fawr·dul·yawn ...
  at the corner
  a saroknál o sho·rawk·naal
  at the traffic lights
  a közlekedési o keuz·le·ke·day·shi
  lámpánál laam·paa·naal
  left/right
  balra/jobbra bol·ro/yawbb·ro

north	észak	ay·sok
south	dél	dayl
east	kelet	ke·let
west	nyugat	nyu·got

HEALTH
Where's the nearest ...?
Hol a legközelebbi ...? hawl o leg·keu·ze·leb·bi ...
  dentist
  fogorvos fawg·awr·vawsh
  doctor
  orvos awr·vawsh
  hospital
  kórház kāwr·haaz
  medical centre
  orvosi rendelő awr·vaw·shi ren·de·lēū
  (night) pharmacist
  (éjszaka nyitvatartó) (ay·so·ko nyit·vo·tor·tāw)
  gyógyszertár dyāwd'·ser·taar

I have a headache.
Fáj a fejem. faa·y o fe·yem
I have a sore throat.
Fáj a torkom. faa·y o tawr·kawm
I have (a) ... ... van. ... von
  asthma Asztmám ost·maam
  diarrhoea Hasmenésem hosh·me·nay·shem
  fever Lázam laa·zom
  nausea Hányingerem haan'·in·ge·rem

EMERGENCIES

Help!
Segítség!   she·geet·shayg
Could you please help?
Tudna segíteni?   tud·no she·gee·te·ni
Can I use your phone?
Használhatom a   hos·naal·ho·tawm o
telefonját?   te·le·fawn·yaat
Call the police!
Hívja a rendőrséget!   heev·yo o rend·ēūr·shay·get
I'm sick.
Rosszul vagyok.   raws·sul vo·dyawk
Call a doctor!
Hívjon orvost!   heev·yawn awr·vawsht
Where's the police station?
Hol a rendőrség?   hawl o rend·ēūr·shayg
Where are the toilets?
Hol a véce?   hawl o vay·tse
I'm lost.
Eltévedtem.   el·tay·ved·tem
Go away!
Menjen el!   men·yen el

I'm allergic to ...
Allergiás vagyok ...   ol·ler·gi·aash vo·dyawk ...
  antibiotics
  az antibiotikumokra   oz on·ti·bi·aw·ti·ku·mawk·ro
  penicillin
  a penicillinre   o pe·ni·tsil·lin·re

antiseptic
fertőzésgátló   fer·tēū·zaysh·gaat·law
contraceptives
fogamzásgátló   faw·gom·zaash·gaat·law
painkillers
fájdalomcsillapító   faa·y·do·lawm·chil·lo·pee·tāw

LANGUAGE DIFFICULTIES

Do you speak (English)?
Beszél (angolul)? (pol)   be·sayl (on·gaw·lul)
Beszélsz (angolul)? (inf)   be·sayls (on·gaw·lul)
Does anyone speak (English)?
Beszél valaki (angolul)?   be·sayl vo·lo·ki (on·gaw·lul)
I (don't) understand.
(Nem) Értem.   (nem) ayr·tem
What does ... mean?
Mit jelent az, hogy ...?   mit ye·lent oz hawd' ...
Could you please write it down?
Leírná, kérem.   le·eer·naa kay·rem

NUMBERS

0	nulla	nul·lo
1	egy	ed'
2	kettő/két	ket·tēū/kayt
3	három	haa·rawm
4	négy	nayd'
5	öt	eut
6	hat	hot
7	hét	hayt
8	nyolc	nyawlts
9	kilenc	ki·lents
10	tíz	teez
11	tizenegy	ti·zen·ed'
12	tizenkettő	ti·zen·ket·tēū
13	tizenhárom	ti·zen·haa·rawm
14	tizennégy	ti·zen·nayd'
15	tizenöt	ti·zen·eut
16	tizenhat	ti·zen·hot
17	tizenhét	ti·zen·hayt
18	tizennyolc	ti·zen'·yawlts
19	tizenkilenc	ti·zen·ki·lents
20	húsz	hūs
21	huszonegy	hu·sawn·ed'
22	huszonkettő	hu·sawn·ket·tēū
30	harminc	hor·mints
31	harmincegy	hor·mints·ed'
32	harminckettő	hor·mints·ket·tēū
40	negyven	ned'·ven
41	negyvenegy	ned'·ven·ed'
42	negyvenkettő	ned'·ven·ket·tēū
50	ötven	eut·ven
60	hatvan	hot·von
70	hetven	het·ven
80	nyolcvan	nyawlts·von
90	kilencven	ki·lents·ven
100	száz	saaz
200	kétszáz	kayt·saaz
1000	ezer	e·zer

How much? Mennyi?   men'·yi
How many? Hány?   haan'

SHOPPING & SERVICES

Where is ...?
Hol van ...?   hawl von ...
  an ATM
  egy bankautomata   ed' bonk·o·u·taw·mo·to
  a foreign exchange office
  egy valutaváltó   ed' vo·lu·to·vaal·tāw
  ügynökség   ewd'·neuk·shayg
  the market
  a piac   o pi·ots
  a shopping centre
  egy bevásárlóközpont   ed' be·vaa·shaar·law·keuz·pawnt
  a supermarket
  egy élelmiszeráruház   ed' ay·lel·mi·ser·aa·ru·haaz

LANGUAGE

I'd like to ...

Szeretnék ...	se·ret·nayk ...
change a travellers cheque	
bevâltani egy utazási	be·vaal·to·ni ed' u·to·zaa·shi
csekket	chek·ket
change money	
pénzt váltani	paynzt vaal·to·ni

Do you accept ...?

Elfogadnak ...?	el·faw·god·nok ...
credit cards	
hitelkártyát	hi·tel·kaar·tyaat
travellers cheques	
utazási csekket	u·to·zaa·shi chek·ket

Where can I buy ...?

Hol tudok venni ...?	hawl tu·dawk ven·ni ...
I'd like to buy ...	
Szeretnék venni ...	se·ret·nayk ven·ni ...
I'm just looking.	
Csak nézegetek.	chok nay·ze·ge·tek
How much is this?	
Mennyibe kerül ez?	men'·yi·be ke·rewl ez
Could you write down the price?	
Le tudná írni az árát?	le tud·naa eer·ni oz aa·raat
What time does it open/close?	
Mikor nyit/zár?	mi·kawr nyit/zaar

Where's the nearest public phone?
Hol a legközelebbi nyilvános telefon?
hawl o leg·keu·ze·leb·bi nyil·vaa·nawsh te·le·fawn
I want to buy a phonecard.
Szeretnék telefonkártyát venni.
se·ret·nayk te·le·fawn·kaar·tyaat ven·ni
Where's the local Internet café?
Hol van a legközelebbi internet kávézó?
hawl von o leg·keu·ze·leb·bi in·ter·net kaa·vay·zāw

I'd like to ...

Szeretném ...	se·ret·naym ...
check my email	
megnézni az	meg·nayz·ni oz
e-mailjeimet	ee·mayl·ye·i·met
get Internet access	
rámenni az internetre	raa·men·ni oz in·ter·net·re

TIME & DATE
What time is it?

Hány óra?	haan' āw·ra
It's (one/ten) o'clock.	
(Egy/Tíz) óra van.	(ed'/teez) āw·ra von
Five past (ten).	
Öt perccel múlt (tíz).	eut perts·tsel mült (teez)

Quarter past (ten).

Negyed (tizenegy).	ne·dyed (ti·zen·ed')
Half past (ten).	
Fél (tizenegy).	fayl (ti·zen·ed')

now	most	mawsht
today	ma	mo
tonight	ma este	mo esh·te
yesterday	tegnap	teg·nop
tomorrow	holnap	hawl·nop
afternoon	délután	dayl·u·taan
evening	este	esh·te
morning	reggel	reg·gel
night	éjszaka	ay·so·ko

Monday	hétfő	hayt·fēü
Tuesday	kedd	kedd
Wednesday	szerda	ser·do
Thursday	csütörtök	chew·teur·teuk
Friday	péntek	payn·tek
Saturday	szombat	sawm·bot
Sunday	vasárnap	vo·shaar·nop

January	január	yo·nu·aar
February	február	feb·ru·aar
March	március	maar·tsi·ush
April	április	aap·ri·lish
May	május	maa·yush
June	június	yū·ni·ush
July	július	yū·li·ush
August	augusztus	o·u·gus·tush
September	szeptember	sep·tem·ber
October	október	awk·tāw·ber
November	november	naw·vem·ber
December	december	de·tsem·ber

TRANSPORT
Public Transport
Where's the ticket office?

Hol a jegypénztár?	hawl o yed'·paynz·taar
What time does it leave?	
Mikor indul?	mi·kawr in·dul
What time does it get to (Eger)?	
Mikor ér (Egerbe)?	mi·kawr ayr (e·ger·be)
How long does the trip take?	
Mennyi ideig tart az út?	men'·yi i·de·ig tort oz üt
How long will it be delayed?	
Mennyit késik?	men'·yit kay·shik
Please stop here.	
Kérem, álljon meg itt.	kay·rem aall·yawn meg itt
How much is it?	
Mennyibe kerül?	men'·yi·be ke·rewl
local bus station	
helyi buszállamás	he·yi bus·aal·law·maash

long-distance bus station

távolsági autóbusz-	taa·vawl·shaa·gi o·u·tāw·bus
államás	aal·law·maash·

Which ... goes (to Budapest/the Parliament)?
Melyik ... megy (Budapestre/a Parlamenthez)?
me·yik ... med' (*bu·*do·pesht·re/o *par·*lo·ment·hez)

bus
busz   bus
train
vonat   vaw·not
tram
villamos   víl·lo·mawsh
trolleybus
trolibusz   traw·li·bus
metro line
metró   met·rāw

When's the ...?
Mikor megy ...?   mi·kawr med' ...
first
az első   oz el·shēū
last
az utolsó   oz u·tawl·shāw
next
a következő   o keu·vet·ke·zēū

A ... ticket to (Eger).
Egy ... jegy (Eger)be. ed' ... yej (e·ger)·be
one way
csak oda   chok aw·do
return
oda-vissza   aw·do·vis·so

Is this taxi available?
Szabad ez a taxi?   so·bod ez o tok·si
Please put the meter on.
Kérem, kapcsolja be   kay·rem kop·chawl·yo be
az órát.   oz āw·raat
How much is it to ...?
Mennyibe kerül ... ba? men'·yi·be ke·rewl ... bo
Please take me to (this address).
Kérem, vigyen el   kay·rem vi·dyen el
(erre a címre).   (er·re o tseem·re)
How much is it?
Mennyit fizetek?   men'·nyit fi·ze·tek

Private Transport
I'd like to hire a/an ...
Szeretnék egy ... bérelni. se·ret·nayk ed' ... bay·rel·ni
car
autót   o·u·tāwt
motorbike
motort   maw·tawrt

ROAD SIGNS

Autópálya Kijárat	Exit Freeway
Behajtani Tilos	No Entry
Bejárat	Entrance
Egyirányú	One Way
Elsőbbségadás Kötelező	Give Way
Megállni Tilos	No Standing
Terelőút	Detour
Útépítés	Road Work Ahead
Várakozni Tilos	No Parking

Is this the road to (Sopron)?
Ez az út vezet   ez oz üt ve·zet
(Sopronba)?   (shawp·rawn·bo)
Where's a petrol station?
Hol van egy benzinkút? hawl von ed' ben·zin·küt
Please fill it up.
Kérem, töltse tele.   kay·rem teult·she te·le
I'd like ... litres.
... litert kérek.   ... li·tert kay·rek

petrol/gas
benzin   ben·zin
diesel
dízel/gázolaj   dee·zel/gaa·zo·lay
leaded
ólmozott   āwl·maw·zawtt
LPG
folyékony autógáz   luw·yay·kawn' o u tāw gaaz
regular
normál   nawr·maal
premium unleaded
ólommentes szuper   āw·lawm·men·tesh su·per
unleaded
ólommentes   āw·lawm·men·tesh

(How long) Can I park here?
(Meddig) Parkolhatok itt?
(*med·*dig) por·kawl·ho·tawk itt
I need a mechanic.
Szükségem van egy autószerelőre.
sewk·shay·gem von ed' o·u·tāw·se·re·lēū·re
The car/motorbike has broken down (at Sopron).
Az autó/A motor elromlott (Sopronnál).
oz o·u·tāw/o maw·tawr el·rawm·lawtt (shawp·rawn·naal)
The car/motorbike won't start.
Az autó/A motor nem indul.
oz o·u·tāw/o maw·tawr nem in·dul
I have a flat tyre.
Defektem van.
de·fek·tem von

TRAVEL WITH CHILDREN

Is there a ...?
Van ...?
von ...

I need a/an ...
Szükségem van egy ...
sewk·shay·gem von ed' ...

baby change room
babapelenkázó szobára
bo·bo·pe·len·kaa·zāw saw·baa·ro

baby seat
babaülésre
bo·bo·ew·laysh·re

(English-speaking) babysitter
(angolul beszélő) bébiszitterre
(on·gaw·lul be·say·lēü) bay·bi·sit·ter·re

booster seat
gyerekülésre
dye·rek·ew·laysh·re

disposable nappies/diapers
eldobható pelenkára
el·dawb·ho·tāw pe·len·kaa·ro

highchair
etetőszékre
e·te·tēü·sayk·re

potty
bilire
bi·li·re

stroller
ülő gyerekkocsira
ew·lēü dye·rek·kaw·chi·ro

Are children allowed?
Beengedik a gyerekeket?
be·en·ge·dik o dye·re·ke·ket

Do you mind if I breastfeed here?
Megengedi, hogy itt szoptassak?
meg·en·ge·di hawd' itt sawp·tosh·shok

Also available from Lonely Planet:
Hungarian Phrasebook

Glossary

Can't find the word you're looking for here? Try the Language chapter (p394) or the glossary in the Food & Drink chapter (p60).

ÁEV – Állami Erdei Vasutak (State Forest Railways)
ÁFA – value-added tax (VAT)
Alföld – same as *Nagyalföld* and *pustza*
aluljáró – underpass
Ausgleich – German for 'reconciliation'; the Compromise of 1867
autóbusz – bus
autóbuszállomás – bus station
Avars – a people of the Caucasus who invaded Europe in the 6th century
ÁVO – Rákosi's hated secret police in the early years of communism; later renamed ÁVH

bal – left
bejárat – entrance
bélyeg – stamp
benzin – petrol
BKV – Budapest Közlekedési Vállalat (Budapest Transport Company)
bokor tanyák – bush farms
bolhapiac – flea market
borozó – wine bar; any place serving wine
Bp – commonly used abbreviation for Budapest
búcsú – farewell; also, a church patronal festival
büfé – snack bar

centrum – town or city centre
čevapčiči – spicy Balkan meatballs
Compromise of 1867 – agreement that created the dual monarchy of Austria-Hungary
Copf – a transitional architectural style between late baroque and neoclassicism (*Zopf* in German)
csárda – a Hungarian-style inn or restaurant
csatorna – canal
csikós – 'cowboy' from the *puszta*
csomagmegőrző – left-luggage office
cukrászda – cake shop or patisserie

D – map/compass abbreviation for *dél* (south)
Dacia – Latin name for Romania and lands east of the Tisza River
db or **drb** – piece (measurement used in markets)
de – in the morning, 'am'
dél – south
du – in the afternoon/evening, 'pm'

É – map/compass abbreviation for *észak* (north)
Eclectic – an art and architectural style popular in Hungary in the Romantic period, drawing from sources both indigenous and foreign
élelmiszer – grocery shop or convenience store
előszoba – vestibule or anteroom; one of three rooms in a traditional Hungarian cottage
em – abbreviation for *emelet* (floor or storey)
emelet – floor or storey
erdő – forest
érkezés – arrivals
észak – north
eszpresszó – coffee shop, often also selling alcoholic drinks and snacks; strong, black coffee; same as *presszó*
étkezde – canteen that serves simple dishes
étterem – restaurant

falu – village
fasor – boulevard, avenue
felvilágosítás – information
fogas – pike-perch like fish indigenous to Lake Balaton
földszint – ground floor
folyó – river
forint – Hungary's monetary unit
főkapitányság – main police station
főváros – main city or capital
főzelék – a traditional way of preparing vegetables, where they're fried or boiled and then mixed into a roux with milk
fsz – abbreviation for *földszint* (ground floor)
Ft – forint; see also *HUF*

gázolaj – diesel fuel
gulyás or **gulyásleves** – a thick beef soup cooked with onions and potatoes and usually eaten as a main course
gyógyfürdő – bath or spa
gyógyszertár – pharmacy
gyógyvíz – medicinal drinking water
gyorsvonat – fast trains
gyűjtemény – collection
gyula – chief military commander of the early Magyar

hajdúk – Hungarian for *Heyducks*
hajó – boat
hajóállomás – ferry pier or landing
ház – house
hegy – hill, mountain
hegyalja – hill country
helyi autóbusz pályaudvar – local bus station
HÉV – Helyiérdekű Vasút (suburban commuter train in Budapest)

Heyducks – drovers and outlaws from the *puszta* who fought as mercenaries against the Habsburgs
híd – bridge
HNTO – Hungarian National Tourism Office
hőforrás – thermal spring
honfoglalás – conquest of the Carpathian Basin by the Magyars in the late 9th century
HUF – international currency code for the Hungarian forint
Huns – a Mongol tribe that swept across Europe under Attila in the 5th century AD

Ibusz – Hungarian national network of travel agencies
ifjúsági szálló – youth hostel
illeték – duty or tax
indulás – departures

jobb – right (as opposed to left)

K – abbreviation for *kelet* (east)
kamra – workshop or shed; one of three rooms in a traditional Hungarian cottage
kastély – manor house or mansion (see *vár*)
kb – abbreviation for *körülbelül* (approximately)
kékfestő – cotton fabric dyed a rich indigo blue
kelet – east
kemping – camping ground
képtár – picture gallery
kerület – city district
khas – towns of the Ottoman period under direct rule of the sultan
kijárat – exit
kincstár – treasury
kirándulás – outing
Kiskörút – 'Little Ring road' in Budapest
kocsma – pub or saloon
kolostor – monastery or cloister
komp – ferry
könyvesbolt – bookshop
könyvtár – library
konzumlányok – 'consume girls': attractive young women who work in collusion with bars and clubs to rip off unsuspecting male tourists
kórház – hospital
körülbelül – approximately (abbreviation kb)
körút – ring road
korzó – embankment or promenade
köz – alley, mews, lane
központ – centre
krt – abbreviation for *körút* (ring road)
kúria – mansion or manor
kuruc – Hungarian mercenaries, partisans or insurrectionists who resisted the expansion of Habsburg rule in Hungary after the withdrawal of the Turks (late 17th/early 18th centuries)

lángos – deep-fried dough with toppings
lekvár – fruit jam
lépcső – stairs, steps
liget – park

Magyarország autóatlasza – road atlas of Hungary
Mahart – Hungarian passenger ferry company
Malév – Hungary's national airline
MÁV – Magyar Államvasutak (Hungarian State Railways)
megye – county
menetrend – timetable
mihrab – Muslim prayer niche facing Mecca
MNB – Magyar Nemzeti Bank (National Bank of Hungary)
Moorish Romantic – an art style popular in the decoration of 19th-century Hungarian synagogues
mozi – cinema
műemlék – memorial, monument
munkavállalási engedély – work permit

Nagyalföld – the Great Plain (same as the *Alföld* and *puszta*)
Nagykörút – 'Big Ring road' in Budapest
népművészeti bolt – folk-art shop
Nonius – Hungarian breed of horse
nosztalgiavonat – vintage steam train
Ny – abbreviation for *nyugat* (west)
nyitva – open
nyugat – west

ó – abbreviation for *óra*
önkiszolgáló – self-service
óra – hour, 'o'clock'
orvosi rendelő – doctor's surgery
osztály – department
OTP – Országos Takarékpénztár (National Savings Bank)
Ottoman Empire – the Turkish empire that took over from the Byzantine Empire when it captured Constantinople (Istanbul) in 1453, and expanded into southeastern Europe

pálinka – fruit brandy
palota – palace
pályaudvar – train or railway station
Pannonia – Roman name for the lands south and west of the Danube River
panzió – *pension*, guesthouse
part – embankment
patika – pharmacy
patyolat – laundry
pénztár – cashier
pénzváltó – exchange office
piac – market
pince – wine cellar
plébánia – rectory, parish house
polgármester – mayor

pörkölt – stew
porta – type of farmhouse in Transdanubia
presszó – same as *eszpresszó* (coffee shop; strong, black coffee)
pu – abbreviation for *pályaudvar* (train station)
puli – Hungarian breed of sheepdog with shaggy coat
puszta – literally 'deserted'; other name for the Great Plain (see *Alföld* and *Nagyalföld*)
puttony – the number of 'butts' of sweet *aszú* essence added to other base wines in making Tokaj wine

racka – sheep on the Great Plain with distinctive corkscrew horns
rakpart – quay, embankment
rendőrkapitányság – police station
repülőtér – airport
Romany – the language and culture of the Roma (Gypsy) people

sebesvonat – swift trains
Secessionism – art and architectural style similar to Art Nouveau
sedile (pl **sedilia**) – medieval stone niche with seats
sétány – walkway, promenade
shahoof – distinctive sweep-pole well found only on the Great Plain (Hungarian: *gémeskút*)
skanzen – open-air museum displaying village architecture
söröző – beer bar or pub
spahi – name given to a member of the Turkish irregular cavalry. The officers of the spahis were granted fiefs by the Sultan, and were entitled to all income from the fief in return for military service to the Sultan.
stb – abbreviation of '*s a többi*' (and so on) equivalent to English 'etc'
strand – grassy 'beach' near a river or lake
sugárút – avenue
szálló or **szálloda** – hotel
székesegyház – cathedral
személyvonat – passenger trains that stop at every city, town, village and hamlet along the way
sziget – island
színház – theatre
szoba kiadó – room for rent
szűr – long embroidered felt cloak or cape traditionally worn by Hungarian shepherds

Tanácsköztársaság – the 1919 Communist 'Republic of Councils' under Béla Kun
táncház – folk music and dance workshop
tanya – homestead or ranch; station
tartózkodási engedély – residence permit

távolsági autóbusz pályaudvar – long-distance bus station
templom – church
tér – town or market square
tere – genitive form of *tér* as in Hősök tere (Square of the Heroes)
tilos – prohibited, forbidden
tiszta szoba – parlour; one of three rooms in a traditional Hungarian cottage
tó – lake
toalett – toilet
Trianon Treaty – 1920 treaty imposed on Hungary by the victorious Allies, which reduced the country to one-third of its former size
Triple Alliance – 1882–1914 alliance between Germany, Austria-Hungary and Italy – not to be confused with the WWI Allies (members of the *Triple Entente* and their supporters)
Triple Entente – agreement among Britain, France and Russia, intended as a counterbalance to the *Triple Alliance*, lasting until the Russian Revolution of 1917
turul – eagle-like totem of the ancient Magyars and now a national symbol

u – abbreviation for *utca* (street)
udvar – court
ünnep – public holiday
úszoda – swimming pool
út – road
utca – street
utcája – genitive form of *utca* as in Ferencesek utcája (Street of the Franciscans)
útja – genitive form of *út* as in Mártíroká útja (Street of the Martyrs)
üzlet – shop

vá – abbreviation for *vasútmegálló* (train station)
vágány – platform
vár – castle
város – city
városház or **városháza** – town hall
vasútállomás – train or railway station
vendéglő – a type of restaurant
vm – abbreviation for *vasútállomás* (train station)
Volán – Hungarian bus company
vonat – train

WC – toilet (see *toalett*)

zárva – closed
Zimmer frei – German for 'room for rent'
Zopf – German and more commonly used word for *Copf*

Alternative Place Names

On a lot of bus and train timetables, Hungarian-language names are used for cities and towns in neighbouring countries. Many of these are in what once was Hungarian territory, and the names are used by the Hungarian-speaking minorities who live there. You should at least be familiar with the more important ones (eg Pozsony for Bratislava, Kolozsvár for Cluj-Napoca, Bécs for Vienna).

ABBREVIATIONS
(C) Croatian, (E) English, (G) German, (H) Hungarian, (R) Romanian, (S) Serbian, (Slk) Slovak, (Slo) Slovene, (U) Ukrainian

Alba Iulia (R) – Gyula Fehérvár (H), Karlsburg/Weissenburg (G)

Baia Mare (R) – Nagybánya (H)
Balaton (H) – Plattensee (G)
Banská Bystrica (Slk) – Besztercebánya (H)
Belgrade (E) – Beograd (S), Nándorfehérvár (H)
Beregovo (U) – Beregszász (H)
Braşov (R) – Brassó (H), Kronstadt (G)
Bratislava (Slk) – Pozsony (H), Pressburg (G)

Carei (R) – Nagykároly (H)
Cluj-Napoca (R) – Kolozsvár (H), Klausenburg (G)

Danube (E) – Duna (H), Donau (G)
Danube Bend (E) – Dunakanyar (H), Donauknie (G)
Debrecen (H) – Debrezin (G)

Eger (H) – Erlau (G)
Eisenstadt (G) – Kismárton (H)
Esztergom (H) – Gran (G)

Great Plain (E) – Nagyalföld, Alföld, Puszta (H)
Győr (H) – Raab (G)

Hungary (E) – Magyarország (H), Ungarn (G)

Kisalföld (H) – Little Plain (E)
Komárom (H) – Komárno (Slk)

Košice (Slk) – Kassa (H), Kaschau (G)
Kőszeg (H) – Güns (G)

Lendava (Slo) – Lendva (H)
Lučenec (Slk) – Losonc (H)

Mattersburg (G) – Nagymárton (H)
Mukačevo (U) – Munkács (H)
Murska Sobota (Slo) – Muraszombat (H)

Northern Uplands (E) – Északi Felföld (H)

Oradea (R) – Nagyvárad (H), Grosswardein (G)
Osijek (C) – Eszék (H)

Pécs (H) – Fünfkirchen (G)

Rožnava (Slk) – Rozsnyó (H)

Satu Mare (R) – Szatmárnémeti (H)
Senta (S) – Zenta (H)
Sibiu (R) – Nagyszében (H), Hermannstadt (G)
Sic (R) – Szék (H)
Sighişoara (R) – Segesvár (H), Schässburg (G)
Sopron (H) – Ödenburg (G)
Štúrovo (Slk) – Párkány (H)
Subotica (S) – Szabadka (H)
Szeged (H) – Segedin (G)
Székesfehérvár (H) – Stuhlweissenburg (G)
Szombathely (H) – Steinamanger (G)

Tata (H) – Totis (G)
Timişoara (R) – Temesvár (H)
Tirgu Mureş (R) – Marosvásárhely (H)
Transdanubia (E) – Dunántúl (H)
Transylvania (R) – Erdély (H), Siebenbürgen (G)
Trnava (Slk) – Nagyszombat (H)

Uzhhorod (U) – Ungvár (H)

Vác (H) – Wartzen (G)
Vienna (E) – Wien (G), Bécs (H)
Villány (H) – Wieland (G)
Villánykövesd (H) – Growisch (G)

Wiener Neustadt (G) – Bécsújhely (H)

Behind the Scenes

THIS BOOK

The first three editions were written by Steve Fallon. He was joined by Neal Bedford for the fourth edition and this fifth edition. This guidebook was commissioned in Lonely Planet's London office and produced by the following:

Commissioning Editor Fiona Buchan
Coordinating Editor Lutie Clark
Coordinating Cartographer Hunor Csutoros
Coordinating Layout Designer Margaret Jung
Assisting Editors David Andrew, Monique Choy, Kristin Odijk
Assisting Cartographers Csanad Csutoros, Anneka Imkamp
Cover Designer Nic Lehman
Managing Cartographer Mark Griffiths
Project Manager Brigitte Ellemor
Language Content Coordinator Quentin Frayne

Thanks to Yvonne Byron, Hunor Csutoros, Sally Darmody, Bruce Evans, Nancy Ianni, Adriana Mammarella, Alan Murphy, Wibowo Rusli, Liz White, Celia Wood

THANKS
STEVE FALLON

Special thanks to my good friend Bea Szirti for all her helpful suggestions and to Erzsébet Tiszai, who helped with the research of the Budapest, Transport and Directory chapters and has the patience of Job. Péter Lengyel showed me once again the way to the wine roads, and Gerard Gorman where the birds fly; I am very grateful. As always Dr Zsuzsa Medgyes of M&G Marketing in Budapest came forward with all those wonderful little details during a very difficult time. Brandon Krueger and

Anna Reich of the Central European University, László Józsa of TV2 and Eric D'Amato of Pestiside .hu added insights into what's on in Budapest after dark. Ildikó Nagy Moran was as welcoming and helpful as always. It was a pleasure working again with my coauthor Neal Bedford.

As always, my share of *Hungary* is dedicated to Michael Rothschild, with love and gratitude.

NEAL BEDFORD

First and foremost, my biggest thanks goes to my friend and co-ordinating author Steve Fallon, who always had an encouraging word and a couple of cold *sör* for me whenever I needed them. For joining me in the far-flung Northern Upland hills and adding her support into the fray, *Danke* to Tiffany. For her translation skills, and all-round Hungarianness, *Köszi* must go to Zsuzsa.

A couple of people went the extra distance to help in the research of this book, and for this you have my eternal thanks: Emese Sziklay and his staff at the Hullám Hostel on the Balaton; Henrietta Harcsa at the EU Information point in Debrecen; David Kendall of 'David's National Anthem' fame (more than you'll ever need to know about national anthems, see david.national-anthems.net); Andrew Ruttkay for his added extras on Szeged and Gyula; and Györgyi Tóth with her insights from the NANE Women's Rights Association (www.nane.hu).

While on the road, the helpful staff in a zillion Tourinform offices lightened my workload time and time again, as did many a local. And a very special thanks goes to the guys who welded my car muffler back on in Hajdúszoboszló – you saved my bacon.

THE LONELY PLANET STORY

The story begins with a classic travel adventure: Tony and Maureen Wheeler's 1972 journey across Europe and Asia to Australia. There was no useful information about the overland trail then, so Tony and Maureen published the first Lonely Planet guidebook to meet a growing need.

From a kitchen table, Lonely Planet has grown to become the largest independent travel publisher in the world, with offices in Melbourne (Australia), Oakland (USA) and London (UK). Today Lonely Planet guidebooks cover the globe. There is an ever-growing list of books and information in a variety of media. Some things haven't changed. The main aim is still to make it possible for adventurous travellers to get out there – to explore and better understand the world.

At Lonely Planet we believe travellers can make a positive contribution to the countries they visit – if they respect their host communities and spend their money wisely. Every year 5% of company profit is donated to charities around the world.

OUR READERS

Many thanks to the many travellers who used the last edition and wrote to us with helpful hints, useful advice and interesting anecdotes:

Bev & Joe Atiyah, Leonardo Aversa, Bruce Bachman, Janita Bannister, Deborah Bogenhuber, Geoff Brandwood, Pauline Brennan, Angela Budai, Cass Chan, Marie Corn, Sally Coshow, Andras Czvek, Henry Dawson, Jack DeLuca, Bruce Denner, Ian Donchi, David Doughan, Olivier Dubarry, Med Lars Floter, Michael Fox, Geer Furtjes, Patrick Gallagher, Norman Gamble, Nathanael Genet, Prue Gifford-Ellis, Jane Gilmour, Peter Gilyen, Gudrun Gisladottir, P Goldsmith, Tom Grevatte, Laura Grignani, Matt Hartcher, Howard Hodges, Joan Joesting-Mahoney, Jeannie Jones, Judy Kell, Damian Klepaczek, Melissa Kluger, Mark Koltun, Laura Konig, Cees Krommenhoek, Viktoria Ladanyi, Roland Landor, Pászthory László, Helen Mannhart, Mirek Marut, Anna Mccreadie, J S McLintock, Susan Meek, Pat Metharom,

Joanne Michaels, Kevin Miles, Jordan Mitchell, Anna Morris, Beth Mylius, Axel Nelms, Carrie Ng, Liz Pal, Matti Paljakka, Mathilde Philippe, Erin Propas, Nick Quantock, Eric Reber, Lisa Redfern, Lois Robey, David Route, Andy Ryan, Korino Sango, Keela Shackell, Fergus Smith, Simon, Judy & Matthew Smith, Damian Spellman, Susanne Stoelting, Amy Szabados, Karin Thorneman, Marjan van Denhoeck, Wim Vandenbussche, Judith Vasey, Jonathan Wickens, Chad Williams, David Wood, Rebecca Wood, David Woodberry, John Woods, Caroline Woolf, Carolyn Yohn, Sarah Zarrow

ACKNOWLEDGMENTS

Many thanks to the following for the use of their content:

Dr Caroline Evans whose material was adapted for the Health chapter.

Globe on back cover Mountain High Maps Copyright ©1993 Digital Wisdom, Inc.

BEHIND THE SCENES

Index

000 Map pages
000 Photograph pages

INDEX

000 Map pages
000 Photograph pages

000 Map pages
000 Photograph pages

000 Map pages
000 Photograph pages

INDEX

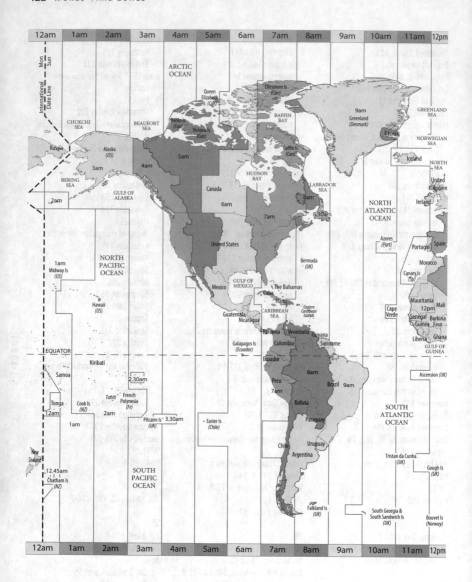

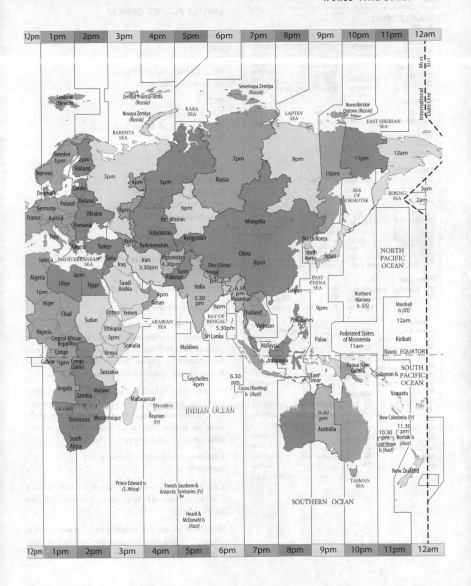

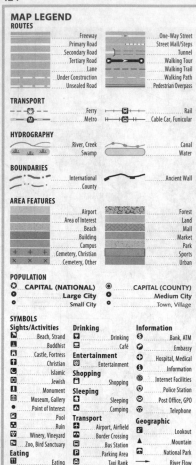

MAP LEGEND

ROUTES

Freeway
Primary Road
Secondary Road
Tertiary Road
Lane
Under Construction
Unsealed Road
One-Way Street
Street Mall/Steps
Tunnel
Walking Tour
Walking Trail
Walking Path
Pedestrian Overpass

TRANSPORT

Ferry
Metro
Rail
Cable Car, Funicular

HYDROGRAPHY

River, Creek
Swamp
Canal
Water

BOUNDARIES

International
County
Ancient Wall

AREA FEATURES

Airport
Area of Interest
Beach
Building
Campus
Cemetery, Christian
Cemetery, Other
Forest
Land
Mall
Market
Park
Sports
Urban

POPULATION

○ CAPITAL (NATIONAL)
● Large City
○ Small City
◉ CAPITAL (COUNTY)
● Medium City
○ Town, Village

SYMBOLS

Sights/Activities	Drinking	Information
Beach, Strand	Drinking	Bank, ATM
Buddhist	Café	Embassy
Castle, Fortress	**Entertainment**	Hospital, Medical
Christian	Entertainment	Information
Islamic	**Shopping**	Internet Facilities
Jewish	Shopping	Police Station
Monument	**Sleeping**	Post Office, GPO
Museum, Gallery	Sleeping	Telephone
Point of Interest	Camping	**Geographic**
Pool	**Transport**	Lookout
Ruin	Airport, Airfield	Mountain
Winery, Vineyard	Border Crossing	National Park
Zoo, Bird Sanctuary	Bus Station	River Flow
Eating	Parking Area	
Eating	Taxi Rank	

LONELY PLANET OFFICES

Australia
Head Office
Locked Bag 1, Footscray, Victoria 3011
☎ 03 8379 8000, fax 03 8379 8111
talk2us@lonelyplanet.com.au

USA
150 Linden St, Oakland, CA 94607
☎ 510 893 8555, toll free 800 275 8555
fax 510 893 8572
info@lonelyplanet.com

UK
72–82 Rosebery Ave,
Clerkenwell, London EC1R 4RW
☎ 020 7841 9000, fax 020 7841 9001
go@lonelyplanet.co.uk

Published by Lonely Planet Publications Pty Ltd
ABN 36 005 607 983

© Lonely Planet Publications Pty Ltd 2006

© photographers as indicated 2006

Cover photographs: Swimmers at public baths in the Hungarian capital of Budapest, Adam Woolfitt/APL/Corbis (front); Traffic trails on the Széchenyi Chain Bridge, Jonathan Smith/Lonely Planet Images (back). Many of the images in this guide are available for licensing from Lonely Planet Images: www.lonelyplanetimages.com.

Printed through Colorcraft Ltd, Hong Kong.
Printed in China